Jewish
Resistance
against
the
Nazis

Jewish Resistance against the Nazis

Edited by Patrick Henry

 The Catholic University of America Press
Washington, D.C.

Library of Congress Cataloging-in-Publication Data

Jewish resistance against the Nazis / edited by

Patrick Henry.

pages cm

Includes bibliographical references and index.

ISBN 978-0-8132-2589-0 (pbk. : alk. paper)

1. World War, 1939–1945—Jewish resistance.

2. World War, 1939–1945—Participation, Jewish.

3. Holocaust, Jewish (1939–1945)   I. Henry, Patrick

(Patrick Gerard), editor of compilation.   II. Lang,

Berel, author. Why didn't they resist more?

D810.J4J49 2014

940.53'18—dc23   2013041583

For Mary Anne, Anne, Nathan, June, and Irene

You wish to praise the heroes, fine,
but please don't do it at the expense
of the victims; don't separate them
in the flames and the ashes. Even
the heroes were victims and the
victims, too, were heroes.

—Elie Wiesel

In memory of all those murdered during the
Shoah and for all the Jewish people who,
already sentenced to death by virtue of their
birth, risked their lives to save the lives of other
Jews throughout occupied Europe during the
Nazi genocide

Contents

Contents

Acknowledgments

I am profoundly indebted to the contributors to this volume, almost none of whom knew me personally when I contacted them and asked if they would be willing to write an essay about Jewish resistance against the Nazis in a specific geographical location. The fact that just about everyone I asked immediately agreed to do so strengthened my confidence in the importance of this work. I am particularly grateful to those contributors who persisted despite trying family health situations, and to three contributors, Debórah Dwork, Nancy Lefenfeld, and Richard Middleton-Kaplan, who helped me out significantly in many other ways.

For various reasons, I also want to thank the following people: Elliott Abramson, Chana Arnon, Barbara Barnett, Beth Benevides, Alan Berger, Holly Case, Catherine Epstein, Martin Goldman, Sandy Goodhart, Dan Gordon, Peter Hayes, René Lichtman, Bob Moss, Kenneth Moss, Larry Mulkerin, Irena Polkowska Rutenberg, Stephanie Seltzer, Timothy Snyder, (the late) Ted Stein, Susan Suleiman, Lynne Vieth, and Zev Weiss.

I am indebted as well to the former director of the Catholic University of America Press, David McGonagle, who oversaw the beginnings of this project, and the current director, Trevor Lipscombe, who has brought it to fruition. At the press, I am also grateful to Theresa Walker, Brian Roach, Tanjam Jacobson, and two insightful anonymous readers of the penultimate draft. I would also like to thank Nancy Halsey for doing a superb job of copyediting this unruly manuscript and Denise Carlson for compiling the index.

Once again, Kristin Vining has prepared the text with her usual intelligence, patience, flexibility, insight, goodwill, and creativity. I could not be more grateful for her inspired assistance.

Finally, there is always my sweetheart and forty-year companion, Mary Anne O'Neil, who has patiently engaged every argument, listened carefully to every anecdote, and encouraged me at every step. I'd be lost without her on paper and everywhere else.

Patrick Henry

Introduction Jewish Resistance against the Nazis

Although the myth of Jewish passivity during the Holocaust has been thoroughly discredited in the scholarly world, it lives on in the popular mentality and is often expressed in such phrases as "the Jews were led to the slaughter like sheep."[1] The myth still finds its way into the media and often goes unchallenged. Most recently, in the 2010 film *The Debt* (directed by John Madden), we hear the fictional Nazi Dieter Vogel, known also as the "Surgeon of Birkenau," insidiously proclaim: "You Jews never knew how to kill, only how to die.... So I knew that you people had no right to live." It is important to understand not only the role that Nazis played in the dissemination of this myth, but that, in the twisted Nazi psyche, this blaming of the victim somehow exculpates the killers from their crimes. This myth also served to justify the bystanders. If the Jews did nothing to save themselves, why should others have risked their lives to help them?

The reality of Jewish resistance against the Nazis, however, and the diverse forms it assumed have been elucidated not only in specialized monograph studies but even in the most general works on the Holocaust.[2] In 1968, to choose an

1. See, for example, the continuously updated *Jewish Resistance: A Working Bibliography* online at The Miles Lerman Center for the Study of Jewish Resistance at the United States Holocaust Memorial Museum (*www.ushmm.org*).

2. This information is readily available in the standard histories, dictionaries, and encyclopedias of the Holocaust. I have profited from four such texts: Abraham J. Edelheit and Hershel Edelheit, *History of the Holocaust: A Handbook and Dictionary* (San Francisco, Calif.: Westview Press, 1994); Jack R. Fischel, *Historical Dictionary of the Holocaust* (Lanham, Md.: Scarecrow Press, 1999); Donald Niewyk and Francis Nicosia, *The Columbia Guide to the Holocaust* (New York: Columbia University

early example, Yuri Suhl, determined to fight "the myth that the Jews did not resist," edited, translated, and published an anthology of texts dealing with concrete examples of Jewish resistance against the Nazis.[3] Entitled *They Fought Back: The Story of Jewish Resistance in Nazi Europe*, Suhl's collection offers stunning examples, several of them first-hand accounts, of male and female Jewish resistance in camps, ghettos, and cities such as Berlin and Paris. In the margins, Suhl militates against Raul Hilberg, whom he considers "the leading exponent of the theory of Jewish passivity," claiming that Hilberg found little evidence of Jewish resistance because, rather than seek out Jewish sources in Hebrew and Yiddish, he relied mainly on German sources.[4]

Almost forty years later, the Museum of Jewish Heritage published *Daring to Resist: Jewish Defiance in the Holocaust* which, like *They Fought Back*, contains many first-hand accounts written during the Shoah by courageous Jews, male and female, who, among many other forms of resistance, were fighting back in the ghettos, forests, and camps. This illuminating and beautifully edited volume also contains retrospective essays that offer sagacious advice on how to approach this terrible moment in Jewish history. David Engel suggests that we "measure the Holocaust in Jewish time ... [which] means identifying the stages through which Jews came to dismiss their initial sense that under Nazi rule they were reliving their past."[5] While some Jews immediately fled from Germa-

---

Press, 2000); and, above all, the four-volume *Encyclopedia of the Holocaust*, Israel Gutman, editor in chief (New York: Macmillan Publishing Company, 1990). Bob Moore's recent *Survivors: Jewish Self-help and Rescue in Nazi-Occupied Western Europe* (Oxford: Oxford University Press, 2010) includes sections on Jewish "self-help" in the rescue process in several German-occupied countries in Western Europe.

3. Yuri Suhl, ed., *They Fought Back: The Story of Jewish Resistance in Nazi Europe* (London: Macgibbon and Kee, 1968), 15. One of the most interesting people Suhl writes about (214–21) is David Szmulewski, a Polish Jew and member of the Auschwitz underground, who survived the war. Szmulewski took photographs of naked women being led to the gas chambers and of the *sonderkommandos* dragging gassed corpses to open pits for burning. These photographs, both of which appear in Suhl's book, were smuggled out of Auschwitz and were the first ones demonstrating Nazi atrocities inside Auschwitz to be seen by the outside world. In *Hitch 22: A Memoir* (New York: Twelve, 2010), Christopher Hitchens claims that Szmulewski was "my ancestor-in-law ... a sort of great uncle" of whom he was obviously proud. Hitchens describes Szmulewski's life before and after Auschwitz (368–72) and, citing David's memoirs, *Resistance in the Auschwitz-Birkenau Death Camp* (written in Yiddish but read by Hitchens in English translation), he describes a Yom Kippur service that Szmulewski helped organize in Auschwitz.

4. Ibid., 73, 74, 265–66. Hilberg's views can be found in *The Destruction of the European Jews* (Chicago, Ill.: Quadrangle Books, 1961).

5. David Engel, "Resisting in Jewish Time," in *Daring to Resist: Jewish Defiance in the Holocaust*, ed. Yitzchak Mais, Bonnie Gurewitsch, Barbara Lovenheim (New York: Museum of Jewish Heritage, 2007), 11, 13.

ny in 1933, most remained, thinking that the situation would improve. In Eastern Europe, we should recall, ghetto life was nothing new for Jews. Initially, during the Hitler years, it might well have seemed like a return to past history rather than the prelude to a totally unprecedented genocide. Reiterating David Engel's wise suggestion, Yitzchak Mais urges us, if we wish to see things in a Jewish perspective, to "suspend our historical hindsight."[6] The Jews in Europe from 1933–1945 simply did not have the benefit of that retrospective viewpoint.

The Jews were victims, objects of hateful Nazi ideology, but they were also subjects, with extremely limited choices, seeking ways of survival for themselves and their families in a situation rife with collaboration and structured overwhelmingly for their demise. For one thing, when it was still possible, Jews fled for their safety from countries such as Poland, Germany, Austria, and France: well over 400,000 German and Austrian Jews left their countries between 1933 and 1939; in Germany, unbelievably, 83 percent of Jews under the age of twenty-four managed to emigrate by 1939;[7] among them were roughly 10,000 children who left on kindertransports to England and the Netherlands.[8] More than 300,000 Polish Jews fled to Soviet-occupied Poland, and, after June 1940, many other Jews in France and Italy sought refuge in Spain and Switzerland. The American Jewish Joint Distribution Committee was the major source of funding for the emigration of Jews from Europe and for subsidizing rescue operations in German-occupied countries. The first major form of Jewish resistance was flight and there is nothing passive about flight.

Tens of thousands tried to emigrate after 1939 but rarely found an exit. Borders were closing rapidly, exit visas were difficult to obtain, and tickets, sponsors, and entry visas were also required. Jewish refugees were restricted from entering England and Palestine as well. Without a valid passport, one could go nowhere. Despite these restrictions, many Jews managed to get out of Europe: the *ha'avara* (transfer) agreement between Nazis and Zionists opened up places in Palestine for besieged Polish Jews. As a result, during the first years of German rule, "the number of Jews in the *yishuv* ["settlement," the organized, prestate of Israel Jewish community in Palestine] doubled from 200,000 to 400,000."[9] But

6. Yitzchak Mais, "Jewish Life in the Shadow of Destruction," in *Daring to Resist*, ed. Mais, Gurewitsch, Lovenheim, 19.

7. Debórah Dwork and Robert Jan van Pelt, *Flight from the Reich: Refugee Jews, 1933–1946* (New York: W. W. Norton, 2009), 127–28.

8. Debórah Dwork and Robert Jan van Pelt, *Holocaust: A History* (New York: W. W. Norton, 2002), 128–29.

9. Dwork and van Pelt, *Flight From The Reich*, 36.

this escape route was soon closed by the British. In 1940, roughly 37,000 Jews managed to emigrate to the United States and some 10,000 to other countries overseas.[10] This number kept dwindling and soon the United States and Cuba also closed their doors to refugee Jews. "The harsh reality," Tony Judt notes, "is that Jews, Jewish suffering and Jewish extermination were not matters of overwhelming concern to most Europeans (Jews and Nazis aside) of that time. The centrality that we now assign to the Holocaust, both as Jews and as humanitarians, is something that only emerged decades later."[11]

Jews offered armed resistance in the ghettos, the camps, the forests, and in organized resistance movements throughout occupied Europe. Understandably, violent Jewish resistance against the Nazis increased as it became clear that the Jews of Europe were experiencing not a return to the Middle Ages, but rather a state-sponsored genocide.[12] This genocide took place in some areas before others, because the Einsatzgruppen's Holocaust by bullets preceded that of the gas chambers. The Bielski brothers were fighting in the forests of Belorussia in December 1941, months and even years before all the various ghetto uprisings and camp rebellions would take place. Within the ghettos of Eastern Europe, where the populations were weakened by starvation and disease, there were two major uprisings. These revolts, in the Warsaw and Bialystok ghettos, were undertaken without any hope of forcing the Germans to change their plans regarding Jews. The only hope was that some of the ghetto dwellers might escape to join the partisans. Generally these heroic and futile acts of resistance against insurmountable odds were immediately crushed, although the Jews in the Warsaw ghetto held out for four months, longer than some national armies did. Timothy Snyder notes in *Bloodlands: Europe between Hitler and Stalin*, that this open act of Jewish resistance in the Warsaw ghetto "worked powerfully against the anti-Semitic stereotype, present in the Home Army and in Polish society, that Jews would not fight."[13] Additionally, there were armed revolts in dozens of other ghettos in occupied Poland and the Soviet Union, in Cracow, Vilna, Minsk, Bedzin, Czestochowa, and Kovno, for example.

10. Ibid., 196.

11. Tony Judt (with Timothy Snyder), *Thinking the Twentieth Century* (New York: Penguin, 2012), 22.

12. In the November 8, 1940 insert to his diary, Emanuel Ringelblum notes: "We are returning to the Middle Ages." It was roughtly two years later, sometime between July and December 1942, after the truth of Treblinka was known, that he lamented the fact that they had not resisted with violence up to that point. Emanuel Ringelblum, *Notes from the Warsaw Ghetto: The Journal of Emanuel Ringelblum*, ed. and trans. Jacob Sloan (New York: Schocken Books, 1974), 82, 310, 321, 326–27.

13. Timothy Snyder, *Bloodlands: Europe between Hitler and Stalin* (New York: Basic Books, 2010), 286.

There were also Jewish underground resistance groups in many of the concentration camps, including Maidanek, Dachau, and Buchenwald, and three major armed revolts within the death camps. "In every instance," notes Primo Levi, these armed uprisings "were planned and led by prisoners who were privileged in some way and, consequently, in better physical and spiritual condition than the average camp prisoner."[14] At Treblinka in August 1943, 750 prisoners escaped but only seventy survived the war. At Sobibor in October 1943, more than 300 prisoners escaped, many of whom were later killed. The Germans liquidated the camp after executing all the remaining prisoners. Finally, in October 1944 in Auschwitz II Birkenau, a group of Jewish sonderkommandos, prisoners assigned to work inside the gas chambers and the crematoria, aware that they were soon to be liquidated and having only explosives for weapons, blew up Crematorium 4. All participants were executed, including the women who provided the explosives. This was an act of pure rebellion with death to the participants assured in advance, an act of heroism, of choosing to die otherwise than as their captors planned, and of leaving a legacy of resistance.[15] "Hanging from the gallows," one of the women, Rosa Robota, shouted, "'Hazak V' Amatz,' [Be strong and courageous], the biblical words that Moses had said to Joshua as he assumed leadership."[16] With one exception, these Jewish-initiated uprisings were the only uprisings against the Nazis in the camps.[17]

When we speak of organized armed Jewish resistance in occupied Europe, it is important to emphasize that we are not dealing with massive numbers. But the numbers of non-Jews resisting the Nazis were also minimal and, not being held in ghettos and camps, their opportunities for resistance were far greater. In France, to choose but one example, Robert Paxton estimates that only "roughly 2 percent of the adult population" were members of the active Resistance.[18]

14. Primo Levi, "Afterword," in *The Reawakening*, trans. Stuart Woolf (New York: Simon and Schuster, 1965), 217.

15. Tim Blake Nelson's film, *The Grey Zone* (Vancouver, Canada: Lions Gate Films, 2001), suggests that the revolt of the sonderkommandos was intended, at least by some of the participants, to halt the slaughter of the recently arrived Hungarian Jews.

16. Michael Berenbaum and Yitzhak Mais, *Memory and Legacy: The Shoah Narrative of the Illinois Holocaust Museum* (Skokie, Ill.: Illinois Holocaust Museum and Education Center, 2009), 109.

17. Yehuda Bauer points out that of the seven prisoner rebellions in concentration and death camps, six were by Jews (Krszyna, Krychow, Kopernik, Sobibor, Treblinka and Auschwitz); the exception was led by "Soviet prisoners of war at Ebensee at the end of the war." See Yehuda Bauer, "Forms of Jewish Resistance During the Holocaust," in *Holocaust: Religious and Philosophical Implications*, ed. John K. Roth and Michael Berenbaum (St. Paul, Minn.: Paragon House, 1989), 143.

18. Robert O. Paxton, *Vichy France: Old Guard and New Order* (New York: Columbia University Press, 1972), 294–95.

Likewise, the fact that many attempts at resistance failed is not an argument against their having taken place. Powerlessness is not synonymous with passivity. The odds against success were insuperable in all cases, even when it involved the youngest, strongest, and best trained individuals. When asked, after the war, why he did not escape, Primo Levi spoke about the barbed wire, the electrified grills, the dogs, and the armed sentinels. Then he added: "[We were] demoralized ... weakened by hunger and maltreatment; ... shaved heads, filthy clothes were immediately recognizable; wooden clogs made a swift and silent step impossible.... [We were] foreigners with neither acquaintances nor viable places of refuge in the surroundings."[19] We should also note that resistance by other prisoner groups was no greater than that of the Jews. Roughly 3 million Russian soldiers, for example, died in German captivity during World War II and 22,000 Polish army officers, police officers, and members of the Polish intelligentsia were slaughtered in April and May 1940 by Soviet secret police in the Katyn Forest in Russia and elsewhere without noticeable resistance. To this should be added Primo Levi's observation that "the gas chambers at Auschwitz were tested on a group of three hundred Russian prisoners of war, young, army-trained, politically indoctrinated, and not hampered by the presence of women and children, and even they did not revolt."[20] We are therefore compelled to ask with Berel Lang: "To whom are the Jews being compared when the questions 'Why didn't they resist *more?*' and 'Why didn't *more* of them resist?' are asked?"

In Eastern Europe, Jews escaped from the ghettos to join guerilla outfits struggling against the Germans. Interestingly, Yehuda Bauer informs us that the much-maligned Jewish ghetto police were part of the resistance in fourteen cases: "In Kovno, for instance," he writes, "the police were at the heart of attempts at armed resistance and attempts to smuggle young people into the forest to participate in partisan fighting." [21] In these partisan forest brigades, Jewish resistance was successful and thousands of Jewish participants survived the war. It has been estimated that roughly 30,000 Jews fought in partisan units in the forests of Belorussia and the western Ukraine alone. Jewish partisan groups also fought with the partisans in Yugoslavia, Bulgaria, and Greece. All of these groups derailed trains, destroyed bridges, and committed various acts of sabotage that took the lives of thousands of Germans.

19. Primo Levi, *The Drowned and the Saved*, trans. Raymond Rosenthal (New York: Vintage Books, 1989), 153.

20. Levi, "Afterword," in *The Reawakening*, 219.

21. Yehuda Bauer, *Rethinking the Holocaust* (New Haven, Conn.: Yale University Press, 2001), 144.

In Western Europe, where there were few ghettos and where the Jewish population was much smaller than in Eastern Europe, there was, proportionately speaking, a large percentage of Jews in the underground Resistance in France, Italy, Greece, and Belgium. Jews also joined the Resistance in North Africa in large numbers and helped prepare the massive U.S.-led invasion of North Africa in November 1942. "Of the 377 members of the underground who participated in the events of November 7–8, 315 were Jews."[22] Jews were also soldiers in every army fielded by the Allies. In the Red Army, as Timothy Snyder points out, Jews were "more likely to have been decorated for bravery than Soviet citizens generally."[23] Finally, there were over half a million Jews in the United States armed forces during World War II and, among the Allies, Jews constituted by themselves "an army more than 1.5 million strong."[24]

When we consider, on the one hand, the extent of Jewish resistance throughout occupied Europe (in every German-occupied country, in the forests, the ghettos, and the camps) and, on the other, the hopelessness of the situation in most quarters (the lack of arms, of training, of a home country, the general indifference or hostility of the surrounding populations of non-Jews) and the vicious, stunningly disproportionate reprisals taken by the Nazis, it is less surprising that not all Jews resisted than it is that so many did in so many different places and in so many different ways. After all, the war against the Jews was, as Elie Wiesel words it: "A war in which the enemy had at his disposal generals, soldiers, tanks, scientists, technicians, engineers, theoreticians, psychologists, and millions and millions of sympathizers—while the Jews had nothing but their bare hands."[25] In her most recent study, Deborah Lipstadt points out that the 1961 Adolf Eichmann trial in Israel "fostered a different perception of the victims" than the prevailing one that they "had gone like sheep to the slaughter."[26] There is a wonderful symmetry to the fact that Abba Kovner, a commander of a partisan unit in the Vilna Ghetto who, in December 1941, urged resistance by stating, "Let us not go like sheep to the slaughter," would offer an anguished testimony at the Eichmann trial in which he claimed that "not resisting was the

22. Robert Satloff, *Among the Righteous: Lost Stories from the Holocaust's Long Reach into Arab Lands* (New York: Public Affairs, 2006), 40.

23. Snyder, *Bloodlands*, 342.

24. Edelheit and Edelheit, *History of the Holocaust*, 107. See too Deborah Dash Moore, *GI Jews: How World War II Changed a Generation* (Cambridge, Mass.: Harvard University Press, 2004).

25. Elie Wiesel, "A Plea for the Survivors," in *A Jew Today* (New York: Random House, Inc., 1978), 243.

26. Deborah E. Lipstadt, *The Eichmann Trial* (New York: Schocken, 2011), 195.

rational thing to do." "Rather than demean the victims," Lipstadt writes, Kovner urged contemporary generations to recognize that it was "astonishing" that "there was a revolt [in Vilna]." Gideon Hausner, chief prosecutor of Eichmann concurred: "The real wonder ... was that there *had* been so much organized and widespread resistance."[27] Given the preponderance of evidence of Jewish resistance, it is simply unconscionable to continue to speak in general terms of "Jewish passivity." Doing so violates the historical record and plays into the hands of antisemites who claim that Jews brought their misfortunes upon themselves.

One major goal of our volume is to expand the notion of resistance to include not only violent resistance but nonviolent resistance as well. Resistance mounted by Jews against the Nazis and their collaborators included many different types of actions. While some were violent and confrontational in nature, many were nonviolent, defensive, or clandestine. In all cases of resistance, armed and nonviolent, we consider Jewish resistance to be resistance by Jewish persons in Jewish organizations and by Jewish persons working within non-Jewish organizations. In Germany, for example, as soon as Jewish artists were fired, a Jewish Cultural Association was founded to provide employment for these artists. Jewish schools were also created there when Jewish professors and students were no longer allowed to teach or study in public education. Other Jewish schools were formed for the teaching of agriculture and manual trades in the hope that these skills would give young Jewish men and women better prospects for immigration papers.[28]

In the ghettos of Eastern Europe, where people were starving to death and diseases were rampant, Jewish organizations promoted educational and cultural activities. Here, more generally, nonviolent forms of resistance would have included any life-sustaining activities or actions that fostered human dignity in the face of a cruel machine designed to extinguish it : smuggling in and sharing food, clothing, and medicine; putting on plays, poetry readings, and art exhibits; creating orchestras, orphanages, study groups, and other morale building acts of solidarity; publishing underground newspapers, founding schools, establishing religious activities, and documenting one's experiences (in diaries, for example). In this regard, we have no greater example than Janusz Korczak, pediatrician, teacher, and radio personality in Poland who had every opportunity to escape but chose to remain with the 200 orphans he cared

27. Ibid., 84, 82.
28. Dwork and van Pelt, *Holocaust: A History*, 83–85.

for in his orphanage, which was eventually moved into the Warsaw ghetto. Korczak died in the gas chamber with his orphans. When asked what he would do if he were to survive the war, he replied: "Take care of German orphans."[29] Thinking along these richly humanitarian lines, Yehuda Bauer uses the Hebrew term *amidah* ("standing up against") to define a broad range of resistance that includes both armed and unarmed resistance:

What does *amidah* include? It includes smuggling food into ghettos; mutual self-sacrifice within the family to avoid starvation or worse; cultural, educational, religious, and political activities taken to strengthen morale; the work of doctors, nurses, and educators to consciously maintain health and moral fiber to enable individual and group survival; and, of course, armed rebellion or the use of force (with bare hands or with "cold" weapons) against the Germans and their collaborators.[30]

In the camps too, but much more strikingly, any attempt by sick, starving human beings to stay clean, to care for the dying, to pray, to observe *shabbat*, to say *kaddish* for their fallen relatives and friends, to read, or to remain physically, intellectually, culturally, theologically, and morally alive constituted resistance to Nazi restrictions, which were designed to demolish individuals, to destroy their souls and their wills, and as Primo Levi has written, to "annihilate us first as men in order to kill us more slowly afterwards ... to kill [us] first in our spirit long before our anonymous death."[31] It was only by fierce rebellion against the laws of life in the camps, the intractable laws of anonymity and conformity, that Jews were on occasion able to create communities of resistance.

Outside the camps, nonviolent resistance focused largely, although not exclusively, on rescue. Throughout all of German-occupied Europe, Jews, particularly Jewish children, were sheltered in non-Jewish institutions, homes, and farms, and smuggled into neutral countries such as Switzerland, Spain, and Sweden. It has been estimated that somewhere between 5 percent and 10 percent of the 3,000,000 Jews who survived the Shoah in Europe were rescued.[32] Despite all the attempts to save children, however, 1,500,000 Jewish children were slaughtered by the Nazis. Only 11 percent of European Jewish children

29. See *Korczak*, the 1990 Polish film (with English subtitles) directed by Andrzej Wajda, and more generally, Betty Jean Lifton, *The King of Children: The Life and Death of Janusz Korczak* (New York: Farrar, Straus and Giroux, 1988).

30. Bauer, *Rethinking the Holocaust*, 120.

31. Primo Levi, *Survival in Auschwitz: The Nazi Assault on Humanity,* trans. Stuart Woolf (New York: Macmillan, 1993), 51, 55.

32. Peter Hayes, "The Shoah and Its Legacies," in *The Cambridge Guide to Jewish History, Religion and Culture*, ed. Judith R. Baskin and Kenneth Seeskin (Cambridge: Cambridge University Press, 2010), 250.

alive in 1939 survived the war.[33] As regards hidden children throughout occupied Europe, we can never overemphasize the fact that the first rescuers were Jewish parents. Separating oneself from one's children on the mere hope of their being rescued (and, for reasons of safety, almost always without knowing where one's children would be hidden) was at once the most courageous and anguished choice Jewish parents had to make and the ultimate act of resistance against the annihilation of European Jewry.

Here in the realm of rescue, particularly when compared to the acclaim granted non-Jewish rescuers, the tremendous role played by Jews in the rescue of other Jewish persons, often working in Jewish organizations and in conjunction with non-Jews, has not received sufficient academic study and appropriate public recognition.[34] We will highlight the fact that rescue was another form of resistance, that Jews played an active and significant role throughout occupied Europe in the rescue of other Jews, and that, like collaboration, rescue had many faces: hiding in one's home country, in adjacent forests, or crossing borders to safety. Even armed resisters recognized the importance of rescue and other forms of unarmed humanitarian resistance which, in the final analysis, saved more Jews than armed resistance. Take, for example, the case of Tuvia Bielski who, with his brothers Asael and Zus, saved 1,200 Jews of all ages in the forests of Belorussia in what became known as "Bielski's Shtetl." When asked about his activities, he clearly expressed his preference for rescue over combat against the Nazis: "So few of us are left, we have to save lives. To save a Jew is much more important than to kill Germans."[35] In addition to the depiction of the ghetto fighters and the forest warriors, perhaps future iconography of Jewish resistance against the Nazis will include images of Jewish couples entrusting their children to Jewish humanitarian workers in the internment camps and ghettos throughout Europe, workers who risked their lives to find shelter for those children, as well as images of Jewish men and women, crossing borders and leading other Jewish people to safety in places such as Switzerland, Spain, Sweden, and Turkey.

33. Debórah Dwork, *Children with a Star: Jewish Youth in Nazi Europe* (New Haven, Conn.: Yale University Press, 1991), xi. Child here means from one day old through sixteen years of age.

34. There is, for example, no program in place at Yad Vashem for the recognition of Jewish rescuers. In this regard, see Patrick Henry, "Righteous Jews," *Shalom: The Jewish Peace Fellowship Newsletter* 39 (February 2010): 10–11 and, more recently, Mordecai Paldiel's insightful, informed, and guardedly hopeful "Righteous Gentiles and Courageous Jews: Acknowledging and Honoring Rescuers of Jews," *French Politics, Culture & Society* 30 (Summer 2012): 134–49.

35. Nechama Tec, *Defiance* (Oxford: Oxford University Press, 1993), 112.

Our goal is not only to demonstrate that Jews resisted everywhere, but to indicate that how they resisted was contingent upon many factors, including temporal ones, internal politics, geography, and shifting Nazi policies. As they move from country to country, readers of our volume will make significant comparisons and will understand why resistance took one form here and another there, and one form at one point in time and something quite different at a later moment. If we take the situation in France as an example, we see that things changed radically in August 1942, when Vichy police started rounding up Jewish children in the still Unoccupied Zone and then, even more so when, in November of the same year, after the Allies had landed in North Africa, the Germans descended to occupy the entire country. It was no longer possible to leave large numbers of Jewish children in homes set up for them in places like Chabannes, by Jewish charitable organizations such as the Oeuvre de secours aux enfants (OSE). Thanks to funding from the American Joint Distribution Committee, OSE had set up eight homes for children in the Unoccupied Zone.[36] These homes now had to be dismantled and the children dispersed for their own safety. That it was prudent to disassemble these homes was tragically confirmed by what happened on April 6, 1944, at Izieu, in a home then being dismantled. Led by Klaus Barbie, a Gestapo raid captured forty-four children and the staff. Only one staff member returned from the camps. Once the option of the OSE homes was no longer viable, the two other options became even more crucial. The first, the placing of children in non-Jewish families and religious institutions, had always been operational but now increased significantly. Non-Jewish groups such as the Quakers, the Red Cross, the YMCA, and the Unitarians helped Jewish groups accomplish this work. The second option, smuggling children into Switzerland, was extremely dangerous. Consequently, it was limited while children were relatively safe in the Unoccupied Zone. After August 1942, smuggling children became a good alternative. Between May 1943 and June 1944, more than 1,500 children and adolescents were smuggled into Switzerland and, as Nancy Lefenfeld's contribution makes clear, this rescue mission, like so many others described in our volume, was ecumenically executed.

36. On the situation in Chabannes, see Lisa Gossels's outstanding 2000 documentary, *The Children of Chabannes*, which studies in depth the excellent care that the 400 children lodged there received from Jewish social workers from OSE. On the general situation in the south of France in August 1942 and the months following, consult Patrick Henry, *We Only Know Men: The Rescue of Jews in France during the Holocaust* (Washington, D.C.: The Catholic University of America Press, 2007), 90–93.

Patrick Henry

The first section of our volume, "Myths and Facts," contains three essays. In "The Myth of Jewish Passivity," Richard Middleton-Kaplan detects the origins of the myth in stereotypes and oversimplifications later reinforced by photographs and films of Holocaust victims lined up waiting with their children and their belongings at deportation sites and in the camps. Most of this footage comes from Nazi propaganda films and continues to be shown today as background to documentaries and even fiction films dealing with the Holocaust, without any explanation whatsoever. Middleton-Kaplan eruditely traces positive "sheep to slaughter" imagery back to Isaiah, Psalms, the Talmud, and the Christian scriptures and depicts its distortion into an image of Jewish passivity. He also discusses the role that Jewish intellectuals such as Victor Frankl, Bruno Bettelheim, Raul Hilberg, and Hannah Arendt played in popularizing the idea of Jewish passivity vis-à-vis the Nazis. Berel Lang questions the validity of the question, "Why Didn't They Resist *More?*" which admits that Jews did resist but wonders whether they resisted enough or whether enough of them resisted. Lang elucidates the "mischievous" character of both questions, "Why Didn't The Jews Resist?" and "Why Didn't They Resist *More?*" seeks the possible motives of those who ask these questions from both inside and outside the Holocaust, and tries to imagine standards by which one might justify the question "Why Didn't They Resist *More?*" Finally, without completely transcending the questions addressed by Middleton-Kaplan and Lang, Nechama Tec presents a panoramic overview of Jewish resistance against the Nazis in "Jewish Resistance: Facts, Omissions, and Distortions." Tec concentrates on armed resistance and "unarmed humane resistance," particularly in Eastern Europe. Her essay focuses on three interrelated issues: how Jewish underground activities and resistance emerged and what forms they took; what conditions promote resistance and to what extent these conditions were available to the Jews; and how Jewish and non-Jewish underground efforts and resistance compare.

The eight essays of our second section deal with Jewish resistance in France, Belgium, Italy, Greece, Holland, Scandinavia, and the Yishuv. In 1940, France had by far the largest Jewish population (somewhere between 320,000 and 350,000) among Western European countries studied here and, Italy excepted, the lowest percentage of Jewish victims slaughtered by the Nazis (76,000; roughly 25 percent). France's Jewish population was, comparatively speaking, more than five times that of Belgium and more than seven times that of Italy. As previously mentioned, geography played a big role in France and, particularly after November 1942, when there was no longer an Unoccupied Zone,

Jews escaped over the Pyrenees into Spain and over the Alps into Switzerland. Approximately 44,000 did so between 1940 and 1944 and another estimated 30,000 found temporary shelter (until September 1943) by fleeing to the eight départements left in the hands of the Italians in November 1942. In "Up in Arms: Jewish Resistance against Nazi Germany in France," Nathan Bracher focuses on armed resistance and explains how resistance, both armed and unarmed, evolved over time according to the changing realities of war and the status of Germany's occupation of the country. He underscores the fact that in France Jews resisted in greater numbers than their non-Jewish counterparts, noting that in London, for example, in La France Libre with General Charles de Gaulle, Jews were six times more numerous than they were in the French population. Jews in all groups—native-born Jews (40 percent), foreign Jews living in France (40 percent) and naturalized Jewish-French citizens (20 percent)—were active resisters against the Nazis in armed combat and clandestine resistance, in the maquis and in all-Jewish outfits such as the Armée juive. Bracher brings to light the interesting fact that certain famous Jewish resisters, such as Pierre Mendès France, Marc Bloch, Raymond Aubrac, and Jean Cavaillès, to name only a few, made it abundantly clear that they were resisting in the name of the democratic institutions of the French Republic, not as members of a separate group. For her part, Nancy Lefenfeld demonstrates that "unarmed humanitarian resistance" was much more widespread in France than armed resistance and constituted the chief means of resisting the enemy within the country itself. In "Unarmed Combat: Jewish Humanitarian Resistance in France during the Shoah," she first underscores the massive legal "relief work" performed by Jewish organizations during the first two years of the Occupation (1940–42) and then, while this legal "relief work" continued, the illegal, clandestine "humanitarian resistance" that would begin in mid-1942 and continue until the end of the war. This humanitarian resistance, most often in conjunction with non-Jewish organizations, clergy, and lay helpers, included making false papers, hiding Jewish people "in plain sight" (under a different identity), and helping other Jewish persons to cross borders into safer areas in France and into countries that were not persecuting Jews. Lefenfeld maintains that the longer the war lasted, the more sympathy the average French person had for the plight of the Jews and, compared to other countries, Jews hiding in France fared well.

Of Belgium's 1940 Jewish population which numbered between 56,000 and 60,000, 94 percent were foreigners. They were, therefore, an especially vulnerable group. Poor and with little government protection, living mainly in Brussels and Antwerp, 45 percent of them would be slaughtered by the Nazis. But, as Suzanne Vromen reports in "Unique Aspects of Jewish Armed Resistance and Rescue in Belgium," hundreds of these foreign Jews, often Communists or Communist leaning and always anti-Fascist, fought fiercely in Jewish groups or Communist organizations to obstruct the German war machine in every way possible, working in intelligence, running clandestine presses, sabotaging factories, garages, and offices, and assassinating collaborating mayors and even a Jewish member of the Association des Juifs en Belgique (AJB), deemed a collaborator for facilitating deportations by establishing files of Belgium's Jews and sending out bogus "employment cards." Vromen narrates one gripping tale after another of rescue and resistance, including the May 1943 rescue of fourteen girls and their monitor from the Convent of the Holy Savior in a suburb of Brussels by partisans belonging to the Front de l'Indépendance (FI), which considered saving Jews part of its work, and the attack on the XXth deportation convoy on April 19, 1943, which was headed from Belgium to Auschwitz. This relatively unsuccessful attack constituted the only attempt anywhere in Europe to halt a train heading to the gas chambers. Particularly noteworthy in Belgian resistance was the sustained, courageous work of the Comité de Défense des Juifs (CDJ), a Jewish organization with ties to the FI, that issued false papers and ration cards and, with the help of non-Jews, often priests, nuns, and lay persons, succeeded in rescuing at least 2,400 children and helping an estimated 10,000 adults.

At approximately 47,000 in 1938, the Jewish population in Italy was comparable in size to that of Belgium, but the proportion of Jews killed (16 percent) was far less. Unlike Belgium's Jews, Italy's were overwhelmingly citizens of their country and, as Ariella Lang stresses in "Resistance and Italian Jews in Wartime Italy," they collectively experienced a "culture of belonging," which not only meant that, unlike their fellow Jews in France and Belgium, they did not form a separate Jewish resistance, but they did not normally react as a function of their ethnicity. To make her point, Lang indicates that the same proportion of Italian Jews became Fascists (one out of three adults) as non-Jewish Italians. Nonetheless, the number of Jews who opposed Fascism from the beginning, insisting on social justice and practicing "political resistance," was proportionately greater than that of the general population. In September 1943, after Mussolini was deposed and resistance against the Nazis began, Jewish identity was a factor in getting Jews to resist. There was, for example, a disproportionately large number of Jews, roughly 1,000, in the armed resistance.

But the greatest number of Italian Jews fought primarily as Italians and for the end of Fascism and the reconstitution of the state of Italy, which had accepted Jews and other minorities. Let us note too that hundreds of Italian Jews and foreign Jews living in Italy joined Italian partisan bands and Communist partisan groups and aided in clandestine operations for British and American intelligence services while, on the home front, many other Italian Jews were involved in relief services for the Jewish community and in the hiding of Jews in non-Jewish homes and institutions.

Eighty percent of Greece's Jews (64,000 of the prewar total of 80,000), two-thirds of whom lived in Salonika, were murdered by the Nazis. But Steven Bowman argues passionately in "Greek Responses to the Nazis in the Mountains and in the Camps" that this slaughter had nothing to do with passivity on their part. On the contrary, they embodied the fierce fighting spirit of the Greeks and their strong nationalism. As in Italy, no separate Jewish resistance developed in wartime Greece; Jews and gentiles fought side by side. Among the 16,000 who survived the Shoah, 10,000 fled to the mountains, male and female, young and old, to resist with partisan groups. Roughly 1,000 men and women fought with the partisans; thousands of others served the Resistance as doctors, nurses, translators, agricultural specialists, laundresses, recruiters, cooks, and social workers. Bowman reports that 300 Greek Jews were among those who prepared the October 7, 1944, revolt in Birkenau that resulted in the destruction of Crematorium 4, and that, in July 1944, 400 others from Corfu chose the gas chamber rather than serve as sonderkommandos. No other group has this distinction.

A large proportion of the 102,000 Jews living in Holland (78 percent) also perished. Unlike France and Greece, there was no place to hide, no escape routes, and a lack of mountains and forests in which partisan bases could be established. But, as Yehudi Lindeman and Hans de Vries make clear in their essay entitled "'Therefore Be Courageous, Too': Jewish Resistance and Rescue in the Netherlands," Dutch Jews did resist, even if they lacked strong resistance leaders and had a deep respect for authority that ultimately worked against their safety. Like the Jews in Greece, it was not passivity on their part that accounted for their demise. First of all, 1,600 Jews managed to escape to England. Then, in early 1941, hit squads (*knokploegen*) were organized to fight Dutch-Nazi thugs attempting to rob Jews and destroy their property. During the first two years, there was little Dutch resistance for Jews to join. By mid-1943, 80 percent of Dutch Jewry had already been deported. Nonetheless, progressively, in Jewish groups and much more widely in Communist organizations and in secular

Patrick Henry

Dutch resistance networks, Jews resisted by making false papers, attacking prisons and liberating prisoners, raiding registration facilities and destroying files, assassinating Dutch Nazis and collaborators, and rescuing an estimated 2,000 children and adults, including somewhere between 700 and 1,100 Jewish babies and young children over a nine-month period from a day care center in Amsterdam.

In the Scandinavian countries, the focus has always been on the Danes and the Swedes, not on the Jews. In "Between Accommodation and Awareness: Jewish Resistance in Scandinavia under Nazism," Cecilie Felicia Stokholm Banke underscores this point and the glaring lack of attention to Jewish resistance in Denmark and Norway and to Jewish support of resistance in neutral Sweden. Before the October 1943 rescue by which 7,000 Danish Jews found refuge in Sweden, the Jewish community in Denmark was lying low, trying not to provoke antisemitic feelings and jeopardize their situation while attempting to help recently arrived Eastern European Jewish refugees. The Danish Jewish community established a center that provided financial assistance to 1,300 refugees. When, with Danish help, the Jews fled to Sweden, they were not passive passengers. They took pains to safeguard their properties and helped to organize their transportation. Many did not make it and were arrested and sent to Theresienstadt. Banke also points out that some young agricultural students escaped to Palestine, while the "Brothers Bohr" (Niels and Harald) were highly successful in their efforts to get German Jewish scientists and mathematicians out of Germany and into Denmark. Norway's Jewish population of 2,100 was the smallest of any occupied country; there German action was quick and unexpected. Even though the Jewish community had little time to mobilize, over 60 percent (1,300 people) managed to reach Sweden, many with the help of an underground network organized by Jews in Norway. Others resisted by not registering and hiding their true identities. With regard to Sweden, Banke particularly underscores the decisive role played by the Jewish community in Stokholm, which helped more than 500 Jewish children brought from Germany and a nearly equal number of German Jewish agricultural students many of whom would move on to Palestine and other countries.

Finally, in "Organizing Jewish Resistance: The Decision-Making and Executive Array in Yishuv Rescue Operations during the Holocaust," Tuvia Friling tracks the executive echelon that dealt with the Yishuv's attempts to rescue European Jews from the Holocaust. He mentions the great Yishuv successes in this area (helping Jews survive in hiding; sending 30,000 men and women to fight in the British Army; the development of paramilitary partnerships with British and American intelligence services) but, citing the internal problems of the Rescue Committee, the rigidity of the British Mandate, and indigenous opposition to mass immigration of Jews into Palestine, he focuses more generally on the failure of the grand rescue projects aimed at bringing hundreds of thousands of Jewish children to Palestine, failures that occurred despite the fact that these projects were entrusted, contrary to popular wisdom, to the finest servants the Yishuv had to offer.

The third section of our volume contains three essays and is entitled "Children as Resisters and Music as Resistance." In the literature of the Holocaust, the focus has primarily been on adults. As Debórah Dwork made abundantly clear in 1991, "children are conspicuously, glaringly, and screamingly silently absent."[37] But not here. Two of our essays deal solely with children's resistance. In "Raising Their Voices: Children's Resistance through Diary Writing and Song," Dwork analyses the diaries of six European Jewish children under German rule, boys and girls twelve to fourteen years of age when they began writing, of rural and urban origin, from all parts of Europe. These diaries were written at home, in hiding, in ghettos, in transit camps. Three of the children survived; three did not. Despite all these differences, what the children wrote about is remarkably similar. They kept a record of their experiences, thinking them through, trying to learn to cope, as if they were speaking to a close friend. They describe daily life in the places where they are, at once joking about the stars they wear, relating the terrible suffering of those around them, and attempting to create a semblance of normality in a life gone mad. They write about their education having been interrupted and their attempts to learn from the plays, music, and lectures in the ghettos and transit camps. All these children talk about their parents, whether they are still living with them or without them while hiding alone in non-Jewish homes. Their diaries suggest that the most common cultural activity in which children engaged was making music and singing. They sang out loud, even in Hebrew during *Oneg Shabbat* (the Jewish welcoming of the Sabbath) in camps and ghettos, and often while being deported, as if, Dwork suggests, to affirm their existence, and by saying "we are here," their resistance. The children's attempts to educate themselves, to prepare for the future, and to cultivate relationships with their parents and friends demonstrate the failure of the Nazi project of dehumanization. The writing it-

37. Dwork, *Children with a Star*, 253.

self, and what it reveals, affirms what the Nazis denied: the Jewish children's worth as human beings. Joanna Beata Michlic, for her part, in "An Untold Story of Rescue: Jewish Children and Youth in German-Occupied Poland," presents what she considers "the most under-researched aspect of Jewish self-help," namely, the moral and physical support older children and youth, male and female, bestowed on other, generally younger, children. She makes her case by mining "ego documents" (memoirs, diaries, letters, interviews, and oral histories) of Jewish children and teenage survivors. This type of physical and moral support included gathering and sharing food, finding shelters and hiding together, general camaraderie and emotional support, teaching younger children how to survive, how to behave, how to recite Christian prayers, where to find food and clothing, and sometimes even providing them with false identity papers; and, at great risk, smuggling them out of the ghetto into Christian orphanages. Because they could steal food, run fast, and move more easily in and out of the ghettos, children often became providers for their own families.

In "Music as Resistance," Nick Strimple surveys the importance of music as a vehicle for resistance in prewar Germany, in Eastern European ghettos, in Western transit and civilian internment camps, in forced labor and death camps, and, finally, in Terezin, which housed so many of Prague's artists and musicians. Even under horrific conditions, where people were slowly starved to death, men and women could not live on bread alone. They hungered for culture as well, and art and music often found an important place in their lives. Strimple focuses on the instances when music provided the impetus to move beyond basic survival and "actually shake a collective fist in the face of National Socialism." The large ghettos all had organized concerts and cabarets; street performances were a vital part of Yiddish culture. Just before the mass deportations from Warsaw to Treblinka in June 1942, a large children's chorus performed a farewell concert in the Moriah Synagogue. Strimple underscores the importance of the sixteen performances of Verdi's *Requiem*, given by inmates of Terezin under the direction of Raphael Schaechter between September 1943 and October 1944. These performances confronted Nazi officers in attendance with the specter of a Judgment Day. As a Terezin survivor told me recently in Portland, Oregon: "We were able to sing to the Nazis what we could not say to them." Music in the camps and the ghettos provided an emotional escape as well as a defiant reaffirmation of one's humanity in the presence of those who would deny it.

The nine essays that constitute the final section of our volume address Jewish resistance in Central and Eastern Europe. Dieter Kuntz's "Jewish Resistance in Nazi Germany and Austria, 1933–45" provides a detailed, chronological account of the evolution of resistance activities. Most German Jews strongly identified with their homeland and were patriotic. They joined anti-Nazi Socialist and Communist organizations, not as Jews but as Germans. Yet, even in pre-1933 Germany, there were all-Jewish groups combating anti-Jewish activity. Kuntz focuses on the Central Association of German Citizens of the Jewish Faith (CV) which numbered 70,000 in the 1920s and worked with Social Democratic groups and Christian organizations to fight against the growing antisemitism. During the first two years of German rule (1933–34), some 60,000 Jews fled Germany. The Jews who remained resisted in numbers greatly out of proportion to their numbers within the German population. Jewish resistance was greater in 1933–34 before the 1935 Nuremberg Laws, but clandestine Jewish resistance activities continued until the end of the war. Kuntz looks closely at the workings of the Herbert Baum Group and the amazing rescue tactics at the Jewish Hospital in Berlin. He estimates that more than 3,000 German Jews resisted the Nazis between 1933–45, 2,000 of whom, male and female, were actively involved in the leftist resistance groups that he studies. Also, by 1935, more than half of all young German Jews had joined Jewish youth movements. Many identified with Zionism: between 1933 and 1936, 7,000 German Jews emigrated to Palestine. This was no longer possible after October 1941. In Austria too, the changed political situation (after the 1938 Anschluss), marked by increased discrimination and surveillance, made it more difficult for Jews and non-Jews to resist the new regime. Almost immediately, 130,000 Austrians, mostly Jews, fled the country. Many of those Jews who remained continued to resist Nazi efforts to disenfranchise, expel, and annihilate them by engaging in subversive, underground activities, by crossing borders, and by helping young Austrian Jews escape to Palestine. An estimated 600 to 700 Austrian Jews survived in hiding, mostly in Vienna.

In Eastern Europe, Jews were rounded up and herded into ghettos, city blocks that were physically separated from surrounding areas by means of barriers. Ghettoization was employed by the Nazis as a means of facilitating forced labor, dehumanization, and physical weakening of the Jewish population; and it was a prelude to deportation and death. Life in the ghetto was characterized by severe overcrowding (several families sharing a single apartment), lack of sanitation, lack of food, and prevalence of disease. The ghettos established in Warsaw, Vilna, Lodz, Minsk, and Theresienstadt were the largest. Dozens of others existed in occupied Poland and the Soviet Union (for example, in Lvov,

Patrick Henry

Lublin, Bedzin, Czestochowa, Bialystok, Kovno, Cracow, Piotrków, Riga, and Dvinsk). In "'Three Lines in History?' Modes of Jewish Resistance in Eastern European Ghettos," Dalia Ofer lets us hear the voices of the ghetto inmates who resisted in the midst of death, disease, and starvation. She relates tales of bravery by armed Jewish resisters in the ghettos in Warsaw and Cracow, who fought to redeem Jewish honor. One such resister, Dolek Liebskind of Cracow, expressed the sentiments of many: "We did not want to be led like sheep to the slaughter." But Ofer concentrates on examples of "passive resistance" found in the daily life of ghetto inmates, who, defying Nazi intentions, did their best to lead normal lives. She finds such examples in ways of dealing with forced labor, in securing provisions (smuggling food and medicines into the ghettos), in living spiritually (cultural and educational activities, reading, keeping diaries), and explains clearly how this system of accommodation and avoidance, compliance and defiance, which, because of the inmates' refusal of total resignation, enabled them to see themselves correctly, not as passive victims, but as active fighters. Ofer's gender awareness adds another level to her contribution as she studies the family unit under Nazi oppression and women in the underground.

In "Jewish Resistance in the Warsaw Ghetto," Avinoam Patt tackles the largest mass revolt in a major city in German-occupied Europe and the defining symbol of Jewish resistance to Nazi oppression during World War II. From the outbreak of the war to the creation of the ghetto, the formation of the Judenrat and the establishment of a grass roots system of social welfare within the ghetto, Patt meticulously paints in detailed chronological fashion the broader underground activity which eventually laid the groundwork for the organization of armed resistance, largely by the leaders of youth movements who had been engaged in multiple forms of nonviolent resistance up to the point when it finally became clear that the Nazi plan was for the total elimination of the Jews. We are introduced to all the key, youth-led movements (Hashomer Hatzair, Akiva, Dror, Betar, and the Bund) and meet all the central players: Adam Czerniakow, head of the Judenrat under the Nazis; Emanuel Ringelblum, organizer of the underground Oyneg Shabes Archive; and dozens of youth leaders, including Marek Edelman, Antek Zuckerman, and Mordecai Anielewicz. In addition, Patt elucidates the innumerable nonviolent acts of resistance (cultural, religious, and educational) that took place in the ghetto on a daily basis for months before the April to May 1943 uprising. Finally, he offers a moving account of the uprising itself, led by the underequipped and outnumbered Jewish warriors of the ZZW and the ZOB who, with no chance for victory against the overpowering and vicious German war machine, struggled to the end to exact some revenge and to die with honor.

In "Courage to Defy: Jews of the Independent State of Croatia Fight Back, 1941–45," Esther Gitman analyzes Jewish resistance against the Axis powers and their local collaborators, the Croatian Ustaše, in the Independent State of Croatia (NDH), which, at that time, after the partition of Yugoslavia in April 1941, included Bosnia and Herzegovina. She points out that most Jews were poorly advised by their leaders and stayed put, not taking Hitler or the anti-semitism of their countrymen as seriously as they should have. Yet Nazi racial ideology prevailed and within four months, the Ustaše government had implemented many of the policies that would destroy the Jews economically, cultur-ally, and finally physically. Based on interviews she conducted with Jewish World War II survivors from the area, and diaries and memoirs she examined, Gitman elucidates the forms of resistance she encountered. For one thing, more than 1,600 Jews joined the partisans; some fought, others served as doctors, nurses, teachers, journalists, or cooks. Jews who remained in the cities mount-ed vigorous relief programs, providing food and clothing for the impoverished in their own communities, for Jews imprisoned in nearby concentration camps, and for Jews on passing transports. Finally, these same organizations sought various ways of rescuing children via Turkey into Palestine.

Romania joined the Axis in November 1940. But thousands of its Jews were killed first by their fellow countrymen (led by the fascist Iron Guard party) and then by the Romanian army, before the Germans got to them. Ultimately 270,000 of Romania's prewar 609,000 Jews were slaughtered during World War II. Ştefan Ionescu points out that there was no Jewish armed resistance against the Ion Antonescu regime because there was no armed resistance whatsoever. The regime was popular and any armed Jewish revolt would have been immedi-ately and savagely defeated. Instead, Jews employed a series of strategies of re-sistance: conversion, spiritual resistance, and intra-communitarian aid (rescue and emigration). But in "Legal Tools Instead of Weapons: Jewish Resistance to the State Takeover of Urban Real Estate and Businesses during the Antonescu Regime, 1940–44," Ionescu focuses on Jewish resistance to Antonescu's anti-semitic policies, namely, his attempt at the Romanianization or Aryanization of urban Jewish real estate and businesses. His study is based on official docu-ments and personal narratives that demonstrate that Jews used legalities (judi-cial contestation) and illegalities (sabotage and camouflage) to hang on to their homes, real estate, and businesses. Their failure to do so would have removed them from the economy and led to starvation, homelessness, and deportation to Transnistria. These cases took time and there were, for example, tens of thousands of them regarding homes and apartments. Over time, the situation in Romania changed radically. When, toward the end of 1942, Antonescu believed that Germany would lose the war, his tactics changed accordingly. He canceled his plans to deport Romanian Jews to the Belzec death camp and made new plans to send them to Palestine. The shifting fate of the Axis may have also accounted for the luck Jews were having in the courts fighting to retain their properties. In any event, we see, once again, that the fate of the Jews and how the Jews themselves reacted, in some places at least, had a lot to do with how the war was going.

For his part, Yehuda Bauer refuses the term "passive resistance," because the word "resistance" implies activity of some sort. In "Jewish Resistance in the Ukraine and Belarus during the Holocaust," Bauer includes all resistance, armed (with either firearms or "cold" weapons) and unarmed (spiritual, educational, religious, smuggling of food and medicines) as active resistance. Only 1 to 2 percent of Jews living under German rule in Belarus and the Ukraine survived the war. The Jews here were taken by surprise, and the annihilation of tens of thousands of them by the Einsatzgruppen and Ukrainian militias was rapid and took place before the Jews had time to become fully aware of their fate, much less organize any opposition. In an atmosphere where there was little, if any, chance for either armed or unarmed resistance, Bauer finds two striking cases of unarmed communal resistance. One took place in Shargorod (a small town in southern Ukraine) where the Romanian Jewish community's Bucharest center helped the inmates in Shargorod's ghetto to establish a livable situation in the midst of a typhoid epidemic. The second occurred in the town of Mogilev Podolski but with much greater numbers. Here health care, soup kitchens, and fairness in forced labor details saved hundreds of lives. In eastern Belarus's capital, Minsk, a large ghetto was set up, in which Jewish groups practiced armed and unarmed resistance (setting up a hospital, welfare services, and a school). In what Bauer considers "arguably, numerically the most significant case of Jewish armed resistance during the Holocaust," the Minsk Jewish underground smuggled 7,500 Jews into the surrounding dense forest, where many of them joined the Soviet partisans. Bauer estimates that of the roughly 23,000 Jews who escaped into the Belorussian forests, some 15,000 fought as partisans while the rest tried to survive in hiding.

More than two-thirds of Slovakia's Jews were annihilated by the Nazis. In "Jewish Resistance in Slovakia, 1938–45," Hana Kubátová analyzes the resistance activities of the entire Jewish community in Slovakia. She covers the period from the declaration of Slovakian autonomy to the fall of the wartime state. Her goal is to present historical evidence that argues against the cooperation and collaboration of the victims. She does so chronologically, elucidating the immediate efforts of Zionist groups of various political persuasions to arrange emigration to Palestine for all those interested. More generally, she explains how these same groups provided vocational training to facilitate emigration, not only to Palestine but to countries, like Hungary, which offered relative safety until 1944. She includes early baptism as a method of resistance that managed to save entire families and, as we have already seen in Romania, Jewish attempts to remain economically stable so as to fight off the increasing process of Aryanization, concentration, and deportation. When the first wave of deportations took place, between March and October 1942, more Jews fled the country and others went into hiding. Two Jewish religious organizations wrote letters of protest to President (and Catholic priest) Josef Tiso, as did the rabbis of Slovakia. There were also efforts to bribe key officials to stop the deportations and the Working Group attempted to bribe the Germans to allow 7,000 Jews to emigrate to Switzerland. Finally, when the Slovak National Uprising took place in September 1944, 1,500 Jews joined the partisans and fought the Germans on all fronts and 250 Jewish men from the Novaky forced labor camp formed an entirely Jewish partisan unit.

More than 500,000 Hungarian Jews were slaughtered by the Nazis, but armed Jewish resistance in Hungary during the Holocaust was basically nonexistent. In "Defying Genocide: Jewish Resistance and Self-Rescue in Hungary," Gábor Kádár, Christine Schmidt van der Zanden, and Zoltán Vági explain why. Hungarian Jews had no arms and, like the situation in Romania, there was no relevant non-Jewish anti-Nazi resistance that Jews could join. In addition, the gentile population was largely indifferent, and, as in Holland, the countryside lacked dense forests, where one might hide. Perhaps, above all, there was no time. When Germany occupied Hungary, in March 1944, the country still had a Jewish population of 800,000 and Eichmann went to work with a fury. As swift as lightning, Jews were singled out, crowded into ghettos, and deported: in fifty-six days, from May 15 to July 9, unbelievably, 437,000 Jews were deported. Nothing like this occurred anywhere else in occupied Europe. Nevertheless, as our authors make clear, tens of thousands of Hungarian Jews did resist German orders and intentions by hiding, escaping, supplying, and rescuing themselves and fellow Jews. Thirty thousand Hungarian Jews survived the war in hiding, mostly in Budapest. There were even a few examples of armed Jewish resistance in Hungary by labor servicemen and young Zionists who bought their arms on the black market, as well as armed resistance by Hungarian Jews in the French Resistance and those 450 Hungarian Jews in the sonderkommando unit that rebelled in Birkenau. But, in Hungary, it was mainly unarmed Jewish resistance, mostly accomplished by a network of left-wing Zionist youth organizations which provided false documents, hid Jewish people all over the country, and helped thousands of Hungarian Jews to reach Slovakia, Romania, and Yugoslav areas. The Jewish Council established in Budapest in 1944 may have been tragically mistaken but it worked to ease the situation of the Jews by offering health care and spiritual and religious care as well. It also cooperated illegally in the rescuing of Jews.

Fittingly, our volume ends in the camps, where the victims of Nazi oppression had their last chance to resist. In "Resistance in the Camps," Robert Jan van Pelt takes a full-range approach by first studying the onslaught that the inmates suffered in the various camps and which they sought to resist. His typological analysis seeks to understand the reality of the camps by comparing and contrasting different ideal types: Paradise, Hades, Purgatory, Hell, and Gehenna. Paradise, according to van Pelt's categories which build on those of Hannah Arendt, included German betterment camps, created by the Nazi regime to reeducate and resocialize German youth and from which Jews were forbidden. Here individuals were encouraged or forced to surrender some of their rights to a larger community. In Hades, one's legal rights were suspended; more generally, the juridical person was annihilated. Resistance here included all efforts to restore the rights of the inmates and all attempts by the inmates to maintain their psychic health (keeping a diary, going to religious services). Hades would include internment camps established to get rid of undesirables, such as refugees, asocials, and stateless people, especially Jews who were not considered human. Purgatory, the site of the classical concentration camp, was where the moral person also comes under attack. Inmates were divided into groups (politicals, gypsies, homosexuals, Jews) designed to pit everyone against everyone else. All attempts to create solidarity in a situation that militated against its very possibility (sharing food, blankets, pairing off in twos) constituted resistance. The death camps constituted Hell where, finally, after the death of the juridical and moral persons, one's individuality was at stake.

The tattoo in Auschwitz replaced one's name and all attempts to avoid a bestial existence (washing one's face, walking erect, praying) constituted resistance. In Gehenna, the place of physical death, van Pelt discusses the revolts of the sonderkommandos in Treblinka in August 1943, in Sobibor in October 1943, and in Auschwitz-Birkenau in October 1944. He also records as resistance the escape from Auschwitz of two persons who sought to warn the Hungarians of their impending slaughter, and to one of whom, Rudi Vrba, he dedicates his essay.

This volume is nothing if not a collaborative effort. We have tried to cover almost all the occupied countries with as little repetition as possible, to look carefully at the ghettos, forests, and camps, and to consider the special status of children of the Holocaust and various forms of artistic resistance to Nazi oppression. Our collective task was not only to put to rest the myth of "Jewish passivity" during the Holocaust but to elucidate and enumerate the various forms of Jewish resistance, violent and nonviolent, during the Shoah, indicating that how the Jews resisted was in large part contingent upon where they were located, how the war was advancing, and how indigenous non-Jewish populations were disposed toward them. In each particular country and within each locale, Jewish resistance was shaped by political, military, social, economic, geographic, and legal realities. Types of actions feasible in one area were not feasible in another. Similarly, what was necessary and achievable at one point in time was judged not to be so at another point in time. Jewish resistance did not occur in a vacuum; the attitudes, actions, and support of the non-Jewish population could render certain forms of resistance possible or impossible. The fact that reliable information was generally unavailable to the persecuted also must be kept in mind.

Our ultimate goal has been to produce a reasonably comprehensive handbook on Jewish resistance against the Nazis, an indispensable guide for Holocaust scholars as well as general readers. Our volume enters a world where the idea of Jewish passivity, as Richard Middleton-Kaplan notes, has "hardened into received wisdom." Despite the failure of earlier attempts to dislodge this myth from the popular mentality, we hope somehow to offset its tenacious persistence.

First of all, as they move from country to country, from ghettos to forests to camps, our contributors have compiled the most convincing, complete, and authoritative mass of evidence ever advanced in one volume in opposition to the myth of Jewish passivity during the Holocaust. Secondly, our volume enters a world where, roughly seventy years after the liberation of the camps, Christian apologies to the Jews and burgeoning examples of interfaith reconciliation offer a ray of hope that whatever residue of anti-Judaism and antisemitism still embedded at the heart of this myth might be eliminated.[38] It is into this world of interfaith dialogue, reconciliation, and peace building, that we send our volume to be read, studied, and discussed by entire communities, to educate, not simply clerics and scholars, but students of all belief systems and all ages.

38. *"Dabru Emet"* (Speak the Truth), *New York Times*, September 10, 2000, 23, without negating the history of Christian anti-Judaism nor the fact that "without the long history of Christian anti-Judaism and Christian violence against Jews, Nazi ideology could not have taken hold nor could it have been carried out," urges Jewish people to relinquish their fears of Christianity and to acknowledge church efforts since the Holocaust to amend Christian teaching about Judaism. Consult too: Patrick Henry, "The Art of Christian Apology: Comparing the French Catholic Church's Apology to the Jews and the Vatican's 'We Remember,'" *Shofar* 26 (Spring 2008): 87–104. As regards post- 9/11 efforts at Jewish, Christian, and Muslim solidarity, consult the following documents: "A Common Word Between Us and You" (October 11, 2007) at www.acommonword.com; "Loving God and Neighbor Together. A Christian Response to 'A Common Word Between Us and You'" in "Week In Review" (New York Times, November 18, 2007, 4); "A Call to Peace, Dialogue and Understanding Between Muslims and Jews" (February 25, 2008) at www.mujca.com/MuslimsandJews.htm, and "Seek Peace and Pursue It" (March 3, 2008) at www.wfn.org/2008/03/msg00012.html.

Part 1

Myths and Facts

Richard Middleton-Kaplan

1   The Myth of Jewish Passivity

One aim of our volume is to demonstrate definitively that Jews during the Holocaust did not go passively like sheep to slaughter. One might ask why such a project is necessary given the voluminous evidence attesting to the fact that Jews resisted the Nazis whenever, wherever, and however it was possible. The compelling evidence has simply done little to change a nearly universal perception. Built from stereotypes and simplifications, reinforced by the ever-looming iconography of emaciated victims staring out helplessly from behind concentration camp barbed wire, and perpetuated through cinema, the muddled supposition that Jews went like sheep to slaughter has hardened into received wisdom, petrifying into a rock-solid wall of common belief seemingly impervious to demolition, no matter how much historical evidence can be marshalled against it.

My intent is not to disprove the myth, but rather to explore its roots and tenacious persistence. If that still-standing wall is ever to collapse, we must understand the reason it has such a strong foundation in our imagination and in our reason. To do so, we must explore the origins of the myth—origins which give the idea of Jews going like sheep to slaughter a cultural hold that predates the Holocaust.

Origins: The Bible to the Ghetto

Just as Hitler's anti-Judaism drew on centuries of antisemitic stereotypes that took on a new form during the Holocaust, so too the idea of Jews going like sheep to slaughter has a long history. The image dates back to the Hebrew Bi-

3

ble, from Isaiah 53:7, where we find an account of a favored servant of the Lord who: "was oppressed, though he humbled himself / And opened not his mouth; / As a lamb that is led to the slaughter, / And as a sheep that before her shearers is dumb; / Yea he opened not his mouth."[1] The passage does not construe the lamb-like servant's silence as a failed protest against slaughterers but rather as praiseworthy because there was no "deceit in his mouth" (Isaiah 53:9).

Rabbi Abraham Joshua Heschel cautions against being misled here: "Yet, Second Isaiah does not passively accept Zion's lot. Far from being silent, he challenges the Lord." In subsequent verses, Isaiah "voices his bewilderment at the silence of the Almighty" and protests because "Israel's misery seemed out of all proportion to her guilt."[2] Heschel's commentary suggests a poignant awareness of Isaiah 53:7 in relation to the Holocaust.

The image of going like sheep to slaughter is positively presented elsewhere in the Jewish *Holy Scriptures*. For example, Psalm 44 describes the suffering and martyrdom of people whom God "hast given ... like sheep to be eaten" (Ps 44:12). Despite this, the people do not forsake God or seek another deity. Rather, they maintain faith unto death: "Nay, but for Thy sake are we killed all the day; / We are accounted as sheep for the slaughter" (Ps 44:23).

This psalm ends with a plea that seems chillingly prophetic in the aftermath of the Holocaust:

> Awake, why sleepest Thou, O Lord?
> Arouse Thyself, cast not off for ever.
> Wherefore hidest Thou Thy face,
> And forgettest our affliction and oppression?
> For our soul is bowed down to the dust;
> Our belly cleaveth unto the earth.
> Arise for our help,
> And redeem us for Thy mercy's sake. (Ps 44:24–27)

Here, becoming sheep for slaughter does not imply passive acceptance of fate, but is coupled with a cry to arouse a slumbering God, a demand for explanation, and a call upon God to act.

Observant Jews say the words "sheep to slaughter" two times a week. The liturgy for morning prayers (*Shacharis*) on Mondays and Thursdays before the Torah reading includes a prayer called *Tachanun*, which adapts wording from Psalm 44:23: "Look from heaven and perceive that we have become an object

---

1. *The Holy Scriptures, According to the Masoretic Text* (Philadelphia: Jewish Publication Society of America, 1955), Isaiah 53:7, 605. Subsequent biblical quotations are from this edition.

2. Abraham Joshua Heschel, *The Prophets* (1962; New York: Harper Perennial, 2001), 185–87.

of scorn and derision among the nations; we are regarded as the sheep led to slaughter, to be killed, destroyed, beaten, and humiliated. But despite all this we have not forgotten Your Name—we beg You not to forget us."[3]

The phrase also occurs in relation to Jewish martyrdom in the Babylonian Talmud, in Tractate Gittin, Folio 57b, which recounts the heroism of Jewish children who threw themselves into the sea rather than be carried off by Romans for immoral purposes. A sage in the Talmudic discussion remarks, "Of them the text says, Yea, for thy sake we are killed all the day long, we are counted as sheep for the slaughter."[4] In being so counted, they are comforted: "since we are dying for the sake of God's name, our deaths bother us no more than the slaughter of sheep."[5]

Rabbi Yisrael Rutman discusses the positive implications of the phrase:

The Maharsha in his classic commentary on the Talmud explains the phrase "sheep to the slaughter" in a manner strikingly different from what we are used to. It had nothing to do with humiliating passivity. It means that death to these giants of faith was something that they faced as casually as sheep going to the slaughter, free of the dread and terror otherwise associated with a violent demise. Theirs were acts of faith and courage, not cowardice and despair.[6]

As Christianity developed, going to death like "sheep to slaughter" retained a positive connotation, though for different reasons. Whereas Talmudic sages had interpreted it as indicative of martyrdom, for Christians the phrase embodied the virtue of meekness and prefigured Christ's sacrifice of himself as lamb of God. Nineteenth-century Presbyterian pastor Albert Barnes, for example, contemplated the "pains and sorrows" Jesus bore and concluded that "the fact that he did not open his mouth in complaint was therefore the more remarkable, and made the merit of his sufferings the greater."[7] He celebrated Christ's "perfectly quiet, meek, submissive, patient" endurance of agonies, and marveled at Isaiah 53:7 as prophetic typology: "How strikingly and literally was this fulfilled in the life of the Lord Jesus! It would seem almost as if it had been

3. *The Complete ArtScroll Siddur: Weekday/Sabbath/Festival*, trans. Rabbi Nosson Scherman, ed. Rabbi Nosson Scherman and Rabbi Meir Zlotowitz, ArtScroll Mesorah Series (Brooklyn, N.Y.: Mesorah, 1990), 135.

4. *Babylonian Talmud: Tractate Gittin*, Gittin 57b, par. 4, accessed July 4, 2011, http://www.come-and-hear.com/gittin/gittin_57.html.

5. Ibid., note 28. I am grateful to Rabbi Yossi Brackman, Rohr Chabad Jewish Center at the University of Chicago and Hyde Park, for assistance with Talmud and *Tachanun* passages.

6. Rabbi Yisrael Rutman, "Like Sheep to the Slaughter," par. 4 of "History of a Phrase," accessed June 21, 2011, http://www.aish.com/ho/i/48954636.html.

7. Albert Barnes, *Notes on the Bible*, 1834, Notes on Isaiah 53:7, par. 2, accessed July 9, 2011, http://www.sacred-texts.com/bib/cmt/barnes/isa053.htm.

written after he lived, and was history rather than prophecy."[8] In the twentieth century, this typology directly influenced Christian views of the Holocaust. The innocent hanged child of Elie Wiesel's *Night*, for example, becomes a reminder that suffering alongside him on the gallows is "that other Jew, his brother—the Crucified, whose Cross has conquered the World."[9]

"Like sheep to slaughter" remained a familiar phrase during the eighteenth and nineteenth centuries through commentaries such as Barnes's. But praise for Christian meekness was hardly what General George Washington had in mind when addressing officers on March 15, 1783, at army headquarters. He warned that if men are prevented from speaking freely on serious matters, "the freedom of speech may be taken away, and dumb and silent we may be led, like sheep, to the Slaughter."[10] His use of the phrase has acquired a cultural history of its own, as his remark now appears on a wide range of merchandise including t-shirts, mouse pads, maternity wear, coasters, aprons, and even, bizarrely, "Like Sheep to Slaughter" Teddy bears.

This merchandise signifies a life for the idiom "like sheep to slaughter" quite separate from its association with the Holocaust; it seems doubtful that those who buy these items have the Shoah in mind. Their profusion and popularity suggest that the caution against going like sheep to slaughter resonates deeply, its biblical overtones harmonizing with national pride in the echoing spirit of revolutionary resistance. They also demonstrate, although the context differs drastically from Holocaust memory, the phrase's continuing power to conjure the spirit of proud defiance against tyranny and perhaps also a contempt for those who are silenced.

In the context of World War II, "like sheep to slaughter" came from Abba Kovner, a resistance fighter from Vilna. On January 1, 1942, Kovner proclaimed: "We will not be led like sheep to slaughter. True we are weak and helpless, but the only response to the murders is revolt. Brethren, it is better to die fighting like free men than to live at the mercy of the murderers. Arise, Arise with last breath. Take Courage!"[11] Kovner's words were communicated by couriers to

8. Ibid., par. 3.

9. François Mauriac, "Foreword," *Night*, by Elie Wiesel, trans. Stella Rodway (New York: Bantam, 1960), x. For the view of Christ suffering alongside the victims, see also Jürgen Moltmann, *The Crucified God* (Minneapolis: Augsburg Fortress, 1993).

10. *The Writings of George Washington, from the Original Manuscript Sources, 1745–1799*, ed. John C. Fitzpatrick (Washington, D.C.: USGPO, 1938), 26:225.

11. Quoted in Michael Berenbaum and Yitzhak Mais, *Memory and Legacy: The Shoah Narrative of the Illinois Holocaust Museum* (Skokie, Ill.: Illinois Holocaust Museum and Education Center, 2009), 113.

other ghettos, inspiring leaders there to make similar proclamations and take up arms.[12] Dolek Liebeskind of Cracow's underground declared, "For three lines in history that will be written about the youth who fought and did not go like sheep to the slaughter it is even worth dying."[13]

How should we regard Kovner's statement? He was not characterizing other Jews, but trying to inspire those alongside him to revolt. Michael Berenbaum and Yitzchak Mais write that such imagery "is not the judgment of history, not the judgment that can be made by those who were not there, who did not face the circumstances."[14] As Yehuda Bauer suggests, "It was a means of causing people to rebel. [Kovner] meant 'Let us not be like sheep, let us not go to slaughter.' But he didn't see himself or the others as sheep ... by using that metaphor, he tried to cause a rebellion against the very use of that term. I think that was the purpose of using such metaphors during the Holocaust."[15]

Kovner's words became twisted after the Holocaust, when they were erroneously taken as meaning that Jews had gone like sheep to slaughter. A cautionary phrase used acceptably by Kovner became offensive when used judgmentally by others after the Holocaust: "When people used [such metaphors]," Bauer continues, "it was something quite different, and very objectionable. Jews were not sheep. Jews were Jews, Jews were human beings; they were not led to slaughter, but to being murdered, which is something quite different. Therefore, I don't think that we, today, should use a term that was used during the Holocaust with quite a different connotation."[16]

How did this distorted connotation arise? How did going to death like sheep to slaughter change from stirring admiration for brave martyrdom and defiance of oppression to encapsulating victim-blaming contempt for a dehumanized mass thought to have passively accepted—and even aided in—their own destruction? To seek the answer, we must turn to the myth's postwar evolution.

12. Yitzchak Mais, Bonnie Gurewitsch, Barbara Lovenheim, eds., *Daring to Resist: Jewish Defiance in the Holocaust* (New York: Museum of Jewish Heritage, 2007), 108.

13. Quoted in Yehuda Bauer, *Rethinking the Holocaust* (New Haven, Conn.: Yale University Press, 2001), 140–41.

14. Berenbaum and Mais, *Memory and Legacy*, 114.

15. "Like Sheep to the Slaughter?" excerpt from interview with Yehuda Bauer by Amos Goldberg, January 18, 1998, Shoah Resource Center of Yad Vashem, accessed June 15, 2011, http://www.yadvashem.org.

16. Ibid.

The Myth Gains Traction

The perception of Jewish passivity was doubtless seared into the popular mind by newsreel footage of skeletal concentration camp prisoners, as well as the iconic photograph of a Jewish boy from the Warsaw ghetto with his arms raised in surrender—an "indelible image" which "reinforces the perception of Jews going 'like sheep to slaughter.'"[17] Further reinforcement came via images from Nazi propaganda films that were often recycled in postwar Western documentaries because no other footage was available, but without their source as Nazi propaganda identified.

Other groups were imprisoned in concentration and death camps, yet something about the myth makes it adhere particularly to Jews, although the Jewish response to Nazi persecution was not more passive than that of others. On the contrary, of the seven prisoner rebellions in concentration and death camps, six were enacted by Jews; the only other was by Soviet prisoners of war. The myth attaches only to Jews partly because those images of death camp prisoners reinforced centuries-old cultural memory and stereotypes of Jews as sacrificial victims and as weak, passive, and feminine. The Bible mentions idolatrous Jews who willingly sacrifice their children to the god Moloch by burning them in fire (Jeremiah 7:31).[18] Matthew Biberman traces the "conflation of femininity and Judaism" in English Christian culture back to the Renaissance.[19] Other scholars have noted similar conflations in other cultures. Martin Cohen, in following the deleterious effects from the Inquisition to the present, said that "The image of the passive Jew is a generalization that has helped create our false concept of the Holocaust Jew."[20] Nor have such notions faded into the past: In *The Jewish Body* (2009), Melvin Konner posits a direct link between centuries of Jewish bodily weakness and the Holocaust, lamenting, "They tried weakness—oh, how they tried; indeed, they were better versed in it than anyone else on earth. Strength is better."[21] Thus, when images of the Holocaust surfaced, the

17. Eva Fogelman, "On Blaming the Victim," in *Daring to Resist*, ed. Mais, Gurewitsch, Lovenheim, 134.

18. I am grateful to Anthony Levin, Holocaust writer and researcher in English and Related Literature at the University of York, U. K., for alerting me to this reference.

19. Matthew Biberman, *Masculinity, Anti-Semitism and Early Modern English Literature: From the Satanic to the Effeminate Jew* (Hampshire, U.K.: Ashgate, 2004), 1.

20. Martin Cohen, "Culture and Remembrance: Jewish Ambivalence and Antipathy to the History of Resistance," in *Resisting the Holocaust*, ed. Ruby Rohrlich (Oxford: Berg, 1998), 28.

21. Melvin Konner, *The Jewish Body*, Jewish Encounters Series (New York: Nextbook/Schocken, 2009), xiii.

stereotypes were there, ready at hand, capable of absorbing the shocking new photographs into the old mythology of Jews as willing, or at least nonresisting, participants in their own deaths.

Prejudices seamlessly accommodate diametrically opposed characterizations of the feared group—for example, Nazi propaganda demonizes Jews as Bolsheviks and capitalists—and the stereotype of passive Jews is no different. At the same time the slaughter of Jews was underway, the 1940 propaganda film *Der ewige Jude* [*The Eternal Jew*] graphically depicted the Jew as the heartless slaughterer of an innocent creature in the notorious, hauntingly disturbing scene that purports to document kosher butchering.

Nazi propaganda during and after the war promulgated the image of passive Jews. The notion of Jewish passivity as it emerged after the war, however, was not solely the fabrication of rabid Jew haters; rather, Jews themselves, including prominent intellectuals, discussed it. Dan Bar-On reports: "The only ones who had the legitimacy to talk during the fifties, in Israel for example, were the Ghetto Fighters and the partisans ... as they had done something to stop the killing. The other survivors were looked down upon as 'going like sheep to slaughter.'"[22] According to Michael Marrus, "for more than fifteen years after the liberation of Europe, professional historians scarcely touched the subject," leaving writing about resistance as an open field ventured into mainly by "those who had experienced it first hand."[23]

Frankl, Bettelheim, Hilberg, and Arendt

Taking the topic to a mass audience was *Man's Search for Meaning* by the Jewish psychiatrist and survivor Viktor Frankl. Published in German in 1946, then in English in 1959, the book maintained that some camp prisoners "were able to retreat from their terrible surroundings to a life of inner riches and spiritual freedom"; moreover, the author notes, "only in this way can one explain the apparent paradox that some prisoners of a less hardy make-up often seemed to survive camp life better than did those of a robust nature."[24] In so

22. Dan Bar-On, "Using Testimonies for Researching and Teaching about the Holocaust: Importance of Testimonies in Holocaust Education," *Dimensions: A Journal of Holocaust Studies* 17 (Spring 2003): par. 1, http://www.adl.org/education/dimensions/importance.asp.

23. Michael R. Marrus, "Jewish Resistance to the Holocaust," *Journal of Contemporary History* 30, no. 1 (Jan. 1995): 85.

24. Viktor Frankl, *Man's Search for Meaning*, English translation 1959, revised and updated (New York: Washington Square, 1984), 55–56.

saying, even if unintentionally, Frankl implied that, as Lawrence Langer puts it, "survival [was] a matter of mental health."[25]

Despite Frankl's qualifying statements, the tenor of his book implied that volition, religious conviction, and a positive attitude could increase one's chance of survival. He suggests that those who fought hard enough to survive could do so; the corollary is that those who perished did not fight. Here Frankl paved the way for the contentions of Hannah Arendt and Raul Hilberg that Jews were partly responsible for their own destruction because they failed to fight back. Such an allocation of responsibility assumes that people could influence their fates by their attitudes and actions. But as Timothy Pytell observes in assessing Frankl's contribution to Holocaust studies, "we know the reality of Auschwitz is that attitude mattered little for survival."[26] Frankl created the misleading impression that attitude did matter, and this view reached a substantial readership, as evidenced by sales of more than 10 million copies in twenty languages.

In 1960, another Jewish survivor, psychoanalyst Bruno Bettelheim, asked why did the Jews "throw their lives away instead of making things hard for the enemy? Why did they make a present of their very being to the SS?" He claimed that, "Like lemmings, [millions] marched themselves to their own death" because they succumbed to a death tendency or instinct.[27] He attacked what he called their "ghetto thinking," and in "The Ignored Lesson of Anne Frank" claimed that the Franks (and by extension other Jews) hastened their own destruction by living in denial and failing to possess a gun. Bettelheim minimized the murderers' role and shifted responsibility to the victims when he concluded *The Informed Heart* with this extraordinary claim: "That the SS then killed them is of less import than the fact that they marched themselves into death, choosing to give up a life that was no longer human."[28] Like Frankl's work, Bettelheim's became an acknowledged, popular classic.

Many Holocaust scholars were not persuaded. They disagreed vociferously, pointing out Bettelheim's excesses, insensitivities, and victim blaming—none more than Langer who argues that "Bettelheim transforms Jewish genocide

25. Lawrence L. Langer, *Versions of Survival* (Albany, N.Y.: State University of New York Press, 1982), 26.

26. Timothy E. Pytell, "Viktor Frankl (1905–1999)," in *Holocaust Literature: An Encyclopedia of Writers and Their Work*, ed. S. Lillian Kremer (New York: Routledge, 2003), 1:379.

27. Bruno Bettelheim, "Foreword," in *Auschwitz: A Doctor's Eyewitness Account*, by Dr. Miklos Nyiszli, trans. Tibère Kremer and Richard Seaver (1960; New York: Arcade, 1993), vi–vii.

28. Bruno Bettelheim, *The Informed Heart: Autonomy in a Mass Age* (New York: Free Press of Glencoe, 1960), 300.

into a form of Jewish suicide, thus diminishing the role of the agents of atrocity and transferring the major responsibility for their extermination to the victims.... This version of Jewish compliance, not invented by Bettelheim but eagerly espoused by him, heaps scorn on the passive victim and virtually ignores the murderer."[29] Why would Bettelheim adopt such a view, and why would so many be persuaded by it? Is it more consoling to blame the victims than to admit the reality of genocide? When viewed as attempts to come to terms with their circumstances and survival, the narratives of Frankl and Bettelheim are understandable; the general reading public, however, did not distinguish between the authors' authenticity as surviving witnesses and their lack of expertise as historians of Jewish resistance.

In 1961, historian Raul Hilberg published his *Destruction of the European Jews*. Following quickly on the heels of Frankl and Bettelheim, here was another Jewish intellectual giving credence to the notion that Jews contributed to their destruction by not resisting. The public took note. Describing the importance of Hilberg's tome, Christopher R. Browning writes that "no book has been more central in inaugurating this field of study, more long-lasting in its authoritativeness, more widely disseminated in numerous translations."[30] Hilberg insists that Jews had "unlearned the art of resistance" and "speeded the process of destruction" by complying automatically with German orders.[31] Jewish culture itself had aided the destruction.

Evidence of Jewish resistance, both throughout the preceding two millennia and during the Holocaust, may have been comparatively scant in 1961. But even as other historians progressively found evidence of Jewish resistance to nineteenth-century pogroms and Nazi persecution, Hilberg's views remained unchanged. In the 1985 edition, an unswayed Hilberg found additional support for his views in Emanuel Ringelbum's note from June 17, 1942, reporting a talk with a friend from a social relief organization who asked, "How much longer will we go 'as sheep to slaughter?' Why do we keep quiet? Why is there no call to escape to the forests? No call to resist?"[32]

Hilberg sees no significant resistance because he construes it narrowly as or-

29. Langer, *Versions of Survival*, 44.

30. Christopher R. Browning, "Spanning a Career: Three Editions of Raul Hilberg's *Destruction of the European Jews*," in *Lessons and Legacies, Volume VIII: From Generation to Generation*, ed. Doris L. Bergen (Evanston, Ill.: Northwestern University Press, 2008), 200.

31. Raul Hilberg, *The Destruction of the European Jews* (Chicago: Quadrangle, 1961), 667, 665.

32. Quoted in Raul Hilberg, *The Destruction of the European Jews*, revised and definitive edition (New York: Holmes and Meier, 1985), 2:500.

ganized armed resistance. He characterizes the Warsaw Uprising as *sui generis*: "In Jewish history ... the battle is literally a revolution, for after two thousand years of a policy of submission the wheel had been turned and once again Jews were using force."[33] In the 1985 edition, Hilberg recounts revolts at Sobibor and Treblinka, a protest in front of an Auschwitz gas chamber by prisoners from Upper Silesia, and the revolt of the Auschwitz Sonderkommando. Despite these acknowledgments, he does not alter his judgment regarding Jewish resistance, which he deems relatively insignificant. Over the nearly 1,200 pages of text that make up the 1985 edition, "resistance" is discussed on only twenty.

Eight years after the revised *Destruction of the European Jews*, Hilberg published *Perpetrators Victims Bystanders*. Here he devoted more attention to resistance—sixteen pages out of 268—covering ghetto uprisings, escape, sabotage, and partisan activity. Even so, he did not find room in his title for a fourth category consisting of resisters or rescuers. He never disavows previous statements. His view remains that the stance and structure of Jewish communities inhibited resistance. Despite strong criticisms of his thesis, Hilberg has had his defenders. Notable among these is Richard Rubenstein in *The Cunning of History* (1975). Rubenstein agrees with Hilberg on the role of Jewish councils, on viewing resistance monolithically in terms of organized armed resistance, on seeing resistance as virtually nonexistent, and in averring that "One of the elements conditioning the compliant Jewish response to the process of extermination was their own history," claiming that Jews have survived by "developing a culture of surrender and submission."[34] Even if it were true—that there was something uniquely Jewish in two millennia of religious conditioning—how would one explain the point that Rubenstein himself concedes, that the Nazis also managed to slaughter large numbers of Gypsies, Poles, and Russian prisoners of war? Rubenstein is honest enough to raise this question but fails to pursue its implications, ultimately evading the question of why Jews alone are associated with passive self-destruction. For his part, Browning offers this assessment: "My own sense is that Hilberg is correct concerning the minimal occurrence and impact of Jewish resistance but is unpersuasive in attributing the lack of Jewish resistance primarily to the crippling effects of diaspora culture.... What is needed is a tragic rather than an accusatory framing of the issue."[35]

---

33. Ibid., 499.

34. Richard L. Rubenstein, *The Cunning of History: The Holocaust and the American Future* (1975; New York: Harper and Row, 1978), 70, 71.

35. Browning, "Spanning a Career," 199. For Bauer's assessment of Hilberg, see *Rethinking the*

Hannah Arendt stands foremost among those influenced by Hilberg, "on whose work she heavily relied and which she often quoted (but to whom she gave less than proper credit)."[36] In Arendt's 1963 articles for the *New Yorker* covering the Eichmann trial, and in the book *Eichmann in Jerusalem* that followed, she comments on "how pitifully small ... resistance groups had been, how incredibly weak and essentially harmless—and, moreover, how little they had represented the Jewish population." As one who despised passivity and had advocated for a Jewish army to fight Hitler, she contends that if Jews had been "recognized by the Nazis as belligerents ... they would have survived, in prisoner-of-war or civilian internment camps." Such a passage draws a direct line between the victims' nonbelligerence and their deaths. As though speaking directly to Jewish authorities in the ghettos, she asks why they cooperated in the destruction of their own people. She then adds that: "To a Jew this role of the Jewish leaders in the destruction of their own people is undoubtedly the darkest chapter of the whole dark story." Most damningly and memorably, Arendt pronounces: "The whole truth was that if the Jewish people had really been unorganized and leaderless, there would have been chaos and plenty of misery but the total number of victims would hardly have been between four and a half and six million people."[37]

Clarifying her views in a "Postscript," Arendt says she dismissed the question "of whether the Jews could or should have defended themselves" as "silly and cruel, since it testified to a fatal ignorance of the conditions at the time." In a letter to Gershom Scholem, she defends herself by saying, "I never asked why the Jews 'let themselves be killed.' ... There was no people and no group in Europe which reacted differently under the immediate pressure of terror."[38] For Arendt, then, the problem was not so much (or exclusively) Jewish passivity, but rather the passivity of the entire world. As a result, whenever she actually acknowledged their existence, she had the highest admiration for resistance fighters, who were accomplishing what most considered impossible.

Arendt's defenders include the late journalist Amos Elon, who wrote that

---

Holocaust, 142, 166, and "Forms of Jewish Resistance during the Holocaust," in *Holocaust: Religious and Philosophical Implications*, ed. John K. Roth and Michael Berenbaum (St. Paul: Paragon, 1989), 138–40, 146.

36. Deborah E. Lipstadt, *The Eichmann Trial*, Jewish Encounters Series (New York: Nextbook/Schocken, 2011), 176.

37. Hannah Arendt, *Eichmann in Jerusalem: A Report on the Banality of Evil*, Penguin Classics Series (1963; New York: Penguin, 2006), 122, 117, 125.

38. Ibid., 283. Hannah Arendt, "'A Daughter of Our People': A Response to Gershom Scholem," in *The Portable Hannah Arendt*, ed. Peter Baehr (New York: Penguin, 2000), 394.

Arendt never made "the victims responsible for their slaughter 'by their failure to resist.' In fact, she bitterly attacked the state prosecutor who had dared to make such a heartless claim." According to Elon, "Her quarrel was not with the murdered Jews but with some of their leaders and with the Israeli prosecution."[39] Nevertheless, as Deborah Lipstadt concludes, "much of what [Arendt] said about Jewish victims and the manner in which she said it is disturbing ...," particularly "her description of Jews going to their death with 'submissive meekness,' 'arriving on time at the transportation points, walking on their own feet to the places of execution, digging their own graves, undressing and making neat piles of their clothing, and lying down side by side to be shot' is riddled with the same contempt that she claimed Hausner [the prosecutor] showed for the victims."[40] Writing a half century after the trial, Lipstadt offers a measured evaluation that acknowledges the strengths of Arendt's work but finds significant flaws: an inability to acknowledge Jewish resisters, seeing "symmetry between the Nazis and their victims where there was none," and combining "ahistorical comments about the Judenrat" with "haphazard treatment of historical data." On the whole, Lipstadt concludes that Arendt's "accusations were simply not supported by the data."[41]

Arendt's inaccurate characterization of victims reached a wide audience—as had the works of Frankl, Bettelheim, and Hilberg. Elon claims that three years after the publication of *Eichmann in Jerusalem*, "No book within living memory had elicited similar passions," and Lipstadt maintains that Arendt's "perspectives on both perpetrators and victims continue to constitute the prism through which many people's view of the Holocaust is refracted." Evaluating the broad influence of Arendt's reporting, Lipstadt notes that "R. H. Glauber, writing in *The Christian Century*, used her theory both to absolve Christianity for having fostered and legitimized anti-Semitism and to blame the victims."[42] As popularly understood, the writings of Frankl, Bettelheim, Hilberg, and Arendt lent credence to the idea that Jews went to their death like sheep to slaughter. Who in the general public could disagree with these experts? This became the dominant paradigm. Ironically, though, despite Arendt's inability to acknowledge Jewish resistance, the Eichmann trial brought the voices of survivors to the wid-

39. Amos Elon, "Introduction: The Excommunication of Hannah Arendt," in Arendt, *Eichmann and Jerusalem*, ix, xix.

40. Lipstadt, *The Eichmann Trial*, 169, 163.

41. Ibid., 175, 184, 185.

42. Elon, "Introduction: The Excommunication of Hannah Arendt," vii. Lipstadt, *The Eichmann Trial*, 149, 174.

er world for the first time, allowing them to emerge as more than just images in liberation footage. Simultaneously, testimonial and documentary evidence accumulated, attesting to the extent of Jewish resistance. Historians and philosophers alike cast critical scrutiny upon accusations of Jewish passivity, exposing it as a myth. Yet it would retain its tenacious hold on public perception.

Historians Confront the Myth

Postwar failure to appreciate the extent of Jewish resistance is understandable. Few people heard stories of resistance because "so few Jewish resisters survived" and because their efforts were carried out in secret.[43] Also, historians focused on Nazi documents in the postwar years—documents which present a distorted perspective of Jewish behavior. Records chronicling resistance came to light slowly, but as they surfaced, a clearer picture of Jewish resistance emerged.

Books about Jewish resistance had come out in the 1940s and 1950s.[44] K. Shabbetai published *As Sheep to the Slaughter? The Myth of Cowardice* in 1962, Yuri Suhl's *They Fought Back* appeared in 1967, and a major conference on "Manifestations of Jewish Resistance" was held at Yad Vashem in 1968. In 1970, Lucien Steinberg brought out *La Révolte des justes: les Juifs contre Hitler, 1933–1945*; it appeared in English that year as *The Jews against Hitler: The Seminal Work on the Jewish Resistance*, and then in 1974 with the title *Not as a Lamb: The Jews against Hitler.* Isaiah Trunk's 1972 *Judenrat* led to broader definitions of resistance beyond armed confrontation. Reuben Ainsztein's *Jewish Resistance in Nazi-occupied Eastern Europe: With a Historical Survey of the Jew as Fighter and Soldier in the Diaspora* appeared in 1974. By then, the idea that Jews had gone like sheep to slaughter had gained enough widespread acceptance that it was confronted directly in both the English title of Steinberg's book and in a chapter titled "Like Sheep to Slaughter" in Bauer's *They Chose Life: Jewish Resistance in the Holocaust* (1973) where the author writes: "Slaughtered they were, but not like sheep. And where they were able to choose resistance over helpless despair, life over death, they probably drew, consciously or unconsciously, on the sources of strength that had always sustained their forebears."[45]

---

43. Marrus, "Jewish Resistance to the Holocaust," 96. See too Yehuda Bauer, *They Chose Life: Jewish Resistance in the Holocaust* (New York: American Jewish Committee, 1973), 25.

44. See *Jewish Resistance: A Working Bibliography*, 3rd ed. (Washington, D.C.: USHMM, 2003).

45. Bauer, *They Chose Life*, 57.

Bauer explores the "commonly held view" that Jews were docile, that "they did not fight back, passively or actively, even when they were carted away to their doom." Directly confronting the claim that Jews hastened and multiplied their destruction by passive compliance, he writes that: "In Poland, after the war had begun, German rules were so brutal that, had the Jews passively acquiesced—even though every infringement of Nazi law was punishable by death—they would have died out in no time at all."[46] Bauer also introduced an expanded conception of resistance rooted in "the Hebrew term *amidah*, which in this context means, roughly, 'standing up against.'"[47] He has continued to make major contributions to the study of resistance, giving the topic sustained attention in *The Jewish Emergence from Powerlessness* (1979), *A History of the Holocaust* (1982; revised 2001), *Rethinking the Holocaust* (2001), and in many other books and articles.

While research intensified and progressed, resistance received renewed attention in Israel. Opposing the portrayal of Jewish communities as "passive actors," historians, "especially Israelis in the late sixties and seventies, [began] to detail the inner organization and functioning of Jewish communities, thus presenting them as the active and attentive publics that they indeed were."[48] Up to the early 1970s, some Israelis had embraced images of the macho *sabra* and the robust, victorious Israeli soldier embodying a state that would not be defeated; with that came distancing from what had supposedly been weak, passive Holocaust victims. However, increased interest in survivor testimonies and the 1973 Yom Kippur War combined to create "a shift in the Israeli thinking about *heroism*: Now just to remain alive became a legitimate way of coping with war and was retrospectively attributed also to Holocaust survivors."[49]

Wiesel, Levi, and Fackenheim

How did survivors cope over the years with hearing the common characterization that they and their families had accepted slaughter like sheep? In his

---

46. Ibid., 23, 34.

47. Yehuda Bauer, "The Problem of Non-Armed Jewish Reactions to Nazi Rule in Eastern Europe," in *Lessons and Legacies, Volume VI: New Currents in Holocaust Research*, ed. Jeffry M. Diefendorf (Evanston, Ill.: Northwestern University Press, 2004), 57. See also Bauer, *Rethinking the Holocaust*, 120.

48. Dina Porat, "Jewish Decision-Making during the Holocaust," in *Lessons and Legacies, Volume II: Teaching the Holocaust in a Changing World*, ed. Donald G. Schilling (Evanston, Ill.: Northwestern University Press, 1998), 85.

49. Dan Bar-On, "Using Testimonies," par 3.

1975 essay "A Plea for the Survivors," Elie Wiesel uses the term "passivity"—not in relation to those who perished, however, but to "leaders of free Jewish communities" whose "passivity ... lack of vision and daring, of anger and compassion," whose "collective weakness" he cannot understand, rationalize, or justify. "There is reason to be ashamed," he insists, not of the victims' conduct, but of the failed response of Jewish and non-Jewish world leaders.[50]

As for the victims, immediately following the Holocaust "nobody was explaining to the dead how they should have gone to their deaths." But after a few years, people began asking questions: "Fierce discussions and debates took place in newspapers, magazines and drawing rooms: Why the *Judenräte*? Why a Jewish police? Why Jewish Kapos? Why did the victims march to the slaughterhouse like cattle? Why this and not that? The height of irony and cruelty: the dead victims needed to be defended, while the killers, dead and alive, were left alone." Worst of all, "They accused us, often by implication, of having willingly endured the concentration-camp experience, perhaps even of having brought it upon ourselves. Of having accepted it, therefore, of having desired it."[51] For Wiesel, these insensitive, brutal, and ignorant attacks showed contempt for the victims, increased their torment, and repeatedly renewed their murder.

In his essay "Stereotypes," Primo Levi also addressed frequently asked questions such as "Why did you not escape? Why did you not rebel? Why did you not avoid capture 'beforehand?'" Because these questions are both inevitable and increasing, he claims, they require our attention. Levi answers each question in detail, helping us to understand that such queries are based on "a stereotyped and anachronistic conception of history, more simply put, of a widespread ignorance and forgetfulness, which tends to increase as the events recede further into the past."[52] He recounts his exchange with a fifth-grade boy who earnestly instructs Levi on how he could have escaped—and could do if he should find himself in a similar situation again—thereby subtly suggesting that our notions on the subject might be just as naive and uninformed as the boy's. Levi emphasizes that our failure of knowledge is compounded by failures of empathy and imagination. His entire essay is a salutary caution to beware of hindsight judgments and stereotypical thinking—the very sources of the myth of passivity.

---

50. Elie Wiesel, "A Plea for the Survivors," in *A Jew Today*, trans. Marion Wiesel (New York: Vintage, 1979), 225, 228.

51. Ibid., 238, 242–43.

52. Primo Levi, "Stereotypes," in *The Drowned and the Saved*, trans. Raymond Rosenthal (New York: Summit, 1998), 151, 161.

Emil Fackenheim writes that one cannot ask how victims allowed themselves to be reduced to a state of the living dead "without gratuitous, posthumous insult to all" of them. Like Wiesel and Levi, he attacks the question itself: "rather than be quick to raise the question of resistance, one may well ask how one can raise it at all." Following public discussions he had with Hilberg and Bauer, Fackenheim approached resistance not from the standpoint of military effectiveness, but rather from an expanded, deeply spiritual one. This new form of resistance Fackenheim characterizes as "resistance *in extremis* to an assault with an extremity of its own" which leaves the thought of anyone who grasps it "radically, permanently astonished" and creates a new "*ontological category.*"[53]

To illustrate such resistance, Fackenheim turns to the testimony of Pelagia Lewinska, who in the filth of Auschwitz perceived the camp's underlying destructive logic, and who was thereby motivated to feel "'under orders to live.... And if I did die in Auschwitz, it would be as a human being, I would hold onto my dignity.'" Her "historic statement" constitutes a "monumental discovery"— an example of resistance *in extremis* that astonishes us and brings us in touch with "an Ultimate." All forms of Jewish resistance are "interrelated" and "unprecedented," Fackenheim argues, for in all of them resistance became not a way of "*doing*" but a way of "*being.*" Finally, he arrives at this: "*the maintenance by the victims of a shred of humanity is not merely the basis of resistance but already part of it. In such a world ... life does not need to be sanctified: it is already holy.* Here is the definition of resistance sought after for so long."[54] With this redefinition, resistance is understood as widespread, and victims are dignified rather than degraded.

With historians having unearthed ample factual evidence to discredit the myth of Jewish passivity, and with eloquent voices such as Wiesel's, Levi's, and Fackenheim's having undermined the myth's logic, we might wonder that it still stands. It has not collapsed partly because of its deep cultural roots, but also because it receives continual reinforcement—sometimes from surprising sources and for surprising reasons.

53. Emil L. Fackenheim, *To Mend the World: Foundations of Post-Holocaust Jewish Thought* (New York: Schocken, 1989), 216, 205, 201, 248.

54. Ibid., 217, 218, 223, 224, 225.

"Never a Trace of Resistance": The Case of *Jakob the Liar*

In *Jakob der Lügner* (1969) by the East German novelist Jurek Becker, the narrator reflects back on a Nazi-administered Jewish ghetto in Eastern Europe in 1944: "go ahead and condemn us ... there was never a trace of resistance. I suppose I should say that I believe there was no resistance. I am not omniscient, but I base this assertion on what is called probability bordering on certainty. Had there been anything of the kind, I would have been bound to notice it." Aware that readers will be familiar with a history of heroic resistance, the narrator insists: "I can tell you that I have since read with awe about Warsaw and Buchenwald—another world, but comparable ... we remained passive until the last second.... Where I was, there was no resistance."[55] Becker's lived experience prevents us from dismissing this troubling passage as stemming from ignorance, antisemitism, or fictional fantasy; he was Jewish and spent 1939 to 1945 in the Łodz ghetto and the Ravensbruck and Sachsenhausen concentration camps. Nor can we dismiss the passage as coming from a minor, obscure work of literature; it received two major literary prizes and gained great popularity in both Germanies. Becker's translation with Leila Vennewitz received a prestigious prize for outstanding translation of a work from German to English.

How do we account for such a passage in an esteemed literary work by a well-informed Jewish writer? Robert Holub places the novel's insistence on Jewish passivity in the context of cold war political ideology: "Becker's novel goes against the grain of GDR injunctions for writers not only because it focuses on the Jewish Holocaust but more importantly because it refuses to indulge the reader in the clichéd poignancy of heroic struggle against National Socialism." According to Holub, Becker's defiant resistance of the reigning orthodoxy that Communists heroically resisted Hitler constituted "a turning point in the portrayal of the Holocaust in postwar German literature."[56] Regrettably, it did so at the expense of those Jews who did resist the Nazis. The novel perpetuated the image of passive Jewish victims; that image was sustained for millions of viewers through an East German film adaptation that aired on television and theaters in the GDR, followed by international acclaim and an Academy Award nomination for Best Foreign Language Film of 1975, and a highly publicized 1999 U.S. movie starring Robin Williams (although the U.S. version took pains to depict some resistance).

55. Jurek Becker, *Jakob the Liar*, trans. Jurek Becker and Leila Vennewitz, 1990 (New York: Penguin/Plume, 1999), 80–81.
56. Robert C. Holub, "Jurek Becker (1937–1997)," in *Holocaust Literature*, ed. Kremer, 1:115.

The case of *Jakob the Liar* serves as a reminder that claims about absence or prevalence of resistance must be evaluated with knowledge of local factors, including politics. A comprehensive history of the myth of Jewish passivity would chronicle its development and persistence by tracing its history in the specific contexts where it flourished, thus enhancing our understanding of how a myth gains traction, becomes intractable, and then influences actions at the individual and collective levels.

The Influence of Cinema

While *Jakob the Liar* stems from a unique political context, the GDR film is perfectly ordinary in cinematic history in its insistence on Jewish passivity. Judith Doneson finds a disturbing, persistent pattern from movies in the immediate aftermath of the war. These include films such as the 1948 Polish feature *The Last Stop* where Jews other than the central character are seen "marching silently into the gas chambers"; the 1949 Czech film *The Distant Journey*, in which a "strong, gentile male is the savior of the feminine Jew"; and on through to *Schindler's List*, which contains "no references to resistance." Instead, *Schindler's List* presents the "category of Jews Bettelheim describes … at the expense of truth," in which "Jews remain the perfect victims—weak, ineffectual, incapable of helping themselves, the stereotype of women." These and many other films she discusses—including *The Diary of Anne Frank*, *The Pawnbroker*, *The Shop on Main Street*, *Voyage of the Damned*, and *Julia*—continually "restate the portrayal of the Jew as a weak, feminine character in need of protection by the strong, male, Christian/Gentile, a portrayal that, by this time, one suspects, should have faded."[57]

Doneson demonstrates that films have continued to recycle the nineteenth-century stereotype of the Jew as weak and effeminate: "And so it is with Jewish imagery in Holocaust films, ostensibly altered and changed from a different age, yet persistent in the analogous motifs that help to form a picture of the Jew in the collective mind." Despite the evidence of Jewish resistance amassed by historians, the image in the collective mind remains the same, underpinned by centuries of stereotype and continuously reinforced by seventy-five years of indelible iconography from Nazi propaganda footage to present-day feature films that present the Jew as "the prince of weakness." Unfortunately, Doneson, who

57. Judith E. Doneson, *The Holocaust in American Film*, 2nd ed. (Syracuse, N.Y.: Syracuse University Press, 2002), 200, 205–6, 207, 201.

passed away in 2002, did not live long enough to see *Defiance*, the 2008 film based on Nechama Tec's book about the Bielski partisans. She did, however, identify a reason for the myth's persistence in its appeal: "the weakness during World War II that found European Jewry in a situation of dependency for survival might still be preferred in the post-Holocaust climate by the Christian/ gentile world."[58] Hence the continuing image of the weak Jew in need of Christian rescue, as in *Schindler's List*. The myth endures because of other appealing factors as well.

The Myth's Appeal

The difficulty of stripping out the deeply ingrained myth of Jewish passivity comes partly from its deep cultural roots, partly because it plays into Christian ideas of meekness as positive, partly because many people do not have an informed understanding of what was a complex historical situation, and partly because of the comforting reassurance it offers.

Fackenheim discerns a lapse into escapism among those who characterize Jews as passive victims: "Certainly all the loose talk about 'sheep to slaughter' and 'collaborationist' Judenräte stems, not only from not knowing about the Holocaust assault, but also not wanting to know: it is more comfortable to blame the victim." While accusing Bettelheim of turning "escapism [into] a system," Fackenheim finds that escapism also characterizes "the professional case" of psychologists, philosophers, historians, and theologians who write about the Holocaust. We must struggle to not lapse into escapism: "*Thought ... must take the form of resistance*," he says, so we must translate the resistance practiced by victims into our own lives as "*overt, flesh-and-blood action and life*."[59]

Eva Fogelman identifies a different comfort derived from preserving the myth. The urge among American Jews in the 1940s to exaggerate Jewish resistance came from not wanting "to feel helpless or show the world that they were weak victims." For contemporary Jews, "many of whom have been brought up to feel that they can do anything, [by focusing on the victim they] often defend themselves against feelings of passivity and helplessness, feelings that are disparaged in our society. They avoid imagining themselves in an overwhelmingly dangerous situation and avoid confronting the question: What would I have done? And would I have survived?" Fogelman's view dovetails with Levi's

58. Ibid., 202, 203, 214. See too Cohen, "Culture and Remembrance," 22–24.
59. Fackenheim, *To Mend the World*, 227, 229, 239.

21

regarding failures of knowledge, imagination, and empathy, and with Wiesel's concern about the damage inflicted: "By blaming the victim, we lose any possibility of fathoming the psychological mindset of a person who lives under total terror. When we belabor victims with questions about why they didn't resist, we distance ourselves from them.... Blaming the victims not only distorts history; it also perpetuates their victimization." While questioners thoughtlessly inflict agony on the already victimized, they insulate and reassure themselves by propping up the illusion of free will that Langer found so pronounced in Frankl and Bettelheim: "Many of us downplay resistance because we know we do not possess the abilities needed to resist, or we exaggerate the importance of resistance because we want to believe that we have the ability to control our own fate."[60] Or that we would have acted more boldly. Finally, perhaps a world that stood by while Jews were murdered exonerates itself by displacing and projecting its own passivity onto the very victims it failed to protect. Blaming presumed Jewish passivity of the past for mass slaughter of Jews confers comfort by diverting our attention from our own positions as passive bystanders amid the continuing genocides in the present; after all, if it is the responsibility of Bosnian Muslims, Tutsis, or Sudanese to resist, then we are not responsible for their deaths.

The Myth's Intractability

Given the evidence that exists to disprove the myth, a historian might consider the issue to require no further discussion. But if Jewish resistance has been amply demonstrated to specialists, public perception remains unaware of the proof. Does the myth really still need countering? Evidently yes, judging by these works from the last two decades:

- In the introduction to *Defiance* (1993), Tec says the silence about Jews who saved other Jews constitutes a "distortion [that] is the common description of European Jews as victims who went passively to their deaths."[61]
- *Resistance: The Warsaw Ghetto Uprising* (1994) features a blurb from Daniel Goldhagen: "Some truisms about the Holocaust are actually misconceptions. The one to which this sober book supplies a corrective is encapsulated in the maddening, oft-heard phrase 'like sheep to slaughter.'" Author Israel Gutman addresses the myth of Jewish passivity at length in his conclusion, where he asserts, "The Uprising confirmed that Nazi ideology and

60. Fogelman, "On Blaming the Victim," 137, 135, 137.
61. Nechama Tec, *Defiance: The Bielski Partisans* (New York: Oxford University Press, 1993), vii.

definitive plans for the destruction of the Jews fueled the 'final solution,' not Jewish passivity."[62]

- *The Holocaust Encyclopedia* (2001) begins its entry on "Resistance in Eastern Europe" by acknowledging the still-prevalent misconception: "Most discussions about Jewish resistance during World War II raise the same questions: Why did the Jews go like sheep to the slaughter? Why did they refuse to fight? The assumptions behind the questions are that European Jews went to their death passively, and that the conditions for resisting existed but Jews failed to take advantage of them." The entry immediately counters these "false assumptions" and informs the reader that "Jews actively resisted their Nazi oppressors."[63]
- The first words on the front cover inside flap of *Daring to Resist: Jewish Defiance in the Holocaust*—a 2007 companion volume to an exhibition at New York's Museum of Jewish Heritage—are: "This important companion book challenges the stereotypical view that Jews were passive victims of Nazi oppression." In the first paragraph of his preface, David Marwell engages the "oft-repeated question" of why Jews went like sheep to slaughter, and then counters it in the second:

> This question, in and of itself, is evidence that the public, including many Jews, has confused Jewish powerlessness during the Holocaust with passivity. People conclude, wrongly, that because Jews were not able to mount significant, sustained, and effective opposition to Nazi persecution, they did not resist at all. The question, based as it is on a false premise, requires an answer that calls for layers of understanding and, yes, an appreciation of context.

Then in the volume's lead essay, Yitzchak Mais writes, "True the Jews were slaughtered, but clearly not like sheep!"[64]

The fact that writers and publishers of these recent works feel compelled to confront immediately the myth of passivity is itself testimony to the myth's enduring life. These statements would not appear if the myth no longer commanded widespread belief.

62. Israel Gutman, *Resistance: The Warsaw Ghetto Uprising* (Boston: Mariner/Houghton Mifflin, 1994), i, 254.

63. Nechama Tec, "Resistance in Eastern Europe," in *The Holocaust Encyclopedia*, ed. Walter Laqueur (New Haven, Conn.: Yale University Press, 2001), 543.

64. David G. Marwell, "Preface and Acknowledgements," in *Daring to Resist*, ed. Mais, Gurewitsch, Lovenheim, 8. Yitzchak Mais, "Jewish Life in the Shadow of Destruction," in *Daring to Resist*, 19.

Moreover, the myth receives continuing reinforcement in popular culture. Indeed, the highly acclaimed 2011 film *The Debt* states the myth baldly. In the film, Doktor Vogel, a Nazi war criminal known as the "Surgeon of Birkenau," is kidnapped in 1966 by three Mossad agents. While they hold him captive and scramble to arrange his transport to Israel for trial, he says to the female Mossad agent, "You Jews never knew how to kill. Only how to die." She responds by taping his mouth shut and then retreating to vomit. Soon after, Doktor Vogel provokes another of his captors, an agent named David who is the son of Holocaust victims, by asking, "Why do you think it was so easy to exterminate you people? Your weakness. I saw it. Every day I saw it.... Why do you think it only took four soldiers to lead a thousand people to the gas chambers? Because not one out of thousands had the courage to resist. Not one would sacrifice himself, not even when we took their children away. So I knew then that you people had no right to live. You had no right...."[65] Vogel's speech is halted by David, who beats the doctor into silence.

Doktor Vogel's words encapsulate the charge of Jewish passivity with striking clarity. They also echo Arendt's reports of Eichmann's claim that "he could see no one, no one at all, who actually was against the Final Solution" and of Robert Pendorf's assertion that "without the cooperation of the victims, it would hardly have been possible for a few thousand people ... to liquidate many hundreds of thousands of other people.... Over the whole way to their deaths the Polish Jews got to see hardly more than a handful of Germans." Fifty years after Arendt reported these statements, moviegoers hear nearly identical words from a fictional Nazi character, and while viewers might be expected to judge a Nazi's words unsympathetically, contemporary audiences are also accustomed to villains uttering uncomfortable truths. Arendt understood that "the question 'Why did you not rebel?' actually served as a smoke screen for the question that was not asked."[66] In *The Debt*, however, the silver screen does nothing to unveil the smoke screen, and it leaves the real questions both unasked and unanswered; the film does nothing to debunk Doktor Vogel's statements. His characterization of Jewish compliance is not refuted with facts; rather, putting tape on his mouth might be seen as a way of trying to silence an unpleasant truth, while David losing his professional aplomb and exploding into a violent rage suggests that

65. Matthew Vaughn, Jane Goldman, and Peter Straughan, *The Debt*, directed by John Madden, performed by Jessica Chastain, Jesper Christensen, Marton Csokas, Ciarán Hinds, Helen Mirren, Tom Wilkinson, and Sam Worthington (Hollywood, Calif.: Universal, 2011).

66. Arendt, *Eichmann in Jerusalem*, 116, 117, 124.

the accusations have hit home. To an audience conditioned by a lifetime of hearing that Jews went passively like sheep to slaughter, the incoherent responses provoked by the doctor's accusations may actually lend credence to them, as if the Mossad agents are sickened and enraged by the truth of what the doctor says but powerless to rebut it factually. Contrasted against presumed Jewish passivity is the doctor's own resistance as he fights against his captors, kicking, spitting in their faces, laughing at their authority, and ultimately escaping; in short, he does everything that Jews are assumed not to have done. The audience is left to wonder why, if this old doctor was able to escape from his captors, Jews were not able to fight back and escape theirs.

The Debt stands as one example that the myth of Jewish passivity retains its currency in the popular imagination and on the cultural landscape. It is no surprise, then, that some historians (such as those cited above in this section) feel the necessity of continuing to confront the myth explicitly; indeed, it is a reminder of the immense challenge that still faces all who write and teach about the Shoah.

Education and the Future

Peter Hayes writes that "nothing in the literature on the Shoah is more unseemly than the blame cast by some writers on an almost completely unarmed, isolated, terrified, tortured, and enervated people for allegedly failing to respond adequately or correctly to the cataclysm that befell them."[67] Sadly, such unseemliness continues to surface in writing—and even when not voiced, in print or conversation, for many people the questions underlying that blame linger on. What if anything can be done to hasten the demise of the myth, so that the myth itself does not outlive the last survivor? Ongoing research into Jewish resistance is crucial, but if it were merely a matter of factual information, the myth would long since have ceased.

Addressing one aspect of this problem, Marwell observes, "The myth that all Jews went passively to their deaths persists, in part, because there has been little effective public education that relates to this very complex issue with an appropriate context and perspective."[68] We do not need a mythology that

67. Peter Hayes, "The Shoah and Its Legacies," in *The Cambridge Guide to Jewish History, Religion, and Culture*, ed. Judith R. Baskin and Kenneth Seeskin (Cambridge: Cambridge University Press, 2010), 253.
68. Marwell, "Preface and Acknowledgements," 8.

romanticizes or hyperbolizes Jewish resistance.[69] Rather, we need a more nuanced, balanced, accurate view of Jewish resistance to supplant the still-dominant paradigm. No model should sacrifice historical truth.

Educational outreach efforts focusing on Jewish resistance—such as those by Holocaust museums, including the materials on the USHMM and Yad Vashem Web sites, and by Facing History and Ourselves National Foundation and especially the Jewish Partisan Educational Foundation in providing curricular materials and teacher-training workshops—may offer the best hope of cultivating a new understanding that will relegate the myth of Jewish passivity to the heap of discredited ideas from the past.

69. See Bauer, *Rethinking the Holocaust*, 142, 165–66.

Berel Lang

2 Why Didn't They Resist *More?*

"Why didn't they resist *more?*" first appeared as a briefer and still more damning question: "Why didn't they resist?" Both questions recur still in relation to the Holocaust, and there can be no doubt against that background about the "they" to whom the questions refer. It is the Jews of Europe whose alleged actions—that is, *in*actions—are criticized: the approximately 6,000,000 who died in the Holocaust, victims of the design for genocide that evolved in Nazi hands into practice as well as principle. Even before the details of the genocide began to be assembled and more intensely afterwards as the manner of the killings became known through accounts of the massacres and "death factories" in the countries under German rule, as photographs and films of bodies left in the camps crumpled together in piles came into public view, one reaction in particular appeared simultaneously with shock and horror at the enormity itself. This was the sense of wonder expressed in the apparently simple question "How could it happen?" That is, how could it be that an act beyond what until then were the limits of the human imagination had not been stopped—or before that, how it had even started.

This encompassing question itself soon turned in two directions. First, pointing at the people most immediately responsible for the murders, beginning with the proximate source in Germany, a traditional seat of European "high culture"; then also extending to the collaborators whom the Nazis found in virtually all the occupied countries: how could they have not only initiated it, but then enabled and amplified it? Second, pointing at the victims themselves, the Jews of Europe, two-thirds of whom had become victims and whose anonymous faces appeared and reappeared in the narrative aftermath and then in the photographs of groups standing in rows or lines, waiting in city or village squares or in open fields, at railroad stations and sidings, clutching children and belongings, but always waiting—essentially passive, it seemed, frozen in space, failing to react against what was so evidently happening to them. The retrospective knowledge of the fate in store for these masses sharpened the edge of this response: why didn't they *do* something? That is, do something instead of standing and waiting for an outcome that seems now to have been crystal clear and, so the claim, should have been only slightly less so then. Surely, *anything* would be more instinctive, more logical, more plausible psychologically, more honorable morally than what they did or didn't do, even if it amounted only to hitting out, throwing oneself on the guards, joining with one or two fellow sufferers, perhaps only attempting to flee. However small the chances of success in these gestures, surely they were larger than the certainty of death in the alternative.

The reasons for the emergence of the question "Why didn't they resist?" in countries outside German rule—for it is among them that the question arose early and in force—were varied. But often—considered now—the question was self-serving. "*Self-serving*?" Yes, as the question's implication of a failure and thus blame of the victims, minimizes the responsibility of those bystanders living in countries outside Nazi rule who might otherwise be charged with *their* inaction. What, after all, could they have been expected to do if the people at risk did not attempt to help themselves? This was a disingenuous counterpart to the question that the bystanders themselves were asking about the supposedly unresisting victims. Other, theoretical reasons drew on associations with ideology or custom. For many versions of Zionism, passivity in the European Jews attested further to the ghetto "mentality" that the new Jew of an emergent Jewish state would displace—additional justification for building that state as a means both of collective defense and of creating a new sense of Jewish personhood, independent and self-assertive. For movements in the Diaspora inclined to the goals of assimilation or acculturation, here was compelling evidence for viewing Judaism exclusively as a religion, with no claims on cultural or political—or biological—identity beyond that. From this perspective, Judaism, viewed as a faith or creed like Catholicism or Lutheranism, would not—could not—have provided a basis for Nazi racial doctrine.

These claims seem in retrospect both conceptually questionable and morally callous: Was the planning and implementation of the "Final Solution" only a logical error on the part of the Germans or a ready consequence (harsh but nonetheless) of Jewish self-deception? But historical causality does not move in step with reason or conscience more than it does with compassion, and the formulation of these "lessons" from the Holocaust is still being repeated. On the other hand, it was not only "external" sources that raised the question "Why didn't they resist?" It was also asked *inside* the Holocaust where the question became "Why don't *we* resist?" That reaction was epitomized in the broadsheet of December 31, 1941 issued by Abba Kovner and his group in Vilna, proclaiming the urgency of resistance and challenging the community to refuse to go "like sheep to the slaughter." That phrase echoed subsequently in contexts that typically failed to mention its initial formulation as primarily a call to action, not a descriptive criticism.[1]

How widespread was that sense of the imperative of resistance within the Jewish communities—or then of efforts to take action? That question itself encloses a nest of legitimate historical issues to which the essays in our volume respond in some detail. But the initiating question of "Why didn't they resist?" has quite a different standing. For one thing, it is a compound or (technically) a "complex" question which assumes as a premise that the Jewish populace destined for death and then murdered *did not* resist: only on that basis does the question of "Why didn't they … ?" make sense. But the prior question, "*Was* there Jewish resistance?" had not been answered or even studied before the other question was posed, a question that turned out to be a *question-begging* question. Few of those asking why the Jews did not resist had considered the "begged" question worth investigating, an attitude that was to some extent understandable psychologically if not logically: was not the fact of 6,000,000 dead prima facie evidence in itself that if there had been resistance, or at least more resistance, it would not have happened?

But of course it is *not* obvious what the mass deaths were evidence of—at least no more than of the extraordinary calculation and brutality of their perpetrators. Indeed it required years after the Holocaust's formal end in May 1945 for the details of its means and causality to take fuller shape, with that research still ongoing and certain to continue. The results, moreover, have come to include evidence not only of the process of murder but also of resistance to it, in

---

1. The statement itself in Yiddish read: "Lomir nit lozn sich firn vi shof tsu der skhite"—"Let us not allow ourselves to be led like sheep to the slaughter." (The statement in Hebrew stood next to this.) See Dina Porat, "Abba Kovner," in the *YIVO Encyclopedia of Jews in Eastern Europe* (New York: YIVO, 2009). YIVO Encyclopedia of Jews in Eastern Europe. Porat, Dina. 2010. Kovner, Abba. http://www.yivoencyclopedia.org/article.aspx/kovner_abba.

various ways that the Jewish populace in the countries occupied by Germany, and in Germany itself, attempted to counter Nazi policies, decisions, and actions. The essays here provide proof of both the occurrence of such resistance and its extent; it should also be noted that in providing this proof, they open the possibility that additional evidence may be forthcoming.

Together with this empirical foundation, certain conceptual issues have had to be addressed, foremost among them the issue of what actions should *count* as resistance. This is more than only a semantic matter, as is evident, for example, in the difference between defining resistance as involving physical acts of violence or force; or, on the other hand, including actions like living in concealment in defiance of Nazi orders; or, given the Nazis' intent when organizing the ghettos and camps of ultimately destroying their inhabitants, of escape from them or of survival *in* them; or of rescue from outside. All these means of resistance as well as others have been proposed at times, but there is no need to attempt to decide the matter here: whatever definition is accepted, it would necessarily include physical resistance. The evidence of such resistance provided by the essays in our volume is more than sufficient to disprove the assumption underlying the question "Why didn't they resist?" as fully as any historical claim can be. Admittedly, such disproof, now widely accepted, has not silenced references to the question itself—whether in its first form or second iteration—but this says more about the motivation behind the questions than about the questions themselves.

A number of related issues remain, furthermore, *about* the recorded acts of resistance. For example, it would be valuable to know what proportion of the Jewish populace (in individual countries or en masse) engaged in physical resistance. That issue, directed to the nine million Jews of Europe includes both those who died and those who survived (among the latter, those untouched directly by the Holocaust like the British Jews).[2] Determining the proportion of the Jewish population that resisted would have to make exceptions for members of the group who were below or above an age when physical resistance was an option and, separately, for those otherwise incapacitated. We might for the purposes of argument stipulate as a starting point a (probably high) figure of 1 percent (90,000) of the European Jewish populace as actively involved in resistance (fighters, couriers, administrators). If we started with that estimate, the question

---

2. With the exception of the few British Jewish residents of the Channel Isles, which were the only part of Great Britain occupied by the Germans. See Hazel R. Knowles Smith, *The Changing Face of the Channel Isles Occupation* (London: Palgrave Macmillan, 2007).

of whether the number was smaller than it could or should have been shifts the focus of discussion to the second question mentioned above of "Why didn't they resist *more?*" or, as an alternative, "Why didn't *more* resist?" These questions intersect with an issue that requires simultaneous consideration with them.

This corollary issue concerns the effects of Jewish resistance that may now be acknowledged and asks more specifically what difference that resistance made to Nazi policies or actions in relation to the Jews, or to the general course of the war. Although the two are sometimes conflated, this is a separate question from that of how much resistance there was; analogously a distinction has also to be drawn between Jewish resistance and resistance as such. At times, especially in the countries of Western Europe but to an extent also in Eastern Europe, Jews individually were members of "integrated" resistance or partisan groups; in these cases, it is difficult to trace the "ownership" of specific acts of resistance. The essays here allude to many of these mixed groups, as well as to exclusively Jewish ones.

Aside from these formal limitations, attempts to measure the effects of specific military actions face difficulties; this would be true even if the lines between opposing forces or the records they left were more distinct, fuller, and more accessible than is the case for most resistance or partisan groups. A tentative conclusion about Jewish resistance can nonetheless be ventured: that in terms of casualties or damage inflicted, the net effect of resistance by Jewish groups on Nazi actions or policies vis-à-vis the Jews and a fortiori on the war as a whole, was slight. The Warsaw Ghetto Uprising that began in January 1943, and grew to full force in April, is the act most often cited as evidence of Jewish resistance. It came at a time when the populace of the ghetto, that at one time had reached more than 400,000, was approximately 50,000, of whom between 400 and 1,000 would then be active combatants. According to German records, the total number of casualties inflicted on German forces was seventeen dead, ninety-three wounded; the estimate based on Resistance sources was about three times those numbers. Clearly, the German military did not anticipate the resistance encountered in the ghetto or that its "liquidation" would require four weeks of sustained fighting. These developments were markedly disturbing to the local German command, but in the end, even if the numbers from ghetto sources are accepted, the German casualties (in the scope of the war) were slight and the ghetto itself was razed. Although a small remnant of resistance fighters escaped, the larger number of resistance fighters and other ghetto inhabitants were killed in or after the fighting, or deported to the camps. That the uprising has figured so prominently in Jewish memory and the historiography of the Holocaust is it-self indicative of the practical consequences of Jewish resistance more generally; this was the most notable and efficacious of those acts—and *yet.* . . .

The question of what the effect of Jewish resistance would have been had it occurred on a larger scale remains unanswered and probably unanswerable. Some Holocaust historians (e.g., Gerhard Weinberg, Yehuda Bauer) have con-cluded that *nothing* the Jewish communities of Europe might have done in the way of resistance would have significantly altered the course of the "Final Solu-tion." (Even assuming this counter-factual as true does not, of course, answer the question of what increased resistance could or should have been *attempt-ed.*) Resistance as a whole in some of the German-occupied countries—notably in Poland, France, Italy—demonstrably affected the German war effort and its planning. That those activities intensified and were most consequential in the later days of the war when its outcome was beyond doubt (and, it should be noted, when the number and condition of Jewish survivors were at their weak-est) does not detract from their overall impact.

The account here has so far addressed the question "Why didn't they re-sist?" on its own terms, disputing its premise that there was no Jewish resis-tance and pointing to issues unacknowledged in the question or in the conven-tional responses to it. That the counter evidence to its premise is so substantial has undoubtedly contributed to the second iteration of the question "Why wasn't there *more* resistance?" But it seems relevant before addressing the lat-ter on *its* own terms to consider a shared feature of the two questions: what I have called elsewhere their "mischievous" character.[3] By that term I refer to a combination of the intent and likely consequences of the two questions. Both of these are basically misleading and thus harmful to understanding the Jew-ish reaction during the Holocaust (thus misleading about Holocaust history as such) and problematic morally. The latter feature appears clearly in the ques-tion's implication that, although "they" failed to resist or to resist sufficiently when they could have, the person posing the question and separating himself from the "they" would have responded differently—presumably more effective-ly and more courageously. This follows because of the tacit norm assumed in the question of what could or should have been done in the particular situa-tion, an assumption which intensifies the "mischief" in the two questions on

3. Berel Lang, "Undoing Certain Mischievous Questions about the Holocaust," *Post-Holocaust: Interpretation, Misinterpretation, and the Claims of History* (Bloomington, Ind.: Indiana University Press, 2005), 86–99.

historical grounds as well: the absence of contextual reference to the extreme character of the Nazi repression, the conditions in which the victims found themselves, and any comparison between the response of the Jews and the response of other victims of Nazi persecution.

These mischievous aspects disclose in the questions much more than a neutral historical inquiry, going well beyond the substantive historical issues of what the nature and proportions of Jewish resistance were. The self-serving part of the questions that claim for the questioner superiority to those judged, is as much an ethical and psychological as historical matter, but that distortion on the part of hindsight is also familiar from the genre of "counterfactual" historical accounts of which it is an instance. Other people who found themselves in the same or similar historical circumstances might indeed have reacted to those circumstances differently; but for the person raising the question to imply that he or she would have been among the brave is personally gratuitous and, on a broader scale, historically suspect.

The charge of ahistoricism or antihistoricism involved in the failure to consider the historical context of resistance in its specific and comparative appearances overshadows even the other elements of "mischief"; that it has recurred in shaping and responding to the questions of resistance arguably goes beyond "mischief" to something much more serious. For to judge the conduct of a group in a given setting is to assume a baseline of normalcy against which to measure the judgment; that is, the norm is drawn from comparison with the conduct of other groups or individuals in the same or closely similar circumstances. This requirement would apply to the assessment of group reactions not only when a group is under stress, but for group conduct as such. In judging Jewish resistance to Nazi persecution, this would entail a comparison between that response and the response of other persecuted groups in the same or similar circumstances; without *some* such contextual reference, even if we assume the historical accuracy of the specific data, the evaluation of Jewish resistance in that appearance—including what it could have or should have been—loses the traction it might otherwise have. Any conclusions would have ignored relevant considerations, such as the power or force confronting (and evoking) the resistance and the conditions affecting the "resisters" before and while they took action, and would also have ignored—the comparison of all those aspects to other groups in the same or similar circumstances. In the absence of this contextual information, reports of the acts of resistance (or their absence) appear in an explanatory vacuum analogous to the interpretation of reading a thermometer without having information of what the thermometer has been set to measure the temperature *of*.

One comparative situation in particular is notably revealing for assessing Jewish resistance. In June 1941, Nazi Germany broke its "peace" pact with Soviet Russia, invading territories conceded to Russia by Germany in the pact and threatening Russia itself. In the ensuing four years of war on that Eastern Front, the Germans took approximately 5,700,000 Russian soldiers prisoner. Of those, 3,100,000 to 3,300,000 are estimated to have died in captivity, about two million of them in the first year of the conflict. That mortality rate has been shown to have been intentional; a large percentage of those killed died of starvation—imposed famine in the "holding" camps, a policy severe and widespread enough to have led also to the practice of cannibalism in those camps.[4] (The Nazis argued that since the Soviet Union was not a signatory to the Third Geneva Convention of 1929 on the treatment of prisoners of war, they were not bound by restrictions on the treatment of Russian prisoners. This was a problematic claim, of course, although not the immediate issue here.)

This sequence of events and circumstances bears on the phenomenon of Jewish resistance in two ways. One relevant feature is that the Soviet POWs had been trained as soldiers and were at least initially fit enough to serve in the armed forces—neither of these qualifications significantly present in the Jewish populace. The second feature is that recorded resistance among the Soviet POWs ultimately killed provides evidence of few, if any, group acts of revolt. Admittedly, records about the camps for Soviet POWs are less detailed than those assembled from the "standard" concentration camps (a small percentage of the Russian POWs were sent to these as well). But this alone would not account for the absence of reference in German or Russian sources to Russian resistance in this distinctive context.

The question then arises of what if anything follows from this "finding" on the reaction of Russian POWs. Is it reasonable to infer from their lack of "resistance" what was typically inferred, and indeed present, in the same question asked about Jewish resistance: that it reflected a failing of some sort in those who became victims. Was there a lack of will because of a cultural tendency toward accommodation, a tendency toward denial amounting to self-deception, or even more straightforwardly, of cowardice? Such possibilities cannot be ruled out,

4. On the German treatment of Russian prisoners of war, see Timothy Snyder, *Bloodlands: Europe between Hitler and Stalin* (New York: Basic Books, 2010), 175–82, and Christian Streit, *Keine Kameraden: Die Wehrmacht und die Sowjetischen Kriegsgefangenen 1941–1945* (Bonn: Dietz, 1978).

but surely a more proximate, less speculative explanation would call attention first to the conditions in which those who subsequently fell victim were held and which, in the given setting, were obviously disabling, physically and psychologically. The imposed famine on Russian POWs would understandably undermine those subjected to it, including even their will to resist. Those measures were more radical than the deprivation practiced in the ghettos and concentration camps where the Jews were kept alive as forced laborers. But in those cases also, except in unusual instances, the food rations (cited in German records specifically in terms of calories) were intentionally designed for debilitation and death. (These measures, of course, had no bearing on the hundreds of thousands of Jews killed upon arrival in the death camps; for them there would be no question of "debilitation.")

The egregious example of the Russian POWs among numerous possible comparisons shows clearly the "mischievous" character of the two questions, "Why didn't they resist?" and "Why didn't they resist *more?*" Both questions imply the possibility of resistance by the Jews and their failure to mount it, with no reference to the conditions under which that resistance would have had to be initiated. Shifting the question to why there was not *more* resistance among *both* the Russian POWs and the Jewish "Haftlinge" in the ghettos and camps alters at least the invidious character of the initial question and its successor. It also shifts the analysis to consider the *conditions* confronting those threatened, the eventual victims, as well as to the question of how still other groups reacted to Nazi brutality—making clear through the extent of this context how crucial such information is prior to drawing any conclusion about the role of resistance in responses to Nazi persecution. No other group was destined by the Nazis for total annihilation as the Jews were, but the threat of death was real in all the occupied countries as well as in Germany and its annexed lands. It was, of course, more than a threat—with an estimated death toll, for example, of 2,000,000 non-Jewish Poles in addition to the 3,000,000 Polish Jews.

By the time World War II ended, none of the countries occupied by Germany was without its underground or resistance movements—some, like Poland and France, on a large scale; others, like Norway, on a smaller scale. Here again, however, context is relevant in relation to the question of Jewish resistance. Specifically, the circumstances of those who undertook to fight in their own land, familiar with and to the territory and its inhabitants and language, were different from those of the Jews who had often been deported and found themselves in dangerous surroundings even if they succeeded in escaping immediate threat. Then, too, there was the single most fundamental factor in understanding the geosocial character of resistance to the Nazi regime, in and outside of Germany itself: the evidently limitless brutality of the Nazis in the retributive and preventative measures they were willing to take.

A number of these "measures" have become symbols of the Nazis' more general disposition, although the repetition of those instances shows that they were not intended only as symbols: the razing of the Czech village of Lidice and the killing of all its male residents after Reinhardt Heydrich's assassination in 1942; the massacres at Oradour-sur-Glane in France (1944) and in the Ardeatine Caves in Rome (1944) where the Germans exceeded the ratio they had themselves settled on, of ten hostages killed for each German death. In Germany itself, there were the vivid examples of the execution in 1942 in Berlin of members of the Herbert Baum group, made up of both Jews and non-Jews, for the attempted arson of an anti-Soviet and antisemitic exhibition in the city; and the guillotining in early and mid-1943 of members of the Munich "White Rose" group (non-Jews) for the offense of distributing anti-Nazi flyers. Neither of the latter acts had caused any loss of life.

The question remains as to how strongly motivated the German populace would have been for resistance even if the regime had been less extreme in its reprisals, but those reprisals clearly had a strong effect that continued even after the outcome of the war was evident within Germany as well as outside it. The failed July 20, 1944, plot to assassinate Hitler, initiated by German military and government officials, was punished by the execution of about 5,000 Germans, many of them only tangentially related (if at all) to the plot. Even in the closing days of the war, the number of German soldiers executed for "desertion" was in the thousands. The total number executed for that reason during the war is estimated to have been 30,000, an extraordinary figure in military terms.[5]

In sum, then, assessing resistance in any setting can be meaningful *only* as it takes account of two contextual factors: the character of the regime against which resistance would be directed and the reaction of other groups in the same or similar circumstances. The question "Why didn't they resist?" in its original form took for granted that the "normal" reaction of a populace faced with a mortal threat would be to opt for resistance. But in making that assumption in order to explain the supposed lack of Jewish resistance, the highly un-

---

5. Richard J. Evans, "Into Dust," *London Review of Books* (September 8, 2011), 13.

usual—not normal at all—circumstances of the Nazi regime and the intensity of its persecution of the Jews (and of its "enemies" more generally) were simply ignored. These included the cloak of secrecy and deception under which the "Final Solution" and its mechanism were hidden, extending to the prohibition on the public use of the term itself; the family ties and dependencies that inevitably weighed in making personal decisions about resistance, the hopes, whether reasonable or illusory, for change in Nazi policies or of rescue from them; and the apparently limitless brutality of the Nazi regime, especially through independent authority of the SS. All of these reasons demand consideration by anyone attempting to decide, whether at that time or now, retrospectively, what was warranted or required in the way of response.

Then, too, for any overall judgment there remains the comparative issue—of how, against the background of the ghettos and the concentration and death camps with their cumulatively debilitating effects, other captive populaces reacted in similar circumstances. Thus, the original, ostensibly reasonable and innocent historical question was, in the form posed, not reasonable or innocent at all, ignoring what any responsible analysis would take into account as a matter of course in tracing historical causality. Much of that failing has carried over into the second, later iteration of the question—"Why wasn't there *more* resistance than there was?"—since here again the issue of context is crucial. A pertinent and dramatic example of the importance of that comparison appeared relatively early in the Nazi persecution of the Jews, in an exchange between Gandhi and Martin Buber, after Gandhi recommended passive resistance as a policy for the Jews in relation to both the Arab populace of what was then Palestine and the Nazi threat in Germany. Buber, one of a small group of binationalists in Palestine's Jewish "Yishuv" and generally inclined also to pacifism, wrote in response to Gandhi (February 24, 1939) that Gandhi's "solution" simply ignored the basic difference between British rule in India, against which passive resistance had proved effective, and the Nazi regime's capacity for brutality and its demonstrated indifference to human life. Buber described it as the "diabolic universal steamroller" against which, he argued, passive resistance would have been worse than futile. (Note that Buber was writing in these terms before the "Final Solution" was even adopted as policy, let alone implemented.)

The second iteration of the original question—its reformulation as "Why didn't they resist *more?*"—avoids the main fault of the early version by acknowledging that there had indeed been some resistance. But it adds a problematic aspect of its own in the implication of its request for "more" as it assumes that for whatever reason (insufficient, if not bad), what resistance there had been was *too little*. What is problematic here is on one side a formal issue: it is difficult to envisage any instance of moral conduct where a similar question might not be raised of why the effort expended could not have been greater—more—than it was. So, for example, in the giving of charity or in parental care of children: could even those who have given generously not have given *more?* At some point, to be sure, absolute limits do appear: one cannot donate to charity more than one possesses, time itself is limited by the twenty-four-hour day—and life of course is the "supreme" sacrifice.

In relation to more conventional possibilities, however, the question's second version conveys its own mischief. It implies that "more" should have been done in the way of resistance, but without even attempting to say what more that was and, beyond that, without proposing any means for determining what circumstances would interrupt or put an end to the otherwise endless question of "Why not more?" That is, what in the way of resistance *would* have been sufficient? Certain measures of resistance related to the Holocaust that might have been initiated but were not have often been brought up, frequently as they involve the bystander nations—for example, the possibility of the bombing of the death camps and the kind of political or moral pressure that could have been exerted in bringing that about. (Resistance in this sense would have been directed against the prevailing political climate shaping wartime strategy.) But here, in fact and unsurprisingly, there was division of opinion on the part of those most closely related to the camp victims about what actions should be taken—a degree of discord largely screened out in the simplification of historical hindsight. The difficulties in deciding this particular instance would not necessarily apply to all such possibilities, but all would together face the objections pertinent to any conclusion of counterfactual history: that of verifiability as measured against what is known to have happened in fact.

Where, then, do these reflections leave the question of Jewish resistance as it was; that is, as distinct from what it could or *should* have been? On the issue of what it was, the essays in our volume give a compelling summary of widespread Jewish resistance in all the countries of Europe to which the Nazi persecution extended. The essays also describe, albeit in lesser detail, some of the difficulties that mobilizing Jewish resistance consistently faced. Could or should there have been *more* resistance? The inclination to answer "Yes" to that question whatever the context or circumstances in which it may be raised is understandable; and even aside from that, one might answer "yes" to the question even as asked specifically about Jewish resistance in the Holocaust. To reject the question or to answer it in the negative (*not* my intention here) would imply that everything that could have been done *was* in fact done. There is ample evidence that that was not the case, and few writers on the Holocaust have argued otherwise. But also without doing that, one can leave room for asking—in relation to the present as much as to the past—what more could have been done that wasn't, but without at the same time finding collective, let alone intrinsic fault in the responses of the Jewish communities.

Finally, any answer to the question of "why wasn't there more resistance?" can be responsible in its force only as it first sees and acknowledges the conditions within which such resistance would have had to be initiated. Nobody should need reminding that human limitations—including the fact that heroism is rare, that heroism is precisely what goes "above and beyond the call of duty"—extend into the past as well as into the present. This does not at all insert into the analysis an all-purpose excuse for anything that was not done which might or should have been done. It only makes explicit what is necessary as a condition for understanding even commonplace decisions and actions, as well as what is necessary for assessing those that are not.

Nechama Tec

3 Jewish Resistance

Facts, Omissions, and Distortions

There are many more questions than answers concerning Jewish resistance during World War II. Most discussions of the subject evince myriad forms of the same queries: Why did the Jews go like sheep to their slaughter? Why did they not stand up to the Germans? Why did they refuse to fight?

Behind each of these questions are unexamined assumptions. Each claims that European Jews went to their death passively, without a struggle. Each alleges that conditions necessary for resisting existed but that the Jews failed to take advantage of these conditions. This sort of reasoning may easily lead to some predictable conclusions: If opportunities existed to thwart Nazi aims but the Jews chose not to rely on them, they must bear some responsibility for what happened to them. These arguments amount to blaming the victims. Blaming the victims, in turn, relieves the perpetrators of some responsibility for their crimes. Such questions and their implications can be settled only by a careful examination of historical facts.

Even a cursory glance at available evidence shows that the assumptions upon which these arguments are based are false. First, favorable conditions for Jewish resistance under the German occupation were virtually nonexistent.

Research for and writing of this article were supported by a Senior Research Fellowship from the Miles Lerman Center for The Study of Jewish Resistance, at the United States Holocaust Memorial Museum, in Washington, D.C. I am most grateful to the Miles Lerman Center for giving me the opportunity to engage in this study. I am indebted to my friends and colleagues Professor Pat Cramer, Dr. Jürgen Matthäus, and Professor Daniel Weiss for their careful readings of and valuable comments about this study.

Second, despite the absence of such conditions, there was a significant amount of Jewish resistance during that period. For example, in Poland and other parts of Eastern Europe, Jewish underground organizations were set up in seven major ghettos (Bialystok, Cracow, Czestochowa, Kovno, Minsk, Vilna, and Warsaw) and in forty-five minor ghettos. Jewish armed uprisings took place in five concentration camps and in eighteen forced-labor camps.[1] An understanding of Jewish resistance will be enhanced if examined within the context of non-Jewish resistance. Before this is done, however, the meaning of resistance in general and Jewish resistance in particular calls for some preliminary clarification. Henri Michel, an authority on European resistance movements during World War II, notes that resistance started with gestures of malicious humor and moved on to more explicit refusals to submit. With time, these refusals became organized and sometimes eventually led to actual battles. While every resistance movement developed in stages, each underground group had its special characteristics. These characteristics varied with the attitudes of the occupying forces to a particular country or group, with the physical and cultural attributes of a country or group, and with the kind of assistance received from the Allies. An offer of assistance, in turn, depended on whether the Allies saw a country or a group as important.[2]

The literature about resistance to the German occupation usually refers to collective, organized forms, which are further differentiated in terms of passive or active, armed or unarmed, spiritual or nonspiritual, as well as with many other characterizations.[3] By their very nature, all underground activities are

1. Yehuda Bauer, "Forms of Jewish Resistance during the Holocaust," in *The Nazi Holocaust*, ed. Michael R. Marrus (Westport, Conn.: Meckler, 1989), 34–48, states that in at least sixty of the ghettos there were armed rebellions or attempts at rebellion. Similarly, he cites six concentration camps in which there were Jewish uprisings. Both the places and the number of uprisings differ somewhat from those presented by Yisrael Gutman and Shmuel Krakowski, *Unequal Victims: Poles and Jews during World War II* (New York: Holocaust Library, 1986), 106.

2. Henri Michel, *The Shadow War: European Resistance 1939–1945* (New York: Harper & Row, 1972), 13.

3. While most students deal with collective resistance, they disagree on several aspects when defining resistance in general. For example, Roger S. Gottlieb, "The Concept of Resistance: Jewish Resistance During the Holocaust," *Social Theory and Social Practice* 9:1 (Spring 1983): 31–49, thinks that the effectiveness of resistance should not be a part of a definition. In contrast, Raul Hilberg's formulation relies heavily on this idea. This is clear when he says that "measured in German casualties Jewish armed opposition shrinks into insignificance." See Raul Hilberg, *The Destruction of the European Jews* (New York: Holmes and Meier, 1985), 3:1031. Yehuda Bauer emphasizes the need for distinguishing between armed and spiritual Jewish resistance. He notes that the main expression of Jewish resistance could not be armed or violent for many complex reasons. See Yehuda Bauer, *A History of the Holocaust* (New York: Franklin Watts, 1982), 246–77. Later I will discuss different forms of resistance.

dynamic, appearing under a variety of guises. The inherent secrecy of underground activities makes the identification of participants by name and ethnic affiliation difficult. This applies particularly to Jews who joined non-Jewish underground groups. As a matter of definition then, do such individuals count as "Jewish" resisters or not?

In most resistance groups, at different stages of the war, Jews were prevented from organizing into separate units. One notable exception was the French maquis, where the Jews formed their own underground sections. In this instance it appears that even though the Jews made up less than 1 percent of the French population, an estimated 15–20 percent of the French maquis was Jewish.[4] Among other exceptions was the Slovakian underground.

The situation was very different for those who, for many valid and not so valid reasons, would not identify themselves as Jews.[5] This applied to the main Polish resistance movement, the Armja Krajowa (AK) or Home Army. As the official military arm of the Polish government-in-exile, in London, each of its many AK subgroups was an extension of one or another of the political parties that made up this government. Some of these parties pursued antisemitic policies while others supported Jews. Depending on the political policy of an AK subgroup, a Jew who wished to join its ranks could be accepted, rejected, or murdered. Because the political ideology of most AK groups was not widely publicized, some Jews concealed their ethnic identity when seeking entrance into the AK. Those accepted into the Polish underground movement as Jews often were faced with discrimination. An unspecified number of Jews participated in the smaller Polish underground, the Polish Communist organization (PPR).[6]

Some Czech Jews joined the Czech elitist underground, which operated in urban centers. Many of these Jews were assimilated and wholeheartedly identified with the Czech nation. Others had severed their ties to Judaism long before the German takeover. Most of them, however, did not deny their ethnic origin. As a rule, the operations of the Czech group were limited to the collection and distribution of illegal materials. By 1942, when the Germans stepped up the

---

4. Leon Poliakow, "Jewish Resistance in France," *YIVO Annual of Jewish Social Studies* (1953): 261.

5. These issues have been elaborated upon by Yehuda Bauer in *The Jewish Emergence from Powerlessness* (Toronto: University of Toronto Press, 1979), 32–33.

6. Shmuel Krakowski describes the attitudes and several attacks upon the Jews by members of the AK. See *The War of the Doomed: Jewish Armed Resistance in Poland, 1942–1944* (New York: Holmes and Meier, 1984), 41–42, 52–55, 67. Krakowski also documents attacks by Soviet partisans. See pages 28, 30, 37.

persecution of Jews, Jewish participation in that underground organization was lessened.[7]

During the early stages of the development of the Russian, Belorussian, Lithuanian, and Ukrainian partisan movements—1941–43—antisemitism with its accompanied mistreatment of Jews was common. Loosely organized and poorly equipped partisan bands roamed the forests in those occupied areas. Undoubtedly, some Jews who joined these units preferred to keep their ethnic origin secret. Others, who were admitted as Jews, suffered from antisemitic consequences. By mid-1943, when the Soviet Union was in a better position to establish and exercise control over most of the partisans in these forests, the Jews were officially shielded from antisemitic excesses.[8]

Also different was the fate of Jewish resisters apprehended as members of non-Jewish underground units. Primo Levi joined an Italian partisan unit. When his group was arrested and interrogated by the Fascist militia, Levi chose to identify himself as an "Italian citizen of the Jewish race."[9] The case of Masha Bruskina, a Jewish girl from the Minsk ghetto, is both similar and different. Already at the beginning of the German occupation, in July 1941, the seventeen-year-old Masha had become a member of a Communist underground group outside the ghetto. Composed mostly of Belorussian non-Jews, these resisters helped hospitalized Soviet POWs recover from their war wounds. With an improvement in health, they were supplied with clothes and documents and led into the surrounding forest to organize partisan units. After a while, this Minsk underground group was denounced by one of the POWs. Members of this unit, together with Masha Bruskina, were imprisoned and tortured. Without their having revealed any secrets, on October 26, 1941, Masha Bruskina and eleven resisters were publicly hanged.

Photos taken by the Germans show her with two of her male comrades being led from the prison through the streets of Minsk; other photos show their execution. As visual documentation of the first public execution of resisters, these photographs were and continue to be widely displayed in museums and similar institutions and are included in encyclopedias and historical books. Viewers of these photos are moved by what they see as a quiet, dignified pride of the condemned. They are particularly touched by the poised yet defiant

7. Livia Rothkirchen, "The Defiant Few: Jews and Czech 'Inside Front' (1938–1942)," *Yad Vashem Studies* 14 (1976): 40.

8. On issues related to antisemitism and the Soviet partisan movement, see Hersh Smolar, *The Minsk Ghetto: Soviet-Jewish Partisans against Nazis* (New York: The Holocaust Library, 1989), 119–37.

9. Primo Levi, *Survival in Auschwitz* (New York: Collier Books, 1959), 10.

Masha Bruskina. Over the years, these photographs have captured the hearts and the imagination of many. Shortly after their deaths, the two Belorussian men photographed with Masha Bruskina were identified by name. Yet despite what many believe to be overwhelming evidence that supports the identity of the girl in the picture as Masha Bruskina, Soviet authorities insisted that she is unknown; more recently officials in Belarus have continued to adhere to this position.[10]

Regardless of how Jews had joined a non-Jewish underground group and no matter how they felt about their Jewishness, being Jewish inevitably affected them. Jews who concealed their ethnic affiliation had to be concerned about the possibility of discovery. Those who entered a non-Jewish group as Jews were treated differently from others in their organization. As a consequence, the experiences of Jews and non-Jews in non-Jewish underground units varied considerably. Ethnic distinctions, particularly as they applied to Jews and non-Jews, so central under the German occupation, had their reflections in the underground. Whether the resisters wanted it or not, whether they identified themselves as Jews or not, whether they were assimilated or not, their Jewishness must have dominated their lives. But does it necessarily follow that Jews who participated in any underground activities were Jewish resisters? Actually, in differing degrees, the same sorts of observations and characterizations can be made about other economic or national groups. A Pole, for example, who joined the French Resistance was considered a Polish resister.[11] In short, as long as the community sees an ethnic or national affiliation as a significant personal attribute and acts upon it, this has an impact upon one's experiences.

Recognizing the complexity of the concept of resistance and the need for further specification, I am guided here by the broad definition that "acts of resistance are motivated by the intention to thwart, limit or end the exercise of power of the oppressor over the oppressed" and that "the goal of resistance must be to lessen the total quantity of oppression."[12] To gain an understanding of Jewish resistance, our discussion will examine communal life as forced upon the Jews by the German occupation. Concentrating mainly on Eastern Europe, the principle focus of annihilation of the Jews during World War II, I will deal with three interrelated issues. First, how did Jewish underground activities and

10. Nechama Tec and Daniel Weiss, "A Historical Injustice: The Case of Masha Bruskina," *Holocaust and Genocide Studies* 11:3 (Winter 1997): 366–77.

11. I wish to thank Professor Pat Cramer for giving me this example.

12. Gottlieb, "Concept of Resistance," 34–35.

resistance emerge and what forms did they assume? Second, what conditions promote resistance and to what extent were these conditions available to the Jews? Third, how do Jewish and non-Jewish underground efforts and resistance compare? These comparisons focus on the shared characteristics of Jewish and non-Jewish underground activities.

How Did Jewish Underground Activities Emerge and What Forms Did They Assume?

Answers to this question depend, to a large extent, on the kind of German anti-Jewish policies employed in specific instances. The German occupation of Europe was oppressive, but the degree and forms of oppression varied from country to country and from group to group. This variation was in part determined by "racial" affinities. For example, as a rule, the Nazis defined Slavs as of only slightly greater racial value than Jews. In contrast, the highest racial rank was reserved for the Germans, followed by the Scandinavians, who bore a close physical resemblance to the Aryan prototype valued by the Nazis. The other European peoples fell somewhere between these two extremes.

The Jews were defined as less than human. Officially recognized as a race, all Jews came to be targeted for total biological extinction. Nevertheless, anti-Jewish governmental policies were imposed in different countries at different times. For Jews who lived in Poland and its surrounding countries, the last quarter of 1941 signaled the beginning of the end. Only in 1943, however, did the Nazis decide to move against the Danish Jews by ordering their deportation to concentration camps.[13] Regardless of the particular timing, mass murder of Jews was preceded by a carefully orchestrated sliding scale of destructive measures. In the first phase, laws were introduced defining and identifying who was and who was not a Jew. Thereafter the Germans confiscated Jewish property and denied gainful employment to Jews. The next important phase was signaled by the removal of Jews from their homes to specially designated areas, usually sealed-off ghettos, often out of sight of Christian populations. The later the date at which these measures were introduced, the more quickly did the destructive measures follow each other. In Lithuania and in other parts of the former Soviet Union, mass murder of Jews preceded the subsequent formation of ghettos.

The initial establishment of ghettos took place after the 1939 conquest of

13. Nechama Tec, *When Light Pierced the Darkness: Christian Rescue of Jews in Nazi-Occupied Poland* (New York: Oxford University Press, 1986), 6–9.

Poland. It was followed by a 1941 phase of ghetto building, after the German occupation of previously Soviet-held territories. Each ghetto was designed as a temporary community, as a step leading to the final murder of the Jews, either through mass killings or transfer into concentration camps. In Western Europe, Jews were forced into special houses. From these they were transported eastward, to ghettos and to concentration camps.

All ghettos were located in the most dilapidated parts of urban centers, where overcrowding, epidemics, starvation, and death were a normal progression. The longer a ghetto lasted, the more coercive was the domination, the more extensive were starvation and death. German laws and directives continuously rained upon the ghettos. Severe punishment, usually death, followed disobedience of any of them. Frequently these sanctions incorporated the principle of collective responsibility. For example, in the General Government, on October 15, 1941, a new law mandated the death sentence for any Jew who made an unauthorized move outside the Jewish quarters. A violation of this law would result in the juridical murder of not only the "guilty" party but also a similar official murder of unspecified numbers of other ghetto inhabitants who had no connection to the deed.[14]

Rigid enforcement of discriminatory orders brought the Germans closer to the main goal: annihilation of the Jews. This aim was paralleled by a series of secondary objectives: humiliation and degradation of the Jews before they died. Physical, social, and psychological measures were mixed in a variety of ways. The Germans excelled in inventing the most diabolical tortures, varying in degree of subtlety.[15] Accompanying these steps were orders leading to cleavages and conflicts within the ghetto population. Among those measures was the forced transfer of Jews from surrounding communities into larger ghettos. Also forced into these confines were Gypsies and Jews who had converted to Christianity, as well as Jews transported from Austria, Germany, Holland, and Hungary. The social dissension created by their arrival inevitably led to serious economic problems.

Most of these newcomers were penniless, with no prospects for gainful em-

14. Ibid., 52–69; Lucy S. Dawidowicz, ed., *A Holocaust Reader* (New York: Behrman House, Inc., 1976), 67.

15. For a few examples of German brutality, see Jean Améry, *At the Mind's Limits* (New York: Schocken Books, 1980), 21–40; Christopher R. Browning, *Ordinary Men: Reserve Police Battalion 101 and the Final Solution in Poland* (New York: Harper Perennial, 1991); Terrence Des Pres, *The Survivor: An Anatomy of Life in the Death Camps* (New York: Oxford University Press, 1976); Daniel Jonah Goldhagen, *Hitler's Willing Executioners: Ordinary Germans and the Holocaust* (New York: Alfred A. Knopf, 1996).

ployment. Many were reduced to begging, and these became an ever-growing proportion of ghetto populations. Usually these unfortunates were the early victims of starvation and disease, leading to death.[16] In addition, higher-class Jewish men often were singled out for especially debasing treatment. Rich factory owners and intellectuals were forced to clean toilets; rabbis became road workers. These assaults caused the entire system of social privilege to be inverted. The wealthy and the intelligentsia became the lowest strata.

Another consistent Nazi practice was the periodic issuing of documents that seemed to give to only a select few the right to live. From Vilna ghetto, Mark Dworzecki tells how he and his friend appealed for these life-saving passes. "Both of us sat in the dark office corridor … waiting for the judgment upon us. We talked together but at the same time we knew that a life voucher for one of us meant a death warrant for the other…. And here the life voucher was issued to me and my friend was condemned. I was ashamed to raise my eyes but nonetheless I took the document."[17]

A work assignment and appropriate documents did not, as a rule, translate into adequate food rations. Officially, in occupied Poland, ghetto inmates were entitled to fewer than 400 calories per day.[18] Added to effects of hunger were the severe problems caused by cramped living conditions, with seven to fifteen people in a single room. The absence of electricity, running water, and adequate toilet facilities led to terrible hygiene and epidemics. Overcrowded hospitals lacked basic equipment and medication. The Jewish hospital staff was required to report all patients with chronic and contagious diseases. If identified, it was common for such patients to be put to death.[19] Prohibitions extended

16. Emanuel Ringelblum, *Notes from the Warsaw Ghetto* (New York: Schocken Books, 1975), 204–20.

17. Mark Dworzecki quoted in Yitzhak Arad, *Ghetto in Flames* (New York: Holocaust Library, 1982), 146. The specific reference to Dworzecki's publication is not clear.

18. Jewish doctors in the Warsaw ghetto hospital studied the effects of hunger on different illnesses. The results were published in *Choroba Glodowa: Badania Kliniczne Nad Glodem Wykonane W Getcie Warszawskim W Roku 1942* [Starvation illnesses: Clinical research about hunger conducted in Warsaw ghetto in 1942] (Warsaw: American Joint Distribution Committee, 1946). Important observations about the psychological effects of hunger are offered by Leo Eitinger, "Auschwitz—A Psychological Perspective," in *Anatomy of the Auschwitz Death Camp*, ed. Yisrael Gutman and Michael Berenbaum (Bloomington, Ind.: Indiana University Press, in association with the United States Holocaust Memorial Museum, 1994), 469–82; and in Ringelblum, *Notes from the Warsaw Ghetto*, 204–9.

19. Charles G. Roland, *Courage Under Siege: Starvation, Disease and Death* (New York: Oxford University Press, 1992); Adina Blady Szwajger, *I Remember Nothing More: The Warsaw Children's Hospital and the Jewish Resistance* (New York: Touchstone, 1990). Tonia Tortkopf (Blair) movingly describes how the extreme suffering intermingled with the self-sacrificing help of the Jewish patients and the Jewish hospital staff. Tonia, a nurse, worked in the hospital in the Lódz ghetto until 1944 (personal interview, New York, 1994).

to school attendance, to private instruction, and to religious observance. All these were a part of the Nazi process of humiliation and degradation.

Faced with these continuously expanding assaults on freedom, dignity, and survival, most Jewish Judenrat leaders and many other caring individuals refused to submit. Collectively and individually they organized a variety of fund-raising events: lectures, theatrical performances, and contests. The leadership imposed taxes on the few ghetto inhabitants who still had money. With these funds they established soup kitchens for the destitute and bought medications to combat the spread of epidemics. There was also a morale-building dimension to these responses: in larger ghettos special committees devoted themselves to establishing and sustaining theatrical presentations, libraries, and educational institutions. Illegal schools flourished in the ghettos of Estonia, Poland, Lithuania, and Latvia.[20] From Vilna ghetto, the teenager Yitskhok Rudashevski underscored the value of these efforts. "Finally I have lived to see the day. Today we go to school. The day passed quite differently. Lessons, subjects, both [of the] sixth classes were combined. There is a happy spirit in class. Finally the club too was opened. My own life is shaping in quite a different way! We waste less time. The day is divided and flies by very quickly.... Yes, that is how it should be in the ghetto, the day should fly by, and we should not waste time." Murdered by the Germans, the author left a diary.[21]

Particularly active in the Eastern European ghettos were youths who, before the war, belonged to Zionist and non-Zionist movements that covered the entire political spectrum from left to right. At the beginning of the German occupation many of these youngsters saw the war only as a passing phase. They concentrated on their own education and that of others, hoping to diminish the demoralizing effects of the deteriorating situation. They were preparing for a better, more just future.[22]

With a worsening of ghetto conditions, these group members implemented their educational plans by devoting themselves to the teaching of children, to lecturing adult audiences, and to the advancement of cultural activities, including the production of theatrical events. From there, quite naturally their

---

20. Bauer, *A History of the Holocaust*, 169–91; Mark Dworzecki, "The Day-to-Day Stand of the Jews," in *The Catastrophe of European Jewry*, ed. Y. Gutman and L. Rothkirchen (Jerusalem: Yad Vashem, 1976), 386–99; Israel Gutman, *Resistance: The Warsaw Ghetto Uprising* (Boston: Houghton Mifflin, in association with the United States Holocaust Memorial Museum, 1994), 71–98.

21. Yitskhok Rudashevski, *The Diary of the Vilna Ghetto, June 1941–April 1943* (Tel Aviv: Beit Lohamei Haghetaot, 1973), 65.

22. Gutman, *Resistance*, 120–32.

efforts expanded into the promotion of social welfare. These young activists seemed at once more daring and more realistic than many of the older generation, including the prewar leaders of the political parties.

By 1942, members of various political youth groups recognized that the Germans aimed at the total biological annihilation of the Jewish people. When this conclusion was reached, many of their leaders began to prepare for other forms of resistance. Initially the Jewish public was to be educated about its impending fate, this through the preparation and distribution of illegal publications. These efforts were accompanied by a collection of arms. While eager to fight the Germans, youthful resisters were realistic about the inevitable outcome of any armed encounters. Knowing well that they could not stop the destruction of Jewish lives, they hoped that through armed resistance, they would, at the very least, salvage the honor of the Jewish people.

In large ghettos, in particular, preparations for resistance commonly led to the cooperation of various political groups on matters such as the timing and location of future confrontations. Around 1942, rumors about forest partisans began to circulate. In ghettos surrounded by forests, such news suggested an option: one might fight inside the ghetto or one might attempt to reach and join the partisans. Most of the youth of the underground were reluctant to leave the ghettos. They felt responsible for their imprisoned communities and feared that by leaving they would be abandoning their people.[23]

At times, the attitudes of the general ghetto populations toward the young resisters tipped the scale in favor of staying or leaving. Older, more traditional ghetto inmates, including some members of the Judenräte, were suspicious of the young. Many of them thought that Jewish contributions to the German war economy could save, if not all, at least the working part of the Jewish population. For them the prospect of a fight in the ghetto or of a mass escape into the forest would portend the destruction of an entire community.

---

23. Ibid., 146–76. See also a transcript from a meeting of the underground in Bialystok. It contains the documents of the arguments used for and against a breakout from the ghetto. See "Facing Death in the Bialystok Ghetto, February 1943," in *Document Reader*, 347–54; Oswald Rufeisen, a Jewish youth who was passing as half-Pole and half- German, and who organized the breakout at Mir ghetto, convinced the Jewish underground youths that they should give up the idea of conducting a battle within the ghetto. For a historical account of the Mir ghetto breakout, see Nechama Tec, *In the Lion's Den: The Life of Oswald Rufeisen* (New York: Oxford University Press, 1990), 134–48. The Minsk Jewish ghetto underground was one of the few exceptions that did not seriously consider fighting inside the ghetto. In part this was due to the political homogeneity that prevailed in and out of the ghetto, and the close contacts that had been established between the Communist Party and the ghetto underground. Hersh Smolar talked to me about these events (in Tel Aviv, in 1989 and 1990), and wrote about it in his *The Minsk Ghetto*.

To be sure, plans about the place, form, and timing of resistance changed often. Some leaders of the underground compromised and made accommodations to the vacillating Judenrat leadership. This happened in the Bialystok ghetto. After considerable soul-searching and after consultations with Ephraim Barash, the head of the Judenrat, the resistance group decided that they would attack the Germans during the final phase of the liquidation of the ghetto. They hoped that their attack would be followed by a mass escape into the forest. But the liquidation of the ghetto began unexpectedly, on August 16, 1943. A desperate, predictably uneven battle ensued. In the end, only a few fighters reached the Aryan side and the forest.[24]

As was the case with most resistance movements, the Jewish underground in Cracow consisted of a coalition of youth organizations. A strategic partner in this assemblage was Akiva, a politically moderate Zionist group initially dedicated to nonviolence and to cultural pursuits. Following the previously described pattern, the Cracow Jewish underground first concentrated on member and community self-improvement, eventually manifested in involvement in the cultural and welfare activities of the ghetto. Soon they turned to the collection and dissemination of information, printing illegal newspapers; they also forged documents, including passes and train tickets.

As in other ghettos, by 1942 young underground leaders in Cracow became convinced that all Jews were destined for destruction. This led to the procurement of arms and to closer ties with the Polish underground, the more accessible Communist Polska Partia Robotnicza (PPR), who were more willing to cooperate with Jews than were most Polish nationalist organizations. Among the dedicated leaders of Akiva was the couple Szymek Draenger (whose *nom de guerre* was Marek) and Gusta Draenger (Justyna), as well as Aharon Liebeskind (Dolek).

The fate of the Cracow Jewish underground was dictated partly by its failure to gain widespread acceptance among the ghetto population and their desire not to endanger the very existence of the entire ghetto. Through the cooperation with the PPR, Akiva obtained the underground's first two pistols and ammunition. They tried to establish contact with forest partisans, but failed. Out of the

24. Chajka Grossman, *The Underground Army* (New York: Holocaust Library, 1987). Chajka was an underground courier for the Bialystok ghetto underground. Her book is both a wartime memoir and a historical account of the Jewish underground in Bialystok. B. Mark, *Ruch Oporu w Getcie Bialystockim* [The underground in the Bialystok ghetto] (Warsaw: Zydowski Instytut Historyczny, 1952). Among the members of the underground who were caught during the liquidation of the Bialystok ghetto and who later escaped into the forest and became partisans was Eva Kracowski (personal interview, Tel Aviv, 1995).

six men who left the ghetto for the forest, only one returned. With the failure of a forest option, this blow tipped the scale in favor of urban operations. Among their daring accomplishments was the December 22, 1942, grenade attack upon Cyganeria, a Cracow coffee shop frequented by Germans. The shop was damaged and several Germans were killed and wounded. This attack was followed by arrests of Jewish resisters, among them Gusta and Szymek Draenger, Aharon Liebeskind, and many others. Liebeskind was executed. Gusta, Szymek, and the rest were imprisoned. During Gusta's incarceration, she recorded on toilet tissue the history of the Cracow ghetto underground. Eventually smuggled out of the prison, that fragile document is one of the important primary sources for an understanding of these events. On April 29, 1943, husband and wife staged separate escapes that also freed other comrades.[25]

After the prison escape the group published and distributed the magazine, *Hehalutz Halohem* (The fighting pioneer); they also resumed urban sabotage actions. But their idealism and courage in these clandestine operations were betrayed by their inexperience. In the fall of 1943 the Draengers were caught again. Nothing else is known about them. By November 1943, the Cracow Jewish underground ceased to exist.[26] Only a few survived. Among them was the heroic courier Hela Rufeisen-Schüpper, who today lives in Israel.[27]

Through the establishment of ghettos, the Germans isolated Jews from the local gentile populations, and also other Jewish communities. Jewish resistance groups, particularly those in large ghettos such as in Bialystok, Cracow, Vilna, and Warsaw, set up illegal communication networks that came to include some smaller ghettos, some work camps, and some partisan groups in the forests. Through these lines of communication, the Jewish underground transferred information, money, goods, and arms.

All these clandestine transfers were accomplished by special couriers, most of whom were young women whose appearance did not betray their Jewish-

---

25. Arieh L. Bauminger, *The Fighters of the Cracow Ghetto* (Jerusalem: Keter, 1986); Gusta Davidson Draenger, *Justyna's Narrative* (Amherst: University of Massachusetts Press, 1996).

26. Ibid. For a historical account of the Cracow underground from the perspective of a young Polish woman who cooperated with the group because of her close attachment to one of the members who perished, Hesio Bauminger, see Janina Bogaj, Testimony/14461 in Pomoc Polakow, 1–180, at the Jewish Historical Institute (ZIH), Warsaw.

27. Much of the history of the Cracow group and its relationships with other resistance groups is described in Hela Rufeisen-Schüpper, *Pozegnanie Mileji 18: Wspomnienia Laczniczki Zydowskiej Organizacji Bojowej* [Good-bye to Mila 18: Memoirs of a courier of the Jewish fighters organization] (Cracow: Beseder, 1996). In personal interviews conducted in Bustan Hagalil, Israel, in 1995, she also shared some of her stories.

ness. The effect of their not stereotypically Jewish looks was matched with their fluency in the Polish language. Known for their courage and daring, many couriers disappeared without a trace. Some were apprehended and sent to concentration camps; others were executed.[28] After the liquidation of numbers of ghettos, most of the surviving couriers continued clandestine efforts in the forbidden gentile world. Some of them devoted themselves to helping Jews who lived in hiding among Christians. Others continued to work as links between the remaining ghettos and work camps.[29]

One of these couriers, Ania Rud, a former member of the Bialystok ghetto underground, lived in the city, passing as a Belorussian. She helped maintain contact between various couriers, the local underground, and forest partisans. A number of Jews who needed temporary lodgings stayed in Ania's rented room.[30] Another courier was Marylka Rozycka, a Jewish girl from Lodz; a member of the Communist Party; she became a wartime legend. In Bialystok, Marylka, whose looks and manner were more typical of those of a Polish peasant, established contacts between the Communist Party and the ghetto underground. After the liquidation of the ghetto, she maintained close ties with the underground in the "Aryan" side and with the forest partisans, some of whom had been resisters in the ghetto. Modest, compassionate, and fearless, she insisted that all jobs were important and none was too dangerous. Marylka survived the war and settled in Bialystok. Ironically, in 1992 she died in a car accident.[31]

Because of the tireless dedication of Jewish couriers such as Rozycka, some ghetto underground organizations served as stepping-off points for the establishment and continuation of settings of armed and unarmed resistance. Illegal life on the Aryan side and in the forests were manifestations of activities in two such newly created settings.[32] Estimates of the number of Jews who partici-

28. Bronka Klibanski, "In the Ghetto and in the Resistance," unpublished paper delivered at the International Workshop on Women in the Holocaust at the Hebrew University of Jerusalem, June 1995; see also Bronka Klibanski, Yad Vashem Testimony, No. 033/1351; Bela Chazan (Yaari) was arrested as a Polish resister and survived the rest of the war in Nazi concentration camps (personal interview, Tel Aviv, 1995).

29. Liza Chapnik, "Grodno Ghetto," unpublished paper delivered at the International Workshop on Women in the Holocaust at the Hebrew University of Jerusalem, June 1995; Vladka Meed (personal interview, New York, 1995) and Vladka Meed, *On Both Sides of the Wall* (New York: Holocaust Library, 1993).

30. Ania Rud (personal interview, Tel Aviv, 1995); Eva Karacowski benefited from her help (personal interview).

31. B. Mark, *Ruch Oporu w Getcie Bialystockim*, 94; most of the couriers talk about Rozycka with a great deal of admiration. Among them are Rud, Karacowski, and Klibanski.

32. Tec, *When Light Pierced the Darkness*, 40–84; Szwajger, *I Remember Nothing More*; Grossman, *The Underground Army*.

pated in the Soviet partisan movement range from 20,000 to 30,000.[33] Of the Jews who fought within those ranks, an estimated 80 percent perished.[34]

Much of western Belorussia was covered by large, thick forests, parts of which were inaccessible. This terrain made the area particularly suitable as an important center of the Soviet partisan movement. The need for this movement began on June 22, 1941, when Hitler launched an attack upon the Soviet Union. It was a sudden, massive onslaught that caused the collapse of several Red Army divisions. Because of the chaotic retreat of that army, many soldiers were left without secure escape routes. The majority of these were taken prisoner, with large numbers falling in mass executions while others died a slow death, often of starvation or from overwork in German camps. Yet some of the Soviet troops who were left behind had succeeded in making their way into the Belorussian forests. There they ultimately received some of their comrades who managed to escape from German captivity.

By 1942, the ranks of the former Soviet soldiers were reinforced by young Belorussian men who wanted to elude compulsory transportation for forced labor in Germany.[35] Later on they were supplemented by some Poles, Ukrainians, and Lithuanians. Referring to themselves as partisans, these forest dwellers formed small groups. Undisciplined as a rule and lacking effective leaders and arms, they roamed the countryside competing for the meager resources. Sometimes competition among the groups led to conflict, violence, and even death.[36]

In 1942, ghetto runaways also reached these forests. Most of these fugitives were former city dwellers, unused to outdoor life. Many of them were older people, women, and children. These Jewish fugitives were confronted by the early partisans who, preoccupied with their own survival, were crude; often they were also antisemitic. Many of the early non-Jewish partisans saw in the disheveled and hungry Jews a threat to their own existence. Some of them robbed the Jewish fugitives of their meager belongings. Some chased them away. Oth-

33. Rueben Ainsztein, *Jewish Resistance in Nazi-Occupied Eastern Europe* (New York: Barnes and Noble, 1974), 394–95.

34. Krakowski, *War of the Doomed*, 301.

35. The Belorussian population only gradually reacted to the Nazi persecution. See Nicholas P. Vakar, *Belorussia: The Making of a Nation* (Cambridge, Mass.: Harvard University Press, 1956), 191.

36. Ainsztein, *Jewish Resistance in Nazi-Occupied Eastern Europe*, 307–38; Bauer, *History of the Holocaust*, 271; Bryna Bar-Oni, *The Vapor* (Chicago: Visual Impact, 1976); Shalom Cholawski, *Soldiers from the Ghetto* (New York: Herzel Press, 1982), 147; Krakowski, *The War of the Doomed*, 28; Dov Levin, *Fighting Back: Lithuanian Jewry's Armed Resistance to the Nazis, 1941–1945* (New York: Holmes and Meier, 1985), 206–07.

ers abused and killed them. Doctors and nurses, and young Jewish men with their own guns, usually had a chance of being accepted into these non-Jewish partisan groups. Only a minority of these partisans treated the runaway Jews with compassion and offered them help.[37] In these jungle-like forests a jungle-like culture emerged; it placed a high value on physical strength, perseverance, and fearlessness. The early partisans did not associate any of these features with the Jewish fugitives. Only toward the end of 1943, after the arrival of special partisan organizers from the unoccupied territory of the Soviet Union, did the forest anarchy diminish.[38]

Faced with threatening and unpredictable forest environments, Jews devised unusual strategies of survival. While some of them had successfully cooperated with non-Jewish partisans, others formed their own units. At times these newly created detachments were transformed into family camps, varying in composition, size, and ability to withstand the overpowering dangers.[39] One of these Jewish groups, known as the Bielski *otriad* (a Russian word for partisan detachment), took on the dual role of rescuers and fighters. With time, it grew into the largest armed rescue of Jews by Jews, numbering over 1,200 indi-

37. The literature is filled with descriptions of abusive behavior toward the Jews by Russian and other partisans. For a few examples see Ainsztein, *Jewish Resistance in Nazi-Occupied Eastern Europe*, 307–08; Nachum Alpert, *The Destruction of Slonim Jewry* (New York: Holocaust Library, 1989), 290–98; Shalom Cholawsky, "Jewish Partisans—Objective and Subjective Difficulties," in *Jewish Resistance during the Holocaust*, Proceedings of the Conference on Manifestations of Jewish Resistance (Jerusalem: Yad Vashem, 1971), 323–34; Krakowski, *The War of the Doomed*, 28–58; Dov Levin, "Baltic Jewry's Armed Resistance to the Nazis," in *Anthology of Armed Resistance to the Nazis, 1939–1945*, ed. Isaac Kowalski (New York: Jewish Combatants Publishing House, 1986) 3:42–48; Levin, *Fighting Back*, 206–27; Joseph Tenenbaum, *Underground: The Story of a People* (New York: Philosophical Library, 1952), 292.

38. John A. Armstrong and Kurt De Witt, "Organization and Control of the Partisan Movement," in *Soviet Partisans in World War II*, ed. John A. Armstrong (Madison, Wis.: University of Wisconsin Press, 1964), 73–139; Tadeusz Bor-Komorowski, *The Secret Army* (London: Victor Gollancz, 1951), 119–20; Michel, *The Shadow War*, 219.

39. For illustrations of the instability and precarious position of these different camps, see Yitzhak Arad, "Jewish Family Camps in the Forests: An Original Means of Rescue," in *Rescue Attempts During the Holocaust*, Proceedings of the Second Yad Vashem International Historical Conference (Jerusalem: Yad Vashem, 1977), 333–53. Lea Garber Kowenska, a member of a small family group in the Lipiczanska forest, touchingly describes how great suffering and mutual caring intermingled in the lives of that group. See Lea Garber Kowenska, "Dos Fos Hot Sich Fargidenk Of Aibik" (What is remembered forever), *Jurnal Fun Sovietisher Heimland* [Journal of the Soviet homeland] 4 (1971): 92–102. In an unpublished Yiddish memoir made available to me by her daughter, Lea Garber Kowenska further describes her life in the forest. In her group of fifteen people, there were seven children. Some of them were orphans whom she and others picked up on the way to the forest; Yehuda Merin and Jack Nusan Porter, "Three Jewish Family-Camps in the Forests of Volyn, Ukraine, during the Holocaust," *Jewish Social Science* 156, no. 1 (1984): 83–92. Also see Tenenbaum, *Underground*, 404.

viduals. The founders of this otriad were the three Bielski brothers, Asael, Tuvia, and Zus. They belonged to a very small minority of Jewish peasants. Born in an isolated village, they were poor, with very limited schooling. Familiar with the countryside, and independent, the three brothers refused to submit to Nazi terror and escaped into the countryside in the summer of 1941.

With the help of Belorussian friends, the Bielskis acquired a few weapons. In the summer of 1942, they became convinced that the Germans were determined to murder all the Jews. With more than thirty followers they formed a partisan unit and appointed Tuvia Bielski as its commander. A strong and charismatic leader, from the start Tuvia insisted that all Jews, regardless of age, sex, state of health, or any other condition, would be accepted into their otriad. Tuvia's open-door policy met with internal opposition that saw in this position a threat to the existence of the group. Tuvia argued that large size meant greater safety. He never budged from this position. On the contrary, as the Germans stepped up their annihilation of the Jews, Tuvia became more determined and more inventive, devising new means of Jewish rescue.

Not only did the Bielski partisans accept all Jews who reached them, but they sent guides into the ghettos to help Jews escape to join the otriad. Bielski scouts would also locate Jews who roamed the forest and bring them to their unit. Many Jewish partisans who had suffered from antisemitism as members of Soviet detachments eventually learned that they could find shelter in the Bielski otriad. In addition, the Bielski partisans punished local collaborators who were denouncing runaway Jews. After a while most anti-Jewish moves by local peasants ceased, making the forests safer for fugitive Jews. Suspended in a hostile environment, Tuvia Bielski neutralized some of the surrounding dangers by cooperating with the Soviet partisans. This cooperation extended to food collection and to joint anti-German military ventures, and later included economic cooperation.

From 1942 until 1943, the Bielski partisans led a nomadic existence, moving from place to place. Toward the end of 1943, their number having grown to about 400 individuals, they established a more permanent home in the huge, swampy, partly inaccessible Nolibocka forest. At this stage the camp came to resemble a *shtetl*, a small town, with many "factories" and workshops. The establishment of these production units transformed part of the Bielski detachment into a supplier of goods and services to the Soviet partisan movement. This change helped neutralize some of the antisemitic complaints that the Jews ate too much without contributing anything of value. In addition, the exchanges that were made possible by the workshops and factories improved the economic situation in the Bielski unit, diminishing the burden on the young men who had to go on dangerous food expeditions.[40]

Unlike the Bielski partisans, who focused on saving lives, some other Jewish partisans and their courageous leaders concentrated on waging war. Dr. Icheskel Atlas, Alter Dworecki, and Hirsz Kaplinski, for example, distinguished themselves as fighters. However, by the end of December 1942, each had been killed in action. The three had operated in and around the huge Lipiczanska forest of western Belorussia. With its thick undergrowth, patches of swamp land, and its few and poorly built country roads, this forest promised relative safety to many of the persecuted. Many Jews fled to that refuge. Atlas, Dworecki, and Kaplinski identified strongly with the Jewish plight. They knew that the survival of the fugitives depended on mutual protection and aid. Nevertheless, the three did not focus on saving Jewish lives. The help they offered to the Jewish fugitives was sporadic; it was not organized, and it was not very effective.

For these leaders, commitment to wage war took precedence over the desire to curtail Jewish destruction. Their preoccupation with fighting the enemy left virtually no room for saving Jews. It is reasonable to conclude that they believed, in the long run, that fighting would save more people. Tuvia Bielski may be compared with those who were committed primarily to armed struggle, each representing different important symbols of Jewish resistance: a Jewish fight for existence, and a Jewish fight for revenge.[41]

More so than ghettos, Nazi concentration camps were places of degradation, coercion, economic exploitation, and murder. Some, such as Treblinka, Sobibor, and Belzec, were built with the sole purpose of putting Jews to death, while in camps such as Auschwitz slave labor was to be extracted from some before their murder. Despite the horrendous circumstances under which they were made to live and die, Jews did organize several armed revolts. Well-documented Jewish

40. Nechama Tec, *Defiance: The Bielski Partisans* (New York: Oxford University Press, 1993).

41. For activities of these leaders, see *Sefer Hapartisanim Hajehudim* [The Jewish partisan book] (Merchavia: Sifriath Paolim Hashomer Hatzair, 1958), 1:375–82, 337–43; Samuel Bornstein, "The Platoon of Dr. Atlas," in *The Fighting Ghettoes*, ed. Meyer Barkai (New York: J. B. Lippincott, 1962), 217–40; Lester Eckman and Chaim Lazar, *The Jewish Resistance* (New York: Shengold, 1977), 51–58; Leonard Tushnet, "The Little Doctor—A Resistance Hero," in *They Fought Back: The Story of the Jewish Resistance in Nazi Europe*, ed. Yuri Suhl (New York: Schocken Books, 1975), 253–59; *Pinkas Zetel: A Memorial to the Jewish Community of Zetel*, ed. Baruch Kaplinski (Tel Aviv: Zetel Association in Israel, 1957) contains several articles about Lipiczanska and other forests and provides information about the two leaders Dworecki and Kaplinski. In addition, Hersh Smolar talked to me at length comparing these different leaders (Tel Aviv, 1989–1990).

uprisings took place in Treblinka, Sobibor, Auschwitz, Janowska, Chelmno, and in eighteen different work camps.[42]

Auschwitz, initially designed as a center to contain political opposition, was gradually transformed; its purpose became the total domination of internees, their economic exploitation, and sooner or later their destruction. The camp had an underground in which influential Polish political prisoners shared power with political prisoners from other countries. The Auschwitz underground maintained contact with the Polish AK, and with the Polish government-in-exile in London. By 1944, the Auschwitz underground had begun to plan a revolt to be coordinated with an outside uprising. The internal uprising was to include Jewish Sonderkommando, a group of men whose task it was to burn the bodies coming out of the gas chambers. As a rule, such groups were allowed to live five to six months (some accounts say three months). After that, they were sent to the gas chambers and another group was selected to take their place.

The Sonderkommando in this case were aware of the ultimate fate planned for them, and were eager to participate in the coming revolt. But soon it became clear that the non-Jewish underground leaders were delaying. Their reluctance was based on several factors. Couriers with plans had been caught; new plans had to be developed. The Germans increased their vigilance. Massive deportations of Poles to other concentration camps followed. In mid-August 1944 it became clear that the Polish uprising in Warsaw was failing. Other underground failures followed, and the idea of coordinating the concentration camp uprising with outside resistance was increasingly seen as unrealistic. Finally, too, the AK and the Polish government in London urged that no revolt should take place unless the prisoners were to face immediate death. Unlike the Sonderkommando, non-Jewish prisoners were not confronted with total destruction. They waited.[43]

42. Alexander Donat, ed., *The Death Camp Treblinka: A Documentary* (New York: Holocaust Library, 1979); Richard Glazar (personal interview, Basel, 1995); Richard Glazar, *Trap with a Green Fence: Survival in Treblinka* (Evanston, Ill.: Northwestern University Press, 1995); Miriam Novitch, *Sobibor, Martyrdom and Revolt: Documents and Testimonies* (New York: Holocaust Library, 1980); William Glicksman, "The Story of Jewish Resistance in the Ghetto of Czestochowa," in *They Fought Back*, ed. Suhl, 69–76; Leon Wells, *The Janowska Road* (New York: Macmillan, 1963); Gitta Sereny, *Into that Darkness: From Mercy Killing to Mass Murder* (New York: McGraw-Hill, 1974); Filip Müller, *Eyewitness Auschwitz: Three Years in the Gas Chambers* (New York: Stein and Day, 1979); Nathan Cohen, "Diaries of the Sonderkommando," in *Anatomy of the Auschwitz Death Camp*, ed. Gutman and Berenbaum, 522–34; Hermann Langbein, *Against All Hope: Resistance in Nazi Concentration Camps 1938–1945* (New York: Paragon House, 1994).

43. Yitzhak Arad, "The Jewish Fighting Underground in Eastern Europe," in *Major Changes within the Jewish People in the Wake of the Holocaust*, ed. Yisrael Gutman and Avital Saf (Jerusalem: Yad

Time was running out for the Sonderkommando. On October 7, 1944, the Jewish Sonderkommando, with some help from Soviet prisoners, staged an armed revolt in Auschwitz II (Birkenau). The uprising began with the dynamiting of Crematoria IV, and continued with a fight in the nearby grove. These prisoners were massacred.[44] In no time the entire guard force of the camp was mobilized against the rebels. Bullets were flying all over the place. SS with dogs were chasing the Jewish and Soviet rebels, many of whom fell while trying to escape. Others took shelter in a nearby forest. When they realized that they had no chance of survival, they set the forest on fire. Another group did the same in another nearby forest in which they hid. As the day was coming to an end, Auschwitz was surrounded by guards and fires. The crematorium was burning against a dark sky, as were small forests on opposite sides of the camp. The ground was covered with the dead bodies of the members of the Sonderkommando.[45]

During the revolt 250 prisoners lost their lives. Later, as a reprisal, the SS shot another 200 Sonderkommando members. No prisoners were saved through escape. The German losses were two or three dead and at least a dozen wounded. This uprising had been made possible by male and female cooperation. Explosives for the final confrontation had been smuggled by Jewish women who worked in a nearby munitions factory. On January 6, 1945, less than three weeks before the Soviet liberation of Auschwitz-Birkenau, four young Jewish women—Roza Robota, Ella Gaertner, Esther Wajcblum, and Regina Safirsztain—accused of supplying the gunpowder were publicly hanged. As the trap door opened, Robota shouted, "Revenge!" Before the execution the women were interrogated under torture. Whatever compromising evidence they possessed died with them.[46]

Vashem, 1996), 337–57; Shmuel Krakowski, "Legend and Reality in the Mutual Relations between the Jewish and the Polish Resistance Movements," in *Major Changes within the Jewish People in the Wake of the Holocaust*, 377–83.

44. Henryk Swiebocki, "Prisoner Escapes," in *Anatomy of the Auschwitz Death Camp*, ed. Gutman and Berenbaum, 503–21.

45. Betti Ajzensztajn, ed., *Ruch Podziemny w Ghettach i Obozach* [Underground movement in ghettos and camps, documents] (Warsaw: Centralna Zydowska Komisja Historyczna w Polsce, 1946), 199.

46. Irena Strzelecka, "Women," in *Anatomy of the Auschwitz Death Camp*, ed. Gutman and Berenbaum, 393–410; Sara Nomberg-Przytyk, *Auschwitz: True Tales from a Grotesque Land* (Chapel Hill, N.C.: University of North Carolina Press, 1985), 58–62; Yuri Suhl, "Rosa Robota—Heroine of the Auschwitz Underground," in *They Fought Back*, ed. Suhl, 219–25.

What Conditions Promote Resistance? Which of These Conditions Were Available to East European Jewry?

Under the German occupation of Europe extensive wooded areas and mountains became settings with a variety of imports. In part the relative inacces-
sibility of woodlands and mountains and the mystery often associated with
them identified them alternatively as sustaining ground for rebellion and as
havens for some of the persecuted. These polar views were held respectively
by the German authorities and by their prospective victims. Propelled by dis-
trust and fear, the Germans warred against civilians who had sought refuge
in the forests and mountains when the conduct of the war gave them cause to
perceive imminent threat. By and large, Eastern Europe had much more terrain
suitable for this purpose than did Western Europe.

No matter how favorable for resistance physical conditions are, all resistance responses require time to mature. The start of the Soviet partisan movement can be traced to the summer of 1941, the outbreak of the Russian-German
war, when the Germans invaded. Yet, despite continual urging from Stalin, it
took the movement about two years to achieve a semblance of order. Similarly,
Tito's Yugoslav operation became a significant force only after the capitulation
of Italy in September 1943.[47] Both the French maquis and the Dutch underground projected a readiness only in late 1943.[48]

With the passage of time, the changing fortunes of war made muscled resistance more appropriate. Thus, only in 1944, after the Germans were weakened by the Allies, would responsible European leaders advocate open armed
resistance; the French, Polish, and Slovak uprisings that year are examples.[49]
This leadership had been given ample warnings of the consequences of pre-
cipitous armed opposition. The assassination of Reinhard Heydrich, planned by
the Czech underground and executed by them on June 5, 1942, was extremely
costly: all the men in the village of Lidice were massacred, and the elite of the
Czech underground themselves were subject to a wave of arrests and murders.[50]

47. Henri Michel, "Jewish Resistance and the European Resistance Movement," in *Jewish Resistance during the Holocaust*, 365–75.

48. Borwicz argues that no responsible European leader would have urged resistance before the
Germans were weakened by the Allies, which was in 1944. See Michal Borwicz, "Debate," in *Jewish
Resistance During the Holocaust*, 335–36.

49. Arad, "The Jewish Fighting Underground in Eastern Europe," 339–41; Bauer, *The Jewish
Emergence from Powerlessness*, 39; Rothkirchen notes that from London the Czech resistance re-
ceived orders not to engage in hazardous actions because they were too costly. See Rothkirchen,
"The Defiant Few," 46–47.

50. Rothkirchen, "The Defiant Few," 46–47.

In contrast, one can point to a successful uprising in Paris. It happened when the Germans were on the verge of collapse.[51] If preparation time is an important precondition to the building of an effective underground movement, it clearly is only one element of the equation, and it does not guarantee success. During the Polish Warsaw uprising, which began in August 1944, 200,000 Poles lost their lives. Afterward 90 percent of Warsaw lay in ruins. Political miscalculations account for this failure, notwithstanding that it happened rather late in the war, when the Germans were in general retreat.[52] On the other hand, in the early days of the Polish AK, in 1939, it lacked unity and organization. At times, its many constituent political parties worked at cross purposes, undermining the effectiveness of the entire underground. Only with time did the Home Army (AK) become one of the most powerful of European resistance organizations. By 1943, its registered membership had grown to 268,000.[53]

In sharp contrast to these and other national underground groups, Jews had no time to prepare. In 1942, in Eastern Europe, the Germans stepped up the annihilation of the Jews. By autumn of 1943, virtually all the ghettos were depopulated.[54] Additionally, if resistance is to emerge and function it must have a strategic base of operation. Such a base, by providing adequate space, promotes mobility. Guerrillas need to be able to vanish and blend into the local population. Making that possible, a strategic base helps compensate for the relatively small numbers of rebels and for their inadequate supply of arms.[55]

51. Arad, "The Jewish Fighting Underground in Eastern Europe," 341.

52. Norman Davies, *Heart of Europe: A Short History of Poland* (Oxford: The Oxford Clarendon Press, 1984), 76–100; Jan Karski, *The Great Powers and Poland, 1919–1945: From Versailles to Yalta* (New York: University Press of America, 1985), 488–91, 521–31. The 1944 Warsaw uprising and the destruction that followed was a reflection of Stalin's determination to dominate Poland. For an additional, excellent account of these events, see Janusz Z. Zawodny, *Nothing but Honor: The Story of the Warsaw Uprising 1944* (Stanford, Calif.: Hoover Institute Press, 1979). To humiliate and destroy the leadership of the Polish underground, the Soviets sometimes would put into the same prison cell Nazi criminals and AK (Home Army) leaders. This happened, for example, to the arrested Polish leader Kazimierz Moczarski. He was placed into a prison cell with Jürgen Stroop, the general in charge of the destruction of the Warsaw Ghetto Uprising in 1943. Moczarski wrote a book based on his imprisonment with Stroop. See Kaziemierz Moczarski, *Rozmowy Z Katem* (Warsaw: Panstwowy Instytut Wydawniczy, 1978), also published as *Conversations with an Executioner* (Englewood Cliffs, N.J.: Prentice-Hall, 1981).

53. Krakowski, *The War of the Doomed*, 7.

54. Philip Friedman, "Jewish Resistance to Nazism," in *Road to Extinction: Essays on the Holocaust*, ed. Ada Friedman (Philadelphia: Jewish Publication Society of America, 1980), 392; and Filip Friedman, "Zaglada Zydow Polskich W Latach 1939–1945," *Biuletyn Glownej Komisje Badania Zbrodni Niemieckiej W Polsce* [The destruction of Polish Jews in 1939–1943] 6 (1946), 165–206. By 1943, most of the European Jews who were destined to be murdered were dead.

55. Friedman, "Jewish Resistance to Nazism," 388–89. Guerrilla fighters, because they are usu-

Closely connected to these conditions is the ability to count on local help for shelter and clothing, and for overall protection of the resistance network. All non-Jewish underground groups relied on such help.[56]

Few, if any, Jewish resisters were so situated. Confinement in scattered ghettos automatically deprived them of a strategic base. Limited exchanges, even of information between these ghettos were maintained only by couriers. And neither the couriers nor other Jews could count on the supportive attitudes of local populations. Except for a handful of Christians who risked their lives to save Jews, local collaborators were busy undermining the chances of Jewish resistance and survival.[57]

Possession of an encompassing leadership and of arms supplies are two additional preconditions for effective resistance. Several national underground organizations had direct contact with their political leaders abroad, who established governments in exile. These leaders supplied their underground with advice and arms. In some cases, arms reached a national underground through the Allies. For example, Tito received such assistance from Britain.[58] Eastern European Jews suffered from lack of these resources as well. The want of leadership continued to grow. Jewish leaders who left Eastern Europe in 1939 failed to organize a unified front. Moreover, during the first stage of the German occupation, many Jewish leaders had been murdered. Of the remaining prewar leaders, some were recruited by the Occupation authorities into the German-mandated Jewish councils, the Judenräte. With continuously changing council membership, powerless, and often ambiguous toward resistance, only a few of these Judenrat leaders wholeheartedly supported the Jewish underground. Among those who did, however, were the leaders in Minsk, Kovno, Iwje, Pruzany, and Lachwa.[59]

---

ally fewer in number than those who are part of conventional forces, have to have more freedom to move. In part, greater mobility and familiarity with the environment tend to counteract the disadvantages that stem from small size and inadequate military equipment. See Armstrong and De Witt, "Organization and Control of the Partisan Movement," 73–139; Michel, "Jewish Resistance and the European Resistance Movement," 365–75; Michel, *The Shadow War*, 13; Jack Nusan Porter, ed., *Jewish Partisan: A Documentary of Jewish Resistance in the Soviet Union During World War II* (New York: University Press of America, 1982), 9; Tenenbaum, *Underground*, 385.

56. Friedman, "Jewish Resistance to Nazism," 388–89; Michel, "Jewish Resistance and the European Resistance Movement," 368–69.

57. Jan Karski, *Story of a Secret State* (Boston, Mass.: Houghton Mifflin, 1944); Walter Laqueur, *The Terrible Secret* (Boston, Mass.: Little, Brown, 1980), 101–56; Tec, *When Light Pierced the Darkness*, 70–84; Tec, "Altruism and the Holocaust," *Social Education* 59:6 (October 1995): 348–53.

58. Friedman, "Jewish Resistance to Nazism," 390–91; Michel, *Shadow War*, 371.

59. For a discussion of Judenrat leaders and their attitudes toward armed resistance, see Isaiah

The existing leadership gap was filled in part by the young heads of the local branches of the various youth organizations. Most of these underground commanders were idealistic, and eager to protect and fight for the Jewish people.[60] Also, as in most periods of social upheaval, during the German occupation there appeared a few charismatic leaders such as Tuvia Bielski.[61] All of these new leaders, though anxious to relieve the Jewish plight, were inexperienced. As we have already seen, at times their idealism coupled with inexperience curtailed their effectiveness.[62]

As regards resistance, in practical terms the Allies had virtually no interest in the Jews. This indifference translated into a rejection of all known Jewish pleas, including those requesting arms and ammunition. It goes without saying that the Jews experienced a chronic arms shortage.[63] Additional hindrances to effective resistance were the pervasiveness of antisemitism among most of the conquered indigenous populations and the virtually continuous flow of debilitating anti-Jewish measures promulgated by the occupying power. Inevitably, because of these measures and those of the Germans, the Jews became physically and emotionally depleted. Hunger, disease, and the loss of all that was dear to them sapped their energy.[64] Indeed, the more deprived people are, the less fit they are for resistance. The heterogeneity of the Jews was accentuated by their overcrowding and their inability to move, further curtailing their ability to organize and stand up to the enemy. However the issues are examined—whether in terms of day-to-day life, factors promoting resistance, or specific opinions created by the Germans for the Jews—the situation was grim. Lucjan

Trunk, *Judenrat: The Jewish Councils in Eastern Europe under Nazi Occupation* (New York: Stein and Day, 1977), 451–74.

60. For some of the young, idealistic leaders in the Cracow ghetto, see the information contained in footnotes 22–24. Commander of the Bialystok resistance, Mordechai Tenenbaum, may be so characterized, as may a number of other leaders, including Arye Wilner (Jurek), Mordechai Anielewicz, the commander of the Warsaw Ghetto Uprising, Yitzhak Zuckerman (Antek), and Zivia Lubetkin. For a discussion of these and other youthful leaders, see Grossman, *Underground Army*; Zivia Lubetkin, *In the Days of Destruction and Revolt* (Tel Aviv: Beit Lohamei Haghettaot, 1981); Yitzhak Zuckerman, *A Surplus of Memory: Chronicle of the Warsaw Ghetto Uprising* (Berkeley, Calif.: University of California Press, 1993).

61. General theoretical insights into charismatic leadership are offered by Max Weber, *Essays in Sociology* (New York: Oxford University Press, 1953), 245–51. For a discussion of charismatic leadership, see Tec, *Defiance*, 204–09.

62. Tec, *Defiance*, 80–93.

63. Friedman, "Jewish Resistance," 387–92; Michel, "Jewish Resistance and the European Resistance Movement," 369–72.

64. Eitinger, "Auschwitz—A Psychological Perspective," 469–82; Primo Levi describes movingly how starvation transforms the living into the living dead. See *Survival in Auschwitz*, 82.

Dobroszycki captured the Jewish options in the following question: "Has any-one seen an army without arms; an army scattered over 200 isolated ghettos; an army of infants, old people, the sick; an army whose soldiers are denied the right even to surrender?"[65]

How Do Jewish and Non-Jewish Resistance Activities and Underground Efforts Compare?

All countries in Nazi-occupied Europe engaged in a variety of resistance activities. However, beyond their shared rejection of German oppression, each country developed its own style of organized response. The characteristics of these movements varied with the attitudes of the occupying forces toward the conquered. Resistance also was influenced by physical and cultural features of the particular country or group, as well as by the amount and quality of as-sistance the resistance received from the Allies. The nature of this assistance depended on whether the Allies saw a country or a group as important. The diversity of the national resistance movements and their inherent secrecy blocked their integration. Each country had a distinct underground; there was no such thing as a unified European resistance. Just as across the continent, so inside each country factors bearing on political, social, and economic issues interfered with the integration of various resistance groups into a single entity. An authority on European resistance, Henri Michel, argues that "the best re-cruiting agents for resistance were the savagery of the SS, the ineptitude of the occupying regime, and the severity of the economic exploitation."[66]

The situation in Poland provides an example. From the beginning, the Ger-mans set out to destroy Poland's cultural institutions. Polish universities and high schools were closed. These actions coincided with the prohibition of all forms of political expression. The Germans wanted to destroy the male Polish elite, targeting the intellectuals, professionals, clergy, and army officers. Many of them were murdered; others were sent to concentration camps. The majority of the early inmates of Auschwitz were members of the Polish elite.

---

65. Lucjan Dobroszycki, "Polish Historiography on the Annihilation of the Jews of Poland in World War II: A Critical Evaluation," *East European Jewish Affairs* 23:2 (1993): 47.

66. Michel, *The Shadow War*, 185; Vakar echoes Michel's statement, also adding that all early partisans in the Belorussian forests, the Russian former military men, the former Soviet POWs, the Belorussian men, and the Jewish ghetto inmates, had one thing in common, namely, they were pro-pelled into the forest by the wish to survive and not by an ideology or desire to fight. See Vakar, *Belorussia*, 192–94.

Some emergent Polish underground organizations established illegal schools of higher learning; others facilitated clandestine lectures and promoted the writing of prohibited literature. The AK, the largest Polish resistance movement, concentrated on the illegal collection and dissemination of proscribed information. The AK also accumulated weapons and ammunition against the day they might be used to confront the occupying forces.[67]

Almost until the summer of 1944, the time of the Warsaw uprising, AK operations resembled the activities of other urban underground groups in Eastern Europe. All concentrated on the collection and dissemination of illegal materials, on forging documents, and on the accumulation of arms for future battles. Only a few armed uprisings—French, Polish, and Slovak—took place in 1944, when the Germans had been considerably weakened by the Allies. Most of the anticipated battles between the resistance movements and the Germans never materialized. Much of the accumulated weaponry had been collected in vain.

In contrast to the urban underground activities, various partisan groups used arms as early as 1941. Some scholars believe that early partisans in Belorussia—including former Soviet soldiers, Belorussian men, Jewish fugitives, and others—were propelled into the forests by the desire to live and not by ideological conviction or a genuine desire to fight.[68]

Coordinated anti-German military moves by Soviet partisans began to take place in the latter half of 1943. That movement claimed responsibility for 3,000 acts of railway sabotage, with attendant destruction of tracks, and sixteen German battalions immobilized. Not all of these claims can be verified.[69] As the largest, most powerful body, the Soviet partisan movement underwent many changes. At the end of 1943, it was partially controlled by three power centers: the Communist Party, the NKVD, and the Red Army.[70]

As the German military reverses became more serious and more sustained, participation in resistance to the Nazis became more attractive to larger numbers all over occupied Europe. Many were eager to join the illegal opposition forces. Among these latecomers some were former Nazi sympathizers and some former collaborators. On the other hand, the Allies only occasionally relied on European underground organizations. Contrary to what often has been claimed, European resistance movements did not win the war. Moreover, much

67. Arad, "The Jewish Fighting Underground in Eastern Europe," 339–40; Krakowski, *The War of the Doomed*, 7.

68. Refer to information in footnote 66.

69. Michel, *The Shadow War*, 279.

70. Armstrong and De Witt, "Organization and Control of the Partisan Movement," 133.

of the postwar talk about the wartime importance of the various resistance movements was exaggerated.[71]

As a people targeted for systematic degradation and total biological annihilation, Jews reacted uniquely to the German occupation. But as was the case with resistance by other Europeans, Jewish reactions to the Germans were influenced by changes in their situation. To recall, the definition of resistance guiding this discussion refers to efforts "to thwart, limit or end the exercise of power of the oppressors over the oppressed." Given the German objective toward the Jews, some scholars have argued that Jewish efforts merely to stay alive and maintain their moral traditions conform to this definition of resistance.[72] Others believe that this approach lacks appropriate precision and that it interferes with a disciplined understanding of resistance.[73]

Through their daily ghetto activities Jews had rejected most German prohibitions. For Jews, all measures to preserve their own lives and those of others constituted forms of opposition. Such efforts undermined the achievement of Nazi goals and seem to qualify as resistance. Yet, their day-to-day survival efforts clearly are an order of activity different from derailing trains or participating in an armed uprising. Since in their daily lives the Jews were responding to extreme and unprecedented conditions, it is fair to represent Jewish reactions as a special form of resistance.

Vladka Meed, a courier in the Warsaw ghetto, who continuously risked her life to promote all forms of Jewish resistance, supports this view. Aware that a few Warsaw ghetto internees behaved in selfish and dishonorable ways, she nevertheless feels that the ghetto majority, "in the middle of hunger, epidemics and suffering ... tried to retain their humanity. Under the most difficult conditions of unexpected pain, they would stick to ... traditional Jewish ethic[s]. Their resistance [resided] ... in the minute aspect[s] of everyday life."[74]

Vladka's mother was one who lived her resistance. Despite extreme hunger that caused swelling under her eyes, each week this woman put aside two slic-

71. Michael R. Marrus, "Varieties of Jewish Resistance: Some Categories and Comparisons in Historiographical Perspective," in *Major Changes within the Jewish People in the Wake of the Holocaust*, 271; Michel, *The Shadow War*, 358.

72. Some examples of this position are found in: Mark Dworzecki, "The Day to Day Stand of the Jews," in *Jewish Resistance during the Holocaust*, 152–89; Nachman Blumenthal, "Sources for the Study of Jewish Resistance," in *Jewish Resistance during the Holocaust*, 46–59; and Bauer, *The History of the Holocaust*, 277.

73. Raul Hilberg thinks that resistance should refer only to armed resistance. See his *The Politics of Memory: The Journey of a Holocaust Historian* (Chicago: Ivan R. Dee, 1996), 134–37.

74. Vladka Meed (personal interview).

es of her bread and hid them under her pillow. Once a week an old man came to their room to give Bar Mitzvah lessons to Vladka's younger brother. The mother's bread paid for the lessons. They never had the Bar Mitzvah.[75] A Vilna ghetto inmate, too, feels that "the resistance of the anonymous masses must be affirmed in terms of how they held on to their humanity, of their manifestation of solidarity, of mutual help and self-sacrifice, and the whole constellation subsumed under the simple heading of 'good deeds.'"[76]

In the ghetto, humanitarian activities on behalf of others required extraordinary moral strength. Such efforts contributed to the perpetuation of Jewish life while challenging the validity of Nazi policies of annihilation. As I have said, these activities seem to constitute resistance of a very special kind, without hope and without resources. Affirming traditional moral values without the "muscular" or violent connotations usually attaching to the notion of resistance, let us call this response unarmed humane resistance. In addition to unarmed humane resistance, the ghetto underground collected and distributed illegal information, forged documents, and prepared for armed resistance by collecting and manufacturing arms. To show the presence or absence of Jewish resistance comparisons *must* be made in terms of shared features of the Jewish and non-Jewish underground and not in terms of the specifics that divide them.

Still, Jewish and non-Jewish undergrounds had different chronologies. When non-Jewish resistance movements became well-organized, most Eastern European Jews already were dead or in concentration camps. But Jewish and non-Jewish resistance groups did engage in a number of similar activities: the collection and dissemination of information, the forgery of a variety of documents, and the collection of arms.

Non-Jewish political inmates of concentration camps established significant resistance groups in Buchenwald, Dachau, and Auschwitz. According to Hermann Langbein, an underground political leader in Auschwitz, their illegal activities involved the collection and destruction of incriminating materials, and the transfer of prisoners to better jobs. Often, the beneficiaries of these transfers were members of the Communist Party. Occasionally the underground helped in prisoners' escapes.[77] Resistance of non-Jewish concentration camp

75. Ibid.

76. Dworzecki, "The Day to Day Stand of the Jews," 174.

77. Josef Garlinski, *Fighting Auschwitz: The Resistance Movement in the Concentration Camp* (Greenwich, Conn.: Fawcett Publications, 1975); Eugen Kogon, *The Theory and Practice of Hell* (New York: Berkeley Books, 1980); Langbein, *Against All Hope*; Krzysztof Dunin-Wasowicz, *Resistance in the Nazi Concentration Camps 1933–1945* (Warsaw: Polish Scientific Publishers, 1982).

prisoners resembled in many respects the sorts of resistance pursued by Jewish ghetto inmates prior to armed rebellion. There were several armed Jewish uprisings in concentration camps, but that cannot be said of the non-Jewish underground groups in the camps.

When Michel raises the issue of comparing Jewish and non-Jewish resistance, he identifies the Jews as the most handicapped in their ability to become engaged in underground operations. He then continues to search for answers by examining the following seemingly comparable groups: non-Jews forced into slave labor in Germany, Soviet prisoners of war, and non-Jewish concentration camp inmates. Each of these groups was exposed to environments that in terms of threats to life, at least, resembled the environments that the Nazis created for the Jews. But neither the forced laborers nor the POWs engaged in any organized armed resistance. Except for a few attempts to escape, they complied with German orders. Acknowledging that the non-Jewish concentration camp undergrounds promoted mutual help, Michel notes that the Buchenwald underground planned an uprising toward the end of the war, but it never took place.

Michel concludes that "Jews were placed by Nazis in conditions in which it was difficult for them not to succumb and not be rent to pieces. Nevertheless, one can honestly conclude that the Jewish resistance movement played an honorable role in European resistance and that in some respects its role was exemplary."[78] Historical evidence shows that open armed resistance was more frequent for Jewish than non-Jewish underground groups. As noted earlier, in concentration camps non-Jewish underground groups did not fight openly. Other, armed non-Jewish uprisings took place in 1944. While exact figures about Jewish participation in non-Jewish resistance movements are elusive, most estimates show that, proportionately, many Jews became active partisans and others joined most of the urban underground groups. History tells that the Jews in these resistance movements behaved at least as bravely as their non-Jewish counterparts. Finally, too, when historical records about non-Jewish and Jewish resistance are compared, they refute any assumption that European Jews were passive. On the contrary, when comparisons take chronology and special circumstances into account, Jewish resistance to the unprecedented evil demonstrates a special kind of moral boldness.

78. Michel, "Jewish Resistance and the European Resistance Movement," 374–75.

Conclusion

Because of the inherent secrecy of underground operations, knowledge about resistance activities is incomplete. Specifically too, exact numbers, names, and ethnic identities of the resisters are unavailable. The paucity of evidence is compounded by the competition among various underground movements, each eager to take credit for Germany's ultimate demise. Indeed, scholars of European resistance warn that knowledge about this subject is incomplete. They also tend to agree that both collectively and singly, World War II underground movements cannot be credited with crushing the enemy. Finally, they admit that, as an area of study, the history of World War II resistance leaves us with many more questions than answers.

Comparing Jewish and non-Jewish resistance, I have studied organized opposition that aimed at the elimination of German oppression. A part of this opposition appeared as a series of steps, starting with the collection and dissemination of information and moving to the accumulation of arms and the preparation of armed resistance. However, the overwhelming power of the German occupation and its use of brutal force were largely responsible for the infrequent appearance of open armed resistance. Significantly, the evidence reviewed here shows that, although targeted for total annihilation, Jews more frequently than other oppressed groups engaged in open armed resistance.

In addition, I have argued that resistance in general and Jewish resistance in particular are complex concepts. The present examination of some relevant historical facts consistently demonstrates the presence of diverse forms of resistance. This examination has also shown that within the context of general anti-German strategies, armed resistance played a modest role. Nevertheless, those who refer to resistance, more often than not, think of fighting, of physical opposition, of the actual hurting of the enemy.

Why this concentration and seeming admiration of armed resistance to the exclusion of spiritual resistance? Why the relative disregard of resistance devoted to helping prospective victims overcome persecution and death? Observations made by two Holocaust heroes seem relevant. In conjunction with the twenty-fifth anniversary of the Warsaw Ghetto Uprising, Yitzhak Zuckerman, second-in-command of the revolt, replied to a question about its military lessons:

I don't think there is any need to analyze the uprising in military terms. This was a war of less than a thousand people against a mighty army and no one doubted how it was likely to turn out. . . . If there is a school to study the *human spirit*, there it should be a major subject. The really important things were inherent in the force shown by Jewish youths, after years of degradation, to rise up against their destroyers and determine what death they would choose: Treblinka or Uprising. I don't know if there is a standard to measure that.[79]

Similarly, when two weeks before his death, in 1987, I interviewed Tuvia Bielski and asked how he explains his devotion to saving lives rather than to fighting the Germans, he answered, "It was simple.... The enemy made no distinctions. They took anyone [any Jew] and killed him or her.... It did not pay. To me it made no sense. I wanted to save and not to kill."[80] Indeed, during Bielski's stay in the forest, as a commander of a unit that took on the dual role of rescuers and fighters, again and again Bielski urged his people, "Don't rush to fight and die. So few of us are left, we have to save lives. To save a Jew is much more important than to kill Germans."[81]

Preoccupied with the examination of different forms of Jewish resistance, I have paid scant attention to the varieties of resistance among non-Jewish groups. Only in passing have I mentioned that under the German occupation, the Polish underground was engaged in supporting the country's cultural institutions, among them different schools and universities. Omitted from my discussion was the help offered by the main Polish underground, the AK, to those who were singled out for special persecution: former Polish officers, concentration camp political prisoners, and Jews. Indeed, by 1942, the Polish underground had a special section, "Zegota," devoted to rescuing Jews.[82]

I have described the humane resistance of the Jews in ghettos—a response that included cultural programs and economic support of the needy. Excluded from this discussion was my earlier research about the rescuing of Jews by Christians. In two more recent research projects about the rescue of Jews by Jews, I examined the actions of Oswald Rufeisen and his selfless protection of both Jewish and non-Jewish victims.[83] I also examined the actions of a group of Jewish partisans commanded by Tuvia Bielski—the largest armed rescue of Jews by Jews during World War II. Results of this research point to the significance of rescue as a form of resistance.[84]

79. Yitzhak Zuckerman, *A Surplus of Memory: Chronicle of the Warsaw Ghetto Uprising* (Berkeley, Calif.: University of California Press, 1990), xiii.

80. Tec, *Defiance*, 48.

81. Ibid.

82. Teresa Prekerowa, *Konspiracyjna Rada Pomocy Zydom w Warszawie, 1942–1945* [Aid to Jews, 1942–1945] (Warsaw: Panstwowy Instytut Wydawniczy, 1982).

83. Tec, *In the Lion's Den*.

84. Tec, *Defiance*.

Selfless rescue as a form of resistance has important implications for an understanding of moral opposition to oppression and has potentially far-reaching implications for views about other resistance forms, including Jewish and non-Jewish opposition to oppression. In short, further attention to rescue as a form of Jewish and non-Jewish resistance would broaden and enlighten our views of the whole topic of resistance.

Dare we hope that soon, a more caring society would show greater support and attribute more value to the rescuing of victims rather than to the killing of enemies?

Part 2

Western Europe
and the Yishuv

Nathan Bracher

4   Up in Arms

Jewish Resistance against Nazi Germany
in France

The story of Jewish resistance against the Nazis in France is in fact composed
of an entire set of interrelated, multifaceted narratives. First, this resistance
evolved over time. Jews adapted their opposition to the Third Reich in response
to the changing realities of the war and the German occupation of France, as
they successively faced the outbreak of hostilities; the defeat and the armistice;
Vichy's collaboration in excluding, pillaging, arresting, and detaining the
Jews in internment camps; and finally, a long list of ever-increasing persecutions and deportations that we now recognize as part of the Nazis' enterprise
of total annihilation. Second, different components of the Jewish population in
France opposed Nazi Germany and its collaborators in numerous ways, which
varied according to the perceptions, cultural habits, and historical experiences
specific to each group. Both armed and unarmed Jewish resistance thus varied
according to contexts that evolved significantly from one stage of the war and
Occupation to another.

    We must moreover be mindful of the geopolitical dimensions of the Occupa-
tion, particularly in the first phase from June 1940 until November 1942, when
France was divided into a number of areas, each subjected to a different set of
dangers and restrictions: in addition to the major split between the Northern
or Occupied Zone, which found itself directly facing the German military command, and the Southern or Unoccupied Zone relegated to Vichy, three départements of the Alsace-Lorraine region, le Bas Rhin, le Haut Rhin, and la Moselle,

had been annexed by the Third Reich, while the northernmost tip of France, the départements of le Nord and le Pas de Calais were declared a forbidden zone. The widely revered World War I "Victor of Verdun," Marshal Philippe Pétain, took over as the overtly paternalistic head of the "French State" at Vichy. Pétain quickly scuttled democratic institutions and immediately set out to stigmatize egalitarian ideals and so-called "non-French" elements of the population. Jews were conveniently blamed for the disastrous defeat accompanied by an equally calamitous collapse of civil society known as the "exodus," when millions had chaotically sought to flee the rapidly advancing Wehrmacht in France. First in line for such scapegoating were prominent Jewish politicians such as Léon Blum, Pierre Mendès France, and Jean Zay, who had championed labor reform and social justice in the late 1930s.

Even under the terms of the humiliating, burdensome, and dishonorable armistice agreement that required French authorities to surrender refugees from Nazi Germany, Vichy peremptorily claimed to embody French sovereignty. From the very outset in late June 1940, however, a previously little known army officer who had gone to London as a liaison to Churchill, General Charles de Gaulle, vigorously denied the legitimacy of both the armistice and the Vichy regime, which in turn lost little time in condemning him to death in absentia. That the very foundations of legal authority were sharply contested created a significant degree of ambivalence and confusion, particularly in the earliest phases of the Occupation, as resistance in the Northern and Southern Zones developed according to contrasting perceptions of events. Resisters in the Northern Occupied Zone tended to see the ubiquitous Germans as their unique enemy and set about organizing acts of sabotage and networks that could gather intelligence and provide escape routes for Allied aviators. Resisters in the Southern Unoccupied Zone tended to have a more political focus that insisted on keeping France in the war on the Allied side in spite of the Armistice and Pétain's demand that France must seek to renovate itself while collaborating with the Germans.[1] Geographical realities added another set of critical factors conditioning Jewish resistance to Nazi Germany: the large expanse of territory, with its sparsely populated rural areas, numerous forests, and major mountain chains offered space for the maquis and armed resistance movements and shelter for refugees within France's mainland borders, while the contiguous

---

1. Dominique Veillon and Olivier Wieviorka, "La Résistance," in *La France des années noires, vol. 2, De l'Occupation à la Libération*, ed. Jean-Pierre Azéma and François Bédarida, 65–73 (Paris: Éditions du Seuil, 1993).

presence of two nonbelligerent countries, Switzerland and Spain, on France's eastern and western borders, offered the possibility of getting the refugees to a safe haven.

At the beginning of World War II, the Jewish population in France was relatively small, numbering from 320,000 to 350,000, but far from homogeneous. Although they shared many common interests and faced a common mortal enemy that would in the end unite them in both military action and rescue operations, foreign immigrant Jews and Jewish French nationals formed two distinct groups with significantly contrasting backgrounds and outlooks. The resurgence of virulent antisemitism in the 1930s had tended to make foreign Jews lightning rods for xenophobia even though they only comprised some 5 percent of the three million immigrants living in France in 1939. Approximately half of these noncitizen Jews had immigrated in the 1920s and the 1930s, coming to fill the need for industrial and agricultural workers created by France's huge loss of manpower in World War I. Many others streamed in later, seeking to escape the increasing danger as Hitler's arrival in power, followed by harsh anti-Jewish legislation in Nazi Germany, the Anschluss in Austria, the annexation of the Sudetenland, and Krystallnacht sent successive waves of Jewish immigrants in search of safety west of the Rhine.

Neither for the French-born Jews perfectly assimilated to the culture and society of their native land, nor for those who had more recently arrived in France, however, can the allegation of passivity in the face of the Nazi onslaught withstand even a cursory examination of the historical record. In order to have a clear understanding of that record and appreciate its multiple dimensions, it is crucial not to project the perspectives and priorities that are ours now, some seventy years after World War II, onto people of another era whose understanding of themselves and of their times was quite different, and understandably so, since such historical self-knowledge was by definition fragmentary and incomplete. To point out that any given historical account is necessarily written in response to the demands and sensitivities of the historian's own context may now be a commonplace, but it remains particularly important when dealing with the war, the Holocaust, and Jewish resistance in France. Our own era presently understands racism to be central to Nazi ideology to the point of having determined strategic Nazi decisions that set in motion the unprecedented and previously unimaginable industrial enterprise of total annihilation. As a result, we tend to seek a distinct and specifically Jewish response to what we now recognize as the rapidly encroaching forces of destruction, beginning with

75

the measures of exclusion, persecution, and spoliation enacted as early as the summer of 1940 in France.[2]

For French Jews in 1940 and 1941, however, the notion of a specifically if not exclusively Jewish form of resistance to Nazi Germany would have been incongruous for several important reasons. It was after all France that in 1791 had been the first in Europe to grant Jews full rights as equal citizens. The Third Republic had welcomed Algerian Jews as citizens in 1871 and, when all was said and done, had finally vindicated and even rehabilitated Alfred Dreyfus in spite of the turpitude on the part of a number of army officers and the resurgence of a fearfully virulent antisemitism in the late 1890s and early 1900s. Grateful for emancipation and trusting in the rule of law for the ongoing protection of their rights, assimilated Jews were therefore on the whole strongly committed to proving themselves model citizens, loyal to France's heritage, scrupulously obedient to its laws, and zealous in service to its ideals and to the defense of its security. Rather than emphasizing their specificity as Jewish, they insisted on presenting themselves as French citizens among many others, relegating Jewishness to the private realms of religious belief and family heritage. This affirmation of a French identity was all the more adamant in the 1930s and 1940s in that antisemites were not only stressing the singularity of Jews as supposedly foreign and unassimilable, but were also presenting Jews as warmongers creating unnecessary and dangerous hostilities between France and Germany.

Penned after the disastrous fall of France in May and June of 1940 that had brought to power Marshal Philippe Pétain and ushered in the Vichy regime that immediately began stripping away legal protections and excluding Jews from many sectors of public life, the famous words written by historian Marc Bloch, the founder of the renowned Annales school of history, are emblematic of the assimilated Jews' devotion to France and the Third Republic. The passage bears citing at length:

I am Jewish, if not by religion—which I do not observe, no more than I do any other religion—at least by birth. I draw neither pride nor shame for that, being, I hope, a good enough historian to know that racial predispositions are a myth and that the

---

2. The demand for a specifically Jewish resistance dates in fact from the 1970s, just as the Holocaust was beginning to be much more widely understood as a highly specific, unprecedented occurrence at the very center of the Second World War, and as, in the wake of the Six Day War, European Jews began to focus on their own specific identity. See Denis Peschanski, "Comment parvenir à faire reconnaître la mémoire des combattants juifs de France dans leur singularité et leur combat commun," in *Les Juifs ont résisté en France, 1940–1945* (Paris: AACCE [l'Association des Amis de la CCE (Commission centrale de l'enfance), 2009]), 242.

notion of a pure race is a particularly flagrant absurdity when people claim that it applies, as is the case here, to what was in reality, a group of believers who had been recruited earlier from the Mediterranean world of Turko-Khazars and Slavs. I never stake a claim to my origins except in one situation: when I am facing an anti-Semite. But people who will be opposed to my testimony may perhaps seek to undermine it in calling me a "mutt." I will calmly reply that my great grandfather was a soldier in 1793; that, in 1870, my father was in the army during the siege of Strasbourg; that he and my two uncles voluntarily left their native Alsace region after it had been annexed by the Second Reich; that I have been raised to revere patriotic traditions, which the Israelites of the Alsatian exodus had always kept up the most fervently of all; and that, finally, while certain people would gladly conspire to have me expelled today from France, and perhaps (who knows?) will succeed, France will, whatever may transpire, remain the homeland in which my heart is rooted. I was born here, I have drunk at the wellsprings of her culture, I have made her past mine, I breathe easily only under her skies, and I have, in turn, striven to defend her to the best of my ability.[3]

These eloquent lines taken from *L'Étrange défaite*, which remains one of the most rigorous assessments of the catastrophe of 1940 even though it was written only weeks after the events, are emblematic of assimilated Jews' attachment to French culture and to the Republic: Bloch insists that he is above all a French citizen whose patriotism is demonstrated by a long personal and family record of military service in times of war. He refers to his specifically Jewish identity only in response to those trying to portray him and Jews in general as not authentically French, and goes on to add that Alsatian Jews were the most fervent of French patriots. Throughout *L'Étrange défaite*, Bloch considers the war not as a problem for Jews in particular but for all of France, which now finds itself overrun by an aggressor whose ideology is anathema to the Republic.

We should take care to notice what makes Marc Bloch emblematic of resistance to Nazi Germany on the part of assimilated French Jews. In the first place, we observe that fierce loyalty to the French Republic led Bloch not to passivity in the face of danger, but on the contrary to armed combat and clandestine resistance. Initially revoked as a professor with the Université de Strasbourg by virtue of Vichy's anti-Jewish legislation, Bloch was able to retain his post after colleagues had obtained an exemption for him on the basis of outstanding scholarly achievement. Deciding against emigration to the United States, he became one of the leaders of the armed resistance in the Lyon region. Captured on March 8, 1944, he was brutally tortured and sent before a Nazi firing

3. Marc Bloch, *L'Étrange défaite* (Paris: Gallimard, 1990), 31–33. Here, as throughout, the translation is my own.

squad: he was executed on June 16, 1944, but not before comforting a younger comrade in arms who had also been condemned to death.[4]

It would be anachronistic to ask what may have been specifically or singularly Jewish in Bloch's unrelenting armed opposition to the Third Reich. Marc Bloch was one of the most illustrious of the many French Jews who became leaders of the French Resistance. Like his counterparts, he refused to differentiate between the cause of Jews and the cause of France, even though he was well aware that Nazi ideology had always targeted Jews in particular. The clear fact of the matter is that, without calling attention to their particular status or grouping themselves together under some separate banner, French Jews resisted in greater proportions than their non-Jewish counterparts, doubtless due to the persecutions that targeted them, but in spite of the greater dangers they faced since they could be arrested and deported either as Jews or as resisters.[5] Indeed, there were a significant number of French Jews who from the early moments of the Occupation became founders and leaders of resistance movements on the French mainland, including Raymond Aubrac (*Libération Sud*), Jean Cavaillès (*Libération Nord*), Jean-Jacques Bernard (*Combat*), Maxime Bloch-Mascart (*Organisations Civile et Militaire*), Daniel Mayer (a Socialist party leader named to the *Conseil National de la Résistance*), Léo Hamon (first with *Combat,* then *Ceux de la Résistance,* and finally the *Comité parisien de Libération*), and Jean-Pierre Lévy (*Franc-Tireur*).[6] Many have echoed Marc Bloch's words, insisting that they fought as French citizens defending the territorial integrity and democratic institutions of the French Republic, not as members of some separate community. Their thinking is summed up aptly in the words of Raymond Aron, who went to London to support Charles de Gaulle and *La France Libre*: "If the Germans won the war, Jews would disappear from France and from Europe. If they lost, [Vichy's] Jewish Statutes would not last: they would vanish with the war."[7] Léo Hamon, a prominent leader of the resistance on the mainland, expressed a similar perspective on the question of specifically Jewish causes in the organized military opposition to the Nazis: "That question was in an entire set of problems: we were fighting against all of

---

4. "Marc Bloch historien et homme d'action," official website of L'Association Marc Bloch: http://www.marcbloch.fr/bio03.html.

5. Renée Poznanski, "La Résistance Juive en France," *Revue d'histoire de la Deuxième Guerre mondiale* 137 (Jan. 1985): 10–11.

6. David Douvette, "Participation des Juifs de France à la Résistance et panorama de la Résistance juive en France 1940–1944," in *Les Juifs ont résisté en France*, 55.

7. André Kaspi, *Les Juifs pendant l'Occupation* (Paris: Éditions du Seuil, 1997), 300–303, 308.

them."[8] While intent on fighting the Nazi menace that had long targeted Jews, they refused any notion of a separate war "for the Jews," particularly since antisemitic propaganda had long depicted them as warmongers pushing France to engage in another useless and catastrophically destructive war with Germany. Even with heightened personal motivation, they identified their combat with that of France and the Allies in general.

The same identification of intense personal commitment to oppose Nazi Germany with the combat of France and of the Allies in general can be found among Jews who went to London to join General Charles de Gaulle in *La France Libre* (Free France). Indeed, Jean-François Muracciole points out that Jews were six times more numerous in de Gaulle's *France Libre* than in the French population in general.[9] It was after all Charles de Gaulle, in his now famous *appel du 18 juin* (call of June 18, 1940), who first summoned the French to "resistance": "Whatever may come to be, the flame of French resistance must not and will not die out."[10] To be sure, we must once again avoid anachronisms: when de Gaulle exhorted his compatriots to fuel the flame of "resistance," he was not thinking of the insurrectional commandos, nor even teams of saboteurs and intelligence gatherers lurking in the shadows. He was instead focused on maintaining France and France's official armed forces in the war. He was categorically refusing the armistice that had officially removed France from the struggle and put the country under the thumb of the Germans. De Gaulle's *appel du 18 juin* and his subsequent war campaign can thus be inscribed in both the categories of the continuity of the French Republic and a daring, radical break. For while de Gaulle was calling for the continuation of the struggle by France's official "legal" army, he was at the same time boldly stepping outside the established order. For that he would be declared an outlaw and condemned to death by Vichy.

Pierre Laborie has defined resistance as an action undertaken within an organized, collective framework, guided by the goal of harming or thwarting the enemy and involving a break with or transgression of the established order.[11] This definition clearly applies to those who enrolled in *La France Libre*, and

8. Cited by Pierre Laborie, "La Résistance et le sort des juifs, 1940–1942," in *Mémoire et Histoire* (Toulouse: Éditions Privat, 1995), 258.

9. Jean-François Muracciole, *Les Français libres. L'autre Résistance* (Paris: Tallandier, 2009), 162.

10. Bruno Leroux, "18 juin 1940: l'appel du général de Gaulle," in *Dictionnaire Historique de la Résistance*, ed. François Marcot, Bruno Leroux, and Christine Levisse-Touzé (Paris: Robert Laffont, 2006), 592.

11. Pierre Laborie, "Qu'est-ce que la Résistance?" in *Dictionnaire Historique de la Résistance*, 37.

all the more so for those who were Jewish. Jean-Louis Crémieux-Brilhac notes that just as de Gaulle had been condemned to death as an insubordinate and an outlaw, so all those who came to join his fight were stripped of their citizenship and condemned as criminals. One moreover had to accept separation from friends, family, familiar surroundings, and be willing to forego financial support.[12] The commitment to de Gaulle's movement therefore involved a paradox, particularly for Jews during World War II: they had to break with what was recognized as the prevailing legal order in France in order to remain faithful to the values of the Republic. On the level of individual private life, the choice could be termed "heroic" in view of the courage and resolution required.

Pierre Mendès France offers one of the most illustrious examples of an assimilated French Jew whose ardent commitment to the French Republic naturally led to highly active resistance to Nazism. Mendès France had had to withstand overtly antisemitic attacks, questioning the authenticity of his French ancestry, in order to become the youngest representative ever elected to the National Assembly at the age of twenty-five in 1932.[13] It was precisely such attacks that spurred him to volunteer for active duty at the outset of the war in 1939. Stunned and disheartened by the defeatism of Pétain's June 17 speech announcing an end to France's battle against the German invasion, Mendès France was galvanized by de Gaulle's call to continue the fight. With other like-minded political and military colleagues, he boarded the ill-fated ship, Massiglia, with the intent of pursuing the fight from the French stronghold in Morocco, where his military unit had been transferred.[14]

A month after his arrival at Casablanca, Mendès France, along with a number of other prominent Jewish personalities of the Popular Front, was charged with desertion and subjected to the humiliation of arrest and detention in a squalid jail. The worst was yet to come, as Mendès France's original faith in the judicial institutions of the French Republic was sorely wounded, first when Vichy's own Jewish Statutes denied him his seat in the National Assembly and then when, after more than a year of detention and legal proceedings, he was finally convicted of desertion, stripped of his officer's commission, and condemned to six years in prison.[15]

Having no intention of going gently into the night of infamy that Vichy had

12. Jean-Louis Crémieux-Brilhac, *La France Libre I* (Paris: Gallimard, 1996), 43, 123–25.

13. Geoffrey Adams, *Political Ecumenism: Catholics, Jews, and Protestants in De Gaulle's Free France, 1940–1945* (Montreal: McGill-Queen's University Press, 2006), 155.

14. Éric Roussel, *Pierre Mendès France* (Paris: Gallimard, 2007), 114–21.

15. Ibid., 122–34.

prepared for him, Mendès France lashed out openly, addressing first the presiding judge, and then Pétain:

An innocent man has just been convicted out of political hatred. This is not France's justice. It is Hitler's. Do not give up on France. Mr. Government Commissary, added Mendès France, I hope that your conscience gives you rest. You have done your job for Hitler and worked well for your promotion.

No one has been fooled. It is not the officer that you wanted to punish. It's the politician, the Leftist representative to the National Assembly, and the Jew that was targeted.... Well, Marshal Pétain, what is to be my attitude?[16]

Outraged at seeing his loyalty, patriotism, and military service impugned purely on the basis of political prejudice and antisemitism, Mendès France escaped from detention and finally reached London after passing through Switzerland and then Portugal. Received warmly by de Gaulle, Mendès France immediately joined the all-volunteer unit whose mission was to fly low-altitude, high-risk bombing and reconnaissance missions over occupied France. When in late 1943 de Gaulle finally formed a provisional government in Algiers, he tapped Mendès France's political and economic expertise for the role of Minister of Finance.[17]

It was precisely the antisemites' repeated attempts to portray him and his fellow Jews as fundamentally different and separate from other French citizens that spurred Pierre Mendès France to join Charles de Gaulle and La France Libre and to participate in the military fight against Nazi Germany. Mendès France was adamant in his determination to show that he was serving his country and fighting for its democratic institutions, not fighting on behalf of a specific group. At the same time, he neither renounced nor dissimulated his socioethnic origins. Like Marc Bloch, he proudly proclaimed his Jewish identity when facing those who sought to attack him on that ground, not only at the conclusion but at the very outset of his trial, as he so eloquently relates in Marcel Ophüls's documentary film, *Le Chagrin et la pitié*: "Your honor, I am a Jew and a Socialist, but I am not guilty of desertion. Let the proceedings begin."

To be sure, Mendès France was part of the "elite" of de Gaulle's intelligentsia and military forces. He was by no means an anomaly: there would be much to say about the action of such figures as Jacques Bingen, Joseph Kessel, Romain Gary, Maurice Druon, André Gillois, André Weil-Curiel, and Jean Pierre Bloch. Like Mendès France, all were emblematic of the Jews seeking to pursue the

16. Ibid., 135, 138.
17. Ibid., 140–67.

fight against Nazi Germany with *La France Libre*. Engaging in the Resistance under the auspices of *La France Libre* allowed French Jews both to affirm their loyalty to the French Republic and to combat Nazi Germany as full-fledged citizens of France.[18]

At the same time, tens of thousands of immigrant Jews who did not enjoy French citizenship were also eager to prove their attachment to the country that they considered a refuge and a beacon of human rights, particularly since the rising xenophobia of the late 1930s had often portrayed them as dangerous subversives or unwanted economic burdens who were weakening French society and undermining domestic and international political stability. Coming from European countries with a history of pogroms or a recent German takeover, many immigrant Jews remained wary of state institutions and officials exercising power.[19] In spite of the insults, prejudice, and harassment that they often encountered in France, they maintained a positive attitude toward the country that, more than any other, offered freedom and the chance for a decent life.[20] Those who did not have their papers in order nevertheless faced expulsion. For all these reasons, and because of the clear and present danger posed by Nazi Germany, foreign Jews were ardent supporters of France's war effort. They translated that support into action by volunteering massively for military service at the outbreak of the conflict in early September 1939: as many as 30,000 of the estimated 150,000 to 160,000 noncitizen immigrant Jews sought to enroll in the French Army, and some 24,000 were accepted.[21]

These foreign Jews volunteering to join the ranks of the French army and fight against Nazi Germany were not exactly welcomed with open arms. At first, all that was open to them was the French Foreign Legion, where they were indignant to find themselves in an outfit commonly regarded as a safe haven for thugs and thieves. On September 16, 1939, two weeks after France had mobilized, however, then Finance Minister Paul Reynaud issued a decree creating special units for foreign volunteers. Sent to the front lines of the battle for iron ore in Narvik, Norway in the spring of 1940, these units, along with France's colonial troops, were also stationed on the front lines when France was invaded in May 1940. Despite the fall of France in June, they distinguished themselves

18. Renée Poznanski, "Juifs dans la Résistance (les)," in *Dictionnaire Historique de la Résistance*, ed. Marcot, Leroux, and Levisse-Touzé, 897.

19. Poznanski, "La Résistance Juive en France," 5.

20. Susan Zuccotti, *The Holocaust, the French, and the Jews* (New York: Basic Books, 1993), 28.

21. Ibid., 31–32. See David Douvette, "L'engagement volontaire des Juifs étrangers dans l'armée française 1939–1945," in *Les Juifs ont résisté en France*, 51–52.

by their fierce combativeness and accordingly heavy losses.[22] Tragically, Vichy did not honor the French Republic's promise to exempt those who enrolled in the armed forces and also their families from internment and expulsion: under the Occupation, many were first sent to French camps and then handed over to the Germans, who deported them to Auschwitz.[23]

Many others, however, would become some of the most active members of the armed mainland resistance which, like *La France Libre*, included a disproportionately large number of Jews among its ranks, precisely because Jews were the first targeted by propaganda, despoliations, detention, and deportation. Previous hardships and persecutions had in a sense predisposed many immigrant Jews for armed opposition by placing before them tough choices requiring courage and clear commitment. Many had also already faced hostile, oppressive regimes and even had to operate clandestinely.[24] Most active of all were those who, even while they were scorned in almost all other sectors of French society, had been taken in by the French Communist Party and grouped together in language groups in the 1920s.[25] Under the Occupation, they contributed to the ranks of the FTP-MOI (*Franc-Tireurs Partisans-Main d'Oeuvre Immigrée* or Partisan Sharp-Shooters—Immigrant Manual Labor), who distinguished themselves as the most active resistance group in Paris. Even though their numbers were modest in absolute terms, numbering about 200 in the Paris region, sixty-five of whom actually conducted raids, they carried out some of the most daring and dangerous operations: From September 1942 until May 1943, the second Jewish detachment of the MOI, often using bombs and grenades, led some fifty attacks against the Germans in Paris. Unlike mainland resistance groups made up of French citizens, these foreign Jewish resisters could not, given their accent and often severe lack of social connections, function like fish in a pond; they instead had to rely on themselves and live totally clandestinely. Their ranks were decimated by Vichy's deployment of some 200 special inspectors working in conjunction with the city police of Paris.[26]

At first blush, one might be tempted to conclude that foreign Jews engaged in more specifically Jewish forms of resistance than French Jews. The reality is

22. Douvette, "L'engagement volontaire des Juifs étrangers dans l'armée française 1939–1945," 52–54.

23. Zuccotti, *The Holocaust, the French, and the Jews*, 31–32.

24. Poznanski, "La Résistance Juive en France," 4–5, 9.

25. Kaspi, *Les Juifs pendant l'Occupation*, 310.

26. Adam Rayski, "Rassemblement des résistants progressistes et stratégie du secteur juif de la MOI," in *Les Juifs ont résisté en France*, 96–98.

actually much more complex. Because of their common political orientation, many foreign Jews active in the mainland resistance were attracted to groups organized or led by the French Communist Party. Unlike most French assimilated Jews, who identified their fight with that of the French Republic upon which their plight presumably depended, these foreign Jews tended to consider the fruits of the Communist revolution in Soviet Russia as holding the greatest hope for destroying the Nazis who were threatening them and mankind in general.

It was Hitler's invasion of the Soviet Union on June 22, 1941, that prompted the French Communists to engage in armed resistance. One of the first actions undertaken by Jewish Communists and Zionists in Paris was to pressure Jewish artisans either to refuse to produce goods such as warm clothing for Germans or to sabotage their production by making those goods prone to failure.[27] The goal of these actions was to help the USSR by hampering the German war effort. Even the FTP-MOI units did not seek to further specifically Jewish goals or to target the personnel or the infrastructure responsible for arresting and deporting Jews. They rather sought to hasten the defeat of Nazi Germany with spectacular operations such as train derailments or the assassination of prominent officers of the Wehrmacht, including Julius Ritter, who was in charge of recruiting French workers and sending them to forced labor in Germany.[28] There again, the objective was to weaken the German war machine by squeezing the supply of workers.

While differing in background, political ideology, and often strategy from their counterparts in *La France Libre* and in the mainland non-Communist resistance, foreign Jews active with the Communist French resistance movements as well as in a number of entirely Jewish individual units, all participated in a common struggle to defeat Nazi Germany and to restore France's territorial integrity and political autonomy. De Gaulle opposed assassinations and random attacks on German soldiers, preferring to reserve military action for systematically organized efforts to liberate French territory, while the Communist resistance groups favored immediate violent attacks. All, however, were intent on showing the Germans and the Allies that instead of remaining passively subdued, France could still actively oppose the Nazis in the war. At the same time, it was crucial to mobilize French public opinion in view of the effort to bring

27. Poznanski, "La Résistance Juive en France," 12.
28. Kaspi, *Les Juifs pendant l'Occupation*, 316–18.

about liberation from the Nazis.[29] That is why both the non-Communist groups, in November 1942, and the Communist groups, in January 1943, united under the umbrella of Le Front National, ultimately recognized Charles de Gaulle as the official leader of the French Resistance.[30] Even the Zionist group, *Organisation Juive de Combat*, which was made up entirely of Jews and focused on getting Jews out of France in order to populate Palestine, was counting on the authority of Great Britain and remained determined to contribute to the Allied victory over Nazi Germany.[31]

The Jewish contribution to the French Resistance proved invaluable, as evident in the prominent examples such as those that follow here, among many others. Out of the twenty-three members of the FTP-Manouchian group who were arrested after a long series of spectacular attacks against the Germans, twelve were foreign Jews. The Germans attempted to turn French public opinion against them by portraying the group as alien terrorists, first in a newsreel film of their trial, and then on the infamous *Affiche rouge* (red poster). The images of youthful, courageous faces having visibly endured torture produced instead the opposite effect, and went on to inspire one of Louis Aragon's most famous poems, later set to music by Léo Ferré, and then made into a film, first by Frank Cassenti in 1976 (*L'Affiche rouge*) and again in 2009 by Robert Guédiguian.[32] While the considerable interest generated by the various dimensions of *L'Affiche rouge* over the years has made the Manouchian group the most well-known, there were even more FTP-MOI combat units made up essentially of Jews in provincial cities, including the Caramagnole batallion that played a key role in the Villeurbanne insurrection of August 24–26, 1944, in preparation for the liberation of Lyon a few days later.[33]

In 1943, the leaders of the Jewish sections of the FTP-MOI created two organizations, the UJJ (*Union des Jeunesses Juives* or Union of Jewish Youth,) and the UJRE (*Union des Juifs pour la résistance et l'entraide* or Union of Jews for Resistance and Mutual Aid). These groups were to fight specifically for the sur-

---

29. Denis Peschanski, "Actions de Propagande et articulations avec les opérations directes des résistants de la MOI," in *Les Juifs ont résisté en France*, 132–33.

30. Jean-Louis Crémieux-Brilhac, "La France libre, la Résistance et la France," in *Dictionnaire Historique de la Résistance*, ed. Marcot, Leroux, and Levisse-Touzé, 16.

31. Poznanski, "La Résistance Juive en France," 16.

32. See *http://www.herodote.net/histoire/evenement.php?jour=19440221* and *http://www.lefigaro .fr/festival-de-cannes/2009/05/11/03011-20090511ARTFIG00573-guediguian-un-film-pour-devenir-soi-meme-resistant-.php*

33. Claude Collin, "L'UJJ, une organisation de jeunesse liée à la section juive de la MOI," in *Les Juifs ont résisté en France*, 117.

vival and the future of the Jews. Those recruited into these groups underwent political and military training. In view of the increasingly grave dangers facing Jews, and in particular Jewish children during the latter phase of the German occupation of France, however, they devoted considerable energy to lead as many Jewish persons as possible to safety, either by hiding them in France or by escorting them across the borders to Switzerland or Spain. They published articles in underground newspapers calling attention to the grave dangers posed by the intensifying persecutions, collected food ration tickets, thwarted transportation, attacked the storefronts of known collaborators, gathered arms, and even executed "traitors." While armed action against the Nazi war machine remained their priority, they were clearly intent on protecting Jews who were not directly participating in military action.[34]

There were moreover uniquely Jewish maquis in the département of Le Tarn, near the Pyrenees, who rallied under both the French flag and the Zionist flag with the blue Star of David. In addition to their physical workouts, they engaged in the study of the Bible, Jewish history, and Jewish cultural traditions, and observed the rites of Jewish worship on the Sabbath. The *Armée juive* was formed by Abraham Polonski and Lucien Lublin in January 1942 and eventually counted some 2,000 members.[35] The EIF (*Éclaireurs Israélites de France*, Jewish Boy Scouts) maquis merged with the *Armée juive* to form the *Organisation Juive de Combat* on June 1, 1944. Resisters in these groups even wore armbands with the Star of David to make sure that the Nazis and their collaborators knew that Jews were standing up to them. During the liberation of Paris in August 1944, a group of their shock troops stormed the Drancy camp in the suburbs, which had served as the antechamber to Auschwitz. Tragically, it was precisely from Drancy that a group of their leaders, having been trapped by the Gestapo, had been deported only a few days before in the last train to leave the camp on August 17, 1944.[36]

Our survey of the various groups of Jews directly involved in the armed mainland resistance thus leads us to what in fact historians recognize as the most important component of their opposition to Nazi Germany: namely, the numerous individuals and organizations devoted to rescuing Jews in France by getting them out of camps, hiding them in various shelters, supplying them

---

34. Ibid., 113–21.

35. Patrick Henry, *We Only Know Men: The Rescue of Jews in France during the Holocaust* (Washington, D.C.: The Catholic University of America Press, 2007), 86.

36. Kaspi, *Les Juifs pendant l'Occupation*, 363–72.

with food, fabricating entire sets of identity and rationing documents, and transporting them across the Swiss or Spanish border.[37] As we have seen, Jews were proportionately much more active in all the branches of the armed resistance operating in mainland France as well as with de Gaulle's forces under *La France Libre*. It is true that the armed Jewish resistance groups, in particular the UJRE and the FTP-MOI, all contributed in various ways to saving Jewish children. But many more Jews were directly engaged in strictly nonmilitary rescue operations.[38] The major debate within the armed resistance was whether, as the Communist groups insisted, to engage in immediate, isolated armed attacks aimed mainly at destabilizing the enemy psychologically and arousing public opposition to the Nazis, or, as preferred by the non-Communist movements, to gather intelligence, stock weapons, and prepare instead for the major battles that would follow the Allied invasion. Within the Jewish resistance, the debate centered on whether the best strategy for saving Jews from arrest, detention, and what was known to be a highly dangerous deportation, was to work within legal channels or to go underground.[39] Given their fierce loyalty to the French Republic and their habit of proving themselves model citizens, these organizations staffed mainly by assimilated French Jews worked largely in the open, using official legal channels.

It is in this light that we can best approach the sensitive matter of the UGIF (*L'Union Générale des Israélites de France*), the compulsory umbrella organization for all Jews and all Jewish organizations that was first demanded by the Nazis and finally created by Vichy in November 1941. Funded not only by mandatory contributions from its unwilling members, but even more painfully, by the proceeds gathered from the systematic despoliation of Jewish businesses under the "Aryanization" program, the UGIF was from the outset and remains today the subject of fierce criticism, as has been the case for other umbrella organizations in other countries occupied by the Germans. Yet it is important to keep in mind that prominent Jews who occupied important positions in the UGIF strongly protested from the beginning that its very creation violated the law of 1905 separating church and state, and that, more seriously, the creation

37. Poznanski, "La Résistance Juive en France," 22. See Kaspi, *Les Juifs pendant l'Occupation*, 339, 371; Joseph Kastersztein "La réalité historique dément une représentation passive des Juifs face à l'extermination," in *Les Juifs ont résisté en France*, 34–37; Douvette, "Participation des Juifs de France à la Résistance et panorama de la Résistance juive en France 1940–1944," 55.

38. Douvette, "Participation des Juifs de France à la Résistance et panorama de la Résistance juive en France 1940–1944," 55.

39. Poznanski, "La Résistance Juive en France," 12.

of the UGIF put the Jews on the margins of society, outside the national community.

It is also important to understand what led Raymond-Raoul Lambert and Jacques Helbronner to accept leadership positions in the UGIF. Far from blind passivity or desire for personal gain, it was for Lambert a courageous affirmation of his citizenship: as a decorated veteran of World War I as well as of the battles of May and June 1940, Lambert refused out of patriotism to leave France for the United States. While strongly disapproving of the creation of the UGIF in principle, Jacques Helbronner finally concluded that the organization offered the best hope of channeling aid to those Jews who now found themselves isolated, abandoned, and deprived of the most basic necessities. Robert Gamzon, founder of the EIF, the Jewish Boy Scouts of France, figured among the UGIF's board of directors before going on to head up one of the main components of the Jewish maquis. Both Lambert and Helbronner, along with André Baur, who had equally protested against the exclusion of the Jews from the national community, ended up being deported to Auschwitz with their families: none survived.[40]

It is also true that all the branches of the armed resistance were, from our present-day perspective, slow to understand the grave threats closing in on Jews in France before the momentous events of the summer of 1942. As Pierre Laborie points out, it is important to remember that, for all the courage and resolution that the Resistance surely exemplified, those actively opposing Nazi Germany nevertheless shared the historical and psychological limits of the early phase of the Occupation: as was the case for *La France Libre* and the Allies, the French armed Resistance, including its Jewish components, saw the persecutions of the Jews as one problem among many others, rather than according it the centrality we give to the Holocaust with our current knowledge of World War II.[41]

It is useful to recall that the very word "genocide" had to be coined in 1944. Even someone as astute and as relatively well informed as Raymond Aron, who during the Occupation had gone to London to support de Gaulle and *La France Libre*, admits in his *Mémoires* that he had for a long time failed to seize the enormity of the ongoing disaster: "the gas chambers, the industrial murder of human beings, no, I admit, I did not imagine that, and because I wasn't able to imagine it, I did not know about it."[42] If the Nazi machinery of death was sim-

---

40. Kaspi, *Les Juifs pendant l'Occupation*, 323–49.

41. Laborie, "La Résistance et le sort des juifs, 1940–1942," 249, 257.

42. Cited in Stéphane Courtois and Adam Rayski, *Qui savait quoi? L'extermination des juifs, 1941–1945* (Paris: Éditions de la Découverte, 1987), 13.

ply unimaginable for Aron, who after the war would prove to be one of France's most astute political minds, how much more difficult it must have been for those working clandestinely in mainland France, where they only had access to fragmentary, often confused and contradictory versions of what was happening elsewhere: people had to do the best they could with the limited, incoherent knowledge available. Madeleine Dreyfus thus ruefully reflected on the plight of her friend Simone Kahn, who, after accepting to escort children to safety, was arrested and ultimately deported to her death: "We didn't know, we who asked her to do so [to take care of the children], that, in a way we condemned her to death. How could we have possibly imagined the gas chambers?"[43]

As we observed at the outset, Jews in France resisted Nazi Germany in numerous ways ranging from documenting the crimes perpetrated against them, to fostering a spirit of Jewish communal identity in the face of systematic stigmatization, exclusion, and persecution, to rescuing and hiding children, to armed commando raids against military targets. We are now poised to reflect further on the very nature and definition of resistance in the context of the Holocaust and World War II in France. As Joseph Kastersztein along with François Bédarida and others have observed, there is something fundamentally problematic in the notion that it was somehow incumbent on Jews to "save their honor" by mounting armed resistance.[44] The stereotypical image of "sheep being led to slaughter" is both a historical falsehood and a vicious stereotype, for it suggests that there was something shameful about being targeted for systematic murder. But on exactly what grounds does one demand that those who have been made most vulnerable by despoliation, exclusion, and scapegoating (not to mention children, the elderly, and the infirm) display armed resistance to have dignity?

The problem stems in part from the very narrow understanding of the Resistance forged in the immediate postwar era, at a time when French national identity was being reconstructed around the ideal of unified resistance to the Nazi aggressor. In spite of having been specifically targeted for systematic murder on the basis of identity, Jews were simply lumped together with all the other "victims" (such as hostages, forced labor deportees, and those killed, wounded or made homeless by the bombing of cities), all of whom took the backstage to those who had engaged in armed military combat: both members of the armed

43. Henry, *We Only Know Men*, 77.
44. Kastersztein, "La réalité historique dément une représentation passive des Juifs face à l'extermination," 34.

resistance and those serving in regular military units were celebrated as heroes who had liberated French territory and saved the honor of the nation after
the humiliating defeat of June 1940. It was in that context that Jews, having
been marked as irremediably alien and unassimilable to the French nation by
the flood of vicious propaganda unleashed as early as August 1940, when Vichy abrogated the Marchandeau Law banning racial attacks in the press, insisted on identifying themselves as French instead of calling attention to the
specificity of their situation. Such was even the case for the many foreigners
who had been active in the Resistance: they were considered to have become
"naturalized" French citizens by virtue of their combat. In postwar France, national unity and Jewish integration were thus forged at the expense of Jewish
identity and of a clear recognition of all that Jews had done to resist the Nazis.[45]

Furthermore, due in large part to the French Communists' insistence on presenting the Resistance as a popular insurrection, resistance activity was until
the 1980s most commonly conceived as being limited to spectacular raids and
acts of sabotage carried out by armed commandos, while the myriad unarmed,
but terribly dangerous efforts to hide and rescue Jews from arrest and deportation were ignored and forgotten, even though they had in fact constituted the
earliest and most widespread component of Jewish resistance.[46] Yehuda Bauer's oft-cited definition of resistance was any group action seeking deliberately
to oppose anti-Jewish laws and to thwart the Nazis' plans for total annihilation.[47] This definition clearly applied to all those who worked not only to protect the present and future lives, but also to preserve Jewish values and identity from destruction. In the many ways that we have outlined, Jews in France
demonstrated that, far from being resigned or passive, they strove to live and
preserve their children's future. Tzvétan Todorov has pointed out that, in the
face of the Nazis' systematic, many-faceted attempts to take away not only the
lives but even the very humanity of those that they destined for the camps, to
live and preserve one's humanity was in and of itself to resist.[48] In refusing the
piece of bread thrown to her by a guard and by rebuffing a sordid offer of food
for sex, Madeleine Dreyfus resisted by maintaining her dignity even in the face

45. See Denis Peschanski, "Comment parvenir à faire reconnaître la mémoire des combattants
juifs de France dans leur singularité et leur combat commun," 241–43.

46. Poznanski, "La Résistance Juive en France," 13; Douvette, "Participation des Juifs de France
à la Résistance et panorama de la Résistance juive en France 1940–1944," 55.

47. Kastersztein, "La réalité historique dément une représentation passive des Juifs face à
l'extermination," 34.

48. Tzvétan Todorov, *Face à l'extrême* (Paris: Points-Seuil, 1994), 190–97.

of extreme psychological and physical duress.[49] To go into hiding or to escape from capture was also a form of resistance, adds Renée Poznanski.[50] Susan Zuccotti takes us one step further: to survive as a Jew, to escape with one's life and one's humanity was to resist; to think of and care for others in such circumstances was heroic.[51]

49. Henry, *We Only Know Men*, 78.
50. Poznanski, "La Résistance Juive en France," 12.
51. Zuccotti, *The Holocaust, the French, and the Jews*, 226.

Nancy Lefenfeld

5 Unarmed Combat

Jewish Humanitarian Resistance in France
during the Shoah

Much has been written on the general subject of Jewish resistance during the
Holocaust and on Jewish resistance in specific countries. While some accounts
appeared in the immediate aftermath of the war, each decade since has seen
the publication of substantial new scholarship that has significantly enriched
our knowledge in this regard.[1] Yet, Jewish resistance remains an alien concept.
Until recently, only one image of a Jewish resister had firmly implanted itself in
the popular imagination—that of the ghetto fighter, specifically Jewish fighters
martyred in the Warsaw Ghetto Uprising. The success of the 2008 film *Defiance*

1. The website of the Center for Advanced Holocaust Studies of the United States Holocaust Memorial Museum (www.ushmm.org) presents a lengthy working bibliography—ninety-seven books
and thirty-seven articles—on the general subject. It also presents bibliographies for each of twenty-
four countries. A few examples of English language sources are: Marie Syrkin, *Blessed Is the Match:
The Story of Jewish Resistance* (Philadelphia: Jewish Publication Society of America, 1947); Zvi
Szner, ed., *Extermination and Resistance: Historical Records and Source Material*, trans. I. M. Lask
and J. Adler (Haifa: Ghetto Fighters' House, 1958); Yuri Suhl, ed. and trans., *They Fought Back: The
Story of Jewish Resistance in Nazi Europe* (New York: Crown Publishers, 1967); Meir Grubsztein, ed.,
*Jewish Resistance during the Holocaust: Proceedings of the Conference on Manifestations of Jewish
Resistance, Jerusalem, April 7–11, 1968*, trans. Varda Esther Bar-on, et. al. (Jerusalem: Yad Vashem,
1971); Yisrael Gutman and Efraim Zuroff, eds., *Rescue Attempts during the Holocaust: Proceedings of
the Second Yad Vashem International Historical Conference, Jerusalem, April 8–11, 1974*, trans. Moshe
Gottlieb, et. al. (Jerusalem: Yad Vashem, 1977); Isaac Kowalski, ed., *Anthology on Armed Jewish
Resistance, 1939–1945* (Brooklyn, N.Y.: Jewish Combatants Publishers House, 1984); Nechama Tec,
Defiance: The Bielski Partisans (New York: Oxford University Press, 1993); Yitzchak Mais, Bonnie
Gurewitsch, and Barbara Lovenheim, eds., *Daring to Resist: Jewish Defiance in the Holocaust* (New
York: Museum of Jewish Heritage, 2007); and Debórah Dwork and Robert Jan van Pelt, *Flight from the
Reich: Refugee Jews, 1933–1946* (New York: W. W. Norton, 2009).

planted a second image—that of partisans in the forests, fighting for survival and striking out against the oppressor.

The case of France is as extensively documented but as poorly understood as that of any other country. Neither of the popular images of resisters cited above has a great deal of relevance for France. The image of the ghetto fighter has no relevance at all. Although Jews were interned in camps, mainly French-administered installations in rural settings, they were not confined to urban ghettos. The partisan in the forest image has some relevance. During the last year of the Occupation, Jews took up arms and fought in maquis groups. A small number of maquis groups were specifically Jewish, having been formed by the Armée juive (AJ; Jewish Army) and the Sixième-Éclaireurs israélites de France (Sixième-EIF; Sixth-Jewish Scouts of France).[2]

Of an estimated 330,000 Jews living in France on the eve of the Occupation, 250,000 evaded deportation and survived.[3] It would be fallacious to draw conclusions about the extent or effectiveness of Jewish resistance based on survival rate; survival was the result of a complex interplay of factors, of which resistance was one. Nevertheless, it is clear from the historical record that far fewer Jews in France would have survived if they had not taken action to resist arrest and deportation. Many engaged in humanitarian resistance, which I consider a form of unarmed combat. Among Jews and Christians alike, humanitarian resistance was much more widespread in France than was armed resistance.

What does humanitarian resistance look like? Who were the unarmed equivalents of the ghetto fighter and partisan? The case of France points to the need for a new paradigm of Jewish resistance and a better understanding of the forms of humanitarian resistance.

2. The *Sixième* was the underground arm of the Jewish Scouts. It was established in August 1942 and was an outgrowth of the *Service social des jeunes* (SSJ; Young People's Social Service), which formed the sixth division of the Fourth Directorate of the UGIF. For a discussion of the formation of the Sixth, see: Alain Michel, *Les Éclaireurs israélites de France pendant la Seconde Guerre mondiale: septembre 1939-septembre 1944: action et évolution* (Paris: Édition des E.I.F., 1984), 123–28; and Susan Zuccotti, *The Holocaust, the French, and the Jews* (New York: BasicBooks, 1993), 348 (note 35).

3. There are no definitive statistics on the number of Jews living in France in 1940. Reputable sources cite estimates of between 300,000 and 350,000. The estimate of 330,000 is discussed by Susan S. Zuccotti, "Surviving the Holocaust: The Situation in France," in Michael Berenbaum and Abraham J. Peck, eds., *The Holocaust and History: The Known, the Unknown, the Disputed, and the Reexamined* (Bloomington, Ind.: Indiana University Press, 2002), 492.

France on the Eve of the Occupation

Specific aspects of the situation in France on the eve of the Occupation warrant mention because they differed markedly from those in other countries and had a direct bearing on the development of Jewish resistance. First, the Jewish population was comparatively large—five times that of Belgium and seven times that of Italy.[4] Roughly two-fifths were native-born Jews, two-fifths were foreigners (both foreign nationals and stateless persons), and one-fifth, naturalized French citizens. In 1940, the many Jewish immigrants who had come to France in the twenties and thirties were joined by an estimated 40,000 Jewish refugees who fled their homes in Belgium, Holland, and Luxembourg.

France's Jewish population was extremely diverse in terms of country of origin, language, culture, religious customs, appearance, and demeanor. Immigrants tended to organize themselves around their *landsmanshaften*, associations formed by those who shared a common place of origin, language, and customs. Native-born Jews tended to identify more strongly with their French Christian neighbors than with their foreign-born coreligionists. Lazare notes that "internal divisions deprived this group of all homogeneity."[5] Yet it is also true that a fundamental division existed between native and foreign-born Jews. "The popular idiom of the day distinguished between the two groups by calling native-born Jews *Israélites* and foreign-born Jews, naturalized or not, *Juifs*," writes Ousby. "The first term was polite; the second was not."[6]

Second, France was the only conquered nation allowed to forego surrender and granted an armistice. The Germans did this because it was in their own best interest to do so. From June 1940 to November 1942, the German army occupied only the northern half of France and the Atlantic coast.[7] The Northern Zone (also referred to as the Occupied Zone) was separated from the Southern Zone (also referred to as the Free Zone or Unoccupied Zone) by a line of de-

4. For a discussion of estimates of Jewish population by country prior to the Second War World and of estimated minimum and maximum losses "incurred by the Jews of Europe as a direct result of Nazi persecution," see part 6 of the appendix, "Estimated Jewish Losses in the Holocaust," in Israel Gutman, ed., *Encyclopedia of the Holocaust: Volume 4* (New York: Macmillan Publishing Company, 1990), 1797–1802.

5. Lucien Lazare, *Rescue as Resistance: How Jewish Organizations Fought the Holocaust in France*, trans. Jeffrey M. Green (New York: Columbia University Press, 1996), 13.

6. Ian Ousby, *Occupation: The Ordeal of France, 1940–1944* (New York: Cooper Square Press, 1997), 180.

7. Germany annexed the three departments comprising Alsace-Lorraine (Moselle, Bas-Rhin, and Haut-Rhin). Two departments (Nord and Pas-de-Calais) were placed under the jurisdiction of the German military governor in Belgium.

marcation that could not be crossed without authorization. The French government, headquartered in Vichy, was the government of all of France. In the earliest days of the Occupation, acting independently and without German pressure, the French government embarked on a program of legislated antisemitism. Marrus and Paxton emphasize that the antisemitism mounted by the French was not intended to work in tandem with that of the Germans but to rival it.[8] Whether French or German, antisemitic legislation and decrees were formulated to identify, isolate, surveil, and impoverish Jews.

Third, despite the fact that xenophobia and antisemitism had swept France in the thirties, the French people adhered to fundamental beliefs in human rights. Catholics as well as Protestants had suffered persecution for their religious beliefs in modern France. Two years after the emancipation of Protestants in 1789, France became the first European country to emancipate Jews. In the nineteenth century, there were constant efforts to define the proper role of religion in society and the relationship between civil and religious institutions. German occupation authorities well understood that French Israelites were highly assimilated, geographically dispersed, well-educated, deeply rooted in their communities, and respected by their Catholic and Protestant neighbors. Particularly after the July 1942 roundups in Paris, increasing numbers of French Catholics and Protestants began to see Jews—even foreign-born Jews—in ways that contradicted Nazi propaganda. This made a tremendous difference to many hunted Jews who sought their help.

Relief Work and Humanitarian Resistance

From the earliest days of the Occupation, German authorities diverted large amounts of food, labor, and other resources from France in order to further the war effort. This resulted in serious privation for the general population. Subjected to state-implemented discrimination and persecution, Jews suffered double privation. They had their businesses taken away and their bank accounts frozen. They were systematically dismissed from their jobs, subjected to special censuses and curfews, and barred from public places.

Oeuvre de bienfaisance, meaning "charity" or "relief work," was a well-established tradition among Jews in France. During the thirties, Jewish organizations in Paris set up soup kitchens, medical clinics, and clothing dispensaries

---

8. Michael R. Marrus and Robert O. Paxton, *Vichy France and the Jews* (Stanford, Calif.: Stanford University Press, 1995), 12.

to help the thousands of poor immigrants from Eastern Europe, particularly Poland, who had settled there. In June 1940, several prominent organizations moved their headquarters from Paris to cities in the south. They not only continued to provide relief services but expanded their efforts, working to meet the needs of a population being forced into poverty. Most of the ways in which Jews helped other Jews during the first two years of the Occupation were legal and above ground. I use the term "relief work" to refer to such forms of assistance.

Although circumstances prompted some organizations to enter into illegal, underground work earlier, the real sea change occurred in the summer of 1942. The massive *rafles* (roundups) carried out by the Paris police on July 16–17, referred to today as the "Vel d'Hiv" roundups, resulted in the deportation of 12,884 people, including over 4,000 children. In late August, following directives from Vichy, local and regional authorities launched raids throughout the Southern (Unoccupied) Zone, rounding up Jewish men, women, and children. Arrests of Jews continued into the fall, and, by the end of October, French authorities in the Southern Zone had handed over to the Germans approximately 10,600 Jews.[9]

"Deportation to forced labor in the East" was an enigmatic phrase that entered the lexicon in December 1941. Few in France had any idea what it meant. Prior to July 1942, individuals deported from that country had been relatively few in number, nearly all male, and predominantly foreign-born.[10] The large-scale, indiscriminate deportations initiated throughout France in the summer of 1942 shocked many Jews and Christians. From then on, Jewish organizations continued doing relief work but also crossed the boundary from legality to illegality and engaged in humanitarian resistance.[11]

9. See, for example, Serge Klarsfeld, *Le calendrier de la persécution des Juifs en France, 1940–1944* (Paris: Les fils et filles des déportés juifs de France and The Beate Klarsfeld Foundation, 1993), 470–75.

10. On the number of individuals deported from France prior to July 1942, see Serge Klarsfeld, *Memorial to the Jews Deported from France, 1942–1944: Documentation of the Deportation of the Victims of the Final Solution in France* (New York: The Beate Klarsfeld Foundation, 1983), xxvi (Table III: Chronology of Deportation Convoys) and narrative information presented on pages 42–43 pertaining to Convoy 5. (The information presented on pages 42–43 indicates that the convoy included thirty-four women, although this fact is not reflected in Table III.) The tabular data and narrative information indicate that, prior to July 1942, five deportation convoys with 5,149 persons left France for Auschwitz. Of that number, 98 percent were men. Included in the deportation convoys were many men who had been seized during two mass arrests carried out in Paris in 1941—the first on May 14 and the second on August 20. For a discussion of these early mass arrests, see, for example: Renée Poznanski, *Jews in France during World War II*, trans. Nathan Bracher (Hanover, N.H.: University Press of New England for Brandeis University Press in association with the United States Holocaust Memorial Museum, 2001), 56–57 and 208; and Klarsfeld, *Le calendrier*, 69–83; 123–36.

11. See, for example: Hillel J. Kieval, "Legality and Resistance in Vichy France: The Rescue of

As used here, the term "humanitarian resistance" refers to illegal activities carried out clandestinely to thwart an oppressor for the purpose of saving human lives. The systematic murder of European Jews was not an unfortunate result of a cataclysm, like an earthquake. Nor was it an unintended effect of a military operation. It was a primary objective of the Nazi regime. Efforts by Jews to thwart this primary objective and save human beings constituted resistance to the Nazi program.

Forms of Humanitarian Resistance in France

The various forms of Jewish humanitarian resistance in France during the Occupation were directed toward a common end—making Jews targeted for arrest and deportation disappear, thereby eluding the grasp of German and French authorities and their agents. There were three basic ways that one might disappear: (1) go into actual hiding; (2) hide in plain sight; or (3) move beyond the oppressor's reach.

The first approach—confining oneself to a place where one would not be seen or detected—conjures up the popular image of Jews hidden in attics and cellars, dependent on a host or outside provider for food and other necessities and unable to venture outside for fear of arrest. This approach was not widely used in France and has limited applicability to this discussion.

Hiding in plain sight entailed shedding one's identity and assuming, as completely as possible, the identity of a real or fictitious individual who did not belong to the targeted group. In France, the lives of thousands of children and adults were saved by hiding in plain sight under Aryan identities. Jewish organizations hid thousands of children in Christian homes and institutions. Many families and institutions who received the children knew that they had been targeted as Jews. In many cases, Christian clergy and lay people actively helped Jewish resisters find suitable hiding places, place children in hiding, and maintain them until the Liberation. Jewish organizations also played a crucial role in hiding adults, some with children, under assumed Aryan identities in small towns and villages and the rural countryside throughout France.

Not all of the individuals and families who were Aryanized and hidden in plain sight survived the Occupation. However, as compared with other German-

---

Jewish Children," in *Proceedings of the American Philosophical Society* 124, no. 5 (October 1980); and Adam Rayski, *The Choice of the Jews under Vichy: Between Submission and Resistance*, trans. Will Sayers (Notre Dame, Ind.: University of Notre Dame Press, 2005).

occupied countries, Jews in hiding in France fared well. Local residents who knew or suspected that newcomers were Jews exhibited a range of reactions. While some denounced them and others risked their lives to help them, most maintained what Zuccotti calls a "benevolent indifference."[12]

Hiding in plain sight was rarely an easy matter. It entailed leaving behind familiar surroundings, taking the necessary steps to assume an Aryan identity, entering unfamiliar surroundings, and working to maintain the new identity. It was not unusual for the individual or family hiding in plain sight to move from one place to another because of fears that the Aryan cover had been compromised. Assuming a new identity entailed costs of travel, relocation, and procuring false documents. It required a willingness to engage in deception and assume risks.

An essential prerequisite was to obtain forged documents that would establish one's Aryan identity and stand up to scrutiny. The single most important document was the *carte d'identité* (identity card); anyone sixteen years or older was required to produce one upon demand. Identity checks were a routine part of everyday life, carried out in all types of public places and on all forms of public transportation. Anyone who looked or sounded foreign drew attention and was more likely to be singled out. Men who were not elderly were routinely asked to produce papers showing that they had been demobilized or exempted from military service. Other types of forged documents, such as marriage licenses and baptismal certificates, were often necessary for establishing one's cover. Ration cards and the validating stamps known as "tickets" were required in order to purchase food. Because such documents were so critical to survival, several Jewish groups developed in-house facilities and expertise so that they could produce large quantities of good quality forgeries.[13]

During the first two years of the Occupation, moving beyond the oppressor's reach most often meant illegally crossing the line of demarcation that separated the Northern (Occupied) Zone from the Southern (Unoccupied) Zone. Mass arrests of foreign-born Jewish men in Paris in May and August 1941 prompted many immigrant Jews to leave that city and move to the Southern Zone in the hope of finding safety. Crossing the line of demarcation was not an easy matter, particularly for immigrants who were not fluent in French or who stood out be-

12. Zuccotti, "Surviving the Holocaust: The Situation in France," 504.

13. The Comité de la rue Amelot (Amelot Street Committee), Mouvement de jeunesse sioniste (MJS; Zionist Youth Movement), Armée juive, and Sixth-Jewish Scouts were among the Jewish groups that developed expertise in the production of false papers. Their work in this regard is addressed subsequently. Lazare, *Rescue as Resistance*, 166–71, provides an excellent discussion of the manufacture of false papers.

cause of their manner or appearance. They looked to Jewish organizations for a variety of kinds of help—false documents, train tickets, instructions on where to go, and the name of a trusted smuggler.

In November 1942, the military situation in France underwent a profound change. This affected the movement of Jews seeking to evade arrest. After the Allies landed in French North Africa, on November 8, 1942, German troops occupied most of what had been the Unoccupied Zone. At the same time, Germany ceded the southeastern portion of France to their Axis partner Italy. German and French authorities expected Italian soldiers to arrest and deport Jews living in their occupation zone, but Italian soldiers acted benevolently, even stepping in to protect Jews whom French authorities sought to deport. By February 1943, word had spread among Jews in France that the Italian Occupation Zone was a safe haven. Thousands of Jews made their way from various regions to Nice, Grenoble, Chambéry, and other cities and towns under Italian jurisdiction.[14]

In reading or listening to testimonies of Jews who survived the Shoah in France, one is struck by the frequency with which Jews changed residence in an effort to evade arrest and maximize the chances of survival. Often, the change of residence required that family members separate from one another for some period of time. It was not uncommon for the male head of the household to move in advance of other family members, scouting out a safe location and suitable living arrangement. Such moves were necessary, yet dangerous. The French government had instituted restrictions on Jews seeking to change domicile.[15] Violating these restrictions when they moved, Jews placed themselves in jeopardy. Arriving in a new place, they might be arrested and interned or directed to leave. Jews in flight had little choice but to use public transportation. However, police frequently boarded trains and buses and checked the documents of those on board.

14. See, for example, Poznanski, *Jews in France*, 387; and Marrus and Paxton, *Vichy France and the Jews*, 319.

15. Marrus and Paxton, *Vichy France and the Jews*, 148, summarizes the restrictions: "Local authorities were supposed to know at all times where Jews were living. A ministerial circular of 18 April 1942 required elaborate reporting procedures for Jews entering and leaving communes; a law of 9 November 1942 forbade foreign Jews to leave the commune where they lived without special documents issued by the police. Since 30 May 1941, all Jews had been required to report any change of address, even when moving within a commune." Restrictions in Paris had been enacted even earlier. Jacques Adler, *The Jews of Paris and the Final Solution: Communal Response and Internal Conflicts, 1940–1944* (New York: Oxford University Press, 1987), 11, states: "On 10 December 1941, the Paris prefect of police, Admiral François-Marie-Alphonse Bard, announced that any change of address by Jews had to be reported at local police stations and that no Jew was permitted to leave the Seine department without police permission."

The fact that France shares borders with Switzerland and Spain, neutral during the war, also created possibilities for moving beyond the oppressor's reach. These possibilities were exploited to a limited extent during the first two years of the Occupation and more fully during the last two years. Crossing the border from France into either of those countries was illegal. Neither country welcomed Jewish refugees. Depending on the time and place, those seeking to enter either Switzerland or Spain illegally could be expelled back into France or arrested and placed in the hands of German or French authorities and deported. Moreover, crossing the border was physically difficult. The international boundaries are predominantly mountainous areas. Only the able-bodied could attempt traversing the Pyrenees into Spain or the Alps into Switzerland. Attempts were perilous during the winter months and in bad weather; even in good weather, one needed a knowledgeable and trustworthy guide. Along the Swiss border, where the canton of Geneva meets the French department of Haute-Savoie, there are areas of flat terrain. Multiple rows of barbed wire and routine patrols rendered these areas difficult although not impossible to cross. In early 1943, when Swiss Federal officials issued clear directives on categories of illegal entrants who would be allowed to remain in the country, Jewish groups identified and exploited opportunities for placing people, mainly children, out of harm's way.

Individual and Organized Humanitarian Resistance

In the early days of the Occupation, few Jews in France were inclined to venture outside the bounds of legality; most judged that strict adherence to the letter of the law afforded them the greatest measure of protection. Thus, nearly all Jews living in the Northern Zone followed the strictures of the German ordinance issued on September 27, 1940, and submitted to a special Jewish census. Foreign-born Jews, targeted for wholesale arrest and deportation earlier than native Jews, shed their illusions about the protective capacity of French law earlier than native Jews. On May 13, 1941, 6,694 Jewish men received "green notes," each summoning the receiver to report to a specific location for an "examination of his situation." Most of the recipients were Polish, but some were Austrian, Czech, or stateless. Only 55 percent responded as instructed. The 3,710 men who reported were arrested and sent to French internment camps in the Loiret.[16] When the Paris police fanned out across the city on the morning

16. The men were interned in two camps—Pithiviers and Beaune-la-Rolande. See Klarsfeld, *Le calendrier*, 69–83, and Poznanski, *Jews in France*, 57–61.

of July 16, 1942, they carried lists of foreign-born Jews targeted for arrest. An unknown proportion of Jews had been warned by members of Jewish Communist organizations, the Amelot Street Committee, and French policemen that a secret action was imminent. Of a total 27,361 Jews whose names appeared on the lists, 13,152 or 48 percent were seized, indicating that many took evasive action.[17]

By the fall of 1942, tens of thousands of foreign-born Jews in France had made the decision to live outside the bounds of the law. One year later, the same held true for native-born Jews. Whether foreign- or native-born, a Jew forced to live a fugitive existence constantly had to confront problems and challenges, make difficult decisions without reliable information, endure physical hardships and psychological stress, seek and receive help from others, and engage in humanitarian resistance.

Humanitarian resistance was the chief means by which Jews fought oppressors in France. Many who engaged in humanitarian resistance judged it more effective than armed resistance as a means of saving lives. As early as 1941, individuals willing to engage in acts of humanitarian resistance were aided by organized Jewish groups that can be divided into two categories. One category encompasses relief agencies that worked legally and above ground for some period of time but transitioned to humanitarian resistance in response to changing circumstances. The second category encompasses humanitarian resistance networks that came into existence illegally and clandestinely under the Occupation and carried out their work in that manner. This essay profiles two Jewish relief agencies that transitioned to humanitarian resistance and two Jewish resistance networks born into illegality. None of the four worked in isolation; each worked hand in hand with other Jewish, Catholic, Protestant, and nonsectarian groups.

In the realm of unarmed combat, certain members of Jewish groups served on the front lines. Their work generally fell into three categories: producing and distributing false papers; preparing people to hide in plain sight, placing them in hiding, and maintaining them through periodic visits; and helping people to cross international borders. The main source of funding for humanitarian resistance work was the American Jewish Joint Distribution Committee (JDC; commonly known as "the Joint").

17. In this regard, see, Poznanski, *Jews in France*, 260–61; Rayski, *The Choice of the Jews under Vichy*, 85–88; and Lazare, *Rescue as Resistance*, 145–48.

From Legality to Illegality: Two Jewish Relief Agencies under the Occupation

The histories of the Comité de la rue Amelot (Amelot Street Committee) and Oeuvre de secours aux enfants-Sud (OSE-Sud; Children's Rescue Network-South)/réseau Garel (Garel Network) under the Occupation are complex and have been explored in numerous books and articles.[18] These profiles are intended to give an overview of each organization's activities and its transition from legality to illegality. Although not profiled here, several other Jewish organizations in France went through similar transitions. Three are mentioned in the discussion—the Sixth-Jewish Scouts, the Paris branch of WIZO (Women's International Zionist Organization), and OSE-Nord (OSE-North).

Le Comité de la rue Amelot

The Jewish community that resided in Paris under the Occupation was markedly different, in size as well as in composition, from the community that had existed there on the eve of war. Paris had been home to two-thirds of all Jews living in France. Its Jewish population of roughly 200,000 was diverse in terms of socioeconomic status. This changed dramatically after the middle of May 1940. Jews left Paris in great numbers, part of what the French would come to call "*l'exode*," the flight of two million people toward the south by car, truck, train, bicycle, and on foot. Adler estimates that, by the time German soldiers occupied the capital, only 50,000 to 70,000 Jews remained.[19] Poor immigrants were the least likely to flee. They not only lacked the resources necessary to travel but had little familiarity with the rural countryside. Many Jewish institutions closed their doors.

18. On the Comité de la rue Amelot, see, for example: A. Alpérine, et al., *L'un des trente-six* (Paris: Kyoum, 1947); Jacqueline Baldran and Claude Bochurberg, *David Rapoport: "La Mère et l'enfant", 36 rue Amelot* (Paris: Mémorial de la Shoah/CDJC, 2007); Jules Jacoubovitch, *Rue Amelot: aide et résistance*, trans. Gabrielle Jacoubovitch-Bouhana (Paris: Éditions du Centre Medem, 2006); Adler, *The Jews of Paris*; Lazare, *Rescue as Resistance*; and Rayski, *The Choice of the Jews under Vichy*. On OSE, see, for example: Katy Hazan and Georges Weill, *Andrée Salomon, une femme de lumière: textes établis et annotés d'après ses mémoires* (Paris: Le Manuscrit, 2011); Kieval, "Legality and Resistance in Vichy France"; Martine Lemalet, ed. and author, *Au secours des enfants du siècle: regards croisés sur l'OSE* (France: Nil Éditions, 1993); Vivette Samuel, *Rescuing the Children: A Holocaust Memoir*, trans. Charles B. Paul (Madison: University of Wisconsin Press, 2002); Sabine Zeitoun, *L'Oeuvre de secours aux enfants (O.S.E.) sous l'Occupation en France: du légalisme à la résistance 1940–1944* (Paris: Éditions l'Harmattan, 1990); and Sabine Zeitoun, *Ces enfants qu'il fallait sauver* (Paris: Albin Michel, 1989).

19. Adler, *The Jews of Paris*, 242n18.

It was in this atmosphere of disruption and disorientation that the Amelot Street Committee was formed. On June 15, the day after German troops entered Paris, a dozen men and women gathered for an emergency meeting. They represented five immigrant organizations—the Fédération des sociétés juives de France (Federation of Jewish Associations of France), the Bund, the Poale Sion de gauche (Left Poale-Zion), Yiddische vinkl (Yiddish Corner), and Colonie scolaire (School Colony). Four operated "canteens" (i.e., soup kitchens); Colonie scolaire operated a medical clinic and clothing dispensary, La mère et l'enfant (Mother and Child). The meeting had been called because two of the canteens and the clinic and dispensary were shut down due to a lack of personnel and supplies. The representatives formed a committee and pooled their resources. Within several days, they had reopened the shuttered facilities. No name was given to the committee; because it met at the offices of the Colonie scolaire, at number 36 on the rue Amelot, it became known as the Comité de la rue Amelot. From that point on, the five constituent organizations worked cooperatively but remained semi-autonomous.[20]

In September 1940, David Rapoport (b. 1883, Proskurov, Ukraine), a founder of the Colonie scolaire who had left Paris during the exodus, returned to the city and accepted the position of secretary-general. His background opens a window on what contributed to the willingness of immigrant Jewish leaders to enter the realm of humanitarian resistance. Rapoport was born in Proskurov (now Khmelnitsky), in western Ukraine. At the age of 23, he emigrated to France, worked in an import-export business in France and England, married, and started a family.[21] In 1914, he returned to Proskurov alone to spend a few weeks with his parents. The outbreak of the First World War, the October Revolution, and Russian Civil War prevented his return to France until 1921. During his enforced stay, he witnessed the effects of what have become known as the Petlyura massacres—the murder of tens of thousands of Jews and destruction of numerous Jewish communities carried out by rampaging soldiers and civilians in Ukraine in 1919.[22] Rapoport dedicated himself to helping survivors of the massacres resettle or emigrate. Upon his return to France, he continued

---

20. Regarding the origins of Amelot, see: Jacoubovitch, *Rue Amelot*, 15–19; Baldran and Bochurberg, *David Rapoport*, 26–30; and Adler, *The Jews of Paris*, 165–68.

21. Baldran and Bochurberg, *David Rapoport*, 228–30.

22. See, for example, Elias Heifetz, J. U. D., *The Slaughter of the Jews in the Ukraine in 1919*, published for the Jewish People's Relief Committee of America (New York: Thomas Seltzer, 1921), 1. This 424-page Red Cross report begins with the statement that the massacres "set the whole land aflame" and "cannot be compared with the pogroms in the eighties and during the first decade of our century."

helping Jewish refugees. In 1926, he and Jules Jacoubovitch (b. 1891, Lodz, Poland) founded the Colonie scolaire, an organization whose original mission was to provide holiday outings for children of Jewish immigrants. In the thirties, they expanded its reach, establishing La mère et l'enfant to improve the health and welfare of mothers and children.

Rapoport is representative of a number of Jewish leaders in France who, having come from Eastern Europe, had had their eyes opened to the horrors of state-sanctioned persecution. Under the Occupation, they were willing to go outside the bounds of legality when necessary. Consequently, they often initiated and oversaw humanitarian resistance efforts.

For a time, the provision of hot meals was Amelot's main focus. Jews were barred from city-operated canteens, but they could find a filling meal at a canteen run by Amelot, the Jewish Communists, or the Association consistoriale des Israélites de Paris (ACIP; Consistorial Association of the Israelites of Paris).[23] Amelot canteens served an average of 40,000 meals per month.[24] In addition to carrying out traditional relief activities, Amelot expanded into new areas, such as helping people obtain the papers they needed to emigrate or to regularize their legal status. On the eve of the Occupation, OSE moved its headquarters to the south; it subsequently split geographically, creating OSE-Sud (OSE-South) and OSE-Nord (OSE-North). The directors of OSE-Nord, Dr. Eugène Minkowski (b. 1885, Saint Petersburg, Russia) and Falk Walk (b. 1883, Bialystok, Poland), worked closely with Amelot.

In November 1940, Amelot established contact with Jewish men imprisoned in the Tourelles barracks, on the eastern edge of Paris. The men were immigrants who lacked proper legal documentation.[25] Learning that their food rations were below subsistence levels, Amelot obtained permission to have two food runners deliver meals. The contacts led to the development of escape plans. Freeing prisoners was only the first step in executing a successful escape. In order to avoid subsequent arrest and incarceration, it was necessary to furnish them with false identity documents and have them and their families smuggled across the line of demarcation. Rapoport found a means of obtaining fabricated documents and, working with the food runners, effected the escapes. Lazare calls this Amelot's "first experience of active resistance, in order to rescue victims who had already fallen into the hands of the enemy or his auxiliaries."[26]

23. Poznanski, *Jews in France*, 50. 24. Adler, *The Jews of Paris*, 170.
25. Lazare, *Rescue as Resistance*, 45. 26. Ibid., 46.

Amelot was soon called upon to expand its capabilities in secretly helping Jews reach the relative safety of the Southern Zone. After the first mass arrest in France, on May 14, 1941, nearly four thousand Jewish men were sent to internment camps in the Loiret. Food was scarce and living conditions harsh in these primitive installations. Prisoners were not allowed to have visitors or correspond with their families. Through the intermediary of the French Red Cross, Amelot delivered parcels of food, clothing, and blankets and established a correspondence service. The Red Cross also provided cover for Amelot workers, enabling them to gain entry to the camps. The workers helped prisoners seeking release as well as those attempting to escape. Amelot is the only group credited with supplying escaped prisoners with the false identity documents essential to evading rearrest.[27]

In the wake of the first mass arrest in May and a second in August, many Jews decided to leave Paris and head south. They looked to Amelot not only for false documents but also for advice and instructions about each aspect of the trip—where to go, how to travel, how to dress, how to comport themselves, and, most importantly, where and how to make contact with a trusted smuggler who would take them across the line of demarcation.

From the beginning of the Occupation, German authorities had been intent on creating a Judenrat in France. By early 1941, they had pressured the chief rabbi of Paris into organizing the Comité de coordination des oeuvres de bienfaisance israélites du Grand Paris (the Coordination Committee of the Israelite Charities of Greater Paris). Amelot leaders were cautious about establishing ties with the Coordination Committee; they feared it would be used by the Germans to further their own objectives. By the end of November 1941, the Coordination Committee had been replaced by a new entity established by the Vichy government, the Union générale des Israélites de France (UGIF; General Union of French Israelites). The UGIF was under the direct control of Vichy's Commissariat-général aux questions juives (CGQJ; Commissariat General for Jewish Affairs). Although all Jewish relief organizations were required to operate within the UGIF framework, Amelot refused. In order to keep its canteens stocked, it

27. Ibid., 88; Poznanski, *Jews in France*, 60. At times, prisoners left the camps with authorization to work on nearby farms or on short-term furlough, or they managed to escape. Cash, valuables, and identity documents were confiscated upon internment, making it especially difficult for prisoners on the outside to make their way to safety without help. See also Henry Bulawko, "Où commence (et où finit) la résistance juive en France," *Le monde juif*, no. 118 (new series), April–June 1985 (Paris: La revue du Centre de documentation juive contemporaine), 69.

worked in tandem with the UGIF, but it did not disclose information regarding the identities of its clients.[28]

By the time Jews in the Northern Zone were required to wear the distinctive yellow star, on June 7, 1942, rumors of an impending *grande rafle* were circulating. Amelot had already suffered losses of personnel; so Rapoport and Jacoubovitch, Amelot's second in command, asked a UGIF representative if their workers could carry the same identification cards that protected UGIF workers from arbitrary arrest and deportation. Such cards had not yet been received by July 16, when Paris police fanned out across the city with lists of Jews in hand. Several Amelot workers were among those arrested and deported. The organization temporarily closed its canteens and dispensaries.

Amelot could have gone completely underground, but it was loath to take such action. Half of the 27,000 Jews targeted for arrest had evaded capture; unable to return to their homes, forced to live outside the law, they waged a daily struggle for survival. Amelot considered permanently shuttering the canteens, which could be raided at any time. Even that precaution was rejected because leaders felt that deprivation posed a greater threat than police raids. In early August, when Amelot workers received UGIF cards, they reopened the canteens and dispensaries. Although Amelot did not go underground, it shifted its main emphasis from relief work to humanitarian resistance.

Foremost among its resistance activities was the hiding of Jewish children. Hundreds of Jewish children in Paris were in need of care. Some had been abandoned or left with friends and neighbors by parents who had been arrested and deported. Others were relinquished by parents or relatives who had eluded arrest but were living as fugitives and had little means of support. Children who became wards of Amelot generally did so in one of two ways. First, they might be directly entrusted to the organization by a parent, relative, friend or acquaintance. Second, they might be sent to Amelot via complicit UGIF officials. Juliette Stern (b. 1893, Paris), the director of the Paris branch of WIZO, was also the director of the social services division of the UGIF, responsible for children in need of care. Some children were placed in UGIF children's homes. Others were placed in foster homes through what was known as "Service 42," supervised by Joséphine Getting (b. 1877, Paris). Stern and Getting developed a clandestine service, "42b," that transferred children to groups that would place them in hiding. Many of these children were entrusted to Amelot and the two

28. Richard Cohen, *The Burden of Conscience: French Jewish Leadership during the Holocaust* (Bloomington, Ind.: Indiana University Press, 1987), 102.

organizations with which it worked most closely—Dr. Minkowski's OSE-Nord and a semiclandestine, nonsectarian group, Entraide temporaire (ET; Temporary Mutual Assistance). The latter was formed in 1941 by Lucie Chevalley-Sabatier (b. 1882, Le Petit-Quevilly, France), founder and president of the Service social d'aide aux émigrants (SSAE; Society for Aid to Immigrants), a legally sanctioned charity. The activists of ET, who were both Jewish and Christian, used the cover of the SSAE to carry out their underground work.[29]

Prior to the Vel d'Hiv roundup, a young Amelot worker named Henry Bulawko (b. 1918, Lyda, Lithuania) had set up a rudimentary shop for producing forged documents.[30] After that event, Rapoport charged him with stepping up the operation, producing larger numbers of better quality forgeries. Berthe Dutruel (née Zysman, b. 1920, Poland), one of several who assisted in this effort, is credited with obtaining essential rubber stamps from a contact in the mayor's office of Pantin, a Paris suburb.[31] The documents were used by individuals and families seeking to leave Paris as well as by those who remained in the city and hid in plain sight under assumed Aryan identities. Bulawko was arrested in November 1942 and later deported, but the forgery operation that he had established continued to operate. By early 1943, many of the false identity cards and other documents produced were used by individuals and families fleeing to the safety of the Italian Occupation Zone.

The reluctance to separate relief work from humanitarian resistance posed major risks to the safety of Amelot personnel and led to the demise of the organization. Those who received illegal assistance were cautioned not to name Amelot as the source. It is not clear what other precautions, if any, were taken to shield resisters from being implicated. In May 1943, aware of the mounting threat, Jacoubovitch and his family moved to Grenoble. On June 1, Gestapo agents arrested Rapoport on charges of distributing false papers. Amelot leaders halted relief operations, but some personnel refused to leave their posts and they too were seized. On June 28, the CGQJ dissolved Amelot and placed its canteens and dispensaries in the hands of the UGIF. Most of the remaining

29. Chevalley-Sabatier also served as liaison between Amelot and Jewish leaders in the Southern Zone, transporting money and sensitive documents. Jules Jacoubovitch, *Rue Amelot: aide et résistance*, 84, 106. For further reading, see Limore Yagil, *Chrétiens et Juifs sous Vichy (1940–1944): sauvetage et désobéissance civile* (Paris: Éditions du Cerf, 2005), 531–33.

30. Henry Bulawko, *Les jeux de la mort et de l'espoir: Auschwitz-Jaworzno* (Paris: Montorgueil, 1993), 39. In the chapter entitled "Les nazis à l'oeuvre en France Occupée," 34–43, Bulawko speaks of his activities during the Occupation prior to his arrest in November 1942.

31. Les Anciens de la Résistance juive en France, *Organisation juive de combat: résistance/sauvetage, France 1940–1945* (Paris: Éditions Autrement: Collection Mémoires n° 85), 234–35.

Amelot personnel went underground and worked clandestinely with activists of OSE-Nord, ET, and other organizations to maintain the children in hiding and safeguard information on their identities and locations. Some of the children whom Amelot had hidden were transferred to a team of activists belonging to the MJS and the Sixth-Jewish Scouts, who smuggled them into Switzerland. In ensuing months, key individuals who had worked with Amelot, including Walk and Getting, would also be arrested and deported.

David Rapoport, Falk Walk, and Joséphine Getting were among many Amelot, OSE-Nord, and WIZO personnel who lost their lives.

Oeuvre de secours aux enfants (OSE-Sud)/réseau Garel

Prior to the start of the Occupation, OSE (pronounced "oh-zay") was already a well-known and widely respected child welfare organization in France. OSE was established in 1912 by a group of doctors in Saint Petersburg, Russia. Its initials originally stood for Obshchestvo sdravochraneniya evreev, Society for the Health of the Jewish Population. In the aftermath of the Russian Revolution, OSE relocated its headquarters, first to Berlin and then to Paris, where it kept its acronym but adopted a new name, Oeuvre de secours aux enfants.[32] (In French, this abbreviation, "ose," means "dare.") OSE professionals provided a variety of services (medical, dental, psychological, psychiatric, and social) and dispensed medicines, clothing, and food and nutritional supplements to children of all ages. They also instructed mothers on proper hygiene, nutrition, and disease prevention.

Between 1938 and 1940, OSE broadened its mission and expanded its operations. The organization began to receive and shelter Jewish children sent to Paris from parents in Germany and Austria. It made the decision to house the children collectively in *maisons d'enfants* (children's homes) and, by August 1939, had opened four children's homes just north of Paris.[33] The declaration of war on September 1 engendered fear among the population that Paris would be subjected to aerial bombardments, and OSE leaders decided that it would be

32. On the history of OSE, see: Archives et histoire de l'OSE, *Une mémoire pour le futur: l'Oeuvre de secours aux enfants, 90 ans d'histoire; A Legacy for the Future: 90 Years of the Oeuvre de secours aux enfants* (Paris: Somogy éditions d'art and Association Oeuvre de secours aux enfants, 2003); Lemalet, *Au secours des enfants du siècle*; and Dr. L. Wulman, ed., *In kamf farn gezunt fun Idishn folk* (*50 yor "Oze"*); *In Fight for the Health of the Jewish People* (*50 Years of OSE*) (New York: World Union OSE and The American Committee of OSE, 1968).

33. The four homes, all in the Val d'Oise, were Les Tourelles, La Villa Chesnaie, La Petite Colonie, and Villa Helvetia.

more prudent to house children away from the capital. Between November 1939 and June 1940, it hurriedly opened six children's homes in the south-central part of the country; three of these—Le Masgelier, Chabannes, and Chaumont— were châteaux in the department of La Creuse. Even before the organization had a chance to transfer the refugee children out of greater Paris to the newly established homes, some beds were filled by children orphaned, abandoned, or turned over by parents living in France.

On the eve of the Occupation, OSE transferred its headquarters from Paris to Vichy and then to Montpellier. Most OSE directors and staff relocated to the Southern Zone. Whereas the organization had previously delivered services in a highly urbanized setting, it now sought to reach a Jewish population dispersed over a wide geographic area. A portion of this population had fled Paris; others had fled Belgium, Luxembourg, and Holland; and still others had been forcibly displaced from Alsace and Lorraine. Regardless of their origins, virtually all families had been uprooted from their homes and had resettled in unfamiliar places where they hoped to find a measure of safety. Many Jewish families installed themselves in Toulouse, Limoges, Lyon, Marseille, Grenoble, and other cities in the Southern Zone. Some with little or no means of support ended up in *centres d'accueil* (reception centers), temporary camps erected on the outskirts of cities. Others sought and found places to live in remote towns and villages, on farms, or in the mountains. OSE developed ways to deliver its health and social services to this dispersed population. It established a network of "medical-social centers" in cities and dispatched mobile teams to visit families in outlying areas.

Immediately after the armistice, the French government had moved quickly to intern large numbers of foreigners, including many foreign Jews. Statistics presented by Poznanski indicate that, in mid-1941, seven large internment camps in the Southern Zone held a total of 24,300 people, 13,800 (57 percent) of whom were Jews.[34] Between the spring of 1941 and the spring of 1942, OSE focused much of its effort on ameliorating the harsh conditions that prisoners faced. Wherever possible, it installed social workers inside the camps and set up canteens, clothing dispensaries, medical clinics, infirmaries, and nurseries. Working with other groups, including the Quakers and the Secours suisse aux enfants (Swiss Aid to Children), OSE supplemented the meager diets of the children, which helped reduce high mortality rates.

34. Poznanski, *Jews in France*, 174. The camps were Argelès, Gurs, Rivesaltes, Le Vernet, Noé, Récébédou, and Les Milles.

By early 1941, it had become clear to OSE officials that children interned for prolonged periods of time would suffer deleterious psychological and physical effects. They sought authorization to remove as many as possible from behind the barbed wire. Securing such authorization entailed two steps: obtaining permission from the French government; and securing certificates of domicile from prefectures of departments willing to receive children. Approval of the French government was secured with relative ease. It proved difficult, however, to find prefectures that would issue certificates. Fortunately, the prefect and the secretary-general of the Hérault Department, Jean-Baptiste Benedetti and Camille Ernst, agreed to provide as many certificates as needed.[35] OSE established a transit shelter at Palavas-les-Flots, near Montpellier and, in the summer of 1941, began transferring children out of the camps to the shelter.[36] After a brief stay, the boys and girls were sent to children's homes in other departments. OSE gave high priority to getting children out of the camps. By July 1942, more than 1,000 had been freed and few remained behind barbed wire.

This unconventional form of relief work led to early instances of humanitarian resistance. Social workers could not gain the release of adolescents sixteen years of age or older because they lacked identity cards. Charles Lederman (b. 1913, Warsaw), an OSE worker in Rivesaltes internment camp, was expelled by camp officials in October 1941, suspected of promoting escapes.[37] Within a few months, his replacement, Vivette Samuel (née Hermann, b. 1919, Paris) had devised a more subtle strategy for liberating older teens: she falsified their ages. Once liberated, they were transferred to departments in which officials were willing to issue new identity cards.[38]

OSE continued to expand its inventory of children's homes, sheltering children freed from the camps and those relinquished by parents facing severe economic hardship, ill health, or other difficult circumstances. By August 1942, the organization had fourteen children's homes under its direct control, and these homes sheltered approximately 900 children.[39] It also helped support

35. Debórah Dwork, *Children with a Star: Jewish Youth in Nazi Europe* (New Haven: Yale University Press, 1991), 58; 148.

36. Asher Cohen, *Persécutions et sauvetages: Juifs et Français sous l'Occupation et sous Vichy* (Paris: Les Éditions du Cerf, 1993), 103.

37. Vivette Samuel, *Sauver les enfants* (Paris: Liana Levi, 1995), 48. Samuel states that Lederman was accused of having "*favorisé des évasions.*" This leaves open the question of whether he was accused of having facilitated escapes or encouraged escapes.

38. Vivette Samuel, "Journal d'une internée volontaire," entry of February 10, 1942, *Évidences* 14 (November 1950): 7–12, 10.

39. Zeitoun, *L'Oeuvre de secours aux enfants (O.S.E.) sous l'Occupation*, 124.

and administer facilities operated by other organizations. New beds were filled as quickly as they became available.

Why did OSE house the children in this manner rather than disperse them throughout the countryside? Prior to the summer of 1942, OSE officials did not fear for the safety of the children in its institutions. They reacted to the nature of the threat apparent at the time but did not feel the need to take preemptive action. The organization was predisposed to supervise directly the moral and educational upbringing of its wards, and this could only be accomplished if children were sheltered collectively.

The beginning of OSE's transition from legality to illegality is associated with events that occurred at the end of August 1942. On August 26, French authorities launched massive roundups of foreign Jews throughout the Southern Zone. In the Rhône Department, approximately 1,200 men, women, and children were confined to an unused military barracks in Vénissieux, a suburb of Lyon. Ministerial directives allowed parents slated for deportation to leave their children in France. A "screening commission" comprised of members of OSE, the Jewish Scouts, and Amitié chrétienne (AC; Christian Friendship), an interdenominational refugee aid organization, spent many agonizing hours trying to convince parents that their children would have a better chance of surviving in France than in an unknown destination "in the East."[40] On August 29, as Jewish relief workers were preparing to evacuate approximately 100 children, new instructions arrived mandating that children be deported with their parents. Priests who were members of Amitié chrétienne intercepted the instructions and helped representatives of OSE and the Jewish Scouts spirit away and hide the children. The next day, the departmental prefect attempted to undo what had been done. He ordered that the deportation train, approaching the line of demarcation, be halted; and he demanded that the children be handed over. The priests defied the prefect's demand and provided adequate cover for the Jewish leaders involved.[41]

Dr. Joseph Weill (b. 1902, Bouxwiller, France), an Alsatian physician who served as medical director of OSE-Sud, and Charles Lederman, then an administrator in the OSE bureau in Lyon, were members of the screening commission

---

40. In each internment camp and holding center, a screening commission reviewed each case file to determine whether the individual or family was subject to or exempt from deportation. Poznanski, *Jews in France*, 280–82 provides an excellent discussion of screening commissions.

41. For detailed accounts of this ecumenical action, see, for example: Lazare, *Rescue as Resistance*, 188–91; Lemalet, *Au secours des enfants du siècle*, 67–69; Samuel, *Sauver les enfants*, 98–101; and Zuccotti, *The Holocaust, the French, and the Jews*, 130–32.

at Vénissieux. A friend of Lederman's, Georges Garel (né Garfinkel, b. 1909, Vilnius, Lithuania), had also been present and witnessed the unfolding of events. Before the buses filled with children had left the holding center, Weill recognized the enormity of the threat and the need to take radical action. Speaking privately, he asked Garel to build a clandestine network, operating outside of the legal apparatus of OSE, that would Aryanize, scatter, and hide children. Garel, a brilliant electrical engineer, had no prior involvement in Jewish causes or relief work. Therefore authorities would not be able to link his name to OSE or any other Jewish organization. Moreover, he had adopted his French-sounding name years earlier and could pass as a Christian. As a first step, with the help of Lederman, Garel met with the Archbishop of Toulouse to seek his advice and support.[42]

The meeting between Garel and the archbishop was pivotal, laying the groundwork for the underground branch of OSE that would become known as the réseau Garel. The seventy-two-year-old, partly paralyzed Monsignor Jules-Géraud Saliège (b. 1870, Mauriac, Cantal, France, 1870) had been the first Catholic priest to object publicly to the treatment of foreign Jews in France. He voiced his objections in a pastoral letter read in all parishes of the diocese in late August 1942.[43] Saliège lent his full support to Garel, providing him with a letter of introduction that opened the doors of many Catholic institutions. The Oeuvre de Sainte-Germaine, a charity based in Toulouse, was the first to receive a group of Jewish children threatened with deportation and to disperse them in private homes and institutions.

With the support of institutions and organizations, both religious and non-sectarian, Garel developed a secret network that extended throughout the Southern Zone. From his base in Lyon, he maintained contact with four regional directors. Each director oversaw a cadre of young, female social workers, both Christians and Jews who posed as Christians. The women made periodic visits to Jewish children living under Aryan identities in private homes and institutions, many of which were Catholic orphanages and boarding schools.

42. Multiple sources indicate that Lederman had met with Archbishop Saliège on at least one previous occasion. Lederman had established contacts with Alexandre Glasberg and Pierre Chaillet, two Catholic priests who founded Amitié chrétienne. Through them, he met Father Henri de Lubac. In the summer of 1942, de Lubac arranged for Lederman to meet with Saliège to inform him of the scale and nature of deportations underway. This along with information provided by others prompted the archbishop to issue the pastoral letter read on the last two Sundays in August.

43. On this letter and its dissemination, see, for example, Marrus and Paxton, *Vichy France and the Jews*, 271. For a fuller discussion of Archbishop Jules-Géraud Saliège and the moral leadership he exhibited under the Occupation, see Yagil, *Chrétiens et Juifs sous Vichy*, 363–70.

Through the visits, they looked after the physical and psychological well-being of the children and delivered ration cards and tickets, shoes, clothing, medicines, payments to cover living expenses, and whatever else was needed. With an engineer's precision, Garel designed the administrative apparatus of the network so that the identities of the children would be safeguarded even if he or other personnel were captured.

OSE continued to function as a government-sanctioned organization under the auspices of the UGIF-Sud. Operating above ground exposed OSE staff and wards, particularly those living in its children's homes, to potential risks. However, the directorate deemed it necessary to conduct relief work in much the same manner it had done previously because the extent of need was so great. Not all of the children entrusted to OSE could be hidden via the réseau Garel. The network did not have the capacity to absorb a large number of children. Also, not all Jewish children could blend into a French Christian milieu.

The picture of OSE that emerges in 1943 is one of an organization using all possible means, legal and illegal, to maintain and safeguard as many Jewish children as possible. Children's homes continued to serve as the mainstay of the organization's relief work. Most OSE homes remained open and occupied until November, sheltering an estimated 1,300 wards; and OSE continued to house children in adjunct facilities. Also operating legally was a family foster care service supervised by the organization's director of social services, Andrée Salomon (b. 1908, Grussenheim, France). Referred to internally as "Circuit B," Salomon's network placed approximately 1,000 children in Jewish and Christian homes throughout the Southern Zone. The children were not hidden; they retained their actual names and identities. The cadre of social workers who maintained contact with the children and foster parents carried the protective identity cards of the UGIF. The réseau Garel, which comprised "Circuit A," emerged as the mainstay of the organization's humanitarian resistance. It also extended throughout the Southern Zone; by the fall of 1943, it camouflaged approximately 1,600 children. OSE launched a second important humanitarian resistance effort in February 1943, when it began smuggling groups of unaccompanied children into Switzerland. Its medical-social centers continued to function legally and above ground but also provided cover for various types of illegal activities, such as the distribution of false documents.

Events at the end of October 1943 forced the OSE directorate to abandon its work as a legal entity and go completely underground. On October 20, Gestapo agents raided La Verdière, a UGIF children's center administered by OSE in

La Rose, a suburb of Marseille. All of its residents—approximately forty children and adults—were deported. At the same time, German officials had begun pressuring OSE-Sud for complete information on children and staff in its homes.[44] Over the next three months, with the assistance of the Sixth-Jewish Scouts, OSE managed to evacuate its homes and disperse the threatened children. The formal end to the organization's legal existence came on February 8, 1944, when the Gestapo raided OSE headquarters in Chambéry and arrested Alain Mossé, a director and OSE representative to the UGIF-Sud, along with seven staff members and numerous visitors. Similar raids were carried out on OSE offices in Lyon and Grenoble. OSE directors ordered homes, clinics, and offices still operating to be shut down immediately. One adjunct facility, an OSE-supported home located in the remote mountain village of Izieu (Ain Department), was still open on April 6, 1944, when Klaus Barbie sent a Gestapo team from Lyon to conduct a raid. Forty-four children and seven adults were arrested and deported.

According to Poznanski, "From February 1944 until the Liberation, the OSE continued in a totally clandestine manner to care for some six thousand children."[45] An estimated three-quarters of those children were in the Southern Zone.[46] Fewer than 100 children under the care of OSE-Sud were captured by German and French authorities.[47]

Alain Mossé was one of many OSE-Sud personnel who lost their lives.

Born into Illegality: Two Resistance Networks

The MJS and Service André are two of several Jewish groups that came into existence illegally and engaged in humanitarian resistance.

Mouvement de jeunesse sioniste

During the 1920s and 1930s, numerous Zionist youth organizations from Eastern Europe established groups in France. Each group reflected a particular political or ideological orientation. Competing with one another for new

---

44. Cohen, *The Burden of Conscience*, 142.

45. Poznanski, *Jews in France*, 398. Kieval, "Legality and Resistance in Vichy France," 364, makes the same point: "For the next six months [following Alain Mossé's arrest in February 1944] OSE ceased to exist and at the same time secured the lives of some six thousand children."

46. Lazare, *Rescue as Resistance*, 204. The data presented by Lazare in this regard do not refer specifically to wards of OSE but to "wards of Jewish organizations saved from extinction."

47. Ibid., 206.

recruits, none experienced significant growth. The movement remained fractured during the first two years of the Occupation. In May 1942, Simon Lévitte (b. 1912, Dniepopotrova, Ukraine), a national leader of the Jewish Scouts, convened a Zionist Unification Congress in Montpellier and convinced delegates to disband their respective groups and unite under the banner of a new organization, the Mouvement de jeunesse sioniste.[48] Those assembled voted not to register the MJS with French authorities but to operate outside the confines of the law. They chose Lévitte to lead them.

Simon Lévitte was a highly self-disciplined individual, an ardent Zionist, and a devoted educator. After publishing a book on modern Zionism in 1936, he and his wife made *aliyah* and worked on a kibbutz in the upper Galilee.[49] They returned to France on the eve of war. During the first two years of the Occupation, Lévitte's efforts as a leader of the Jewish Scouts focused on leadership training.

The mission of the MJS was to provide young men and women with the Jewish and Zionist education, physical training, and vocational skills they would need to create successful communities in Palestine. However, almost immediately after the Unification Congress, foreign Jews in France were targeted for arrest and deportation, and the MJS was called upon to engage in both relief work and humanitarian resistance. Many MJS members and their parents were themselves targeted because they were foreign-born.

In 1943, under the protection of the Italian army and in conjunction with members of the Sixth-Jewish Scouts and the Armée juive, the MJS developed into an effective resistance network.[50] Soon after the Germans took up positions in much of the Southern Zone, Lévitte transferred the organization's head-

48. For a discussion of the Unification Congress, see Lazare, *Rescue as Resistance*, 67–70.

49. Simon Lévitte, *Le Sionisme: quelques pages de son histoire* (Paris: Éditions des Cahiers juifs, 1936).

50. I know of no comprehensive accounts that chronicle the growth and development of the MJS or its humanitarian resistance efforts during the Shoah. However, the subject is addressed to varying degrees in numerous published and unpublished accounts written by individuals who were themselves MJS members or who were members of groups that worked with the MJS. For further reading, I would recommend: Hélène Gorgiel-Sercarz, *Memoirs of a Jewish Daughter* (Tel-Aviv:H. Gorgiel-Sercarz, 1990); René S. Kapel, *Un rabbin dans la tourmente (1940–1944)* (Paris: CDJC: 1986); Anny Latour, *The Jewish Resistance in France (1940–1944)*, trans. Irene R. Ilton (New York: Holocaust Library, 1981); and Georges Schnek, "Être jeune en France, 1939–1945," an address presented at the Colloque international de Grenoble in January 1997 and reproduced in Dereymez, Jean-William, ed., *Être jeune en Isère (1939–1945)* (Paris: L'Harmattan, 2001), 59–64. See too: David Knout, *Contribution à l'histoire de la Résistance Juive en France, 1940-1944* (Paris: Éditions du Centre, 1947), 126–31; and unpublished testimonies of Tony Gryn (Centre de documentation juive contemporaine DLXI–35) and Toto Giniewski (today, Eytan Guinat) (Centre de documentation juive contemporaine DLXI–31).

115

quarters from Montpellier to Grenoble. *"Gdouds"*—Hebrew for "brigades"—had been established and were functioning in various cities in the Southern Zone; but, after the German invasion, many MJS members found their way to Grenoble and Nice. Not all MJS members were involved in or had knowledge of the resistance work in which the group was engaged; a subgroup of MJS leaders and activists carried out illegal, underground work using the cover name "Éducation physique" (Physical Education). The Jewish Scouts had been operating both legally, under the umbrella of the UGIF, as well as illegally, through its underground arm, the Sixth. In January 1943, German authorities outlawed the existence of the Jewish Scouts, who then went completely underground. From that point on, the scouts and Zionist youth were integrated and worked together to carry out resistance activities.[51]

During the relative peace of the Italian interlude, the Grenoble *gdoud* developed a sophisticated laboratory for producing high-quality false documents. Eytan Guinat (né Otto Giniewski, b. 1920, Vienna) , an MJS leader and doctoral student in chemistry at the University of Grenoble, perfected the art of creating what was called a *synthé*, a document based on the identity of a real person.[52] He trained fellow MJS member and chemistry student Georges Schnek (b. 1924, Warsaw) to be his assistant. The *faussaires* (forgers) were supported by a network of two dozen or so MJS activists and scouts, young men and women who made their way, sometimes on bicycle, to mayoral offices throughout the countryside to get the information and materiel needed. Sympathetic clerks and secretaries allowed them to work peaceably in their offices and supplied them with official stamps and copies of blank birth certificates, marriage licenses, and baptismal certificates. By the summer of 1943, the operation was producing hundreds of high quality documents.

In February 1943, OSE had begun smuggling groups of unaccompanied children from France into Switzerland. Swiss directives issued in late 1942 defined certain categories of people whom they regarded as "hardship cases" and who, having entered the country illegally, would not be sent back to France.[53] Unac-

---

51. Poznanski, *Jews in France*, 401–02.

52. See, for example: testimony of Toto Giniewski (today, Eytan Guinat) (Centre de documentation juive contemporaine DLXI–31); and Georges Schnek, "Être jeune en France, 1939–1945," in *Être jeune en Isère (1939–1945)*, 59–64.

53. Independent Commission of Experts Switzerland—Second World War, *Die Schweiz und die Flüchtinge zur Zeit des Nationalsozialismus* (Bern: Distributed by BBL/EDMZ, 1999), 122; 133. The document is generally referred to as the *Bergier Report*. Categories of hardship cases were first defined in late August 1942, following a wave of protests that occurred after the Swiss Federal government closed the border. Initially, categories of hardship cases were broadly defined and included:

companied children younger than sixteen and families with children younger than six were among those deemed hardship cases. In August 1943, when it became apparent to Jewish leaders that Italian troops were going to withdraw from some or all of their occupation zone, Andrée Salomon of OSE asked Simon Lévitte to organize a second network, separate from that of OSE, to smuggle children across the border. Lévitte chose two young MJS leaders, Tony Gryn (b. 1921, Lublin, Poland) and Mila Racine (b. 1919, Moscow), to lead this operation.[54] The two quickly organized a small team and took convoys of unaccompanied children from Saint-Gervais and Megève, the principal centers of assigned residence in the Italian Occupation Zone, to the Swiss border.[55]

In early September, as Italian soldiers retreated and German soldiers swept in, Gryn and Racine established a base in Annecy (Haute-Savoie Department) and began receiving children brought from other parts of France. The Annecy team sheltered the children briefly, prepared them for the border crossing, organized them into groups, and took them to an area outside of Geneva. Both the MJS and OSE *réseaux* (networks) received essential help from Catholic and Protestant resisters in the Haute-Savoie and from paid guides—*passeurs*—who knew the local terrain and movements of the border patrols.

During the second week of September, the Germans unleashed a reign of terror against Jews in Nice more brutal than anything previously seen in France.[56] No distinction was made between native and foreign-born Jews; anyone suspected of being Jewish was seized. Jewish relief agencies shut down their operations, and underground networks struggled to aid as many people as possible. Members of the Nice *gdoud* worked hand in hand with those of the

---

unaccompanied children less than sixteen years of age; parents with their own children less than six years of age; the sick; pregnant women; elderly persons over sixty-five; those with immediate family members living in Switzerland; and those with other close ties to the country. In December 1942, the Federal government tightened criteria defining hardship cases. Significant to this analysis is the fact that the criterion regarding families with children was changed—henceforth, only families with children younger than six were classified as hardship cases and permitted to remain within the country.

54. Tony Gryn testimony (Centre de documentation juive contemporaine DLXI–35).

55. Nancy Lefenfeld, *The Fate of Others: Rescuing Jewish Children on the French-Swiss Border* (Clarksville, Md.: Timbrel Press, 2013), 52–74. Archives of the State of Geneva, collection Justice et Police—specifically, personal dossiers of Jewish children smuggled from France into Switzerland in August, September, and October 1943—form the primary basis of this work.

56. See, for example, the following: Daniel Carpi, *Between Mussolini and Hitler: The Jews and the Italian Authorities in France and Tunisia* (Hanover: University Press of New England, 1994); Serge Klarsfeld, *Nice: Hotel Excelsior: Les rafles des Juifs par la Gestapo à partir du 8 septembre 1943* (Paris: Les fils et filles des déportés juifs de France, 1998); and Léon Poliakov and Jacques Sabille, *Jews under the Italian Occupation* (New York: Howard Fertig, 1983).

Sixth-Jewish Scouts and the Armée juive to fabricate and distribute false documents and find safe places for those camouflaged under Aryan identities.[57] Jacques Wajntrob (b. 1920, Tarczyn, Poland) was the young, dynamic leader of the Nice brigade. Before his arrest in late September, he and his wife, Léa (née Eisenbaum, b. 1921, Ostrowiec, Poland) worked feverishly to transfer Jewish children secretly from Nice to the MJS team in Annecy. The first step in accomplishing this difficult work was to convince desperate parents that their children stood a better chance of reaching safety in Switzerland than of evading arrest and deportation in Nice and that they should entrust them to a network of resisters—persons whom they did not know.

At the beginning of October, OSE temporarily suspended its smuggling operation, but the MJS group based in Annecy continued on and redoubled its efforts.[58] On October 21, a convoy led by Mila Racine and a fellow MJS activist, Roland Epstein (b. 1922, Szczncin, Poland), was seized at the border, and the *réseau* was shut down for the winter. In the spring of 1944, the MJS and OSE networks resumed smuggling operations. In 1943–44, the activists of MJS and OSE smuggled approximately 1,000 unaccompanied children from France into Switzerland.[59] They also aided an unknown number of families with young children in making their way across the border.

Jacques Wajntrob and Mila Racine were among many MJS resisters who lost their lives.

Service André

Tall, broad, and supremely confident, Joseph Bass (b. 1908, Grodno, Belarus) has been described by many as larger than life.[60] At the age of sixteen, he trav-

---

57. Lazare, *Rescue as Resistance*, 233–34; Les Anciens de la Résistance juive en France, *Organisation juive de combat*, 38; and testimony of Henri Pohorylès, leader of the Armée juive in Nice during the period (Centre de documentation juive contemporaine DLXI–76). In June 1944, the Armée juive changed its name to the Organisation juive de combat (OJC; Jewish Combat Organization). Subsequently, other groups engaged in resistance placed themselves under the OJC banner. The volume referenced above—*Organisation juive de combat*—presents brief biographies of men and women who identified themselves with the AJ, MJS, OSE-réseau Garel, Amelot, Sixth-Jewish Scouts, les Hollandais, les aumôniers (chaplains), réseau Marcel, and réseau André. Resisters' biographies can also be accessed on the website of the Mémorial de la Shoah (www. memorialdelashoah.org). As indicated there, many resisters identified themselves with more than one group. Pertinent to this point is the fact that some members of the MJS team based in Annecy also identified themselves with the Sixth-Jewish Scouts.

58. Lefenfeld, *The Fate of Others*, 129–31.

59. Centre de documentation juive contemporaine, OSE (II)-307, "Liste des enfants partis en Suisse en 1943–1944."

60. Two sources in particular provide colorful portraits of Bass: Denise Siekierski, "Joseph

eled, alone and without resources, from Belarus to Paris. Performing manual labor to support himself, he completed university studies in law and engineering and went on to oversee an industrial patents and property office. Not long after serving in the French army during the *drôle de guerre*, he found himself interned in Le Vernet, a punitive camp in the department of Ariège. He escaped and made his way to Marseille.

In the fall of 1942, Bass began organizing an underground network to help those threatened with arrest and deportation. The group would become known as the Service André. His savoir-faire, audacity, and powers of persuasion enabled him to recruit Jewish and Christian men and women, including several prominent clergy.[61]

From the outset, Bass felt it was essential that Jews leave the city and disperse throughout the rural countryside. Pastors in Marseille put Bass in touch with Pastor André Trocmé (b. 1901, Saint-Quentin, France) of the Reformed Church of France in Le Chambon-sur-Lignon, on the Vivarais-Lignon plateau (Haute-Loire Department). Inspired by the example of André Trocmé and his wife, Magda (b. 1901, Florence, Italy), French Huguenot communities on the plateau were already sheltering Jews who had shown up of their own accord or had been brought there by members of the Garel Network. Bass established a *filière d'évasion*, an escape channel, between Marseille and Le Chambon. Throughout the remainder of the Occupation, the Service André relied more heavily upon this particular region than any other as a place to hide Jews in plain sight.

Despite her youth, Denise Siekierski (née Caraco, b. 1924, Marseille) played a significant role in the Service André. She described the group's work as comprising six key elements: fabricating false papers; researching hiding places in regions far from Marseille; escorting people to hiding places; paying monthly visits to those in hiding; serving as *agents de liaison* to transport sensitive and valuable materials; and transferring people to resisters prepared to smuggle them across the Swiss border.[62]

Sporadic acts of resistance broke out in Marseille after German troops occupied much of the Southern Zone in November 1942. In January 1943, German

---

Bass," *Revue d'histoire de la Shoah, Le monde juif*, no. 168, January–April, 2000 (Paris: La revue du Centre de documentation juive contemporaine), 140–74; and Léon Poliakov, *L'auberge des musiciens: mémoires* (Paris: Mazarine, 1981).

61. The prominent clergy included the Capuchin monk Père Marie-Benoît, Dominican prior Father de Perceval, and pastors Roland Leenhardt, Jean-Séverin Lemaire, and Marcel Léon Heuzé.

62. Siekierski, "Joseph Bass," 143–44.

and French police carried out reprisals, conducting raids and strict identity controls, arresting thousands of "undesirables," and destroying the Vieux-Port neighborhood, where many immigrants lived. French as well as foreign Jews were swept up. Bass and his team focused their efforts on the embattled Jews of Marseille during the first part of the year and then extended their work to other cities, including Aix-en-Provence, Avignon, Orange, Nîmes, and Lyon. In September 1943, when the Italian Occupation Zone fell and Germans unleashed a reign of terror in Nice, members of the Service André worked together with those of the MJS, the Armée juive, and the Sixth-Jewish Scouts, placing themselves at great risk to save as many people as possible.

Several men and women of the Service André not specifically mentioned above lost their lives.

What can we call these unarmed combatants other than forgers, camouflagers, and smugglers? Law-abiding people shrink from the use of these pejorative labels. Therefore, it is imperative to remember that the Jewish men and women who engaged in humanitarian resistance did so when French law not only failed to protect them but was used as a weapon to speed their destruction.

Recognizing the nature and importance of Jewish humanitarian resistance does not detract in any way from honoring the many French Christians who came to the aid of Jews, often at the risk of their own lives. Indeed, it is an essential step in understanding that the humanitarian resistance efforts that saved the lives of tens of thousands of Jews in France during the Shoah were, above all, ecumenical in nature.

Suzanne Vromen

6 Unique Aspects of Jewish Armed Resistance and Rescue in Belgium

On July 25, 1942, four armed men stormed into the new offices of the Association des Juifs en Belgique (AJB). Two of the men herded the employees into a room and castigated them about working for this organization, established by the Nazis to transmit and execute their orders within the Jewish community. In an adjoining room, the two other men quickly set fire to AJB files containing the names and addresses of all Jews to be called up for so-called labor in the East. This occurred two days before the opening of the Malines (Mechelen) transit camp, from which the assembled Jews were to depart. Unfortunately, the intruders did not realize that the files they destroyed were duplicates; the originals already had been transmitted to the Gestapo. The fire was intended not only as an obstacle to the call-up but as a warning to ignore the AJB's instructions.

A month later, on August 29, 1942, Robert Holzinger was shot and killed on a Brussels street. A German Jewish member of the AJB's central committee, Holzinger was responsible for sending out the deceptive "employment cards" that facilitated the orderly assembling of Jews in the Dossin barracks at Malines prior to their transfer to the East. The cards included a fake assurance that the recipients were not being deported. In actuality, Holzinger and other AJB notables carrying out this work were acting as the mailmen of the Final Solution.[1]

1. Maxime Steinberg and José Gotovitch, *Otages de la terreur nazie: Le Bulgare Angheloff et son groupe de Partisans juifs Bruxelles 1940–1943* (Bruxelles: Uitgeverij VUBPRESS, 2007), 85.

These two episodes represent the first concerted efforts of Jewish armed resistance against the massive deportations in Belgium, which began in the summer of 1942. The men who took part in these actions belonged to the mobile corps of partisans sponsored by the Front de l'Indépendance (FI), a resistance organization set up by the Communists a year earlier and shortly after Germany invaded its former ally, the Soviet Union. Until then, the Belgian Communist Party had remained uneasily neutral toward the country's German occupiers. Now, the party was outlawed and its militants relentlessly persecuted. With a goal of liberating the Belgian homeland, the FI organized as a broad national resistance coalition. Its strategy was twofold: armed actions by partisans and civil resistance through alliances with different social and political groups. The FI mobilized support for resistance among workers, farmers, police officers, judges, teachers, doctors, and youth organizations. It eventually developed into "an energetic and diversified movement."[2]

Let us place the two events described above in context. On the eve of Germany's invasion of Belgium on May 10, 1940, estimates of the country's Jewish population ranged between 56,000 and 60,000, with 94 percent of these foreigners. As a result, it was a vulnerable population that felt little entitlement to government protection. On the contrary, it preferred to avoid any scrutiny by legal authorities. Most Jews had arrived either during the 1920s, fleeing poverty and pogroms in Eastern European countries, or in the 1930s, as refugees from Nazi Germany. Living mainly in Brussels and Antwerp, this immigrant community included a poverty-stricken urban proletariat confronted by xenophobia and (especially in Antwerp) blatant antisemitism. An active minority was Communist or expressed Communist and militantly anti-Fascist sympathies. In fact, 200 Belgian Jews fought in the International Brigades in the Spanish Civil War.[3] Their experience proved good preparation for fighting the Nazi occupiers.

The partisans in the mobile corps were members of the Main d'Oeuvre Immigrée (MOI), the clandestine Communist organization of foreigners whose ranks were primarily Jewish. Before the war, the MOI recruited immigrant workers into the Communist Party and enlisted members who were already Communists. Within the MOI, Jewish immigrant workers living on the margins of Belgian society and not always readily accepted by Belgian workers (nor by the Belgian Communist Party itself) could maintain both their Communist beliefs and their

2. Pieter Lagrou, "Belgium," in *Resistance in Western Europe*, ed. Bob Moore (New York: Berg, 2000), 50.

3. Rudi Van Doorslaer, *Enfants du Ghetto: Juifs révolutionnaires en Belgique (1925–1940)* (Bruxelles: Editions Labor, 1997), 210.

Jewish identities. The MOI was divided into sections by language groups and nationality. Though the mobile corps in Brussels counted just twenty-four members at its inception, it was organized into three companies following a similar protocol. The first company was made up of immigrants from Poland who spoke Yiddish. The second company included Jews from Hungary, Czechoslovakia, Yugoslavia and the Balkans. Less attached to their Jewish identity and more assimilated, its members spoke Hungarian. The third company counted a few Bessarabians who spoke mainly Russian but also Yiddish. Being a small group, they were eventually absorbed into the second company.

Todor (Theodor) Angheloff served as commander of the mobile corps. Of peasant background, he was a veteran Communist from Bulgaria who had fought in the International Brigades during the Spanish Civil War. Though not a Jew, Angheloff had spent time militating among the Jewish immigrants as the MOI's political secretary, which reportedly gave him a solid and sympathetic understanding of them. He recruited the mobile corps' partisans himself; at least a quarter of them also had fought in Spain.[4] They formed "triangles" of three people and often employed women couriers as liaisons. To ensure secrecy and efficiency, the groups should have operated with no knowledge of each other. In practice, they fraternized.

In the beginning, the mobile corps' main aim was to obstruct the activities of Jewish collaborators, in this way sabotaging the German war machine. Economic collaboration was their primary target. For example, they worked to thwart Jewish furriers who specialized in sewing rabbit-skin linings into vests that were shipped to Nazi soldiers on the Eastern Front. When the furriers' enterprises were liquidated, they worked at home for Aryan firms or for their own "Aryanized" firms. This allowed them to remain exempt from deportation to forced labor camps—first in northern France and later in the East. They wound up paying heavily for this Nazi protection.[5]

At first, mobile corps partisans used flyers, letters, and graffiti to discourage this economic collaboration. When these efforts failed, they repeatedly attacked enterprises working for the Germans, destroying machines, burning vests and skins, and seizing money from safes. They also extorted money from Jewish economic collaborators. On June 20, 1942, they shot and killed a Jewish collaborator who threatened to denounce them. It was the first killing by the mobile corps. *Le Drapeau Rouge*, the Communist Party's clandestine newspa-

4. Steinberg and Gotovitch, *Otages de la terreur nazie*, 69.
5. Maxime Steinberg, *La traque des Juifs 1942–1944* (Bruxelles: Editions Vie Ouvrière, 1986), 2:38.

per, subsequently wrote that the murder was the mobile corps partisans' way of commemorating the date on which the Germans invaded the Soviet Union. The paper muddled history: the invasion occurred on June 22, 1941.[6]

Angheloff's group targeted collaborators because it wanted to shatter the illusion that conformity was normal and collaboration acceptable behavior. But the two actions described at the beginning of this paper—the burning of AJB files and the murder of Robert Holzinger—had the added intentions of striking against the deportations and delegitimizing AJB notables. Holzinger, a Jew, was killed by a Jew. As Steinberg points out, the partisans did not kill SS officer Kurt Asche, who gave the order to disseminate the employment cards. Instead, they gunned down the German Jew most engaged with the SS officer for Jewish affairs. By letter they threatened other notables with the same fate.[7] The killing was precisely timed. A growing number of Jews ignored the cards with their fake reassurances, so to fill the fourth convoy to Auschwitz the SS carried out two large nighttime roundups in Antwerp, brutally removing more than 2,000 people from their homes. Holzinger was killed the day after the second roundup. Jews in Brussels were rounded up a few nights later. The majority of the remaining Jewish population then lost all illusions about the AJB's legal role and plunged into hiding.

As noted, in their early activities the partisans rarely engaged in killing but resorted to sabotage, in effect serving as urban guerillas. As the historian José Gotovitch expressed it, they had not yet taken the step from powder to bullets.[8] From the beginning, though, the partisans extended their activities beyond the Jewish community. They sabotaged factories and garages and repeatedly damaged the extensive Belgian railroad network. Violence grew in the second half of 1942, as they stepped up lethal attacks against collaborators: the lackeys of the occupiers were seen as traitors to be terrorized. A series of collaborationist mayors were assassinated and power plants blown up.

The mounting violence brought about severe reprisals and unrelenting pursuit. Between November 1942 and January 1943, sixty-eight hostages were shot. Most—including Angheloff, who was captured in January 1943—were Communist partisans who fell into German hands.[9] Hostages were not necessarily killed for their own actions but for what their presumed comrades had done. Partisans were sometimes arrested as Jews and deported in racial convoys. On other occasions, they were seized as resisters, defined as "terrorist hostages,"

6. Steinberg and Gotovitch, *Otages de la terreur nazie*, 82.
7. Steinberg, *La traque des Juifs*, 2:43.
8. Steinberg and Gotovitch, *Otages de la terreur nazie*, 13.
9. Ibid., 32.

incarcerated in Breendonk (the infamous prison camp), tortured, and eventually executed or deported to German camps.

Though no partisan of the mobile corps was arrested before November 1942, its members were ruthlessly pursued. The corps lasted only about a year; by early 1943 its ranks had been decimated. Two-thirds of the fighters did not survive arrest, captivity, or deportation. The remaining members were amalgamated with the other FI partisans, among whom were many Jews. In assessing the Communist resistance, Gotovitch appraised the mobile corps in the following way: "the Jewish partisans of the MOI with their commander Todor Angheloff will have played in this concert a sacrificial overture, a heroic one."[10] In the mobile corps the partisans maintained their Jewish identity and trusted their own people. With their attacks, they upheld a sense of Jewish pride and, at the same time, put into practice their political beliefs by carrying out the directives of the Communist Party. A different aspect of Jewish resistance is the remarkable work dedicated to the rescue and survival of Jewish children. It was carried out by the Comité de Défense des Juifs (CDJ), which was established under the auspices of the FI and became one of its most effective groups. The CDJ's name has double meaning: a committee to defend Jews and a Jewish defense committee. In other words, it implies a need both to protect Jews and to empower them to defend themselves. To a large extent, the CDJ succeeded on both fronts.

Ghert Jospa, a Jewish engineer of Bessarabian origin and a founding FI member, and his wife, Yvonne Groisman-Jospa, established the CDJ after Jews were mandated to wear the Star of David. Their situation rapidly deteriorated, culminating with their roundup beginning in the summer of 1942. Among the eight individuals who initially joined Jospa and his wife in the CDJ were seven Jews and one non-Jew—Emile Hambresin, a left-wing Catholic who had long fought against racism with his friend Jospa. (He later perished in one of the Nazi camps.) Another important CDJ founder was the Jewish philosopher Chaim Perelman. A faculty member at the Free University of Brussels, he was also a Zionist militant who enjoyed a high intellectual standing in Jewish and non-Jewish circles. Perelman's cooperation was vital and enabled the CDJ to make rapid progress in establishing a resistance committee. Eventually, nearly all of Belgium's Jewish organizations were represented on the CDJ. It was an important achievement to unite people from opposite ends of the political spectrum: Communists, Zionists of all persuasions, and Belgian and foreign Jews. It is important to note that the CDJ was a committee, not a movement: all who joined were allowed to preserve

10. Ibid., 43.

their own political identities. Clearly, members of the FI considered the rescue of Jews an integral part of their work.

The CDJ clandestinely installed an extensive administration. It also included a service for forging identity papers and rationing cards; a network of hiding places for children systematically separated from their parents; a service offering assistance to impoverished Jewish adults without resources and help to go underground; and departments for a clandestine press, propaganda, and finances. The department for forged documents was so efficient and skillful that it generated a supply beyond the CDJ's own needs. It wound up providing false papers to labor draft evaders and selling quality forgeries to wealthy individuals. The proceeds were used to finance CDJ activities. Newspapers in French, Flemish, and Yiddish were printed specifically for Jewish readers and carried warnings against following AJB directives.

When deportations began on a large scale, parents at the least tried to save their children. Some found hiding places on their own, but this proved insufficient for the large number of children needing help. Providing an efficient response to the racist deportations, the CDJ developed a systematic, consistent, and responsible way to provide safe placement—first for those children who were abandoned due to their parents' deportation and then those threatened by deportation themselves. Though the committee began to function officially in September 1942, the rescue of children was so pressing that it started operating prior to its formal organization. Soon afterward, adults who escaped the first roundups also were helped to enter the underground so they too could evade the Final Solution.

Historian Maxime Steinberg has argued that the hidden Jews could not have survived clandestinely without the organized Jewish defense.[11] At the height of the CDJ's activities, the names of about 2,400 children it had spared from deportation were listed in carefully coded and hidden notebooks. This represented about half the children the Nazis were unable to deport. As successful as this seems, many more children fell victim to Nazi barbarism: 5,093 children under the age of sixteen were deported. Of these, 145 were younger than two years of age, with the youngest just thirty-nine days old.[12]

Some members of the CDJ also held official positions in the AJB. Acting as double agents, they engaged in secret resistance activities while enjoying rela-

11. Steinberg, *La traque des Juifs*, 2:20.
12. Maxime Steinberg, *Un pays occupé et ses juifs: Belgique entre France et Pays-Bas* (Gerpinnes, Belgium: Editions Quorum, 1998), 98.

tive protection within the AJB. For example, Maurice Heiber had the main responsibility for the children's section of the CDJ, while the AJB assigned him the task of establishing an orphanage in Wezembeek-Ophem for children of deported parents. Officially, these children were labeled as abandoned and registered by the Germans. Because the orphanage was an official venture, it also came under the purview of the Oeuvre Nationale de l'Enfance (ONE), a governmental agency created in 1919 to promote children's health and reduce child mortality. The ONE, in turn, was dependent on Belgium's Ministry of the Interior and the Family.

Heiber confided to Yvonne Nèvejean, head of the ONE, that he was worried about German intentions toward these children. She promised to protect them if need be. Heiber's fears were soon confirmed. In October 1942, the children and their caretakers were suddenly rounded up and brought to the Dossin barracks to fulfill a deportation quota. A non-Jewish housekeeper in the orphanage alerted Nèvejean, who immediately appealed to Queen Elizabeth, the Queen Mother, to intercede with German authorities. Other interventions took place as well. Those arrested were eventually freed and returned to the orphanage.

From then on, Nèvejean devoted herself to the CDJ's rescue mission. She used all of her resources to find placements and provide subsidies. She intervened at a time when the CDJ was running out of money. (While some placements were free, many required payment.) Nèvejean also provided safe helpers whom she chose from her intimate circle. Later, she formally joined the CDJ as a member of the children's section. She also sat on its finance committee.[13]

The rescue of Jewish children owes much to Yvonne Nèvejean-Feyerick (as she was known after her marriage). As head of the ONE she held a key official position that gave her oversight of a large number of children's institutions. She was thoroughly aware of what hiding places were available across the country, and she used her wide network of connections to seek placements. Through her own organization she provided financial assistance; she also raised considerable funds from banks and clandestinely from the Belgian government-in-exile in London. While it is true that she joined an existing rescue organization that counted many devoted members, her boundless support was crucial to the CDJ's expansion and overall success. When Nèvejean died in 1987, Yvonne Jospa eulogized her: "Nèvejean was driven by her love for children, her an-

13. Ibid., 132–36.

tipathy towards any form of discrimination, and her ... defiance against the Nazi occupation. Her paramount concern was to provide the same opportunities for Jewish children as for non-Jewish ones."[14] Nèvejean provided Jewish children with more than equality of opportunity: she gave them the gift of life. In February 1965, she became the first Belgian woman to be honored as a Righteous Among the Nations. In 1996, the Belgian postal authority issued a stamp in her memory.

On the one hand, the CDJ provided a striking example of Jews saving Jews: it empowered itself to rescue Jews, then initiated and carried out a plan to ensure success. At the same time, the CDJ illustrated the existence of a profound collaboration with non-Jewish organizations. One non-Jewish group that played a significant and remarkable role in safeguarding Jewish children was the grassroots Roman Catholic clergy. Convents throughout the country, often through the help of parish priests, sheltered many children.[15] Historian Bob Moore is right to assert that: "The cooperation between different welfare and resistance organizations in Belgium during the Occupation, coupled with the willingness of Jewish and non-Jewish groups across the political spectrum to work together provided the basis for an organization *unique* in Western Europe."[16]

Many women were actively engaged in the CDJ's efforts to rescue children. It is not surprising they were essential to this mission: the rationale for their tasks was rooted in their traditional gender roles. Protecting children, feeding and clothing them, checking up on their well-being, paying for their keep—all were feminine occupations. Some skills, however, such as assessing hiding possibilities and breaking up families, had to be learned, and the risks of leading secret lives accepted. Women were essential in separating children from their families; they were trusted as surrogate mothers, even if only temporary ones. Organizing the rescue in all of its facets went far beyond traditional gender roles. In contrast to many other resistance organizations, women in the CDJ's children's section occupied decision-making positions from its inception.

The rescue of Jewish children is a clear example of successful civilian resistance, in the way Jacques Semelin has conceptualized it.[17] In contrast to those

14. Dan Michman, ed., *The Encyclopedia of the Righteous Among the Nations: Rescuers of Jews during the Holocaust. Belgium* (Jerusalem: Yad Vashem, 2005), 194–95.

15. Suzanne Vromen, *Hidden Children of the Holocaust: Belgian Nuns and Their Daring Rescue of Young Jews from the Nazis* (New York: Oxford University Press, 2008).

16. Bob Moore, *Survivors: Jewish Self-Help and Rescue in Nazi-Occupied Western Europe* (Oxford: Oxford University Press, 2010), 175 (emphasis mine).

17. Jacques Semelin, *Unarmed against Hitler: Civilian Resistance in Europe 1939–1943* (Westport, Conn.: Praeger, 1993).

using armed resistance, civilian resisters had no intention of attacking the enemy directly. They sought to foster survival by thwarting the occupiers' murderous intentions and preserving the values threatened by the Nazi regime. The civilian resistance in Belgium developed ideological dimensions through the underground press, and its appeals for help increasingly sensitized the wider population. As mentioned earlier, the CDJ unified different political factions under one umbrella and ensured that organizations opposing the occupiers saw saving Jews as an integral aspect of resistance. It successfully avoided divisive ideological issues and, in this way, provided the social cohesion that Semelin deems essential for the emergence and efficient functioning of a civilian resistance movement. The survival of Jews and thousands of others who evaded the Nazi labor draft promulgated in October 1942 remained a major challenge for the civilian resistance until the liberation.

Another unique aspect of the Jewish resistance in Belgium is the attack on the XXth deportation convoy on April 19, 1943. It was an attempt to stop a deportation train, open its wagons, and allow the escape of as many deportees as possible. Thousands of deportation trains rolled across occupied Europe, yet this presumably was the only attempt to halt one. By coincidence, it occurred on the same day as the onset of the Warsaw Ghetto Uprising. The XXth convoy was to travel to Auschwitz from the Dossin barracks in Malines, located midway between the two largest Jewish population centers of Brussels and Antwerp. It was the first train made up of cattle cars. Previous convoys used regular third-class railroad carriages, from which a handful of deportees had escaped.

The XXth convoy was not part of the first wave of deportations. From summer to fall 1942, 30 percent of Belgium's Jewish population had been deported to Auschwitz. In 100 days, seventeen convoys each carrying an average of 1,000 deportees left Malines.[18] But then, with the help of the CDJ, the Jewish population went into hiding and became more difficult to round up. As the pace of deportations slowed, it became impossible to meet quotas with customary rapidity. With the XXth convoy scheduled for April 19, 1943, the number of deportees was nearing a total of 20,000 Jews.

The CDJ was moved to rescue by a sense of urgency. Its leaders were convinced that the deportees would never return. The CDJ's clandestine paper, *Le Flambeau*, stated bluntly in its March 1943 issue: "Nazi deportation means death." The idea for stopping a deportation train originated in discussions with-

18. Maxime Steinberg and Laurence Schram, *Transport XX Malines-Auschwitz* (Bruxelles: VUB-PRESS, 2008), 9.

in the CDJ between Ghert Jospa and two new members, Maurice Bolle and Roger Van Praag. They realized they lacked the ability and the experience—not to mention the weapons—to carry out such an audacious plot. Jospa knew that many former partisans who had been rounded up were scheduled to be deported by the XXth convoy, so it was crucial to enable them to escape. He approached Jean Terfve, a leader of the FI partisans, and asked for his support. Terfve considered it too risky and too rushed. Still, Jospa did not abandon his idea.

Through Bolle's daughter, he eventually recruited Youra (Georges) Livshitz, a recent medical school graduate. Livschitz's brother was a FI partisan, but he had recently been wounded in action. Livschitz at first tried to obtain the cooperation of Group G, a resistance movement made up of scientists and engineers, former students from the University of Brussels, where he had connections. Group G specialized in carefully planned industrial sabotage and in causing extensive damage to the country's transportation network and electricity supply. Armed action was not part of its agenda, and its leaders did not endorse the plan. However, one Group G member, Richard Altenhoff, gave Livschitz a small revolver and a handshake and wished him luck. Finally, Livschitz asked two friends, Jean Franklemon and George Mastriau, to join him. Neither was Jewish, nor had they been engaged in a resistance movement up to this point. Yet both agreed to help.

In preparation for the operation, the men covered a lantern with red paper. Their plan was to place it on the rails, signal of an obstruction further down the line that would entice the engineer to stop. Once the train was halted, Livschitz would immobilize the engineer by threatening him with his revolver while Franklemon and Mastriau would open the cattle cars with pliers and distribute fifty-franc bills (secured from the CDJ) to facilitate the escapees' flight to safety.

Under cover of darkness the men bicycled to a railroad intersection about a dozen kilometers from Malines. Almost immediately, their plans went awry. They had expected the German police escort to be in its usual place, in the train's rear cars. However, this time officers were also sitting at the front of the convoy. They started shooting as soon as the train came to a halt. Livschitz and Franklemon were forced to flee immediately. Mastriau managed to open one car with his pliers. Seventeen deportees jumped out and dispersed; seven were rounded up and did not survive a second deportation. (Through the testimony of the ten surviving escapees, the event was carefully reconstructed after the war.)

The three young plotters made it safely back to Brussels, but some time later Livschitz was denounced, arrested, and condemned to die for having fired at

Germans. He was shot as a terrorist hostage in February 1944, a week before his brother met the same fate. Jean Franklemon was deported to Sachsenhausen. Mastriau joined Group G after the attempt but was eventually captured and deported to Buchenwald and other camps. Both he and Franklemon survived the war. Richard Altenhoff was caught and shot for having provided the revolver.

The freeing of seventeen deportees is not the end of this story. As noted previously, the XXth convoy included many partisans. With the complicity of workers at the assembly camp, some partisans smuggled tools onto the train. They cut floorboards and bars and jumped whenever the convoy slowed down. People escaped from nearly every car; the youngest escapee was eleven years old.[19] This deportation train was larger than usual—it carried 1,636 people, the oldest over ninety, the youngest thirty-nine days old. On the way to Auschwitz, it "lost" 232 deportees. Of these, 119 were never caught, eighty-seven were recaptured and deported on subsequent convoys, and twenty-six lost their lives.[20] This was a train of rebels against the Final Solution, people who helped themselves with much courage and determination.

Thirty years after the war, Mastriau judged the attempt youthful and foolhardy. In fact, it was the trio's lack of experience that led them to take risks that more seasoned resistance fighters refused to consider. By spring 1943, the partisans had incurred immense losses. As noted above, the mobile corps at that point was decimated. Clearly there was a desire to preserve forces and abstain from operations with poor odds. Also at that time, the tide of war had begun to turn against the Germans. Armed resistance efforts focused on sabotaging and harming the Nazis were deemed more essential than trying to save deportees. As the Germans began to lose the war, repression against the Resistance was more fierce than ever, so risks had to be weighed carefully. No attempt was made to stop the eight subsequent deportation trains from Belgium. Nor, presumably, was any other deportation train ever attacked in all of occupied Europe.

After the war, the tale of the attack acquired mythical dimensions and easily slipped into exaggeration. The three young men were often mistakenly hailed as liberators of over 200 deportees. The occurrence of the attack coinciding with the start of the Warsaw Ghetto Uprising also helped it to acquire symbolic value. Every year on April 19 the Jewish population in Belgium commemorates simultaneously a unique local feat and an event that has become emblematic of Jewish resistance during the Holocaust.

19. Ibid., 18–24.
20. Ibid., 35.

The CDJ's strong ties to armed FI partisans proved vital in another episode of Jewish resistance in Belgium. In May 1943, just a month after the attack on the deportation train, fourteen Jewish girls and their monitor, placed by the CDJ in the Convent of the Holy Savior in Anderlecht (a suburb of Brussels), were discovered and denounced by "Gros Jacques," the alias of Icek Glogowski, a notorious Jewish traitor employed by the Gestapo to detect Jews.[21] The girls ranged in age from twenty months to twelve years. Sister Marie-Aurélie, the head of the convent, talked the Nazis into postponing the arrests for a day so she could prepare the children for their departure and pack their belongings. When the Gestapo left, she alerted a parish priest, Father Jan Bruylandts, who was sheltering several Jewish boys. Also hearing the dreadful news, Bernard Fenerberg, one of the boys, in turn informed Paul Halter, a member of the FI partisans. That evening, the partisans came to whisk away the children, staging the flight to appear as if it had been accomplished by force. To create the appearance that the nuns had resisted, they bound and gagged the women, cut the telephone lines and overturned the furniture. By the time the Gestapo arrived the next day, the girls had been safely dispersed in hiding places throughout Brussels with the help of the CDJ. Because Fenerberg had acted so rapidly and decisively, Halter allowed him to become a member of his group, though he was only seventeen years old.

The Nazis tended to avoid confrontations with Catholic clergy; so the nuns suffered no consequences for their brave stand. However to show their anger, the occupiers arrested Maurice Heiber, who was in charge of the AJB's official orphanages, as well as his wife, Esta, whom they considered his accomplice. (The occupiers were not aware that the Heibers were also prominent members of the CDJ and in charge of its children's section.) The couple was interned in the transit camp in Malines and put in charge of transient children there. They were never deported, probably because the AJB intervened and used its influence and bribes.

After the war, this audacious rescue also acquired mythical dimensions, with many people claiming that they had taken part in it. Eventually the actual participants felt the need to set the record straight. In 2003 the Jewish Welfare Service, the Hidden Child Association and former FI partisans ceremoniously installed a plaque on the building where the convent had been located. The plaque's text recounts the rescue of the girls from deportation and certain

---

21. Steinberg, *La traque des Juifs*, 2: 191–94, 211–13.

death. It names the members of the Resistance who took part, among them An-drée Ermel, the sole woman in the group. But Sister Marie-Aurélie, who made the rescue possible by arguing and negotiating with the Nazis, is not men-tioned at all.

Clearly, the intent was to set the historical record straight. To those respon-sible for the plaque and to those who might read it, the people whose names are inscribed on it were responsible for accomplishing this dramatic mission. Though a photograph of Sister Marie-Aurélie is displayed in the Museum of Deportation in Malines, in Anderlecht itself the nun's bravery appears to have been entirely forgotten. It is the dramatic armed resistance feat that is com-memorated, not the quieter, enabling act that made it possible.

The episodes related in this essay were selected to highlight resistance by Jews in organizations in which they were predominant. Resistance in Belgium, however, was fragmented into a large variety of dissimilar groups, and Jews participated in many of them. Some with Belgian citizenship and military training also succeeded in escaping to Great Britain, where they enlisted in the Belgian forces organized by the government-in-exile or in the British forces.

The *Dictionnaire Biographique des Juifs de Belgique*, more a history book than a dictionary, contains more than 700 individual references. Among these are 138 resisters belonging to the partisans, the FI and the Communist Party; eighty-six resisters engaged in other resistance groups, networks and clandes-tine press activities; and twenty-eight people serving in forces from abroad. While these numbers only partially reflect Jewish participation in the Resis-tance, they throw light on the *variety* of participation.

For example, Jews fought in the Mouvement National Belge (MNB), partici-pating in its escape and intelligence networks, and very actively in its clandes-tine press. The MNB was founded at the end of 1940 on a platform of patrio-tism, conservatism, and virulent anti-German feelings rooted in the memory of World War I. Its members were mostly middle class, French speaking, and at-tached to the existing regime. It launched a clandestine but widely distributed newspaper, *La Voix des Belges*, in 1941 and participated in escape networks. Thanks to members' ties with the country's administration, it was able to aid the labor draft evaders who went underground in 1942. Other MNB members who were postal workers intercepted denunciation letters and saved many lives. The organization also engaged in some sabotage. An attempted alliance with the FI did not succeed because of the organizations' political differences. (The MNB feared FI domination.) The MNB was badly hurt by enemy infiltra-

133

tors in 1944 and therefore was unable to play a significant role in the days leading up to liberation.

Jews actively participated in escape networks. For example, Maurice Bolle and Beno Nykerk, both of Dutch origin, helped labor draft evaders, Allied pilots, and Jews to escape from the Netherlands and Belgium to Switzerland or Spain, an endeavor that required extensive organization and entailed great risks.[22] To move their escapees safely through France, they collaborated with the evasion network Dutch-Paris, created by Jean Weidner, a Dutch businessman living in France. Bolle and Nykerk received help from the head of the Dutch Reformed Community in Brussels and financial support from Dutch diplomats in Bern. As well as organizing escapes, both men also were members of the CDJ. As noted above, Bolle helped Jospa in planning the attack against the deportation train. In addition, he was involved in manufacturing explosives for Group G.[23] Arrested in July 1943, he was taken to the infamous Breendonk prison camp and later deported to Buchenwald; he survived the war. A Zionist, Nykerk was invited to join the CDJ at its inception and served as its treasurer until December 1943. During that period he slipped into Switzerland to seek funds. While on a mission for the Dutch-Paris escape network, he was arrested in Paris in spring 1944 under a false identity and deported to Neuengamme, from which he did not return. The number of people Bolle and Nykerk helped to escape is unknown, but the Dutch-Paris network with which they were affiliated and worked closely is credited with saving around 1,000 people, among them 100 Allied airmen.[24]

Intelligence was vital for effective resistance. For the British, it provided information about military targets and was essential in planning the Allied invasion. For the Belgian government-in-exile in London, it was the sole source of information about what was happening in the country and about the morale of the inhabitants. Sending this information safely across the English Channel was a major problem until radios were parachuted in and reliable routes for microfilmed reports established.[25] Eventually, a total of thirty-seven intelligence networks functioned in Belgium.[26] (Lagrou mentions forty-three.)[27] One of the

22. Lucien Steinberg, *Le comité de défense des Juifs en Belgique* (Bruxelles: Editions de l'Université de Bruxelles, 1973), 123–26; Moore, *Survivors: Jewish Self-Help and Rescue*, 60–64; Jean-Philippe Schreiber, *Dictionnaire biographique des Juifs de Belgique: Figures du judaïsme belge XIX–XX siècles* (Bruxelles: Editions De Boeck Université, 2002), 64, 262.

23. Schreiber, *Dictionnaire biographique des Juifs de Belgique*, 64.

24. Moore, *Survivors: Jewish Self-Help and Rescue*, 63.

25. Lagrou, "Belgium," 36.

26. Fabrice Maerten, *La Résistance* (downloaded manuscript provided by author, 2004), 21.

27. Lagrou, "Belgium," 35.

most important was Zéro, whose 3,000 members included businessmen, industrialists, and lawyers, among them Jews. In 1943, the lawyer Maxime Van Praag, Jewish and Belgian born, became the fourth person to head the network after the first three leaders fled to London to avoid arrest. In July 1944, Van Praag fell victim to enemy infiltrators, was arrested, and tortured in the hell of Breendonk. Deported to a series of camps in Germany, he died at Nordhausen in April 1945. Nevertheless, Zéro continued to provide information until the liberation.

Patriotism was the major motive for working in intelligence. Those engaged in it were middle class, patriotic bourgeois with relatively easy access to information. Many were employed in communications, the postal services, and railroads. Historian Fabrice Maerten noted that, on the whole, intelligence work was undertaken by people who were Catholic or liberal. A few were Socialists, but none were Communists.[28] Maerten does not need to explain the Communist absence: in general, Communists carried out resistance activities in accordance with directives from the Soviet Union, which pursued its own information goals. In a recent study, Maerten points out that about fifteen Jews, mostly of Polish origin, constituted half of the Belgian group within the Red Orchestra, the intelligence service of the Soviet army for Western Europe, whose main center of activity was in Belgium between the end of 1940 and the summer of 1942. It was headed by Leopold Trepper, a Jew from Poland.[29] The actions of Trepper and the Red Orchestra were commemorated by the European Parliament in Brussels *for the first time ever* on December 6, 2011, the seventieth anniversary of the first German raid on the group's headquarters.[30] Clearly, Jews in Belgium were involved in intelligence work across the entire political spectrum.

Just as in World War I, soon after the capitulation of Belgian forces in 1940, a clandestine press developed to sustain the population's morale and debunk German propaganda. It also provided a basis for cohesion from which many resistance groups emerged. Newspapers were created by political parties, by movements, and as independent protests. During the Occupation, about 675 newspapers appeared, engaging more than 12,000 resisters, among whom 1,650 died as a result of their participation. The risks were so high that on average a newspaper lasted one year; only about twenty managed to continue pub-

28. Maerten, *La Résistance*, 21.

29. Fabrice Maerten, *Les Polonais dans les mouvements de résistance en Belgique occupée: entre intégration et particularisme* (downloaded manuscript provided by author, 2011), 12.

30. Accessed online on December 25, 2011: http://www.lpbrussels.com/remembering-leopold-trepper-the-brussels-based-spy-ring-"the-red-orchestra"/.

lication throughout the entire Occupation. These newspapers were produced primarily, but not only, in Brussels.[31]

The content of the clandestine newspapers may be divided into two major categories. Writings emanating mainly from the Communist Party and the FI urged the need for active resistance and merciless attacks against collaborators. Newspapers reflecting moderate left or right ideologies favored less violent resistance, such as help for labor draft evaders and intelligence work. These publications relied on the postwar justice system to handle the collaborators. If one asks to what extent the persecution of Jews was mentioned in the clandestine press, the answer is rarely.[32] Some concerns appeared in print in spring 1942, when the wearing of the yellow star was decreed, and again that summer, when the roundups occurred. Most newspapers expressed pity but did not call for resistance or advise the general population to help Jews. On the whole, Jews were marginal to the concerns of the underground press. The clandestine Communist and FI press was the exception. Early on, it denounced the anti-Jewish measures and warned against collaborating with the AJB. For example, *Les Temps Nouveaux*, the organ of Communist intellectuals, accused the AJB of playing "the Nazi game" and asserted that "the Jewish association cannot be trusted by the population."[33]

Not only did Jews work in the general underground press, they also produced clandestine newspapers in Yiddish. This was of vital importance for a Jewish population that was 94 percent foreign-born. *Unzer Wort* [Our Word] was the organ of left-wing Zionists and the first Jewish publication during the Occupation. It appeared in December 1941, immediately after the AJB was established by the Nazis. The paper launched a double appeal to the Jewish people, urging them to "defend human and national honor" and not "to help the occupier establish an organized community in which membership will be compulsory (i.e., AJB)."[34] A later tract called the AJB "a direct agent of the Gestapo within the Jewish community." *Unzer Kampf* [Our Fight], published by the Communist Party urged Jews to join the armed fight. In June 1943 it proclaimed that "staying hidden and waiting for others to avenge by risking their lives and blood is more than a crime." Reacting to the killing of Jews in Poland,

31. Maerten, *La Résistance*, 26.

32. José Gotovitch, "Resistance Movements and the 'Jewish Question,'" in *Belgium and the Holocaust: Jews Belgians Germans*, ed. Dan Michman (Jerusalem: Yad Vashem, 1998), 274.

33. Steinberg, *La traque des Juifs*, 2:114.

34. Maxime Steinberg, "The Jews in the Years 1940–1944: Three Strategies for Coping with a Tragedy," in *Belgium and the Holocaust*, ed. Michman, 362.

the paper stated that it was inconceivable that "a Jew could … stay aloof, quietly eating and drinking while in Oswiecim his father, mother, brother and sister are burned."[35] It was especially important to produce newspapers in Yiddish; morally, it was like defying the enemy. By denouncing and condemning the collaboration of AJB notables, these newspapers shaped and affirmed a specific Jewish resistance.

As historian Pieter Lagrou has pointed out, Communist Jews in Belgium were in "the vanguard of partisan resistance and the first target of the occupier's repression."[36] They were also the only ones to act decisively against the massive deportations. Jews of various political beliefs can be found throughout the disparate resistance organizations, in sabotage, in escape networks, in intelligence, and in the underground press. However, just as with non-Jews, those involved in resistance activities were a small minority. In 1943, Pierre Broder used the pages of *Unzer Kampf* to exhort his fellow Jews to join the armed fight, arguing that it was an existential necessity and a Jewish duty of dignity.[37]

Half of the Jewish population in Belgium survived the war, many more than in the Netherlands, fewer than in France. They did so by going underground through their own initiative, with the help of the CDJ and the local population. The success of the CDJ in rescuing at least 2,400 children and helping about 10,000 adults is undoubtedly the most important achievement of the Jewish resistance in Belgium. This civil resistance was initiated as Jews saving Jews and succeeded because it managed to transcend political ideologies, included charismatic personalities, and linked up effectively with non-Jewish organizations.

The National Memorial to the Jewish Martyrs of Belgium was dedicated in 1970 in a suburb of Brussels. The six walls of the monument facing inward contain the engraved names of nearly 25,000 deportees. Nine years later, an addition was made, this time on the side of a wall facing the street. There were inscribed the names of 243 Jewish resistance fighters. Daniel Dratwa questions whether locating the memorial in this way reveals both embarrassment—that Jews "went like sheep to the slaughter"—and pride.[38] One thing is clear: this volume helps lay to rest the myth of Jewish passivity.

35. Ibid., 353.
36. As discussed in Moore, *Resistance in Western Europe*, 47.
37. Steinberg, *La traque des Juifs*, 2:12.
38. Daniel Dratwa, "Genocide and Its Memories: A Preliminary Study on How Belgian Jewry Coped with the Results of the Holocaust," in *Belgium and the Holocaust*, ed. Michman, 552.

Ariella Lang

7 Resistance and Italian Jews in Wartime Italy

As a case study in wartime resistance, Italy proves to be unique in a number of ways. First, the existence of the Fascist regime in Italy, and its alliance with Hitler, meant that armed resistance against the Nazis began only in September 1943, when the armistice with the Allies was signed, and when Germany invaded its former ally. Indeed, after September 8, 1943, Italy was essentially split in half, with the Allies controlling southern Italy and the Axis controlling the North. This divide proved fateful for Italian Jews, who lived almost entirely in central and northern Italy, and who regained their rights only after the Allies entered these areas: Rome was liberated in June 1944 and in August Florence was freed. It was not until April 1945, however, that other, more northern cities were liberated. As Michele Sarfatti notes, in this period about 43,000 "persons of 'the Jewish race' were being hunted down in north-central Italy, consisting of about 8,000 foreigners or stateless ex-Italians and about 35,000 Italian citizens."[1] German actions against Italian Jews, often with the collaboration and assistance of the Italian police, began immediately following the September 8 armistice, when Germany annulled the agreement it had made with Italy's

1. Michele Sarfatti, *The Jews in Mussolini's Italy: From Equality to Persecution* (Madison: University of Wisconsin Press, 2006), 179. In 1938, the Direzione Generale Demografica e Razza census counted Italy's Jewish population at 46,593, most of whom would have been considered members of the middle class. This number, of course, cannot be considered completely trustworthy, since the census was hardly scientific in its counting methods. Not only was the Italian Jewish community small, it was a largely secular, assimilated community that had a generally remote connection to Jewish ritual apart from the High Holidays and lifecycle events. Liliana Picciotto Fargion, "Sul contributo di ebrei alla Resistenza italiana," *La Rassegna Mensile di Israel* XLVI, no. 34: 132–46.

Fascist government not to deport Italian Jews, located in areas under German control, to the territory that Germany controlled in the East.[2]

While many Jews were caught unaware of the terrible shift in policy that occurred with the September 8 armistice, the final months and years of the war mark a period of remarkable involvement of Jews in the Resistance. To some degree this response should come as no surprise: "Since Jews were engaged in the defense of their right to life, and since the goals of the Third Reich and of the RSI [Mussolini's puppet government, the Repubblica Socialista Italiana] were to deprive them of this right, it seems legitimate to say that Jews were de facto committed to political action against these regimes."[3] About a thousand Jews participated in the armed resistance, if one includes in resistance activity those who worked with the Allied forces. Considering Italy's tiny Jewish population, and taking into account the ever-diminishing number by the war's end, this figure is significant.[4]

The armed resistance of the period 1943–45, however, is only one part of the story of Jews and resistance in Italy. This final phase of the war emerged as the product of the years of political resistance that preceded it. As Gina Formiggini suggests in her detailed work on Italian Jews and the Resistance, it may be impossible to establish a specific date for the birth of the Italian Resistance, and with it Italian Jewish resistance, but it was unquestionably born with the advent of Fascism itself.[5] Indeed, the Resistance in Italy is best defined as having several phases: from the time Mussolini ascended to power in 1922 to the outbreak of the Spanish Civil War in 1937 marks one phase; from 1937 until Mussolini was deposed in 1943 marks a second stage of resistance. Both of these

2. Sarfatti, *The Jews in Mussolini's Italy*, 184. Sarfatti points out (202) that approximately 7,000 Jews, or 16.3 percent of the Jewish population died after being deported, or were killed on the peninsula. To give an example of the speed with which arrests and deportations began, she writes that on September 12, the chief of German police in the northern province of Bolzano ordered the arrest of that area's Italian and non-Italian Jews. Thirty-five Jews were immediately arrested, almost all of whom were deported to Auschwitz. On September 28, 350–400 foreign Jews were rounded up in the Cueno area and held at the Borgo San Salmazzo camp. 329 of these Jews were later deported to the French camp at Drancy and then to Auschwitz. Actions against Jews in Piedmont, in the area between Lago Maggiore and Novara, resulted in the arrest of fifty-six Italian and foreign Jews who were murdered on the spot (183).

3. Ibid., 208.

4. Ibid., 210. This number is disputed; Gina Formiggini puts the number at over 2,000. Gina Formiggini, *Stella d'Italia Stella Di David: gli ebrei dal Risorgimento alla Resistenza* (Milan: Mursia, 1970), 84, while H. Stuart Hughes suggests between 2,000–3,000 Jewish partisans. H. Stuart Hughes, *Prisoners of Hope: The Silver Age of the Italian Jews, 1924–1974* (Cambridge, Mass.: Harvard University Press, 1983), 64.

5. Formiggini, *Stella d'Italia Stella Di David*, 73.

phases were defined in largely political terms, and will be explored in the following section. The final phase, 1943–45, is marked by the transformation of the political opposition into an armed resistance against both the Fascists and the Nazis, and will be discussed below.

A notable number of Italian Jews were active in resisting Mussolini's rise to power and the Fascist culture that he and his supporters promulgated. Some of these opponents resisted Fascism from its inception; others stepped into the fray later on, when the vitriol and antisemitic tenor of the Italian Fascist movement became more apparent. Interestingly, however, and despite the fact that Jews participated in the political and armed resistance in Italy in disproportionately high numbers, there was by no means a "Jewish" resistance movement in Italy. In this essay, however, I argue that Jewish identity nonetheless provided a crucial underlying motivation in the decision of many Jews to join the resistance movement in Italy.

Before turning to the political activism that often inspired this participation, we need to consider the deep sense in which Italian Jews felt themselves to be Italian—a sentiment and a connection to the peninsula that spoke to the acculturation and assimilation of the great majority of Italian Jews into the community at large. The "culture of belonging" that defined Italy's Jews requires no greater proof than the wide variety of perspectives and positions Jews held in this period, particularly in terms of their responses to the rise of Fascism. Jews became Fascists or anti-Fascists in proportions almost equal to their non-Jewish Italian counterparts. That is, rather than acting as a specific group, defined exclusively by their Jewishness, the political identities of Italian Jews were also formulated based on their social class, their economic standing, their political identity, and even their geographical identification. Just as Fascists found many supporters among the bourgeoisie—a class of citizens who understood the Fascist movement to be a patriotic expression that would bring stability and prosperity to Italy—so too they often found support among the upper middle classes within Italy's Jewish communities. Jew and non-Jew alike, particularly among the bourgeoisie, saw the Fascist regime as forging a new national identity that had been corroded by the individualism and materialism of liberalism. Consequently, the Fascist promise to resolve many of the problems of the liberal regime appealed across religious lines to Jews and non-Jews lining up to support this agenda.

Likewise, geography had considerable weight in terms of who identified with or against the Fascist regime. While even Fascists considered Turin a hotbed of dissent, Giorgio Bassani, the Jewish Italian novelist, claims that he did not know a single Jew who was not a Fascist in his native city of Ferrara.[6] As Alexander Stille remarks, Jewish Fascism was "a real ideological movement, a mass phenomenon, as much as that was possible in Italy's tiny Jewish population of 47,000."[7] Mussolini's March on Rome brought together over 200 Jewish participants from a variety of cities, and at least 700 Jews were among the earliest Italians to join the Fascist party.[8] Prior to the establishment of the racial laws, "more than 10,000 Jews—about one out of every three Jewish adults—were members of the Fascist Party."[9]

But a case can be made on the other side as well. Movements associated with anti-Fascism, and with both political and armed resistance against Fascism and, later, Nazism, attracted many Jews who opposed Fascism from its inception. In fact, "statistically, the number of Jews who opposed Fascism from the beginning was greater than the rest of the Italian population."[10] One must add to these the Jews who may have initially welcomed Fascism to power, but who swung toward the opposition once Mussolini's antisemitic campaign became more public and more severe. Consequently, while Italy may have had the distinction of being the only European country with a significant number of Fascists among its Jewish citizenry, it was also a country for which opposition to Fascism was represented by a disproportionate number of Jews as well. How can one explain this seeming contradiction? In considering the nature of resistance and collaboration in Italy, and Jewish contributions to both movements, it is important to acknowledge the particular circumstances of Italian Jews that, in part as a result of assimilation, and in part as a result of the Jewish sense of belonging to Italian society, led to this strong political identification of such opposite political movements.

We may recall that following unification, and as an expression of their patriotic zeal, Italian Jews participated in significant numbers—more, perhaps, than anywhere else in Europe—in the postunification government, in the

---

6. Cited in Peter Egill Brownfeld, *The Italian Holocaust: The Story of an Assimilated Jewish Community, Issues,* Fall 2003 (online at http://www.acjna.org/acjna/articles_detail.aspx?id =300).

7. Alexander Stille, *Benevolence and Betrayal: Five Italian Jewish Families under Fascism* (New York: Macmillan, 1991), 22.

8. Maria de Blasio Wilhelm, *The Other Italy: Italian Resistance in World War II,* (New York: W. W. Norton, 1988), 149.

9. Stille, *Benevolence and Betrayal,* 22.

10. Iael Nidam-Orvieto, "The Impact of Anti-Jewish Legislation on Everyday Life and the Response of Italian Jews, 1938–1943," in *Jews in Italy under Fascist and Nazi Rule, 1922–1945,* ed. Joshua D. Zimmerman (New York: Cambridge University Press, 2005), 159.

military, and more generally in the civic life of the country. The fact that Piedmont had led the unification process for all of Italy led many Piedmont Jewish families—in Turin in particular—to send their children into the military: "It is highly significant that King Carlo Alberto, the head of the Savoy dynasty, which would become Italy's royal family, literally signed the decree granting religious freedom to Jews in 1848 on the battlefield of Voghera before going off to fight Austrian troops. Thus, the Italian cause and the battle for Jewish freedom were exactly contemporaneous."[11] The most well-known Jewish anti-Fascists came from Tuscany and Piedmont—a fact that is undoubtedly linked to this history: many Jews felt a strong connection to democratic liberalism as the ideology that had supported Jewish emancipation and civil rights and had helped them knock down the ghetto walls. In the second half of the 1800s, Tuscany and Piedmont were among the earliest beneficiaries of emancipation, and the memory of this period was actively commemorated by Italian Jews in later years through a political identification that, at least in these areas, led them to identify with a liberal government and oppose Fascism.

More generally, the result of the simultaneous developments of emancipation and unification meant that Jews were especially devoted to the cause of unification and so established an identity defined by civic commitment, philanthropy, and a sense of duty to society. During the unification period, for example, eight Jews were among the 1,000 soldiers that joined Garibaldi when he sailed off to liberate Sicily.[12] While France was embroiled in the Dreyfus affair, Italy had twenty members of parliament who identified themselves as Jews; in 1910 the prime minister, Luigi Luzzatti, was a Jew from Venice. This civic engagement continued to be displayed during World War I, by which time a significant number of positions of responsibility and leadership both in government and in the military were held by Jews. In other words, civic and political participation was directly connected to Jewish emancipation, and thus became an inseparable part of Italian Jewish identity. Indeed, among such a rapidly assimilating Jewish community, patriotism often became a substitute for traditional religious belief—a religion in and of itself.[13]

Political activism and national identity were thus deeply entrenched elements of Italian Jewish identity; as a consequence, ironic as it might sound,

---

11. Alexander Stille, "The Double Bind of Italian Jews," in *Jews in Italy under Fascist and Nazi Rule, 1922–1945*, 25.
12. Ibid., 25.
13. Stille, *Benevolence and Betrayal, passim.*

Fascism and anti-Fascism should be considered opposing iterations of a similar desire to connect to the political landscape of Italy. One may have supported the ruling ideology or one may have opposed it, but since the emancipation of Italy's Jewish communities in the nineteenth century, when political involvement had become a possibility for Italian Jews, political activism was seen as a means of reaffirming Jewish commitment to Italian society. Ironically, then, the motivating factors for Jewish partisan anti-Fascists and Jewish Fascists were not all that different: a love of country and a patriotic sense of duty, albeit on different sides of the political playing field, inspired both commitments. Thus, while it is clear that Italian Jews joined the Fascist party or the Resistance for different reasons, the simple act of political participation was often motivated in significant ways by the link between Jewish and Italian identity and the sense of civic duty that this identity engendered for many Italian Jews.

On the one hand, the significant participation of Jews in both the Resistance movement and the Fascist movement in Italy can be interpreted as further evidence of the process of assimilation and acculturation that began after emancipation. On the other hand, the act of political participation itself contains an element integral to postemancipation Italian-Jewish identity, suggesting that while there might not have been a Jewish resistance in Italy, Jewish participation in the Resistance *qua* Jews needs to be considered. After all, anti-Jewish legislation in Italy caused only a small number of Italian Jews to detach themselves from the Jewish community completely—even if they supported Fascist ideals. Italian Jews considered themselves citizens with a deep bond to Italy and, regardless of their political orientation, they generally did not see this bond as conflicting with their Jewish heritage.[14]

In thinking about resistance in particular, the memory of the historical alignment of unification and emancipation in a sense led many Jews to champion the liberal ideals of the Italian state and this activity itself exhibits what would become the political participation of Jews during the World War II era. Indeed, in this activity one finds their affiliation to Judaism. As Sergio Parussa suggests, "Judaism can be found in this sense of history as active memory."[15] That is, while a traditional religious identity might be absent, there are oblique ways, often filtered through an active connection to history, that link Judaism

14. Nidam-Orvieto, "The Impact of Anti-Jewish Legislation," 174–75.

15. Sergio Parussa, *Writing as Freedom, Writing as Testimony: Four Italian Writers and Judaism* (Syracuse, N.Y.: Syracuse University Press, 2008), 84. Note that Parussa is examining Natalia Ginzburg's works.

and Jewish identity even for remotely affiliated Jews. We will focus on political and armed resistance among Jews in Italy and suggest that, while many factors contributed to Jewish participation in both armed and political resistance, Jewish identity as linked to the national identity of Jewish participants should not be overlooked. It may not have been the primary reason for a resister to have joined the Resistance, but it was a central (albeit often unspoken) reason that informed, motivated, and inspired a significant number of Italy's Jews to join the Resistance, both in its earlier and later phases.

Political Resistance

As outlined above, the absence of a strong current of traditional Judaism among Italy's Jewish communities meant that many Italian Jews saw political engagement as a way of expressing their cultural and religious identity. Among the anti-Fascist leadership in Italy—a group that included well-known political and intellectual leaders such as Antonio Gramsci, Filippo Turati, and Piero Gobetti—were a substantial number of Italian Jews: Claudio Treves, Nello and Carlo Rosselli, Leone Ginzburg and Carlo Levi, to name just a few. None of these Jews had particularly traditional affiliations to their Jewish communities or to Judaism. Natalia Ginzburg, who herself rarely spoke of her Jewish heritage, suggested that Jewish identity represented a "secret complicity."[16] Her identity as a Jew was one that she felt profoundly despite her secular upbringing, and was an identity that was deepened during the years of persecution leading up to and during World War II.[17] Natalia's suggestion of a silent bond highlights the nature of Jewish identity among many of these early anti-Fascist resisters: on the one hand, it acknowledges a shared heritage, a shared moral system; on the other, this common identity goes unspoken, is implicit, contained in the camaraderie and political ideals that tied these individuals together rather than being articulated in any tangibly "Jewish" way (whatever that might be).

The link between Jewishness and anti-Fascist resistance certainly cannot be overlooked, although members of the Resistance spoke of this Jewish heritage and connected it to their political identity to varying degrees and at times not at all. Claudio Treves who was born into an assimilated, wealthy Turinese Jewish family, founded one branch of Italy's Socialist Party, the Partito Socialista Unitario (PSU) in 1922 (together with the well-known Socialist leader Filippo

16. Cited in ibid., 69.
17. Ibid., 66.

Turati and the future Socialist deputy Giacomo Matteotti). As a secular Jew, Treves had only a remote connection to traditional Judaism, but he was part of a growing number of Jews who found in socialism a resource for their views on social justice, as well as a response to persecution they had suffered in the past as Jews.[18] Treves edited the party's newspaper, *La Giustizia*, until the Fascists closed it down in 1925. In 1926, he fled first to Switzerland and then to France in order to avoid arrest in Italy. During this period, he became a mentor to Carlo Rosselli, an early leader of the anti-Fascist movement, and a key figure in the resistance movement.

The Rosselli family provides a fascinating genealogy of political activism and Jewish identity that, while striking and unique in one way, was also in keeping with the culture of civic duty that was particularly prevalent among Jews in Piedmont and northern Italy. Rosselli's mother Amelia (née Pincherle) came from a family with a long history of civic engagement: a great uncle was a minister in the government of Daniele Manin in 1848–49, and her father defended Venice against the Austrian siege during the unification period as well. Amelia was herself politically active as an anti-Fascist and Mazzinian liberal. While she acknowledged her Jewish heritage, her Italian patriotism was of greater significance to her: "I am certainly Jewish," she was often quoted as saying, "but first of all I am Italian."[19] Carlo Rosselli's father, Giuseppe Rosselli—named after Giuseppe Mazzini no less—was the grandson of Ernesto Nathan, who in 1900 was elected mayor of Rome. At the outbreak of World War I, Ernesto Nathan volunteered for service, serving at the age of seventy as a lieutenant in the infantry.[20] So we see in the Rosselli family a long history of political engagement and support—in varying forms and to varying degrees, of course—of the liberal values associated with the Risorgimento and the emancipation movements which enabled them to participate.[21]

Carlo Rosselli and an older brother, Aldo, also fought in World War I, and Aldo was in fact killed in battle in 1916. When Mussolini seized power in 1922, Carlo was a university student in Florence. Repelled by the Fascist movement, he founded an anti-Fascist cultural group in Florence to express his rejection

18. Formiggini, *Stella d'Italia Stella Di David*, 43–44.

19. Antonella Iovino, "The Italian Risorgimento Seen by its Women. The Key Roles of Sara Levi and Amelia Pincherle Moravia," http://www.i-italy.org/17265/italian-risorgimento-seen-its-women-key-roles-sara-levi-and-amelia-pincherle-moravia

20. http://www.theodora.com/encyclopedia/n/ernesto_nathan.html

21. Mazzini had died in the house of Rosselli's great aunt and uncle. Joel Blatt, "Carlo Rosselli's Socialism," in *Italian Socialism: Between Politics and History*, ed. Spencer di Scala (Amherst, Mass.: University of Massachusetts Press, 1996), 81.

of Fascism. When Mussolini banned public political dissent, Rosselli began a clandestine publication entitled *Non Mollare!* [Don't Give In!], which soon became a model for other clandestine papers in Italy. In addition, while only in existence for ten months before being shut down by the Fascists, *Non Mollare!* "published several devastating documents against the regime," including a report that implicated the highest levels of government in the murder of Socialist politician Giacomo Matteotti.[22]

In 1927, Rosselli was arrested and sent *in confino*, to internal exile, a system of arrest and detainment revived by Mussolini and the Fascists and used frequently for Italians deemed political threats. In this case, Rosselli was sent to the penal island of Lipari as punishment for having helped the Socialist leader, Filippo Turati, escape to France in 1926. While *in confino* Rosselli penned his most important theoretical work, *Liberal socialism*, a text that became influential for its argument in favor of a synthesis of social justice and democratic liberty. The text also points to the connection between Rosselli's Jewishness and his political identity. As he explains in the text, "socialism owed some of its special characteristics to the messianism of Israel: the 'entirely earthly' idea of justice, 'the myth of equality,' 'a spiritual torment that forbids all indulgence.'"[23] In sum, the value and dignity of the individual, the moral system that sustained these ideas, was rooted in Jewish thought, and it was precisely that which was under attack with Fascism.

Carlo's other brother, Nello, likewise described how Judaism infused in him a moral compass, civic duty, and liberal principles. Indeed, he discussed his Jewish-Italian identity at a Zionist youth conference in 1924. Like his brother, his words suggest that his political identity, that is, his Italian identity, was deeply connected to his Jewish heritage:

I am a Jew who does not go to Temple on the Sabbath, who does not know Hebrew, who does not observe any rituals of the faith ... and yet I hold fast to my Judaism.... I call myself a Jew because the monotheistic conscience, which no other religion has expressed with such clarity, is indestructible in me, because I have a very live sense of my personal responsibility ... because every form of idolatry repels me; because I consider with Jewish severity the task of our lives on this earth ... because I love all men as it was commanded in Israel. And therefore I have a social

22. Stanislao G. Pugliese, *Carlo Rosselli: Socialist Heretic and Antifascist Exile* (Cambridge, Mass.: Harvard University Press, 1999), 62.

23. Alberto Cavaglion, "The Legacy of the Risorgimento: Jewish Participation in Anti-Fascism and the Resistance," in *The Italian Refuge: Rescue of Jews during the Holocaust*, ed. Ivo Herzer, K. Voigt, and J. Burgwyn (Washington, D.C.: The Catholic University of America Press, 1989), 91.

conception which descends from our best traditions; because I have that religious sense of the family that, for those who look from the outside, truly appears as the fundamental bedrock principle of Jewish society. I can therefore call myself a Jew.[24]

The Jewish traditions that both anchor Nello's political views and inspire his anti-Fascism are thus linked to his Jewish heritage. It is interesting to note that Nello gave this speech as a challenge to Italian-Jewish supporters of the Zionist movement, in effect arguing for a synthesis of his identity as Italian and Jew, and as an emotional—and for many Italian Jews persuasive—argument against Zionism.[25]

In 1929, Carlo escaped exile to Tunisia, ultimately making his way to France, to the community of Italian anti-Fascists that had established themselves there. Nello remained in Italy and together the Rosselli brothers organized one of the most well-known and effective anti-Fascist Italian political resistance groups, Giustizia e Libertà, which was envisioned as a leftist, non-Communist group that favored abolishing the monarchy and establishing a democratic republic in Italy. When the Spanish Civil War broke out, Giustizia e Libertà organized the first Italian volunteers (among them a number of Jews) to help defend the republican Spanish government against Franco. Carlo Rosselli was among the first to understand that the Spanish Civil War represented resistance to Fascism in Europe more generally. Here again, we see a connection between his political resistance, his activism, and his Jewish identity: "echoing the famous Jewish prayer of the Passover seder, he coined the slogan 'Today in Spain, tomorrow in Italy.'"[26] The expression used in the Passover Haggadah promises a future in Israel. Carlo, like Nello in his challenge to the Zionists, firmly stakes his future in Italy, but with a clear connection to his Jewish heritage nonetheless.

Carlo and Nello Rosselli's articulation of their Jewish identity as a call to civic duty, as a belief in democratic systems, as a moral identity that infuses their political activism exemplifies the way in which Jewishness and resistance worked together in Italy. That is, while their work in the Resistance was not exclusively bounded by work with Jews or on behalf of Jews, nor was their motivation entirely defined by their heritage, the inspiration for their work is

24. Cited in Stanislao G. Pugliese, *The Most Ancient of Minorities* (Westport, Conn.: Greenwood Press, 2002), 6.

25. The Zionists were represented by the well-known Enzo Sereni, who moved to Palestine not long after this congress took place. He returned to Europe toward the end of World War II, fighting in the armed resistance against the Nazis.

26. Alexander Stille, "Outside Party Lines," *New York Times* (December 19, 1999). http://www.nytimes.com/books/99/12/19/reviews/991219.19stillet.html.

nonetheless very much defined by their Jewish-Italian identity. For the Rosselli brothers, Judaism was an anchor to their political identity, and their acts of resistance, just as their personal definition of *italianità*, Italianness, is infused with a sense of Jewish obligation and identity.

Carlo Roselli's call to action in Spain was compelling enough to be of deep concern for Mussolini and his Fascist henchmen. When Carlo developed a medical condition that forced his return to Paris (he commanded a unit in Catalonia), Nello came to visit him. The two brothers were murdered by French Fascist militants, presumably at the behest of Mussolini, while travelling to the French town of Bagnoles-de-l'Orne. The popularity of these two men, and the significance of their contribution to the resistance movement in Italy, was reflected in the fact that their deaths sparked the loudest protests against Fascism and Mussolini since the murder of Giacomo Matteoti.[27] In a speech about the Rosselli family, Tullia Zevi recalls the mother Amelia, and the deep sorrow she lived through with the death of all three of her sons in her lifetime: "Her first son was killed in the Alps and yet never did a note of regret, anger or displeasure issue from her lips—neither for his conduct nor for that of his brothers, already preparing to sacrifice themselves. It was only natural that they should do so; it was their duty. She looked upon them with a trembling heart but never expressed any kind of selfish intransigence. They were her life and yet there was within her a profound and religious democratic [Mazzinian] understanding. Life is given to be lived and spent, and to be continued in others".[28] Once again, one sees in Amelia's response a commitment to liberal Italy deeply rooted in family history.

As a more public legacy, Giustizia e Libertà produced significant ties to the Jewish community and to the Resistance. The movement was particularly popular among Italian intellectuals, many of whom were Jewish, and many Jewish partisans came out of its ranks. Carlo Levi, a protégé of Carlo Rosselli who often visited him in Paris, became the chief Piedmontese organizer for Rosselli's Giustizia e Libertà movement. Along with Leone Ginzburg, he became director of the Italian branch of the movement. Indeed, the leaders of the movement worried that the group had attracted too many Jews. When Vittorio Foa, a young

27. Wilhelm, *The Other Italy*, 166–67.
28. Cited in a speech that Zevi gave at the Circolo Rosselli in Florence on November 15, 1999, in commemoration of the 100th anniversary of Carlo Rosselli's birth. Reprinted in *Quaderni del Circolo Rosselli* 1 (Florence: Alinea Editrice, 2000). Trans. Inga Pierson. http://www.primolevicenter.org/Articles/Entries/2011/1/29_Tullia_Calabi_Zevi_%281919-2011%29__My_Political_Autobiography.html

Piedmontese Jew and another Giustizia e Libertà leader, told Carlo Levi that a friend, Sion Segre, wanted to join, Levi replied: "'Oh no, another Jew!'"[29] Like Rosselli, both Levi and Ginzburg were sent into exile following the well-known Ponte Tresa Affair in 1934. The affair represented a high point of political resistance and activism in Turin, and the large number of Jews involved provides further evidence of just how prevalent the ideals of the Resistance were among Italian Jews, particularly in Piedmont, where the Risorgimento traditions of political involvement and an adherence to democratic liberalism were at their strongest.[30]

The Ponte Tresa Affair was sparked by the resistance activities of two Jews, Sion Segre and Mario Levi, both members of the Turin branch of Giustizia e Libertà. The two young men had been stopped by police while in the act of smuggling anti-Fascist pamphlets over the border from Switzerland into Italy. Levi managed to escape by swimming across to the Swiss border. Sion Segre was arrested, however, along with fourteen others who the Fascists believed to be coconspirators. Eleven of those arrested were Jewish, and included members of both the Levi and Segre families, including Carlo Levi. Leone Ginzburg was also among those arrested for suspected involvement. While those arrested were released shortly afterwards, the affair resulted in a stream of antisemitic articles in the press, where particular emphasis was given to the number of Jews involved in the Resistance, and the questionable loyalty that these actions augured for the Fascist state. These statements proved critical to the Jewish community of Turin, where many Jews saw themselves as anti-Fascists, but where many had yet to become actively involved in the Resistance. As Stille notes, the family of Vittorio Foa had never before considered a connection between its anti-Fascist views and the fact that they were Jews, until the list of those arrested in the Ponte Tresa Affair was published. Jewish Fascists certainly existed, countering the accusations of the Fascist newspaper that Jews were inherently anti-Fascist.[31] But there was also something to be said for the fact that so many leaders of the anti-Fascist movement were Jews: "Claudio Treves and Renato Modigliani, both Jews, were among the principal leaders of the Socialist Party. Umberto Terracini, a Jew, was one of the heads of the Italian Communist Party. The founder of Giustizia e Libertà, Carlo Rosselli, was Jewish,

29. Stille, *Benevolence and Betrayal*, 99.

30. Cavaglion, "The Legacy of the Risorgimento," 80.

31. Indeed, Ettore Ovazza, one of the most ardent of Fascist Jews, used the occasion to establish his Fascist Jewish newspaper, *La Nostra Bandiera*.

as were its leaders in Turin: Leone Ginzburg, Carlo Levi, Vittorio Foa and his friends."[32]

Carlo Levi was arrested again a year later, in 1935, for his anti-Fascist activities and sent *in confino*, exiled first to Grassano, a small village in the Basilicata region, and then, to an even more remote village, Aliano, which served as the inspiration for his memoir, *Christ Stopped at Eboli*. Levi does not refer to his Jewishness in the text; he was exiled as an anti-Fascist, not as a Jew. Nonetheless, there are ways in which we might think of Levi's history, his assimilated Jewish background, his Piedmontese roots, his political activism, and his work with Giustizia e Libertà as connecting his heritage with his modern, political identity as a Socialist and as a member of the Resistance.[33]

In 1938, Leone Ginzburg married Natalia Levi. The couple had met through Natalia's father, Giuseppe Levi, a well-known biologist from Trieste whose own anti-Fascist activities involved the entire family, and whose house was a meeting place for intellectuals who opposed Mussolini: "The famous names of the resistance to Fascism and several prominent figures in the political and cultural life of Italy between the 1920s and 1930s gathered in the sitting room of her [parents'] house: the Rosselli brothers and Adriano Olivetti, Carlo Levi and Cesare Pavese, Filippo Turati and Felice Balbo."[34] Indeed, Natalia's brother Mario had been arrested in the Ponte Tresa Affair, as had her father. While Natalia's childhood was defined by the ideals of socialism and anti-Fascism more than religious identity—her father was Jewish, her mother Catholic—Natalia spoke many years later, in 1992, of her Jewish identity and the impact of the war years on it: "while I did not have any sort of formal Jewish upbringing, I nevertheless felt my Jewishness very acutely during the war years (my first husband, Leone Ginzburg, was a Jew) and after the war, when it became known what had been done to the Jews in the camps by the Nazis. Suddenly my Jewishness became very important to me."[35] The violence and persecution of the war years led many within Italy's assimilated Jewish community to reexamine their Jewish identity, and the persecution of these years was a factor in many Jews' decision to join the Resistance. For Ginzburg, her heritage, the enormous impact of her father's persona and his political involvement, as well as her marriage to a Jew helped sharpen the sense of a "silent complicity" that she shared with other Jews.

32. Stille, *Benevolence and Betrayal*, 102.
33. For more on Carlo Levi's Jewish identity, see Hughes, *Prisoners of Hope*, 55–85.
34. Parussa, *Writing as Freedom*, 63.
35. Ibid., 66.

Two years after Natalia's marriage to Leone Ginzburg, Leone was arrested again—the year was 1940—for anti-Fascist activities. He was exiled to the remote village of Pizzoli in the Abruzzi region until 1943. Unlike Carlo Levi, when Ginzburg was sent to Pizzoli *in confino*, he was labeled as both a Jew and an anti-Fascist: official communications declare him "'l'ebreo Ginzburg Leone,'" ("'the Jew Ginzburg Leone'") and "'straniero di razza ebraica,'" ("'foreigner of the Jewish race'").[36] The double appellation suggested early on that his troubles with the state would be dire. After several months of freedom, Leone was again arrested, this time for editing the anti-Fascist newspaper *L'Italia libera*. After Leone's arrest by the fascist police, he was identified as a Jew and handed over to the SS, who were especially interested in Jewish prisoners.[37] On February 5, 1944, he died under torture while in prison. Natalia, in her characteristically unadorned style, describes this second arrest, which occurred shortly after the family had moved to Rome, in her memoir, *Family Sayings*: "He was arrested 20 days after our arrival, and I never saw him again."[38] While his imprisonments were most directly the result of his anti-Fascist activity, his handover to the SS and his death under torture were also clearly connected to his Jewish identity.[39] As a foreign-born Jew (Ginzburg was born in Russia), his and Natalia's passports had been revoked in 1938. His identity as both a Jew and an anti-Fascist surely contributed to Natalia's sense of identification with her Jewish heritage, and was a bleak reminder to Leone himself of the reasons for his opposition to the Fascist regime.

In describing the anti-Fascist political resistance in Italy, and its deep roots in the country's Jewish community, I have mentioned only the most prominent of protagonists. Eugenio Curiel, Bruno Pincherle, Gustavo Sacerdote and hundreds of other Italian Jews joined Giustizia e Libertà and other political resistance movements, and many suffered dire consequences for this decision, from internal exile to imprisonment, deportation, and death. What I hope to have illustrated is that, despite the fact that resistance in Italy did not have entirely Jewish bands or squadrons, Jewish identity was an enduring reason that inspired many Jews to resist.

---

36. Nadia Castronuovo, *Natalia Ginzburg: Jewishness as Moral Identity* (Leicester, U.K.: Troubador Publishing, 2010), 20.
37. Ibid., 22.
38. Natalia Ginzburg, *Family Sayings* (New York: Arcade Publishing, 1989), 138.
39. Catronuovo, *Natalia Ginzburg*, 22.

Armed Resistance

The second phase of the resistance movement in Italy lasted from 1943 to 1945, and is marked by the transformation of anti-Fascist, political resistance to armed resistance. Like earlier political resistance, the armed resistance that began to organize in 1943 did not generally include a collective Jewish body such as those found in France, Poland, and elsewhere in Europe. There were Jews in Italy who worked almost entirely on behalf of the Jewish community: Rabbi Nathan Cassuto and Rabbi Riccardo Pacifici, for example, both of whom were ultimately arrested, deported, and murdered, were particularly involved in such relief and resistance activities. Likewise, activists, mainly Jews, who worked on behalf of other Jews through the DELASEM (Delegazione per l'Assistenza agli Emigranti), which managed to distribute food, medicine, and clothing to Jews in need, helped many destitute Jews in hiding.[40] These examples are significant, but belong to a rather different category of resistance from that which will be the focus of this discussion—that is, armed resistance. Hundreds of Italian Jews, particularly after the Germans invaded their native cities, joined the partisan bands located near their homes, or near the homes of other family members. Non-Italian Jews who had emigrated to Italy after 1933 also joined Italian partisan groups. Italian Jews who had escaped abroad, such as Gianfranco Sarfatti from Switzerland and Enzo Sereni from Palestine, went so far as to return to the peninsula in order to fight. Sereni and other Italian Jews participated in clandestine operations for the British and American intelligence services; still others helped the Allied forces as they made their way up the peninsula. In the Naples insurrection that occurred almost immediately following the American and British landing in Sicily, for example, Bettino Voghera organized the distribution of arms and Osvaldo Tesoro cycled to the hot spots of battle to lend a hand.[41]

Most Jewish resistance fighters cited their patriotism on equal terms with their self-defense as Jews as inspiration for action. Certainly, many Jews saw their participation in the Resistance as a "'second Risorgimento,'" which, like the first, affirmed their commitment to Italy, and which reasserted their freedom and rights.[42] As Gianfranco Sarfatti writes in a letter to his parents regard-

---

40. Sarfatti, *The Jews in Mussolini's Italy*, 208.
41. For further discussion, see Formiggini, *Stella d'Italia Stella Di David*, 80–83.
42. Ian Thomson, *Primo Levi: A Life* (New York: Metropolitan Books, 2002), 138.

ing his decision to join the partisans, "my way of life and the reason for my life for many months have only been an effort to leap into humanity, to share its existence, hard or easy that it may be. If I did not act this way, I would be renouncing myself, I would remain without a guide, humiliated, prostrated. And thereby I would also be renouncing you who have given me life and nourished me."[43] Emanuele Artom also noted in his diary on September 9, 1943, "The German radio announces that they will come to avenge Mussolini. We shall have to enroll with the forces of one of the [political] parties and I have done so."[44] In other words, Jewish partisans were motivated by their own wartime experience to join the partisans, joining partisan bands in the mountains or countryside more often than those operating in urban areas.[45] While Jews were motivated by their own desire for justice, equality, and solidarity, they were accepted as fighters among general partisan groups, and fought alongside non-Jewish Italians in integrated groups rather than in groups organized around their Jewishness.[46] For the partisan leadership, accepting Jews into the partisans meant that "the anti-Fascist 'parties' restored the historical process that Fascism and the monarchy had sundered with the antisemitic legislation of 1938."[47]

Jews who joined the partisans had strikingly varied social, economic, and political backgrounds. Eugenio Calò owned a machine shop in Arezzo and joined the partisans after his wife and three children were deported to Germany. Eugenio Colorni, a professor of philosophy from Milan, was a head of the Roman resistance and an organizer of the clandestine military center of the Socialist Party, although he had originally been a member of Giustizia e Libertà. Umberto Terracini, became a prominent member of the Communist Party in the 1950s. During the war, he left Genoa for Switzerland, but in the summer of 1944 he returned and joined a Communist partisan band. While most Jewish resistance fighters reflected the secular acculturation of the community at large, some came from more traditional families. Emanuele Artom, for example, was raised in a more traditional Jewish home, and joined the Monte Bracco partisan group in Turin. A Jewish Italian patriot, he referred to his civic pride as a "mission of the Jewish people."[48] Augusto Segre, in his memoir, writes of

---

43. Cited in Sarfatti, *The Jews in Mussolini's Italy*, 211.
44. Ibid., 209.
45. Ibid., 208.
46. Ibid., 210.
47. Ibid.
48. Cavaglion, "The Legacy of the Risorgimento," 77.

celebrating Yom Kippur in the Resistance, and of carrying a prayer book and shawl with him as a partisan. Another religious Piedmontese Jew, Leo Levi, survived interrogations because of his ability to read Hebrew, a language that reads right to left. After the 1934 roundup of many of Turin's Jews, he used his "well-trained eyes" to read backwards the statements made by other prisoners while his interrogators were momentarily distracted.[49]

Despite their varied backgrounds and the different affiliations they may have had—or not had—to their Jewish heritage, there are some undeniable similarities among Jewish partisans. Rosselli's resistance group, Giustizia e Libertà, which had appealed to a large number of Jewish anti-Fascists, was singular in terms of its transformation after the armistice was signed, and in its continued appeal to many Italian Jews. When German troops occupied France in 1940, the public activities of Giustizia e Libertà were forced to come to a halt, and its members fled their Parisian headquarters. In 1942, militants who had formerly belonged to Giustizia e Libertà founded an anti-Fascist political party, the Action Party (Partito d'Azione), that represented the ideological heir to Rosselli's *Liberal Socialism* and which was attractive to liberal Socialists and democrats as an alternative to Communism. Indeed, Tristano Codignola, one of the founders of the Action Party, had been director and editor of *Non Mollare!*, the clandestine newspaper that Rosselli had founded early in his career. The Action Party was close enough to Giustizia e Libertà that, following the armistice with the Allied forces in 1943, partisan brigades formed under it were referred to as Giustizia e Libertà. In fact, the Giustizia e Libertà partisan group was one of the largest non-Communist partisan groups and thus became favored by the Allies, receiving provisions and training that partisan brigades linked to the Communist Party in Italy were denied. Undoubtedly because of its lengthy affiliation with well-known and respected Jews, it was also a partisan group that Jews joined in higher numbers than most other partisan bands.

There are two noteworthy aspects to this development. First, one sees how deeply connected anti-Fascist political resistance was to armed resistance. As Armando Saitta writes: "The antifascism of the early years not only had a great moral significance and a notable political function; it was the *condition sine qua non* for the subsequent rise of the [armed] Resistance. Without the former, there would not have been the latter."[50] Indeed, after the military vic-

49. Ibid., 83.
50. "L'antifascismo dei primi anni non solo ebbe un grande significato morale e una notevole

tory against the Germans and Fascists, the Resistance returned to being essentially a political movement, intent on establishing "a new constitutional, social, and political order."[51] Thus the political roots of the resistance movement had important implications for the formation and disbandment of the armed resistance. Secondly, and in thinking about Jewish resisters specifically, it is noteworthy that many Jewish partisans emerged from their Giustizia e Libertà movement. Again, the reasons behind Jews' decisions to join the Resistance were various, but nonetheless we see here further evidence of the "silent complicity" that bound even assimilated Jews together in terms of the appeal of Giustizia e Libertà as a movement founded by Italian Jews that spoke to Jewish members of the Italian political resistance. In reality, most Jewish members of the Resistance belonged to either the Action Party or the Communist Party and thus belonged to the armed formations designated as either Giustizia e Libertà or Garibaldi, to which at least the 180 Piedmontese Jewish partisans belonged in equal number.[52]

Many Jews held high-ranking positions in the Resistance and in the command structure of the Resistance: Mario Jacchia, for example, became Partisan Military Inspector of Emilia and Commander of the Partisans of Northern Emilia, in a critical area for the Germans. Leo Valiani, a member of the Action Party, and Emilio Sereni, a member of the Communist Party, were chosen to represent their respective parties on the executive committee appointed by the Committee of National Liberation for Northern Italy (CNLA), and were charged with overseeing the imminent partisan insurrection.[53] Jewish partisans were often older than other partisans, perhaps a sign of their commitment to fighting, and their strong desire for freedom and equality.[54] Nonetheless, younger volunteers joined as well. Among the youngest was Franco Cesana, who died before his thirteenth birthday, and was awarded the gold medal of honor—one of Italy's highest awards—posthumously. Cesana was expelled from school at the age of seven, in 1938, as a result of the racial laws. He attended a special school in Rome for Jewish children until he moved to Bologna, where, in December 1943, he was forced to flee due to the German invasion of the city. He joined a Garibaldi partisan unit and was assigned the task of spying on Ger-

funzione politica, ma fu la *condizione sine qua non* per il sorgere posteriore della Resistenza. Senza il primo essa non ci sarebbe stata." Cited in Formiggini, *Stella d'Italia Stella Di David*, 84–85.

51. Ibid.   52. Sarfatti, *The Jews in Mussolini's Italy*, 210.
53. Ibid.   54. Ibid.

man soldiers stationed in the town of Gombola, where he was ultimately killed in an ambush. Most Jewish partisans who died, died in combat or shortly after being captured. Some were taken to the concentration camps of Mauthausen and Dachau as political prisoners, or to Auschwitz and Flossenburg after December 1944, as we shall see with the case of Primo Levi.

Other Jewish partisans included Vito Volterra, a partisan commander who, in early May 1944, attacked the concentration camp at Servigliano after Allied planes bombed the perimeter of the camp. Also known for his courage was Enzo Sereni, born in 1905 to a wealthy Roman Jewish family, who had moved to Palestine in 1927. In 1944, he returned to Europe, parachuting behind German lines to carry out a mission for the British intelligence service. When the Allies landed in Italy, he was posted in Puglia. From there he was parachuted into the middle of German positions in Pratomagno, and was arrested and eventually deported to Dachau, where he was murdered.[55] Not unlike the Rosselli sons, Sereni came from a family with a long history of civic involvement: His older brother, Enrico, a volunteer fighter in World War I, had died young; his younger brother, Emilio, was an anti-Fascist who joined the Communist Party, becoming a Communist deputy in Parliament after World War II. His Italian identity and commitment to liberal ideals drew him back to his roots: "The continuity between the threads of the Italian *Risorgimento* and anti-Fascism was represented for Sereni in Vittorio Alfieri's *Autobiografia*.... The *Risorgimento*, prophetic Judaism, Crocean philosophy, modernism: these are the elements that make up the spectrum of the Jewish Resistance."[56]

The number of Jewish women who joined the Italian partisans was limited, both because of women's traditional role in caring for family members and the household, and because life in wartime, particularly in hiding, was restrictive, complicated, and demanding, making it difficult to engage in sabotage. However, because most male partisans were army deserters, women were able to move about during the day more freely without arousing suspicion. Thus, for example, Marisa Diena, upon fleeing to the mountains after the Germans occupied Turin, became the vice-commander of information for her unit, riding her bicycle around the countryside, collecting information from local informers.[57] Silvia Elfer and Rita Rosani of Trieste and Vanda Maestro of Turin likewise were involved in the armed resistance. Rita Rosani, a teacher in a Jewish

55. Formiggini, *Stella d'Italia Stella Di David*, 84–85.
56. Ibid., 86–87.
57. http://www.jewishpartisans.org/

school in Trieste, received the Italian military gold medal, which was awarded to her posthumously after she was killed fighting.[58]

An early member of the Action Party's partisan brigades *Giustizia e Libertà* was the well-known author Primo Levi, who gives a good sense of what it was like in the early days of the brigade's formation: "We were cold and hungry," he writes in *The Periodic Table*, "we were the most disarmed partisans in the Piedmont, and probably also the most unprepared."[59] Levi came from an assimilated, Turinese Jewish family. In a reference to the first chapter of *The Periodic Table*, Primo Levi talks of Argon as an apt metaphor for his condition as an Italian Jew in Mussolini's Italy: "assimilated and integrated, but not Fascist. Argon is a gas which does not interact with other gases."[60] In *The Periodic Table*, Levi uses Argon to describe his ancestors: noble, inert, "people of Israel."[61] In other words, while Levi was aware of his Jewish heritage, it was an identity anchored in history and memory rather than the present. These reference points developed new meaning with the events leading up to World War II.

Despite the racial laws that prohibited Jews from entering universities, Primo Levi received a degree in chemistry in 1941. He found a job working in a pharmaceutical factory until 1943, when the Germans invaded northern Italy. Following the invasion, on October 1, 1943, Levi joined the Resistance. Fewer than three weeks had passed since Italy publicly announced its armistice with the Allied forces, and organized armed "resistance" did not yet exist. As Ian Thomson notes, "At this early stage the Italian Resistance was extremely chaotic and disorganized. 'We more or less had to *invent* the Resistance,' Levi recalled."[62] Less than three months later, Levi and his *banda* were discovered and arrested by Italian Fascists. "I was not a very good Partisan," Levi told Herbert Mitgang in a 1985 interview: "When my unit was betrayed by an informer, I was interrogated by Italian Fascists and handed over to the Germans. I was put on a train with hundreds of other Jews and sent to Monowitz-Auschwitz, the factory part of the camp that used slave labor."[63]

---

58. For further discussion, see Formiggini, *Stella d'Italia Stella Di David*, 316–21.

59. Primo Levi, *The Periodic Table*, trans. Raymond Rosenthal (London: Abacus Press, 1990), 130.

60. Nancy Harrowitz, "Primo Levi's Science as 'Evil Nurse': The Lesson of Inversion," in *Memory and Mastery: Primo Levi as Writer and Witness*, ed. Roberta S. Kremer (Albany, N.Y.: SUNY Press, 2001), 60.

61. Levi, *The Periodic Table*, 5.

62. Thomson, *Primo Levi: A Life*, 138.

63. http://www.nytimes.com/learning/general/onthisday/bday/0731.html

Levi was handed over to the Germans because of his admission during interrogation that he was a Jew. Interestingly, despite the harsh conditions and the psychological games that were part of the interrogation process, Levi seems intent on emphasizing that his admission was not made because he believed he would receive better treatment, nor because he capitulated, as one might understand, under questioning. On the contrary, he kept to himself the few important names that he knew. His admission of Jewishness was made in part from exhaustion but also out of pride in his origins. The Fascist interrogator, he writes, "alternated moments of simulated cordiality with equally simulated explosions of rage; he told me (probably bluffing) that he knew I was a Jew, but that it was good for me: I was either a Jew or a partisan: if a partisan, he would put me against a wall; if a Jew, fine, there was a collection camp at Carpi, they were not bloody butchers, and I would remain there until the final victory. I admitted to being a Jew: partly because I was tired, partly out of an irrational digging in or pride, but I absolutely did not believe his words."[64]

This is not the first time that Levi speaks of taking pride in his Jewish identity; earlier in the same autobiographical memoir, he writes of the passage of the racial laws and the publication of a new antisemitic magazine, *Le Difesa della Razza*, which made him realize his own "impurity" and take pride in it: "I am the impurity that makes the zinc react, I am the grain of salt or mustard. Impurity, certainly, since just during those months the publication of the magazine *Defense of the Race* had begun, and there was much talk about purity, and I had begun to be proud of being impure. In truth, until precisely those months it had not meant much to me that I was a Jew."[65] His later declaration of pride in his more public assertion of his identity to a Fascist interrogator can thus be considered a culmination of a growing identification with his Jewishness that until that time had remained unspoken—reflected only in his political views and by the few Hebrew words adopted into the Piedmontese dialect that his ancestors spoke. The moment after his arrest, however, he slowly and literally ate "bit by bit" his false identity card.[66] This marks the moment when his identification as a Jew, not a partisan, seems inevitable. Not unlike Natalia Ginzburg, Levi's Jewish identity may have helped compel him to join the partisans. After all, joining the partisans was a means both of resisting Fascism and also of asserting his own identity. But it was the persecution of those years that affirmed his Jewish identity. His experience was not unique: many Jews saw fighting in

64. Levi, *The Periodic Table*, 134.   65. Ibid., 35.
66. Ibid., 131.

the Resistance as a reaffirmation of their loyalty to the Italian state, and a reaffirmation of their belonging as Italian Jews.

While the liberation of Rome and the subsequent reorganization and resumption of activities of the Union of Italian Jewish Communities in Rome were key to the reconstitution of the Italian Jewish community more generally, they also point to the difficulties Jews had in terms of reasserting themselves within the general community, of understanding their identity and where they exactly fit in Italian society after the trauma, violence, and rejection that the Fascist period embodied. As we saw in the evolution of the resistance movement, the identity issue for many Jews was their identification with being Italian and with being Jewish, and a feeling that political participation was the synthesis of these two identities. For many Italian Jews, identification with the Jewish community was reaffirmed by the prejudices and racism of World War II. As the publication *Israel* noted at the time, it hopes that "Jewish citizens" will help rebuild the real Italy, to restore its fortunes, to restore the place of the people of Israel within Italy.[67] In this statement, one sees both a sense of pride in terms of a Jewish identity, but also an equally tangible sense of pride in being Italian and desire to belong that flourished in the post-Fascist period.

Politically, Jews continued to occupy many places on the spectrum, but almost all Jews identified with or felt connected to the partisan resistance in some sense or another. Many Jews saw the Resistance as embodying a renewed emancipation that had been initiated upon the establishment of the modern Italian state, and one that continued to inspire Italian Jews less than a century later.[68] Certainly, the "religion of liberty," as Croce calls the liberal principles of the Risorgimento, appealed to many Jews who joined the Resistance, and Risorgimento liberalism was a "recurring common denominator in the choices that young Jews made before and after 1938."[69] Thus, much like the participation of Jews in the battle for Italian Unification in the nineteenth century, many Italian Jews saw their participation in the Resistance as an affirmation of their patriotism and their Italian identity. Given that Fascism explicitly challenged and revoked the Italian-ness of the country's Jews, the patriotism of Jewish resisters was inherently linked to their Jewishness. That is, as I have maintained,

67. Mario Toscano, "The Abrogation of Racial Laws and the Reintegration of Jews in Italian Society, 1943–48," in *The Jews Are Coming Back*, ed. David Bankier (Jerusalem: Berghahn Books, 2005), 163.

68. For more discussion, see ibid., 148–68.

69. Cavaglion, "The Legacy of the Risorgimento," 78.

Ariella Lang

Italian Jews understood their political activism and their Jewish identity as intricately linked, bound by a history that stretched back to the shared and almost simultaneous events of emancipation and unification in the nineteenth century. Thus, while a "Jewish resistance" per se may not have existed in Italy, those Jews who did join the Resistance—either political or armed—were often motivated in some way by the link between their Jewish and Italian identities.

Steven Bowman

8 Greek Responses to the Nazis in the Mountains and in the Camps

Several factors together single out the Greek experience of resistance during World War II. First and foremost are the fighting spirit of the Greeks and the fierce tradition of nationalism that had infused the spirit of independence in the modern monarchy for well over a century. The Greek Revolution of the 1820s was a model for the Balkan peoples that stimulated the continuing re volts which finally ended Ottoman control on the eve of World War I. Greek nationalism resurrected the ancient idea of collective and individual noble death that Jacob Burkhardt so elegantly chronicled in his *fin de siècle* lectures on classical Greece.[1] Jews, caught up in the jingoism of modern nationalism, imbibed this intoxicating atmosphere of national sacrifice defined as shedding blood on the battlefield to prove one's worth of citizenship, and watched their sons volunteer for service in the expanding state. This was a revolution in the Jewish experience in the Balkans, and indeed throughout the rest of Europe, given the restrictions on Jews in both Christian and Muslim law and practice since late antiquity and the early Middle Ages against service in the armies of the majority religious cultures.[2] Despite the millennial contempt of military and pugnacious societies for nonfighting Jews that continued through the first century and a half of European nationalism, Jews soon found roles in the new military organizations that recognized reluctant uses for their various talents.

1. Jacob Burkhardt, *The Greeks and Greek Civilization* (New York: St Martin's Press, 1998).
2. Much of *shari'ah* law against *dhimmis* developed out of Christian Roman restrictions on Jews.

Jews increasingly found their "return to history" through the violence of modern armies and other irregular forces (e.g., ideological revolutionaries and *andartes* or partisans as well as spies).

An additional factor was age. Modern warfare might be characterized as an aged senatorial class sending professional officers who led large groups of young peasants to be slaughtered by new munitions and other weapons, for example, air ships and gas. This modern slaughter of the innocents perhaps began with the American Civil War and continued through the *aqedot* of World War I in the trenches that ringed Central Europe.[3] It then spread to the civilian and noncombatant populations in the terrible Nazi-Einsatzgruppen massacres and their horrifically efficient death camps in World War II. Both Churchill and Stalin called for and supported partisan resistance activities; Churchill from any source (right or left) and Stalin from his faithful Communist cadres and later from those loyal to Mother Russia. Due to their various skills, which I will enumerate, Jews were to find refuge among republican groups and even more welcome among Communist-led resistance groups, especially in Greece. The point to note here is that young and old, male and female, Jew and non-Jew contributed to the resistance movements and activities in Greece. It was a national effort sullied only by the "collaborators," who proliferated in Greece as they did throughout Slavic and Germanic Europe, which included even Great Britain, and who were especially prevalent in the Arab Middle East where the Nazi Axis was warmly supported. Indeed, from this last perspective, we could argue that every one of the new and old nations of Europe was engaged in civil strife between the Right and the Left during the interwar years and in open combat during the war and postwar years.[4]

Another factor is topography. Traditionally, Greeks have fled to the mountains in the face of invasion and occupation. Conquerors always stayed in the

---

3. Plural for *aqedah* (Hebrew), literally "the binding," refers to the sacrifice of innocents or, in nineteenth-century Hebrew sources, to the mass slaughter on modern battlefields. In Christian jargon, the sacrifice of Isaac is well summarized in "The Parable of the Old Man and the Young," written by the British poet Wilfred Owen (1893–1918) who was killed shortly thereafter in those same trenches: "But the old'man would not so, but slew his son, / And half the seed of Europe, one by one." See Yael Feldman, *Glory and Agony: Isaac's Sacrifice and National Narrative* (Stanford, Calif.: Stanford University Press, 2010).

4. One should note, of course, that both Fascism and Nazism were ideologies on the extreme Left (Nazi = National Socialism) of Socialism, as was Communism and its less virulent predecessor, Socialism. The *ancien régime* of monarchists, and its successor imperialists (including U. S. capitalists), represented the Right. For the social and economic story of the Occupation and its vicissitudes, see Mark Mazower, *Inside Hitler's Greece: The Experience of Occupation 1941–44* (New Haven, Conn.: Yale University Press, 1993).

valleys whose produce of food, fodder, and family was exploited. *Sta Vouna*, "To the Mountains," was the standard response to persecution; in Christian times, it replaced the national suicide of the Hellenic defenders of the *polis* who had chosen death for themselves and their families rather than slavery, degradation, and disgrace in ancient times. The Swiss never had to exercise their well-fortified Redoubt; the Slavic Balkans never had the funds or the organization to construct one. The Metaxas Line in Greece, begun in 1936 and completed in 1940 in time for the German invasion, was modeled on the French Maginot Line and was an impregnable defense whose forts held out until the surrender of the armies in Epirus in April 1941, which left them with no state to defend. Jews, primarily urban dwellers, craftsmen, merchants, and professionals, relied on the hospitality of the mountain villages and the organization of the resistance movements headquartered in these safe havens for the infrastructure that contributed to the survival of the approximately 10,000 who escaped deportation to the concentration and death camps in the occupiers' northern forests.

A fourth factor was the fate of Greece after surrender. Hitler magnanimously rewarded all participants, both those who were Axis allies and the Greek army itself. In his May 4, 1941 speech, Hitler praised the fighting spirit and courage of the Greek soldiers who defended the Rupel Pass and the Rhodope Mountains (the Metaxas Line) as well as Thermopylae and the battlefields of Crete where many of his crack troops, especially his prize parachute corps, were killed in fierce fighting and lie buried in numerous military graveyards. (Mararthon contains about a dozen mass graves, mainly SS troops killed by the Greek Resistance, sleeping peacefully under the Christian cross rather than celebrating their heroism in Valhalla covered by the Nazi Swastika.)[5] Indeed, when costumed Cretan women fighters, who had fiercely resisted General Student's parachutists, were brought to prison in Athens, they were allowed to keep their knives as a show of respect for their valor. All Greek POWs were released by the Germans and the Greek prisons were opened, freeing all those imprisoned by the Metaxas regime, in particular the Communists since Germany and the USSR were still bound by treaty (until June 22, 1941).

Greece itself was divided. Bulgaria's irredentist claims justified the acquisition of Thrace from Greece and western Thrace and Macedonia from the dismantled Yugoslavia. Italy received the bulk of Greece's territory and her innumerable islands in order to contribute to Mussolini's dream of recreating

5. Compare their activity in Greece to that of the Thracians as recorded by Thucydides in his *History of the Peloponnesian War*, trans. Rex Warner (New York: Penguin Books, 1954), 449–50.

a Mediterranean *imperium romanum* ruled by his *fasces,* and to assuage Mussolini's own tarnished performance during his five-month failed campaign against Greece. Germany took Salonika and its environs, part of Crete, and a stretch along the Greek-Turkish border in order to alleviate any potential tensions between neutral Turkey and Axis Bulgaria. A puppet government was installed in Athens that saw three prime ministers replace one another during the three and a half years of occupation. The Greek Orthodox Church, led by its archbishop, remained *autokephalos* (autonomous) and continued its relationship with the Orthodox Patriarch in Istanbul. The Greek Church was a consistent supporter of the Resistance, from mountain and urban monks to the archbishop, save for those clerics who still saw their enemy as encompassing Communists and Jews.

On the other hand, two Greek governments-in-exile functioned: one in London, the other in Cairo, both loyal to the king of Greece who was hosted by the British; the latter also absorbed the considerable Greek merchant marine fleet into its war effort. A semiautonomous government, consisting of a congeries of leftist parties organized under the rubric EAM but in actuality secretly led by the Communist Party (KKE), soon controlled the mountains of central Greece, designated as "Free Greece" during the Occupation. The military arm of EAM was called ELAS (occasionally confused with 'ELLAS, the Greek name for Greece). By summer 1943 it was organized as a regular army with its own officer training school, which included a number of young Jews recommended as candidates by their commanders; ELAS was more directly controlled by the KKE than EAM. A second resistance movement (EDES) emerged in the mountains of Epirus. It consisted of Venizelist republican officers whose leader cagily acknowledged the king in order to garner British support and military supplies. The two factions eventually absorbed or destroyed other regular and irregular resistance groups and continued to fight each other off and on for the duration of the Occupation as a prolegomenon to the Greek Civil War (1946–49). The Germans continued the Italian policy of stirring up ethnic tensions in the north among the various groups contributing to internecine fighting among the Greeks. In addition, the efforts of the Communist and Socialist, republican and monarchist resistance movements were periodically directed by the British in order to create diversionary attacks that would coincide with the broader military strategy in the Mediterranean. Buckets of Greek blood fertilized the tensions.

Where do the Jews fit into this complicated picture? As an educated, polyglot, urban middle class, Jews had a variety of skills which they could and did contribute to the resistance efforts. Intelligence was perhaps a key factor in the overall Mediterranean strategy of the Allies. Local Greek networks could easily report on troop movements and the enemy order of battle through the age old method of "pillow talk" and polyglot. Christians and Jews served nobly. German and Austrian officers of all branches were quartered among the Greek middle and upper classes, and in pre-deportation Salonika primarily among the Jews, a number of whom could speak German or communicate through French and Italian. Additionally, Jewish and gentile Greeks cooperated in underground networks. They rescued British soldiers who had either been left behind during the retreat and evacuation of the BEF (British Expeditionary Force sent in 1940) or who were escapees from POW camps, and Greek officers and recruits seeking to join the official war effort, as well as Greek forces now centered in Cairo. Their agents gathered more than enough information on German troop and supply movements to swamp the intelligence services in Cairo, and their reports are a great boon to later historians and other students of the war years.

As Jews in the German zone were systematically deprived of their rights as Greek citizens, stripped of their property, marked with the yellow star, imprisoned and tortured to reveal their property, ghettoized, and finally deported to death and slavery, many fled seriatim to the mountains, either singly, aided by Greek friends, or recruited by the Communists and other resistance groups. Usually it was the youth who fled, mainly to avoid the man-eating forced labor imposed on the community beginning in July 1942. Of the teenage boys and girls who fled to the mountains, many of them from Socialist and Zionist youth groups, many were to return due to the hardships of "roughing it." The desire to return was strong, especially since they were a population long reduced to starvation level of subsistence, and for whom the intensity of family connections in too many cases superseded the danger of deportation. The Salonika Jews included those of Greek citizenship and those Jews who possessed foreign passports, a long-standing tradition in the Balkans since late Byzantine times. When word came that Jews were being expelled, not all of the latter were deported; they were protected by their local consulates. But many of the Jewish communities of central Greece and other areas under former Italian control fled to the mountains to seek the age-old refuge of the inaccessible villages and the protection of the Resistance, primarily ELAS.[6]

Here the polyglot skills of the Jews proved most handy, for the uneducated

6. Italy left the war in September 1943 and the Germans occupied their zone, co-opting those Fascist units that remained within the Axis.

peasants and the Greek army officers who led them were monolingual for the most part. Skilled Jews received officer status and served on ELAS HQ staff or with the BLO (British liaison officer) command center. Several were recorded on the payroll of the main British SOE (special operations executive) units that proliferated in the mountains as the British assigned their BLO officers to individual commands. Jewish as well as other university students, in particular medical and agricultural students, served in the mountains. They contributed to the efforts of EAM and ELAS to modernize the primitive mountain life; several of the Jewish students established cooperatives which helped to alleviate the dearth caused by the British blockade in tandem with the German occupation policy of living off the land, both of which contributed to the spiraling black market. So devastating was the ensuing starvation that the International Committee of the Red Cross recommended restricting milk supplies to the strongest child in the family so that a breeding stock could survive the war. Some of these cooperative Jewish student organizers translated for the villagers and negotiated with the Italians and later the Germans who frequented the mountain villages on foraging expeditions. Other Jews in ELAS units took on the extremely dangerous task of foraging for their units, which necessitated their visiting occupied towns for food and funds to succor those in the hills. Older and more experienced itinerant peddlers (some self-taught in English) knew the mountain paths and were able to guide BLOs through the seemingly trackless and hostile hills to friendly villages.

Young Jewish girls, many avid Socialists, served in numerous capacities. Many had leadership skills and experiences from their school days and helped to organize support for the resistance in the scattered villages. They collected food and clothing for the fighters; recruited young males for the resistance forces; trained young village girls in basic nursing; and were what could best be described as "cheerleaders" through dance, song, and education in the revolutionary ideologies of Socialism—that unknowingly masked the Communist propaganda that was spreading throughout the mountains. The revolutionary "feminism" that the resistance preached made a significant change in the lives of the women, many of whom spent years, even decades, in prison after the war for refusing to recant their new sense of dignity and worth. The role of women in the resistance has recently come into scholarly purview, although the basic material has long been known from memoirs and reports. Jewish women also carried weapons, and a few rose to leadership positions, or *kapetanissas* (male *kapetans*) as the Greeks called them.

The fighting record is the traditional subject that makes history. Ancillary contributions still remain on the margin of military history and are still somewhat disparaged by professional military men. This attitude has long been changing among scholars, but during the war the disdain for irregulars remained paramount even as the Allies tried to develop such resistance in occupied Europe. The Greek Resistance, divided as it was between the somewhat Communist controlled Left and the republican Right, has suffered historically from this wartime divide. With the support of the British and later the Americans, the postwar persecution of the ELASites lasted until the 1980s' electoral victory of PASOK and the rehabilitation of ELAS fighters and leaders. ELAS fighters who had been branded Communists and persecuted by postwar Greek governments were now allowed to return to Greece. While even today some Greeks still maintain a suspicious political attitude toward the *andartiko*, scholars and politicians have begun the integration of the wartime Left into Greek society and its evolving historical memory of the war. With respect to the Jews, however, the few Communists and the other veterans of ELAS were forced for various internal and external reasons to keep a low profile in Greece as well as in Israel, where a number settled after the war. Only a few remained to return to Greece to visit old comrades in arms during the thaw in the 1980s and subsequent decades. Even so, many of those who went to Israel were debriefed at Yad Vashem and their memoirs reside in its archives on Mount Herzl in Jerusalem and in other research centers. Many Greek Jews who immigrated to the United States have left their memoirs at the United States Holocaust Memorial Museum in Washington and other regional archives. The stories that these memoirs relate have revolutionized understanding of the role of Greek Jews in the various resistance movements in Greece and in the concentration camps in which they were enslaved during the war.[7]

The formal stage of this revision began, however, with the public lecture of Joseph Matsas in 1982, in which he presented his research based on interviews with former *andartes* and his own wartime experiences in the mountains.[8] He succeeded as well in assiduously collecting the names of some 650 fighters, many of whom had died during the war in the mountains in the continuing battles with the enemy. Michael Matsas, Joseph's younger cousin added his

7. See my *Jewish Resistance in Wartime Greece* (London: Vallentine Mitchell, 2006).

8. See my "Joseph Matsas and the Greek Resistance," *Journal of the Hellenic Diaspora* 17 (1991): 49–53 and Joseph Matsas, "The Participation of the Greek Jews in the National Resistance, 1940–1944," *Journal of the Hellenic Diaspora* 17 (1991): 55–68.

own collection of interviews and his personal memoir of a youth who survived with his family in the mountains during the war.[9] My own research elicited from ageing fighters and their relatives additional names and stories. The sum total of our research suggests that at least 1,000 Jewish men and women fought in the mountains and thousands of others, primarily young, dedicated people, some for ideological reasons, others from necessity, fought or otherwise served in the Resistance in Greece during the war years. A general assessment of their contribution and their experiences ranges from those who were *kapetans* and officers in the ELAS army to individual fighters. No Jews served in the upper echelons of ELAS or the KKE during the war years, although Barukh Schibi of Salonika was an active leader in the political leadership in Athens and in the fighting in the Peloponnesus; hence the general stigma of Communist that was attached to everyone who served in the *andartiko* has ill served their postwar memory, despite the handful of actual Jewish Communists who fought in the various ranks of ELAS. The figure of approximately 1,000 Jews (many Jews took Greek *noms de guerre* or Greek pseudonyms to hide their identity for various reasons) compares well with estimates of some 30,000 regular *andartes* and a reserve of several hundreds of thousands of "volunteers" who were called upon to support various missions as determined by the leadership.

Itzhak Mosheh, for example, was a Jew from the Baron Hirsch quarter in Salonika who joined the Communist Party during the labor disputes of the mid-1930s, though not out of ideological conviction: "I debated with myself whether to become a Catholic or a Communist."[10] He and a few friends distributed leaflets to the striking workers and collected money and food during the strikes, especially the infamous tobacco strike of 1936 in Kavala that triggered the August 4 revolution of Ioannes Metaxas and the suspension of the constitution. Many Communists were jailed, or rather exiled to waterless islands where they were totally under the control of the government, or were induced by Konstantin Maniadakis, the Minister of Public Safety, to recant their membership in the KKE. The latter tactic resulted in their expulsion from the party and effectively led to state control of the KKE until the German occupation. Itzhak, among others, was later denied the opportunity to become an officer in the Greek army during the recruitment following the Italian invasion of Greece at the end of October 1940. In his estimation this was due to his affiliation with the Commu-

9. Michael Matsas, *The Illusion of Safety* (New York: Pella Publishing, 1997).

10. On several occasions, I was able to interview him and his wife Daisy (Carasso), who also served in the Resistance. Their prior written interviews are available in the Yad Vashem Archives.

nists. By comparison, the Venizelist (republican) officers had been cashiered by Metaxas who favored the Monarchist officers; so they were not allowed the honor of confronting the invaders. Itzhak served in one of the Salonika companies, nicknamed the "Cohen Company" from the preponderance of Jews in it, in the mountains of Albania. It was nearly decimated there by the suicidal charge across an exposed bridge ordered by its ("antisemitic") Greek commander, during Mussolini's final and failed surge that necessitated the German intervention in April 1941. Later, when a German armored car arrived at the Greek rear in the Albanian mountains and called for surrender, Itzhak, the only Greek there who could speak German, negotiated the surrender. Released after Hitler's speech on May 4, 1941, Itzhak walked home along with thousands of other veterans and succeeded, after numerous adventures and clever escapes, in reaching Salonika.

With the rise of the Resistance in late 1941, Itzhak went to the mountains and was assigned to the region of Naoussa where he and a handful of men raided German supplies in order to assist the local farmers. As he later explained in several interviews, he was in charge of a small band that received its orders from a central leadership; in turn he called for sufficient volunteers among the neighboring villages to complete the mission. When not active, his nucleus hid in the fields where he edited a resistance newsletter and carried on party propaganda. He took the *nom de guerre* Kapetan Kitsos after his commander, who died in his arms after being shot while on a mission. Kitsos remained an active fighter throughout southern Macedonia and participated in harshly hounding the Germans and their collaborators during their retreat from Greece in November 1944. Once he asked his men why they volunteered whenever he called for a mission. They replied, "Because you always bring us back." This testament to his leadership and to his concern for his men, who all knew that he was a Jew, hints at the special place that Jews had during the war. Kitsos then was what the Soviets called a *politruk*, that is, someone officially in charge of the cultural and ideological facets of the unit to which they were assigned. In addition to leading his men into battle (a group including a number of partisan Jews from Yugoslavia who escaped to Greece to fight), Kitsos also edited a newspaper, as did Markos Vafiades, for example, and other leaders. Even after his arrival in Israel, Itzhak Mosheh continued to read the Greek Communist newspaper *Rizopastis* until his demise a few years ago. Few Jews, however, were actively engaged in the Right and Left split that characterized interwar Greek politics and indeed was inherent in the divide among the Greek body politic after independence.[11] Most Jews were forced into the Resistance by the genocidal policies of the Nazis, and so they fought for Greece and for their own survival. Few were part of the ideological struggle that divided Greece during the war, and for a generation following the horrific Civil War in which more Greeks were killed than during World War II. Few of the Jews in the Resistance were aware of the Communist influence in the Resistance and so were even more shocked by the postwar government persecution of ELAS, which contributed to the exodus of survivors mainly to Israel, Great Britain, the United States, Benelux countries, and South America.

Another example of the nationalists who later became unwilling refugees and expatriates can be found in the wartime career of Sarika of Chalkis, the capital city of Euboea. This elongated island, which stretches down the Aegean coast of central Greece, was the gateway to freedom for thousands of Greeks who sought to join the official war effort against the Axis and for about a thousand Jews whom the Greek Resistance, in cooperation with the Palestinian Yishuv's Haganah, ferried to safety. I have briefly explored this complicated story against the background of British efforts to smuggle their men into occupied Greece and to smuggle Greek volunteers out, and the cooperation of the American OSS under the leadership of Major John Caskey. The latter two Allied forces were from their respective bases in the Çesme peninsula of Turkey.[12] Worthy of note is the wartime career of Alberto Amarilio, a prominent Zionist in Salonika who escaped to Athens where he worked with the secret leadership of the community. After the Germans began their persecution of the Jews of Athens in the fall of 1943, he fled to the mountains and then to Euboea where he remained under the protection of ELAS and assisted in the organization of the Aegean rescue service established by the Barki brothers and the Haganah. Amarilio, or "Aleko" as he was known to his ELAS contacts, who also bore heroic aliases, represents the contribution of a trained political and community professional who assisted with the organization of important facets of the resistance in Eu-

11. Symbolized in the national debate over the language: whether the *katharevousa* (purist) Greek preferred by the conservatives or the *demotike* (popular) Greek derived from the *koine* adopted by the Orthodox Church. This language war was fought during the nineteenth century throughout Greek society and finally ended after the electoral victory of PASOK and the defeat of the Junta that still promoted the artificial purist *katharevousa*.

12. Bowman, *Jewish Resistance in Wartime Greece*, chapter 3 and Steven Bowman, *The Agony of Greek Jewry* (Stanford, Calif.: Stanford University Press, 2009), chapter 8. See also Tuvia Friling, "Between Friendly and Hostile Neutrality: Turkey and the Jews during World War II," in *The Last Ottoman Century and Beyond: The Jews in Turkey and the Balkans 1808–1945*, ed. Minna Rozen (Tel Aviv: Tel Aviv University Press, 2002), 2:407–16.

boea. These went beyond the occasional sabotage by the locals and the reeducation of the masses to the revolutionary new order of ELAS. Amarilio's report can be found in the Tel Aviv Haganah Archives.[13] It is a mine of information on Jewish and gentile partnerships in wartime Athens and on the organization of the resistance forces in Euboea. One can easily judge from the quality and content of his report the various skills he could offer his hosts.

Closer to our theme of violent resistance is the wartime career of Sarah Yehoshua (née Yeshurun) of Chalkis, a precocious teenager who forced her widowed mother to send her to school and later, after the Germans quartered a pathological dentist in their home, to escape to the mountains where they could be free from what she perceived as the open German designs on the Jewish community. Sarah escaped from Chalkis with the assistance of her friends in the resistance youth movement. When they agreed to help her, she had already expressed her intent to be a fighter and leader of a unit, but she was assigned to be a cook and washer woman like most other Greek women who joined the resistance forces. She would have none of that and eventually received permission to establish her own group of a dozen young Greek teenage girls whom she mothered and taught to defend their honor and the honor of their country as well as how to shoot. They served as lookouts and decoys, setting off charges to attract the occupiers while the men performed sabotage operations elsewhere. They assisted in capturing collaborators. Sarah, or Sarika as she was known, even avenged her cousin who had been brutally tortured and killed when she was mistakenly identified as Sarika. She received permission from her commander and sought out and shot the collaborator who had organized her cousin's killing. By the summer of 1944, Sarika, dressed in a khaki uniform she had sewn from an army blanket, drilled a special company of *andartes* for the benefit of the American Greek journalist Constantine Poulos, who had been smuggled into Greece by the OSS to report on the Greek Resistance, and for the bevy of reporters who toured the liberated zone under the auspices of the British army.[14] The strength of her nationalist spirit was captured by Poulos in his report: "This is my country. I was born and raised here. The Greeks are my people, their fight is my fight. This is where I belong." But politics intervened. After the British returned the Greek government-in-exile from Cairo to Athens and the Right emerged as the political leadership of Greece for the next generation,

13. Greece—March 1943 to April 1944, Haganah Archives, file 14/51, dated 11.6.44, 84, summarized in Bowman, *Jewish Resistance in Wartime Greece*, 39–43.
14. See his report in Bowman, *Jewish Resistance in Wartime Greece*, 44–46.

Sarika was warned very quickly by the local police chief that she faced arrest for her service in ELAS during the past year. Helped to escape from Greece, she spent her subsequent career as wife, mother, and teacher in the Israeli school system and later contributed a son to the roster of Jewish heroes in Israel's continuing battle for survival.

Sex and rape were two problems that the Communists in World War II had to address. The sexual revolution among menless women in the wake of the man-eating butchery of the World War I trenches loosened the European patriarchal hold over women's sexual morality. In France, for example, many women vied for each single man and the phenomenon was similar elsewhere in Europe. Turkey, too, lost one-quarter of its manpower fighting the Russians in the mountains of Armenia.[15] The other side of the coin was the abandonment in urban Europe and among progressives in the United States of sexual inhibitions—"Auntie Mame" is a popular example in American memory—some for ideological reasons, others for rebellion, an anticipation on both counts of the sexual revolution that swept the West in the 1960s and 1970s. Rape is the vicious underside of the traditional attitude of the fighter toward the enemy noncombatant women he encounters, as we witnessed recently in the Balkans. The fighter's testosterone levels need release and women, if not sheep, are a readily available outlet. Christian practice ranged from barbarity to genocide. Muslim war rules, generally observed in the breach, encouraged the enslavement of captured women for a life of sexual exploitation, which at least guaranteed a roof over the head of the victim and a daily meal. By comparison, see the more humane biblical war rules in Deuteronomy 21:10–14 regarding treatment of female war captives. In any case, the woman's life is totally changed; in the Christian and Muslim examples, she is ruined psychologically and socially, especially if there is a child as a result of the rape. In many cases, she might even be slaughtered afterwards, as Nazis did to their Jewish victims who were otherwise forbidden to them under the racial laws of the Third Reich. Hence the problem in the Greek resistance movements (and among the Communists elsewhere when compared to the other fighting ideologies) was the need to control male sexual aggression—whether rape or seduction—and the perceived necessity for women to trade sexual favors for protection.

15. The estimate is from Howard Sacher's survey of WorldWar I, *The Emergence of the Middle East: 1914–1924* (New York: Alfred Knopf, 1969). It may be an understatement. The 1922 *Encyclopedia Britannica,* 12th ed., vol. 23, has a detailed description of the Turkish campaigns ("Caucasus Front," 802–9) including losses, e.g., in January 1915 the Third Army suffered losses in battle and from typhus of 86 percent and the losses continued until the Russians left the war.

Communist policy was strict in its application of a new moral code and demanded the equality of females in terms of their sexual autonomy. Males in the Resistance were officially forbidden to sleep with coresistance women or to exploit the local women. Rapists were executed. Should a couple, however, desire a liaison, there was always a priest available to marry them! There were many marriages of this type, including some Jewish girls to *andartes* as well to the sons of the peasants who offered the orphaned girls refuge. The problem, of course, was that the girls had to convert to Orthodoxy—whether in Serbia, Greece, or Albania, from which areas I draw my examples—and then either remain Orthodox after the war or suffer the pangs of divorce or widowhood in order to revert to their Jewish heritage and people. Both options exist in the record and in both options there is considerable psychological damage, as reported by my sources, in particular guilt for the conversion.

Sarika, who had promised the peasant mothers of the girls she enlisted in her platoon to protect their daughters' virtue, endured the burden of this responsibility for over a year. She herself had to sublimate any personal feelings toward the handsome young men who shared blankets with their *synagonistes* (fellow fighters) in the mountains. How difficult for a seventeen-year-old virgin commander of younger teenage girls in the rough and tumble life of guerilla society. Her interviews, available at the Jewish Partisan Educational Foundation in San Francisco, record in sufficient detail the pressures she felt in dealing with this added aspect of her decision to become an equal to the fighting men of the Resistance. As for the young girls who had to return to their patriarchal homes after the war, there were other problems to overcome. As part of their training, they were exposed to the lectures of the *andartissas* that taught them about female liberation, equality, and dignity, which replaced and occasionally superseded the patriarchalism that they had experienced at home. After the war, many of these females refused to give up this new self-enhancement and identity and renounce the Communist equality in which they had been indoctrinated. Their conservative fathers were shocked and these young women willingly spent years, even decades, in special female prisons set up by the postwar rightist governments in Greece. Many raised their children in these prisons, lest they lose the freedom of empowerment that was the major contribution of the resistance revolution in the mountains to the new Greek woman. This phenomenon of female revolution and empowerment should be seen in the long tradition of female power within pagan Greece and its survival *sub rosa* under eighteen centuries of Pauline antifeminism. Both are a legacy still evidently at odds with each other in contemporary Greece.

Jewish girls also stemmed from a patriarchal society, that of the Sephardim who brought the attitudes of medieval Spain into their exile and blended them with the local patriarchalism of the Balkans. However, rabbinic Judaism emphasized the biblical sanctity of the family and the inherent rights of women. Despite subservience to her father or husband and the respect due her as a mother equal to the father within the home, it allowed for the development of independence among those women who sought it. When modernism began to infiltrate into the new societies of the Balkans, Sephardi girls were sent to school to learn languages and arts, much like their counterparts among the Ashkenazim of Central and Western Europe. They, too, especially in Salonika, were exposed to Socialist ideas and Socialism's revolutionary attitude toward female emancipation, yet they were tempered with traditional Sephardi respect for the patriarch and his domestic counterpart who was head of the females and dominated the daily life in any multigenerational household. During the war, they too sought refuge in the mountain villages and contributed to the clarion call for resistance and for the participation of the younger girls in whatever they could contribute to the war effort, whether as nurses whom they trained, foragers, recruiters, washers and cooks, cheerleaders and entertainers, or caretakers for families whose sons were off among the fighting units. They were part of the educated Greek female population from urban centers who spent the war in the rural areas. Their education stood them in good stead to be leaders among the social revolution that pervaded the rural parts of Greece and helped bring these neglected areas into the twentieth century.

Constantine Poulos describes the general female contributions after he ends his lengthy encomium of Sarika:

Sarika is one of the incredible number of Greek women who took part in the fierce Resistance Movement. Sometimes it seems as if more women than men were in the mountains.

I have watched organizers, cooks, laundresses, social workers and nurses tirelessly carrying out their tasks under the most difficult of conditions. They worked 10-12 hours a day organizing women's relief committees, schools, nurseries, clinics, and hospitals, in those parts of Greece in *Andarte* hands.

I watched a demonstration of 4,000 women and 17 priests, who had gathered from a 25-mile radius, as they fearlessly approached a Nazi-held village to demand the release of dozens of hostages. They failed, but when I left, they were discussing their tactical errors and were planning a large mass demonstration by calling on more women from other villages.

In Roumeli, Crete, many people told me the story of Ariadne Dalari, a woman dentist from the Greek city of Lamia, who was tortured for fifteen days by the Nazis in an attempt to make her talk about the Resistance Movement. Unable to break her, they stood her against the wall and shot her while a crowd of women stood by, defiantly singing *Andarte* songs.

They also tell the story of another woman from Roumeli, Angelica Montesantou, who was condemned to death for underground activities. On the public scaffold, she placed the noose around her neck herself, tightened it, and shouted, "I die happy because I die for my country."

I watched a woman's relief organization go from village to village collecting food and old clothes for those families whose houses had been burned by the Germans. After the Nazis had passed through, I saw women dig up sacks of wheat from their hiding places under the dirt floors of their homes. In other places, I have seen women carrying food and ammunition to isolated *Andarte* guard posts and garrisons.

Hence when we talk about resistance in general and in this book Jewish resistance, we have to be gender equal in our recognition that everyone contributed from their various skills and that the voluntary effort of men and women and boys and girls should not be differentiated by any preconceived notion of what was more valuable. Anyone in the Resistance was liable to a death penalty which should be considered as the great leveler of one's contribution. Jewish and Orthodox Greek children, for example, used to paint the antioccupation signs on Athens's streets until a few got shot by the Axis patrols. Does age really count in a national uprising against the conquerors and occupiers of one's homeland?

Our volume is, in part, a response to the view that the victims of the Holocaust went "like sheep to the slaughter," an insult that has all but banished the phrase from Israeli discourse.[16] "As sheep to the slaughter" is actually derived from a strident rejection of this idea as expressed by Abba Kovner in his call to fight against the Nazis, whom he determined were set on eliminating all the Jews of Europe. His call to fight was uttered in a speech to the Vilna youth of Hashomer Hatsa'ir on the last night of 1941, just three weeks before the Wannsee conference that was to seal the fate of the Jews in the official Final Solution that stemmed from that meeting.

Kovner uttered his fateful phrase "Let us not go like sheep led to the slaugh-

16. A comprehensive study of the phrase in all of its various Hebrew and English manifestations was presented by Yael Feldman at a Yad Vashem seminar on June 23, 2011 and will be forthcoming as "'*Not* as Sheep to Slaughter': On Trauma, Selective Memory, and the Making of Historical Consciousness," *Jewish Social Studies*, 2014 [in press]. The following is partially based on that lecture. My thanks to Professor Feldman for sharing her work in progress with me.

ter," a phrase that was to resound through the ghettos and camps and forests throughout the remainder of the war before it was negated by both survivors and retractors who first described and later castigated the victims who went "like sheep to the slaughter." Indeed Kovner reports that when he went to the forest, the Soviet resistance leaders there asked him: "Why did your people go like sheep?"[17] Elsewhere Kovner emphasized that the forefront of the battle against the Nazi invaders in Lithuania consisted of Jews, a stunning revelation, supported by the collaboration of many Lithuanian gentiles with their German rescuers from Soviet occupation and Communist persecution. One-fifth of the Jews of draft age fought in the army; Jews fought in the Vilna ghetto, were in the underground in the Kovna ghetto, and were among the partisans in the forests of Vilna and throughout Lithuania. The Lithuanian division in the Red Army was 70 percent Jewish, including officers; and the language was Yiddish.[18]

Several years ago, Professor Yael Feldman and I published an account of Kovner's phrase in the 2007 Hanukkah issue of *Ha'aretz*.[19] In that issue we showed that Kovner did not invent the phrase as scholarship avers and as Israelis generally believe, but rather the phrase was in vogue already at the beginning of the twentieth century among the Jewish self-defense groups in Russia. Indeed they took it from an even older text, namely Sepher Yosippon, a history of the Second Temple period penned by an anonymous historian in tenth-century southern Italy and accepted by Jews and non-Jews as the very work promised by Josephus Flavius to his own people in their own language. In any case, it remained the most popular book in myriad languages and versions for the next millennium until World War II.

In the author's tenth-century rewritten version of the Maccabaean Revolt, he has the priest, Matityahu ben Hasmonai, call to his sons and the Hasidaeans: "We shall no longer mince words. There is nothing other than prayer and fighting. Be strong and we shall prevail and we shall die fighting and not die like sheep led to slaughter!"[20] For the first time, two biblical phrases (from Psalm 44:22 and Isaiah 53:7) are combined here by this unknown scholar to

17. Abba Kovner, *On the Narrow Bridge: Essays* (Tel Aviv: Sifriat Poalim, 1981), 38–39 (in Hebrew). My thanks to Yael Feldman for the Kovner references.

18. See *Abba Kovner—Seventy Years 14.3.1918–14.3.1988*, ed. Ruzhka Korchak-Marla and Yehudah Tubin (Tel Aviv, Moreshet, Beit Edut' al shem Mordecai Anielewicz, and Sifriat Poalim, 1988), 18–19.

19. Yael Feldman and Steven Bowman, "Let us not die as sheep led to the slaughter," in *Haaretz Literary Supplement*, December 7, 2007. The Hebrew version appeared in *Haaretz Literary Supplement* on the same date.

20. *The Josippon (Josephus Gorionides)*, ed. David Flusser (Jerusalem: Bialik Institute, 1981), 1:76.

produce a unique ringing phrase—*lo namut ke-tzon latevah yuval*—that stood at the heart of Jewish nationalism for a millennium, and that during the Shoah of World War II stimulated many groups to revolt against their killers. The latter resisters, especially in the Warsaw Ghetto Uprising, were also influenced by the epic poem "Masada" by Yitzhak Lamdan, which Feldman argued in her recent book is based not on Josephus Flavius's *Jewish War* but is indebted to the sacrificial themes of Sepher Yosippon. Moreover, many prewar youth were inspired by Franz Werfel's *Forty Days of Musa Dagh* (1933), which was translated into Hebrew the next year and puts this stirring phrase into the mouth of an Armenian leader.[21]

In addition to the teaching of Sepher Yosippon in the Judeo-Spanish translation of the eighteenth century, the Jewish youth of Greece were exposed to the secularized national tradition of modern Greece during the nineteenth and twentieth centuries through the school system and curriculum imposed on the Jewish community by the modern Greek kingdom in the throes of its new irredentist policy of *Megali Idea*. The intent of this policy was the recreation of the ancient Greek democracy of the Periclean Age alongside the reconquest of the Hellenic Balkans and Hellenized Anatolia. That *Megali Idea* lasted well beyond the *Katastrophe*, the 1922 defeat of the Greek army and the expulsion of the Orthodox from Anatolia, and still resonates with Greeks today. This "noble death" tradition reinforced for Jews the tradition recorded in Sepher Yosippon of the negation of the phrase *ketzon latevah*, a phrase that appears already in late antique *piyyutim* (liturgical poetry). Christians had already applied the "lamb led to slaughter" of Isaiah 53:7 to Jesus who was crucified on Passover, thus becoming the Paschal lamb sacrifice to expiate his followers' sins.

So who did go like "sheep to the slaughter?" The 50,000 Soviet POWS who marched to Auschwitz to be starved to death so that only 100 survived, to the great respect of their Ukrainian and Gestapo guards? The trainloads of unsuspecting Jews shipped to death camps and to the crematoria of Treblinka, Maidanek, Sobibor, and Auschwitz-Birkenau, to cite but a few of the killing centers? It was not uncommon for Jews to use the well-worn trope of "sheep to slaughter" for the Jewish victims during the war years. However, the phrase became increasingly pejorative after the war when Israel began to celebrate the heroism of those who fought back in the armies of the Allies, in the resistance movements throughout Europe, on the trains to Treblinka, in the concentration

21. My thanks to Yael Feldman for this reference.

camps of the Reich, and in the infamous death camps to which we now turn for the Greek contribution to the armed resistance in Auschwitz.

Among the instances of revolt in the death camps (e.g., Sobibor, Treblinka, Birkenau) by the slaves who serviced the crematoria in the special squads called Sonderkommando, it appears that the teenagers and young men were unable as well as unwilling to rebel, until there appeared among them former military officers with organizational and military skills. At that stage, plans were made and implemented in a number of killing sites, as these death factories were in the process of closing down due to lack of further raw material—that is, Jews—in the area.[22] Auschwitz was no different. During the summer of 1944, nearly half a million Hungarian Jews were transported to Auschwitz and gassed, shot, or thrown alive into the ovens and burning pits of Birkenau. Hungary was the last great reservoir of Jews in the Reich's empire. Birkenau or Auschwitz II would soon have to close down. Auschwitz I, the POW, experimental, and industrial camp, would continue to the end of the war and perhaps after; Auschwitz III, the major manufacturing center for German industry would remain as a huge industrial park after the war. The Communist resistance in Auschwitz, consisting of Poles and Germans, had been planning to revolt for some years, although they were waiting for the Soviet advance before implementing what otherwise would have been a suicide effort. The Jewish resistance committees were in touch with the main Resistance as an auxiliary and counted on the Sonderkommando to lead the revolt. The youth of the Sonderkommando were well fed for the heavy work they had to do during the three months of their tenure, until their killing and replacement by a fresh group of youth. Even without that, they would have had the strength and nerve to sacrifice themselves in the vanguard of a camp-wide revolt to shut down Himmler's hell on earth.

In the summer of 1944, the best organized group in the Sonderkommando was the Jewish Greek contingent that had been added as a replacement for the Xth Sonderkommando workers gassed in June. A group of some 400 (or 435) incoming young Greeks were selected upon arrival in Birkenau but they refused when the job was explained to them. They went willingly to their death rather than desecrate the memory and honor of their families, whom they would have had to feed to the crematoria. Other young Greeks sent to the Sonderkomman-

---

22. This is not the venue to critique the arrogant reference to the Sonderkommando "revolt" by Hannah Arendt in her *Eichmann in Jerusalem: A Report on the Banality of Evil* (New York: Viking Press, 1963), 189. See Bowman, *Jewish Resistance in Wartime Greece*, chapter 7, for more details of the uprising.

do included some 300 who were connected with the preparation for the revolt. Some thirty-two or perhaps many more of the Greeks, whose entry forms into Auschwitz I discovered in YIVO, all had military experience in the Italo-Greek war of 1940–41 in the mountains of Albania.[23] Their inspiration in Birkenau was Joseph Varouh, as he signed his name, a thirty-four-year-old field officer in the Greek regular army who also fought with the Resistance before his capture and deportation to Auschwitz. Were these Greeks led "like sheep to slaughter?" Did they know they were going to their deaths or exploitation prior to destruction? Once they got to their new assignment, however, it did not matter. As Leon Cohen put it, no matter how many died—even half or more—they had to stop the mass killings.[24]

The camp-wide revolt led by the Sonderkommando was set to break out on August 15, a Second Temple holiday (15 Ab) that had been rededicated to Mary by the church. The guards were usually drunk on that date and so the revolt had a better chance of initial success. Unfortunately the kapo in charge, a former military officer, was betrayed and thrown into an oven. The plan was shelved and shelved again, and possibly even a third time, for various reasons. On Saturday, October 7, at roll call, the numbers of the Greeks were called, a clear indication that they were to be culled and gassed to reduce the complement of the Sonderkommando. Joseph Varouh called out the traditional cry of the Greek officer and they charged the guards. After some initial success, the main forces of the guards arrived and put down the revolt. Those who were captured during the revolt were executed on the spot.[25]

The Greeks who barricaded themselves in crematorium 3 sang the Greek national anthem and the Jewish national anthem and then blew up the crematorium in typical Greek tradition, thus honoring the memory of the heroes of 1821 who blew up the Sikou Monastery, the heroic act of Geogakis Olympios still taught in the Greek schools and commemorated in the well-known painting of Peter von Hess. These Greeks also honored the memory of Matityahu the Hasmonean who called for the revolt against the Syrian persecutor in the immortal words they learned in Hebrew school: "Nor shall we die like sheep led to slaughter." So the young warriors fought and died according to the precedents

23. See Bowman, *The Agony of Greek Jewry*, 271–72 note 6.

24. Leon Cohen, *From Greece to Birkenau: The Crematorium Workers' Uprising* (Tel Aviv: Salonika Jewry Research Center, 1996).

25. See my "The Greeks in Auschwitz," in *The Holocaust Odyssey of Daniel Bennahmias, Sonderkommando*, ed. Rebecca Fromer (Tuscaloosa: University of Alabama Press, 1992), xi–xxv.

of their two respective nationalist traditions of "noble death," that is as free men who controlled their own deaths rather than surrender to the enemy who would torture and kill them anyway.

Other slaves who revolted, who had been "sheep led to slaughter," were the Salonikan Jews, many of whom were stevedores from the port and market who were selected for slave labor upon arrival in Auschwitz for their legendary strength. But not all revolted or lived long enough to resist. Some 3,000 were sent to Jaworzno to open coal mines so that the mines could be later worked by experienced Polish miners. Only a handful survived the experience. Others were sent to numerous work camps and most died from the harsh winter and the brutality of the guards. Only a few survived the war.

Others were among the thousands sent, beginning in September, to recycle the ruins of the Warsaw ghetto which had been destroyed in the spring of 1943 during the famous Warsaw Ghetto Uprising, led by the nuclei of the various youth movements which had been left in the depleted ghetto. As with the inter-war generation of youth in Palestine, all of these youths were imbued with the sacrificial and fighting ethos of Isaac Lamdan's epic poem "Masada," which is based on the author's reading of Sepher Yosippon. The cry "Masada shall not fall again" resonated in the ghetto fighting and became the slogan of the state of Israel's army. That the Warsaw youth did not die in vain is stressed most recently by Moshe Arens in his book on the uprising.[26]

In July 1944, most of the surviving workers in the ghetto project were sent back to Dachau, first on a death march and later by train. One who was not evacuated was the heroic Saul Shaul, a Salonikan who had immigrated to Palestine and was sent back as a missionary (*shaliah*) to his native city where he was trapped by the war. Deported to Birkenau, he was part of the labor force sent to Warsaw. There, his leadership skills enabled him to assist and even save his fellow slaves. Following the failure of a sophisticated attempt to escape with the aid of the Polish underground, he was hanged, but not before giving a stirring speech to the assembled slaves. Only some 280 of the evacuated Greeks reached Dachau. The remaining 150 or so slave laborers, mainly Greeks, were required to break down the camp before being returned to the prewar Reich, which was now in full retreat in an effort to regroup and defend the homeland.

26. Moshe Arens, *Flags Over the Ghetto* (Tel Aviv: Yedioth Ahronoth and Chemed Books, 2009). See above the influence of Franz Werfel's, *Forty Days of Musa Dagh*, which is also mentioned as an influence on the suicidal plan to fortify the Carmel range against the Nazi genocidal threat prior to the Battle of Al-Alamein. My thanks to Yehudah Bauer for his comments on this plan.

Naturally the Gestapo took as many slaves as could survive the death marches which averaged heavy losses along the way, in some cases well over 90 percent! Finally the opportunity presented itself for revenge. The approach of the Soviet army to the shores of the Vistula triggered the revolt of Ber Komorovski against the remaining German occupiers. The surviving Greeks seized the opportunity to escape and join the fray where they made considerable contributions. After all, they had military experience whereas the young Poles did not. Who could drive the captured tank? Who could fire the cannon? Who would charge into the face of heavy fire as the Greeks had learned against the Italians in Albania? Having divided into several groups so that some Greeks could survive to report their story and the fact that they flew the Greek flag during battle, only a third of the approximately eighty who fought remained alive by the end of October to return to Greece or other destinations. And the Soviet army? It remained on the Vistula waiting, according to Stalin's order, for the Germans and the Poles to slaughter each other before the imminent Soviet occupation of the detritus of Poland. Well rested, the Red Army then pushed on to grapple with the dying yet still deadly snake of Hitler's forces. Their no-holds-barred, unconditional surrender advance continued through the merciless bombardment of Berlin in revenge for the rape of Russian culture and the slaughter of some 20 million Soviets. According to reports, not one female between the age of six and seventy escaped violation by the savage Asian hordes in the vanguard of the armies that descended upon the population in their victorious march westward.

The study of resistance in the camps has begun to consider new facets in recent years: what constitutes resistance other than fighting? Is survival in the face of a death process in which slaves were expected or assisted to die within three weeks resistance? Is courage in the face of certain death resistance? In other words, how do human beings labeled "sheep to slaughter" react to the butcher's knife or the killing ramp? Such research has begun to reread the memoirs and debriefings of survivors of the various camps.

Unfortunately such was not the methodology until recent years and the questions asked of earlier survivors were not quite on target for the results sought today. Notwithstanding the methodological weaknesses and the lack of more extensive material and continued research, we do have a sufficient nucleus of material to outline various kinds of resistance within the camps to accompany our description of violent resistance among the Greek Jews who were sent off like "sheep to slaughter."

Upon arrival and during the selection process that sent about 10 percent of the deportees to slave labor and the remaining 90 percent—elderly and infirm, women accompanied by children or obviously pregnant, or those unsuited for work in the eyes of the often inebriated doctor who made the selections—to the gas chambers. During this selection process and later during the weekly and special selections among the slaves, there were numerous instances of individuals jumping the line to be with family, not knowing whether the line was for imminent or delayed death. The acts of these new arrivals in the camps were a continuation of the family solidarity that brought youth to accompany aged parents into exile. In the later rhythms of selection, one has to probe the motivations of the individual. Was it a case of accompanying a family member to the gas chamber out of love or despair? What of individuals already at the end of their tether who voluntarily substituted themselves for one selected for some minor reason? What, too, of the instances of clerics in Dachau where the majority of those interned sacrificed themselves on behalf of another by substituting their number to the *Schreiber*. "For greater love hath no man than to sacrifice himself for another," and a number of Jewish survivors benefited from this ancient Jewish teaching now practiced by Christian clerics. These types of resistance may be characterized as rejection of the Nazi system that was aimed at the total demoralization of the human being and the destruction of one's ethical self-identity. What, too, of the many physicians who worked in unbelievable conditions, often without any medication, who developed new techniques to operate and otherwise treat the sick and dying slaves? How many suborned SS personnel to save their patients from selection or otherwise bent the rule to introduce more patients into the so-called hospitals? Or the women who brought to term their unborn babies who were then drowned by the midwives so that the mother would survive, since otherwise her pregnancy was an automatic death sentence?[27]

Greeks had a huge repertoire of songs that they learned in their homeland or perpetuated as an inheritance from preexilic Iberia. Both males and females communicated with each other through substituting conversation or information for the traditional words of the songs. Men would sing to the women to give messages; women would sing songs to announce who lived. Indeed the women, whose angelic voices calmed the savagery of the guards who congregated to listen to their Mediterranean melodies, continually sang their special songs

---

27. This policy changed sometime in 1944 and babies were allowed to live.

of resistance. A particular favorite was the wildly popular song "Mama," which they sang as they marched off to work or at night in the barracks, to build up spirits. Individual women of talent would sing or dance to entertain their fellow slaves and to strengthen the camaraderie or "sisterhood," encouraging mutual assistance over the Hobbesian competition that more often characterized the men's barracks. Among the Greek men, however, as Primo Levi noted, there was a civility and group solidarity which emphasized "their aversion to gratuitous brutality, their amazing consciousness of the survival of at least a potential human dignity" that "made of the Greeks the most coherent national nucleus in the Lager, and in this respect, the most civilized."[28]

The will to survive and to assist others to survive was a form of resistance that gave strength to the slaves and the hope that there would be a future for them or for their memory. Those whom starvation had reduced to the stage of catatonic withdrawal, whom the prisoners called *Musselmann*, a camp term that may have derived from a disparaging description the Italian Fascists gave to the Muslims in North Africa, literally gave up and died, or were selected for the gas chamber during periodic attempts to reduce the numbers of slaves or to eradicate typhus and malaria outbreaks. Even so, among those uncritically designated as *Musselmänner* or Muslims, one finds examples of self-respect and initiative that belie the arrogance or indifference of (primarily male) prisoners who too quickly applied the term to those weaker than themselves. By contrast, in one moving incident a truckload of women selected for the crematorium erupted in the Zionist anthem *Hatikvah* as a gesture of defiance against their killers.

"Sheep to slaughter" is a metaphor drawn from the richness of biblical tropes. There are many varieties of this phrase in Hebrew, all with different intent, interpretations, nuances, and consequences. At some point during the war, the phrase began to be used in a deprecating way in regard to the victims of the accelerating slaughter, until eventually it became a pejorative term used to insult the memory of the victims of the Holocaust. Yet there were those who fought, especially in Greece where the sense of self superseded the threat of death. The Jews born and raised there absorbed this tradition. Resistance has also developed numerous nuances beyond the call for irregular military related action, for example sabotage and spying, by the Allies. Among the conquered

---

28. Primo Levi, *Survival in Auschwitz* (New York: Collier Books, 1971), 72; quoted in Bowman, *The Agony of Greek Jews*, 132.

nations and the victims of the ensuing Holocaust or Shoah—as the preferable Hebrew term that has been adopted to distinguish the Jewish disaster from the bankruptcy of its postmodern proliferation—resistance has come to designate a variety of survival tactics. Among the Greeks, violence was an ancestral tradition that the Jews learned about during their increasing Hellenization in school and from service in the Greek national army. The Greek sense of independence and tradition of "noble death" were ancient traditions and the Jews had similar, albeit dormant, independent sources in their own tradition that were activated by their Hellenic environment. But most of all the Jewish sense of family and solidarity was an important basis for the self-help they shared among themselves, as witnessed by numerous testimonies, and that served them well in their resistance to the aggressively pursued policy of mass killing on the part of their captors.

Yehudi Lindeman and Hans de Vries

9   "Therefore Be Courageous, Too"

Jewish Resistance and Rescue in the Netherlands

> I know that those who have known me really well will not feel sorry for me.
> Therefore be courageous, too.
>
> Hans Katan, in a letter to his family, September 30, 1943

By most accounts, about 102,000 Jews were murdered in the Netherlands during World War II. That amounts to 75 percent of the prewar Jewish population, a percentage unmatched in Western Europe. In comparison to France, for example, where 25 percent of the country's estimated 320,000 Jews perished, the Dutch mortality figures are stunningly high. We may well ask what went wrong in the Netherlands. In the early postwar years, roughly from 1945 to 1960, the issue of how this could have happened was hardly raised in public discussions of the war. The emphasis was on collective survival and reconstruction. The specific experience of the Dutch Jews in wartime and their unparalleled losses, while acknowledged, were readily subsumed into the theme of national Dutch loss and rehabilitation. Pondering the question of how a calamity of such deadly dimensions could have occurred remained mostly a Jewish preoccupation.

Why were so many Jews killed? The issue has in recent decades come to occupy the center of Dutch historiographical discourse about World War II.[1] A

With thanks to the dedicated staff of NIOD, and especially to Hubert Berkhout.

1. See, for instance, Bob Moore, *Victims and Survivors: The Nazi Persecution of the Jews in the*

number of different explanations have been given to account for the catastrophic fate of the Dutch Jews, who had lived in conditions of reasonable harmony with their gentile neighbors since their first arrival in the early 1600s. To make sense of what happened to them, here are a few of the most cited factors: first, a civil occupying regime, with the SS in charge, rather than the Wehrmacht, and a Reichskommissar responsible only to Berlin; second, an accommodating judiciary and a subservient network of police, mayors, and municipal administrations; third, the geographic particulars of the Dutch countryside that worked against the Jews with its lack of mountains, escape routes, or hiding places; fourth, a Jewish population that lacked non-Jewish connections, deferred to authority, and was governed by a *Joodsche Raad* (henceforward Joodse Raad, Jewish Council) that promoted obedience and discouraged escape.

While these political, social, and geographic factors emphasize the vulnerability of the Dutch-Jewish population, they do not take into account the aims and conduct of the targeted victims, or the strategies available to them. For the record, within months of the German invasion of May 1940, Jews became outlaws in their own country. Stripped of all legal protection, what self-defense mechanisms did they devise? Did they actively develop networks of resistance, both separately and together with others who were not Jewish, not only to save themselves, but also to place the country on the path to a new and better postwar existence? The provisional answer, as we will see, is that they did just that and much more, even though history has been slow in acknowledging their actions.

One explanation for the unequaled losses of the Jews of Holland ties their low survival rate to the behavior of the victims themselves. According to this mode of thinking, the Jews did not stand up to the Germans and did not resist, either as individuals or as a victimized group. If only they had fought back, they would not have "gone like lambs to the slaughter," as the saying goes.[2] In

---

Netherlands, 1940–1945 (London: Arnold, 1997). Although somewhat dated now, the introduction gives a good summary of the historiography. See also, among other publications, Henk Flap and Marnix Kroes, eds., *Wat toeval leek te zijn maar niet was: De organisatie van de jodenvervolging in Nederland* [That which appeared to be but was not an accident: The organization of the persecution of the Dutch Jews] (Amsterdam: Het Spinhuis, 2001), 12.

2. Dutch historian Jacques Presser used the term "like cattle to the slaughter," in an article that lies at the basis of much of the thought expressed in this chapter. His main conclusion is that "on the basis of historical research, the Jews were present at every type of Dutch resistance." See Jacques Presser, "Het verzet van Joden in Nederland 1940–1945" [The Resistance of Jews in the Netherlands 1940–1945], in Jacques Presser, *Schrijfsels en Schrifturen*, (Amsterdam: Moussault, 1961), 139; 141–42. Discussing the term "like lambs to the slaughter" and its origins, Bob Moore refers to a number of authorities, including Hannah Arendt, Raul Hilberg, Emanuel Ringelblum, and Abraham Lewin.

response, we intend to show the fabricated nature of such statements, to explain why they maintained their currency and still persist today, and to draw a detailed map of the many pockets of actual Dutch Jewish resistance.

Because of its geographical status, Holland was not a country of maquis or partisans. Symbolic images, such as those of the Warsaw Ghetto Uprising or the armed partisans of Eastern Europe are entirely absent. Clearly, this kind of eye-catching resistance did not take place in the Netherlands, or for that matter in many other countries. But Jewish resistance in Holland did include participation in the underground press, attacking prisons, raiding central population registration facilities, assassinating Dutch Nazis and collaborators, and, last but not least, rescuing Jewish children and adults.

Given our scope, we will not speak of acts and events within Jewish cultural or communal life, of what the historian Richter Roegholt called "*klein verzet*," small acts of resistance taking place inside people's homes or at political and cultural gatherings, even inside camp Westerbork. Is it resistance when people read the underground press, listen to the illegal radio, and pass on the information to neighbors and friends? Is it resistance when actors give secret performances, or when artist Lin Jaldati, with her sister and friends, gives recitals in Amsterdam of songs by Kurt Weil and Bertolt Brecht? The answer is surely yes, but although this is an area of research where much work still needs to be done, these activities lie outside our present range.[3]

In what follows we will observe how active Jewish participation in the Resistance was reluctantly acknowledged by post-World War II Dutch society. Next, we will see how a century-old integration process crumbled following the German occupation and the start of deportations in 1941–42. Along the way, we will present landmarks of Dutch Jewish resistance and profiles of individual Jewish men and women in the Dutch underground. We will not define Jewish resistance other than signaling (a) that the rescue of Jews by Jews, though very important, was not the single focus of Jewish resistance activities, and (b) that while many Jews operated illegally within Jewish frameworks, many more Jews functioned individually within the broader context of secular Dutch resistance networks.

See *Survivors: Jewish Self-Help and Rescue in Nazi-Occupied Western Europe* (Oxford: Oxford University Press, 2010), 2.

3. Richter Roegholt, "Nee, nee en nog eens nee!" [No, no and once again, no!], in Richter Roegholt and Jacob Zwaan, eds., *Het verzet 1940–1945* [The Resistance 1940–1945] (Haarlem: Fibula-Van Dishoeck, 1985), 13–14 and Ben Braber, *Zelfs als wij zullen verliezen: Joden in verzet en illegaliteit 1940–1945* [Even if we shall lose: Jews in the Resistance and underground 1940–1945] (Amsterdam: Balans, 1990), 17.

It has been well documented that during the first fifteen to twenty years after the war Dutch Jews found themselves excluded from Dutch national memory. Whatever recollections they had of their experiences were theirs alone to consider, but were publicly wrapped in silence. The collective Dutch experience of the war widely prevailed and this narrative left no room for the specific fate of the Jews. During the 1960s, this picture began to shift. Eloquent accounts of national victory over oppression yielded to more problematic images of failure and shared guilt over the country's inability to protect the Jewish minority. The fate of the Dutch Jews came to occupy center stage in all discussions about the war, and Auschwitz became the central metaphor. With a new openness to collective failure at the national level, there was now, in the words of one historian, room for "thinking about those groups and those emotions that had always been excluded from the dominant images of history."[4]

If the subject of Jewish resistance received attention at all during those postwar decades, it did not merit any public discourse or historiographical debate. The country had to be reconstructed and people needed to rebuild their own lives. Following the liberation of May 1945, many issues of the utmost national importance appeared on the Dutch political agenda, including the impending decolonization of the Dutch East Indies. Within the dynamics of a postwar society, few claimed public attention for a relatively minor topic like the fate of the Jews.

Plausibly, the need to call for such attention did not exist because the notion of Dutch Jewish passivity was socially comfortable and served to relieve the guilt feelings of the non-Jewish majority. That way, painful questions about the Dutch authorities' inability to prevent or slow down the deportations could be conveniently avoided by blaming the victim. Besides being convenient, the label of Jewish passivity also reinforced the stereotype of the Jews as a cowardly people, which had been passed on through the ages.[5]

If non-Jews were not interested in examining the state of Jewish self-help

4. Frank van Vree, "Een verleden dat niet verdwijnen wil" [A past that won't go away], *Icodo-Info* 20, no. 1 (June 2003): 28–29. See also Robert van Ginkel, "4 en 5 mei" [May 4th and 5th] and Conny Kristel, "Het Monument Joods Verzet 1940–1945" [The Jewish Resistance monument 1940–1945], in *Een open zenuw* [An open nerve], ed. Madelon de Keizer and Marije Plomp (Amsterdam: Bert Bakker, 2010), 35–36; 385–87 and Yehudi Lindeman, ed., *Shards of Memory: Narratives of Holocaust Survival* (Westport, Conn.: Praeger, 2007), xxi.

5. We are aware that this bias does not apply exclusively to the Netherlands, but it is one of the intentions of this chapter to put it to the test in the Dutch context. For a recent publication about anti-Jewish bias, see Anthony Julius's book about the reputation of the Jews in England, *Trials of the Diaspora: A History of Anti-Semitism in England* (Oxford: Oxford University Press, 2010).

and resistance, one might expect such a call to originate from within the Jewish community itself, but this was not the case. Too few Jews had survived. Estimated at no more than 28,000 in 1947, Jews in the Netherlands constituted less than 0.5 percent of the population and lacked the social and cultural power to put their issues on the public political agenda. Plainly, their experiences during the Occupation had not coincided with those of the non-Jews. Moreover, like their non-Jewish compatriots, Jews had other things on their minds, as they set about rebuilding their lives.

This deafness and silence at the national level does not imply that the facts about Dutch Jewish resistance could not be known. On the contrary, there was plenty of available documentation. Three examples from the early 1950s will help make the point: Abel Herzberg's book about the persecution of the Dutch Jews from 1940–45, Ben Sijes's study of the February Strike of 1941, and Lydia Winkel's volume about the Dutch underground press during German occupation.

Abel Herzberg's *Chronicles of the Persecution of the Jews*, first published in 1950, was well reviewed and often reprinted. Herzberg helpfully differentiates between Jewish resistance initiatives and the underground activities of individual Jews performed in a non-Jewish context. His first example of Jewish resistance concerns the rescue work of the so-called *chalutzim* or "Palestine Pioneers." Herzberg's second example of Jews saving Jews is the rescue by Jewish Council officials of more than seven hundred children from the so-called *crèche* opposite the *Hollandsche Schouwburg* (henceforward Hollandse Schouwburg). We will come back to the work of these two groups.[6]

In 1954, historians Ben Sijes and Lydia Winkel, both staff members of the already well-established Netherlands Institute for War Documentation (*RIOD*), published studies about the February Strike of 1941 and the underground press, respectively.[7] In his fourth chapter, "Fighting in the Capital," Sijes looks at the violent events of early 1941, when bands of Dutch Nazis began attacking Jews in the center of Amsterdam. The Amsterdam police were helpless, but groups of Jewish toughs stood their ground, sometimes forcing the national Socialist gangs to retreat. These clashes were a prelude to the 1941 February Strike that we will discuss below. Lydia Winkel's book focuses on newspapers and peri-

---

6. Abel Herzberg, *Kroniek der Jodenvervolging* [A chronicle of Jewish persecution] (Amsterdam: Boeken, 1950), 227–29.

7. B. A. Sijes, *De Februari-staking. 25–26 Februari 1941* (Amsterdam: H. J. W. Becht, 1954); Lydia E. Winkel, *De ondergrondse pers 1940–1945* (Amsterdam: Marinus Nijhoff, 1954).

odicals from 1940–45 that defied the German domination of the press. Many of those underground publications, including the Social-Democratic *Het Parool*, the Communist *De Waarheid*, the independent Socialist *De Vonk,* and the revolutionary Marxist *Spartacus* had Jews working for them as editors, journalists, managers, and distributors.

Even though these three books established that large numbers of Jews had participated in the Resistance, it was still too early for the silence to be broken. Meanwhile, in the words of sociologist Robert van Ginkel, "for lack of listening ears, the survivors and the sons and daughters of those killed, cloaked themselves in silence and tried all alone to absorb their memories and traumas."[8] Effectively, Jews found themselves excluded from the prevailing narrative of a collective Dutch fate, and even the word Jew itself was outlawed.

Growing up in Amsterdam as a young survivor of the war, one of the authors of this essay (Yehudi Lindeman) recalls that one quickly sensed that the word "Jew" was heavily charged with embarrassment and even fear. Of the nine Jewish classmates in his elementary school, not one ever admitted to being Jewish, let alone to being a survivor. None of them ever alluded to the experience of having survived in hiding. To do so would have unmasked them as different or possibly excluded, and they were all much too eager to integrate and belong. Did they have a past that they could own? Not in any public sense. Only at home did they talk freely about these matters. That is, for those of them lucky enough to have returned to a place called home. In society as they knew it, there was clearly no interest in what they had been through and it was the same in the fifties, in high school. Silence reigned.

Then something changed. Between 1960 and 1965, historian Loe (Louis) de Jong, the director of the *RIOD*, presented his nationally broadcast TV-series *De Bezetting* [The Occupation], which intended to offer the Dutch population for the first time an all-embracing picture of its whereabouts during the Occupation. It was a bombshell of sorts, an extended happening of national significance. This was also the period of the Eichmann trial (1961) and the Auschwitz Trials (1963–65). Both focused attention on the fate of the Jews under German occupation. So did several key publications, including Raul Hilberg's *The Destruction of the European Jews* (1961), and Hannah Arendt's *Eichmann in Jerusalem* (1963).

In the series *De Bezetting*, de Jong paid much attention to the Resistance in

8. van Ginkel, "4 en 5 mei" [May 4th and 5th], 35.

its many shapes. He certainly mentioned a number of individual Jews as former resistance fighters. However, he did not explicitly identify any of them as "Jews." Apparently, de Jong did not consider the resistance of Jews, individually or collectively, as a topic to be dealt with separately. Another factor limiting the perceived Jewish share in the national resistance is that Jews working in solidarity alongside non-Jews for a common cause were hard to distinguish from their colleagues, and may not have wanted to make such a distinction. But if resistance by Jews was hard to distinguish from general resistance, surely that does not mean that it did not take place.[9]

The national silence was only broken in 1965 with the publication of *Ondergang* [The Destruction of the Dutch Jews], historian Jacques Presser's comprehensive two-volume publication about the *Shoah* in the Netherlands. In an urgent plea to pay special attention to the resistance of Jews, Presser is both blunt and explicit: "After the war, the Jewish part in the Resistance was played down by many people both at home and abroad—the reader must decide for himself how much of this, too, was due to anti-Semitism. But even among those who cannot be suspected of this bias, many have deplored the fact that Jews apparently failed or feared to fight back."[10]

Presser's claim squarely confronts us with the question of how and to what degree the minority Jewish community was integrated into Dutch society at large. Like many other Western European countries, the Netherlands had experienced a process of rapid and fundamental economic change since the last quarter of the nineteenth century. Modern capitalism brought in a different class structure with an ever more important petty bourgeoisie. In this emancipation process Jews took part as well as non-Jews. As lawyers, teachers, physicians, and small entrepreneurs, Jews newly and successfully occupied certain time-honored professions. But if Jews now had access to all occupational categories, their social reality was quite different. Especially in Amsterdam, where the majority lived, Jews occupied only a narrow range of vocations, and many of them toiled at or near the bottom of the poorest classes. There was a big social gap between the well-off bourgeoisie and the "impoverished proletariat."[11] In the hundreds of small towns where the Jews had lived for centuries, the so-

9. See Jacques Presser, *Ondergang: De vervolging en verdelging van het Nederlandse Jodendom 1940–1945* [Destruction: The persecution and extermination of the Dutch Jews 1940–1945] (Amsterdam: SDU Uitgevers, 1965), 2:3–4. See too Braber, *Zelfs*, 21.

10. Jacques Presser, *The Destruction of the Dutch Jews*, trans. Arnold Pomerans (New York: Dutton, 1969), 279, and Presser, *Ondergang*, 2:6.

11. See Moore, *Survivors*, 210.

called "*mediene*," their occupations were different, but of an equally limited range.

Jews in the Netherlands constituted a small minority. Throughout the nineteenth and early twentieth century they amounted to less than 2 percent of the total population. The Jewish population of about 140,000 (plus 20,000 so-called half-Jews) was not equally spread all over the country. The great majority, 60 percent, lived in Amsterdam. Some 80 percent lived in the two western provinces of the Netherlands. Generally speaking, the community had witnessed strong tendencies toward integration, assimilation, and secularity, but these social processes clearly had their limits. Few Jews were actually baptized or had formally become Christian, and mixed marriages did not exceed 20 percent.[12] This does not mean that maintaining their own religion played an important role, because with few exceptions it did not. The absence of influential rabbis also indicates the high level of integration and assimilation into Dutch society. Until the eve of the German invasion of May 1940, there were no national, charismatic Jewish authorities or community leaders.

One notable exception to this leadership vacuum was the lawyer Lodewijk Visser, a highly regarded member of the Dutch Supreme Court and, since 1939, its Supreme Justice. Forced to retire from the bench by the Germans in November 1940, Visser became the trusted president of the Coordination Committee, which looked after the interests of the Dutch Jews. In contrast to the Joodse Raad, founded at the command of the German occupiers, the Coordination Committee received its mandate from the official Dutch Jewish community. Historian Jacques Presser sees Lodewijk Visser as an early representative of Dutch Jewish resistance. In this, he agrees with Abel Herzberg's notion that "in the Netherlands, resistance was most strongly heard in the voice of L. E. Visser." But Presser adds that this kind of position was only possible during the early part of the war. Herzberg is probably right in believing that, had he lived long enough, Visser surely would have been killed or deported to a concentration camp.

A frequent contributor to the illegal newspaper *Het Parool*, Lodewijk Visser vehemently opposed the formation of the Jewish Council, and rejected its policy of cooperation with the German occupying authority, deeming it illegal. As the historian Ben Braber puts it: "The anti-Jewish measures were, in his eyes,

12. In October 1941 and August 1942 an estimated 20,000 mixed marriages existed (two-thirds ot them Jewish men with non-Jewish women). From March 23, 1942 onward, entering into a mixed marriage was strictly forbidden.

in conflict with the Dutch constitution that did not allow making any distinctions between citizens, and he therefore raised his voice against the policy of the occupiers."[13]

Visser tried hard and courageously, but in vain, to intercede with the Germans on behalf of the Dutch Jews sent to Mauthausen. His greatest fear was that the Jewish Council would become the manager of German oppression. Eventually the Germans abolished the coordinating committee. Visser died of an illness in February 1942 in his hometown Den Haag.[14]

Later on, after the start of the deportations, the absence of natural Jewish leaders would prove to be a handicap. Jews traditionally showed a strong adherence to the Dutch national authorities, the monarchy, and the parliamentary democracy, and saw themselves as Jewish Dutchmen rather than Dutch Jews. The Zionist perspective appealed to only a minority and there were no national Zionist leaders. But a good part of the Jewish population of Amsterdam and Rotterdam supported the Socialist cause which fueled much activity in clubs and organizations associated with the prewar Socialist party, the SDAP, and its affiliated trade unions.

Like most of their fellow Dutchmen, the majority of Jews were not particularly concerned about political developments in Nazi Germany. A "Jewish Question" was not supposed to exist in the Netherlands. Only the immigration of more than 15,000 refugees from Germany and Austria, who brought with them their experiences of antisemitic terror, caused some ripples of change in that rather laid-back attitude. As a neutral country during World War I, Holland lacked the experience of being invaded and living under foreign occupation, so that the invasion of May 1940 came as a shock. On the other hand, small numbers of Jews, as well as non-Jews, clearly saw what was about to happen. About 1,600 Jews managed to get away to England. In Amsterdam alone, over 200 Jews committed suicide.

For the Jewish population, the first few months of the Occupation seemed to pass rather quietly even as, in an almost undetectable way, the first measures directed against them were introduced. To the vast majority of the increasingly segregated Jews, it seemed best to do just as they were told. This is how historian Louis de Jong put it:

13. Braber, *Zelfs*, 48.
14. See Presser, *Ondergang*, 1:42 , 82, 92–93; 2:8–11. Herzberg, *Kroniek der Jodenvervolging*, 189–201.

Apparently it was as hard for Jews as it was for non-Jews to imagine that a persecution of Jews identical to the one that had manifested itself in Germany from 1933 till 1939, would take place in the decent Netherlands.... Nearly all Jews did what they had always done: they obeyed the authorities and did so even more readily since, at every step along the way, official Dutch state institutions were involved in the implementation of each new German measure.[15]

As deceptively quiet as the situation may have been in these early months of the Occupation, during the same period two anti-Jewish decrees were issued that would be of crucial significance for the deportations to come. In October 1940, Jews were ordered to let their businesses be registered (Verordnung 189/40). This order was of primary interest because it anticipated the future spoliation of Jewish property. Still, the most important section, hidden inside one of the paragraphs, was its introduction of a definition of the concept "Jew." January 1941 witnessed a second decree of major importance: the registration of Jews (Verordnung 6/41). These two decrees would provide the Germans with the basic administrative data needed for the execution of their future deportation policy. From this moment on, Jews were completely registered and identifiable. On top of this, they would receive a "J" in their ID (January 1942) and would have to wear a star (May 1942).

The political quietness was only at the surface. From mid-December 1940, the situation would change drastically. In January and early February 1941, Dutch Nazis repeatedly attacked and provoked Amsterdam Jews, invaded their neighborhoods, smashed down their front doors, beat them, and stole or destroyed their properties. In reaction, a few hundred Jews, sometimes aided by their non-Jewish neighbors or buddies from their sports clubs, defended themselves and fought back. These young Jewish men, loosely organized in *knokploegen* (hit squads), represent the earliest example of Jewish resistance during the Occupation.

Clashes between the opponents increased in February 1941. Members of the WA (Dutch uniformed Nazis) began evicting Jews from public places, especially cafés and restaurants, while forcing business owners to install signs saying "*Verboden voor Joden*," (Prohibited for Jews). Next, WA men, aided by members of the extreme NSNAP, started to remove Jewish men and women forcibly from public transport. A streetcar conductor witnessed several Dutch Nazis physically abusing a Jewish passenger. One of the attackers choked him from be-

---

15. Louis de Jong, *Het Koninkrijk der Nederlanden in de Tweede Wereldoorlog* [The Dutch kingdom during World War II] (Amsterdam: Martinus Nijhoff, 1974), 5:510.

hind, while he "knocked him deliberately, repeatedly and with great force in his face, as if from below, while one of the other men hit the Jew deliberately and repeatedly in the middle of the face, with well-aimed blows."[16] This was the atmosphere that prevailed in central Amsterdam during the early part of the year. Supervised by the occupying authorities, the Amsterdam police stood idly by.

The tensions between the Dutch Nazis and a number of different Jewish *knokploegen* culminated in major street battles during the day and evening of February 11, 1941, mainly in and around the old Jewish Quarter. Early that evening, about forty WA men entered the neighborhood in formation, marching to the centrally located Waterloo Square. Bennie Bluhm, accompanied by a friend, saw them arriving and remembers: "It was a damp and foggy evening, we let them come, because we knew that further along, in the streets and alleys, at least eighty of our men were waiting."[17]

During one of the scuffles, a Dutch WA-man, by the name of Koot was fatally wounded. Piet Wertheim, known as "Black Pete," Toontje Prenger, and Jo Heide, nicknamed "Red," all of them Jews, participated in the fights. Jo Heide survived the war and recalls some of the details: "Yes I was there. First he [Koot] had an argument with someone. He shouted that he would exterminate the Jews, the lot of them. We shouted back and told him to bring it on. There were a whole bunch of us, and we were ready. At the moment when the first one of them started to fight, we all joined in." At the end of the short battle, the WA beat a hasty retreat, leaving behind Koot, who would die from his injuries. There were a small number of injured Jews and about twenty wounded WA men. Based on eyewitness accounts by three of the surviving participants, at least 125 Jewish men had actively participated in that day's street fights in the center of Amsterdam. In reality, their number may have been much larger.[18]

The Germans instantly reacted with severe measures, almost all of them targeted at Jews. Their most important step was the formation of a Joodse Raad. Through this body they aimed to keep the Jewish population under control by having them be ruled by their own representatives.[19] One of the means by which they hoped to accomplish this was through *Het Joodsche Weekblad* [The

---

16. Sijes, *De Februari-staking*, 65.   17. Braber, *Zelfs*, 62.
18. Ibid., 58–65, 154–55.

19. It is important to note that in the Netherlands an East-European-modeled *Judenrat* was installed and not, as in Belgium or France, a German-style *Reichsvereiniging der Juden*. The latter was able to operate far more independently from the authorities than the former.

Jewish Weekly]. This periodical, though censored by the Germans, would be published under the supervision of the Joodse Raad.[20]

Meanwhile, further incidents took place in Amsterdam. On February 15, new clashes broke out, this time in the south of the city, in and around an ice cream parlor and pastry shop called Koko. The Dutch Nazis possibly targeted it because it was a hangout for many young Jews, as well as older German Jewish immigrants, for whom it served as a community center. Some of the clients decided to organize themselves as self-defense groups, and purchased improvised clubs and metal rods to prepare for battle. As Sijes notes, the militants were all Dutch, while the German-Jewish immigrants kept their distance. "They [the immigrants] apparently had an idea about how the occupying power might react."[21]

This time, too, the Dutch Nazis were chased away. The owners of the Koko ice cream parlor and a sister store, also named Koko, a bit to the north, were two German Jewish businessmen, Kohn and Cahn. A few days later, during the evening of February 19, Dutch Nazis were reported to be on the move again and the young Jewish men prepared for a fight. But instead of the expected Dutch Nazis, a contingent of Germans, the dreaded *Grüne Polizei* (Green Police), arrived in a patrol car. They had probably been tipped off. After forcing their way in, the Germans claimed they had been attacked, and that ammonia was squirted in their faces. They then arrested a number of men from the Jewish self-defense groups, as well as the ice cream parlor's two owners.

This relatively small incident was exactly what the Germans needed. Many arrests followed as the prisoners were brought to trial the next day. Eight of them received lengthy prison and hard labor sentences. One of the defendants, Ernst Cahn, one of the two German Jews who co-owned the parlor, was sentenced to death. His execution, the first in the Netherlands, took place on March 3, 1941 in the dunes near The Hague.[22]

The German reaction did not confine itself to the arrest of individuals involved in the Koko incident. On February 22 and 23, during an exceedingly violent roundup, they arrested about 425 able-bodied Jewish men. This first *Aktion*

20. The weekly appeared from April 1941 until September 1943, when the Joodse Raad was abolished.

21. Sijes, *De Februari-staking*, 101.

22. After this execution a second followed. Again, the victim was a Jew. Leendert Schijveschuurder, a presser, took part in the February Strike and was preparing for another one, when he was arrested. The background of the third execution, with another Jewish victim, is still unknown. Simon Klein, a bookseller, was executed on March 10 or 11. His resistance is unclear, although there is some indication that he was in touch with the British intelligence service.

or *razzia*, the term used by the Dutch, was the German reaction to the clashes in the center of Amsterdam that led to the death of Koot, the WA man. Within days, almost all of the arrested men were deported to Buchenwald concentration camp and from there to Mauthausen, where all but two of them perished quickly. A few weeks after their deportation, the first death reports were delivered to the Joodse Raad, which passed them on to the family of the deceased.

In shocked reaction to these roundups, tens of thousands of Amsterdam's state and municipal employees, transport personnel, factory workers, longshoremen, and many others called a major citywide strike known as the February Strike. In this, the Communists took the lead.[23] It was violently repressed, but whatever its lasting political value, the February Strike was a collective act of great solidarity. It most certainly let the Jews feel and know that they did not stand alone.

Other mass arrests of Jews soon followed. As in February, the Germans only arrested young men. They too were deported to Mauthausen and they too perished quickly. The roundups continued in 1942. In all, in 1941 about 800 Jewish Dutch men were murdered in Mauthausen, including some in Buchenwald, and another 400 Jewish Dutch men and women would follow in 1942.

The events of these two years showed the Jewish population that any resistance would be severely punished. Hence for the Dutch Jews, on the verge of the deportations to Poland which started in July 1942, it seemed more advantageous to obey the German orders, rather than avoid or resist them. The Joodse Raad, for its part, urged Jews to stay calm and heed the German directives. This was in keeping with its policy of "accommodation and compliance with the German instructions," and to "avoid something worse" (meaning Mauthausen), says historian Bob Moore. Unlike the AJB in Belgium and even the often-maligned UGIF in France, the structures of the Amsterdam Jewish Council "provided no opportunities for organized opposition."[24] The Joodse Raad in Enschede, in the eastern part of the Netherlands, was alone in officially advocating rescue. The representatives of the Jewish Council of Enschede, writes Louis de Jong, are the only example we know of "that systematically promoted going into hiding."[25]

23. During the Molotov-Ribbentrop Pact which lasted until June 1941, the official Dutch party line was complicated. Because of the Molotov-Ribbentrop Pact (August 1939), the official Dutch party line was not to resist the German invaders; but individual Communists, among them many Jews, certainly did.

24. Moore, *Survivors*, 214–15.

25. de Jong, *Het Koninkrijk*, 6:1:252. See too Marjolein J. Schenkel, *De Twentse Paradox: De Lot-*

We may conclude that the prospects of any Jew who resisted were far from favorable. To this we will add another element, which is the resistance of non-Jews. For as sociologist Nechama Tec correctly points out, "An understanding of Jewish resistance will be enhanced through an examination within the context of and a comparison to non-Jewish resistance."[26] What about non-Jewish resistance in the Netherlands? The massive German repression did not only touch Jews, but also non-Jews. On March 13, 1941 eighteen resistance fighters were shot, fifteen from the resistance group *De Geuzen* and three participants in the February Strike. The Geuzen was the first major resistance group in the Netherlands. Their leader, Bernard Ijzerdraat, published an underground newspaper and organized sabotage in the greater Rotterdam area that included destroying telephone lines. The execution led to the composition of the best-known Dutch war poem, "The Song of the Eighteen Dead," by Jan Campert. Campert, himself a member of the Resistance, would perish in Neuengamme. The long poem, illustrated and printed as a broadsheet, was distributed and sold by members of the Dutch underground, and was so successful that it helped finance the rescue of Jewish children.[27]

"A cell measures only seven by seven" is the first line of "The Song of the Eighteen Dead." In the opening scene, the poem's protagonist reflects on the actions that brought him there and on his fate. It captures well the dilemma that many Dutch men and women faced early on in their relation not only to the German occupiers, but also to the Jews who were, whatever their misgivings about them, their fellow countrymen and often, in a more mundane sense, their neighbors. What were they to do? To look away and give in to the fear of retaliation that the Germans were such masters at evoking? That would be the rational thing to do. Or to call a halt, and "fight the battle, even if it is in vain," as Jan Campert's poem puts it?

There is a whole genre of Dutch World War II poetry known as *verzetspoëzie* (poetry of resistance). Printed in broadsheets and underground magazines, some of it reiterates themes and images of the old struggle for freedom against the Spanish. In a long poem by Yge Foppema, "Ballad of One Sentenced to Die,"

---

gevallen van de joodse bevolking van Hengelo en Enschede tijdens de Tweede Wereldoorlog (Zutphen: Walburg Pers, 2004).

26. Nechama Tec, *Jewish Resistance. Facts, Omissions, and Distortions*, Paper of the Research Institute of the USHMM (Washington, D.C., 1997).

27. For an explanation of how the broadsheet financed transportation and other expenses for the child rescue workers, and for an English translation of the poem, see Bert Jan Flim, *Saving the Children* (Bethesda, Md.: Program of Jewish Studies, Cornell University, 2005), 77–79.

the protagonist similarly considers his fate, weighs the decision that led him to resist the occupiers, and achieves some comfort in the notion that "the country called, and I answered that summons." Thousands of those who received that call stood up against the Germans by saying, in the words of journalist and underground writer Evert Werkman, "*Nee, nee en nog eens nee!*" (No, no, and once again, no!). That motto, later adopted by the previously mentioned Richter Roegholt, sums up rather well the mentality of those who risked their lives for the cause. Did they save the honor of the Dutch people, as Roegholt puts it? Probably. But can we blame all the others who just looked on, or looked away? That was the dilemma. The Dutch leadership, including its top civil servants, both inside the country and in London, far from encouraging resistance, did not provide any model that might inspire or guide ordinary citizens. Therefore, one's personal attitude, the position one took, was all-important. It became a matter, as the Dutch said then, and many still say today, of "Goed of fout," that is, of right versus wrong. That was the theory. But fear served as a terrible deterrent. The reality was that even if many thousands decided to join the Resistance, the vast majority of the Dutch remained on the sidelines, not to mention those who joined the Nazi party or chose to collaborate.[28]

One of the captured Geuzen and one of the first Jews to be tried for resistance activity was Bill Minco, an eighteen-year-old high school student. According to the prosecution at his trial, Minco had been drawing maps of military installations in and around Rotterdam. Accused, on February 20, 1941, of espionage and giving active assistance to the enemy, he was sentenced to death. Certain that he would die, but pardoned only hours before his execution, on account of his young age, he would make the rounds of German concentration camps (Münster, Untermassfeld, Mauthausen, Auschwitz, Gross-Rosen, Dachau) and live long enough to write about it. Kept in a solitary cell for the first seven months, he learned Goethe's *Faust* by heart. Minco claims that he owes his survival, first, to meeting the Jewish boxer Leen Sanders, and second, to being treated as a political detainee, rather than as a Jew. Sanders, a former national boxing champion, was arrested and deported on account of underground activities. In Auschwitz he had a reputation for supporting fellow inmates and sharing the extra food that his position as a boxing instructor and prominent person earned him. Sanders protected Bill Minco, a fellow Rotterdammer, from the glacial con-

---

28. It is estimated that 22,000 Dutch men and women participated in nonviolent resistance against the Germans, and 3,000 in paramilitary activities. See "Verzet" [Resistance] in *Winkler Prins Encyclopedie van de Tweede Wereldoorlog* (Amsterdam: Elsevier, 1980), 608.

ditions outdoors by getting him a job in a munitions factory. Twice selected for the gas, Minco was twice sent back to his barracks because of his status of political criminal:

[In Auschwitz] I ended up in the department of a Kapo who wore a green triangle, which is, as I mentioned before, the mark of all criminals. Consequently I also wore one. Because he thought that we were kindred spirits, he appointed me foreman over a group of ten men. This had the advantage that I did not have to work, and that I did not get beaten.... It seems as if the SS were eager to preserve me. They feared an epidemic and on top of that, as a *Schutzhäftling* (in protective custody), I was not allowed to be gassed, nor to become seriously ill.[29]

Only in early 1945, at the start of his evacuation from Gross-Rosen to Dachau, was Bill marked as a Jew: "Fifteen minutes later all the Jews had to step forward. We were about 1,500 men." In spite of his seeming bravado, the main impression left by Minco's immediate postwar account, written while he was recovering from lung disease in Davos, is that of a resilient young man feeling terribly alone.[30]

Partly because of the fear of savage German retaliation, the national Dutch resistance was far from developed during 1941 and 1942. As a result, any substantial help to the Jews did not start before mid-1943, when about 70 percent of the Jewish population had already been deported to the camps.[31] Even moral support was hard to come by during the first two years of the war. The national Dutch authorities, including the judiciary, police, and mayors, obediently stuck to the German orders and hardly showed any solidarity with the Jews. Even the Dutch Red Cross largely abandoned the Jews. Exceptions were some churches and some universities. If moral support failed at home, it did not come from abroad either. Neither the queen nor the government in exile, both residing in London, paid any attention to the deportations of hundreds of Jewish Dutchmen to Mauthausen.[32]

It is fair to say that after the February Strike Jews factually stood alone and

29. Bill Minco, *Koude Voeten* [Cold feet] (Nijmegen: Sun, 1997), 101, 107. See also Braber, *Zelfs*, 98–99.

30. Minco, *Koude Voeten*, 117 and Braber, *Zelfs*, 98.

31. The period of deportations through the transit camp Westerbork and Vught lasted for more than two years (mid-July 1942-mid-September 1944). In this period about 107,000 people were deported (including the Mauthausen deportees and all those arrested in Belgium and France), i.e., about 75 percent of the target group.

32. On November 28, 1941, a day on which the fate of the murdered Jews in Mauthausen was already well-known in the Netherlands, Queen Wilhelmina, in her broadcast over *Radio Oranje* (Radio Orange), only spoke of "victims of German terror." Her speech, which lasted more than thirteen minutes, did not contain any specific references to the deported Jews.

became isolated from society at large. When the deportations to the death camps started, in mid-July 1942, Jews of course had to disappear from the public arena. If by showing themselves in public they took great risks, the danger increased five-fold once they decided to participate in resistance work. In his preface to the account of the Jewish resistance fighter Jacques van de Kar of the Hollandse Schouwburg resistance group, the previously mentioned Evert Werkman sums up how vulnerable those Jewish men and women were, and how brave: "What they did was extremely risky and they were aware of it. Any Jew caught in the act of sabotaging any installation of the German authorities, would at once be transported to Westerbork as an 'S-case' [the German word is *Straf*, i.e., punishment] and from there directly to Poland.... Jews who participated in the Resistance knew that once they were arrested, nothing would be able to save them.[33]

In other words, Jews who decided to resist took enormous risks. But if they had to enter a brand-new life in which they had to adopt a completely new, false identity, this new state had its advantages too. It meant contacts with people who knew how to forge documents and could even lead to the permanent availability of one or more hiding places. It invariably involved meeting previously unknown gentiles who were ready to help. Certain Jews already had such access because theirs was a mixed marriage, or on account of their ties with non-Jewish prewar networks.

Aware of the dangers involved in resistance activities, at least three distinct Jewish groups followed the route into illegality. Their principal goal was rescuing and hiding people, and providing for them. They also liberated Jews from the Schouwburg and the Westerbork transit camp. We will examine their activities below. In addition, hundreds of Jews resisted in the context of non-Jewish resistance groups. With their traditional integration and assimilation at risk, and their protection by the national authorities gone, at least this new situation gave them an opportunity to join their fellow countrymen.

Joining was not always easy. Since Jews presented an extra risk for resistance groups, their non-Jewish comrades were not always eager to accept them. There were even cases of outright antisemitism. But in general the cooperation between Jews and non-Jews worked out pretty well. In Jacques Presser's words: "In our country, Jewish resistance, by and large, was part and parcel of the common struggle against the enemy."[34] In our view, Presser is correct in sig-

---

33. Jacques van de Kar, *Joods Verzet* [Jewish resistance] (Amsterdam: Stadsdrukkerij van Amsterdam, 1984), 5.
34. Presser, *The Destruction of the Dutch Jews*, 278

naling that the "struggle against the enemy" was the crucial common element here, rather than an overriding concern with helping fellow Jews.

Jewish contributions cover the entire range of organized resistance and include operating the underground press, rescuing Jewish children and adults from deportation and caring for them, printing and distributing forged I.D.s and other documents, collecting weapons, participating in sabotage, attacking population registration and prison facilities, and killing key Dutch Nazi officials and collaborators. Jewish resistance workers were involved in all of these, in keeping with Presser's observation that there "existed no branch of the Dutch resistance in which Jewish men and women were not active."[35] These Jewish resisters hailed from all walks of life and from the left, middle, and right of the political spectrum.

Is it an impressive record? Certainly. Yet we may want to take a moment to step back and observe that, quantitatively speaking, Dutch Jewish resistance or resistance by Dutch Jews, was small, perhaps even marginal. It helped save many hundreds of lives and that is enough of a justification, but in the overall perspective of things, it did not diminish German power, nor did it change the course of the war. Nor, for that matter, did general Dutch resistance. But qualitatively speaking, Jewish resistance was of great significance, not only as "an important component of Jewish memory," as Yehuda Bauer puts it, but also as a component of Dutch Jewish memory and, for that matter, human memory and human decency.[36] In what follows, we will look in greater detail at some examples of Jewish resistance.

The revolutionary MLL-Front with its influential underground publication, *Spartacus,* stood on the fringes of the CPN, the illegal Communist Party, but was independent from it. Prior to the war, it was known as the RSAP, and most of its members were Trotskyists. Its leader was the charismatic Henk Sneevliet. Its second in command was a Jew, Ab Menist. He was born and grew up in Amsterdam as the son of an Orthodox father, a shopkeeper, with whom he had a conflicted relationship.

Ab Menist's first political act was his refusal, in 1916, to report for military service. As a result, he spent ten months in prison. After World War I, he started working in construction as a mason, decidedly not a very Jewish vocation, and joined the Communist Party. Having moved to Rotterdam in 1924, he assumed

35. Ibid., 283

36. See Yehuda Bauer, *Rethinking the Holocaust* (New Haven, Conn.: Yale University Press, 2001), 119–66.

a leadership role in the construction workers' trade union. Dissatisfied with the Communist Party line, Menist cofounded the Revolutionary Socialist Labor Party. Representing the RSAP, Menist was elected to the province of South Holland's governing body, the *Provinciale Staten*. He was also a member, for the RSAP, of the Rotterdam city council and was much in demand as a public speaker in the impoverished neighborhoods of the city.

During the early months of the Occupation, Menist, a good organizer, set up the Resistance within his party, and succeeded in recruiting 400 men and women, dividing them into active cells of five persons each. In 1941, Menist, already one of the principal editors of *Spartacus*, became responsible for the distribution of its 5,000 copies. The paper had been fiercely critical of the anti-Jewish events of early 1941, and played a role in organizing the February Strike. A year later, it blasted the Germans for the inhumane *razzias* of early 1942: "They pursue the Jews like animals, and treat them in the most revolting ways. On Saturday 10 January more than a thousand Jews were hunted down and shipped like cattle to the camps."[37]

Arrested in March 1942, along with many others, Menist had few illusions about what awaited him. To his German captors he admitted: "I realized that my acts were punishable, but I believed that I was fighting for a just cause." On April 9, along with seven others, he was sentenced to death. In his summary, the presiding judge said that "Menist, as a Jew and communist, is a dangerous agitator who fanatically sticks to his Marxist and Leninist ideas and is dedicated, as a so-called trade union leader, to the working classes." Menist wrote moving farewell letters to his family, including his children. To his wife he wrote that he felt at peace with the sentence, and about his firm belief in the Socialist ideal "for which I now have to die, because I could not act in any other way." To his father he confessed that the years had not distanced them from each other, but on the contrary brought them closer. He begged his father to "be strong, assume and carry this burden, and share some of my equanimity." On April 13, 1942, after singing the *International* together in their small underground prison, the eight men were brought out in two groups of four, and shot.[38]

The main force on the left was the illegal CPN (Netherlands Communist Party) with its newspaper *De Waarheid* [The Truth], whose editor Paul (previously

---

37. Braber, *Zelfs*. 121

38. See Braber, *Zelfs*, 121–22; Dick de Winter, *Ab Menist* (Amsterdam: Eburon, 2010), 207, 209; and Emil Henssen, "Het verzet van links" [Resistance on the Left], in *Het verzet 1940–1945*, ed. Roegholt and Zwaan, 89.

Saul) de Groot was a Jew. He survived the war in hiding. The paper and several of its subsidiaries were founded in November 1940. Many Jews were committed party members. Although we lack concrete numbers, it is fair to say that a lot of Jews were active in the Communist movement. Sometimes their illegal activities had started already in the 1930s, when they helped political refugees and Jews from Nazi Germany to stay in the country. Early editions of *De Waarheid* were mimeographed at the house of Hirsh (Herman) Ohringer in the Blasius Street in Amsterdam. Hirsh Ohringer, Dubi Jurgrau, and David Friedman and their wives were all active in the Resistance. As Communists, they were a minority in the Yiddish speaking culture and labor group Anski, which consisted of Jewish immigrants from Russia and Poland. Many of them had arrived in Holland in the 1920s, or even earlier. Though it accommodated joint cultural events, Anski, founded in 1921, was largely a Socialist organization, and was dominated by Bundists.[39]

Among those of the Anski group active in the Resistance were Ernst Levy, Max Rubinstein, David Weinrieb, and Ben Foerster. Ernst Levy was an active Communist and one of the three principal leaders of the Groep-van Dien at the Oosteinde home. He and Rubinstein were also involved in many illegal escapes from the Schouwburg, where they worked together with Jacques van de Kar. Levy had experience in prewar anti-Fascist activities. One thing he taught the others was not to open the door when the bell was rung. "Let that person whistle a song," he advised them. The selected tune was the Yiddish song "Bei mir bistu shein," or in German "Bei mir bist Du schön."[40]

Still on the left, but hugging the middle, was the resistance paper *Het Parool*. Social-democratic but not following any party line, *Het Parool* was one of the largest and most widely read underground newspapers. At one point in 1943, it had a circulation of 40,000. Started as a newsletter, it soon broadened into a major newspaper. It followed a hard anti-German line and was implacably opposed to any cooperation with the occupying authority. A number of Jews were involved in getting the newspaper written, printed, and distributed, including Hans Warendorf, Jaap Nunes Vaz, Maurits Kann, and Jaap Melkman. Warendorf, Nunes Vaz, and Kann served on the editorial board. Of the four, only Warendorf survived the war by escaping to England in late 1942. Jacob

39. Yehudi Lindeman's interview with Mirjam Ohringer (June 1, 2011).
40. Van der Kar says that the same tune is still used by his family as their family whistle. Van de Kar, *Joods Verzet*, 56–57; Braber, *Zelfs*, 89; Ben Braber, *Passage naar vrijheid* [Passage to freedom] (Amsterdam: Balans, 1987), 110–11.

Melkman was arrested in February 1942 and after being imprisoned in Amsterdam, Scheveningen, and Utrecht, was sentenced to death at the "First Parool Trial" on December 19, 1942. He was executed on February 5, 1943, along with twelve others from the group. It is striking that several other Jewish illegal workers for "Het Parool" were not brought to trial but deported instead. Nunes Vaz was murdered in Sobibor in 1943.[41]

There were a number of militant resistance groups in the Netherlands, with different targets. Some used violence to raid government and local data banks and central registration facilities in order to destroy as many documents as possible, usually by burning the entire facility. By destroying the records of Jews registered in the data centers, the attacks aimed to protect them from deportation. One group affiliated with these actions was the so-called "Persoons Bewijzen Centrale" (PBC, literally the Center for Personal I.D.s). Its best known representative was the non-Jewish sculptor Gerrit-Jan van der Veen, Holland's emblematic resistance hero. Van der Veen had connections with many Jews, and his organization found the means to supply many of them with forged identity papers and ration card I.D.s. One of van der Veen's colleagues was Gerhard Badrian, a German-born Jew. A raid on Amsterdam's central municipal registration facility, on March 27, 1943, though successful, led to multiple arrests, including those of four young Jewish participants, Rudolf Bloemgarten, Karl Gröger, Coos Hartog, and Henri Halberstadt. Editors of an underground periodical, "Rat Poison," they had already tried to derail a train on the main rail route between Amsterdam and Haarlem. After a lengthy trial, all four of them faced a firing squad, as part of a large-scale execution on June 30, 1943.

When Gerrit-Jan van der Veen was arrested and executed, after a daring attack on the main Weteringschans prison of Amsterdam, Gerhard Badrian was one of the men who took over the leadership of the PBC. Badrian had the reputation of being a daredevil. In April 1943, dressed up in the uniform of the German SS, he had led a raid on the state printing facility of the Netherlands in The Hague. The successful attack netted thousands of valuable blanks for national I.D.s. Legends about "Blonde Hans," (Fair-haired Hans) and his activities sprang up around him, including his talent for engineering escapes. According to various sources, the Jewish Badrian once brazenly entered the central police headquarters of Amsterdam. Dressed in his SS uniform, with German documents in hand, he demanded the transfer to a German facility of two prisoners.

41. Henssen, "Het verzet van links," 80–81; and Braber, *Zelfs*, 103–06.

On his way out, in the courtyard, he slapped one of them in the face. Only after they were safely inside the car that the resourceful Badrian had organized for the escape did the two newly liberated resistance men realize what had happened. Badrian did not survive the war. Facing a number of German police, and after shooting down one opponent, he died in a hail of bullets, on June 30, 1944.[42]

Hans Katan and Leo Frijda were two young Jewish students at the University of Amsterdam. They belonged to the Group CS-6, named after a house at 6 Corelli Street in Amsterdam, where their fellow group members Jan Karel and Louis Boissevain lived with their family. Hans Katan, who had served in the Dutch army, was a student of biology and an editor of an illegal Communist periodical. Though CS-6, started in mid-1942, cooperated with the Communists, on whom it relied for arms and logistics, it remained independent. The goal of the group was to engage in active sabotage and do maximum logistical damage to the German occupiers. They targeted some especially harmful Dutch Nazis. Among those killed were General Seyffardt who was in charge of recruiting young Dutchmen for the eastern German front, and H. Reydon, a Dutch deputy minister. Concentrating on spectacular assaults, members of CS-6 tried to derail a deportation train, attacked a German storage facility filled with the radios confiscated from Dutch Jews, set fire to the Hollandse Schouwburg, and raided a student home for Dutch Nazis. They attacked the main Amsterdam unemployment office and, in January 1943, largely destroyed the Rembrandt movie theater in Amsterdam, where German propaganda films were routinely shown.

The group succeeded in killing several more Dutch Nazis before most of its members, including Katan and Frijda, were arrested in the late summer of 1943. When he was caught, Katan was preparing the assassination of the notorious Dutch Nazi Mussert, the "Dutch Führer." The prosecution claimed that Hans Katan had been "the leader and mastermind behind the attacks on the railroad and setting of fires that the terrorist group had instigated." The German judge found all the members of the group guilty and sentenced them to death on September 30, 1943.

In an early letter to his family dated May 11, 1943, Hans Katan, after giving practical and detailed advice to his parents, shifts gears and searches for words to explain his activities and place them in a larger perspective:

---

42. There is a memorial plaque honoring Badrian's name and actions in the Rubensstraat in Amsterdam. See de Jong, *Het Koninkrijk* 7:719–29 and Braber, *Zelfs*, 123–26.

Don't give in to hatred. Instead, look at all of this in the perspective of world history, rather than just in the light of yourself or myself. Above all, the things we have aimed to accomplish will not remain without consequences. The generations after us will continue to build on the foundations that we, in the fervor of our thoughts, first laid down. [He continues in French] I have great faith in the future because I know that I have not yet accomplished all that I am capable of.

His final letter, dated September 30, 1943, is principally addressed to his mother:

The inevitable blow has been struck. We have been sentenced and ... we have only a short time left. I realize that this is worse for you than it is for me. All I can think of telling you, by way of apology, is about my deep realization of having more than fulfilled my duty here on earth, in spite of my young age. So far, I am feeling quiet. My best wishes for the future of yourselves, and that of the Netherlands and the world.

[He adds a P.S.] I have been in detention since August 19. They treat me reasonably well.... I have known many people and loved many people. I know that those who have known me really well will *not* feel sorry for me. Therefore be courageous, too, and be happy when you think of your son.

Though he has been sentenced to die, the parting impression we get of the twenty-four-year-old Hans Katan is one of equanimity, and a quiet attachment to his fate. His final demand, tender but clearly articulated, is for others to be as brave in the face of his death as he had been in facing his destiny. He was executed in Overveen near Haarlem on October 1, 1943, along with Leo Frijda and seventeen other men.[43]

Appearances to the contrary, resistance by Jews also took place on the right side of the political spectrum. One example is the activity of ex-army officers and other noncommissioned men that included many Jews. Demobilized after the Dutch defeat of May 1940, the ex-army men, members of the so-called OD, were involved in various resistance activities, including sabotage, armed attacks, and transferring information to London. At the first so-called Stijkel trial, one of the OD-affiliated trials, Mozes Hes and Barend Davidson were accused of espionage and passing information to the British. Both were sentenced to death and executed. Numerous other Jewish ex-military men were involved in similar resistance activities. Among those who were sentenced and killed were Salomon Vaz Dias, Rudolf Hartogs, Rudolf Lewin, Abraham Wijn-

---

43. NIOD Doc I, file 1763a; de Jong, *Het Koninkrijk*; Henssen, "Het verzet van links," 98–100; Braber, *Zelfs*, 110–12.

berg, Abraham Jakobson, Jakob Lopes de Leao Laguna, Maurits Kann, André Polanus, and Levie de Groot and Hugo Samkalden.

According to the accusations, Hartogs and Lewin had been stockpiling weapons and preparing the assassination of a Jewish dentist who worked for the Gestapo. Another Jew, Abraham Wijnberg, 29, a successful business manager and the father of a nine-month-old child, was asked to help kill a notorious Dutch Nazi. When the man arrived home from a party to celebrate Hitler's birthday, on April 20, 1942, Wijnberg struck him with the back of his revolver. One of the others finished him off. All of the men escaped, but the Germans were able to track down most of them. When he was arrested, Wijnberg was carrying two guns. Wijnberg was shot on July 29, 1943 close to Camp Amersfoort. Maurits Kann, besides being an editor of the illegal *Het Parool*, had served as a captain in the Dutch army in 1940, and was a member of the OD. Before the war, he had been the respected editor of *De Groene Amsterdammer*. He was married and the father of four children. Like several of the other accused, he was sent to Germany where he was murdered. Polanus and de Groot were sentenced to short prison sentences, but being Jewish, were deported after the termination of their sentences. Polanus was killed in Auschwitz in 1944. Hugo Samkalden was accused of espionage and passing information to the British. Though sentenced to death, in August 1942 the sentence was converted to life in prison. But unlike his codefendants, the Jewish Samkalden was forced to serve his sentence in Mauthausen where he perished. Many other Jewish OD men were captured and killed. Jules Gerzon and Herman Speyer were among the few who were able to escape arrest. Speyer escaped to London where he worked for the information service.[44]

Surprisingly, numerous other underground initiatives have either been forgotten or are almost unknown today. It was recently revealed that Hans Keilson, the author and psychiatrist, was active in a very delicate kind of resistance work. On behalf of the umbrella organization *Vrije Groepen* (VG, Free Groups), a network of small resistance groups that did not want to join the national rescue organization, the Jewish Keilson gave frequent consultations to Jews in hiding who were deemed to be in need, or struggling with special problems. "In that capacity, I traveled all over the country, wherever the organization sent me," he recently wrote. But Keilson was a cautious man. He only started doing the work, which included running errands for the VG as a courier, af-

44. See Braber, *Zelfs*, 50–55; discussed in Roegholt and Zwaan, *Het verzet 1940–1945*, 25–28; NIOD Doc. II, file 583.

ter obtaining a "foolproof" counterfeit I.D. through his contact with a friendly Dutch policeman.[45]

Surprisingly, only in 2001 did substantial new information become available about the so-called "P. P. Groep," part of the *Vrije Groepen Amsterdam* (VGA), which included many Jews, usually of mixed marriage, who provided other Jews with hiding places and further care. After the war it became apparent that about 20 percent of the P. P. Group's members were Jewish.[46] There are many more cases of individual or group Jewish resistance. Jacques Presser, reporting in 1965, says that he encountered "several hundreds of names" during the research for his book.[47] Clearly, much work on the subject still needs to be done.

Of the three Jewish groups that stood up in resistance, the first two were the Group Oosteinde and the Palestine Pioneers. A third network, known as the Schouwburg Group, saved Jewish adults and children imprisoned in the Hollandse Schouwburg and the *crèche*. The operations of these three Jewish networks most closely fit the label of Jewish resistance. Many of the men and women in the Group Oosteinde were Communists, and most of them were German Jews who had come to Holland as immigrants or refugees during the 1930s. For many, their illegal activities had already started in Germany. In Amsterdam, their main goal was to help fellow German Jews to stay in the country. Other members were Dutch Jews active in assisting German Jewish refugees, especially if they were illegal and penniless, as many were. Thus, the house at 16 Oosteinde (after which the group was named) was already a center for illegal activities prior to the German invasion. The main people in charge were three German immigrants, all of them dedicated Communists. Alice Heymann-David was a kind of warden who had the daily responsibility for running the "Heim." Nathan Notowicz was a slight, intense man of great intelligence and musical talent, who arrived with his family in the mid-thirties from Düsseldorf. The already mentioned Ernst Levy was a tall, elegant businessman from Hamburg

---

45. Hans Keilson, *Daar staat mijn huis* [There stands my house] (Amsterdam: Athenaeum Boekhandel, 2011), 88, and Yehudi Lindeman's telephone interview with Marita Keilson (May 27, 2011). Other books by Keilson include *Comedy in a Minor Key* (New York: Farrar, Straus and Giroux, 2010) and *The Death of the Adversary* (New York: Farrar, Straus and Giroux, 2010).

46. See Loes Gompes, "Porgel en Perulan in het verzet," [Porgel and Perulan in the Resistance] in *De Groene Amsterdammer* (May 5, 2001).

47. See Presser, *Ondergang*, II, 7; and Braber, *Zelfs*, 15. In addition, Presser compiled an "Honor List" of those Jewish men and women who were killed or executed, and who especially distinguished themselves in the Resistance. See NIOD Doc. I, file 9980. A version of it appears as Appendix I in Braber, *Zelfs*, 144–53.

who was, according to reports, smart and funny. Arriving in 1935 to help run his father's German import-export business, he had stayed in Holland to organize aid and collect money for German Jewish refugees. The main goal of the Groep-van Dien, as the Oosteinde "Heim" was later known, was to offer support. After the start of the deportations, people were very conflicted, says Alice Heymann-David. "One of my principal tasks in those days was to tell them, 'Make sure you stay out of the claws of the Nazis.'"

If starting with the 1940 invasion the "Heim" became a center of anti-German activity, the deportations in July 1942 marked a departure. From then on, it aimed to hide, assist, protect, and liberate members of the group caught in the German web by any means necessary. The group created hiding places, provided counterfeit I.D.s, and helped friends and colleagues escape from the Schouwburg, the deportation trains, and camp Westerbork.[48] There was a well-oiled illegal connection linking the organization in Amsterdam to that of Westerbork. The key person in the camp was Werner Sterzenbach. His resistance is a good example of "amidah," a Hebrew term that can be loosely translated as "standing up to."[49] Stertzenbach, in camp Westerbork since 1941 (when it was still administered by the Dutch Justice Department), gathered a resistance group of fifteen people around him that became involved in many escapes from deportation.[50]

Werner Stertzenbach had come to the Netherlands in 1933 as a twenty-four-year-old refugee from Germany. Suspected of being a Communist, he was arrested in March 1933 and served six months in prison. To avoid future arrest, he fled to Amsterdam where he found an office job with the Jewish Refugee Committee at the Oosteinde address. Unable to keep his refugee status, he was arrested by the Dutch authorities as an illegal alien, and sent to prison. When the Germans invaded in May 1940, he was still in Dutch detention. When the Gestapo were unable to find proof of his prewar Communist activities, the Dutch authorities interned him at Westerbork. Here Stertzenbach set up an extension of the Oosteinde resistance group inside the camp, helped organize many illegal activities and was responsible for at least twenty escapes.

Escaping from Westerbork was not easy, he says:

48. Braber, *Zelfs*, 89 and van de Kar, *Joods Verzet*, 56–57.
49. See Bauer, *Rethinking the Holocaust*, 120.
50. For the discussions of the Groep-van Dien, see Braber, *Zelfs*, 89–91 and especially Braber, *Passage naar vrijheid*, 16–2, 72–76 and *passim*.

It took forged papers, money, reception in Amsterdam, and a hiding address.... The Westerbork group was able to organize these things in various ways.... Joseph Mahler, a member of the Group Oosteinde, worked in the mailing room.... The Group in Amsterdam sent parcels with illegal newspapers, blanks for I.D.s, stolen documents and money to a fictional character in the camp, Karel Merksma, which Mahler was able to fish out of the mail bag before it went to the censor.... The couriers of the Jewish Council, who traveled back and forth between Amsterdam and the camp, were another way of smuggling materials into Westerbork.[51]

Sometimes Dr. Fritz Spanier, the Chief Medical Officer of Westerbork and a Jew, helped set up an illegal telephone contact between the Oosteinde Group and the Westerbork group, by allowing Stertzenbach to receive urgent messages from Alice Heyman-David.

During one particular escape, Stertzenbach, who as a plumber had permission to work outside the barbed wire fence, transported a young woman, Bella, out of the camp in a large wheelbarrow, after covering her with some metal plating. A woman from the Oosteinde Group met her and accompanied her on the train back to Amsterdam. At the same time, the resistance network inside the camp needed to remove the card with Bella's name from the administrative file of camp inmates. Sometimes Stertzenbach hid someone inside a small truck that he used to take bodies of the deceased to the crematorium, which was situated outside of the camp. Another easy but nerve-racking way was to free someone just before they boarded the deportation train. At that point, the deportee hid inside the camp and was smuggled out the next day. The SS did not worry about that person any more, because in Auschwitz nobody would be consulting lists of names any longer. After an especially bitter experience in the camp, Stertzenbach decided to get out. Using the same escape method that he himself had developed, he left the camp in September 1943. Hiding in Amsterdam, at the house of Alice Heymann-David, he worked in the Resistance until the end of the war. He eventually married Alice Heymann-David.

The so-called *chalutzim*, or Palestine Pioneers, were young Jewish people with a strong Zionist orientation. There were several Pioneer chapters in the Netherlands, but our focus is on the rescue of forty-eight youngsters living together with their leaders and counselors at the so-called Youth Aliyah House, in the small village of Loosdrecht twenty miles southeast of Amsterdam. Like the people in the Oosteinde Group, most of these young people were of German Jewish origin, and had come to the Netherlands to escape persecution in Ger-

51. Ibid., 72–73.

many. As refugees preparing for a future life in Eretz Yisrael, they did not fit in with any of the mainstream Dutch Jewish communities. As historian Igal Benjamin put it, "The *chalutz* movement and its *hachsharot* in Holland had little in common with Dutch Jewry, even with its Zionists."[52] With no strong ties to the community, and a nonconformist attitude to authority, they operated outside of the parameters of Dutch Jewish society, which would prove to be an asset.

To go or not to go had been the question on the minds of the leadership at the Youth Aliya House of the Loosdrecht *chalutzim* in late July 1942, as it emerged that the young people in their charge would shortly face deportation. In early August, after long discussions, the counselors decided in favor of hiding the members of the group, but they did not know how to go about it.[53] Their challenge was how to find hiding places for forty-eight boys and girls. At a loss, they turned to Miriam Waterman who came from an assimilated Jewish family and had many contacts in the non-Jewish community. She had been a teacher at the nearby progressive "Werkplaats" school, but because she was Jewish, she had been forced to give up her job in November 1940. After consulting two of her former colleagues, a few hiding places were found, but it was not enough. In desperation, they turned to Joop Westerweel, a former teacher at the "Werkplaats." Westerweel, who was known for his ability to get things done, was now a school principal in Rotterdam. With his help and that of his wife Wil, places for all of the children were located within three days. The non-Jewish Joop Westerweel soon developed a close personal relationship with the Jewish Joachim "Schuschu" Simon of the Loosdrecht Pioneers.

On August 15, the leadership received a phone call from their contact within the Joodse Raad with the news that the Germans would raid the Loosdrecht Aliyah House the next Monday. That evening the two leaders, Menachem Pinkhof and Schuschu Simon, told the young people of their plans. They were deeply disappointed and reluctant to hide, for they had expected to travel to Poland

---

52. Igal Benjamin, "Faithful to their destiny and to themselves: The Zionist Pioneers' Underground," in *The Netherlands in War and Holocaust* (Ramat Efal, Israel: Beit Lochamei Hagetaot, 1998). Apart from an "abstract in English," this book is written in Hebrew.

53. For what follows, see NIOD II, file 1283 which contains a large number of personal documents written by and about members of the Palestine Pioneers. It is based on the German "Vom Ringen des holländischen Hechalutz" (1954) and the Hebrew *Hamachteret hachalutzit beholland hakevushah* (Tel Aviv, 1969). See also Ineke (Chaja) Brasz, *De Jeugdalijah van het paviljoen Loosdrechtsche Rade, 1939–1945* [The youth aliyah of the Loosdrechtse Rade pavilion, 1939–1945] (Hilversum, Netherlands: Verloren, 1998) and Yehudi Lindeman, "Against All Odds: Successes and Failures of the Dutch Palestine Pioneers," in Jeffry M. Diefendorf, ed., *Lessons and Legacies VI* (Evanston, Ill.: Northwestern University Press, 2004), 88–111.

together as a group. They believed their chances for survival were good, for they were young, healthy, and used to hard physical work as part of their preparation for life in a kibbutz. They also shared a strong sense of solidarity. After Schuschu addressed the group, and reminded them of his own experiences in Buchenwald, the young people gave in. Within hours after the meeting, a number of youngsters were taken to nearby hiding places. By Sunday, all the children had found a place. Schuschu was satisfied but realized how much remained to be done. He was also quite pessimistic about the future.[54]

In the autumn of 1942, when friends and colleagues from the Amsterdam chapter of the Palestine Pioneers wanted to share the benefits of Schuschu's new network, Schuschu decided to branch out. He believed that it was impossible to stay within the Dutch borders because of the high degree of treason and the difficulty of finding sufficient hiding places. For him, the future of the movement lay across the border in France and Spain, and he was able to convince others of his plans. It was a bold vision. Schuschu himself volunteered to go abroad and make the first contacts. He left in early October 1942. His second mission was to search for reliable French underground networks, which he considered essential in order to cross the Pyrenees successfully into Spain. During several more visits to France, between October and January, he made useful contacts with an organization of Jewish scouts and with a Zionist youth group, the *Mouvement de la jeunesse sioniste*. But in January, Schuschu was arrested while crossing the Dutch-Belgian border. Rather than risk the betrayal of his friends, he took his own life in a Dutch prison on January 27, 1943.

Schuschu's valuable contacts with the Jewish French underground were now lost and it would be another four months before his group's contacts with foreign groups, including the Toulouse-based *Armée juive*, would lead to the first crossings of the Pyrenees. After Menachem Pinkhof, Joop Westerweel continued the work and made several successful crossings to the south of France. After he was arrested and sent to Camp Vught, the group continued to function under the leadership of Kurt Reilinger. Of the other leaders, Menachem Pinkhof and Miriam Waterman were arrested during an attempt to liberate Westerweel from Camp Vught. They would survive the Bergen-Belsen concentration camp. Joop Westerweel was executed on August 11, 1944.

Joachim Simon grew up in Berlin and Frankfurt. In 1937, he joined the German group of Palestine Pioneers. In 1938, following *Kristallnacht*, he was ar-

---

54. For details about Schuschu Simon, see NIOD II, file 1283.

rested and sent to Buchenwald. After being released, he moved to Holland where he became a group counselor at the Loosdrecht Aliyah House and joined the board of the national Pioneer organization. He had studied sociology and philosophy, and continued his studies in Loosdrecht. In a letter to a friend, written on November 20, 1942, Schuschu speaks of his motivation for doing resistance work and his fears and misgivings about its future success:

I do my utmost to succeed, but who knows, maybe it is too late, and I won't be able to do what needs to be done.... But even if everything appears almost hopeless, we may still be able to achieve something.... We have the ability to struggle against our destiny, even if it means that we will lose. And if tomorrow something should happen to me, I can be at peace. I won't regret what I did for one moment. We had the courage to fight, and even if we failed, that is our fate. And the fact that we did not fight for ourselves only is an encouraging thought.[55]

As a result of the escape route first opened by Schuschu Simon and Joop Westerweel, about one hundred members of the Dutch Pioneers found refuge in France. Seventy of them successfully crossed into Spain. Sixty-one pioneers boarded two different ships in Spain and arrived in Haifa in February and November 1944. Among them were eleven of the original Loosdrecht *chalutzim*. Of the remaining thirty-seven Loosdrecht youngsters in hiding, fourteen would be captured, deported, and killed. The others would emigrate to Palestine and Israel after the war. Yad Vashem honored Joop Westerweel posthumously as a Righteous Gentile. A monument to Schuschu Simon inside the Joop Westerweel forest in Israel constitutes a permanent reminder of the friendship between the two men, and what they aimed to accomplish.

Our third example of Jewish resistance by Jewish groups is the extended rescue operation at the Hollandse Schouwburg in the center of Amsterdam. Officials working for the Jewish Council helped remove at least 700 and possibly as many as 1,100 young children and babies from the *crèche* (daycare center) over a period of about nine months. The individual Jewish officials and daycare workers who supported the operation all acted illegally, and without any formal Jewish Council support. The *crèche* was situated opposite the Hollandse Schouwburg, a large former theater used by the Germans as a temporary holding pen for Jews on their way to being deported. Each week at least two transports left the facility for transit to camp Westerbork in the north of the country. Out of 61,000 Jews deported from Amsterdam, about 15,000 may have

---

55. NIOD II, file 1283. See also Braber, *Zelfs*, 86.

passed through the Schouwburg or the *crèche*. The once-beautiful theater was an overcrowded, unhygienic, and exceedingly noisy prison with barely enough space for the often young families to lie down. Because of this, the Germans decided to move the youngest inmates to the daycare annex on the other side of the avenue. Although the new location made escapes easier, the enterprise of saving the children was complex, as it involved a delicate interplay between Jewish Council personnel, Jewish daycare workers, non-Jewish members of at least two fledgling resistance groups, and students and staff at the Protestant teacher training college next door to the *crèche*. As this rescue operation has been well documented, our account will be relatively short.[56]

Essentially there were three ways of smuggling out Jewish children. In registering a family, an official of the Jewish Council in charge of registration routinely listed the names of two instead of three children. "One of the three children," says Sieny Cohen-Kattenburg, who was a daycare worker at the annex, "was now staying illegally in the Hollandse Schouwburg."[57] Walter Süskind, the head of registration for the Jewish Council, always contacted the *crèche* ahead of time through its director, Henriette Henriquez Pimentel. That way Ms. Pimentel knew exactly when the next transport would leave, and the names of the children who would have to go. That same day, one of the most trusted of the thirty or so daycare workers contacted the parents in question, to explain the situation and ask them if they were willing to leave one child in their care to be saved, and which child that should be. It was a heart-rending situation for all concerned. If the parent or parents were uncertain or confused, they were given until 4 p.m. to decide. At that time, the daycare worker would return to the Schouwburg to get the final go-ahead. Transports to Westerbork usually left in the evening. Once a parent agreed, the youngster would be handed over to a non-Jewish resistance worker who would take the child into hiding. No children were ever removed from the *crèche* without full parental permission.

If, on arrival in the Schouwburg, the child had been registered, the situation presented a different challenge. One often-used method was for the mother to leave the Schouwburg holding a doll wrapped in a blanket, both provided by a daycare worker. "That evening, the parents entered the deportation van with a

---

56. For the rescue of children at the *crèche*, see Flim, *Saving the Children*, 46–70; Debórah Dwork and Robert Jan van Pelt, *Holocaust: A History* (New York: W. W. Norton, 2002), 342–46; and Moore, *Survivors*, 304–11.

57. Marcel Prins and Peter Henk Steenhuis, *Andere Achterhuizen* [Other secret annexes] (Amsterdam: Vitgeverij Athenaeum, 2010), 76.

doll in their arms," observes Sieny Cohen-Kattenburg, so that "those children were now, as it were, hidden in the *crèche*."[58] That way, the baby could be safely taken into hiding.

With older children, things were more complicated. To remove them from the registration list, Walter Süskind, helped by his assistant Felix Halverstadt, had designed a dangerous but, as it turned out, foolproof method. In each case, they were able to remove the card of the child in question from the card file. Next, they had to fix the record of the Germans' central registration facility so that there too the number of children on the official list matched the number of children present in the Schouwburg and the *crèche*. Surprisingly, Süskind's ingenious doctoring of the records never failed. Giving presents and bribes to the SS seems to have helped the situation.

Toddlers and young children could be smuggled out of the *crèche* in a backpack or in any other reasonably portable device. Older children were taken for a walk, which the Germans allowed at certain hours of the day. Often two or three fewer children returned to the *crèche* than had left half an hour earlier. A resistance worker, most often from the NV or "Trouw" group, waited at an agreed-upon spot. Sometimes an older child simply disappeared with a resistance worker when a streetcar, during a short stop at the intersection, blocked the view of the German guard stationed in front of the Schouwburg. All of these activities were risky, but in spite of some close calls, none of them ever went awry. In addition, starting in April 1943, personnel at the Protestant teacher training college next door to the daycare center helped make the enterprise of hiding children a lot safer. With full support of the school principal, Johan van Hulst, large numbers of Jewish children were saved. This was done by moving them through the college's back yard which, with German permission, was used as a playground.[59]

In July 1943, following major *razzias* in the city, most of the children and adults were deported to Westerbork. In a situation that brings to mind that of the Polish physician Dr. Janusz Korczak, the daycare center's director Henriette Henriquez Pimentel was also deported, along with all of the daycare staff and the remaining children. Only two workers, Virginia (Virrie) Cohen, who received a last minute exemption through her father Professor David Cohen, the copresident of the Joodse Raad, and Sieny Cohen-Kattenburg, by then married

58. Ibid., 77.
59. See Flim, *Saving the Children*, 46–72 and Moore, *Survivors*, 304–11.

to Harry Cohen, a courier for the Joodse Raad, were allowed to stay. The Germans, who called Sieny "the cheeky bitch" (*das freche Weib*), had appointed her to be in charge of the children who still kept on arriving as a result of the intensified and often successful hunt for Jews throughout the city of Amsterdam. She deferred to the older and more experienced Virrie Cohen, who assumed the position of director.

But by now the days of the Schouwburg and daycare center were numbered. Both would be closed on September 29, 1943, the eve of Rosh Hashanah, the Jewish New Year. Aided by Süskind who knew about the imminent closure, dozens of children were saved during the last few days of the *crèche*'s existence. All the remaining Jewish children were sent to Westerbork, along with all the remaining adults. On the final day of the Schouwburg, the Jewish Council was abolished, and its last remaining members were deported, including Professor David Cohen. Walter Süskind was deported too, and would be murdered in Auschwitz. Felix Halverstadt went into hiding and survived the war. So did Virrie Cohen.

That morning of September 29, Harry and Sieny decided to go into hiding as well, and walked out. A German guard stopped them, and asked for their I.D.s. Fortunately, Harry was able to pull out the right documents with the large black "J" stamped on them, because they were still wearing the Jewish star on their clothes. In his other pocket he carried two recently acquired counterfeit I.D.s, without a "J" on them. They explained to the guard that they were on official business and were taking a walk around the block before returning to work. He let them go. "And walk we did," says Sieny. "Both of us were petrified. Only our legs moved." When they were near their destination, she says, "we moved closer to each other and then carefully took off the stars, which we had already loosened a bit. Then our time in hiding began."[60]

There is, alas, a legend that stubbornly survives, says Evert Werkman. According to it, "The Jews generally submitted freely to the measures imposed by the Germans and even brought about their own destruction by cooperating with those measures. Anyone who bothers to study closely what really happened, will arrive at a different conclusion, but the legend refuses to be destroyed."[61] Although through the years the general view has definitely changed, one cannot say that the legend or myth has disappeared completely.

---

60. Flim, *Saving the Children*, 70.   61. See van de Kar, *Joods verzet*, 5.

How could it? As we said before, in the first two decades after the war the question of whether Jews had resisted, or resisted enough, did not become a matter of public discussion or historiographical debate. At that time both non-Jews and Jews had their reasons not to talk about it. Though the social situation is completely different now—Holland is a prosperous, rather easy-going country—"blaming the victims" has not been affected by these social changes. "Blaming the victims" continues to give non-Jews the relaxed feeling that it was not all their fault. However, in the last few decades new historical research has made it abundantly clear that, within the overall frame of Nazi policy, Dutchmen were involved in the implementation of the deportations. Dutch policemen very often arrested the Jews, dragging them out of their homes; Dutch streetcar drivers transported the arrested Jews to the Hollandse Schouwburg in Amsterdam or to one of the railway stations. Dutch railway personnel transported the Jews to the transit camps, Westerbork and Vught. In Westerbork, Dutch military policemen guarded them and returned them to the camp after they managed to escape.[62] Moreover, Dutchmen not only played their part in the deportations, they also took part in the concomitant spoliation of the Jews. Of course, on a macro level this organized looting was the sheer implementation of German policy. Jewish moveable property was supposed to be transported to Germany to give some comfort to the population of the bombed cities. But that will not cover the micro level. How much money disappeared into the pockets of non-Jews as a result of this spoliation? Even more simply, how many neighbors were not ready to return to the surviving Jews their rightful properties? It is clearly not our intention here to talk about guilt. At the most, we are talking about examples of non-Jewish Dutch responsibility for the fate of the Jews, which might provide ample reason for feelings of guilt. In other words, as we said in the beginning, it remains a comforting and reassuring thought that Jews were themselves partly responsible for their destiny.

It is important to note that this conspicuously biased view of nonresisting Jews lived not only in people's minds. It can be found on other levels as well. An institutionalized and considerably milder form of it can be traced in the enforcement of two laws that enable people to get a pension or other benefits

---

62. There is a large and still increasing amount of documentation reflecting on the role played by the Dutch authorities, especially that of the police. One of the most recent publications is Ad van Liempt and Jan H. Kompagnie's *Jodenjacht: De onthutsende rol van de Nederlandse politie in de Tweede Wereldoorlog* [Hunting for Jews: The perplexing role of the Dutch police during World War II] (Amsterdam: Balans, 2011).

because of health damage caused by their sufferings during the war. A very modest number of Jews qualified for the *Wet Buitengewoon Pensioen* (Extraordinary Pension Act) that was enacted in 1947 in order to give financial support to former members of the Resistance or their surviving spouse and offspring. Although in principle Jews can apply for benefits under this law, they are more or less supposed to apply for the *Wet Uitkering Vervolgingsslachtoffers* (Benefit Act for Victims of Persecution, 1972) which, as the name clearly indicates, defines the applicants as victims of persecution, meaning passive people having been terrorized by others.

The institutionalized biased view can also be found in the limited representation of Jews in the nationally acclaimed *Erelijst der Gevallenen* [List of Honor of Those Who Fell] and other memorial publications for fallen resistance fighters. Altogether, this incompleteness provides serious problems for future researchers, the more so as concrete sources about the participation of Jews in the Resistance simply are absent. To sum it up in one theoretical example: it is possible in principle, but extremely hard to prove in practice, that somebody who perished in Auschwitz in say 1942 (and is hence to be considered and remembered as a "victim of persecution") did actually resist in the period prior to their deportation.

Although Jacques Presser's appeal certainly led to a change of opinion, it did not lead to the complete disappearance of the legend or myth. That could not have been expected: after all, at least part of the life of a myth is its capacity for stubborn survival. As far as we could establish, the question of passivity and hence of abrogating one's own responsibility has not been addressed to survivors of other genocides. It seems to be a Jewish privilege.

Cecilie Felicia Stokholm Banke

10 Between Accommodation and Awareness

Jewish Resistance in Scandinavia under Nazism

It might seem paradoxical at first to speak of Jewish resistance in Scandinavia, especially in the case of Denmark, since one usually refers to the escape of the Jews in October 1943 as an act of rescue rather than resistance. Indeed, if we examine the stories told by those who fled, it is clear how much they, themselves, felt that they were rescued and how grateful they were for the help they received. The escape was not experienced as a particularly Jewish act—let alone an act that the fleeing Jews helped arrange. On the contrary, it was said to have been initiated through the interaction of the resistance movement, Danish politicians, and local civil actors, whose names, if not completely forgotten, are often only partially remembered—a first name or an anonymous "Mr. Jensen."

Norway, on the other hand, was different. There was no resistance to prevent the deportation of the 772 Jews to concentration camps, most of whom were murdered in Auschwitz. Indeed, between 30 and 40 percent of the Norwegian Jewish population—a total of 766 Jews—were slaughtered during the Holocaust. A review of the literature on the fate of the Norwegian Jews—deportation and escape—reveals little about Jewish resistance, especially if one defines resistance as active opposition to deportation, armed defiance, or open criticism of the German regime.

Resistance of this type is not found in Sweden either, where such activity would have been far more possible than in neighboring Norway or Denmark. In Sweden, resistance first emerged during the second half of 1942 in the form of help, first to the Norwegian Jewish refugees and later, in 1943, to the Jewish refugees from Denmark. Given all of this, how shall we evaluate Jewish resistance in Scandinavia? Did Jews in Denmark, Norway, and Sweden resist Nazi Germany's discrimination and persecution? Did the Jewish community or individual Jews protest? What was the general attitude of the Jewish communities in Denmark, Sweden, and Norway?

To answer these questions, we must first examine the term, "Jewish resistance," and discuss what is meant by resistance. Then we will discuss the situation in Denmark, where there was very little actual Jewish resistance. Indeed, the general policy of the Jewish community in Denmark was *not* to attract attention or influence in any way the cooperation between the German occupation forces and Danish politicians and civil servants, which, from a Danish Jewish point of view, was considered beneficial, if risky. Until the "rescue" of October 1943, the cooperation policy managed to protect the Jews from Nazi persecution—and from deportation.

There were, however, some exceptions, as described by Jørgen Hæstrup in 1987: for example, the group of about fifty young agricultural students who, at the start of 1943, insisted on investigating the possibilities of an escape route from German-occupied Europe to Palestine.[1] The members of this group made a series of death-defying attempts to cross the continent to Turkey in an attempt to reach Palestine. The first was Bertil Grass who, in order to test whether it was possible, hid between the wheels of a train carriage, supplied with both food and drink. He traveled all the way from Copenhagen to Sofia. On his way back, Grass was captured by the Germans in Hamburg, and was never able to share his experience with the group. He died in Auschwitz. Later, another escape route was tested, when three members of the Danish *Hechaluz*, in March 1943, sailed on a fishing boat from Bornholm to Simrishamn in Sweden. In spite of everyone's presumptions to the contrary, they proved that it was possible to escape to Sweden by sea.

From Denmark we move to Norway, where the question of Jewish resistance becomes even more difficult to answer. The action against the Norwegian Jews happened quickly and unexpectedly. There was therefore not much possibility for Norwegian Jews to oppose the decision. At the same time, the Norwegian Jewish community hoped until the end of the war that those who were deported would return. This attitude indicates that resistance was not an option gener-

---

1. Jørgen Hæstrup, "The Danish Jews and the German Occupation," in *The Rescue of the Danish Jews: Moral Courage under Stress*, ed. Leo Goldberg (New York: New York University, 1987), 39–42.

ally accepted. Soon after the German invasion of Norway in April 1940, the Jewish community experienced the arrests of Jews who had publically expressed criticism of National Socialism before the war—for example: Moritz Rabinowitz from Haugesund, who had written in Norwegian newspapers about the "Nazi danger," was arrested in December 1940 by the German security police and sent to the Åneby camp; and Ephraim Wolff Koritzinsky from Trondheim, also known as an anti-Nazi, was arrested in December 1941 and sent to the Falsted camp, where he was physically abused and later died.[2]

Thus, both Rabinowitz and Koritzinsky were made examples to prove that people should not express criticism or oppose anti-Jewish measures, but should rather keep a low profile and, as far as possible, attempt to adapt. Again, it must be remembered that the Norwegian state participated in the implementation of the anti-Jewish policies in Norway. The strategy of adapting had greater success in Denmark than in Norway where, from the very beginning, the German occupation had a completely different character. In Norway, the Germans met resistance, while in Denmark they did not. In Norway, a national government was established under the leadership of Quisling and with members of the Norwegian National Socialistic party. In Denmark, the government resigned after the strikes in August 1943.

The question can, of course, be asked why the Norwegian Jews did not arrange to flee early, or why some of those who actually did flee in connection with the German occupation returned after about a month when the commotion had died down and things seemed to have returned to normal. But, as Irene Levin, among others, indicated, the Jews in Norway tried to manage as best they could and, at the same time, adapt to the situation. Also, the German occupation did not have any immediate impact, and it could well have seemed that it was safe enough to stay put. The anti-Jewish measures came gradually, making it easier to adapt, and it was difficult to imagine that the Jews in Norway were also in danger. Even after Jewish men were arrested on October 25–26, 1942, Jewish women reacted by obeying the German order to gather at the police station every day. They did not, as might have been expected, try to save their own lives and flee to Sweden. Instead, the women provided moral and emotional support by sending packages and greetings to the prisoners.[3]

2. Irene Levin, *Flukten. Jødenes flukt til Sverige under annen verdenskrig,* Temahefte nr. 2 (Oslo: HL-seneret, Senter for Studier av Holocaust og livssynsminoriteter, 2007); Per Olof Johannson, *Oss selv nærmest. Norge og jødene 1914–1943* (Oslo: Gyldendal Norsk Forlag, 1984). See also Irene Levin, "Taushetens tale," *Nyt Norsk Tidsskrift* 4 (2001).

3. Levin, *Flukten,* 24.

Both Norwegian and Danish Jews found refuge in the neutral neighboring country, Sweden, which made possible the rescue of 7,000 Danish Jews (and some non-Jewish spouses) and about 1,300 Jews from Norway. Sweden's reception of the Norwegian and Danish Jews has been well described by historians, especially in the work recently published by a new generation of Swedish historians, like Karin Kvist Geverts's 2008 dissertation, *Ett främmande element i nationen. Svensk flyktingpolitik och de judiska flyktingarna 1938–1944* [A Foreign Element in the Nation] and Mikael Byström's 2006 *En broder, gäst och parasit* [A Brother, Guest and Parasite].[4]

Common to these works is their lack of focus on Jewish resistance in Sweden as a separate subject. Therefore, I will provide a definition of Jewish resistance and also point out some deficiencies in this research, which could have benefitted from more detailed descriptions of those who helped both Danish and Norwegian refugees. From Denmark and Norway, we will move to neutral Sweden and describe how the Swedish Jewish community reacted to Nazism, how it felt little prepared to provide extensive help and residence, and how it chose a very pragmatic course, which included adapting to the Swedish state's official political line in relation to Nazism.

Resistance

In the standard literature on the Holocaust and Scandinavia, relatively little is found regarding the Jewish community's reaction to the Nazi persecution of Jews. Most works describe state policies toward Germany, how the states dealt with the Jewish refugees from Germany, and the prevalence of antisemitism in Denmark, Norway, and Sweden. Specific Jewish resistance is only given in individual instances, which can be explained by the small size of the Jewish communities and their assimilated nature. Bob Moore writes, for example, in *Survivors: Jewish Self-Help and Rescue in Nazi-Occupied Western Europe* that, contrary to what happened in other countries where Jews participated actively

4. Karin Kvist Geverts, *Ett främmande element i nationen.Svensk flyktingpolitik och de judiska flyktingarna 1938–1944* (Uppsala: Acta Universitatis Upsaliensis, 2008); Mikael Byström, *En broder, gäst och parasit. Uppfattningar och föreställningar om utlänningar, flyktningar och flyktningpolitik i svensk offetlig debatt 1942–1947* (Stockholm: Acta Universitatis Stockholmiensis, 2006); Paul Levine, *From Indifference to Activism. Swedish Diplomacy and the Holocaust: 1938–1944* (Uppsala: Uppsala University, 1996) and Steven Koblik, *The Stones Cry Out: Sweden's Response to the Persecution of the Jews 1933–1945* (Stockholm: Norsteds Förlag, 1987); Lars M. Andersson and Karin Kvist Geverts, eds., *En problematisk relation? Flyktingpolitik och judiska flyktingar i Sverige 1920–1950* (Uppsala: Opuscula Historica Upsaliensia 36, 2008).

in organizing escape and rescue, the "story of rescue in both Norway and Denmark is one where, with very few exceptions, the Jewish populations were the passive recipients of aid from friends, motivated individuals and organized resistance, rather than contributing much in the form of self-help."[5]

The Danish historian Sofie Lene Bak does point out that although Jews in Denmark were helped to escape, they were not "passive victims of the occupation forces' assaults." On the contrary, they were actors who took their fate into their own hands. They did what they could to safeguard their property, arrange for funds for their flight, and also participated in organizing transportation to Sweden.[6] Even though Bak points out these facts, we know little about Jewish resistance. There are several reasons for this. First, as Moore also writes, it was not possible to resist, either in connection with deportation of the Danish Jews in October 1943 or regarding the actions against the Norwegian Jews. The nature of the German occupation in both Norway and Denmark also played a major role. The Jewish communities in both countries did as little as possible to provoke the Occupation forces or attract attention. Finally, as Irene Levin mentions, the anti-Jewish policies were basically understood as something happening far away that would not affect the small Jewish communities in the north.

One aspect that seems remarkable in the existing research, however, is the lack of recognition that resistance could be specifically Jewish, or rather, that resistance could be conceived of from a Jewish point of view. This phenomenon can be explained in part by the desire of the Jewish communities in Scandinavia to be considered equal members of the nations to which they belonged and not exceptional in any way. The Jewish communities in Denmark and Sweden in the 1930s did much to stress that they were first Danes and Swedes, and to emphasize assimilation as a strategy to avoid antisemitism. Another explanation involves the term "resistance" itself. Resistance is identified in many minds with armed resistance, and Jewish resistance would, therefore, necessarily be understood as Jews participating in armed conflict against Nazi Germany. An example of this kind of resistance can be found in Norway, where Jews participated in the struggle against the German occupation, and where Bernhard Goldberg was the most highly decorated Norwegian Jew in the Allied armed services.[7]

5. Bob Moore, *Survivors: Jewish Self-Help and Rescue in Nazi-Occupied Western Europe* (Oxford: Oxford University Press, 2011), 97.

6. Sofie Lene Bak, *Ikke noget at tale om. Danske jøders krigsoplevelser 1943–1945* (København: Dansk Jødisk Museum, 2010), 33.

7. Bjarte Bruland, "Jødeforfølgelserne i Norge" in *Danske tilstande, norske tilstande 1940–45,*

But it is still unclear why so little research actually exists regarding what Jews did to react against the situation in which they found themselves. In this context, international research is a step ahead of Scandinavian scholars, having already produced works that focus on Jewish resistance and thus confront the usual conception of Jews as passive victims of the Holocaust.[8] As Sofie Lene Bak also points out in relation to the flight to Sweden, it is more meaningful to speak of flight rather than rescue, as is often done in the early literature.[9] The distinction in terminology is important—"rescue" suggests passivity, whereas "flight" indicates action. The approximately 7,000 people with Jewish background who fled from Denmark to Sweden in October 1943 acted on their own initiative in order to avoid deportation, and although history has emphasized, for good reasons, the efforts of the individuals who helped them flee, the refugees were not just passive passengers. Their flight was a choice with consequences.

If we were to employ the broader definition of Jewish resistance of Israeli historian Yehuda Bauer with his use of the Hebrew word *amidah* (which means "to stand up against"), we could consider unarmed actions against the Germans as resistance as well.[10] We could include actions meant to help keep individual Jews alive and to help ensure the community's survival. Resistance in this sense, therefore, would include efforts to maintain Jewish life, religious practice, culture, and tradition. Resistance might be the seemingly simple action of continuing to teach children about Judaism, and to celebrate Jewish rituals and holidays in spite of prohibitions and difficult circumstances. Resistance could mean saving others from starvation and caring for the sick and the elderly. Resistance could mean helping Jews to reach Palestine. This perspective on Jewish resistance—on *amidah*—allows a social-historical view of the

ed. Hans Fredrik Dahl, Hans Kirchhoff, Joachim Lund, and Lars-Erik Vaale (København: Gyldendal, 2010) and Bjarte Bruland and Mats Tangenstuen, "The Norwegian Holocaust. Changing Views and Representations," *Scandinavian Journal of History* 36, no. 5 (December 2011): 587–604.

8. See, for example, Nechama Tec, *Defiance: The Bielski Partisans* (New York: Oxford University Press, 1993); James M. Glasse, *Jewish Resistance during the Holocaust: Moral Uses of Violence and Will* (Houndmills, U.K.: Palgrave Macmillan, 2004); Yitzchak Mais, "Jewish Life in the Shadow of Destruction" in *Daring to Resist: Jewish Defiance in the Holocaust*, ed. *Yitzchak Mais, Bonnie Gurewitsch*, and *Barbara Lovenheim* (New York: Museum of Jewish Heritage, 2007).

9. See, for example, Leo Goldberger, ed., *The Rescue of the Danish Jews: Moral Courage under Stress* (New York: New York University Press, 1987); Harold Flender, *Rescue in Denmark* (New York: Simon & Schuster, 1963); Leni Yahil, *The Rescue of Danish Jewry: Test of a Democracy* (Philadelphia, Pa.: Jewish Publication Society, 1969).

10. Yehuda Bauer, *The Death of the Shtetl* (New Haven, Conn.: Yale University Press 2009), 6–8, and *Rethinking the Holocaust* (New Haven, Conn.: Yale University Press 2001).

Jewish community's internal reaction to the Holocaust, and thus raises questions about the relationship between the Jewish community and the majority society, not only in the past, but also in the present.

Danish Resistance Heroes and Jewish Adaptation

In a book about his flight to Sweden, written by the lawyer and former tax minister Isi Foighel a few years before his death, the author asks: "Who could imagine that a whole population—known and unknown and with their own lives at risk—could unite in what no country could ever agree to, to protect and save its Jews?" Foighel's question is not only moving, it also expresses the deep gratitude that most of those helped to flee to Sweden felt, and continue to feel, toward those who aided in their rescue. For Foighel, the flight to Sweden was nothing less than a miracle. Fleeing with his brother and a fellow Boy Scout, Foighel was helped first by his scout leader, Frode Fald, and then by Pastor Knud Ballin, who arranged to send the three boys to members of the Catholic congregation in Brønshøj, where Foighel was housed by a bookbinder. By this point, several volunteers had already aided the boys in their flight. However, they failed to find help to continue their escape. Unable to advance further, the teenagers decided to "try for themselves," as Foighel remembers it; they decided to take the train to Aalsgaarde (a small city on the coast of Denmark and a convenient disembarkation point to Sweden), where they knew that someone might help them to sail to Sweden.[11]

In Aalsgaarde, they found their way to Mr. Nicolaysen's house, where they were given a bath and a meal. When Nicolaysen was warned that the Germans were on their way, the three boys, not wanting to cause trouble for the family, left the house and hid in the woods during the night. They had once more made a choice. The following day, Mr. Nicolaysen arranged for a boat with a local fisherman, who sailed the three boys to Sweden. According to Foighel, the trip cost 10,000 DKK—a considerable amount of money at that time—which Mr. Nicolaysen paid. As recent research has shown, the motives of the fishermen were not purely selfless when they sailed refugees to Sweden; they exposed themselves to a certain risk and wanted compensation.[12]

In Sweden, Foighel and his brother were reunited with their mother, who

11. Isi Foighel, *Miraklet i Danmark* (København: Christian Ejlers Forlag, 2007).
12. Rasmus Kreth and Michael Mogensen, *Flugten til Sverige. Aktionen mod de danske jøder oktober 1943* (København: Gyldendal, 1995).

had come over in another way, and the family remained there until the end of the war. For Foighel, there was no doubt that what the three boys had experienced, along with other Jews from Denmark, was exceptional. He remained deeply grateful for the rest of his life. Whereas this feeling of gratitude is clearly understandable, it has helped to overshadow other aspects of the history of the Holocaust in Denmark, including that the refugees themselves played a role in their own escape and that their flight had its consequences. Families were disrupted; children were left behind; and life as an exile in Sweden was not without its insecurities. Testimony from persons who as children had been left behind with relatives, neighbors, or even strangers has provided insight into the consequences that the choices of those who escaped could have had on those closest to them.

The Danish Jewish Museum has recently documented the cases of at least 133 Jewish children who had been hidden in Denmark, left behind by their parents who had either fled to Sweden or been deported to Theresienstadt. This figure represents 10 percent of all the Jewish children exposed to Nazi persecution in Denmark. For a parent, leaving a child behind must surely be among the most difficult choices imaginable. One must consider, however, that no one knew what the future would bring. Most felt that their stay in Sweden would be brief, and flight itself carried significant risks that could not only imperil the child, but also the safety of those with whom one was fleeing.

This act of resistance that some parents performed by hiding their children in Denmark naturally had an effect on the children who, in some cases, were taken in by non-Jewish foster parents. Some children later abandoned their religion and did not consider themselves Jews. But flight could also have its consequences. Flight to Sweden could affect someone's identification with Judaism. At least eighty-three people withdrew their membership from the Danish Jewish community after returning home to Denmark, provoking Rabbi Marcus Melchior to write angrily in the congregation's journal, accusing these people of succeeding where "Goebbels and Streicher" had failed by striking this blow against the community.[13]

That some should reject Judaism after their return from Sweden could have several causes. First, realization of the enormity of the murderous crimes against Jews caused some to renounce belief in God. In addition, for most refugees, their stay in Sweden meant a withdrawal from Jewish life and practice.

13. Bak, *Ikke noget at tale om*, 174.

However paradoxical it may seem, the action that can be interpreted as active Jewish resistance led in some cases to the end of one's practice of Judaism. What we know about the refugee's living conditions in Sweden is still limited, but Michael Mogensen believes it can be shown that there existed, if not antisemitism, then a widespread negative attitude toward Jews.[14] At the same time, the refugee administration in Sweden made it difficult to lead an observant Jewish life. On the grounds of not wishing any controversies between the various refugee groups or of provoking the local population, the authorities, according to Bak, made it clear that Jews should not draw attention to themselves.[15] As a consequence, many families no longer observed Jewish rituals to the same extent as before the flight.

Over the years, the flight to Sweden has been thoroughly described, both through research and by the refugees themselves.[16] The same holds true for the deportation of the nearly 500 Jews from Denmark, who did not succeed in reaching Sweden but were arrested by the Germans and sent to Theresienstadt. They now have a place in Danish history so that our picture of the fate of Danish Jews during World War II includes more than the dramatic escape to Sweden.[17] We do not, however, know enough about how the Jewish community in Denmark responded to Germany's anti-Jewish policies.

In general, one can say that the Jewish community in Denmark was careful to adapt to the general policy laid out by the Danish authorities, both in

14. Michael Mogensen, "Antisemitisme i det danske flygtningesamfund i Sverige 1943–45" in *Antisemitisme i Danmark?* ed. Michael Mogensen (København: Dansk Center for Holocaust- og Folkedrabsstudier, 2002), 101–14.

15. Bak, *Ikke noget at tale om*, 127.

16. For personal stories, see among others Ina Rohde, *Da jeg blev jøde i Danmark. Nogle erindringsblade fra besættelsesårene* (København: C. A. Retizels Boghandel A/S, 1982); Marcus Melchior, *Levet og oplevet. Erindringer* (København: Statens Bibliotek og Trykkeri for Blinde, 1965) and Olly Ritterband, *Jeg ville overleve*, (København: P. Hasse & Sons, 1984). For Danish research on the flight to Sweden, see Sofie Lene Bak, *Jødeaktionen oktober 1943. Forestillinger i offentlighed og forskning* (København: Museum Tusculanums Forlag, 2001); Hans Sode-Madsen, ed., *Føreren har befalet. Jødeaktionen oktober 1943* (København: Samleren, 1993); Gunnar S. Paulsson, "The Bridge over 'Øresund.' The Historiography on the Expulsion of the Jews from Nazi-Occupied Denmark," *Journal of Contemporary History* 30, no.3 (1995): 431–64.

17. Hans Sode-Madsen, *Dengang i Theresienstadt. Deportationen af de danske jøder* (København: Det Mosaiske Trossamfund, 1995); Hans Sode-Madsen, Reddet fra Hitlers helvede. Danmark og De Hvide Busser 1941–45 (København: Aschehoug, 2005); Elias Levin: Mine erindringer om mit ophold i Theresienstadt (København: Dansk Center for Holocaust- og Folkedrabsstudier, 2001); Silvia G. T. Fracapane: "Fakta og fortielser om fangerne i Theresienstadt" (København: Information, 29 March 2007), and "Myter og misforståelse om deportationerne til Theresienstadt," *Rambam. Tidsskrift for jødisk kultur og forskning* 17 (2008): 56–66. See also the newly developed educational material available for students at http://www.theresienstadt.dk/. This material was developed by the Danish Institute for International Studies and financed by the Danish Ministry of Education.

relation to Nazi Germany and in relation to the German Jewish refugees. The Jewish community did not wish to attract too much attention to these refugees or help too many come to Denmark. The community assisted as much at it could, but until the war broke out, the general strategy was to lie as low as possible and not provoke any kind of anti-Jewish sentiments. The Danish refugee policy toward German Jewish refugees has recently been described in a comprehensive study that also provides insight into how the Jewish community reacted to the refugee question.[18] The so-called refugee problem was not surprisingly followed and commented on in the community's magazine, *Jødisk Familieblad* where, among others, Rabbi Marcus Melchior regularly reported about the developments under the heading "From the Jewish World." In his often moving and increasingly concerned reports, Melchior provided the Danish Jewish community with updates and news about European developments. In that sense, the community was informed about the situation of Jews outside Denmark, which can also be seen from the way other members of the community responded to the situation of the Jews in Germany. Though there was an understanding of the seriousness of the situation in Germany, the Jewish community in Denmark did not consider itself able to help the refugees if it would jeopardize their own situation.

Nonetheless, the Jewish congregation established an aid committee, Committee of 4 May 1933, which, like the other aid committees in Denmark, had close contacts with the international aid work for Hitler refugees, including HICEM and the American Joint Distribution Committee (the "Joint") which financed the transport of German refugees to the United States. Internal records show that, during the period from 1933 to 1939, the committee helped support 1,300 persons economically, including help for agricultural students who came to Denmark through the *Hechaluz* movement and the *Alijah* children. In total, the aid amounted to 900,000 DKK, with all but 200,000 coming from the community.[19] The Committee of 4 May 1933 cooperated with the other refugee com-

18. Lone Rünitz, *Af hensyn til konsekvenserne. Danmark og flygtningespørgsmålet 1933–1940* (Odense: Syddansk Universitetsforlag, 2005); Cecilie Felicia Stokholm Banke, *Demokratiets skyggeside. Flygtninge og menneskerettigheder i Danmark før Holocaust* (Odense: Syddansk Universitetsforlag, 2005); Hans Kirchhoff, *Et menneske uden pas er ikke noget menneske* (Odense: University of Southern Denmark, 2005); Hans Kirchhoff and Lone Rünitz, *Udsendt til Tyskland. Dansk flygtningepolitik under besættelsen* (Odense: Dansk Institut for Internationale Studier, 2007). See also Cecilie Felicia Stokholm Banke, "Welfare, Refugees and Rescue. Denmark and the Jewish Question from 1933 to 1945" (DIIS Working Paper no. 2007/11), and Lone Rünitz, "The Politics of Asylum in Denmark in the Wake of the *Kristalnacht*" (København: Danish Institute for International Studies, 2003).

19. Kirchhoff, *Et menneske uden pas er ikke noget menneske*, 83–85.

mittees in Denmark and in general followed a very defensive policy in order to avoid antisemitism and opposition to the official line in Danish refugee policy.

From the congregation's magazine, we can also follow the community's attitude toward the settlements in Palestine. During the public debate of the 1930s, Palestine had been viewed, not only among Jews but also among the general Danish population, as a means of solving the problem of the Jewish refugees from Germany.[20] In the congregation's magazine, both Chief Rabbi Max Friediger and Rabbi Marcus Melchior expressed support for the settlements, not because Danish Jews should participate or become involved, but because Palestine was the place where Jews who could no longer remain in their homelands could go. Friediger's enthusiasm was thus aroused both by the belief that Palestine was a necessity and the conviction that Palestine could now "once more be a dynamic center for millions of people."[21] In 1935, Friediger himself had visited Palestine and, after returning home, described his experiences enthusiastically, first on the radio and then in a travel book, *The Country That Is Being Rebuilt*, published in 1936.

For Marcus Melchior, Palestine represented a hope for the Jewish world. In 1934 he returned to Copenhagen from his post as rabbi in the German city, Beuthen, and wrote diligently in *Jødisk Familieblad*. During the 1930s, Melchior agitated for a more positive attitude among the community's members toward the Jewish settlements in Palestine. He wrote that Palestine was a Jewish reality. It was an "enormous Jewish responsibility" and meant everything to those who no longer had any opportunities in their former homelands. Therefore, Jews could only show understanding for the strong longing for Palestine that characterized German Judaism. Without this hope for the future, the German Jews "would be doomed to death by spiritual and bodily starvation."[22] In that

---

20. Banke, *Demokratiets skyggeside*, chapter 3.

21. Max Friediger, *Landet der genobygges* (København: Berlingske Forlag, 1936). Several travel books from Palestine were published in the interwar years, among them E. O. Clausen's *Det nye Palæstina* [The new Palestine] in 1918 and Inge Hofman-Bang's *Strejflys. Rids fra Palæstina* [Rays of light. Sketches from Palestine] in 1925. Later came others, such as Ditlef Nielsen, *Hellig Jord* [Holy ground, 1928], Marie Petersen, *Meine Reise nach Palästina* [My journey to Palestine, 1934] and Ernst Harthern's *En Jøde rejser til Palæstina* [A Jew travels to Palestine, 1934]. A Danish version of Chaim Weizmann's *The Jewish People and Palestine* came out in 1936. In 1937, Ella Melbye published a practical handbook for "Tourists and Others," *Rejs til Palæstina* [Go to Palestine], containing, among other things, "good advice on footwear and clothing." The number of publications together with a series of newspaper and journal articles indicates the general public interest in Jewish settlements in Palestine. For more on this issue, see Banke, *Demokratiets Skyggeside, passim*.

22. Marcus Melchior, "De tyske Jøder og Sultedøden" ("The German Jews and Death by Starvation"), *Jødisk Familieblad* 9 (May 1935).

sense, both Friediger and Melchior acted as important voices both for the Jewish community and in the Danish public, representing a commitment not only to the congregation in Denmark, but also to the Jewish cause in general.

However, supporting Zionism was not without its problems, and as a Danish Jew, one had to be very careful to balance solidarity with fellow Jews and identity as a Dane. It was important during the 1930s, once one was allowed to enter Denmark and was accepted, not to invite any confusion regarding one's national affiliation. This situation can be illustrated by a debate that arose after an article by Nathan Skorochod. Skorochod was the son of one of the leading Danish Zionists, the Russian immigrant and furniture merchant, Sorac Skorochod. Together with the author Pinches Welner, among others, Sorac Skorochod had founded the Zionist workers' branch of *Avodah* in Denmark.[23] In his article in the November 1933 issue of *Jødisk Familieblad*, his son, Nathan Skorochod, declared assimilation to be bankrupt. The only worthy goal for a Jew was, according to Skorochod, to pursue "a real basis for being able to develop and promote this culture"—Judaism. Jews had a common fate and, for Skorochod, no difference existed between Danish and foreign Jews.[24]

The reaction from the more established members of the Jewish community came promptly. Carl Grün responded in the next issue that, "our fatherland is Denmark—our mother tongue is Danish—and our flag is the Dannebrog."[25] Frans Henriques was more direct in his reaction. Assuming that Skorochod was the spokesman for "the young foreign Jews, who at the moment are living in Denmark," he addressed himself to them. Until the beginning of the twentieth century, there was a Jewish congregation of Danish citizens. It was not large, about 3,000 and the nucleus consisted of families that had immigrated to Denmark 150 to 200 years earlier. The Danish community was, or could be if it wished, "completely assimilated"; it enjoyed "general respect," and no antisemitism worth discussing existed. Henriques described it as almost idyllic. Denmark, had "so hospitably" received "the great new immigration," and it now lay in the hands of the growing group of foreign Jews whether they, and especially their future children, would "peacefully glide into our hospitable country's population." As Henriques put it, "[You will decide] whether you will have peace and work in peace, or by your disobedient, haughty, and challeng-

23. Bent Blüdnikow, *Immigranter. Østeuropæiske jøder i København 1904–1920* (København: Borgen, 1986), 145, 191. See also Morten Thing, *De russiske jøder i København 1882–1943* (København: Gyldendal, 2008).

24. *Jødisk Familieblad* 6, no. 3 (November 1933): 10.

25. *Jødisk Familieblad* 6, no. 4 (December 1933): 10.

ing nature will provoke an antisemitism that will come to threaten your own existence and destroy the Danish Jews' position."[26]

The position of the old Jewish families was therefore clear. The new Jewish immigration from the East should not in the name of Zionism compromise the situation that Jewish immigrants before them had established. A Danish Jew could only have one fatherland and belong to one nation. It was, of course, Henriques argued, understandable that the tragic events in Germany had been traumatic for "the Jewish mentality" and made it react "in accordance with the concept that Mr. S. professes—the national Jew." Henriques could also appreciate this concept's legitimacy. When a family is driven from one country to another, "one is not rooted anywhere" and therefore "one clings to the religion and family tradition one has." But then one must also accept the consequence and admit that a national Jew of non-Danish origin was a guest in Denmark and must behave as a "well-brought-up guest does in a welcoming, hospitable home—and without making any demands."[27]

Several things were in conflict here. The Jewish community was not clear about its position on Zionism and the idea of a Jewish homeland. On the contrary, there was a schism between the "old" Jewish families who enjoyed emancipation and felt equal in Danish society, and the new Eastern European Jews who sympathized with Zionism. How much solidarity could one show for the settlements in Palestine? How far could Jewish community reach? To how great an extent could one publicly, in columns also read by non-Jews, show one's commitment to Zionism? How much should one warn about the increasingly dangerous refugee question? It was not easy for Marcus Melchior, who each month tried to maintain hope for "the Jews in the darkness that had fallen over Europe."[28]

Norwegian Women Stand by Their Men

Since the anti-Jewish process in Norway, once it started, was extremely compressed in time, and since the Norwegian police were also instrumental in this process together with the Norwegian bureaucracy, the possibilities for resistance were very limited. It is, therefore, not surprising that the literature on the persecution of Jews in Norway only sporadically touches the subject of

26. *Jødisk Familieblad* 6, no. 5 (January 1934): 12.
27. *Jødisk Familieblad* 9, no. 6 (February 1936): 3.
28. *Jødisk Familieblad* 6, no. 10 (June 1934): 3.

resistance and that resistance, as such, has not been a theme for any serious, in-depth research. The flight to Sweden is only described to a limited extent in the research and often only in connection with descriptions of the Swedish state's reception of the Norwegian refugees.[29] Thus, Mats Tangenstuen claims that the history of the Jews' flight to Sweden is largely absent in the Norwegian research literature primarily because, in the standard works about the flight, the focus is not on Jews but generally on Norwegians.[30] The aim of this section is therefore, first, to introduce the perspective of Jewish resistance in Norway, and then, through selected examples, point out the potential contribution of a social-historical approach to the Jewish community's reaction to the persecution of Jews in Norway.

Of the countries occupied by the German armed forces during the first three years of the war, Norway had the smallest Jewish population—2,100 at the time of the German invasion. The Jewish minority, representing only 0.8 per thousand of the total population, was in all respects a small religious community which, in its composition, resembled the communities in Denmark and Sweden in relation to its representation in business, its desire for assimilation, and the schism between the more established families and those newly arrived from Eastern Europe. The first Jews who came to Norway in the mid-1800s established themselves primarily in Oslo in the south and Trondheim in the north. The Norwegian Jewish community in 1890 comprised 214 persons, of which more than half lived in Oslo. The Jewish population increased progressively thereafter, reaching a total of 1,359 in 1930. When Hitler came to power in Germany, Norway was also confronted with the problem of German Jewish refugees and, as in Denmark and Sweden, there was concern that the many Jewish refugees would create a "Jewish colony." The number of refugees that could be received was therefore limited and, as described by Per Ole Johanssen, Jewish refugees were discriminated against when compared to political refugees.[31] A total of more than 500 Jewish refugees came to Norway, most at the end of the 1930s, and many eventually left the country again.[32]

In contrast to Denmark, however, the actions against Jews in Norway were more similar to those launched in the rest of German-controlled Western Eu-

29. See, for example, Geverts, *Ett främmande element i nationen.*

30. Mats Tangenstuen, "Også jødene kom for øvrig over grensen høsten 1942," in *Jødiske flyktninger fra Norge i Sverige 1940–1945* (Bergen: Hovedopgave i historie, Universitetet i Bergen, 2004), 6–9.

31. P. O. Johannsen *Oss selv nærmest. Norge og jødene 1914–1945* (Oslo: Gyldendal, 1984).

32. Einhart Lorenz, *Exile in Norwegen: Lebensbedienungen und Arbeit deutschsprachiger Flüchtline 1933–1943* (Baden-Baden: Nomos 1992).

rope. There were, nonetheless, special characteristics to the Norwegian process, which can help explain why resistance was not considered possible. First, the process in Norway, which lasted from the registration of Jews at the start of 1942 to the last deportation in February 1943, was very compressed—less than a year—much shorter than in other places. The registration was initiated far later than in other countries (in the Netherlands, Belgium, and France, for example). Finally, the Norwegian police and bureaucracy participated in carrying out the registration and J-stamping of the Jews' identity cards. The reaction in Norway to the registration of Jews was surprisingly modest. No one in the Norwegian public debate seemed to understand what this action could mean. When the executive order on registration of Jews was announced in Norwegian newspapers on January 20, 1942, only Jews reacted. Many questions arose: Should I comply with being registered? How should the order be understood? What if I do not feel specifically Jewish? What will the consequences be, if I do not comply?

Until recently, it was believed that everyone followed the order and was registered, but it has been shown that this was not actually the case. Some people sensed implicitly what it would lead to and therefore did not comply. This was at least the case among Jews who came to Norway as refugees, but we still do not know much about the more specific motives. Should this refusal, therefore, be considered resistance? Yes, because registration was a prerequisite for the annihilation of the Jews. It was an essential factor in the Final Solution. Others contacted the Quisling regime in order to evade the order, but most people obeyed and filled out the form and their passports were stamped with a J.[33] Few had imagined that registration was a prerequisite for the subsequent deportation to the camps. As mentioned earlier, those in the Jewish community hoped until the end of the war that persons deported in the fall of 1942 and in February 1943 would return home.

Another way to oppose the anti-Jewish policy was to flee. When the most extensive action against the Jews in Norway was launched on October 25, more than half of the 2,100 managed to flee, in many cases under very rigorous and often dangerous circumstances. It was exceptionally cold during that winter. In this respect, we can also characterize the Norwegian Jews' flight to Sweden as resistance. They opposed the anti-Jewish policies. What we know about this flight is still limited, as is our understanding of the choices made by individu-

33. Bjarte Bruland, "Jødeforfølgelserne i Norge" in *Danske tilstande, norske tilstande 1940–45*, ed. Hans Fredrik Dahl, Hans Kirchhoff, Joachim Lund, and Lars-Erik Vaale (København: Gyldendal, 2010), 227.

al refugees.[34] To flee through the woods in October with a baby in a knapsack must have involved considerations related to risks, advantages, and disadvantages. We know, for example, that in December 1942, Ethel Mesner fled with her three-month-old baby, but that it had taken her a long time to decide. Ethel's husband, Hermann, had been arrested and was in a prison camp; so she would not leave Norway. On the contrary, she visited Hermann as often as she could and also smuggled food and medicine to him in prison. Whether he received it is not known. Ethel had therefore postponed her flight. She would not desert her husband but would rather stay and take care of him and keep hoping.[35]

Can maintaining hope be considered resistance? Did the Norwegian women resist Nazism when they insisted on staying with their men? Or were they caught in a trap that kept them and their children near the interned men thereby preventing them from fleeing? We do not know. When a merchant named Israel Steinfeldt was arrested in March 1942 and sent to Falstad after increasing harassment by the Gestapo, his wife, like Ethel Mesner, chose to stay nearby. The family bond was stronger than the fear of death. The Steinfeldt family had even been offered a place on a ship out of German-occupied Norway to an allied harbor, but the fifty-year-old merchant declined the offer. He would not abandon his home and his business. Both Israel and his wife and their two children were murdered in Auschwitz.[36] Nor would the secretary for the Jewish congregation in Oslo, David Goldberg, leave his home. He continued to postpone his journey and was finally taken together with his wife and daughter. This passivity on the part of members of the Jewish community is later explained by Oskar Mendelsohn, himself a refugee, as lack of recognition among the Norwegian Jews of the seriousness of their situation. Most did not believe that the German occupation would last very long, convinced that Norway would be liberated within a few months.[37]

In spite of the late recognition of the character of the anti-Jewish policies,

---

34. Few scholarly publications have appeared on the Norwegian Jews' flight to Sweden. Most existing literature consists of biographical works by the refugees, such as Robert Levin and Mona Levin, *Med livet i hendene* (Oslo: J. W. Cappelens Forlag, 1983); Herman Sachnowitz and Arnold Jacoby, *Det angår også deg* (Oslo: J. W. Cappelens Forlag, 1990 (1976)); Robert Savosnick and Hans Melien, *Jeg vil ikke dø* (Oslo: J. W. Cappelens Forlag, 1986); and Jo Benkow, *Fra synagogen til løvebakken* (Oslo: Gyldendal Norsk Forlag, 1985).

35. Levin, *Flukten.*

36. Johannson, *Oss selv naermest,* 46–48.

37. Oskar Mendelsohn, *Jødedlne i Norge, historien om en minoritet,* bdn. 2 (Oslo: Universitetsforlaget, 1986). See also "The persecution of the Norwegian Jews in WWII" (Norges Hjemmefrontmuseum, 1991).

more than half of the Jews in Norway succeeded in fleeing, among them violinist Ernst Glaser, who refused to leave Norway in the middle of the concert season, relenting only after strong pressure from friends and colleagues. Historian and publisher Max Tau, whose friends had long urged him to flee, but who felt secure because his employer had promised help, if necessary, also refused to leave. Even after the Germans arrested two of his friends, Tau believed he was safe. It was only in the days after October 26 that he understood the seriousness of the situation and departed.[38]

Although disorganized at first, the flight of the Norwegian Jews gradually became systematic as time went by. One of the first networks to help Norwegian Jews to flee was started in the fall of 1941 by the Austrian Jew Wilhelm Rothkopf together with Eger Ollum. Ollum's sister was married to a Norwegian Jew, an airplane mechanic and trade union representative, who in March 1941 was arrested together with other trade unionists and died in a German camp, apparently inspiring Ollum to become involved in helping Jews escape. Through some contacts in the city of Flisa, close to the Swedish border, he arranged an escape route to Sweden and, together with Rothkopf, who operated from Oslo, they brought many Jews to safety. In January 1942, the network was discovered and its members shot by the police. Ollum fled to Sweden, while Rothkopf's fate is unknown.[39] There are other examples of refugee networks that helped Jews and others to escape, operating both before and during the deportations in the fall of 1942.[40] It is important to note that in Norway, unlike other countries, support actions helped people flee rather than go into hiding—only about forty Jews remained in Norway throughout the war.

The question of why everyone did not manage to flee and why so many waited until it was almost too late can only be answered through a closer analysis of the Norwegian Jewish community's character and relationship to Nazi Germany, before and after the German invasion in April 1940. This analysis also ought to include the special circumstances of the anti-Jewish process in Norway, where the Norwegian police and bureaucracy were involved both with the registration of Jews and the subsequent deportations. This involvement is significant in relation to how much resistance the anti-Jewish policy met when it was implemented. We know, for example, that the Jewish community observed

38. Ragnar Ulstein, *Jødar på flukt* (Oslo: Det Norske Samlaget, 1995), 117–37.

39. Ragnar Ulstein, "The Rescue of c.1000 Jews in Norway during Second World War," cited in Moore, *Survivors*, 75, note 19.

40. Bruland and Tangenstuen, "The Norwegian Holocaust," 587–604.

Yom Kippur in September 1942, but we do not know whether this observance was a conscious act of resistance.[41]

Swedish Ambivalence

Although today we conceive of neutral Sweden as providing an important haven for people fleeing from Nazism during World War II, the Swedish position in relation to both the Jewish refugees and Nazi Germany's anti-Jewish policy is not entirely clear. Many researchers have illuminated other aspects of Sweden's friendly attitude toward the Hitler regime in Germany, just as Sweden's restrictive policy toward Jews and its antisemitism have been described in greater detail in more recent research.[42] How the Swedish Jewish community reacted to Nazism has, however, received less focus, and the perspective of specific Jewish resistance is hardly considered. On the basis of the existing research, I therefore attempt to show how, to begin with, the Swedish Jewish community showed ambivalence towards the persecution of Jews. This ambivalence was due to the Jewish community's complex character and the schism between established Jewish families in Stockholm and Gothenburg, who believed in assimilation, and Jewish immigrants from the East, primarily from Russia, who came to Sweden at the start of the twentieth century and who maintained a stronger Jewish identity.

In the beginning of the 1930s, about 7,000 Jews lived in Sweden, mainly in Stockholm, Gothenburg and Malmø. The first Jewish immigrants came from Germany and Holland at the end of the 1700s. They were merchants who settled in the larger cities, and if they were not already well-off, they quickly became so and thus took their place as members of the Swedish bourgeoisie. Their goal was to assimilate and become part of Swedish cultural society. Why they had such a strong desire to assimilate can be traced to the Swedish monoculture in which it was difficult to thrive unless one belonged. As Ingrid Lomfors notes, Swedish nationalism and protectionism contributed to making the relatively

---

41. Ulstein, *Jødar på flukt*, 54.

42. Klas Åmark, *Att bo granne med ondskan. Sveriges förhållande till nazismen, Nazityskland och Förintelsen* (Stockholm: Albert Bonnier Förlag, 2011); Lars M. Andersson and Mathias Tydén, eds., *Sverige och Nazityskland: skuldfrågor och moraldebatt* (Stockholm: Dialogos, 2007); Lars M. Andersson, *En jude är en jude är en jude: representationer av "juden" i svensk skämtpress omkring 1900–1930* (Lund: Nordic Academic Press, 2000); Henrik Bachner, *"Judefrågan": debatt om antisemitismen i 1930-talets Sverige* (Stockholm: Atlantis, 2009); Svante Hansson, *Flykt och överlevnad. Flyktningverksamhet i Mosaiska Församligen i Stockholm 1933–1950* (Stockholm: Hillelförlaget, 2004).

small Swedish Jewish community play down its connection with other Jews, and the community, for example, changed its name from *Judiska Nationen* to *Mosaiska församlingen*—from "The Jewish Nation" to "The Mosaic Community." Through this name change, Swedish Jews could emphasize that although theirs was a religious community, it was part of the Swedish nation and not a nation in and of itself.[43]

With the immigration of a larger group of Jews from the East, the social and cultural patterns in the Swedish Jewish community changed. These immigrants had fled from pogroms in Tzarist Russia, Ukraine, and Lithuania, and they had a very clear understanding of what it meant to be persecuted. They could more directly relate to having to flee. Unlike the established Swedish community, they were poor and generally had deep roots in Orthodox Judaism. While some had given up their religious practice and traditions when they arrived in Sweden, others maintained them and established small Orthodox congregations throughout the country. In contrast to the established Jewish communities in Stockholm and Gothenburg, which gathered in large synagogues, these immigrants met in small, less ostentatious facilities. Some of the Eastern European Jews were also supporters of the Zionist movement; their Jewishness therefore encompassed more than a simple affiliation with a religious congregation. As Lomfors points out, they identified with a more extensive Jewish community.[44]

There was thus a great difference between being a Swedish Jew belonging to a national religious community, and being a newly arrived Eastern European Jew with stronger bonds to Judaism. The fundamental difference in approach to being a Jew not only contributed to creating a division in the Swedish Jewish community, but it also influenced the way in which people reacted to Nazism. For while the old Jewish community was more reserved and supported the restrictive Swedish policy toward Jewish refugees from Germany, the Eastern European Jews basically expressed more solidarity with their fellow Jews. A clear example of this division emerges from an exchange of letters in 1935 between two prominent Swedish Jewish historians, Hugo Valentin and Eli Hekscher, concerning the refugee question and to what extent a Jew had a special obligation to help other Jews. Valentin represented the Eastern European Jewish im-

43. Ingrid Lomfors, *Förlorad barndom, återvunnet liv. De judiska flyktningbarnen från Nazityskland* (Gøteborg: Historiska Institutionen, Göteborgs Universitet, 1996), 80–81. See also Hugo Valentin, *Judarna i Sverige* (Stockholm: P. A. Norstedt,1964); Gunnar Broberg, Harald Runblom, and MattiasTyden, *Judiskt liv i Norden* (Uppsala: Acta Universitatis Upsaliensis, 1988).

44. Lomfors, *Förlorad barndom,*79–88.

migrant group, while Hekscher belonged to the established Jewish community, which supported assimilation.

For Valentin, it was clear that one was obliged to be loyal to the persecuted Jews in Germany, while Hekscher saw no reason to show any special Jewish solidarity. Writing to Valentin, Hekscher indicated that his commitment to others was not because they were Jews. For him, it was because they were old friends, colleagues from his history studies and the university. Yes, even political allies were closer to him "than a German, Russian, Polish or Romanian Jew."[45]

The same form of ambiguity can be seen in the efforts the Jewish community in Stockholm made to bring German refugee children to Sweden temporarily. Sweden functioned in the 1930s as a transit country for refugees who intended to move on, primarily to the United States. For the Jewish community, it was important not to risk the status it had achieved in Swedish society. Therefore, it supported the Swedish government's restrictive immigration policy, while it also tried to help as best it could. Thus, antisemitism in Germany also interfered with internal Swedish Jewish relations and confronted the Jewish community with a series of challenges, which it was not initially prepared to meet. First and foremost, a mental barrier had to be broken in order to show solidarity and help Jews outside Sweden. Then, there was the purely practical organization and fund raising connected with the aid effort. Precisely because the Eastern European Jews had also settled outside the larger cities, the Jewish population was spread out; there was no center where the Jewish effort could be coordinated.

In spite of the restrictive refugee policy, it was possible to bring several hundred Jewish children into the country. It was here that the Jewish community in Stockholm played a decisive role. The congregation gave economic and practical guarantees for refugee children and caused an increase in the quota for the number of Jewish children that could enter Sweden from Germany. Head Rabbi Marcus Ehrenpreis, together with the community's spokesman, Gunnar Josephsen, paid a visit to the Swedish foreign minister, Richard Sandler, immediately after Kristallnacht in 1938, with the aim of increasing the so-called children's quota. A total of 500 Jewish children came to Sweden before the war—not many, especially compared to the 70,000 or so Finnish refugee children who came to Sweden during the war. With the outbreak of the war, it was no longer possible to bring more from Germany. The 500 Jewish refugee children

45. Letter from Eli Hekscher to Hugo Valentin, 22 March 1935, reprinted in Gregorz Flakierski, "Rötter: Den judiska frågan i brevväxlingen mellan Hugo Valentin och Eli Hecksher," *Historisk Tidsskrift* (1982:2): 181. Cited here in Lomfors, *Förlorad barndom*, 84.

who did go to Sweden did so on the condition that the Swedish Jewish community would guarantee their care and maintenance.

In her investigation of refugee children in Sweden, Ingrid Lomfors describes how the first to show interest in these children were Jewish families and others who had acquaintances and relatives in Germany.[46] Many were themselves German refugees or emigrants who could therefore directly relate to the German Jews' fate. The work with the Jewish refugee children was carried out in an interaction between the Jewish congregation in Stockholm, the Swedish authorities, and both Jewish and non-Jewish volunteers. The community arranged for all Swedish Jewish homes to be asked to take care of a refugee child. Rabbi Ehrenpreis encouraged people to open their doors to these children.[47] Valentin and other writers in *Judisk Krönika* asked people to show their solidarity.[48]

Posterity's judgment of the Jewish congregation's efforts has nevertheless been harsh.[49] The community is criticized for not taking a position and for initially speaking out directly against receiving German Jewish refugees. The community only used its influence with the authorities in relation to quotas for transit refugees and refugee children. It was not intended that the Jewish refugees should stay in Sweden, and therefore the community's efforts were consistent with Swedish refugee policy which, throughout the 1930s, became increasingly restrictive.

The same attitude also applies to the *Hechaluz* movement, which fitted well into this pattern and which, from the end of the 1930s onward, became an important element in Swedish refugee policy. *Hechaluz* came to Sweden through veterinarian Emil Glück, who singlehandedly arranged for ten agricultural students to come to Sweden. As described by Malin Thor, Glück continued to be the front figure, but the community in Stockholm would not allow him to choose the students alone; therefore, they joined the effort and also supported the movement financially.[50] By 1937, 170 German Jews had come to Sweden as agricultural students; of these, twenty later went to Palestine and forty-two to

---

46. Lomfors, *Förlorad barndom*.

47. *Judisk Krönika*: 1939:8, 118; quoted here in Lomfors, *Förlorad barndom*, 98.

48. *Judisk Krönika*: 1939:1, 3, 5, 8.

49. Hansson, *Flykt och överlevnad*; Åmark, *Att bo granne med ondskan*. Pontus Rudberg makes a more positive judgment of the efforts made by the Jewish community in Stockholm to help German Jewish refugees. See his "Restriktivitet eller generositet? Flyktingverksamhet inom Stockholms mosaiska församling och hjälpkommittén för Tysklands judar 1938–1940" in *En problematisk relation?* ed. Andersson and Geverts, 209–26.

50. Malin Thor, *Hechaluz—en rörelse i tid och rum. Tysk-judiska ungdomars exil i Sverige 1933–1943* (Göteborg: Växjö University Press, 2005).

other countries. After Kristallnacht, Swedish authorities agreed to increase the quota to 300. A total of 490 German Jews went to Sweden as agricultural students; most were men between eighteen and thirty-five years of age. Women came primarily as the men's partners. Of the 490 agricultural students, 147 emigrated to Palestine and 106 to other countries; 238 remained in Sweden and later made their homes there. At the same time, there was a shift inside the Swedish Jewish community as awareness of the magnitude of the Nazi crime against European Jewry increased. Toward the end of the war, there was no longer any doubt about helping. The readiness to contribute increased, as did the awareness about what a haven Sweden actually had become for Jews who fled. This shift was not least stimulated first by the Norwegian Jews' flight to Sweden in 1942 and then the Danish Jews' flight in October 1943, when Nordic fellowship also came into play as an argument for involvement. That solidarity with other Nordic people played a role can be seen, for example, in a pamphlet issued by *Judisk Tidsskrift* following the action against the Norwegian Jews in October 1942. Entitled *Nordic Voices against Persecution of the Jews and Violence*, this pamphlet was sold for one Swedish crown and the profit went to the "Help for Europe's Jews" fund.

It was precisely this fact—that Nordic Jews had been subjected to Nazi persecution—that Kvist Geverts suggests was key in the Swedish state's willingness to receive refugees from Norway, Denmark, and Finland.[51] Thus, refugee aid in Sweden increased after a slow start to a relatively intensive effort in 1939. In this year alone, the organized refugee aid amounted to at least 942,000 SEK, of which Jewish aid organizations had collected almost half. At the end of the war, the Jewish community's economic contribution to survivors from concentration camps increased markedly to almost twice as much as during the war.

If we were to evaluate the Swedish Jewish community's efforts on behalf of other Jews, it is obvious that it depended greatly on, first of all, the Swedish state's general policy toward Nazi Germany. But it must also be stated that the internal disagreements among Swedish Jews in relation to Jewish identity and the wish for assimilation also influenced the response to Nazi persecution of the Jews. To be sure, individual efforts were important, as in the case of Emil Glück and the *Hechaluz* movement in Sweden, or the Latvian refugee, Gillel Storch, who came to Sweden in 1940, established the Swedish branch of the World Jewish Congress, and contributed to the effort to send food packages to

51. Geverts, *Ett främmande element I nationem*, 183–210.

Jewish prisoners in concentration camps.[52] We must also include Hugo Valentin's efforts to maintain Jewish commitment in the Swedish Jewish community, even though representatives of the Jewish community in Stockholm opposed him, and Daniel Brick, the secretary of the Swedish Zionist Association, who, with photographer Anne Riwkin-Brick, held open house for the Jewish refugees in their apartment in Stockholm and thereby provided a place for Jews to gather where they felt at home.

A deeper investigation of the Swedish Jewish community's reaction to Nazism and its resistance in the form of aid to Jews outside Sweden, as well as through maintaining its Jewish identity under difficult circumstances, would provide greater insight into not only how the Swedish Jewish community reacted, but also how its wartime experience raised its consciousness about what it meant to be Jewish. Such an analysis should also examine how Swedish Jewish intellectuals, who participated in the public debate at the time, reacted to Nazism and its anti-Jewish policies.

Between Accommodation and Awareness.

A general evaluation of Jewish resistance in Scandinavia must, as described above, take as its point of departure the circumstances of the Danish, Norwegian, and Swedish Jewish communities before and during the war. Resistance was, in many cases, not clearly Jewish or motivated by specifically Jewish concerns, but was rather a consequence of existing circumstances. In both the Danish and Swedish cases, the schism between established Jewish families and the newly arrived Eastern European Jews played a role, especially at first, in the way people reacted to the persecution of the Jews in Germany. To a great extent, Jewish involvement in the refugee question was based on the condition that German Jews were not to seek permanent residence in Sweden but rather travel on to either the United States or Palestine. Nevertheless, efforts were made to bring German Jewish children and youths out of Germany, just as help was given to the German refugees who fled to the Scandinavian countries in the 1930s.

Helping people fleeing Nazism was a cause that won broad support and was not exclusively dependent on Jewish solidarity. A well-known dimension of the Danish effort to bring German scientists out of Germany was the initiative of

52. Åmark, *Att bo granne med ondskan*, 534.

Niels and Harald Bohr, as described in the Bohr biography by Abraham Pais, *Niels Bohr's Times*. The Bohr brothers came from a well-known Danish Jewish family but, like many Jews in the 1930s, they had no special affiliation with Judaism.[53] When Hitler assumed power in Germany, both Niels and Harald Bohr became active in the Committee to Aid Intellectuals. They were both members of the committee's board and managed, with the support of, among others, the Rockefeller Foundation and the Rask-Ørsted Fund, to create opportunities for German scientists in Denmark. Niels Bohr helped many German physicists, including Guido Bech, Felix Blox, Otto Frisch, Hilde Levi, George Placzek, Eugene Rabinowitch, Stefan Rozental, Erich Schneider, Edward Teller, Arthur von Hippel, and Victory Weiss-Kopf to come to Denmark, where all except Levi og Rozenthal stayed for a short time as guest researchers and guest professors. Harald Bohr helped many German mathematicians, including Werner Fenchel, who came to Copenhagen during the summer of 1933 and became an associate professor at Denmark's Technical University in 1938. Fenchel fled to Sweden in 1943.[54] Although it is possible that their aid work was rooted in solidarity with these scientists as Jews, it is more likely that the Bohrs were inspired by a feeling of kinship with fellow students and scientists, especially since not all of them had Jewish backgrounds. The Bohr family, like so many other secular Danish Jews, had to flee to Sweden in the fall of 1943.

How do we then evaluate the extent of the various Scandinavian Jewish communities' engagement in the cause of persecuted Jews? It can be concluded that the loyalty of Swedish Jews toward other Jews increased toward the end of the war, and that the mass elimination of European Jewry generally led to a deepening of Jewish identity within the Jewish community. We can only speculate whether this increased loyalty was related to the position generally assigned to Sweden immediately after the war as a nation that sheltered refugees and defended human rights and democracy. But there was a shift within the Swedish Jewish community as a result of the war. On the other hand, as a consequence of their time as refugees in Sweden, many Danish Jews decided to dissociate themselves from the Jewish community in Denmark when they returned home. According to Marcus Melchior, their rejection of Judaism completed the process that Goebbels and others had started by delivering a hard

53. Abraham Pais, *Niels Bohr's Times: In Physics, Philosophy, and Polity* (Oxford: Clarendon Press, 1991), 39.

54. Steffen Steffensen, *På flugt fra nazismen. Tysksprogede emigranter i Danmark efter 1933* (København: C. A. Reitzels Forlag, 1986).

blow to the Jewish community. The fate of the Norwegian Jews was quite different in this respect. Unlike in Denmark, the property of Norwegian Jews was confiscated after they were deported or had fled, leaving the Norwegian Jewish community weakened after liberation.[55] Not everyone wished to return to Norway after living in Sweden. This left the Norwegian Jewish community in 1946 with only 559 members. Postwar efforts to come to grips with the anti-Jewish process lasted for several decades. It was only in the 1990s that the Norwegian Jews could feel somewhat compensated for the losses and suffering that the anti-Jewish process in Norway had caused.

55. For more on the restitution issue in Norway, see the report, NOU 1997:22, *Inndragning av jødisk eiendom i Norgen under den 2. verdenskrig* (Oslo: Statens Forvaltningstjeneste, Statens Trykning, 1997).

Tuvia Friling

11   Organizing Jewish Resistance

The Decision-Making and Executive Array in Yishuv
Rescue Operations during the Holocaust

The Negative Stereotype and Its Roots

It took only until the early 1950s before the debate over what the Yishuv, and
its leadership, did to rescue European Jews from the Holocaust overstepped
the boundaries of a historical debate rooted in a certain context and circumstances; with growing celerity, the debate became an instrument in the ideological struggle for the shaping of Israel's image. Both the general public and
scholars debated the extent of the "purity" of the Zionist revolution, how the
revolution was consummated in practice, and the degree of Israel's legitimacy.[1]

1. Works by people and activists at the time the events took place as they appear in the Department of Oral Documentation, the Ben-Gurion Heritage Institute Archives (hereafter: ABG); Protocols
of the Mapai Secretariat, Mapai Secretariat Labor Party Archives (hereafter: LPA); Protocols of the
Secretariat of the Histadrut Action Committee, Israel Labor Movement Archives at the Lavon Institute (hereafter: ILMAL); and in the daily newspapers. The second source: newspapers, intellectuals,
and research scholars. See Tom Segev, *The Seventh Million: The Israelis and the Holocaust* (New York:
Hill and Wang, 1993); Shabtai Beit Zvi, *Post-Ugandian Zionism in the Crucible of the Holocaust* (Tel
Aviv: Bronfman, 1977) (Hebrew); Yigal Elam, in an interview with Yona Hadari Ramage, "Another
Cup of Water on the Burning Town," *Ha'aretz* (daily newspaper), October 3, 1986; Yigal Elam, *An In-
troduction to Zionist History* (Jerusalem: Lewin-Epstein, 1972) (Hebrew); M. Vazelman, *Sign of Cain:
On the Zionist Movement and the Jewish Agency's Omissions during the Holocaust, 1939–1945*, ed. Me-
nachem Gerlik (Tel Aviv, n.p., n.d) (Hebrew); Roman Frister, *Without Compromise* (Tel Aviv: Zmora
Bitan, 1987) (Hebrew); Michael Dov Weissmandel, *From the Boundary: Memories from 1942–1945* (Jerusalem: published by the author's sons, 1960) (Hebrew); Avraham Fox, *I Called and There Was No
Answer: Weissmandel Cry during the Holocaust* (Jerusalem: self-published, 1983) (Hebrew); Moshe
Shonfeld, ed., *Teheran Children Accuse: Facts and Documents* (Beni-Brak: n.p., 1971) (Hebrew); Shalom Shalmon, *The Crimes of Zionism during the Destruction of the Exile*, (Jerusalem: self-published,

245

Intertwined in this debate are two elements of crucial importance: the status of the leaders whom the Yishuv tasked with the special challenge of rescuing European Jewry and the nature of the professional and executive echelon reserved for this cause.

Both elements derive their centrality from various factors, one of which is that the conventional wisdom about them in the research and public discourses gave rise to a negative stereotype: the idea that the Yishuv was immersed in its own needs and interests, that is, settlement, defense, and the building of power. Since rescue was neither a necessity nor an important interest for the Yishuv, the argument goes, it became the bailiwick of second-rate leaders and junior executives, while those graced with audacity, seniority, and skills busied themselves with other causes and duties.[2] Bundled with this allegation are judgments about the nature of those involved and the attribution of Palestino-centric considerations to the Yishuv and its leadership during the Holocaust.

I will investigate those who made the main decisions about rescue during World War II, track the executive echelon that dealt with attempts to rescue Jews in Europe, and attempt to assess the quality and origin of the foregoing statements about the type of people whom the Yishuv assigned to rescue operations.

The Yishuv and the "Rules of the Game" on the Eve of and during World War II

The Yishuv—the organized Jewish community in pre-Israel Palestine—during World War II was small, highly heterogeneous in its sociopolitical profile and, from the moment the annihilation was officially reported, thrust into a state of great perplexity. From its standpoint and that of others, the internalization of what was happening in Europe, and the correct implications of those events, posed an unprecedented challenge. According to data and estimates

1990) (Hebrew). For other expressions in this spirit, see Shabtai Teveth, "The Black Hole," *Alpayim* 10 (1994): 111–95 (Hebrew). More, in a similar vein: Jim Allen, *Perdition: A Play in Two Acts* (London: Ithaca Press, 1987); Binyamin Harshav (Harshovsky), in a poem published under his literary pseudonym, "Gabi Daniel"; Moshe Zimmermann, introduction to "Fifty Years Later: The Holocaust Influence on Cinema and Culture in Israel," manuscript supplied by the author (Hebrew). The Scholars: Mordechai Friedman, *The Public Political Response of the American Jewry to the Holocaust* (dissertation, Tel Aviv University, 1985) (Hebrew); Hava Wagman Eshkoli, "The Palestine Jewish Leadership's Stand on Rescue of Europe's Jews," *Yalkut Moreshet* 24 (October 1977): 87–116 (Hebrew); Amos Elon in *Timetable* (Garden City, N.Y.: Doubleday, 1980).

2. Beit Zvi, *Post-Ugandian Zionism*, 103–05,130,143. Segev, *The Seventh Million*, 82, 83, 86, 89, 92, 95.

from the Jewish Agency statistics department, there were around 485,000 Jews in Palestine at the end of 1942; 80 percent of them were under the age of forty-four. It was a very small Yishuv by all accounts.

The Yishuv's structure at this time was intricate, complex, and based almost entirely on voluntarism. It had a set of self-rule institutions, all operating by dint of the trust that the public invested in its elected officials, since they lacked the means of enforcement that one ordinarily associates with statehood. The broadest of these institutions was Knesset Israel, which represented 95 percent of the Yishuv, including the Revisionists but excluding Agudath Israel.

Parallel to Knesset Israel was the World Zionist Organization, an entity common to the Zionist parties in Palestine and the Zionist movement in the Diaspora, with the exception of the Revisionist Party, which had seceded from it in 1935. Once the Jewish Agency was established in 1929, allowing non-Zionist personalities connected with the National Home to join the Executive alongside Zionists, the Zionist Executive began to answer to an additional name: "the Jewish Agency Executive."

The Zionist organization tasked the Executive with building and strengthening the National Home. Accordingly, the Executive dealt with organizing immigration—and, as an outgrowth of this function, with Zionist activity in the Diaspora. The executive also considered itself the representative of Zionists in Palestine and the Diaspora vis-à-vis the Mandate government, H.M. Government, and the Soviet Union and the United States.

The Executive was a coalition creature; its various departments, functions, and power centers were divided among its constituent political parties. Needless to say, its main functions remained in the hands of the Yishuv's largest and strongest party, Mapai (Palestine Workers Party). The Executive was chaired by David Ben-Gurion; Moshe Sharett headed the political department, and Eliezer Kaplan minded the treasury and headed the finance department. Yitzhak Gruenbaum (General Zionists A) headed the labor department.

The Executive also had offices in Britain and the United States. The division of functions and powers between them was not totally clear. Once the "Rescue Committee" was up and running, it metamorphosed into a large and cumbersome body. Thus, yet another contentious player was thrust into the parallelogram of forces that operated in the Yishuv—this time directly into rescue affairs.[3]

---

3. For details on the Rescue Committee, see Tuvia Friling, *Arrows in the Dark* (Madison, Wis.: University of Wisconsin Press, 2005), 1:125–35; Dina Porat, *The Blue and the Yellow Stars of David*

The Yishuv's severe heterogeneity in its political parties and movements recurred in other senses: various complexions of nonreligious and religious Jews, town dwellers and rural settlers, older immigrants and recent immigrants; Sefardim and the Ashkenazi majority, and some forty *landsmanshaften* (immigrant organizations based on areas of origin), each looking out for its own people—all operating under self-rule institutions that had no powers of coercion save social suasion. This set of circumstances sheds much light on the focal issue of our question: the ability to execute and lead, leadership and the imposition of leadership, among those at the top of this problematic and contested hierarchy.

At least two additional organizations deserve mention here: the World Jewish Congress and the American Jewish Joint Distribution Committee (JDC). Both figure importantly in our discussion; both maintained diverse relations with the Jewish Agency in matters of relief and rescue; both were paternalistic and extra-Yishuvic bodies not subject to the Executive's authority. Unlike the World Jewish Congress, only six or seven years old when relief and rescue became part of the Jewish people's agenda in its full gravity, the JDC, an American-Jewish philanthropic organization, had amassed much experience before World War II. Personalities such as Paul Baerwald, chairman of JDC at the time, Joseph (Joe) Schwartz, director of JDC-Europe, and Dr. J. L. Magnes, president of the Hebrew University and head of JDC's Jerusalem office, dealt with various aspects of relief and rescue in several centers of activity—New York, Lisbon, Geneva and Stockholm, Jerusalem and Istanbul. Sometimes they were in close and harmonious cooperation with the heads and external functions of the Executive; at other times there was struggle and tension.[4]

Although Ben-Gurion's status as the main power broker in the Zionist movement solidified steadily during this time, the Ben-Gurion of the World War II years was not yet the much more powerful Ben-Gurion of the 1950s. Ignoring this distinction, we would obtain a distorted picture. Instead, we must probe Ben-Gurion's actions and maneuverings as corollaries of his actual power at the time of events.

Another point to bear in mind is this: Palestine was governed under the British Mandate, born at the end of World War I. The nature of the mandatory regime hinged on British policy at large and the way the local regime's factotums

---

(Cambridge, Mass.: Harvard University Press, 1990), 64–71; Arye Morgenstern, "The Rescue Committee's Action During 1943–1945," *Yalkut Moreshet* 13 (June 1971): 60–103 (Hebrew).

4. Regarding the cooperation between the JAE and the JDC, see Friling, *Arrows in the Dark*, 2:151–63, 185, 207.

and agents, foremost the high commissioner, implemented it. During most of the period at issue here (1938–1944), the high commissioner was Sir Harold Alfred MacMichael, an official noted for his rigid and hostile attitude toward the Yishuv and his strict application of the 1939 White Paper policy. His approach, stringent to begin with, toughened even more due to the introduction of emergency regulations when the war broke out.

The brunt of the tension and the collision between the Yishuv leadership and the Mandate authorities during World War II centered on three flashpoints: official restrictions on Jewish land purchases, the deportation policy that the British applied against clandestine immigration ships that managed to break through the blockade and reach the shores of Palestine, and the hunt for secret Haganah arms depots. Once the report on the annihilation of European Jewry was officially published, the closure of Palestine to refugees took on an additional portent: it doomed those who remained in Europe to annihilation.

To understand how the Yishuv leadership pursued rescue during the Holocaust, we should recall that apart from the comprehensive British policy in the Middle East and Palestine, four additional comprehensive policies related to the prosecution of the war had a direct if not decisive impact on the Yishuv's rescue efforts and the fate of the Jewish people. All four were associated with the Allies and, among them, Britain as a central player in the struggle against the Nazis. First, the war effort must focus on defeating Hitler. Exponents of this policy cited it to explain why forces and resources were not being "scattered" and allocated for rescue attempts. Second, the war must end with Germany's unconditional surrender; this made any attempt to negotiate with the enemy, overt or covert, illegal if not treasonous. Third, Britain refused to admit that the Jews had a unique fate in this war. Hence it opposed special action to rescue Jews. Fourth, transfers of money to the occupied territories must not be allowed.

This meant that any large rescue action would clash with the Allies' overt and covert policies and, accordingly, had to be concealed from them. Since large rescue operations entailed Allied political, financial, and logistical support no matter what, it would be naïve if not impossible to assume that such things could be hidden from them. The logic of the growth and, in part, the serpentine modus operandi of the "parallel system" fed on the duality and the internal contradiction that this reality created.

All plans involving the rescue of large numbers of Jews, by their very nature, had to be masked from most of the population in Palestine and elsewhere for at least two additional reasons. The first concerned the policy of Germany and its satellites. Even if some elites among them were willing, at certain stages of the war, to negotiate the liberation of Jews or turn a blind eye to their rescue, no one could guarantee that everyone involved in such a *démarche* would participate in this policy. The second relates to the Palestinian Arabs' attitude toward the possibility of large-scale Jewish immigration from Europe.[5]

The Yishuv Rescue and Aid Operations during World War II

An overview of the Yishuv's rescue actions during World War II shows that, from late November 1942, when the systematic annihilation of Jews in Europe was officially disclosed, the Yishuv pursued relief and rescue along three main avenues:

(1) "Grand rescue" or "grand projects"—actions meant to rescue Jews by extricating them from the occupied areas. This aggregate included programs for the rescue of children and at least three ransom schemes: the Transnistria Plan, the Slovakia Plan (and its derivative, the Europa Plan), and the "goods for blood" proposal, delivered from Hungary by Joel Brand.

(2) "Small rescue" or "small projects"—sundry efforts geared mainly to helping Jews survive the war in the occupied areas: sending money, dispatching parcels of food, clothing, medicines, and forged papers, and arranging "excursions"—smuggling Jews from one dangerous place to another less dangerous place.

(3) Two additional levels of action in the Yishuv—first, more than 30,000 young men and women enlisted in the British army.[6] Second, the Yishuv developed a broad web of secret partnership between its paramilitary operational and intelligence agencies and various players in the British and American intelligence services, military and civilian alike. Partnership for diverse operations emanated from their headquarters and from branches in Jerusalem, Cairo, London, Washington, Ankara, Istanbul, and also Bari, Italy, in late 1944. This cooperation underlay the actions that gave rise to the "parachutists plan," which was but a small element in the overall array of Yishuv attempts to set this furtive cooperation on solid ground.

5. Regarding the mufti, Mohamad Haj Amin Al-Husseini, see Friling, *Arrows in the Dark*, 1:20. See also Yoav Gelber, *Growing a Fleur-de-Lis: The Intelligence Services of the Jewish Yishuv in Palestine 1918–1947* (Tel Aviv: Ministry of Defense, 1992), 278–79 (Hebrew).

6. Yoav Gelber, *The Emergence of a Jewish Army* (Jerusalem: Yad Yitzhak Ben-Zvi, 1986), 3–5 (Hebrew); Friling, *Arrows in the Dark*, 2:200.

Figure 11-1. The Yishuv Rescue and Aid Operations

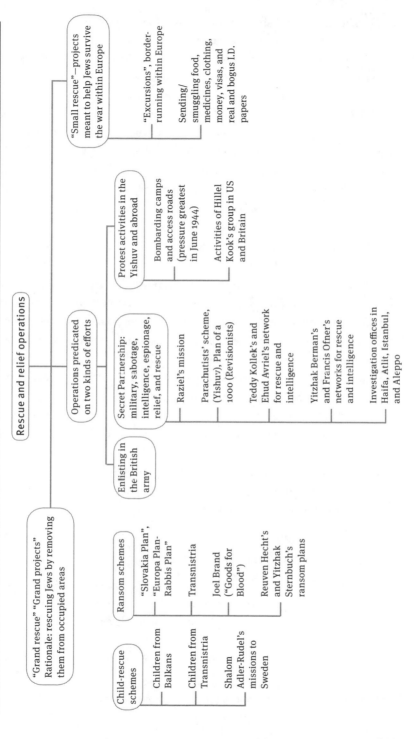

251

At what echelon of Yishuv officialdom was the range of rescue attempts masterminded? Who managed the attempts? Where were the decisions about them made? Who determined where they stood on the Yishuv's scale of priorities? Along what channels were they commanded, supervised, and controlled? Putting the cart before the horse, the answer lies in what is described below as the "parallel system" and the "undeclared triumvirate" at the special operations desk—another name that we made up—at the Jewish Agency political department, and in those associated with it. The members of this leading triumvirate were David Ben-Gurion, Eliezer Kaplan, and Moshe Shertok or Sharett (hereafter: Sharett). It availed itself of an operational body staffed by Reuven (Shiloah) Zaslani, Teddy Kollek, Eliahu Epstein (Elath), Ehud Avriel, and others at the political department, accompanied by additional rescue emissaries and operatives from other organizations and movements: Shaul Meirov (Avigur), Eliyahu Golomb and Zvi Schechter (Yehieli), Ze'ev Schind, Venja Pomeranz (Ze'ev Hadari, representing Hakibbutz Hameuhad movement), Menachem Bader (representing Hakibbutz Ha'artsi or Hashomer Hatza'ir), and others. The triumvirate not only made the decisions and provided the supervision and management; it also gave the operational body public, political, and moral backing for its actions—operations that by nature had to take place far from the eyes of most of the public and, quite often, from those of its elected representatives. That included contacts and relations with "the devil," as the Nazis and their agents were called in the jargon of the time. The operations of this surreptitious matrix usually took place under a system that compartmentalized out a lengthy series of players in the Yishuv—hence a "parallel system," at once formal and informal, that made it possible to engage in various kinds of clandestine and complex rescue operations in a young, fragmented Yishuv that had neither adequate operational and political experience nor a tradition of operational discipline.

Lightning Rod: Establishing the Rescue Committee

In the meantime, broad public pressure was being applied at the internal Yishuv level—directly and via various representatives—to open the ranks of the "club" of future rescue activists to the widest possible membership.[7] Therefore,

7. On the development of the Rescue Committee, see: Morgenstern, "The Rescue Committee's Action During 1943–1945"; Porat, *The Blue and the Yellow Stars of David*, 64–71; Eshkoli-Wagman, "The Palestine Jewish Leadership's Stand on the Rescue of Europe's Jews," 87–116 (Hebrew). About the Committee of Four, see Morgenstern, "The Rescue Committee's Action," 61–62; Chaim Barlas,

the wholesale murder operation underway in Europe posed a fateful challenge to the self-awareness of Zionism, particularly among the Zionists who headed the Yishuv. From this perspective, the Yishuv saw as its main function the preparation of the requisite infrastructure for the accommodation of a good portion of the Jewish people in Palestine.

The Yishuv leadership also understood the importance of rescue from the additional perspective of political power. The leadership of a national movement that asserts the status of leadership over all members of the nation undermines the very justification of its existence—fails the supreme test—if it abandons the nation to its fate and takes no part in actions to save it in its direst hour. Willful abandonment, then, amounted to personal and public suicide. Thus, as they awakened to the disaster and its meanings, the various movements, parties, bodies, and organizations began to ask how they should deploy for relief and rescue. The result was wrestling, bargaining, and within a short time, the establishment of an entity pretentiously titled the "Rescue Committee." The Committee started out with four or five members, but within a few days it had twelve members, and within two months or so—under the pressure of those wishing to join it—it ballooned into a cumbersome thing composed of some sixty members.[8] It was a "parliament" in the derisive judgment of the time.

Historical analogies always blur the uniqueness of the objects of comparison. Their use, however, may demonstrate that the outcome of the Rescue Committee's formation, in which the true will of the public may yield a product that clashes with the same public's true interest, was not an invention of the Yishuv.[9] Therefore, the Rescue Committee could not serve as the central agency for rescue. Even its chairman, Yitzhak Gruenbaum of the General Zionists A Party, could not help it along.[10] For one thing, Gruenbaum had no real political

---

Rescue during the Holocaust (Tel Aviv: Hakibbutz Hameuhad, 1975), 96 (Hebrew). See too National Council Executive, November 23, 1942, Central Zionist Archives (hereafter: CZA) and daily press.

8. The Committee of Four was established soon after the war began and consisted of Yitzhak Gruenbaum, Eliyahu Dobkin, Moshe Shapira, and Emil Schmork. Later on Dr. Dov Joseph, the political department secretary, joined it, possibly to answer two needs: assisting the committee in approaching governments and international organizations and in dealing with the Mandat government; putting the aid and rescue activities under the inspection of the professional and experienced body of the JAE. The name of the committee changed to The Action Committee, meaning acting for the sake of the Jews in occupied Europe. See: Friling, *Arrows in the Dark*, 1:125–27, and compare with Porat, *The Blue and the Yellow Stars of David*, 64–68.

9. About the "parliament," see Porat, *The Blue and the Yellow Stars of David*, 68; Friling, *Arrows in the Dark*, 1:130–32.

10. The results of the twenty-first Zionist Congress election held in August 1939, the last before the war, reflected the party's size. The General Zionists A received 30 percent in the Diaspora and 6 percent in Palestine, and General Zionists B received 10 and 8 percent respectively.

clout in the Yishuv at the time. However, there were at least three additional reasons.

The Mossad le-Aliyah Bet, the Haganah and its spinoffs, Youth Aliyah, the Jewish Agency immigration department, and the people at the Jewish Agency political department were the natural addresses for such operations. The second reason related to the process of the Committee's rapid growth. Amid the atmosphere of emotional mobilization and the problematic sociopolitical structure of the Yishuv, no leader could withstand public pressure from so many sides to act for the rescue of "their" Jews, their home, their *shtetl*, their organization. Paralysis flowed not from unwillingness to rescue or willingness to evade rescue but from the opposite. The third reason relates to the nature of the coalition that took shape in the Committee. Here, too, the torrent did not wash away the heavy residues that affected majority-minority relations between the center and the Revisionists on one extreme and the Agudath Israel and Po'alei Agudath Israel delegates on the other. Later, the major and minor "Saisons" would come about.[11] These were only an external manifestation of the hard feelings and suspicions that boiled and roiled within this entity.

Furthermore, neither side was innocent of the feeling that if rescue actually succeeded, it would mean—insofar as it happened in large numbers—an influx of new "soldiers" for the ranks of the various parties sparring over the nature and control of the formative entity in Palestine following the resolutions of the Biltmore Convention—the "Jerusalem Program."[12] Thus, the Rescue Committee was chaired by a leader whose future was already behind him; furthermore, it was too awkward and poorly structured to carry out any complex and secret operation. Even beyond these factors, however, the Committee's superficiality and operational flaccidity were reflected in three additional ways.

First, the Committee was not allowed to set its budget without the approval of Eliezer Kaplan, treasurer of the Executive and a member of the "triumvirate." Grievances about the Committee's poor budgetary condition and its dependency on the Executive beset the panel throughout its lifetime.[13] Second, perhaps

11. "The Saison," the hunting season, was the name given to the Haganah's suppression of the IZL's uprising against the government of the British Mandate in Palestine. The Haganah collaborated with the British authorities and handed people over. The "Little Saison" refers to actions committed in the spring and summer of 1947, meant to sabotage the IZL and Lehi insurgencies against the British.

12. On the Biltmore Convention, see Friling, *Arrows in the Dark*, 1:41, 44, 53, 63–64, 197–98; 2:198. Compare Shabtai Teveth, *The Road to May* (Tel Aviv: Ministry of Defense, 1986), 208–09 (Hebrew).

13. On grievances about the Committee's poor budgetary condition, see Yehuda Suprasky, National Council Executive, February 15, 1943; Moshe Ichilov, ibid., January 17, 1944; Gruenbaum, JAE, February 7, 1943 and April 4, 1943; Joseph Klarman, the Rescue Committee, March 4, 1943; Binyamin

symbolically, Ben-Gurion never appeared before the Committee to its dying day and, apart from one exception in early 1945, did not see fit to take part in any of its meetings. Perhaps even more symbolically, the one meeting in which Ben-Gurion participated was called to advise the Committee of the Jewish Agency Executive's decision to disband it—an unpleasant duty that Ben-Gurion agreed to take upon himself.[14] Third, the Committee was not given access to all important information that entailed strict secrecy. An eminent example came up during Brand's mission. More than a week after Venja Pomeranz delivered Brand's shocking information to Palestine, Gruenbaum asked Ben-Gurion whether he could share word of the great drama with the heads of the Rescue Committee as well. Ben-Gurion responded by sending him one of those chilling gazes and utterances that he knew how to call forth when necessary. Its gist: Gruenbaum had to make up his mind whether he represented the Rescue Committee vis-à-vis the Jewish Agency Executive or the other way around.[15] Additional examples of compartmentalization abounded during the war, but in this matter the Rescue Committee could find small solace in the fact that the Executive itself had been compartmentalized out and did not know things that Ben-Gurion, Kaplan, Sharett, and their associates in the "parallel system" thought might endanger them if leaked. Consequently, the Jewish Agency Executive plenum— officially the highest executive organ of the Zionist Movement—is another body that need not be researched in the quest for knowledge of what was done or not done to rescue European Jews during the war.

In sum, even if we do not credit every development with forethought, at some stage Ben-Gurion and his close associates in the leadership must have realized that had public pressure not brought such an entity as the Rescue Committee into existence, they might have had to invent it themselves. It was needed to absorb the public's pressure and clear the way for real rescue attempts by other entities, smaller and more professional. Thus, the Rescue Committee played the vital and thankless role of a lightning rod and no more.

Mintz to Gruenbaum, March 29, 1943; Moshe Koldony, Zionist General Council, May 18, 1943—all in CZA. Dan Horovitz and Moshe Lissak, *From a Yishuv to a State: Palestine's Jews under British Rule* (Tel Aviv: Am Oved, 1977), 16–18 (Hebrew).

14. The Rescue Committee meeting, January 15, 1945, CZA, S26/1238, where Mintz said: "if we get to see Mr. Ben-Gurion take part in this meeting for the first time—we should be sorry for the first time in three years that we exist...." Among the persons included in this body who, shortly thereafter, understood its futility, was Dr. Joseph who, in September 1943, asked to be relieved of his membership on the committee for this reason. Joseph to Ben-Gurion, September 13, 1943, CZA, S44/471.

15. Friling, *Arrows in the Dark*, 2:15, regarding the JAE meeting of June 4, 1944. See also Ben-Gurion's words to Gruenbaum in Zionist General Council, January 18, 1943, CZA.

The "Undeclared Triumvirate" and the "Parallel System"

If the Rescue Committee had not been the initiator, planner, and implementer of the main rescue actions, who dealt with such things? If tracking the Yishuv's rescue actions by investigating the large, cumbersome, and implausible body that went by the pretentious title of "Rescue Committee" resembles searching for a lost object under the streetlight instead of where it went missing, where, in fact, should we search? It takes only a quick look, however, at the modus operandi of the Yishuv leaders from the 1930s to the end of Israel's first decade (and perhaps later as well) to find a bold crimson thread that links this system and method with the treatment of a whole set of important, sensitive, and secret matters: the building of power—defense and procurement, the establishment of intelligence services and the crafting of the Yishuv's initial foreign relations, the development of the nuclear option, the creation of covert economic relations with the states of the Communist Bloc, the extrication of Jews from hostile countries, and so on. This crimson thread is the very same triumvirate, that "parallel system" which, for the most part, included the same people. The same system and the same people to whom the Yishuv and, at its outset, the state of Israel "outsourced" such matters as they would to a professional elite, those who dealt with all those Palestino-centric issues on the eve of World War II and afterwards, were the ones who shouldered the burdens of clandestine immigration and rescue action during World War II.

This system, which did the initiating and the planning, the commanding, the controlling, and the implementing, operated around what we call the special operations desk, part of the Jewish Agency political department. It was comprised of Reuven Zaslani (Shiloah), Teddy Kollek, Ehud Avriel, and Eliahu Epstein (Elath) and, to other extents, people such as Yitzhak Kleinbaum, Emanuel Yelan (Vilensky), Gideon Ruffer (Raphael), Eiga Shapira (who did more important things than his title of secretary would suggest), and others. Zaslani-Shiloah, Kollek, and Avriel, directly subordinate to the managing triumvirate or to Ben-Gurion alone, were the ones who directed the operational arm of the "parallel system."[16] During the second half of World War II, Zaslani was the longest-tenured, the most experienced, and the closest to Ben-Gurion among the trio, which was comprised of himself, Kollek, and Avriel. Kollek gradually rose in status but remained Zaslani's runner-up. Avriel was just starting out at the time.

16. On the "parallel system," see Friling, *Arrows in the Dark*, 1:134.

Shaul Meirov (Avigur), head of the Mossad le-Aliyah Bet, and Eliyahu Golomb, commander of the Haganah, also took part in this operational array even though they did not belong to the political department. They entered the system with political status of their own—Golomb as a leading factotum in Mapai and de facto commander of the Haganah until his death in 1945, and Meirov as head of the Mossad le-Aliyah Bet, a senior personality in the Haganah, and a central figure in Mapai and Hakibbutz Hameuhad.[17] Zvi Schechter (Yehieli), who from a certain moment onward figured importantly as the co-ordinator and commander of parachutist operations in the Occupied Zones, was also a member of this circle. Moshe Averbuch (Agami) was there, too; he returned to this circle chiefly as of October 1943 on and was concerned with operations for the rescue of Jews from Greece.[18] Another focus of his work was the rescue of Jews from Romania. Other members of this group—Ze'ev Schind, Venja Pomeranz (Ze'ev Hadari), and Menachem Bader—worked at times as part of the mechanism that led directly from the "field," where things were done, to the top of the political hierarchy. Additional people were co-opted into the system intermittently or on an ad hoc basis: Eliyahu Dobkin, Mordechai Eliash, who set out on missions to Turkey, and others.[19] The system hardly interrelated with the Rescue Committee. Often even the Jewish Agency Executive plenum was unaware of the extent and nature of the secret operations over which it presided.

The group followed the directives of the triumvirate (whose forces were not equally divided), as handed down by Ben-Gurion, Kaplan, and Sharett in that order. This administrative system paralleled the other political systems mentioned above. It was the product of the Yishuv institutions' structural undergrowth and the complexity of control and operation in this tangle and derived its justification from the importance of what it was doing for the Jewish people and the need to do it in a quiet and disciplined way. The triumvirate was visible at the focal point of the main rescue actions, and sometimes, when warranted, the arena of secret control was expanded to include Yitzhak Gruenbaum, the chair of the Rescue Committee and a member of the Jewish Agency Executive, Ben-Gurion's Mapai leadership colleague Berl Katznelson, and occasionally

17. Ibid., 2:205.

18. On Moshe Averbuch and the operations for the rescue of Jews from Greece, see Friling, ibid., 1:342–45, 347.

19. Eliash's first mission was in the beginning of February 1944. He and Herzog reported on it at the JAE meeting of March 5, 1944. Eliash went again to Istanbul on March 26 and arrived there on March 28, 1944. For reports on this journey, see JAE, September 3 and 10, 1944, CZA. See also Friling, *Arrows in the Dark*, 1:253–56, 258–59.

others, but not many others. The inclusion of Katznelson in decision-making should be tested in more than quantitative terms, that is, the number of times that his views were solicited. His moral and political backing for Ben-Gurion and the triumvirate until his death in August 1944 was also immensely important.

The "parallel system" reflected its dualism clearly: it circumvented the formal hierarchic constellation of Yishuv institutions to which it belonged. It did belong to the formal system; after all, it was run by none other than the chairman of the Jewish Agency Executive, the treasurer of the Executive, and the head of the Agency's political department, and the three of them operated as senior political department officials. The heads of the Executive simply developed a chain of command, reportage, and performance that eluded the plenum's control. Its operations presumably were funded under vaguely worded budget lines titled "Kupa Bet" ("Fund B") plus sources outside the current budget.[20] Accordingly, the budgeting of the "parallel system" was also firmly concealed and, thus, it is hard to investigate today.

Here, in any case, is where secret matters were dealt with. The Executive functioned in a mist and was itself misty. It was not fully coordinated and, while relatively disciplined, sometimes it exhibited disorder and even clashing loyalties. Differences of temperament also had an effect as a natural rivalry developed for status and operational prestige in the sphere of power that circled Ben-Gurion. The vertical connections that linked various parts of the system to the managing triumvirate, and especially to Ben-Gurion at its top, sometimes outweighed their horizontal connections—those between Kollek and Zaslani or between Zaslani and Pomeranz, for example. Sometimes a different pattern of relations surfaced, allowing interrelations among those in the field of action to prevail.

Presence of the "Undeclared Triumvirate" and the "Parallel System" in Rescue Operations

The process that routed sensitive and important operations to the triumvirate and its operational extension enters our field of vision from various angles, beginning with the early preparatory stages of the comprehensive rescue schemes. Much the same occurred when attempts to rescue children were

20. On "Fund B" in the Jewish Agency budget, see Friling, *Arrows in the Dark*, 2:133–34, 191.

made—although here, too, other solutions were tried first. The decision to define children in Europe as the first targets for rescue was made when the Yishuv leadership first discussed the matter after officially reporting to the public on the events in Europe. There were several reasons for giving the children priority. They were the most exposed to the ravages of the war, starvation, cold, and diseases; in the discussants' judgment, they were a burden and therefore would be the first victims because the Nazis had nothing to gain from their labor.[21] Conversely, the discussants hoped that the Allies and international relief agencies would agree to help children; expecting humanitarian sentiments to provide an especially strong motive, they thought the Allies would tip in favor of rescue. Moreover, while the British had rationalized their reluctance to rescue Jews by citing the fear of spies, no one could allege that the Nazis had planted informers among child refugees. There was also room for hope that the accommodation of children in Palestine would attract less British and Arab resistance than accomodating adults. After all, children could not bear arms and would be more of a burden to the Yishuv than a threat to its enemies, at least for a few years. Fourth, they thought Jews in the free world would agree to donate larger sums for children than for others and believed that the allocation of funds and entrance visas for the rescue of children would not spark controversy in the Yishuv and the Zionist movement. How would anyone be able to cite a worthier cause on which to spend strained resources?[22]

At the very outset of the discussions, Ben-Gurion proposed to streamline the decision-making process, management, and execution of the operation, which was immediately understood to be complex in every possible sense, foremost regarding logistics. Ben-Gurion explained to his Jewish Agency Executive associates that the existing array of immigrant-absorption institutions—foremost Henrietta Szold's Youth Aliyah—was unsuited to an operation on the scale of the type foreseen; furthermore, given its political and military complexities, it entailed "an institution of the Executive that will deal with this crucial question." He proposed that the Jewish Agency Executive appoint a committee to work up a broad program for the intake of children into Palestine, and he also suggested the composition of the committee, one that reflected not only the importance that he attributed to the matter but also his intention of keeping the

21. On giving priority to saving children, see Friling, *Arrows in the Dark*, 1:143–44, 183–94 and JAE, November 22, 1942, CZA.

22. On the discussions of the question of saving children, see JAE meeting, November 22, 1942, CZA and Mapai Secretariat meeting, November 24, 1942, LPA.

operation under strict control: Ben-Gurion, Gruenbaum, Kaplan, and the co-leaders of the immigration department, Dobkin and Shapira.[23]

The Executive accepted Ben-Gurion's proposal and its subcommittee, the Special Committee for Children's Immigration Affairs, held its inaugural meeting the day after it was appointed. The urgency of the convocation also attested to the intention of making the fastest possible progress in the children's rescue. The five committee members as well as Dov Joseph, secretary of the Executive, discussed the immigration of the "Teheran children."[24] They also discussed the reorganization of the Yishuv's immigrant-absorption mechanisms, cooperation with JDC, the immigration of children from the Balkan countries, and a far-reaching plan for the youngsters' intake.[25] In addition, the committee decided to sever relations between Youth Aliyah and the Jewish Agency's German department and to equip Youth Aliyah with a new administration. Specifically, it proposed to add three members of the Jewish Agency Executive to the panel which was staffed by Henrietta Szold and Dr. Georg Landauer, the two previous heads of Youth Aliyah. The goal was clear: to strengthen the Executive's control of Youth Aliyah.

However, the idea of reorganizing the Yishuv's main immigrant-absorption apparatuses proved touchy; it was linked straight away to accusations that Mapai was trying to seize control of the children. Ways to deflect the tempest had to be found. Ben-Gurion proposed that Szold remain at the helm of Youth Aliyah, presumably to exploit her organizational and pedagogical experience and her connections with Hadassah and American Jewry, but also to neutralize the accusations already in the air. Nevertheless, once it became clear that the Jewish Agency Executive wished to assure itself a controlling majority in the Youth Aliyah administration and the executive organs of other entities that would be engaged in rescue and intake operations,[26] additional players demanded to be represented on the Special Committee for Children's Immigration Affairs.

By the end of 1944, the Committee had grown and changed its complexion.

23. Friling, *Arrows in the Dark*, 1:149 and JAE, December 13, 1942, CZA. On the Executive standpoint, see Joseph's diary, December 13, 1942, CZA, S25/1510.

24. Friling, *Arrows in the Dark*, 1:250 and 2:95–96.

25. The JAE's Special Committee for Children's Immigration met for the first time on December 14, the day after being appointed. The urgency of the meeting is also proof of the intention to advance the issue with all possible expediency. See Friling, *Arrows in the Dark*, 1:150.

26. On the Jewish Agency Executive's growing control of the Youth Aliyah administration, see Friling, *Arrows in the Dark*, 1:150–51.

Various interests demanded to be represented there: political parties, movements, religious circles, kibbutzim, others. Each of them wanted some of the children for its own—the very children who ultimately, and sadly, would not arrive. Thus, the Special Committee became yet another body that swelled until it could no longer be effective. The addition of delegates to the decision-making function set an uncontrolled inflation in motion, just as the Rescue Committee had ballooned to "parliamentary" magnitudes and forfeited any chance of being fit to discuss and carry out sensitive matters. One of the key manifestations of this process was that Ben-Gurion and Kaplan avoided the committee, thereby shifting the main arena of action in this domain elsewhere.[27] As a result, both the Rescue Committee and the Special Committee for Children's Immigration Affairs—and, later on, the Yishuv mission in Istanbul as well—underwent rapid growth that led to rapid emasculation. The natural pressure to be part of the project and participate in the decisions and, under the circumstances, the ability to channel rescue resources to each side's preferred target population ultimately neutralized these entities. The action moved elsewhere.

More of the Reasoning behind the "Triumvirate" Operation

For an outstanding example of the coalescence of the triumvirate and the parallel system, and the ascent of these entities to the top of the pyramid, we will consider Eliezer Kaplan's departure on a mission to Turkey three or four months after the watershed in the Yishuv's consciousness about the events in Europe. His mission again reflected a modus operandi that sheds light on the backstage workings of the Yishuv leadership, the place where the Yishuv went about its secret and important business. Whenever a real possibility of rescue seemed to come into sight, a mission headed by Kaplan or Sharett, Ben-Gurion's associates in the triumvirate, was dispatched to the location.

When it became necessary to explore the possibilities of action in Istanbul, for example, Kaplan was sent to Turkey. The rescue possibilities at this juncture were three: the plan to rescue children and two ransom schemes, the Transnistria plan and the Slovakia plan. Kaplan set out during the first week of March 1943, accompanied by Eliahu Epstein of the Jewish Agency political department. During a previous stint in Turkey and in activities related to secret

27. On the Special Committee for Children's Immigration, see Friling, "Ben-Gurion's Interaction in the Child Rescue and the Absorption Polemic"; Friling, "David Ben-Gurion and the Catastrophe of European Jewry, 1939–1945" (dissertation, 1991) (Hebrew).

partnership with the British in 1940–1942, Epstein had developed connections with foreign diplomats, Turkish government officials and ministers, and British intelligence people who assisted the Yishuv emissaries in rescue-related matters.[28]

Epstein's task was to steer Kaplan to important people and help him carry out another intention of the triumvirate and those in its orbit: to broaden the span of secret Yishuv activities in Istanbul, this being considered one of the primary ways to promote large-scale rescue programs. The Yishuv people and British intelligence officials had signed a cooperation agreement back in mid-January.[29] Nevertheless, Ben-Gurion, Kaplan, Sharett, and their associates believed that a broader net of secret action—based on cooperation with British intelligence authorities and, to the extent possible, with corresponding American authorities—should be cast in Istanbul.

Epstein was a quintessential man in the field who had good connections with intelligence operatives and government officials in various places, including Turkey. In June 1940, he paid the country his first wartime visit in order to form relations with Turkish officials. He also met there with members of the British espionage service, the MI6, known then as the SIS (Secret Intelligence Service).[30] In 1941, he visited Turkey again, met with SIS officers, and on this occasion gained the acquaintance of Commander Walfson, an SIS officer in Turkey, and Colonel Harold Gibson, SIS commander in Istanbul, both of whom had been among the godfathers of the aforementioned January 1943 agreement.

There was a significant exchange when Epstein met with Gibson.[31] Epstein divulged the crux of the idea of infiltrating Yishuv emissaries into the heart of the occupied areas: the Yishuv would establish "more daring contacts with our movements in Nazi-occupied zones," while Gibson would gain "trustworthy

28. See Gelber, *Growing a Fleur-de-Lis*, 455–56, 481–82, 540. On Kaplan and Epstein's joint journey in March 1943, see Epstein's diary from the visit to Turkey, March 23–26, 1943, and "Kaplan's notes from his visit to Turkey, March 1943"—both in CZA, S53/230.

29. Friling, *Arrows in the Dark*, 1:261–65.

30. On the British intelligence organizations, see: Friling, ibid., 1:264; Gelber, *Growing a Fleur-de-Lis*; Shlomo Aronson, *Hitler, the Allies, and the Jews* (Cambridge: Cambridge University Press, 2004); Patrick Howarth, *Undercover: The Men and Women of the Special Operation Executive* (London: Routledge and Kegan Paul, 1980); E. H. Cookridge, *Inside SOE: The Story of Special Operations in Western Europe 1940–1945* (London: Arthur Baker, 1966); Reginald Victor Jones, *The Wizard War, British Scientific Intelligence, 1939–1945* (New York: Coward, McCann & Geoghegan, 1978); Richard Harris Smith, *OSS: The Secret History of America's First Central Intelligence Agency* (Berkeley, Calif.: University of California Press, 1972); Corey Ford, *Donovan of OSS* (Boston, Mass.: Little, Brown, 1970).

31. Friling, *Arrows in the Dark*; Epstein to Sharett, June 24, 1941.

sources of information about what was happening in enemy territory." Gibson accepted the proposal and they decided that the matter would be taken up at another meeting, with the participation of Kaplan, where they would work out the final details.[32] The tripartite meeting took place several days later. Gibson's manner was direct and matter-of-fact: he desired "a quick implementation of the plan regarding co-operation." The meeting ended with agreement and good cheer. They had decided to extend cooperation, share intelligence, co-opt additional people into future missions, and task Ze'ev Schind with establishing an interrogations office in Istanbul patterned after the one already operating in Haifa.[33]

Kaplan and Epstein attempted to establish similar relations with the Americans in Turkey and probe the possibilities of cooperation with them; to this end they met with American intelligence people at the U.S. Embassy in Ankara and officials at the consulate in Istanbul. The modus operandi repeated itself: Epstein made the first inquiries and prepared the way; then Kaplan moved in to hammer out the agreements and the final undertakings. They met with the American consul general in Istanbul, Burton Berry; the deputy ambassador, Robert Kelly; Professor Ernest Wright; and others, including the British intelligence officer Arthur Whittall.[34]

Kaplan returned to Palestine in late March and reported to the Executive what he had learned and done in Turkey. Germany's strength was declining and those who had been confident in Hitler's victory were no longer so sure, he related. Consequently, several satellite countries had a motive to soften their policies toward the Jews and were now willing to allow them to leave or to cross.[35] However, Kaplan then reported that both possible routes from Turkey to Palestine, by land and by sea, were almost totally blocked. The Turkish authorities were unwilling to allow their ships to transport the refugees without British approval and, Kaplan inferred, the British were in no hurry to help re-

32. Friling, *Arrows in the Dark*; Epstein's diary, March 23–26, 1943, CZA, S53/230, 5; See also Shaul Avigur (Meirov), "Our Parachutists," *Magen Baseter* (Secret defense), ed. Zrubavel Gilad, (Jerusalem: Jewish Agency Press, 1948), 195 (Hebrew).

33. Friling, ibid., 1:291–92; Epstein's diary, 5, 17, CZA. Emmanuel Vilensky (Yelan) headed the interrogations office in Haifa. The office dealt with the investigation of refugees arriving from the Balkans, and with collecting military information. Ze'ev Schind was the first head of the Istanbul office, later Teddy Kollek and at the end of 1943—Ehud Avriel.

34. Friling, ibid.; Epstein's diary, 15, CZA; Yehuda Bauer, "Parachutists and the Defense Plan," *Yalkut Moreshet* 1 (November 1963): 88 (Hebrew).

35. Reports on the journey: JAE and the Rescue Committee meetings—both from March 28, 1943, CZA, S26/1237; Mapai Secretariat, March 30, 1943, LPA and Friling, ibid., 1:294.

move children from danger zones, despite their own declarations and the signs of change in their policy. On the success side of the ledger, Kaplan reported the Red Cross's consent to place the vessels under its patronage and the Soviets' consent not to attack refugee ships as they crossed the Black Sea.

Kaplan also reported a series of diverse attempts by the emissaries to establish efficient marine transport of Jewish refugees by leasing or buying ships from various countries. None had worked out. Kaplan then described his impressions of the Transnistria plan. His visit to Turkey, he said, had taught him that there was no room for "sensational operations" and that the Transnistria plan "proved neither serious nor realistic." It had fallen through, he ruled, because it had been "unrealistic from the start." Just the same, Kaplan thought that a more modest plan—to remove the deportees from Transnistria to Romania proper by bribing Romanian officials or exploiting their wish to obtain an alibi ahead of the possibility of a German defeat—stood a chance and might do some good. He expressed this, in practical terms, by ordering the emissaries to seize an opportunity that had come up while he was still in Istanbul and to move 5,000 Jewish children from Transnistria to Romania. The estimated cost of this rescue operation was 75,000–100,000 Palestine pounds. Kaplan instructed the emissaries to take all requisite actions and promised that the Executive would come up with the money. Once back in Palestine he explained, "We've got to continue" with this operation; "Time will tell" whether it would be a first step toward the rescue of additional refugees.[36]

The minutes of the Executive meetings say nothing whatsoever about Eliezer Kaplan's reportage. He may have reported the matter but his remarks were omitted from the minutes due to their sensitivity; alternatively, he may not have reported it at all due to the fear of leaks. Either way, there is no evidence that Kaplan told his colleagues in the Jewish Agency Executive plenum that he and Eliahu Epstein had met with a series of American and British diplomats and intelligence operatives, and had discussed with them modalities of secret partnership that both sides would find useful.[37] In contrast, these contacts were described to Ben-Gurion who, true to form, recorded the gist of what they had said in his diary.

36. JAE and the Rescue Committee meetings—both from March 28, 1943, CZA, S26/1237; Mapai Secretariat, March 30, 1943, LPA; the Committee for the Jews of Occupied Europe, "Modiin," 2–3, copy to Ben-Gurion, March 5, 1943, CZA, S26/1240. On the proposal to transfer 5,000 orphans from Transnistria to Romania, see *Davar*, March 10 and 25, 1943.

37. Epstein to series of diplomats and intelligence operatives in the British and American consulates in Ankara and Istanbul, April 7, 1943, CZA, S25/22674.

Immediately after they returned to Palestine, Kaplan and Epstein kept the wheels of the agreements with Gibson rolling. Epstein, Shaul Meirov, and Teddy Kollek met with an SIS officer in Cairo, Smith-Ross, and an officer from the same organization in Jerusalem, Reed, to coordinate actions and discuss the implementation of the Gibson-Kaplan agreement. The latter meeting was also attended by Hooper, Reed's aide.[38] This stage of the affair, too, finds no expression in the meetings of the Jewish Agency Executive and the Rescue Committee.

Kollek was appointed liaison and Kaplan and Epstein introduced him to their interlocutors.[39] Thirty-two years old and a member of Kibbutz Ein Gev who served with the political department, Kollek was gifted with charisma and the ability to make friends easily, characteristics that would earn him fame in subsequent postings. Smith-Ross was not unfamiliar to Zaslani and his associates; he had already visited Jerusalem in late February to promote the Simmonds-Schind agreements that had led to the training of the first group of parachutists.[40] Reinterrogating Zaslani about the Zionist cells in Bulgaria, Romania, and Hungary, they asked him how circumspect and operational the cells were, since the plan envisaged them as rendezvous and concealment points for the British and their people in those countries. Zaslani assured them that the cells existed and were safe; recently the mission in Istanbul had even managed to establish good contact with them.[41]

In the coordination meeting called in Jerusalem pursuant to the Gibson-Kaplan agreement, the following areas of cooperation were sketched out: (1) collecting information from immigrants to Palestine and other Jewish sources about developments in the Balkans; (2) dispatching emissaries to the Balkans. The relevant British department would assist on the condition that the emissaries' people would also serve the British military authorities (mainly in respect to information). The Jewish Agency would send a special operative to Istanbul to coordinate the collection of information and serve as a general liaison with the British department in all matters relating to the exploitation of the connections of the Jewish Agency and other Jewish circles in the occupied countries.

38. Meeting summary, May 7, 1943, CZA, S25/8884.

39. Ibid.

40. On the agreement, see Tony [Simmonds] and Danny [Schind], January 15, 1943, CZA, S25/8883; Ze'ev Venja Hadari, *Against All Odds, Istanbul 1942–1945* (Tel Aviv: Ministry of Defense, 1992), 259 (Hebrew); Friling, *Arrows in the Dark*, 1:205.

41. [Unsigned, but most likely Zaslani] to Squadron Leader Smith-Ross, February 25, 1943, CZA, S25/8908; at the end of February, Simmonds and his headquarters transferred to Algeria. He notified his friend Zaslani, using his nickname "Zasi," February 28, 1943, CZA, S25/22513.

Kollek's planned activity in Istanbul, the discussants said, should be co-ordinated with the experienced and active interrogations office in Haifa, run by Emanuel Vilensky, who "to this day has presented hundreds of reports that were much appreciated by the British intelligence coordinators in the Middle East and London." They agreed that prospective immigrants to Palestine would undergo a partial interrogation in Istanbul on urgent matters such as movements of forces, whereas the full interrogation would take place in Haifa.

As for the emissary infiltrators, the discussants found a redundancy between the agreement with Simmonds and that with Gibson. While training those who were destined to participate in missions planned by Simmonds had already begun in Cairo, preparations for their departure had begun in Jerusalem. Therefore, the participants in the meeting decided to distinguish between two kinds of infiltrating emissaries. Those to be sent under the Gibson-Kaplan agreement would be "mainly Zionist emissaries." Secondarily, they would carry out missions for the British in return for assistance that Gibson and his people would supply. Those emissaries who would be sent under the Simmonds-Schind agreement, by contrast, would not have "their British mission second in importance." This distinction would also be reflected in their training programs: those training in Cairo would take "very thorough courses indeed," whereas those who would be sent under the new agreement would receive only partial military training. This accord was sent on to Gibson in Istanbul, who approved it.[42] If so, the British—at least such officers as Gibson and Simmonds—agreed that it would be the Yishuv that would define the main mission of some of the emissaries. Epstein furnished Kollek with letters to officials at the British and American embassies and consulates in Istanbul. He described Kollek as "a man of great experience in the operational sphere … ; very reliable … and a personal friend."[43]

Among those people whom Kollek was advised to contact in Turkey, at least three were of particular interest: Gardyne De Chastelain, Ray Brock, and W. Bertholtz.

De Chastelain was the son of a Huguenot family that had settled in England. He directed sales for the Phoenix petroleum and transport company in Romania before the war. It was rumored that in the autumn of 1940 he had helped King Carol II to escape from Romania together with his riches; he had also

42. Meeting summary, May 7, 1943, CZA, S25/8884; Zaslani to Reed, May 24, 1943, ibid., S25/8908; Memorandum, May 8, 1943, ibid., S25/10756.
43. Epstein to Reed, April 7, 1947, CZA, S25/22674.

planned sabotage operations, along with David Hacohen and Yehuda Arazi, two other members of the clandestine cooperation matrix.[44] De Chastelain left Romania after it joined the Axis powers and was placed in charge of the Romanian desk of the SOE office in Istanbul.[45]

Ray Brock was a well-connected journalist in Turkey, a representative of the *New York Times* and an intelligence-gatherer who relayed news to his employer every evening through the Turkish government radio, including coded information from Epstein about the Jews' situation in Europe and events in Palestine. Epstein divulged the code to Stephen Wise, whose daughter, Justine Wise-Polier, would decipher the messages embedded in Brock's relays and convey them to her father and his people.[46] Bertholz, also a well-connected journalist and a frequent guest at the Ankara Palace Hotel, was known to Epstein. He was a non-Jewish Czech representative of a Swedish newspaper in Turkey.[47]

Kaplan took it upon himself to introduce Kollek to Chaim Barlas, the senior Jewish Agency representative in Turkey. As Kaplan later wrote, Kollek was sent "to conduct, on behalf of the Political Department of the Jewish Agency, the operation which was decided upon when I was with E. Epstein in Turkey." He asked Barlas to help Kollek "by equipping him by every means at your disposal and at the disposal of our office in Kushta [Istanbul] in order to facilitate his activity."[48] This underscored Kaplan's important status in Ben-Gurion's intimate operational triumvirate; it also demonstrated how sensitive it was to insert another representative in Turkey, which had been Barlas's almost exclusive fief until several months earlier.

Kollek's activity required budget revisions, since it was necessary to finance not only the establishment of an office but also Kollek's planned network of contacts, most of whom would not be volunteers. Zaslani itemized the expenses in a memorandum to Kaplan: "This matter is fundamentally different from other projects in which we cooperated with various army departments in the past"; those were primarily "general military projects" that obtained their funding from the British as a matter of course. Kollek, in contrast, was by no means a "subcontractor" whom the army hired to carry out its missions; rather,

---

44. See Friling, *Arrows in the Dark*, 1:265–68 (on David Hachoen) and 1:28 (on Yehuda Arazi).

45. Rubin, *Istanbul Intrigues* (New York: Pharos Books, 1992), 90, 258, 265–66; Anthony Cave Brown, *Bodyguard of Lies* (New York: Harper & Row, 1975), 452–53.

46. Eliahu Elath, *The Struggle for Statehood, Washington 1945–1948* (Tel Aviv: n.p., 1979–1982), 1:42 (Hebrew); Eliahu Elath, *San Francisco Diary* (Tel Aviv: Dvir, 1971), 57 (Hebrew).

47. Ibid.

48. Kaplan to Barlas, May 5, 1943, CZA, S53/1987.

he had been placed in charge of a variety of operations that entailed direct Yi-shuv financing. The people involved had been enlisted *ab initio* to undertake a "double mission—a general Jewish mission and a general military mission."

Having demanded and also received "certain rights in running the project," the Yishuv now had budget responsibilities as well. The British had agreed to finance the military side of the project but could not be asked to finance the Jewish side as well. Zaslani estimated that the Yishuv would be asked to allo-cate only 750 Palestine pounds for the coming three months and suggested that Sharett and Kaplan authorize the expenditure.[49]

Thus, by March 1943, the idea jelled of establishing an advance command group in Istanbul that would investigate the events in Europe hands-on, judge the likelihood of successful action, and plan and coordinate the operations in direct contact with the decision-making echelon in Jerusalem. Where nec-essary, this echelon would also be brought to Istanbul to make decisions on the spot. Once Teddy Kollek set out for Istanbul in May 1943, this channel of activity came into even sharper focus. Sharett's visit to Istanbul in June 1943, Ehud Avriel's visit in August of that year, and Reuven Zaslani's "frequent flyer" trips on the Jerusalem-Cairo-Istanbul route were part of this channel, as were the visits of Shaul Meirov (Avigur). Little of this peripatetic activity found ex-pression in the documentation of the Jewish Agency Executive and the Rescue Committee. We do not consider this a coincidence.[50]

Role of the "Parallel System" in Rescue Attempts of the Jews in Hungary

Events surrounding the Brand affair provide another example of the activity of the "parallel system" and demonstrate—perhaps in the most significant way of all—the triumvirate's working methods. In a nutshell, on May 19, 1944, Joel Brand and Bandy Grosz reached Istanbul.[51] There they reported on the ransom

49. Zaslani to Kaplan, copy to Moshe Sharett, May 3, 1943, CZA, S25/8883 and S25/8885.

50. On Kaplan's actions after he returned from Turkey: his meeting with Macpherson the deputy high commissioner on April 2, 1943, and with Mills, head of the Mandatory government's emigration department, see: G. R. Sandford, Palestine Government Chief Secretariat, to JAE, April 2, 1943, ABG, correspondence. For Kaplan's meeting with Richard Casey, the resident British minister for Middle Eastern affairs and the highest ranking British diplomat in the region, see JAE, May 16, 1943, CZA.

51. Memorandum titled "from Joel's words," June 11, 1944, ABG, correspondence; JAE, June 14, 1944, CZA; U.S. Consul, Istanbul, to Foreign Office, June 13, 1944, 862/20200/6, 1344 USA NA (hereaf-ter: NA); Shalom Rosenfeld, *Criminal Case 124/53* (Tel Aviv: Karni, 1955), 81–84 (Hebrew); Yehuda Bau-er, "Joel Brand Mission," *Yalkut Moreshet* 26 (November 1978): 23–60; Bela Vago, "Intelligence Aspects

scheme that goes by the hair-raising title "goods for blood": The Nazis were willing to release a million Jews in return for 10,000 trucks and other merchandise. On May 24, the proposal was presented to Ben-Gurion and Sharett by Venja Pomeranz, whom Kollek chose to deliver the plan from Istanbul to Palestine. That night, the two Yishuv leaders digested Pomeranz's report. The next day, the proposal was presented to the Jewish Agency Executive plenum. On July 19, exactly two months after Brand and Grosz had landed in Istanbul, the offer was stricken from the agenda for all practical purposes; the Americans and the British had leaked it to Western newspapers.[52]

Again in a nutshell, the permits that Brand and Grosz possessed for their stay in Turkey were questionable and problematic. Thus, on May 25, the Turks arrested Grosz on a smuggling charge and Brand for illegal entry. The men were interrogated and placed under restricted movement. On May 31, the Turks announced their decision to deport both of them to Hungary. A short time later, they changed their minds: Grosz and Brand would be allowed to choose between deportation to Hungary via Bulgaria and deportation to Syria.

The emissaries in Istanbul also vacillated, especially after Sharett cabled them an explicit instruction to keep Brand in Turkey and prevent him from reaching Palestine, an area in the British sphere of control. The British, Sharett explained, might arrest Brand, prevent him from returning to Hungary, and thereby defeat his mission.[53]

Barlas, Avriel, Schind, Bader, and others shared Sharett's concern about a British trap: Brand would be arrested, the mission would fail, and the British could breathe easily, their fears of a million Jews inundating Palestine or

of the Joel Brand Mission," *Yad Vashem Studies* 10 (1974): 89–90; Yehuda Bauer, *The Holocaust—Some Historical Aspects* (Tel Aviv: Moreshet-Sifriat Hapoalim, 1982), 148–91 (Hebrew). U.S. Vice-Consul to Foreign Office, Squires's memo, June 17, 1944, NA, OSS, RG 84; Rubin, *Istanbul Intrigues*, 196–97.

52. On July 19 it was published in the *New York Herald Tribune* and the following day it was common knowledge throughout the free world and Palestine. Sharett to Leo Kohn, the source of the leak in Ankara, July 24, 1944, ABG, correspondence; Gruenbaum and Kaplan, JAE, July 23, 1944, CZA; Dobkin, JAE, September 21, 1944, ibid.; Bernard Wasserstein, *Britain and the Jews of Europe 1939–1945* (Oxford: Clarendon Press, 1997), 261–62. The question of who first leaked the information has been investigated by several researchers and is irrelevant to this discussion. The Allies blamed each other, but the leak served them all. See Yehuda Bauer, *Jews for Sale? Nazi-Jewish Negotiations, 1933–1945* (New Haven: Yale University Press, 1994); Friling, *Arrows in the Dark*, 2:3–69; Bela Vago "Hungarian Jewry's Leadership," in *The Leadership of Hungarian Jewry During the Holocaust*, ed. Israel Gutman, Bela Vago, and Livia Rothkirchen (Jerusalem: Yad Vashem, 1976), 61–76 (Hebrew); Israel Kasztner, *The Truth of Kasztner: A Report on the Hungarian Rescue Committee, 1942–1945*, trans. Binyamin Gat-Rimon (Tel Aviv: Association for Eternalizing the Memory of Dr. Israel Kasztner, 1981) (Hebrew).

53. Shertok's report, June 27, 1944, CZA, Z4/14870; Bauer, *The Holocaust—Some Historical Aspects*, 148–86.

the West alleviated. Thus, the emissaries proposed to the British that Brand meet with Sharett in Aleppo. The British operatives in Istanbul expressed their consent. Sharett received a similar go-ahead from the general secretary of the Mandatory Government to Jerusalem and from Brigadier Maunsell, chief of British military intelligence in the Middle East.[54]

On June 5, Brand and Avriel headed for Aleppo on the trans-Turkey Taurus Express. That day, Sharett set out for his appointment with Brand in Aleppo. Brand was allowed to make his way to Aleppo, as promised. When he got there, however, contrary to all their assurances, British intelligence agents arrested him and held him in hiding. After frantic intervention by Zaslani and Sharett, a directive came through from the British Foreign Office: Sharett and Brand would be allowed to meet after all.[55]

Those attending the meeting in Aleppo were among the highest-ranking persons in the Yishuv's secret operational array: Sharett, Avigur, Zaslani, and Zvi Schechter (Yehieli). The loftiness of this delegation is evidence of the importance attributed to the meeting with Brand. Only such a team could review the new information at once and consider how to contend with it.[56]

As soon as Sharett returned from Aleppo, the Jewish Agency Executive began its second special meeting over the ransom proposal.[57] Ben-Gurion, chairing the meeting at his home in Tel Aviv, gave the floor to Sharett straight away. Sharett delivered a detailed account of Brand's reportage and emphasized the main point: "This thing is more complex and intricate than we had imagined, there is no doubt...." He added that "Brand's escort [Grosz] reported the entire mission to the British."[58]

Thus, the task of representing the Executive in regard to Eichmann's proposal and visiting Turkey for this purpose fell into the lap of Sharett, a member

54. Menachem Bader, *Sad Missions* (Mehravia: n.p., 1954), 105 (Hebrew); Bader's letters to Pomeranz, May 27 and June 10, 1944, according to Bauer, "Joel Brand Mission," 37–38; Ehud Avriel, *Open the Gates!* (London: Weidenfeld and Nicolson, 1975), 182–83; Rosenfeld, *Criminal Case 124/53*, 55, 62–64; Vago, "Intelligence Aspects of the Joel Brand Mission," 81.

55. JAE, June 14, 1944, CZA; Shertok's report, June 27, 1944, London, CZA, Z4/14870; Joel Brand, *On Behalf of Those Condemned to Death* (Tel Aviv: Ayanot, 1957), 129–31 (Hebrew); Avriel, *Open the Gates!* 181–85; Rosenfeld, *Criminal Case 124/53*, 55–65; Bader, *Sad Missions*, 105.

56. Avriel, *Open the Gates!* 185–86; Rosenfeld, *Criminal Case 124/53*, 360; Haggai Eshed, *Reuven Shiloah, the Man behind the Mossad: Secret Diplomacy in the Creation of Israel* (London: Frank Cass, 1997), 74–75.

57. See Amos Elon, *Timetable* (Garden City, N.Y.: Doubleday, 1980), 204.

58. JAE, June 14, 1944, CZA; U.S. Consul, Istanbul, to Foreign Office, June 13, 1944, NA, OSS, RG 226, entry 94, box 554, folder 30.

of the triumvirate. The Turks refused to let him enter. Fearing that Brand would not present the affair to the Yishuv's high leadership directly and that he would be deported to Hungary before such a presentation could take place, they decided to meet in Aleppo. Those who went to Aleppo for this purpose were among the very highest members of the "parallel system." It was the complexity and intricacy of the affair, coupled with the fear that unprofessional and inadequately sensitive handling would make it even more complicated than it was, that underlay the dispatch of this team.

The Necessity for Clandestine Operations

An additional event derived from the Brand-Grosz affair carries the imprint of the "parallel system" and the severe compartmentalization that concealed developments from some Yishuv leaders. The development at issue originated in the feeling that the Allies were loath to allow the matter to move ahead or even to create the appearance of negotiations that might buy the Jews some time. The idea was to try to create an independent alternative for action in the event that the Allies were found to be deliberately foiling the scheme.

The possibility bruited was actually an attempt to apply an idea that had already been taken up in discussions over previous ransom plans. The official representative of the War Refugee Board, Ira Hirschmann; the director of JDC-Europe, Joseph Schwartz; and Moshe Sharett met in Cairo and explored the possibility of independent action, if they could prove American and British hesitancy or evasion. They discussed the preparation of a large sum of money in a place where it could be transferred to occupied Europe, so that the Nazis could be paid in coin instead of in trucks and goods. After all, in one of the initial rounds of negotiations in Hungary, the Nazis had agreed to accept cash and had even put forth "price lists."[59]

Schwartz and the American-Jewish relief organization that he represented in Europe had already consented to participate in independent rescue operations even if they broke American law or clashed with American and Allied war policies. Hirschmann was a high-ranking American official, the representative of a panel that had been vested with far-reaching powers to contact representatives of the enemy. He was an American Jew and a senior executive with the

59. On the Hirschmann-Shertok-Schwartz meeting: Shertok's report, June 27, 1944, CZA, Z4/14870, 8–9; Harold MacMichael to Colonial Secretary, May 26, 1944, Public Records Office—PRO, London, FO 371/42758.

Bloomingdale's department store chain in New York, who had in his pocket a personal letter of authorization from President Roosevelt to act for the rescue of such Jews as remained in Europe. It can be conjectured that Hirschmann's official status and self-confidence strengthened Schwartz's willingness to plan and participate in rescue actions of borderline legality.

Sharett, Schwartz, and Hirschmann discussed the idea that JDC would deposit money in a closed account in Switzerland, where it would be ready for payout in lieu of 10,000 trucks and quantities of goods. If so, the head of the Jewish Agency political department, a representative of JDC, and the representative of the U.S. administration's War Refugee Board were studying an alternative to action through ordinary American and British government channels. This semi-independent alternative rested on the assumption that the British and American governments would initially turn a blind eye to the matter and would ultimately cooperate in nailing down the deal.

The *chargé d'affaires* at the American interest section in Egypt at the time, Pinkney Tuck, contributed to the positive atmosphere. As far back as 1942, he had initiated a scheme for the rescue of Jewish children in France.[60] Tuck accompanied Hirschmann to the meetings in Cairo and was supposed to provide logistical and communication services for the alternative being probed. The secret was divulged to JDC's representative in Palestine, Judah L. Magnes; the idea was for him to accompany Schwartz to Istanbul. Wishing to be sure that Schwartz was not overdoing things, he reported the scheme to the chairman of JDC in New York.[61]

Hirschmann also advised the American ambassador in Turkey, Laurence Steinhardt, of the semi-independent alternative being debated in Cairo and asked him to arrange an entrance visa to Turkey for Schwartz. Lord Moyne, a senior member of the British government and the resident minister in the Middle East, was also in on the secret. When Hirschmann asked him what he thought about the viability of the plan, Moyne replied that he did not think his

---

60. In June 1944, Pinkney Tuck, the American *chargé d'affaires* in France, initiated a plan to save Jewish children separated from their parents. His partners in the initiative were the JDC personnel in Europe, clerks in the American Foreign Ministry, Eleanor Roosevelt's Committee for the Care of Children, as well as other groups. The Dominican Republic, Argentina, Canada, and others agreed to accept a number of these children. The Yishuv expressed its willingness to accept them all. See Yehuda Bauer, *American Jewry and the Holocaust: The American Jewish Joint Distribution Committee 1939–1945* (Detroit: Wayne State University Press, 1981), 259–61; Steinhardt to Tuck, June 20, 1944, NA, OSS, RG 84; Shertok's report, June 27, 1944, CZA, Z4/14870.

61. OSS Palestine Branch's memo, August 27, 1944, 4; Magnes to Paul Berwald, June 22, 1944, NA, OSS, RG 226, entry E120.

country would object and then asked whether he could report the idea to London. Hirschmann asked him to refrain from doing so before he could discuss it with Steinhardt and his higher-ups in the American administration.[62]

At the end of the consultations in Cairo, the agreements in place, Sharett returned to Palestine. Immediately afterwards, on Saturday night, June 24, 1944, the Jewish Agency Executive convened in yet another special session—the third extraordinary session called for the discussion of Brand's mission. Sharett was to head for London the next day; Ben-Gurion ran the meeting, which began with a report from Sharett about his actions in Cairo. In his talks with Lord Moyne in the Egyptian capital, Sharett discovered the existence of a real menace: the British Foreign Office intended to issue a statement about Brand's mission. The disclosure of the Transnistria proposal and the dire outcome of that development hovered in the air. Sharett opposed disclosure, of course, on the grounds that it would doom the plan to failure; Hirschmann concurred. Sharett demanded that the British Foreign Office wait for him to reach London. Lord Moyne promised to pass Sharett's request on to London. Therefore, Sharett had to rush to the British capital.[63]

In his reports, Sharett said nothing about the semi-independent initiative that he had discussed with Schwartz and Hirschmann in Cairo.[64] The next day, too, when the Executive held its regular meeting, the business in Cairo was not discussed.[65] The reasons for this are not adequately clear. Perhaps those in on the plan were afraid of leaks to third parties who would wish to torpedo the scheme. Or it may have been another example of the withholding of knowledge of such issues from anyone who had no need to know—those outside the "parallel system."

The Brand affair also gives an indication of how the Yishuv's channels of information worked. The first recipients of the freshest information, always, were Ben-Gurion and the "parallel system" that he had built around himself. Venja Pomeranz reached Palestine on May 24, 1944, and spent all that night reporting to Ben-Gurion and Sharett. According to one of the sources, Sharett first reported to Ben-Gurion upon his return from Aleppo. Gershon Agronsky (Agron), a senior journalist who also served as a courier for the Yishuv leaders, returned

62. Ira Hirschmann, *Life Line to the Promised Land* (New York: Vanguard Press, 1946), 126–27; Bader's weekly review, June 25, 1944, CZA, S25/22465; Shertok's report, June 27, 1944, Z4/14870, 8; Kaplan, JAE, July 28, 1944, CZA; Hirschmann addendum, June 22, 1944, OSS, RG 84.

63. JAE, June 24, 1944, CZA.

64. Ibid.

65. JAE, June 25, 1944, ibid.; Shertok to Dobkin, June 16, 1944; CZA S26/1253.

from London and reported only to Ben-Gurion about Chaim Weizmann's and Mordechai Eliash's contacts concerning the Brand affair and the self-defense plan. This was also the practice of two JDC officials, Judah Magnes and Harry Viteles; Kaplan and Eliash, too, reported to Ben-Gurion when they returned from Turkey. The first information about the invitation extended to Menachem Bader, one of the highest-ranking emissaries in Istanbul, to Budapest for direct negotiations with the Nazis reached Ben-Gurion first and the rest of his coterie later.[66] Regular information to Palestine from London and Istanbul flowed directly to Ben-Gurion even if addressed to Leo Kohn or Eliezer Kaplan. Indeed, for the first time and in a departure from the two previous ransom affairs, despite all the pressures, no information about the secret Executive discussions of Eichmann's proposal and its derivatives was leaked to the public. It may also have been a sign of growing maturity.

Summary: The "Undeclared Triumvirate" and "Parallel System" as Necessary Evils

If the ability to keep information secret was a sign of growing maturity, where were the Yishuv's main decisions about rescue during World War II made? If it were the Jewish Agency Executive plenum, why—apart from the issues described above—was this entity not advised of the August 1943 agreement with JDC, in which JDC undertook to collaborate in illegally transferring funds to the occupied areas, no less? Why did the Executive not debate the question of the secret messenger who had been arrested in Turkey and released under the guarantee of Yishuv officials, almost certainly senior ones? Why was the decision to "contact the devil," in response to the Slovakia plan in early 1943, made by Ben-Gurion, Kaplan, Sharett, and maybe two or three others and not presented to the Executive for debate?[67]

Additional examples of this kind abound, always on the most sensitive of topics. We cannot identify the forum that made the ultimate decision to accept Gruenbaum's proposal that the Allies be implored to bombard the camps and the roads leading to them. In regard to parachutist affairs, too, the eight-mem-

66. Kaplan, JAE, July 23, 1944, CZA; Dr. Eliash, ibid., September 10, 1944; Rosenfeld, *Criminal Case 124/53*, 58, Avriel's testimony.

67. Although a review of the JAE protocols in late 1942 and early 1943 shows that no decision was reached on Slovakia, emissaries and other individuals acted as if someone had instructed them to begin examining various plans; see Bader to Venja and Schind, MAGH, D.1.713.

ber panel that had been established to oversee the parachuting and infiltration operations was sidestepped. The more sensitive and complex the matter
was, the thicker the mist became—and rescue matters were highly sensitive
indeed.[68] If so, in what setting were the decisions made? It seems to us that
the "parallel system" headed by Ben-Gurion, Kaplan, and Sharett provided the
patronage and guidance that not only made the decisions in rescue matters but
also managed the operations in the field. If so, we may now address the question of the documentation needed to reveal what was done to rescue European
Jews. The documentation that counts is not that associated with the entities
at the top of the official hierarchy. Thus, the information we need cannot be
sought in documentation of the Jewish Agency Executive, the Rescue Committee, or the main political parties of the time. These were not the arenas that
mattered; we say this with a great deal of confidence.

One can find some documentation about the rescue operations and their
ramifications in an unlikely place: among the foreign espionage operatives who
kept abreast of what the Yishuv representatives were up to. British and American
sources offer such information; presumably more will turn up among Polish,
Czechoslovakian, Yugoslavian, Romanian, and other sources after the Russian
and former Soviet archives are opened. British and American archives contain
sources of two kinds. One comprises reports, summaries, and correspondence
among intelligence operatives about secret cooperation with the Yishuv and its
emissaries, including assistance that they provided for the rescue operations.
The other, contrarily, was written by the intelligence people who ruled out cooperation with the Yishuv, fretted over what the Yishuv people were up to, kept
them under surveillance, and did their best to frustrate the rescue operations.
At issue, then, is documentation that is difficult to obtain, reveal, and understand, as opposed to stories of actions not taken or realities not extant.

Finally, given the anonymity of important rescue activists and the failure
of the rescue operations, it has been argued that the Yishuv assigned second-
rate people to rescue work. As we have seen, the truth was totally different. Before and after World War II, and even in the early statehood years, people like
Meirov-Avigur, Golomb, Zaslani-Shiloah, Epstein-Elath, Kollek, Avriel, Schind,
Bader, and Pomeranz-Hadari dealt with Palestine-centric matters—weapons,
defense, intelligence. They were among the highest-ranking and most sophis-

---

68. Yehuda Bauer, *From Diplomacy to Resistance* (Philadelphia, Pa.: Jewish Publication Society,
1970), 123–24; Tevet, *The Road to May*, 177, 235.

ticated individuals that the Yishuv and the Zionist Movement had. These were precisely the people who dealt with rescue! Bodies such as the Rescue Committee were indeed packed with back-benchers of the second and third order, but this happened because the Rescue Committee was not the entity that really mattered. The rescue efforts did not fail because they had been entrusted to also-rans, but failed in spite of the fact that they had been entrusted to the finest servants that the Yishuv had to offer. This is evidently a difficult fact to tolerate and to comprehend.

Part 3

Children as Resisters and Music as Resistance

Debórah Dwork

12   Raising Their Voices

Children's Resistance through Diary Writing and Song

Helga Kinsky-Pollack was eight years old when her parents sent her from her native city of Vienna to her father's family in Kyjov, over the border in Czechoslovakia. It was just after the Anschluss in spring 1938 and the faces of their infatuated neighbors told her parents how popular Hitler and his policies would be. A year later, in spring 1939, Helga's mother went to England as a domestic worker. Her plan was to arrange the emigration of her daughter. Time was not with her. The German army marched into Czechoslovakia in 1939, and mother and daughter were separated.[1] Helga's father managed to reach her in Kyjov, and in January 1943 they were deported to the transit camp the Germans called Theresienstadt, and the Czechs, Terezín.

"Sunday 17 January 1943. This is my last day in Kyjov, and we are in a great rush," Helga, then twelve-and-a-half, told her diary. "Now I am sitting at a writing desk, and I am very tired. No matter! The last day at home must be noted down." If she did not grasp the historic nature of the unfolding events, she certainly understood their significance for her. Determined to record what she lived, despite her fatigue, she expressed her feelings as she wrote. "Within twelve hours the whole apartment will be deserted. (No, I shall not leave home hanging my head; I shall hold my head high.)"[2] So secure was she in her defi-

1. Mrs. Pollack-Meisels, interview with author, Vienna, Austria, August 15, 1989.

2. Unpublished diary of Helga Kinsky-Pollack, in her possession. Photocopy in possession of Debórah Dwork. Entry of January 17, 1943. Translation of this and all quoted passages by Pavel Kalvach and Debórah Dwork.

ance that she declared it as a self-evident statement, worthy only of a paren-thetical comment.

Berthe Jeanne (Bertje) Bloch-van Rhijn lived at home with her sister Jeanne-Truus (Jt) and their parents in Enschede, the Netherlands, when she began to keep her diary in February 1942. She, too, expressed defiance, although she did not come to that position immediately. When the star decree was announced on May 1, 1942, Bertje worried that "while a lot of people would be very nice . . . the NSB [Dutch Nazi Party] people would yell, 'Yid, dirty Yid!' at me." Her atti-tude soon changed. "20 May Wednesday. This evening we had a meeting about Zionism" at a friend's house. "Marion came, even Annelies." But, she wrote, if another schoolmate, Halberstadt, knew, "he would stand on his head." She continued with great disdain: "You have never seen such an assimilationist. He always holds his schoolbag in front of the star, and this is sewn so low that one cannot really see it." Within just three weeks, hiding the star had come to mean lack of pride in Jewish identity.[3]

Not all young diarists expressed defiance as unequivocally as did Helga Pol-lack and Bertje van Rhijn. But the act of keeping a diary itself was a form of defiance; of resistance against the Germans' massive campaign conducted in the private and public spheres, indeed in every aspect of children's lives, to undermine their sense of themselves as worthy human beings because they were Jews. Writing offered the diarists a mechanism through which to assert their perceptions and a space in which to maintain their identity. It was a way to raise their voices.

Seventy years later, these documents afford us a window into how young people resisted the Nazi assault. Focusing on six diaries by girls and boys aged twelve-and-a-half to just under fourteen when they began to write (an eigh-teen-month age spread), we shall analyze a spectrum of experiences as report-ed in the journal pages. Helga Pollack kept her diary for six months, from the day before she was deported to Terezín until June 6, 1943. Written more or less clandestinely, it was hidden in the camp by her father when she was shipped to Auschwitz. Like Helga, Pavel Weiner was deported to Terezín. A Prague-born Czech Jew, Pavel, his brother Hanuš (called Handa), and their parents Valy and Ludvik were sent to that transit camp in May 1942. "Now after having spent two years in Terezín, I deeply regret that I haven't kept a diary from the begin-

3. Unpublished diary of Berthe Jeanne Bloch-van Rhijn, in her possession. Photocopy in posses-sion of Debórah Dwork. Entries of May 1 and 20, 1942. Translation of this and all quoted passages by Robert Jan van Pelt and Debórah Dwork.

ning," twelve-year-old Pavel wrote in April 1944.[4] Thus began his record of his third and last year of incarceration; it ended with a final entry on April 22, 1945, shortly before liberation in May. Petr Ginz, born February 1, 1928, was a Prague boy, too. Identified as *Mischlings* by the Nazis because their father was Jewish and their mother gentile, Petr and his sister Eva lived with their parents until each child, in turn, was sent to Terezín at age fourteen. Petr's diary records life at home from September 19, 1941, until August 9, 1942.[5] Yitskhok Rudashevski, also thirteen-and-a-half when he began his two-year diary (June 1941 to April 1943), described his experiences at home and, after his family and community's forced move, in the Vilna ghetto.[6] Dawid Rubinowicz, by contrast, was the son of dairy farmers in the rural village of Krajno. Yet his diary, like Yitskhok's, followed his family from their lives under German occupation at home through their forced removal to the nearby town of Bodzentyn. Twelve-and-a-half at the time of the first entry on March 21, 1940, he was just shy of his fifteenth birthday when the diary broke off in midsentence on June 1, 1942.[7]

Almost certainly, Dawid was murdered in Treblinka. Neither Petr nor Yitskhok survived either. Petr was shipped from Terezín to Auschwitz. Yitskhok and his family secured a hiding place when the Germans liquidated the Vilna ghetto (September 23, 1943) that was discovered a fortnight later; they were murdered in Ponar. Bertje Pollack and her family also hid, and had the great good fortune to survive. During the diary years, Bertje and Jt went from Enschede (where they were hidden for three months), to Apeldoorn (a few weeks), to Beverwijk (three months), and to Leiden (four months). Finally, in May 1943, the sisters and their parents went to Kampen, where they hid in the home of the widowed mother of a university friend of Mrs. van Rhijn. The entire family and the diary—which Bertje carried from place to place—survived. Pavel and his mother were spared because she worked in the mica industry, which the Germans considered essential to their war effort; Handa and Ludvik were deported to Auschwitz and perished in the Dachau subcamp, Kaufering. Helga too was deported to Auschwitz from Terezín. She survived to be reunited with both her father, who had remained in the transit camp, and her mother in England.

The diarists, in short, were girls and boys; rural, town, and city dwellers;

4. Pavel Weiner, *A Boy in Terezín: The Private Diary of Pavel Weiner* (Evanston, Ill.: Northwestern University Press, 2011), 7.

5. Chava Pressburger, ed., *The Diary of Petr Ginz* (New York: Atlantic Monthly Press, 2007).

6. Yitskhok Rudashevski, *The Diary of the Vilna Ghetto* (Tel Aviv: Ghetto Fighters' House, 1979).

7. David Rubinowicz, *The Diary of Dawid Rubinowicz* (Edinburgh: William Blackwood, 1981).

they wrote while at home, in transit camp, in ghetto, and in hiding, and they came from Western, Central, and Eastern Europe. All suffered German occupation; half were murdered. While the immediate contexts of their lives spanned a great range, the subjects they discussed were remarkably similar, starting with each one's choice to keep a diary.[8]

Writing itself was an act of resistance. It required the acquisition of scarce materials—paper, pencils, pens—and called for time, focus, and energy in a situation that claimed all of these for daily life. Then, too, diaries posed a danger if they fell into the hands of the Germans or their allies. Bertje's parents balanced this risk against their daughter's wish to write. They buried her diary in the garden of their hiding home, taking it out from time to time. Bertje wrote her entries, and the diary was returned to its underground spot.[9] If it had been found, the family would have been discovered and the friends who helped them put in jeopardy.

Despite the practical difficulties and the great perils, a number of children kept a diary. Some, like Pavel Weiner, saw their journal as a means to chronicle their experiences; they sought to create a record. He asked, "Wouldn't it be the best remembrance" of a harsh life? "Here one gets to know the harder side of life; one's mother doesn't keep you pampered. One tends to see things with eyes wide open." And he concluded, "I hope that I will be successful and that my diary will fulfill its purpose!"[10] For others, it seems to have been a source of comfort, perhaps even of company. Bertje, for example, chatted to her diary, apologizing for failing to write, as if the diary had feelings and would be hurt by her neglect.

Whether record or friend, the youngsters' journals pertain primarily to their daily lives, the people around them, and themselves. For instance, while still at home in Enschede and attending a newly established Jewish school, Bertje entered three lists. First, she noted her own grades. A list of her friends' grades in relation to her own followed. Third and last, she wrote, "A new series of decrees has been promulgated." And she listed them, with a caveat: "I will write nothing about handing in the bicycles and silver because I think I will remember it

8. See, too, Alexandra Zapruder's important edited collection, *Salvaged Papers: Young Writers' Diaries of the Holocaust* (New Haven, Conn.: Yale University Press, 2002) and Alexandra Garbarini's equally important study of Holocaust diaries (primarily by adult writers), *Numbered Days: Diaries and the Holocaust* (New Haven, Conn.: Yale University Press, 2006).

9. Oral history of Berthe Jeanne Bloch-van Rhijn conducted by Debórah Dwork with Robert Jan van Pelt, Doetinchem, The Netherlands, June 21, 1984.

10. Pavel Weiner, *A Boy in Terezín*, 7.

later, and it really is too dangerous to write down!"[11] In part, youngsters wrote about themselves because they were cut off from the rest of the world. In part, their perspective is simply age appropriate. To see oneself as central, to focus on the mundane details of daily life and, with the onset of adolescence, to become absorbed with one's interior life, are developmentally normal behaviors. And it is precisely this self-absorption that provides a lens on the phenomena of resilience and resistance. How did these youngsters adapt to persecution? How did they manifest their resilience? How, in short, did they resist the Germans' efforts to dehumanize them, to negate their sense of self, and manage to assert themselves as individuals with worries and fears, but also dreams and ambitions?

The diary entries show us some of the mechanisms, like the use of humor, youngsters employed to negotiate the assault they suffered. Their enjoyment of jokes about German measures shines bright. Noting that Jews now had to wear the star emblem, Petr Ginz related, "When I went to school, I counted sixty-nine 'sheriffs,' Mummy counted more than a hundred of them." The language suggests that they had devised a game. He seemed to chortle: "Dlouha avenue is now called 'The Milky Way.'"[12] The same joke circulated among Jews in the Netherlands. Referring to Jewish districts in Amsterdam, Bertje relayed the current quips: "What are the Joden Breestraat and the Waterlooplein called? The Milky Way and the Place d'Etoile!" And, she added, "when you see a Jew fall, you may make a wish."[13]

Through their narratives, the youngsters reveal that they lived on multiple levels simultaneously. They reported the harsh facts of German persecution alongside information about ongoing, life-affirming activities without bridge or segue. "In the morning at the Levituses; they have everything ready for the journey to Poland," Petr noted (October 30, 1941). He continued, "Afternoon in school."[14] Yitskhok Rudashevski moved seamlessly between the horrors he researched in the ghetto and his engagement with the research project. Like many his age in Vilna, Yitskhok belonged to a youth club and he and his companions grew utterly engrossed with the club activities. "We are investigating the history of Courtyard Shavler 4," he explained on October 22, 1942. He elaborated on their system. "Questionnaires have been distributed among the mem-

11. Unpublished diary of Berthe Jeanne Bloch-van Rhijn, entry of July 7, 1942.
12. Pressburger, *The Diary of Petr Ginz*, 28.
13. Unpublished diary of Berthe Jeanne Bloch-van Rhijn, entry of May 8, 1942.
14. Pressburger, *The Diary of Petr Ginz*, 39.

bers, with questions that have to be asked of the courtyard residents.... The questions are divided into four parts: questions relating to the period of Polish, Soviet and German rule (up to the ghetto), and in the ghetto." Yitskhok reported, too, on his experience as an investigator. "The residents answer in different ways.... I got a taste of a historian's task. I sit at the table and ask questions and record the greatest sufferings with cold objectivity. I write, I probe into details, and I do not realize at all that I am probing into wounds, and the one who answers me—indifferent to it: two sons and a husband taken away—the sons Monday the husband Thursday." Perceiving the caesura between the information relayed and his recording of it, he acknowledged, "And this horror, this tragedy is formulated by me in three words, coldly and dryly. I become absorbed in thought, and the words stare out of the paper crimson with blood."[15]

Yitskhok reflected on the importance of this work a fortnight later. "Today we also went to Shavler 4 with the questionnaire for investigating the ghetto. We did not get a good reception. And I must sadly admit that they were right." Yet he remained undaunted. He looked to the future, and envisioned a reckoning. One day, the Germans would be brought to justice. "But I am not at fault either because I consider that everything should be recorded and noted down, even the most gory, because everything will be taken into account."[16]

Club projects served multiple functions. At one and the same time, Yitskhok's research prompted him to pay attention to the misery of ghetto life and, busy with his investigations, inured him to it, kept him intellectually occupied, and nourished his fantasy of postwar power. Pavel Weiner, incarcerated in the Terezín transit camp, had a similar experience. Children accounted for about 10 percent of the population of Theresienstadt. The Germans (happily) took little notice of them, leaving their governance to the Council of Elders. The council's Youth Welfare Department housed the majority of children over the age of four in separate children's homes. At that time many of the Jewish leaders were Zionists, and they had the idea that this collective life would help to instill the values of Zionism while protecting the children from the worst of the brutality of life at Terezín.[17] Assigned to room 7 of building L417, the Czech Boys' Home,

---

15. Rudashevski, *The Diary of Vilna Ghetto*, 73.

16. Ibid., 84.

17. For more on Jewish child life in Terezín, see H. G. Adler, *Theresienstadt 1941–1945: Das Antlitz Einer Zwangsgemeinshaft* (Tübingin: J. C. B. Mohr, 1960), 547–48, 560, 562; Council of Jewish Communities, *Terezín* (Prague: Council of Jewish Communities in the Czech Lands, 1965), 78, 93; Debórah Dwork, *Children with a Star: Jewish Youth in Nazi Europe* (New Haven, Conn.: Yale University Press, 1991), 113–53; Zdenek Lederer, *Ghetto Theresienstadt* (London: Edward Goldston, 1953), 41, 47,

Pavel founded a magazine that, as the room 7 boys called themselves *nešarim* [eagles], he named *Nešar*. Producing the illustrated magazine channeled his energy: writing articles, serving as editor, and encouraging other boys to produce material for it. "I am glad my exams are over and I can devote all my time to *Nešar*," he wrote in his diary on April 4, 1944. "Today I am experiencing a serious crisis with the magazine. There are very few contributions and my head is empty. However, I manage to write two articles: 'Death on the Ship' and 'The Sick Man.'"[18] As for Yitskhok, Pavel's work on the magazine prompted him to pay attention to life in Terezín in order to write about it and, busy with creative production, inured him to it.

The endeavor lurched from struggle to struggle—for good pieces, for readership, for drawings—yet Pavel managed to produce thirteen issues. He spoke of it with pride sixty-five years later. *Nešar*, he said, was like the *New York Review of Books*. The competition, *Rim, Rim, Rim*, was the *New York Post*. One aimed for high culture; the other was popular for its sports reports.[19] The initiative reflected his goals and ambitions. Despite incarceration, and notwithstanding the human resources problem of persuading others to participate, and the practical obstacles of obtaining paper and writing instruments, Pavel pressed forward. He set his sights on "life after." And in the meantime, as his diary entries reveal, he sought to produce some simulacrum of normality.

For youngsters, schooling was crucial to that simulacrum. To go to school meant to preserve a key prewar social norm: children study in order to prepare for the future. Insisting upon their right to an education, maintaining a primary structure of childhood, and keeping their focus on the future, young people carried on alone or in classes—permitted and clandestine—with others. Dawid Rubinowicz, still at home in his village on August 12, 1940, reported on his efforts to continue his education. "All through the war I've been studying at home by myself. When I think of how I used to go to school I feel like bursting into tears."[20] Bertje and Petr, while still at home, went to Jewish schools with other children. Bertje, as we have seen, reported her grades to her diary, and compared them to her classmates'. July 7, 1942: "History 8; Geography 8; Eng-

97, 132–33, 137. For a first-hand account by Gonda Redlich, head of the Jugendfuersorge, see Saul S. Friedman, ed., *The Terezín Diary of Gonda Redlich* (Lexington: University Press of Kentucky, 1992). See too Hannelore Brenner, *The Girls of Room 28: Friendship, Hope, and Survival in Theresienstadt* (New York: Schocken Books, 2009) for a discussion of the Czech girls' counterpart.

18. Pavel Weiner, *A Boy in Terezín*, 7–8.

19. Pavel Weiner, oral history conducted by Debórah Dwork, New York, January 7 and 11, 2010.

20. Dawid Rubinowicz, *The Diary of Dawid Rubinowicz*, 5.

lish 8; Physics 8!; Dutch 7; Biology 9; French 7; German 7; Drawing 7; Algebra 7; Geometry 5; Total: 81 points." Her achievements in relation to others remained important to her. "Herbert 72; Mario 72; Meta 72; Annelies 75; Bertje 81; Marian 82."[21] While the habit of classroom competition may die hard, surely Bertje's comparison of herself with her companions expresses her firm hold on basic tenets of her childhood: she would go to school and would seek to do her best. The German occupation and subsequent regulations that threw her out of the public school system and into a newly established tiny Jewish school did not change her determination. Petr, equally adamant, expressed his commitment to education with a nearly daily log of his school attendance. No matter what measures the Germans took to restrict access to information and knowledge, Petr continued to learn. "In the morning I was in town; there is an announcement on the board in Politika in Wenceslav Square that Jews are not allowed to read newspapers. In the afternoon at school," he reported on March 12, 1942.[22]

Whether at home, in ghetto, in transit camps, or in hiding, the youngsters held fast to education. On September 19, 1942, fifteen months after Vilna fell to the German army (June 24, 1941) and a year after the institution of the ghetto (September 6, 1941), Yitskhok confided his despair to his diary. "It is cold and sad. When in the world will we get back to our studies? When I used to go to my lessons, I knew how to divide the days, and the days would fly, and now they drag by for me grayly and sadly. Oh, how dreary and sad it is to sit locked up in a ghetto." A few weeks later (October 5), his gymnasium (academic high school) classes began and he was delighted. "Finally I have lived to see the day. Today we go to school. The day passed quite differently. Lessons, subjects..... There is a happy spirit in school.... My own life is shaping up in quite a different way! We waste less time, the day is divided and flies by very quickly.... Yes, that is how it should be in the ghetto, the day should fly by and we should not waste time."[23] He didn't. "I often reflect, this is supposedly the ghetto yet I have such a rich life of intellectual work: I study, I read, I visit club circles," Yitskhok reported on March 18, 1943, less than a month before his diary ended abruptly on April 6. By that date, millions of Jews had been murdered. Yitskhok's entries detail German *aktionen* in the ghetto, his family's attempts to hide, their mortal terror, his keen interest in news about the war. Yet he continued to channel his focus on productive activities. "Time runs by so quickly and there is so much

21. Unpublished diary of Berthe Jeanne Bloch-van Rhijn, entry of July 7, 1942.
22. Pressburger, The Diary of Petr Ginz, 90.
23. Rudashevski, *The Diary of Vilna Ghetto*, 56, 65.

work to be done, lectures, social gatherings. I often forget I am in the ghetto."[24]

Pavel, too, worried about wasting time. In his diary, he discussed the subjects the room 7 boys studied, the books they read, and topics they discussed. As everyone maintained the idea that the educational program prepared the youngsters for postwar reentry into the school system, the boys were tested in math, physics, Hebrew, Czech literature, geography, and history. If Pavel was fiercely determined to continue his education, the Jewish administration policies and practices supported his ambitions, as did the social culture of the camp in general and his parents in particular. Still: the energy and drive came from him. He reported in detail on what he learned in classes and the private lessons he enjoyed. His parents paid with food for English-language tutorials and piano instruction for him, and he begged his mother to teach him French. No matter how much he did, he fretted that it was insufficient. "Two years of my life have been lost," he lamented on August 4, 1944. "If I were in Prague, I would be going to theaters, I would read, I would write, but here I have no materials, no opportunity, and no freedom." He resolved: "I will start leading a new life.... I will study, read, and study some more."[25]

Diary writing; constructive activities; education: all of these were expressions of the children's resistance to the Germans' message that they had no future. Yet the lifeblood of the youngsters' existence was their relationships with family and friends. These relationships were their most important form of resistance to the Germans' ever more violent program of dehumanization. At no point did the children stop feeling or caring. At no point did they stop writing about those feelings and cares. Their active emotional lives defied the Germans' plans.

Expressions of love and yearning abound. Writing after she had been in bed for a week with a cold and an eye inflammation, Helga Pollack confessed, "I cried many times as I lay there, mostly from longing for my mom. Now, I don't cry any more because it gave my dad a heavy heart."[26] Sometimes, however, the youngsters' attention to interpersonal relationships served as a screen to protect them against the assault they endured. Bertje, for example, focused on the turmoil of her hiding home rather than the catastrophic situation outside her door. Separated from their parents, Bertje and Jt's first hiding home was with a woman whom she called "aunt" in her diary; her husband, a public

24. Ibid., 135–36.
25. Pavel Weiner, *A Boy in Terezín*, 108–09.
26. Unpublished diary of Helga Kinsky-Pollack, entry of March 3, 1943.

notary, "uncle;" their teenaged son, "Sjors," and the maid, Bep. According to Bertje, "uncle" was a difficult man who fought with his wife. Her first report, a few weeks after her arrival, mentioned the discord briefly. As time went on, her descriptions became increasingly graphic. "Wednesday, 2 September [1942]. We have been having horrible days. Auntie and Uncle had a quarrel." Some ten days later, Uncle went out to consult on a will and the rest of the household had dinner without him. Auntie put the girls to bed and while she was reading a book to them, "Uncle came in, furious, so furious he couldn't get the words out of his mouth, because dinner was not ready. He stormed out, and when he gets back his meal must be prepared. When he returned at 11:30 everything was ready, but of course he did not want anything! The idiot! Bah: he is totally awful." This occurred on a Sunday, and Auntie remained in her room until dinnertime on Tuesday. "He came back from the office at least ten times on Monday morning. He watches everything. Risking our lives, Bep and we brought Auntie her food and coffee. Oh, if he had seen us doing it. He specifically instructed Bep not to do this.... And the worst is that [Auntie] is so afraid of him."[27] Bertje and Jt were the ones in hiding, yet it was Auntie who hid in her room. No word about Bertje's and Jt's fears of the Germans and Dutch Nazis, while Auntie cowered. Through Bertje's experience of the relationships around her, she resisted the Nazi assault: she was not the prisoner; she did not feel fear. On the contrary: she was the rescuer!

By the end of the month, Bertje hardly could keep up with her accounts of the domestic fights. "Tuesday 22 September. I just want to say that we have received no news from Father and Mother, and that yesterday and today there were again quarrels," she began. "Auntie is allowed to do this. Bep must do that, Auntie must do this, Bep must do that. Completely idiotic.... Poor Auntie." In her view, Uncle saw Auntie as "a nice, tough cleaning lady who works herself to death for him, and with whom he can do what he wishes." What did she, Bertje, want? "I must say I would not mind if they would imprison Uncle for a few months!" For Bertje, "Uncle" was the enemy—not the Germans. Indeed, she mentioned the Germans infrequently. Her anxiety arose from, and her anger was directed at, the uncle. It was the domestic—not national or international—situation that shaped her interior life. A key factor was communication with her parents. Her ability to tolerate the household tension was in direct relation to her contact with them. "I really hope a letter will come soon," she

---

27. Unpublished diary of Berthe Jeanne Bloch-van Rhijn, entries of September 2 and 13, 1942.

lamented that same day. "That would cheer us up again." As further entries illuminate, when Bertje did not hear from them, she had difficulty coping; when she received a letter or phone call, the wrangling was of no consequence. "This morning a short violent explosion. The whole day was passed in bitter silence, but it does not bother us. Last night [Father and Mother] phoned ... and today we got a very, very wonderful letter. We just loved it, and we look forward to writing back."[28]

Unfortunately, the comfort Bertje got from her contact with her parents did not sustain her for long. The situation deteriorated. "Thursday 1 October. THE QUARREL. Last night before we went to eat everything was normal, not ordinary, but normal ... and when Uncle slurped his soup, Sjors told him that even without teeth [he wore dentures] it was not necessary to slurp.... When Sjors said this, Uncle got angry and stood up. 'This is a household out of a Jan Steen painting! A Jan Steen household!' ... Auntie was always out on the street, always out of the house, this was a Jan Steen household, etc. [Auntie left on her bike] after this violent quarrel, and [Uncle] locked all the doors so Auntie could not get in any more. But Bep stayed up, and opened the door for Auntie."[29] Bertje felt affection and loyalty for her "aunt," and her identification of her as a victim helped her negotiate her own situation. It was the aunt who was locked out of her own home, not Bertje. Again, no word about the Germans' actions: her "uncle" had bolted the doors. And Bep, the servant, sneaked her in. Thus Auntie eluded danger and Bertje, through her, eluded the dangers of the outside world at war. She was safe.

For Bertje, the relationship between Auntie and Uncle loomed large. Pavel, by contrast, focused on his relationships with the other boys; Frantisek (nicknamed Franta) Maier, the young man who served as the head counselor, or *madrich*, of room 7 in the Czech boys' home; and his parents, his mother in particular. Much of what has shaped Theresienstadt's postwar image—the organization of children's homes and schooling efforts; music and lectures; the Red Cross visit; Geron's propaganda film; the exchange transport to Switzerland and the white buses to Sweden—appears in the pages of Pavel's *Diary*. Famous people (Jews) and infamous figures (Nazis) flit across the pages. Yet his turbulent relationships with the other boys and his parents claim much more of his attention.

In 1944, Pavel quarreled regularly with everybody. The boy who emerges

28. Ibid., entries of September 22 and 23, 1942.
29. Ibid., October 1, 1942.

from the diary was nothing like the even-tempered, good-natured, well-liked adult he became. He adored Franta, and felt slighted when the madrich appeared to favor another. He sought friendship, and felt hurt when the other boy seemed to choose someone else's company. His father annoyed him, even while Pavel worried mightily about his health. He fought with his mother about everything: what he ate; what he wore; what he did; what *she* did; what *she* said. Yet he wanted nothing more than her love and approval. "I go to my mother's in order to study French. When I arrive at my mother's, she refuses to teach me. I am very angry," he raged (April 29). The underlying cause of his distress tumbled out. "It comes to a point when even my mother doesn't believe in me. I feel miserable. It affects my whole disposition. I feel totally abandoned. The worst is when I have an argument with my parents. I am unhappy." Yet: "I don't listen to my mother."[30]

Like the other young diarists, Pavel was an adolescent. He suffered from the mood swings, self-doubts, and self-absorption so characteristic of that stage of life. Even while caught in the Nazi net. Pavel's diary lays bare the maturation of a twelve-year-old boy through his bar mitzvah year at a particular time, 1944–45, and in a particular place, the Terezín transit camp. As he neared his thirteenth birthday, he began to actualize his insights into actions. Perhaps age accounted for this development. Possibly it was due to events. In one month, from September 27 through October 28, the Germans shipped 18,422 people to Auschwitz. The deportations emptied the camp and Pavel, still subject to adolescent turmoil, nevertheless gained greater perspective. "The impact of the circumstances affects one so much that one doesn't know what he is doing and tends to vent one's feelings to the nearest person—in my case, it is my mother even though I love her." Beginning to outgrow the urge to express his anxiety as anger, "This argument quiets down shortly because love towards Mother overtakes me and I calm down." At core, he acknowledged (October 14), "I see in my mother the only friend I have."[31]

It was a pivotal realization. Describing his mother, Pavel's words and tone changed. "I feel sorry for her that she works so hard," he wrote the next day. He walked "through the empty streets." Despair overwhelmed him. "I can see only darkness and in this darkness there is only one bright spot and that is my mother."[32] They continued to quarrel, of course. But he had begun to grow up. The adult this young person would become glimmers in his entries. "I'm only

30. Pavel Weiner, *A Boy in Terezín*, 31.   31. Ibid., 176.
32. Ibid., 177.

13 years old and I can already independently form my views about the world," he reflected on New Year's Eve 1944. "I have grasped what life is about, which is the principal matter and also the most difficult one."[33]

Hundreds of miles to the east, Dawid Rubinowicz reported on his interactions with his neighbors and, most especially, his father. As the Jews' situation worsened and the Germans' actions became increasingly violent, the Rubinowiczes' gentile neighbors' attitude changed. Dawid's report (February 12, 1942) of a particularly appalling incident suggests his sense of betrayal as well as his overriding chagrin. "I recognized the village constable and asked him where he was going. He said he was going to the mayor with notices." The constable lied. "About two hours later the village constable came up and began putting up a notice. It wasn't a notice but a caricature of Jews." In sharp contrast to his typically terse prose, Dawid detailed these Nazi stereotype images. "On it a Jew is shown, mincing meat and putting a rat in the mincer. Another is pouring water from a bucket into milk. In a third picture a Jew is shown stamping dough with his feet, and worms are crawling over him and the dough." The text, Dawid reported, "ran as follows:"

> Dear reader, before your very eyes,
> Are Jews deceiving you with lies,
> If you buy your milk from them beware,
> Dirty water they've poured in there,
> Into the mincer dead rats they throw,
> Then as mincemeat it's put on to show.
> Worms infest their home-made bread,
> Because the dough with feet they tread.

An odious text. Yet it was his neighbors' reaction that Dawid seems to have taken to heart. "Some people came along, and their laughter gave me a headache from the shame that Jews suffer nowadays."[34] Two months later, the family had been removed to Bodzentyn, and Dawid and his father returned (with a pass) to Krajno. He had hoped his former neighbors would give him a little money or food. Few responded. "I meant to collect a few coppers, but it was no use." Whatever solidarity or compassion they might have felt disappeared when the family was forced to move. "While we lived here, it was easier to get things; now people won't put themselves out," Dawid observed. The social fabric had disintegrated. Writing about it, Dawid conveyed what he experienced as

---

33. Ibid., 212.
34. Rubinowicz, *The Diary of Dawid Rubinowicz*, 42–3.

significant in words on paper. He observed, analyzed, and commented. In so doing, he resisted the role allotted him.

Dawid cared about his neighbors' attitudes and actions. But however humiliating or disappointing these may have been, they held little weight in comparison to his father's attitudes and actions. One day Josek lost his temper. As Dawid saw it, Josek was responsible for the situation. Father "began to be very angry at me—why had I scattered the wood all over the wood-shed—and beat me. I told him I hadn't had time to tidy up the wood [because Josek had called him away], and he beat me even more. I was very upset with him for beating me without cause. And finally, when he'd beaten me so hard several times with his belt buckle, I began crying, not so much out of pain as anger." Dawid realized that "but for the war I wouldn't have been at home, I'd have long been out learning a trade," but this was mere backdrop for the real issue: his unjust punishment. From there it was a mere short step to his age-appropriate lament: "Father doesn't love me at all, and he wouldn't be sorry if something happened to me."[35]

As it transpired, Josek was caught first. "6 May. A terrible day!" A Jewish and a Polish policeman, acting for the Germans, seized Jewish men for forced labor in the Skarzysko camp. Dawid caught sight of his father in the back of a truck. "I kept on looking at him until he disappeared around the corner, then I had a sudden fit of crying, and I felt how much I love him and how much he loves me." Dawid realized that what he "wrote on 1st May about him not loving me was a beastly lie," and mourned that "the dearest person in the whole world we had, they've taken from us."[36] To the family's immense relief, Josek was released a month later: "No one can imagine our joy." But there was no happy ending to this story. That was Dawid's last entry; his diary breaks off midsentence. A loving son, bright, energetic, and sensible, he had resisted dehumanization until his last recorded word.[37]

Dawid's diary came to an abrupt end on May 6, 1943. Bertje, in hiding in Kampen, continued to write through liberation in May 1945. Following the war news, she learned that the Allies had mounted "a new offensive at Arnhem and Nijmegen." She knew that this meant "only a few days now," and she began to worry about her return to her hometown. "In my heart I am afraid that we will not be greeted warmly in Enschede. I just cannot imagine walking in the

35. Ibid., 66–7. 36. Ibid., 70.
37. Ibid., 86–7.

streets of Enschede again." Thinking of being seen, of being publicly visible once again, Bertje proceeded to examine herself, to describe how she saw herself in the mirror. She was well aware of German stereotypes of Jews; she'd digested five years of Occupation newspaper reports and articles. Her self-image reflected none of that.

I am rather content with the way I look. I am not so shy any more, thank God. I still blush often, but less frequently than I used to. My hair is nice: short, with two barrettes on each side and a parting. My barrettes are really gone, completely bent out of shape. They do not hold any more, and there are none others left. Now I hold my hair with two pins, which drop out all the time. I have a nice nose if I say so myself, great mouth, chin with little dimples, and freckles over my whole face except my forehead. A good temper, hm., hm., good hands and nails, good legs. In a word, I am content with myself. But it will be great later, when I will be able to buy new dresses again, and nice shoes, and to have a professional haircut.[38]

The liberation of Enschede meant many things to many people. For Bertje it signified that she would leave her hiding place and return home. As she was anxious about the reception she would receive when she went back to Enschede, she consoled herself that she was sociable and pretty. Even her nose, that most reviled of "Jewish" features, was "nice."

Diaries express a private voice. Singing, by contrast, is typically done out loud, in the public realm. While diary writing is a solitary activity and the narrative carries a single voice, singing is often done with others. Children sang to raise their spirits, to express their identity, and simply to pass the time. They sang while still at home, in ghettos, in camps, and in transit from one place to another.

Songs were a means to create bonds and to transmit culture. Adults used song for educational purposes and children used song to educate themselves. Commenting upon the Germans' efforts to shut down education in the Kovno ghetto, the Zionist lawyer Avraham Golub, now deputy secretary to the Jewish Council, applauded one Mrs. Segal. Mrs. Segal, he reported to his diary on March 21, 1943, "pays no heed to the bans and prohibitions. Although the Jewish school has been officially closed on orders from the Germans, this order has yet to reach this courageous and distinguished educator. Every day, children gather in her own small room, where she teaches them the alphabet, to say 'Shalom' in Hebrew, and to sing Hebrew songs." Mrs. Segal's choice of songs and the language in which they were sung are key. Both served a specific pur-

38. Unpublished diary of Berthe Jeanne Bloch-van Rhijn, entry of April 3, 1945.

pose: "She implants in their hearts a love for the Jewish people and a longing for their homeland—the land of Israel."

Devoted to her kindergartners, the redoubtable Mrs. Segal focused on the Jewish holidays to teach them about their history and about moral courage. "Today is Purim," Golub wrote in his diary. "Hitler has promised that there will be no more Purim festivities for the Jews." But in the Kovno ghetto, "our children, our Mosheles and Shlomeles, give lie to Hitler's predictions by celebrating Purim with all their innocence and enthusiasm." Mrs. Segal's kindergartners "have been preparing the Purim festivities for many weeks. They have been learning the Purim songs, the dances, the games.... Who is going to play the part of Mordechai, Haman, Queen Esther and Vashti? The children have been telling their parents all about their Purim preparations, and the parents— if there are any parents left alive—let themselves be drawn in by the festive atmosphere."[39] If the adult, Mrs. Segal, helped the children resist the Germans' assault, the youngsters' enthusiasm helped the adults, too.

Yitskhok Rudashevski's experience in Vilna mirrored the situation in Kovno, although he and his friends were some years older than Mrs. Segal's kindergartners. "Today we had a club holiday," Yitskhok wrote on December 11, 1942. "I look around at the crowd, all of our kind teachers, friends, intimates. It is so cozy, so warm, so pleasant." The youngsters baked a potato pudding, recited poems, and sang. "Until late into the night we sang with the adults songs which tell about youthfulness and hope.... Song after song resounded. " The whole event, and the singing in particular, gave them great joy. "We do not want to go home. Songs kept bursting forth, they simply will not stop." Yitskhok's interpretation was clear and unequivocal. This showed that "we can maintain our youthful zeal. We have proven that from the ghetto there will not emerge a youth broken in spirit; from the ghetto there will emerge a strong youth which is hardy and cheerful."[40]

Singing was a sociable activity enjoyed by many young people in ghettos throughout Nazi Europe. Like Yitskhok, Mania Tenenbaum, a native of Radom, belonged to a youth club, in her case the Zionist organization Masada. Masada continued to function in Radom ghetto, and it served as "a second home" for Mania. A smaller social unit emerged, she explained decades later. "I was in a group of eight people. It was *our* group." As she recalled, "Here we were, a

39. Avraham Tory, *Surviving the Holocaust: The Kovno Ghetto Diary*, ed. Martin Gilbert (Cambridge, Mass.: Harvard University Press, 1990), 253f.

40. Rudashevski, *The Diary of Vilna Ghetto*, 104–5.

group of kids, dancing and singing and playing, so big deal, so there was war outside." Through these activities, they held on to prewar life. "Even when they were killing on the outside, we were sort of oblivious to it. I mean, we heard and it was said, but somehow we lived a semi-normal life." Music was particularly important to them. "We used to spend wonderful evenings listening to music.... My friend [George Krongold] who was an opera singer, would sing, play guitar and sing."[41] Mira Teeman, orphaned in the Lodz ghetto, lived in a small children's home supervised by Chaim Rumkowski, chairman of the Jewish Council. In this group, too, one of the youngsters was an opera singer. "It was wonderful, what we had," Mira remembered half a century later. "Lucy sang opera arias, and taught us to be a choir. So we were singing very much. It was wonderful." Singing together forged bonds and, equally important, brought comfort: "It was in a way a period of quietness."[42]

Singing had a similar function in transit camps. In Terezín, adults organized a range of now famous musical activities for children. They sought to shield the youngsters; to nurture them through song and thus help them resist the Germans' assault on their childhood. And the youngsters appreciated these productions and were eager to participate. Decades later, Helga Pollack remembered these activities very well. "Some children were in choirs singing from Smetana or *Brundibár*, and some were playing theater and some were dancing, because there was a choreographer from the National Opera House.... One of my best friends of those days was Ella [Weisberger] who was in *Brundibár*."[43] She recalled correctly. The composer Karel Reiner worked with children, choreographer Kamila Rosenbaum interpreted Jan Karafiát's "Fire-Flies" as a dance-play for children (it was shown nearly thirty times) and, best known of all, the conductor Rafael Schächter trained a children's choir and produced the enormously popular opera *Brundibár*. As we have seen in the case of Mrs. Segal and her kindergartners in Kovno, Schächter's choice of opera and language are significant. Composed by Hans Krása with libretto by Adolf Hoffmeister in Prague in 1938, *Brundibár* features children, and spins a morality tale of good defeating evil. It was hugely successful, playing fifty-five times in Terezín. For the spectators, the children represented hope in the future, and the youngsters vanquished the evil Brundibár, who had come to represent Hitler.

41. Mania Salinger-Tenenbaum, oral history recorded by Debórah Dwork, Bloomfield, Michigan, January 10 and 29, March 7, 1987.

42. Mira Teeman, oral history recorded by Debórah Dwork, Stockholm, September 6, 1995.

43. Helga Kinsky-Pollack, oral history recorded by Debórah Dwork, Vienna, August 15, 1989.

Children in Terezín sang in such major productions and, as Pavel Weiner mentioned in his diary, they sang as part of their daily education. "4 April 1944. Franta comes to give an exam in singing. During the exam I get angry because Franta keeps saying that I have lost my pitch. I am very worried, but I pass the exam." Groups of boys and groups of girls formed choruses, too. Pavel noted rehearsals and the song composers. "I go to Room 9, where they are singing songs by Voskovec and Werich," he wrote on August 2, 1944.[44] Jiří Voskovec and Jiří Werich founded the avant-garde, anti-Fascist Liberated Theater in Prague, which the Nazis closed. Yet the boys sang their defiant songs in Terezín.

Conditions in other transit camps did not allow for the rich cultural and intellectual life of Terezín. But music, easily organized and needing no special instruments, prevailed as perhaps the most common cultural activity in which children engaged. "I know that we sang songs all the time there," in Westerbork, Esther Levi, then nine years old, recalled.[45] Irene Hasenberg, age thirteen, also remembered singing with others. "I have memories of in the summertime [in Bergen-Belsen in 1944] that there was a group of young people; on a Friday night there would be *oneg shabbat* [Sabbath celebration] and we would sit together between two barracks and sing songs.... I don't remember it happening very many times, but I have the image of sitting out there in the evening in the summertime for *oneg shabbat* and singing Hebrew songs. Hebrew songs and other songs, but I particularly remember that we sang Hebrew songs."[46]

Singing, children expressed their convictions and their identity and, in a range of contexts, sometimes defiance. Helga Pollack, deported by the Germans, joined her companions in song as they were forced to depart. "When the train started to move, Kyjov's youth began to sing—which made the Germans murmur," she told her diary. Children under Georges Loinger's care, by contrast, left France for Switzerland clandestinely, and they sang too. He explained his underground railroad to spirit children to safety: "I went to Lyon to get them, and took them from Lyon to Annemasse, all together as group, by train." The youngsters "were prepared as if they were children who were leav-

44. Pavel Weiner, *A Boy in Terezín*, 9, 107.

45. Esther Levi, oral history recorded by Debórah Dwork with Robert Jan van Pelt, Hilversum, The Netherlands, June 18, 1986.

46. Irene Butter-Hasenberg, oral history recorded by Debórah Dwork, Ann Arbor, Michigan, October 10 and November 7, 1986; March 5 and April 6, 1987; April 16, 1994.

ing for summer camp, and they were like such children, anxious, but gay. They sang and played in the train." Referring to another group that was deported by the Germans, he recalled, "Like the children of Izieu who sang, 'You Will Never Have Alsace and Lorraine' in the truck, these children sang also."[47]

Jack Rubinfeld, who at thirteen was the same age as the youngsters Georges Loinger sought to save, was forced from his village of Bircza, west of Lvóv in Galicia in the summer of 1942. The Jewish population was marched from Bircza to Przemysl; older people, his mother among them, were shot and buried on the side of the road. From Przemysl the survivors were taken to Starochowice; unbeknownst to them, they were scheduled for deportation to Belzec annihilation camp. Jack's sister noticed that the Germans were singling out young people who would be good workers and urged Jack to join them. Although he was not large for his age, he edged near the selected group "and kneeled down next to them. I noticed right after that one of my close friends who I was at school with came and wanted to join that group also, and they just smashed his head in two. Just like that." The group was detailed to the Flugzeugmotorenwerk Reichshof, an airplane motor factory in Rzeszów. Jack did not think about the future; he managed day by day: "You were worrying how you were going to make it for the next day. Will you make it until tomorrow?" He, together with others, "tried to start to do something, singing, just to try to get it out of your mind."[48] It was a way of holding on, of keeping despair at bay. Shortly before his diary ended, Yitskhok Rudashevski described such a moment. The ghetto inhabitants had just learned that five thousand Jews had been shot to death in Ponar. "The children run away from their homes where it is terrible to stay on account of the mood," he reported. "The teachers are also despondent. So we sit in a circle. We rally our spirits. We sing a song." His very last entry, written the following day (Wednesday, April 7, 1943) continued: "Our mood is a little better. A happy song can be heard from the club." Yet, he concluded, "We may be fated for the worst."

Seeking to escape the worst, Herta Heymans and her family hid. Herta's mother was a German Jew; her father a Dutch Jew. They lived in Essen (Germany) until 1937 when they moved to the Netherlands to escape persecution. But the Nazis caught up with them and in 1942 the Heymans were forced to

47. Georges Loinger, oral history recorded by Debórah Dwork, Paris, June 26, 1987. See too Georges Loinger, *Aux Frontières de l'espoir* (Paris: Editions le Manuscrit, 2006).

48. Jack Rubinfeld, oral history recorded by Debórah Dwork, Ann Arbor, Michigan, November 9, 1987.

go underground. Herta, age fifteen, her grandfather, and another elderly man were hidden by an older couple in a "tiny little working-class house." Like Jack Rubinfeld, Herta "just thought of surviving today. You couldn't think as far as tomorrow, you couldn't." Herta remembered her grandfather as "a strict disciplinarian and he would tell me off in no uncertain way if I did something wrong in his eyes." Unable to express affection—"that wasn't done, not in my youth, it wasn't unfortunately"—he was "kind in his own way; he meant well." It was terribly important to her that he was there with her. Fortunately, "he was a very, very musical person." This served both grandfather and granddaughter: "We would have sort of a quiz." Herta challenged him, "Sing me the second movement from Beethoven's First Symphony! And he would sing it. He couldn't play an instrument but he was very musical. Or he would sing arias from operas. That's how we passed the time." All in a whisper.[49] If singing offered a diversion, it was also a means of transmitting a culture both valued. He wanted her to know about opera and classical music, and she wished to learn. The game gave the teenager in hiding and her strict, elderly grandfather a way to communicate and to help each other get through another day. Raising their voices in whispered song, they held on to a canon of knowledge and to each other.

Magda Somogyi and her family were less fortunate than the Heymans; they met the worst. Magda, her parents, two brothers, sister, and grandparents were deported from their small town in Hungary to Auschwitz in the summer of 1944. "We were together, the whole family, but the first day when we arrived in Auschwitz we were selected. My parents, my grandfather, my grandmother, and my little brother all were selected by Mengele and sent to the crematorium. The very first hour," she related many decades later. The sixteen-year-old Magda and her seventeen-year-old sister remained together and, as they looked alike and were thought to be twins, they were sent to the barracks for the twins on whom Mengele and his colleagues experimented.[50] "It was an awful life, because I knew what was happening to me and to the other children. I cannot begin to express, or describe, how awful these experiments were," she recalled. Yet even there, the older inmates used song to alleviate the youngsters' pain. "We had a program for children every day. For instance, in the morning we played a game and we

49. Herta Montrose-Heymans, oral history recorded by Debórah Dwork, Cardiff, Wales, July 21, 1985.

50. For more on the pseudo-medical experimentation at Auschwitz, especially on twins, see: Lucette Matalon Lagnado and Sheila Cohn Dekel, *Children of the Flames* (New York: William Morrow, 1991) and Miklos Nyiszli, *Auschwitz: A Doctor's Eyewitness Account* (New York: Fawcett, 1960), 31–32; 50-6; 100–03.

were singing." There were no classes, "no education. Only singing, only songs. We learned songs." Possibly because youngsters came from so many countries and they needed one language in common, they sang "German songs." Magda remembered the daily routine vividly. "A day's program. Early in the morning we got up and our block *elteste* [head] said, 'Clean the shoes, make the beds.' The older children helped the little children make the beds and clean the shoes." They were permitted to go to the toilet and to "the washroom to wash ourselves with cold water. After this, we went back into the barrack and we made our programs. We were singing or playing games," with, again, teenagers like Magda and her sister looking after the young ones.

What did singing mean in that notorious "medical experimentation" barracks in Birkenau? How are we to understand it? Surely it was a way to pass the time; for the teenagers to occupy themselves and to amuse the youngsters. Still: singing was a choice. A cooperative endeavor, it entailed teaching (and learning) tune and words, and joining in unison. Singing thus brought the children together and created connections between them. They sang out loud. This holds great significance in a place where the slightest sound in the Germans' presence was forbidden and at risk of death. "When the SS came into the block," Magda explained, "all the children were silent, even the tiny children. Every child was silent. When they went out, these SS, then the children began again to play and to sing."[51]

We will never know what the move from silence to sound signified for the children. Thus we cannot make too much of it. Nor should we minimize it. The Germans' command for silence and the children's consciousness of the price of disobedience imbue the song with meaning; the command adds weight and significance to the disobedience. Ordering the children to be mute, the SS minimized and diminished the young prisoners' physical presence. In that context, perhaps raising their voices upon the Germans' departure was a way of saying: We are here.

51. Magda Somogyi, oral history recorded by Debórah Dwork, Budapest, Hungary, July 19, 1987.

Joanna Beata Michlic

13   An Untold Story of Rescue

Jewish Children and Youth in German-Occupied Poland

> In the first years, society could bear to listen only to the bold voices of the underground fighters and the rebels. They resonated clearly in a world that had fought the Nazis, and in a nascent State of Israel in the midst of its own war for existence. It was years until the concept of heroism could also echo in a piece of bread given by one prisoner to another, in a prayer of the "Days of Awe" handwritten by memory in the absence of prayer books, in the ability to love in the camp, in the gallows humor, or in the voice of Primo Levi, who recited Dante on his way to pick up a pot of soup.... Years passed until the guilt of the survivors vis-à-vis the killed, and even more the guilt of society vis-à-vis the survivors, gave way to listening and documentation. At the last moment.
> —Michal Govrin, *Hold On to the Sun. True Stories and Tales* (New York: The Feminist Press, 2010), 221.

Thinking Outside the Box about Rescue

In recent years, scholars have come to realize that they had neglected research on Jews who rescued Jews during the Holocaust and that this has resulted in a limited understanding of Jewish self-help "as a phenomenon of pre-armed stages of resistance and also as counterevidence to the perception of Jewish passivity in the face of their powerlessness."[1] There is an unmet need for analytical concepts to delineate a variety of complex and nuanced indi-

---

1. Michael Berenbaum, "The Rescuers: When the Ordinary Is Extraordinary," in *The Routledge History of the Holocaust*, ed. Jonathan C. Friedman (London: Routledge, 2011), 316.

vidual Jewish responses—terms that should expand our vocabulary of Jewish self-help and complicate our understanding of it. Current lively debates among scholars and Jewish survivors alike and the recent scholarly conferences and publications promise to correct this troubling gap.

Historians have come to recognize individual Jewish self-help during the Holocaust as a multifaceted field for scholarly inquiry whose thorough investigation will undoubtedly lead to a deeper understanding of the history of Jewish individuals and communities, the role of gender under extreme genocidal conditions, and the uncovering of previously unknown historical events. Studying Jewish self-help may also result in meaningful scholarly comparisons with responses of other national and ethnic communities who like European Jews were also subjected to genocide.

This new positive approach toward the subject of Jewish self-help has risen out of research on Jewish nonarmed resistance known as *amidah*.[2] That research has been part of the ongoing process of the redefinition of Jewish resistance. The advancement of the history of Jewish women and families during the Holocaust has also contributed to the study of Jewish self-help, as has a growing frustration with the Yad Vashem criteria for the recognition of rescuers, the Righteous Among the Nations. This important award was created in 1962–63 to be bestowed only on non-Jewish rescuers, with no provision to recognize Jews who rescued other Jews.[3] Another important, perhaps decisive factor is the recent recognition of the validity of a variety of personal testimonies in the reconstruction of Jewish social history during and after the Holocaust. In the words of the historian Omer Bartov, "testimonies can save events from oblivion ... and also provide very different perspectives of events known through conventional documents."[4]

This essay deals with what may be the most underresearched aspect of indi-

2. On the full definition of resistance as *amidah*, see Yehuda Bauer, *Rethinking the Holocaust* (New Haven, Conn.: Yale University Press, 2001), 120.

3. On the history of the commemoration of the Righteous Among the Nations, see Kobi Kabalek, "The Commemoration before the Commemoration: Yad Vashem and the Righteous Among the Nations, 1945–1963," *Yad Vashem Studies* 39 (2011): 169–211.

4. Omer Bartov, "Testimony and History. Setting the Record Straight," *Pastforward* (Spring 2011): 24. See too, Omer Bartov, "Interethnic Relations in the Holocaust: Postwar Testimonies from Buczacz in East Galicia, 1941–1944," *Zmanim: A Historical Quarterly* 98 (Spring 2007): 82–91 (in Hebrew), previously published as: "Les relations interéthniques à Buczacz (Galicie orientale) durant la Shoah selon les témoignages d'après-guerre," *Cultures d'Europe Centrale* 5: "La Destruction des confins," ed. Delphine Bechtel and Xavier Galmiche (Centre Interdisciplinaire de Recherches Centre-Européennes, Université de Paris-Sorbonne, Paris IV, 2005), 47–67.

vidual Jewish self-help, namely the help of older children and youth bestowed on other children. My goals here are to signal key problems, to contextualize the topic within the broader studies of rescue and the history of Jewish childhood during the Holocaust, and to describe a few different examples of self-help among older children and youth. I do not intend to provide a synthetic and in-depth picture of this subject; my rather modest aim is to establish it on the map of the history of Jews rescuing Jews.

There is no doubt that children and youth were able to help each other, but on a smaller scale than Jewish adults because of their age and a number of factors related to it. As young people, they lacked connections with underground Jewish and non-Jewish organizations and did not own property that could provide hiding places for other Jews. Nevertheless, individual older Jewish children helped each other, and their self-help took different forms inside the ghettos and on the Aryan side. We learn about the spectrum of such self-help in the so-called "ego documents" of Jewish child and teenage survivors, such as memoirs, diaries, letters, interviews, and oral histories from different periods, beginning with the wartime and early postwar years. Some of this primary material, especially from the wartime period, is only fragmentary.

In addition to the general problem of lack of scholarly interest in individual self-help of Jews, two specific issues hindered the study of self-help among Jewish children and youth. The first collectors (*zamlers*) of child survivors' testimonies in the early postwar period deemed child survivors' accounts of little value to historians. In their eyes, child survivors' testimonies could not be treated as historical evidence because children at their stage of cognitive development lack the capacity to transmit their lived experiences and general information accurately. This was the position advocated by Genia Silkes (Sylkes) (1914–84), herself a survivor and an active member of the Central Jewish Historical Commission (*Tsentrale yiddishe historische komisye*), a body first established in Poland in August 1944 and transformed into the *Żydowski Instytut Historyczny* (Jewish Historical Institute, ZIH) in October 1947. In 1945, Silkes compiled the instructions for interviewing child survivors that became the guidelines for the newly established Jewish Historical Commissions in Poland. The guide was published in both Polish and Yiddish in Łódź, a major thriving city of Jewish life in post-1945 Poland.[5] It stated that the *children's testimonies were considered*

---

5. On Łódź as a thriving center of Jewish life in postwar Poland, see Shimon Redlich, *Life In Transit: Jews in Postwar Lodz, 1945–1950* (Boston, Mass.: Academic Studies Press, 2010) and the 2008 documentary film by Sławomir Grünberg, *Peretznkis* (LOGTV and Polish TV SA).

valuable material for psychological and educational purposes rather than important documents for historians.[6] "When carrying out precise studies of children, we assume beforehand that they are less valuable than evidentiary material; however, they have a psychological value that can't be reckoned with, which adults are not in the position to give us."[7] Somewhat contradictorily, Silkes, and other like-minded activists of the Jewish Historical Commissions, also viewed the children's testimonies as powerful emotional communications of resistance and heroic acts, demonstrating the young survivors' courage (*mut*), practical survival skills (*lebns hokhme*) and the vigor of their resistance (*vidershtands-kraft*).

The second interrelated problem springs from widespread skepticism that young individuals lacking an adult grasp of reality on a cognitive level would be capable of consciously helping someone else under conditions of war and genocide. Adults in the postwar period shared this skepticism regarding both Jewish and non-Jewish children. Yad Vashem's department for the Righteous Among the Nations, for example, has displayed a continuing hesitancy to recognize children of non-Jewish rescuers as essential helpers, worthy of the title of Righteous Among the Nations. This has been the case despite accounts contained in the testimonies of their parents and those of Jewish survivors, revealing that some children as young as eight to ten years old were consciously engaged in helping feed Jewish fugitives and guarding their shelters. Some adolescents and teenagers were involved in obtaining and smuggling false identity cards for the Jewish fugitives hidden in their families' homes. One critical act of solidarity historians have failed to recognize as rescue was the phenomenon of children providing emotional support to other children. Though non-Jewish children were among the most cruel blackmailers of Jewish children on the Aryan side, some of them of varied young ages played with their Jewish fugitive peers and kept them company, thereby helping them to experience some vestiges of a normal childhood filled with playfulness, laughter, and trust. One

6. *Instrukcje dla badania przeżyć dzieci żydowskich w okresie okupacji niemieckiej*, Seria II. Prace Metodologiczne, vol. 3, Łódź, Centralny Komitet Żydów Polskich, Komisja Historyczna, 1945, 1–16 and *Metodologische onveyzungen tsum dem khurbn fun poylishn yidntum*, no. 5, Łódź, 31–47. For an analysis of the *Instrukcje*, see Joanna B. Michlic, "The Children Accuse, 1946: Between Exclusion from and Inclusion into the Holocaust Canon," in *Zwischen Zwangsarbeit, Holocaust und Vertreibung. Polnische, jüdische und deutsche Kindheiten im besetzten Polen*, ed. Krzysztof Ruchniewicz and Jürgen Zinnecker (Weinheim: Juvenata Verlag, 2007); and *Newsletter of the Society for the History of Children and Youth*, H-Childhood 9 (February 2007), http://www.history.vt.edu/Jones/SHCY/Newsletter9/michlic.html (accessed November 6, 2009).

7. *Metodologische onveyzungen tsum dem khurbn fun poylishn yidntum*, no. 5, 35

moving illustration of this emotional support is conveyed in the testimony of a young Jewish child survivor, Jankiel Zając [Yankel Zayontz]: "When the Germans chased the Jews out of our town [*shtetl*], my father and I escaped to one village and there we hid in a farmer's attic. It was very tiring and sad to sit all day in the attic. The attic was without one small window to look through. My only pleasure derived from the visits of Antek and Wacek, the farmer's two sons. They would climb up to the attic to join me and we all three would sit in one corner and tell each other stories."[8]

Moral and Physical Support among Jewish Children and Youth on the Aryan Side

Both their adult contemporaries and historians have failed to recognize how older Jewish children and youth supported each other morally and physically in different ways: garnering and sharing food with each other, finding shelters and hiding together in the countryside on the Aryan side. Such mutual group support played an important role in the struggle for daily survival, though gatherings of large groups could only last a short time because of safety concerns. Groups numbering more than two or three fugitives were at a higher risk of being discovered by local non-Jewish children and adults, who could not only chase the young Jews away, but also harm them or denounce them to Germans. Nevertheless, spending a week or two or a month in a group of five or ten, hiding together in forests and fields, meant a great deal to Jewish child fugitives. It provided them with a boost of emotional and mental strength to persevere and not give up on living. In addition, Jewish children learned from each other the essential "Bible," that is, how to survive on the Aryan side. They learned whom to approach, for example, for a bowl of soup at the end of the day—here the elderly Polish people, living in isolation on the outskirts of villages were usually considered more sympathetic and considerate than families with children. They shared their knowledge of how to behave in church and in peasants' homes, how to say Christian prayers, how to greet the locals, and where to look for safe shelter.

The long and moving testimony of Abram Sztybel (given on March 3, 1948) serves as a good illustration of what peer support among Jewish children and youngsters meant to those children who had just learned about the liquidation

8. Testimony of Jankie Zając [Yankel Zayontz], The Jewish Children's Home in Lublin, [n. d.], File no. 301/22, 1 (Yiddish), The Collection of Genia Silkes, Record Group (RG) no. 1187, Series 2, Box 2, Folder 30, YIVO Archives.

of their ghettos and the murders of their parents and other relatives by the Germans. Sztybel was born on December 1, 1929, in the small town of Komarów near Zamość in southeastern Poland. Like many other Jewish children in this region, soon after the Germans set up the ghetto in his hometown in the summer of 1941, he began to work for a peasant in order to alleviate the burden of daily life in his family. The living conditions of the local Jewish community drastically deteriorated throughout the second half of 1941, and in the spring of 1942 the first deportations to the Bełżec death camp began. In October and November 1942, the Germans embarked on the final annihilation of the Komarów ghetto, and Sztybel, who at the time worked as a helper to the compassionate peasant Józef Ryciniak in the village Borki, lost touch with his remaining family in the ghetto. At approximately that time the fear of severe reprisals by the Germans for keeping a Jew on one's property made Ryciniak dismiss Sztybel. But the peasant provided the boy with advice and food for the road, and promised that he would take him in again if he was in a desperate situation. It was then that Sztybel encountered a group of orphan Jewish children like himself. Together they began a new stage in a battle for survival in the forests and fields, near Komarów. This is how Sztybel recalls this period:

He [the peasant Józef Ryciniak] gave me bread and ordered me to go wherever I wanted, and said that when I was nearby … and nobody could see, I could approach and get some food. It was very difficult for me, and I didn't know where to go, whom I could get advice from, or what to do. I thought to myself that whatever would be, would be. I didn't go in the direction of the town, but towards the fields, and moreover not on the roads but through the fields themselves. It became dark and I went on alone. There was a pile of hay by the road. It was very cold, and I was freezing. I crawled inside the haystack and fell asleep. I slept deeply, and came out as the day began. I finished eating whatever bread I had left, and went on. I entered a young forest, where I met an entire group of Jewish boys and girls from our town of Komarów, all of whom just like myself had been forced to leave behind their [peasant] bosses and wander around in the forest.

This gladdened me a bit and made my heart lighter. I talked together with them about my mother and brother, but nobody knew anything. We said amongst ourselves that a cat and a dog were better off than us: a cat has a house, and a hound has a doghouse, but we were chased like hares from one place to another. We stuck together in the meantime—we were eight boys and two girls. All of us were young children. The eldest was seventeen years old, and the youngest was a little girl who was perhaps only eight. We lived very well together, dividing the bread amongst ourselves. We were all very sad, and we often cried. It was very difficult for me because I didn't know anything about my mother. I didn't know if she'd already been captured or if she was still hiding somewhere. We slept on leaves in the forest....

We spoke about how we needed to split into small groups, since the children [of] the shepherds from the village might see us and betray us. In addition to this, it was decided that we should go to the houses of shepherds and ask for bread.[9]

Living under constant fear of being abused, denounced, and killed, young Jewish fugitives matured fast on the Aryan side. Some children experienced living in pairs or threes with their peer Jewish fugitives as mutually beneficial on various levels. An encounter with another Jewish child suffering from the same predicament invariably lightened the burden of loneliness and brought moments of happiness and feelings of security. Jewish children quickly recognized that having particular physical and internal attributes and social skills determined their chances of survival. A good physical appearance (that meant blond hair and blue eyes), a good knowledge of the Polish language and the Catholic religion, personal assertiveness, sharpness, and quick-mindedness were considered the most desirable attributes. A good knowledge of the local Christian Polish community among whom the children were forced to beg for food, clothes, and medicine, and a good knowledge of the geographical area in which they hid were also highly desirable.

In her video testimony of March 17, 1996, Chava Meir (born on November 2, 1931, as Ewa Wełna in Serock in Legionowo County in Masovian Voivedship) recalls that her dreadfully lonely life as a beggar girl on the Aryan side became more bearable once she began to share it with two siblings: twelve-year-old Bracha and six-year-old Israel Neimark or Naimark.[10] The children met sometimes toward the end of 1942 after Chava lost most of her adult relatives, who were murdered by the Germans in the Warsaw and Legionowo ghettos and, in the case of her father, by a Polish man with whom he had made financial transactions during the war. Though Chava spoke better Polish than the Neimarks, according to her recollections, they were more effective at begging and stealing food and always shared their portion with her. Chava and the Neimarks cared for each other's hygiene, shared some old rags to dress in the fall and winter, and slept together in dugouts in a forest near Legionowo. The children considered this forest the safest place for them to be at night. After the end of the war, Meir and the Neimarks remained together and continued to care for each other. The

---

9. Testimony of Abram Sztybel, March 3, 1948, Warsaw, 39 pages (original Polish and partial Yiddish translation), Collection of Genia Silkes, RG. No. 1187, Series 2, Box 2, Folder 28, 11–12. (Polish), YIVO Archives.

10. Interview with Chava Meir, March 17, 1996, Petach-Tikva, Israel, Hebrew, File no. 12189, USC, Shoah Foundation Institute (SFI), USC, Tape 3.

children found an empty house that they moved into.[11] The two girls began to collect books, notebooks, and pencils to sell in order to buy food for all three of them. They became the sole breadwinners of their tiny "family unit" since by then Israel Neimark, the youngest of them, lost his ability to walk and had to rest alone in the house. After two months of this new adult-like life, a Jewish woman named Mrs. Sokolov discovered them. Immediately, she took them with her to the newly formed Jewish Committee on Targowa Street in the neighborhood of Praga in Warsaw, from which the children were transported to the Jewish Children's Home in Otwock near Warsaw, the first Jewish children's home in central Poland, run under the auspices of the Central Committee of Polish Jews (CKŻP).[12]

Abram Sztybel recalls that in late 1942, he went into hiding with a boy named Yosele (no family name given) whom he had known from the village Borki where both boys had pastured livestock for the local peasants. Living together on the Aryan side, the boys helped each other cope with the piercing cold in the winter and with constant hunger. At nighttime they usually forced their way into barns and hid under the hay to keep warm, while during the day they begged for food separately. One day, a peasant discovered them in his barn and called the Polish police (*Granatowa policja*). On the way to the police station, Yosele offered the two men money that he had hidden, and they let them go. Abram was grateful to Yosele for saving his life:

I was very happy that I had been saved together with Yosele. We agreed to remain with one another in the future, that God had protected us together. We stuck together even more so than before; we were like true brothers. Even when the wind rustled through the leaves we were already afraid that someone was pursuing us and we'd be taken away. However, sitting in the forest was cold and wet, and later we took to going around to the houses, begging for something to eat. We tried to avoid every barn. We also had to make an effort not to visit too often any of the same householders, and to search out new places constantly.[13]

However, at some point the boys split up. The separation occurred as a result of meeting another young Jewish fugitive who had decided that Abram was a liability to them because of his pronounced semitic features, and should be left behind. The newcomer was older than the two boys. He spoke good Ukrainian, and was blessed with the "good Aryan look." Yosele knew him, and instantly agreed with his decision to abandon Abram:

11. Ibid., Tape, 5.
12. See Joanna B. Michlic, "The Raw Memory of War: Early Postwar Testimonies of Children in Dom Dziecka in Otwock," *Yad Vashem Studies* 37, no. 1 (2009): 11–52.
13. Testimony of Abram Sztybel, 14.

They immediately decided to leave me behind and stick together. Yosele told me that we couldn't always stay with one another and needed to separate. I started to plead with him, but this didn't help. I didn't want to leave them and be alone. I began to cry, but my tears didn't move them. They started to leave. I asked them where they were going, but they didn't want to tell me. I followed after them. They stood still and didn't let me go any farther. The [newcomer] boy hit me and they both began to run. I couldn't keep up with them and remained alone. I was cheerless and wandered around all alone. Later I began to go around begging. I slept in various barns, wherever it was possible. Things got worse and worse, and nobody wanted to help. I was dirty, full of lice, hungry, and totally alone without help. I wandered through the forests and across fields.[14]

This episode suggests that among the motives for self-help in Jewish children and youth living on the Aryan side, we find both positive feelings of friendship and a desire to share and support one another. But we also find pragmatism and selfishness which were nourished by a real fear of German anti-Jewish discriminatory and elimination policies and the local non-Jewish environment in which it was difficult to differentiate friend from foe.

Momentary Assistance: Jewish Children as "Sudden Protectors"

In recent historical works on non-Jews rescuing Jews, we learned about the salient role of the so-called "sudden rescuers-protectors" in life-threatening situations of Jewish children.[15] "Sudden protectors" were strangers as well as acquaintances, who emerged in the most dramatic moments of the Jewish children's lives on the Aryan side, supporting their passing as playing Christian Polish children, and thus protecting them from Polish blackmailers, German gendarmes, and ordinary nosy onlookers, who could also cause them harm. Sometimes, the "sudden protectors" helped with relocation from those rescuers who mistreated the children mentally and physically. In other situations, the "sudden protectors" offered immediate assistance in the form of money, food, and life-saving advice of where to hide next.

Studying Jewish children's testimonies, one also comes across cases of Jewish children who acted as "sudden protectors" for other Jewish children, though the scope of their assistance could not be as expansive as the spectrum

14. Ibid.
15. Joanna B. Michlic, *Jewish Children in Nazi-Occupied Poland: Survival and Polish-Jewish Relations during the Holocaust as Reflected in Early Postwar Recollections*, Search and Research—Lectures and Papers (Jerusalem: Yad Vashem, 2008).

of actions performed by adult non-Jewish rescuers and adult Jewish rescuers. Nevertheless, their actions played an important role in saving lives and even several decades later, in their wartime biographies, the recipients of such help recall those events as crucial. In his interview of March 11, 2011, for the daily Polish *Gazeta Wyborcza*, Jakub Hersz Griner, for example, today a resident of Israel known as both Father Grzegorz Pawlikowski and Zvi Griner, emphasizes that he survived thanks to an unknown Jewish teenager he met on the streets of his hometown Zamość at the age of eleven.[16] The older boy approached Griner, born in 1931, and asked him if he would like to stay alive. Like many other young Jewish fugitives, Griner had a strong drive to live and did not hesitate to answer him in a positive manner. Then, the older boy ordered him to wait and disappeared for a short time into a nearby building. He came back with a Christian birth certificate that provided Griner with a new identity. That document saved his life on many occasions. The first time he used it was in the small labor camp on the outskirts of Zamość where the German gendarmes at first identified him as a Jew. But Griner assertively showed them the false document and was freed.

Rafał (Rafel) Shleger, born in 1931 in Brody (Brod in Yiddish) in the Lviv province, owes his life to his friend's instructions voiced in a whisper at the slaughterhouse where the two boys were about to lose their lives.[17] Germans captured Shleger outside the Brody ghetto and brought him back to an isolated building where they were ready to shoot him with a group of other Jews, both female and male. During the shooting both boys fell down, but were not shot. Shleger was terrified and did not know how to act. Instantly his friend, lying next to him, told him not to move and not to say a word. When the brutal killings were finished, both boys managed to escape from the building to the nearby river.

Another dramatic example of the importance of the actions of a "sudden protector" emerges from the early postwar account of Chava Veicher (born in 1933 in Turka on the Stryj River in western Ukraine). Since the summer of 1942, Chava and her older sister had been living on the Aryan side, fending for themselves in the forest near Turka, assisted from time to time by a friendly peas-

---

16. Zvi Griner, Żołnierz Mesjasza. Rev. Grzegorz Pawlikowski in a conversation with Marcin Bielesz, *Gazeta Wyborcza* (March 11, 2011); http://wyborcza.pl/2029020,75515,9233809.html?sms_code= (accessed August 25, 2011).

17. Testimony of Rafal [Rafel] Shleger (undated, 3 pages), Yiddish, File no. 9, the Central Jewish Historical Commission, Collection of Genia Silkes, RG no. 1187, Series 2, Box 2, Folder 28, YIVO Archives.

ant–rescuer who brought them potatoes and bread, and allowed them to stay in his house from time to time. At a given moment, at the request of the peasant, a group of forty adult Jewish fugitives, hiding in a nearby forest, reluctantly accepted the girls into their camp. When winter began, the group moved into a bunker in the forest that the fugitives had built earlier in late fall. However, the bunker was discovered and they had to flee to the depths of the forest and hide in harsh weather conditions. The group had to move quickly from place to place because the Germans were chasing them. During that time, Chava Veicher's sister, who was barefoot, got severe frostbite and could not walk. At first, adult male Jews carried her on their backs; however, at some point they decided to shoot her since in their eyes she was endangering the lives of other Jewish fugitives. But Chava Veicher strongly opposed that plan: "I did not permit this to happen. I said that they should either shoot the both of us, or neither of us. So they again took pity on her, and carried her on their backs."[18] After that incident, the girls were left at a woman's house in one of the nearby villages. By the summer of 1944, however, they once again had to fend for themselves. Chava Veichler had to beg for food for a month, even after the liberation of the area from the Germans. Then she went to Turka to look for surviving relatives, and eventually she and her sister were transported to the Jewish Children's Home in Bielsk.

A similar case of "sudden protection" resulting in saving an injured thirteen-year-old boy by a young Jewish stranger, himself a fugitive living on the Aryan side, took place in a hideout in Warsaw in the aftermath of the defeat of the Warsaw Uprising of August 1, 1944. This is the story of Nachman Fryszberg (who took the Aryan name Piotr Jablonski during the war and is now known as Peter Jablonski) and Wacek Zalcberg (now called Walter Saltzberg), eleven years his junior, whose life he saved.[19] Saltzberg was born on January 31, 1931, into an upper middle class family in Warsaw and Jablonski was born on October 20, 1920, in Lublin into a family that owned a paper goods factory. Jablonski and Saltzberg met by chance in an empty building in the Warsaw's Mokotów neighborhood where Walter was injured during the German bombing

---

18. Testimony of Chava Veicher, Jewish Children's Home in Bielsk, Poland. (Undated). Yiddish, Collection of Genia Silkes, Record Group 1187, Series 2, Box 2, Folder 29, 3. YIVO Archives.

19. The account of Peter Jablonski's rescue of Walter Saltzberg is based on the videotaped testimony of Walter Saltzberg, File no. 14961, May 8, 1996, tape 3 (English language), the USC SFI, and Peter Jablonski's unpublished postwar memoir *To be or not to be ... ?* I would like to thank the late Peter Jablonski for giving me permission to use his memoir and George Saltzberg, the son of Walter Saltzberg, for making this memoir accessible to me.

of the city that occurred as a reprisal for the Warsaw Uprising. Jablonski immediately transferred the injured boy to a nearby burned-out building at Malczewskiego Street no. 2 where he had already built a special hideout. Two mature male Jewish fugitives, who knew Jablonski, joined them in the new shelter. There they all hid for another five months until the middle of January 1945. One night, when Jablonski returned from his daily trips in search for food, he saw one of the two men, choking the crying Saltzberg. He instantly prevented the man from killing Saltzberg. The pacified would-be killer regarded Saltzberg as a liability and had decided to end his life when the boy began to cry out loud because of the pain caused by the open wounds on his broken leg. As the only Jew in the group who would go out and bring the food for all of them, Jablonski threatened the man that if he were to harm Saltzberg again, he would no longer supply him with food. In addition to feeding and protecting Saltzberg against the anger of the two other fugitives, Jablonski took the best possible care of Saltzberg's wounds by disinfecting them with his urine. Once they were freed to emerge from the hideout in the middle of January 1945, Jablonski did not abandon Saltzberg either. He visited the newly established Jewish organization in Warsaw where he arranged for Saltzberg's transfer to the Jewish Children's home in Otwock, from which the boy immigrated to Canada in 1947. Jablonski, who passed away in July 2011, was also responsible for saving his cousin George (Jerzy, Józef) Mandlebaum (born in Warsaw in 1937). Through his connection with Polish underground organizations, Jablonski smuggled the boy out of the Warsaw ghetto to the Aryan side where a Christian Pole took the boy to a safe shelter. After the war, Jablonski searched for his cousin and with his new wife Sabina, he became the boy's official guardian for two years. Nonetheless, the young Mandlebaum left Poland for Mexico with a group of Jewish children, after which he travelled on to the United States.

Children and Youth as Rescuers of Their Families

Various ego documents inform us that adolescents and teenagers of both genders were determined to protect adult and younger members of their families. They extended their help in different ways. Abram Sztybel, for example, gave his place in a hideout in the Komarów ghetto to his mother during one of the dreaded "German Actions."[20] Another, more common example of children

20. Testimony of Abram Sztybel, 39.

rescuing family members was the taking of one's younger siblings out of the ghetto to the Christian Polish rescuers or to places such as Catholic churches and the front doors of state and Catholic orphanages. These were considered safe public spaces where Christian strangers would most likely take care of the "abandoned" children. In a telephone interview on August 6, 2011, Shulamit Aloni (born Mina Fuchsberg in 1931 in Borysław, near Drohobycz in the Lviv province) recalled that in late 1942, her brother Alexander Fuchsberg, a year and a half her senior, brought her to Christian Polish rescuers, Władysław and Helena Grzegorczyks. Once he brought her to safety, he went to fight with the underground Jewish units in the nearby forests. This was the last time his sister saw him alive.

Some child-rescuers constantly felt worried about the fate of their younger siblings after they had placed them with Christian Poles whom they barely knew. Anxiety about the safety and well-being of one's brother or one's sister was intensified by the fact that, for safety reasons, the child-rescuers often could not maintain any contact with their younger siblings. The early postwar testimony of Rachel Sternshis (born in 1932 in the city of Rivne—Yiddish Rovno—in western Ukraine) contains this account of anxiety regarding the well-being of her younger sibling:

I often wept with longing for my little sister whom I left in the village. I accused myself of separating from her and leaving her with an unknown peasant ... The pain of separation did not leave me for a long time, even when I was liberated, and when I ran away to a Jewish woman from the peasant for whom I had worked [during the war]. I remained with the Jewish woman for a while. She was very kind to me, but I was still tormented by my conscience that I had left Sonia, my baby sister, in unknown hands. There were times when my guilt nearly led me to suicide, but [instead] I decided to look for her. After a long search, I found Sonia—my dear little sister. We are now both in the Jewish children's Home in Bielsk.[21]

Sternshis's case shows that the child-rescuers, who faced high levels of risk to save the lives of their younger siblings during the war, were also determined to recover and be united with them in the aftermath of the war. Thus, these young rescuers took upon themselves parental responsibilities: the older orphans looked after the younger orphans and started life anew together as a reconstructed family unit. Generally this was a complicated trajectory because of the long periods of time during which the siblings were separated and the

---

21. Testimony of Rachel Sternshis, Jewish Children's Home in Bielsk (undated), two pages in Yiddish, Collection of Genia Silkes, RG 1187, Series 2, Box 2, Folder 28, YIVO Archives.

development that took place in the lives of the young children who had only vague memories or none at all of their biological families and their Jewish background. One illustration of such a complicated saga of rescue and recovery of young siblings is the case of Witold Wajnman (Wujnmach, Weinmann), born on November 1, 1927. At the age of fifteen, Witold Wajnman became the sole breadwinner of his family in the ghetto in Skarżysko-Kamienna, a town where the Wajnman family had settled before the war. Prior to the liquidation of the Skarżysko-Kamienna ghetto, in the fall of 1942, Wajnman began to prepare his two younger siblings for their departure to the Aryan side. His sister Danuta was born on January 3, 1936, and the brother Henryk was born on March 23, 1941. In January 1943, he took Henryk to Cracow and, in a seemingly desperate but carefully planned move, left the baby boy at the entrance of the building at 45 Krakowska Street, near a Catholic orphanage. The caretaker of the building took Henryk to the orphanage, where he remained until 1945.[22]

Then Witold Wajnman proceeded to find a refuge for his seven-year-old sister Danuta.[23] He must have been aware that their chances of survival together on the Aryan side were nil, and therefore they had to separate. He thus left Danuta in the Church of St. Jacob at G. Narutowicz Street in Warsaw where he hoped she would find help. Before they separated, he ordered Danuta to say that her real name was Barbara Ślązak, that she came from Mielce, and that she had gotten lost on the way to her relatives in Warsaw:

My brother Henrik [Henryk] was taken by Witold to Kraków and left by a building in which an orphanage was located. He watched from a distance to see that someone picked up the baby. Witold then worked on my new identity. My name was to be Barbara Ślązak, born in Mielce. I also learned Catholic prayers from friends and a priest. In 1943, my brother took me to Warsaw and told me to enter a church— St. Jacob's Church. In the church, before closing time, I told the priest I was lost. I said that I had come to visit my grandmother in Warsaw and played with some children, and now I could not find my grandmother's house. I was taken to the office of the General Care Council [*Rada Główna Opiekuńcza*, RGO][24] where lost children

22. For the history of Henryk Wajnman and his family, see Joanna B. Michlic, "Who Am I? Jewish Children's Search for Identity in Post-War Poland, 1945–1949," *Polin* 20 (2007): 98–121, and Michlic, *Jewish Children in Nazi-Occupied Poland*. At the time of writing these two works, I had not yet found all personal testimonies and other official documents about the survival of Danuta Wajnman [Weinmann] and about the early postwar life saga of the three Wajnman siblings.

23. Testimony of Dana Axelrod, File no. 7786, The Collection of the Righteous Among the Nations, Yad Vashem Archives (YVA), 2–3.

24. On the history of General Care Council (RGO) during the war, see Bogdan Kroll, *Rada Główna Opiekuńcza* (Warsaw: PWN, 1985).

were brought. Stanisław Kornacki was sitting at the desk. After asking me many questions and filling out many documents, he told me not to worry—he would find my parents. He provided food for me and then, after work, took me to an orphanage on the outskirts of Warsaw.[25]

Stanisław Kornacki became the girl's official guardian, and soon after he also turned himself into her dedicated rescuer. She stayed with his family from the winter of 1943 until July 28, 1944, and once again from May 1945 until November 1947. Kornacki officially named her Barbara Kornacka. He also left a note in the church with his address, in case a relative of hers should come looking for her. That enabled Witold Wajnman to track down Danuta's whereabouts in late 1947.[26] He met his sister for the first time on her way to school and took her with him to the Jewish Children's Home in Częstochowa where he and the youngest brother Henryk had already been living for a short-time. Witold, who had survived the war as a farmhand at the family of Jan Skarbek-Tłuchowski who treated him as if he were his own son, did not encounter problems in recovering Danuta. However, in the case of Henryk's recovery, he had to fight a double battle. First, he had a prolonged custody battle with Henryk's adoptive parents, Mr. and Mrs Janowscy, a childless couple who had adopted him in 1945 without knowing his Jewish origins. The second was the battle of minds and hearts with his younger brother who did not wish to be separated from his beloved parents and regarded Witold Wajnman as a stranger and intruder destroying his happy childhood and solid family life. Yet in spite of these challenges, the three siblings were reunited, but by early 1948 Witold Wajnman had to face another battle over keeping his newly reunited family together. This time it was a protracted and frustrating bureaucratic battle with the American immigration office, regarding the reunion of the three siblings with their eldest sister, Ruth Griffith, who had already been living in the United States for some time, and was married to an American.[27]

---

25. Testimony of Dana Axelrod (Danuta Wajnman), File no. 7786, The Collection of the Righteous Among the Nations, 2–3, Yad Vashem Archives.

26. See Stanisław Kornacki, Testimony of September 20, 1958, signed by T. (Tatiana) Berenstein of the Jewish Historical Institute in Warsaw, File no. 301/5635, Archives of ZIH.

27. See the large folder of various documents, regarding Witold, Danuta, and Henryk Wajnman's immigration case, The Collection of the Joint, 1945–1949, File no. 350/387, Archives of ZIH.

Amidah in the Ghettos and Spiritual Forms of Rescue Among Youth

The best-known images of young children attempting to help their families in the Warsaw ghetto are those of the little smugglers of food. Children begged for food on the Aryan side and brought it back to the ghetto at the risk of losing their lives. The activities of the young smugglers were acknowledged and praised during the war. The promising Polish-Jewish poetess Henryka Lazowert, who was murdered in the Treblinka death camp, wrote a poignant poem dedicated to and titled, "To the Child Smuggler":

> Through walls, through holes, over ruins, through barbed wire still I will find a way.
> Hungry, thirsty and barefoot I slither through like a snake: by day, at night, at dawn.
> No matter how hot. No matter how much rain.
> You cannot begrudge me my profit. I am risking my little neck.[28]

Other wartime diaries and newsletters (*Gazetki*) written in the ghettos inform us that older children and youth also embarked on spiritual and cultural rescue, what they understood as protection of the members of their generation from the ongoing psychological and moral degradation of the Jewish community imprisoned inside the ghettos' walls. One illustration of such spiritual and cultural self-help among youth can be seen in the few surviving, fragmentary *Gazetki* newsletters of the young Zionist group headed by Dawid Joskowicz in the infamous Litzmanstadt ghetto.[29] This Zionist youth group, like all other Zionist and Communist youth groups in the Litzmanstadt ghetto, was located in the Marysin neighborhood, where the so-called Marysin Farm was also active between July 1940 and October 1941 for approximately 14,000 younger children. Like other Zionist groups, Dawid Joskowicz's organization was involved in ideological, educational, cultural, and social activities conducted in the spirit of the prewar Zionist vision of settlement in Palestine. On November 28, 1943, the group issued its first handwritten newsletter in which it called upon other youth to join them: "From the editors! Brothers and sisters! Today we are issuing our first *Gazetka* in which we wish to voice our thoughts. This *Gazetka*

28. Henryka Lazowert, "To the Child Smuggler," cited in Samuel D. Kassow, *Who Will Write Our History? Emanuel Ringelblum, the Warsaw Ghetto, and the Oyneg Shabes Archive* (Bloomington: Indiana University Press, 2007), 182.

29. On the history of the Litzmanstadt ghetto, see Gordon J. Horowitz, *Ghettostadt: Lodz and the Making of a Nazi City* (Cambridge, Mass.: The Belknap Press of Harvard University, 2008) and Michal Unger, *Lodz: The Last Ghetto in Poland* (Hebrew) (Jerusalem: Yad Vashem, 2005).

shows that in spite of the poverty and suffering in the Ghetto, we the youth desire to live above all that, and fight for a better tomorrow. We ask you to assist us in our work and send us your articles."[30]

Dawid Joskowicz and his team of writers, consisting mainly of female authors such as Genia Artykiewicz, Pola Szulsztajn, Sala Horn, and Hanka Kuperman—and some authors only known by their first names and initials such as Zachawa A., Izrael G., and Chaim M.—wrote short essays, poems, and stories for the *Gazetka*. The newsletter also contains spare handmade pencil drawings of nature, episodes from life in the ghetto, and Zionist images. The last separate fragmentary entry of the *Gazetka*, a poem dedicated to the famous Hebrew poet, Chaim Nachman Bialik (1873–1934), written by Dawid Joskowicz, carries a June 10, 1944 date, less than two months before the final liquidation of the ghetto in August 1944. The available database of the ghetto's population allows us to infer that Dawid Joskowicz was born in 1929 and lived with his family first at Północna Street no. 26, and next at Wolborska Street no. 35 in Łódź. All the young female authors were pupils at No.10B School at Franciszkańska Street.[31]

All the creative writings are imbued with Zionist dreams and the distinct self-image of the youth group vis-à-vis the rest of the inhabitants of the ghetto. Enthusiasm for building one's home in Palestine and the commitment to remaining morally strong, expressed in a naïve and childlike style were a demonstration of their total dedication and youthful hope against hope. This issue of *Gazetka* records the moral and cultural work within the youth group. Here are three examples of the representations of spiritual rescue recorded by its members:

The inhabitants of the Ghetto are turning sad. They fear the arrival of a harsh and tough winter. After all, we neither have coal to heat nor warm clothes and shoes to wear to protect us from the cold. We suffer from hunger more and more with each day, and there is no way out. We have to work to sustain the Ghetto and survive this cruel time. We work all day long in departments (*resorts*) for the Germans. We, the youth, wish that this situation would soon end; we are wasting our time here. But we forget about all the [ghetto's] rules we have to obey and instead, live with a hope that our future will be better, that our love and our youthful energy will outlive our suffering, and we will build our homeland that we have yearned for so long. Let us try with all our might to survive this terrible war that resulted in so many victims

---

30. "From the Editors," *Gazetka*, no. 1, 28, November 1944, Julian Hirszhaut Papers, 1939–1945, RG, 720, Box. 2, Folder 108, Dawid Joskowicz, 10 (Polish), YIVO Archives.

31. See Children of the Lodz Ghetto: A Memorial Research Project, USHMM http://online.ushmm .org/lodzchildren/name_list.php?letter=K (accessed August 30, 2011).

in our nation. We, the youth, will serve as an example for others, and we will not allow ourselves to become inhuman (*zezwierzęcenie*). Our slogan is to be *Hazak!* (Hebrew word for Strong)[32]

We are ready! We will win over those people. Moses waited forty years in the desert for the old generation to die out and the young one to emerge. Today, in the same spirit we will deal with the resigned masses of the ignorant people. We will win them over! We will convince them! But at first we have to create people ready to sacrifice. We first have to work on ourselves and then on others![33]

The queue was formed in vain, nothing was distributed. And those are the ways of the Ghetto. The allocated portion of food provided for two weeks lasts only a few days, and the rest of the time one has to go about hungry and wait for the next portion of food. But we, the youth, do not think about food, instead we dedicate our time to work on ourselves, on our characters and our souls in order to work for the goodness of our Homeland in the future.[34]

Conclusion

On the eve of the Second World War, Polish Jewry was considered a youthful community and most scholars agree that in 1939, the number of children aged fifteen years or younger was several hundred thousand. In the summer of 1945, the Central Committee of Polish Jews registered five thousand Jewish child survivors.[35] This figure was not final, as it did not include all the young survivors from Nazi-occupied Poland, nor those Polish Jewish children who along with their families had survived the war in the Soviet Union. But it clearly indicated the sheer physical destruction of Jewish children and youth. Next to the elderly, they were the first victims of the Nazi genocidal policies, and many of those who escaped to the Aryan side were also exposed to all kinds of abuse and neglect. Nonetheless, in spite of the great vulnerability of the young ones in the world of adults during the Holocaust, many older children and youth attempted to fight for their survival and made their own decisions even if on a limited basis. Cases delineated in this essay reveal that older children and youth de-

32. Pola Szulsztajn, "Jesień w getcie," *Gazetka*, no. 1, 28, November 1944, Julian Hirshaut Papers, 1939–1945, RG, 720, Box. 2, Folder 108, Dawid Joskowicz, 6 (Polish), YIVO Archives.

33. Dawid J. Untitled fragments of a poem, *Gazetka*, no. 1, 28, November 1944, Julian Hirszhaut Papers, 1939–1945, RG, 720, Box. 2, Folder 108, Dawid Joskowicz, 8 (Polish), YIVO Archives.

34. Sala Horn, "Sytuacja getta," *Gazetka*, no. 1, 28, November 1944, Julian Hirszhaut Papers, 1939–1945, RG, 720, Box. 2, Folder 108, Dawid Joskowicz, 4 (Polish), YIVO Archives.

35. On the history of the reemergence of the remnants of the Jewish community, child and adult survivors, see Lucjan Dobroszycki, "Re-emergence and Decline of a Community: The Numerical Size of the Jewish Population in Poland, 1944–47," *YIVO Annual* 21 (1993): 3–32.

sired to live, fought for their own survival against the Germans and hostile seg-
ments of the Polish Christian community, and were actively and consciously
engaged in helping other Jews. The older children and youth helped relatives,
particularly parents and younger siblings, and friends, as well as strangers.
They extended help inside the ghettos and on the Aryan side. The spectrum of
the self-help among older children and youth includes sharing food, clothing,
medicine, and vital information about the specific human and geographical
environments on the Aryan side, providing shelter for each other, instructing
others how to behave on the Aryan side, securing a potential safe haven for
younger siblings and delivering them to specific Christian Polish rescuers, and
offering one's own place in a hideout in the ghetto to one's parents. Given the
limitations they faced because of their age, including lack of money and lack of
contact with underground networks, young Jews could not extend their help to
others the same way as adults did. Yet, many of them acted as "sudden protectors," saving other children's lives in traumatic life-threatening situations on
the Aryan side. Some not only helped each other during the war, but also continued to support each other after the war. In addition to helping others to save
their lives, in the ghettos, older children and youth were engaged in the spiritual forms of rescuing each other through cultural activities, many of which were
fused with Zionist dreams of the return to the free Jewish state in Palestine.

This subject of individual self-help among older Jewish children and youth
in Nazi-occupied Poland and other occupied states awaits its thorough and
comprehensive treatment. The aim of this work is to show the subject's own
merits and establish it on a map of the history of rescue of Jews by Jews. The
various current developments within the history of the Holocaust, Jewish wom-
en's history, and the history of Jewish childhood, as well as new positive approaches toward ego documents among historians indicate a possible bright
future for in-depth scholarly investigations of the subject. But, in order to document the accounts of young Jews rescuing other Jews, we need to learn to think
"outside the box" about rescue, children, and youth. We need to expand the
vocabulary of rescue and include a spectrum of responses of older children
and youth that ultimately will nuance our understanding of rescue and of the
human condition. This subject should not be treated in a mystifying way, using exaggerated language and embellishments of all kinds. Finally, we have to
bear in mind that some accounts of the young ones who attempted to help others will never be known to us because so many of these young individuals—the
rescuers and the would-be rescued—perished during the Holocaust.

Nick Strimple

14   Music as Resistance

Long after World War II, Norwegian television broadcast an interview with Paul (Rabinowitsch) Sandfort, a survivor of Theresienstadt concentration camp who had been active as a trumpet player there. When asked why music played such an important role in the camp, Sandfort said, "it is because you hunger. You do not hunger just for food." At this point the interviewer interrupted him, saying, "the fact that they hungered for food in the camp is understandable. But that they also had a hunger for culture is almost incomprehensible. Can you say something about that?" Part of Sandfort's reply was, "even though [we] talked about food then, the hunger for culture was just as strong, just because we did not have it. We talked about large dinners, but we only had a small crust of bread; but it tasted good. Nowadays in our society people would let a piece of molded bread, lying in the street, lie. But if you are hungry you pick it up, and then it tastes heavenly. It is like that with music, too, with culture: that if your life really hangs by a thread, then expressing yourself and being able to consume, eat, enjoy and absorb culture is more important, almost more important than food."[1]

Paul Sandfort was expressing, from his own experience, what the Canadian commentator Jean-Jacques van Vlasselaer more recently articulated:

I believe that culture is born the day a human being becomes conscious of his or her mortality. Meaning originates from the presence of closure. Culture is a means of domesticating closure. The artistic gesture is born when one realizes death is inevitable. A work of art tries to tame death, facing it, braving it, in order to better possess it. Culture affirms our mortal humanity. It is an invented source of life.

1. Transcript of undated Norwegian television interview, courtesy of David Bloch.

The concentration camps with their organized violence tried to eradicate words, speech, language, the cultural gesture. They were the ultimate defeat of the human being.[2]

It can be argued, then, that every effort to stay alive in the ghettos and camps was an act of resistance. After all, rabbis in the camps constantly preached to their fellow inmates that they must do whatever was necessary to remain alive. Still, there were many instances when music provided the impetus to move beyond basic survival or the maintenance of ritual observances (even in a culturally secular sense, for instance, concerts), and actually shake a collective fist in the face of National Socialism. Below are examples.

Jewish (and Other) Music as Resistance in Prewar Germany

Among the first acts of the National Socialist government in 1933 was the establishment of concentration camps. These camps were not designed for Jews specifically but rather for political opponents of the Third Reich; and inmates, on stipulation that they leave Germany permanently, could have their freedom purchased by someone on the outside. The earliest example of a camp song is *"Die Moorsoldaten"* ("The Peat Bog Soldiers"), which was composed in the Börgermoor camp. The music, by Rudi Goguel, is typical of marches and cabaret songs popular during the Weimar Republic and later; and the text, by Johann Esser and Wolfgang Langhoff, is similar in tone to later camp songs:

Wohin auch das Auge blicket	Everywhere you watch
Moor und Heide nur ringsam	Bog and marshes all around
Vogelsang uns nicht erquicket	The chirping of the birds does not please us
Eichen stehen kahl und krum	Oaks are standing bare and crooked
Wir sind die Moorsoldaten	We are the Bog soldiers
Und ziehen mit dem Spaten ins Moor	And we move with the spade into the bog
Is das Lager anfgebaut	Is built up the camp
Wo wir fern von jeder Freude	Where we, far from every joy,
Hinter Stacheldraht verstaut	Are locked up behind barbed wire.
Wir sind die Moorsoldaten	We are the Bog soldiers
Und ziehen mit dem Spaten ins Moor	And we move with the spade into the bog

2. *Tracks to Viktor Ullmann* (Vienna: Edition Selene, 1997), 12–22.

The first performance was probably on August 27, 1933, although confusion exists among various accounts—some of them firsthand—concerning its creation, performance, acceptance in the camp, and later subsequent migration throughout Europe. Most agree that the camp commandant banned the song soon after the premiere. While this is most likely the case, it is also obvious that "*Die Moorsoldaten*" quickly became very popular, both inside and outside the concentration camp system, and remained a prominent workers' protest song well into the second half of the twentieth century. By 1935 it was so well-known that Hanns Eisler, then living in London, composed a new version for mixed chorus, retaining certain identifiable elements of the original melody but otherwise making it his own.

Also in 1935, Eisler began writing music for several anti-Fascist poems by Bertolt Brecht, including "To the Fighter in the Concentration Camp," which became part of Eisler's *Deutsche Sinfonie* (1935–57). In 1936, Eisler submitted the two completed portions of his symphony (including "To the Fighter in the Concentration Camp") to a composition contest held in conjunction with the Paris World Exhibition the next year. It won the contest and was duly scheduled for performance as part of the exhibition in 1937. The German government, however, successfully lobbied the French government to cancel the performance. Eisler, who was already living abroad because of a German arrest warrant, moved to the United States. *Deutsche Sinfonie* did not receive its first complete performance until 1959.

A student of Arnold Schoenberg, Eisler was a capable craftsman; each movement of his symphony is based on classical formal structures as if to present his music and political views as a natural and authentic continuation of the musical, cultural, and political achievements of Bach, Beethoven, and Goethe (for example, "To the Fighter in the Concentration Camp" is a passacaglia). But the texts, especially compared to "*Die Moorsoldaten*," are volatile, as can be easily seen in this excerpt of Brecht's poem:

Kaum Erreichbare ihr,	You who can hardly be reached,
In den Lagern begraben,	Buried in the concentration camps,
Abgeschnitten von jedem menschlichen Wort.	Cut off from every human word.
Und ausgeliefert diesen Mißhandlungen.	Subjected to brutalities
Niedergeknüppelte, aber nicht Widerlegte.	Beaten down but not confuted
Oh ihr Verschwundenen, aber nicht Vergessen....	Vanished but not forgotten....

Mit allen unaufhaltsam	Along with all those incorrigibly
Weiterkämpfenden,	fighting
Mit allen kämpfeneden, anaufhaltsam	Now and forever
kämpfenden,	
Die wahren Führer Deutschlands.	The true leaders of Germany.

By 1938, singing or other music-making, at the commandant's pleasure, had become common in concentration camps. Even so, such activities were essentially relegated to performances of folksongs, or other preexisting music, either sung informally by the inmates for their private gratification, or on special occasions as ordered by the camp officials. In two camps at this time, however, important new songs were composed, one on the commandant's order and one secretly. In both cases the songs also became known in other camps as inmates were transferred. Whatever their original intent, by the end of the war these songs, like *"Die Moorsoldaten"* before them, had become symbols of resistance and hope throughout the concentration camp system.

The first of these, *"Buchenwald Lied"* ("Buchenwald Song") was not intended, on the surface at least, as resistance. Rather, the commandant had tired of the Communist inmates' spontaneous singing of the "Internationale" during morning roll call (a statement of resistance *in extremis*) and decided to sponsor a contest for a new song that other inmates could sing, on his signal, in order to drown out and intimidate the Communists. Hermann Leopoldi, a Viennese cabaret composer, and Fritz Löhner-Beda, one of Franz Lehar's operetta librettists, were officially banned from entering the contest because they were Jewish; so their song, *"Buchenwald Lied,"* was entered in the name of a camp guard. It won the contest.[3]

The music is composed in the popular style of a cabaret march; the text walks a tightrope, on one hand expressing thankfulness to be alive in Buchenwald, while at the same time hinting at the deprivations endured and expressing the hope of eventual freedom:

Refrain:

O Buchenwald,	O Buchenwald,
ich kann dich nicht vergessen,	I can never forget you,
Weil du mein schicksal bist.	Because you are my fate.
Wer dich verließ,	Whoever leaves you,
der kann es erst ermessen,	he alone can measure
Wie wundervoll die Freiheit ist!	How wonderful freedom is!

3. David A. Hackett, trans., *The Buchenwald Report* (Boulder, Colo.: Westview Press, 1995), 140–42.

O Buchenwald,	O Buchenwald,
wir jammern nicht und klagen,	we do not lament and wail,
Und was auch unsre Zukunft sei,	Whatever our fate might be.
Wir wollen trotzdem	But we do want
ja zum Leben sagen,	to say yes to life,
Den einmal kommt der Tag,	For someday the time will come
dann sind wir frei!	when we are free!

Leopoldi's freedom was purchased by his family. In 1939 he was released and joined them in the United States. Löhner-Beda, however, was eventually transferred to Auschwitz where he was murdered in 1942.

The second song is *"Dachau Lied"* ("Dachau Song") by Herbert Zipper and Jura Soyfer. Again, the musical style is that of the cabaret march—in fact, the style of these songs is identical to the *"Horst Wessel Lied"* and other Nazi rally songs. But the text blatantly incites resistance through recognition of the evil of National Socialism, using the Nazis' own camp slogan, *Arbeit macht frei*, ("Work makes you free") as a satire against itself:

Refrain:

Doch wir haben die Losung von	But we all learned the motto of
Dachau gelernt,	Dachau to heed
und wir wurden stahlhart dabei:	and became as hardened as stone.
Bleib ein Mensch, Kamerad,	Stay humane, Dachau mate,
Sei ein Mann, Kamerad,	Be a man, Dachau mate,
Mach ganze Arbeit, pack' an, Kamerad,	and work as hard as you can, Dachau mate,
Den Arbeit macht frei!	For work leads to freedom alone![4]

Further, the last verse looks forward to a day in which *"die Arbeit, die wir machen, diese Arbeit, die wird gut"* ("the work we are designing, our work, will be for good").

Whereas *"Buchenwald Lied"* was designed for singing in the presence of Nazis, *"Dachau Lied"* was intended to be performed only for inmates in secret Sunday afternoon concerts organized by Herbert Zipper and held in an abandoned latrine. To accomplish this he and other inmates fashioned guitar-like instruments out of scrap wood secretly gathered from around the camp, and wire obtained by bribing a guard.[5] Both Herbert Zipper and Jura Soyfer were transferred to Buchenwald, where Soyfer died of typhus in 1939; Zipper's fam-

---

4. Translation by Herbert Zipper.

5. Paul Cummins, *Dachau Song: The Twentieth-Century Odyssey of Herbert Zipper* (New York: Peter Lang, 1992), 75–91.

ily managed his release. He traveled to the Philippines where he became the founding music director of the Manila Philharmonic Orchestra. Some years after the war, which he spent in a Japanese internment camp, he immigrated to the United States where he became one of the country's most highly respected and beloved music educators. Many years later, in an interview that appeared in the *Los Angeles Times* on April 9, 1997, Zipper said "I realized in Dachau that the arts in general have the power to keep you not just alive, but to make your life meaningful even under the most dreadful circumstances."[6]

In addition to opening concentration camps in 1933, the National Socialist government also began the relentless, systematic removal of Jews from German society. The Jews were now prohibited from attending public concerts, cinemas, and theaters, and were otherwise becoming increasingly isolated. Berlin's chief rabbi, Leo Baeck, and other prominent community members urged Joseph Goebbels, minister of propaganda, to create an organization for the maintenance of culture within the Jewish community. Goebbels was drawn to the idea because it would not only provide Jews with their own entertainment, thereby helping to keep them docile, but would also provide employment for Jewish musicians and theatrical personnel who were being removed from their jobs in large numbers. Based on an organizational model designed by the Jewish conductor Kurt Singer and provided by him to Hans Hinkel, an SS officer on Joseph Goebbels's staff, the *Jüdische Kulterbund* (Jewish Cultural Organization) was soon producing plays and concerts in Berlin and before long throughout the country.[7]

The *Jüdische Kulterbund* presented works by most of the great German composers (except for Richard Wagner and Richard Strauss) until the summer of 1937 when the Ministry of Propaganda, invoking one of the original 1933 anti-Jewish laws, prohibited the practice. Still, however, the *Kulterbund* was allowed to play works by Jewish composers of any nationality. On at least one occasion a work of Karl Amadeus Hartmann—who, though not Jewish, was on the Nazis *Entartete Kunst* [Degenerate Art] list—was performed without incident.

On February 27, 1941, the *Jüdische Kulterbund* in Berlin presented Gustav Mahler's monumental *Resurrection Symphony* (Symphony no. 2). The music begins with a gigantic, multifaceted funeral march, proceeds through an Austrian ländler and a scherzo, to poignant settings of *"Urlicht"* ("Primeval Light")

6. Matea Gold, "The Chord of Life: At 92 and Ailing, Holocaust Survivor Herbert Zipper Knows the Power of Music," *Los Angeles Times* (April 9, 1997), B 1.

7. The first production in Berlin was the play *Nathan the Wise* by Gotthold Lessing, which took place on October 1, 1933, during the high holy days. The first musical evening was a production of Mozart's *The Marriage of Figaro*, on November 14, 1933.

and *"Auferstehung"* ("Resurrection") by Friedrich Gottlieb Klopstock, and ends in triumphal splendor with a text by Mahler himself:

O glaube, mein Herz, o glaube,	O believe, my heart, o believe,
Es geht dir nichts verloren!	nothing of you will be lost!
Dein ist, ja dein, was du gesehnt,	What you longed for is yours,
dein was du gelibt,	what you loved
Was du gestritten!	and championed is yours!
O glaube,	O believe,
du wardst nicht umsonst geboren,	you were not born in vain!
hast nicht umsonst gelebt, gelitten!	You have not vainly lived and suffered!
Was enstanden ist,	What was created,
das muß vergehen,	that must pass away,
was verganen, auferstehen!	What passed away must rise!
Hör auf zu beben!	Cease to tremble!
Bereite dich zu leben!	Prepare yourself to live!
Aufersteh'n,	Rise again,
ja aufersteh'n wirst du,	yes, rise again you will,
mein Herz, in einem Nu!	My heart, in an instant!
Was du geschlagen,	Your struggle
Zu Gott wird es dich tragen!	Will bear you up to God!

In May 1941, after the *Kulterbund* concert season had ended, the Berlin orchestra's conductor, Rudolf Schwarz, assembled his players to talk about plans for the next season and to play through a work unfamiliar to many of them: the *Inextinguishable Symphony* (Symphony no. 4) of Danish composer Carl Nielsen. According to Martin Goldsmith, Schwarz spoke to his players about this particular piece in these words:

This is music that speaks directly to our situation and that of our listeners. All of us—musicians, electricians, tailors, grocers, mothers, and fathers—need to be reminded that life is paramount. Even where it is stamped out, it eventually returns. Where there is life, there is spirit. And where there is spirit, where there is even one human soul, there is music. We are proof of that. We have suffered, yet we have endured. And we have made music. And that is why I have asked you here this afternoon, to play through this symphony with me and to keep it in your hearts until we meet again to perform it for the public in the fall. Some of you, I know, will not be with us then. But wherever you are, a part of you will always be here. And you will have this music, this inextinguishable music, to remind you of us, always.[8]

8. Martin Goldsmith, *The Inextinguishable Symphony: A True Story of Music and Love in Nazi Germany* (New York: John Wiley and Sons, 2001).

The read-through of Nielsen's magnificent, jagged, angry, and ultimately consoling work apparently had a profound effect on all. But it was never performed for Berlin's Jewish audience. On September 11, just before the new concert season was to start, the *Jüdische Kulterbund* was dissolved.

Music in the Eastern Ghettos

The largely Yiddish-speaking Jewish communities in Eastern Europe had, over many centuries, promoted song almost to a level of elevated speech (a similar phenomenon can be seen in some of the most isolated rural areas of Appalachia). No aspect of life was left untouched by song writers' observations. Each individual's work, even though the origins were usually known, simply became the common property of the community at large. It is no wonder, then, that this environment produced a large body of song—both descriptive and in protest—during the period of Nazi occupation. Additionally, formal musical activities were organized in ghettos, sometimes over the objections of community leadership.

Perhaps the most famous composer of Yiddish songs was Mordechai Gebirtig, a resident of Cracow who would not survive the war. Gebirtig had already written "*S'Brendt*" ("It Burns"), an anguished, angry, firsthand account of the destruction of a *shtetl* during the Polish pogroms of 1935–36. Now, in 1939, this song became a universal cry for vengeance from the collective belly of Jewish communities throughout Poland and the Baltics, as can be seen from its final verse:

Shteyt nit, brider, ot azoy zikh	Don't just stand and look upon it
Mit farleygte hent.	With your folded arms.
Shteyt nit, brider, lescht dos fayer—	Stand not, brothers, while the fire spreads—
Undzer shtetl brent!	Our town burns!

In the small Polish ghetto of Bendzin, Henryk Rozmaryn who, as Henry Rosemarin, would eventually become one of the most sought-after harmonica virtuosi in Hollywood, wrote a heart-wrenching song chronicling the forced removal of a friend's mother, leaving the young boy behind to fend for himself:

Wein nisht mein teirer Itzuś	Don't cry my dear Itzuś
Gib a kish mein kind	Give a kiss my child
Weil ich wehrdoch wysiedlet	I am being resettled
Oi, bleib besindt....	Oh, be well....

Rosemarin performed the song in Bendzin, just after the woman's departure (circa 1943). He did not perform it again until 1993. In Bendzin, Henryk Rozmaryn had functioned with a few other musicians as a kind of lone troubadour. This was typical in the small ghettos; but in large ghettos, such as Warsaw, Vilna, Kovno and Łodz, things were completely different.

Warsaw, especially, maintained a highly sophisticated musical life during the Nazi period. It continued to publish newspapers openly and included in them reviews of recent concerts, as well as notices for upcoming concerts and advertisements promoting popular artists who were performing in the ghetto's supper clubs. Władysław Szpilmann, whose autobiography was adapted for the academy award–winning film *The Pianist*, performed in these clubs, as did the extraordinary young soprano Marysia Eisenstadt, who also performed opera arias with the ghetto's orchestra and gave vocal recitals accompanied by her father, David Eisenstadt, one of Poland's most prominent Jewish composers. In 1942, while attempting to join her parents who were being deported to Treblinka, Eisenstadt was shot dead on the platform in front of them by a Nazi officer.

Attending symphony concerts and clubs was expensive and controversial because, for one reason, there were not enough clubs or organized concerts to accommodate the needs of the ghetto's population. Therefore, many unemployed musicians played and sang on the streets for handouts. Street performances had always been a vital part of Yiddish culture. Whereas orchestra concerts and club entertainment focused on classical, or light-classical repertoire, street musicians upheld the traditions of *klezmer* and Yiddish song. In Warsaw—as in all the other ghettos—new songs were written and old songs, such as Abraham Goldfaden's famous "*Rozhinkes Mit Mandlen*" ("Raisins and Almonds") continued to be performed, sometimes with new words more reflective of the ghetto residents' situation.

Perhaps the most powerful musical events in Warsaw took place in June 1942. The ghetto symphony orchestra had been shut down in April for performing Aryan music. Now, at the beginning of June, a new orchestra was formed by the ghetto's Jewish Police, which managed to give at least one documented concert (on June 7, 1942). Late in the month, just before the mass deportations to Treblinka and other death camps began, a very large children's chorus—possibly consisting of all the various choruses that had been active in the ghetto—performed a farewell concert in the Moriah Synagogue.[9] The last piece on the

9. Shirli Gilbert, *Music in the Holocaust: Confronting Life in the Nazi Ghettos and Camps* (Oxford: Oxford University Press, 2005), 44–46. Gilbert writes that "hundreds of children participated" and

program was *"Hatikvah"* ("The Hope"), a Zionist song which would later become the national anthem of Israel:

Kola de balevav P'nimah	As long as the Jewish spirit
Nefesh Yehudi homiyah	Is yearning deep in the heart
Ul fa'ateymizrach kadimah	With eyes turned to the East
Ayin l'tzion tzo ofiyah	Looking toward Zion
Ode lo avdah tikvetenu	Then our hope, the two thousand
Hatikvah bat shnot al payim	Year old hope, will not be lost:
L'hiyot amchofshi b'artzenu	To be a free people in our land,
Eretz Tzion v'Yerushalayim.	The land of Zion and Jerusalem.[10]

The other large ghettos also presented organized concerts, cabarets, and plays for the inmates. Such activities were almost always controversial. In Kovno, for example, a young woman named Tamara Lazerson, who was apparently involved in some sort of music making, wrote in her diary: "There are some excellent singers and poets. And that is how people forget where they are for one night, transporting themselves to an entirely different world. Although some people angrily object to what we are doing, they are wrong. A lot of people are composing something in the ghetto."[11]

The most interesting musical efforts were those of the street singers and the organized resistance groups within the ghettos. As in Warsaw, street singers in all the large ghettos produced a steady stream of new songs and new ghetto-specific texts for popular preexisting songs. Particularly noteworthy are the songs of Yankele Hershkovitz in Łodz, which do not attack the Nazis directly, but rather skewer Chaim Rumkowski, the strongman who dominated the Jewish Council of Elders and whose iron-fisted policies Hershkovitz opposed.

The songs usually associated with partisans, including the famous *"Zog Nit Keynmol"* ("Never say you're walking your last road"), which was written in Vilna, were mostly composed by people active in resistance groups inside the ghettos, who sang them there. Songs were then circulated by fighters who escaped to join partisan bands operating in the countryside. Some, like *"Yid, Du Partizaner"* ("The Jewish Partisan") may have been written in a partisan

---

cites both the *Ghetto Diary* of Janusz Korczak (New York: Holocaust Library, 1978), 84–85, and the *Warsaw Diary* of Michael Zylberberg (London: Vallentine-Mitchell, 1969), 61–63. Korczak's diary makes no mention of musical events in June 1942.

10. Naphtali Herz Imber wrote the original text in 1878. Schmuel Cohen arranged a Romanian folksong to fit the text in 1888. The lyrics were subsequently altered at the First Zionist Congress in 1897 and later changed into the current form by Zionist settlers in Palestine.

11. Tamara Lazerson, Diary entry of December 11, 1942, in *Hidden History of the Kovno Ghetto* (Washington, D.C.: United States Holocaust Memorial Museum, 1997), 172.

camp. But these songs were almost certainly never sung by partisans in the countryside, the romanticized representations of Hollywood notwithstanding. Yetta Kane, whose family traveled and hid with Lithuanian partisans for the duration of the war, testified unequivocally that noise of any kind—much less singing—was simply not tolerated because the Germans were constantly in close proximity.[12] On the other hand, Szymon Laks's assertion that the songs of the resistance movement were actually written after the war is also incorrect.[13]

Rachel Böhm was a young member of the resistance organization in Łodz. When she was deported to Auschwitz (where she perished in January 1945) she hid a note in the rail car that was recovered by her comrades when the train returned to the ghetto. Böhm briefly listed train stations, travel times, and other information she thought important to send back. Then she wrote: "We keep singing our songs."[14]

Music in Western Transit and Civilian Internment Camps

After their victory in the west, the Nazis established a number of camps in France and the Low Countries for the purpose of gathering and holding Jews for eventual transport to what was euphemistically called "Family Camp in the East." Music in these transit camps was largely, but not exclusively, confined to concerts and cabaret performances organized by Nazi officials to aid in keeping the inmates calm. Etty Hillesum, one of the most articulate witnesses to German occupation in Holland, railed against such concerts in the Westerbork camp, in part because they were always held the night before the invited audience was shipped east: her anger aimed equally at the callousness of the Nazis and the blind naïveté of inmates who always seemed to enjoy the evening's entertainment, apparently without realizing the fatal consequences of their journey the next morning. Nevertheless on October 1, 1942, Hillesum, who volunteered to work in Westerbork for the Amsterdam Jewish Council before she was actually confined there, wrote "There is no hidden poet in me, just a little piece of God that might grow into poetry. And a camp needs a poet, as a bard who is

---

12. Presentation by Mrs. Kane to the author's class, October 26, 2010.

13. Szymon Laks, *Music of Another World*, trans. Chester A. Kisiel (Evanston, Ill.: Northwestern University Press, 1989), 119.

14. Michal Ungar, ed., *The Last Ghetto: Life in the Lodz Ghetto 1940–1944* (Jerusalem: Yad Vashem, 1991), 184–85.

able to sing about it."[15] When she was deported east on September 7, 1943 to Auschwitz, where she would perish, she had come to understand—as Rachel Böhm would understand later in the war—that music could be a weapon of resistance. Etty Hillesum somehow managed to throw a postcard from the moving train. On it she had written, in part: "We left the camp singing."[16]

William (Hildesheimer) Hilsley was a British citizen teaching music at the International Quaker School in Utrecht when the Nazis invaded. After the Dutch surrender, he dutifully answered the order for assembly and deportation and was sent, along with other British non-combatants, to a civilian internment camp in Tost, Germany. These camps were operated according to Geneva Convention rules similar to prisoner-of-war camps; among other small luxuries, the camp was inspected regularly by one of several aid agencies from neutral countries, and inmates were free to send and receive mail. The prisoners were encouraged to develop leisure activities including a variety of educational, theatrical, and musical programs. Since Hilsley was adept at various aspects of musical production and staging, he immediately became involved in preparing concerts and staged cabaret shows.

Early in 1942 he and the other Jewish prisoners were transferred to Kreuzburg. Alarmed at this move, he was happy when his non-Jewish comrades from Tost arrived in Kreuzburg a few days later. They had gone to the Tost commander and threatened to inform the next inspectors that Jewish prisoners had been removed for no apparent reason. In reaction the commandant transferred to Kreuzburg all the British who had been incarcerated with Hilsley. For the remainder of the war, Hilsley and other Jewish prisoners were protected by these men. In thanksgiving, and as a Christmas present for those he considered to be his saviors, Hilsley composed *Missa (in festo Nativitatis)*, a little Mass for unaccompanied men's chorus.[17] A miniature jewel, it is quite unlike any other music to be composed in a German camp (of any kind) during the war. For obvious reasons Hilsley omitted the *Credo*. But this omission opens the work up to inclusivity not otherwise possible, and matches the universality of Hilsley's exquisite musical rhetoric—a rhetoric that cannot be identified as belonging to a specific time or national, ethnic, or religious style.

Perhaps more interesting is a performance recorded by Swedish Radio for its

15. Etty Hillesum, *An Interrupted Life and Letters from Westerbork*, trans. Arnold J. Pomerans (New York: Henry Holt, 1996), 225.

16. Ibid., 360.

17. William Hilsley, *When Joy and Pain Entwine: Reminiscences* (Beverweerd: Syzygy Music, n.d.), 27–34.

internationally broadcast program "From behind Barbed Wire," which documented life in prisoner of war and civilian internment camps by means of recorded musical performances, dramatic readings, and other events, as well as interviews with inmates. For a broadcast from Kreuzburg in July 1944, William Hilsley and fellow inmate Geoffrey Lewis Navada performed an African-American spiritual: "Go down, Moses, way down in Egypt's land. Tell old Pharaoh to let my people go!"[18] After the war William Hilsley returned to the International School in Utrecht where he spent the rest of his life. Until his retirement he continued to stage, with his students, the musicals he had composed in Kreuzburg.

Music in Forced Labor and Death Camps

Herbert Zipper testified that after he was moved from Dachau to Buchenwald in 1938, he could no longer produce concerts in his barrack because security was too tight. However, by 1944, security had either slackened in Buchenwald, or individual barracks were secretly creating musical activities of their own: the great Czech composer Petr Eben, incarcerated for two years as a teenager, remembered composing and performing at least two cabaret songs there.[19] Also, a number of Polish partisan songs with inflammatory texts are known to have been sung in Buchenwald at this time.[20]

In Sachsenhausen similar activities took place, mostly documented by Aleksander Kulisiewicz. One particularly poignant occurrence involved the Holocaust-specific adaptation of the text of a famous Yiddish folksong, "*Tzen Brider*" ("Ten Brothers"). Rather than dying in various ways according to the original, brothers in the shortened Sachenhausen version are led off to the gas.[21]

In the Gross-Rosen satellite of Auschwitz and Birkenau, David Kane, then about eleven or twelve years old, volunteered with five other boys to sing German folksongs on a daily basis for the camp commandant. For this he and his fellow singers shared an extra ration of bread. Prior to the war he had memorized from a recording a number of Hebrew prayers as sung by the great cantor Yossele Rosenblatt. These he occasionally sang in the barracks for fellow inmates. At some point camp guards, having heard him sing frequently for the

18. William Hilsley, *Musik hinterm Stacheldraht: Tagebuch eines internierten Musikers 1940–1945* (Utrecht: Stichtung Matrijs, 1999), 118.

19. Interview with the author, January 6, 1989.

20. Copies of songs sung in Buchenwald are preserved in the National Holocaust Museum in Washington, D.C.

21. Gilbert, *Music in the Holocaust*, 137–41.

commandant, asked him to sing for them. So, with the encouragement of his father, David Kane stood on a small table and, into the faces of the guards, sang Rosenblatt's version of the high holy day prayer *"Elokai ad shelo notzarti"* ("God, before I was created, in countless periods of time in which I did not live, I could not have fulfilled my mission in this world. You therefore waited to create me until the generation arrived in which I would be granted the possibility to act as your agent in this world"). The guards were delighted; and even though they did not understand what was sung, most everyone else within earshot did.[22] David Kane survived to become a cantor and, later, a distinguished rabbi.

Adam Kopycinski, orchestra director in the Auschwitz I camp, went on record as believing that music strengthened the inmates.[23] It is known that children in at least one barrack in Auschwitz kept their spirits up by singing the early nine-teenth-century song "Die Gedanken sind frei, ver kann sie eratten?" ("Thoughts are free; who can erase them?"), which had been prohibited by the Nazis. However, musicians from the Auschwitz II (Birkenau) men's and women's orchestras have stated flatly that they played to stay alive another day. Still, when circumstances were right, these musicians found subtle ways to resist the Nazis.

Szymon Laks, a member of the Birkenau men's orchestra, one day found in the mud a manuscript of anonymous eighteenth-century polonaises. He cleaned it off, kept it safe, and arranged the music for the camp orchestra to play in their barrack, even though the performance of Polish music, according to Laks, was forbidden. Laks wrote, "some of my Polish colleagues congratulated me on this, regarding it as an act of the resistance movement.... In any case, if this episode can be regarded as a sign of resistance, it is the only one I can boast of during a rather long stay in Birkenau."[24]

Alma Rosé, director of the Birkenau women's orchestra, came under withering criticism from Fania Fénelon, one of the orchestra members. Fénelon would become famous after the war for the film version of her memoir *Playing for Time*. Among other things, Fénelon thought that Rosé drove the orchestra mercilessly in an impossible pursuit of musical perfection, which Rosé apparently thought necessary to preserve the lives of her players. Be that as it may, Rosé, who died in April 1944 from what was probably a brain aneurism, was one of only four members of the women's orchestra who did not survive the war.

Also, in January 1944, Rosé and another of her orchestra members, Mar-

22. Presentation by Rabbi Kane to the author's class, October 26, 2010; interview with the author, July 10, 2011.
23. Laks, *Music of Another World*, 117.
24. Ibid., 65–66.

got Anzenbacher Větrovcová, created a song from Chopin's famous *Étude in E* (opus 10, no. 3). Vocal arrangements of the opening section of this piece had been popular since at least 1930, when it was published with French lyrics. Recordings also appeared throughout that decade, not only in French, but in English and German as well, performed by a wide variety of singers, including Richard Tauber, Paul Robeson, and Jo Stafford. While Rosé and Větrovcová may have been familiar with the French words, they seem to have based their new words on a German text by Ernst Marischka, retaining his title, *"In mir klingkt ein Lied"* ("A Song Echoes within Me"). Like other versions, Rosé's, preserved in her own hand, languishes in melancholy. After hearing it, camp officials complained of the song's sadness and forbade further performances unless the text was changed. Apparently Chopin's études, if Laks is correct, were not considered Polish. Rosé refused; so the song simply fell into official disuse. However, the orchestra continued to play and sing it for themselves during rehearsals, when no guards or untrustworthy inmates were present.[25]

Late in 1944, there was an uprising of the Sonderkommando (those inmates who worked in the crematoria) in Birkenau. One of the crematoria was destroyed and many of the Sonderkommando escaped, only to be tracked down and killed. Some were formally executed in front of the other assembled inmates. As the condemned were being taken to the place of execution, they began singing *"Ani Ma'amin"* ("I believe, with unshakeable faith, in the coming of Messiah"). Spontaneously, the entire assembly of prisoners sang with them.

Music in Theresienstadt

Theresienstadt (Terezín) was unique in the Nazi system because, in addition to its purpose of serving as backdrop for a propaganda film, it also functioned as transit camp, labor camp, and ghetto. Much has been written about the exceptionally well-organized musical activities in Theresienstadt where a steady stream of concerts, recitals, operas, and cabaret shows took place from the first night inmates arrived in November 1941 until late October 1944. Several should be mentioned here because inherent in them were unusual qualities of resistance.

Most famous, perhaps, are the several performances of Verdi's *Requiem* which took place from early September 1943 until October 1944. Raphael Schaechter,

25. Richard Newman (with Karen Kirtley), *Alma Rosé: Vienna to Auschwitz* (Portland, Ore.: Amadeus Press, 2000), 292–94.

the progenitor of musical activities in Theresienstadt and mastermind of most of the choral and opera performances there, conceived of this as a way to confront the Nazi officers with the idea of judgment day (*"Dies irae, dies illa"*—"Day of wrath, day of mourning"). He managed, without giving away his true intent, to convince the Jewish Council of Elders to support his presentation of this particular Roman Catholic funeral mass because of its cultural importance. The sixteen performances he eventually conducted were spread over several months because choristers would be transported without notice to Auschwitz, forcing him to reorganize the choir and begin again. But his plan worked and during at least one performance Adolph Eichmann is rumored to have been present.

In the same vein was the August 1944 performance of Mendelssohn's *Elijah* by Theresienstadt's German language choir, under the direction of Karl Fischer. Two brothers from this choir survived and one of them, Henry Oertelt, later wrote about this performance. While his memory proved faulty in regard to some details, his description of the concert's opening is riveting: "The Nazi commander and his SS-uniformed cohorts sat down. The Jewish leaders of the camp, strangely enough, were placed right next to them ... the huge choir of inmates cried out in a strong fortissimo: 'Help, Lord—Help, Lord! Wilt thou quite destroy us?' We knew it was the most beautiful and most meaningful performance that ever took place anywhere!"[26]

A song was created for each children's barrack. Neither text nor music was ever committed to paper because of their subversive nature. They were taught by rote and the melodies were used to identify children when away from the barrack. One of them, *"Byt svetem vladla"* ("Even though a power dominates"), is probably by Raphael Schaechter and his brilliant young associate Gideon Klein. It speaks directly to their predicament and instills a sense of hope by using the last words of the fifteenth-century Czech martyr Jan Huss as a refrain: *"A pravda vítezi!"* ("The truth will prevail!").

Composers also quoted preexisting pieces as a sign of resistance. For example, Pavel Haas (the most famous Czech composer in the camp) had saved his wife, who held a Russian passport that did not identify her as a Jew, and young daughter by divorcing his wife before he entered the camp. After arriving in Theresienstadt, his loneliness and depression crippled his ability to compose for almost a year, even though Schaechter and Klein continually urged him to help them. Eventually he composed *"Al S'fod"* ("Do Not Lament"), a setting for

26. Nick Strimple, *Choral Music in the Twentieth Century* (Portland, Ore.: Amadeus Press, 2002) 109–10.

men's chorus of a poem in Hebrew by the Palestinian Jewish poet David Shimoni. The poem extols the value of work, especially work for the common good. In the music, Haas cleverly hid one of the most emotionally charged Czech patriotic hymns, the Hussite "Saint Wenceslaus Chorale." His last completed work, *Study for Strings*, uses the four-note opening motive from Antonín Dvořák's *Requiem* as the first notes of a fugue subject.

At this point it may be good to remember that the Theresienstadt inmates—at least the privileged ones who got to attend concerts—were largely Czech and, for the most part, completely assimilated into secular Czech society. They were also highly educated. Virtually every prisoner who heard these works of Haas would have easily recognized the Hussite and Dvořák quotations (in fact, the Czech government had interrupted regular radio programming for years by broadcasting Dvořák's piece immediately before important government announcements). Inmates of other nationalities (primarily Germans and Danes) who arrived later also tended to be well educated and culturally astute.

So the various musical quotations in the opera *Der Kaiser von Atlantis* ("The Emperor of Atlantis") should come as no surprise. The composer Viktor Ullmann and his librettist, the talented young artist Petr Kien, labored for considerable time on this allegorical opera; and the urgency with which they worked is noticeable in the surviving manuscripts. They managed to bring it into rehearsal but not performance because, in the end, they and their performers were caught in the last large transports to Auschwitz in October 1944 where most, including the composer and author, were murdered. Kien's story of Emperor Überall, whose warlike ways are such an affront to humanity that Death himself walks off the job, is remarkable. Ullmann adorns this tale with new music that includes well-known tunes, some used in politically incorrect ways. Dvořák's *Requiem* is quoted subtly. But the opening trumpet call is borrowed from Joseph Suk's orchestral piece about the Angel of Death (*Asrael Symphony*); "*Deutschland, Deutschland über alles*" ("Germany, Germany above all") makes an exaggerated appearance; and lastly an altered—even purified—version of Martin Luther's "*Ein feste Burg*" ("A Mighty Fortress") is used for the final chorale admonishing listeners to honor the sanctity of death:

Komm Tod, du unser werter Gast,	Come, Death, our honored guest,
in unsers Herzens Kammer.	enter the chamber of our hearts.
Nimm von uns Lebens Leid und Last,	Take from us life's pain and woe,
führ uns zur Rast nach Schmerz und	lead us to rest after grief and
Jammer.	Sorrow.

Lehr uns Lebens Lust und Not	Teach us to honor in our brothers
in unsren Brüdern ehren.	the joys and sorrows of life.
Lehr uns das heiligste Gebot:	Teach us the most holy command-ment:
Du sollst den großen Namen Tod	Thou shalt not take
Nicht eitel beschwören.	Death's great name in vain.

Petr Kien's conclusion is shocking because, ultimately, the victims and the oppressors share the same redemption. But this last musical quotation is particularly profound because it illuminates another, hidden, meaning. Ullmann was aware of the sophistication of the Theresienstadt audience. He knew that they were at home in secular, even Christian, society; he himself knew absolutely nothing about Jewish liturgy or traditions. Two of the most popular works in the standard repertoire of European ensembles were J. S. Bach's *Ein feste Burg* (Cantata no. 80) and Felix Mendelssohn-Bartholdy's *Reformation Symphony* (Symphony no. 5), both based on Luther's chorale. So it is entirely possible that Ullmann's fellow prisoners, had they gotten to hear it, would not only have understood Kien's text but also have remembered the last verses of Luther's original:

Und wenn die Welt voll Teufel wär	Though hordes of devils fill the land
Und wollt uns gar verschlingen,	All threat'ning to devour us,
So fürchten wir uns nicht so sehr,	We tremble not, unmoved we stand;
Es soll uns doch gelingen.	They cannot overpow'r us.
Der Fürst dieser Welt,	This world's prince may rage,
Wie saur er sich stellt,	In fierce war engage.
Tut er uns doch nicht.	He is doomed to fail;
Das macht, er ist gericht't.	God's judgment must prevail.
Ein Wörtlein kann ihn fallen.	One little word subdues him.
Das Wort sie sollen lassen stahn	God's Word forever shall abide,
Und kein' Dank dazu haben.	No thanks to foes, who fear it;
Er ist bei uns wohl auf dem Plan	For God himself fights by our side
Mit seinem Geist und Gaben.	With weapons of the Spirit.
Nehmen sie den Leib,	If they take our house,
Gut, Her, Kind und Weib,	Goods, fame, child, or spouse,
Laß fahren dahin.	Wrench our life away,
Sie haben's kein Gewinn.	They cannot win the day.
Das Reich muß uns doch bleiben.	The kingdom's ours forever.[27]

27. *Lutheran Book of Worship*, (Minneapolis, Minn.: Augsburg Publishing House, 1978), unattributed translation.

Conclusion

On Sunday, August 20, 1995, the *New York Times* published an article by Alex Ross which dealt extensively with music associated with World War II and the Holocaust. Ross made the point that music itself is morally neutral. After all, both sides in the war used music effectively to promote their own agendas. As has already been pointed out, the musical rhetoric of *"Horst Wessel Lied"* and *"Dachau Lied"* is the same. In Ross's view, "music is adept at the larger, vaguer emotions, like joy and despair. Joy or despair at what, the listener decides: anything more particular, such as political protest, usually falls outside the composer's reach." He goes on to reference Theresienstadt as the "most agonizing example of music's helplessness," citing the use of Haas's *Study for Strings* in the Nazis' unfinished propaganda film *Der Führer Schenkt den Juden eine Stadt* (The Führer Gives the Jews a City): "the music's forceful fugal motion speaks of a defiant spirit. But this astounding vigor is diabolically twisted around for propaganda purposes: the music communicates an illusion of Jewish safety."[28]

While Ross did not mention that such illusion was created more by the film's visual production than by the music, he was correct in his estimation of the inability of music to express other than general emotions. Still, he misunderstood the value that music—often as a vehicle for the projection of words—had for many people in the camps and ghettos at the time, including those pictured in the propaganda film. If we are not ourselves Holocaust survivors, we cannot possibly hear the music from the camps or ghettos the way it was heard then because we have absolutely no frame of reference, at all, for what the concentration camp or ghetto experience was like. While it is true that music was an irritant to some prisoners, for many others it provided not only a means of emotional escape, but also a way to remain human and thereby fight back. Jews have been fighting back through music, poetry, and prayer since the Babylonian captivity and the writing of Psalm 137:

By the waters of Babylon, there we sat down, yea, we wept, when we remembered Zion.
We hanged our harps upon the willows in the midst thereof.
For there they that carried us away captive required of us mirth, saying, Sing us one of the songs of Zion.

28. Alex Ross, "In Music, Though, There Were No Victories," *New York Times* (August 20, 1995): H 25.

How shall we sing the LORD'S song in a strange land?

If I forget thee, O Jerusalem, let my right hand forget her cunning.

If I do not remember thee, let my tongue cleave to the roof of my mouth; if I prefer not Jerusalem above my chief joy.

Remember, O LORD, the children of Edom in the day of Jerusalem; who said, Rase it, rase it, even the foundation thereof.

O daughter of Babylon, who art to be destroyed; happy shall he be that rewardeth thee as thou hast served us.

Happy shall he be, that taketh and dasheth thy little ones against a stone.

The Psalm makes clear that Jews did not sing the songs their Babylonian captors expected, but rather lamented their situation and sang out for justice. Their twentieth-century descendants followed suit. Viktor Ullmann, in one of the essays he wrote while in Theresienstadt, eloquently articulated the imprisoned Holocaust musicians' point of view:

Goethe's saying "Live in the present moment, live in eternity" always represented for me the enigmatic meaning of Art.... Theresienstadt was, and still is for me, the school of form. Before that, when we did not feel the impact nor the burden of material life because they were erased by comfort, that magical accomplishment of civilization, it was easy to conceive artistic forms of great beauty: It is here [in Theresienstadt], when in our daily existence we had to vanquish matter with the help of the power of form, when everything that was related to the muses contrasted extraordinarily with the environment which was ours, that was the true school of mastery. Like Schiller we tried to penetrate the secret of each work of art in an attempt to annihilate matter through form, which is the supreme mission of the human being: the aesthetic one as well as the ethical one.... One has to stress that Theresienstadt contributed to emphasize and did not hinder my musical activities, that in no way whatsoever did we sit down to weep on the banks of the waters of Babylon, and that our effort in the service of Art was commensurate with our will to live, in spite of everything. I am convinced that those who fight, in life as well as in Art, to triumph over matter which always resists, will share my point of view.

Part 4

Central and
Eastern Europe

Dieter Kuntz

15 Jewish Resistance in Nazi Germany and Austria, 1933–45

In 1871, Jews were granted full civil rights within the newly unified German state and over the course of the nineteenth century—and especially during the first three decades of the twentieth century—Germany's Jewish population gradually expanded its participation in Germany's economic development, cultural arena, and social and political life, aspiring ultimately to achieve full assimilation within the German nation. Most German Jews thought of themselves as Germans. As a result of this considerable degree of Jewish self-identification with the interests of the German state and society, an examination of the question of a "Jewish resistance" in Germany to the threat posed by Nazism must necessarily be situated within the broader context of overall German resistance to the Nazi regime during the years 1933–45. Similarly, the definition of what constituted "resistance" must also be analyzed within a much broader framework than many earlier studies that focused narrowly on organized, armed efforts to overthrow Hitler and the Third Reich.

German and Austrian Jews were members of non-Jewish political organizations and cultural groups and clubs that opposed the Nazis. Yet because their oppositional activities often occurred as members of these larger groups—of Communist or Socialist political parties—their actions have not been regarded as specifically "Jewish" resistance or opposition. Just as there were opponents of the Nazis within Germany whose activities ranged from public criticism of the regime, to covert opposition, and finally to active armed resistance, so too was there a range of Jewish reactions to the policies of the Hitler state. Simply to dismiss the Jewish response to Nazism as nonexistent, as some historians have done, fails to note the varied and multifaceted nature of the involvement not only of oppositional groups, but also of individual German and Austrian Jews who engaged in behaviors ranging from simple private nonconformist deeds to more daring acts of refusal and defiance, as well as to open protest that aimed to influence public opinion.[1]

As Yehuda Bauer has shown, resistance must not be defined only as "armed rebellion or the use of force," but must also be seen in the broader context of a multitude of Jewish acts of nonconformism, including "mutual self-sacrifice within the family to avoid starvation or worse; cultural, educational, religious, and political activities taken to strengthen morale; the work of doctors, nurses, and educators to consciously maintain health and moral fiber to enable individual and group survival."[2]

Pre-1933 Jewish Opposition to Nazism in Germany

Despite the degree of assimilation Jews had achieved earlier, the years following World War I were characterized by continued prejudice, discrimination, and even persecution. This was especially pronounced and became increasingly more vociferous within *Völkisch* circles, encompassing the radically racist, right-wing movements within German politics. The growth of the Nazi party (NSDAP) during the years of the Weimar Republic, along with its vitriolic attacks on Jews and other perceived "enemies" it targeted in its early platform, the "Twenty-five Point Program," and in Hitler's ideological manifesto *Mein Kampf*, made it clear that these circles still regarded Jews as outsiders or "foreign" and rejected their inclusion in the *Volksgemeinschaft*, the biologically defined "national community." Although antisemitism had become more pronounced after the war, those who demanded the reversal of Jewish emancipation were nonetheless still largely confined to right-wing fringe elements. Antisemitism was certainly not a new phenomenon and German Jews responded in different ways. Sustained by Weimar's constitutional guarantees, many felt that antisemitism would fade and the anti-Jewish agitation could be endured until it passed. Others, however, responded by organizing within groups and some, like the Central Association (*Centralverein*), recognized the

1. Detlev Peukert, "Working-Class Resistance: Problems and Options," in *Contending with Hitler: Varieties of German Resistance in the Third Reich*, ed. David Clay Large (Washington, D.C.: German Historical Institute, 1991), 36–37.

2. Yehuda Bauer, *Rethinking the Holocaust* (New Haven, Conn.: Yale University Press, 2001), 120.

serious nature of the threat and actively resisted the Nazis even before the NS-DAP (National Socialist German Workers' Party) came to power. The *Centralverein* engaged in behind-the-scenes propaganda campaigns that supported those political parties that attempted to defend Weimar's parliamentary democracy—especially the Social Democrats—working particularly closely with the party's auxiliary organizations, *Reichsbanner* and the Iron Front (*Eiserne Front*).[3]

Already in 1893, the perceived need to counteract antisemitism had initiated the founding of the most influential organization among German Jews, the Central Association of German Citizens of the Jewish Faith (*Centralverein deutscher Staatsbürger jüdischen Glaubens*, or CV). During the 1920s the CV's membership numbered almost seventy thousand, with local branches established in many cities and regions throughout Germany. Through the pages of its widely circulated newspaper, the *CV-Zeitung*, the organization's national leadership was able to communicate news, disseminate policy matters, and coordinate responses to Nazi actions directly from CV headquarters in Berlin to its various local groups.[4] The CV engaged in public propaganda efforts aimed at countering Nazi antisemitism by distributing fliers and pamphlets and protesting Nazi acts in the *CV-Zeitung*, as when in the aftermath of a 1931 SA (Sturmabteilungen) rampage in Berlin that saw storm troopers attacking people who to them "looked Jewish," the paper denounced this "anti-Jewish eruption" and pleaded with the public to show its disapproval and form a "front of decent people" (*Front der Anständigen*).[5]

The CV worked closely with the Social Democratic Party (SPD) although their relationship was necessarily largely not public. This tactical strategy hoped to avoid fueling the Nazi claim that the Socialists were "Jewish shocktroops." Clearly recognizing that the SPD was an important bulwark against Nazism, the CV contributed considerable funding to party coffers; for instance, financing the printing of SPD election posters in Saxony. The CV also made its publications refuting anti-Jewish propaganda available at no cost to the party and its auxiliary organizations and affiliations.[6] The CV similarly cooperated with and supported the SPD's *Reichsbanner* by purchasing uniforms for the or-

3. Arnold Paucker, *German Jews in the Resistance, 1933–1945: The Facts and Problems* (Berlin: Gedenkstätte Deutscher Widerstand, 2003), 11.

4. Jürgen Matthäus and Mark Roseman, eds., *Jewish Responses to Persecution, 1933–1938* (Lanham, Md.: AltaMira Press, 2010), 1:xxxii.

5. Ibid., xxxv.

6. Donald L. Niewyk, *German Social Democracy Confronts the Problem of Anti-Semitism, 1918–1933* (unpublished dissertation, Tulane University, 1968), 261–62.

ganization in some districts and authoring anti-Nazi pamphlets that were distributed as *Reichsbanner* publications.[7] Jews were, of course, themselves also active members of the *Reichsbanner*, an openly confrontational political paramilitary organization that frequently engaged the SA and SS in street battles during the 1920s and early 1930s.

The CV also worked closely with the League for Combating Antisemitism (*Verein zur Abwehr des Antisemitismus*). Originally founded in 1890, the League (a nondenominational, Christian-based organization that also had Jewish members) worked during the Weimar years to counter the image of Jews as racially inferior and frequently in its newspaper, the *Abwehrblätter*, attacked Nazi writings in the NSDAP newspaper, *Völkischer Beobachter*, as well as Hitler's ideas expressed in *Mein Kampf.* In its December 1932 edition, the paper lamented that, despite the NSDAP losses in the November Reichstag election, the Nazis' antisemitism had not diminished:

The decline of the National Socialist Movement has not brought with it the related decline of its anti-Semitic pronouncements, which one might have expected. Indeed, there has instead been—and a quick look back at 1931 confirms this—an increase in its anti-Semitic venom. This is perhaps understandable, because now that their numbers have decreased, the swastika-wearers have to scream louder, and act even wilder, if they want to maintain their image of ever-increasing strength.[8]

In 1933, the newspaper was forced to close, with its last edition appearing on March 3, and the organization dissolved itself shortly thereafter, in June.[9]

Also active in the fight against German antisemitism was the Reich Association of Jewish Frontline Soldiers (*Reichsbund jüdischer Frontsoldaten*, or RjF). At times cooperating with the CV, the RjF sought especially to combat the right-wing charge that portrayed Jews as cowards who shirked their military responsibilities during the war. A RjF flier distributed during the 1932 Reichstag electoral campaigns depicted a Nazi in the stylized figure of a farmer "sowing the seed of hatred and lies." Underneath the figure, Germans were warned about the dangerous falsehood being spread throughout the land:

> A sower passes through the land,
> Spreads hatred and lies with his hand.

7. Ibid., 263.

8. *Abwehrblätter*, Band 42, 1932, 10 December, 232. Bayerische Staatsbibliothek. Digitale Bibliothek, Münchener Digitalisierungszentrum.

9. Barbara Suchy, "The Verein zur Abwehr des Antisemitismus: From Its Beginnings to the First World War," in *Leo Baeck Institute Year Book*: 28:205.

Germans, beware of this poisonous seed!
From it sprouts the slander that during the Great War
the Jews were cowards and shirkers.
12,000 fallen Jewish soldiers bear witness for us,
who defended the Fatherland with their life and property.[10]

Very influential within German Jewry, especially among the young, was the leading representative of the Zionist movement, the Zionist Association for Germany (*Zionistische Vereinigung für Deutschland*), along with its newspaper, the *Jüdische Rundschau*. It was, however, through membership in both Jewish and non-Jewish youth groups during the three decades prior to the Third Reich, that post-1933 rebellious and oppositional attitudes began to form. In reaction to the exclusionist antisemitism of nationalist German youth organizations such as the "Wandering Bird" movement (*Wandervogel*), alienated Jewish youths in search of a Jewish identity in the years after World War I established and found their way into organizations such as the anarchist group, the "Black Heap" (*Der Schwarze Haufen*), the Zionist youth group, "Blue-White" (*Blau-Weiss*), or into the largest non-Zionist group, "Comrades" (*Kameraden*). Fractured by internal divisions, this group disbanded in 1932, splitting into factions with the more prominent group, the left-Zionist "Workmen" (*Werkleute*), organizing underground activities for a brief period after 1933. In the main, its internal activities included intellectual discussions and the crafting of plans for future settlements in Palestine. "Blue-White," the largest Zionist youth group after 1933, would also become involved in covert actions against the Nazi regime, but its pre-1933 activities also centered mainly on political discussions. In 1928, the left-wing Zionist "Young Guard" (*Haschomer Hazair*) was established and would become significant, serving as a training ground for future anti-Nazi dissidents. Similarly, before 1933, this group also engaged largely in discussions of political and social theories.[11]

Resistance against the Third Reich, 1933–38

When the Nazis assumed power in 1933, Germany's Jews confronted a harsh new reality as the regime methodically began to enact its anti-Jewish policies. Jews reacted in different ways. Some 60,000 Jews fled from Germany just dur-

---

10. Jürgen Matthäus and Mark Roseman, *Jewish Responses to Persecution*, xxxiv.
11. John M. Cox, *Circles of Resistance: Jewish, Leftist, and Youth Dissidence in Nazi Germany* (New York: Peter Lang Publishing, 2009), 16–19.

ing the first two years of the Nazi regime. Others clung to the belief that they could persevere, that the regime would not last, and that ultimately their situation would improve. This was especially true of the older generation. Younger Jews, especially those more radical and who had been active in left-wing youth groups, were more inclined to be defiant and looked for a way out of their situation. There were also some not affiliated with political parties or other groups who acted individually. Centralized and organized resistance against the regime, however, was complicated by the fact that Jews came from so many different backgrounds and social classes, and did not share a common ideology or political orientation. Nonetheless, German Jews did resist, and they did so in numbers enormously out of proportion to their numbers within the German population.[12]

Workers' Movements and Leftist Organizations

Jews played leading roles in the underground activities of a variety of anti-Fascist organizations and many of the political prisoners initially sent to the early Nazi concentration camps were Jews. Because of racial persecution, resistance by Jews was, in fact, more difficult than anti-Nazi resistance by non-Jews. Heinz Galinsky observed in 1947 that "Jewish heroism proved itself in circumstances of special severity: they were marked men, constantly under police surveillance, surrounded by people ready to denounce them, often as political opponents of the Nazi regime under the obligation to report regularly to the police."[13] Yet despite this close surveillance, the danger of discovery by the Gestapo, and the inevitably harsh punishment, many young Jews particularly were moved to participate in covert operations.

After 1933, the proportion of Jews participating in oppositional activity of the newly illegal leftist parties and the prohibited workers' movement was considerable—especially in proportion to their overall representation within workers' parties during the Weimar era. It has been estimated that of the more than 3,000 Jews who resisted the Nazis at different times between 1933 and 1945, some 2,000 were actively involved in the most important leftist resistance groups and were members of organizations such as the banned Social

12. Helmut Eschwege, "Resistance of the German Jews against the Nazi Regime," in *The Nazi Holocaust: Jewish Resistance to the Holocaust*, ed. Michael Marrus (Westport, Conn.: Meckler Corporation, 1989), 7:387–88.
13. Ibid., 391–92.

Democratic Party (SPD) and Communist Party (KPD), or belonged to the German Communist Party Opposition (KPO), the Socialist Workers' Party (Sozialistische Arbeiterpartei or SAP), the Trotskyists, or the International Socialist Militant League (*Internationaler Sozialistischer Kampfbund*). The leadership of the leftist splinter group consisting of disillusioned former SPD and KPD members, New Beginning (*Neu-Beginnen*, also known as the *Org*), as well as much of its membership, also consisted of Jews.

Because the Gestapo quickly discovered many of these illegal resistance organizations, many of their members were arrested and imprisoned in concentration camps. Many were released between 1936 and 1939 on the condition that they leave Germany permanently; yet some came back, crossing the border to resume their oppositional work.[14] Among Jewish Communists, for example, Alexander Abush, editor of the Communist daily newspaper, *Ruhr-Echo*, emigrated to Paris where he edited the *Brownbook on the Reichstag Fire and the Hitler Terror* that was distributed throughout Germany. Herman Axen joined the Communist Youth Organization in 1932 at the age of sixteen, and in 1933 immediately began to engage in underground activities. Imprisoned for three years and then expelled from Germany, he continued his anti-Nazi activities with Communists in France and again fell into the hands of the Gestapo, whereupon he was sent to concentration camps. In Buchenwald in 1945, he participated in the fighting to liberate the camp. The artist, Lea Grundig, a KPD member and founding figure in the "Association of German Revolutionary Artists," continued after 1933 to produce anti-Fascist art critical of the regime and to document the growing fear within the Jewish community. Arrested in 1938 and imprisoned on charges of high treason, she was released in 1939 and expelled from the Reich, whereupon she made her way to Palestine and there created drawings and sketches that illustrated the persecution of Jews in Germany. Published in book form under the title *In the Valley of Death*, this compilation of her work was released in England in March 1945 and helped draw attention to the abysmal plight of the Jews at the hands of the Nazis. KPD member, Bruno Baum, who after the war would become a leading member of East Germany's ruling Socialist Unity Party, was sentenced to thirteen years of hard labor for his work in the Resistance.[15] In 1936, the Gestapo discovered and smashed the resistance group around Jonny Hüttner, alias Nathan Hirschtritt.

---

14. Arnold Paucker, *Deutsche Juden im Kampf um Recht und Freiheit* (Berlin: Verlag Hentrich und Hentrich, 2004), 214–17; Paucker, *German Jews in the Resistance*, 18–19.

15. Eschwege, "Resistance of the German Jews against the Nazi Regime," 403–06.

This was an offshoot group of the KPD propaganda circle, The Red Mouthpiece (*Das rote Sprachrohr*), that had formed illegally in 1933.[16] Hüttner spent the years 1936–45 incarcerated in the Nazi camp system and became involved in resistance movements inside the camps.

There were also a number of KPO-affiliated resistance groups. One such group operating in Breslau until 1937 was made up primarily of Jews who were former members of the German-Jewish youth group *Kameraden*. Their activities included distributing leaflets and smuggling reports from the Reich into Czechoslovakia, as well as bringing political material back into Germany. One of these activists, Helga Beyer, joined the resistance group at the age of thirteen and smuggled papers across the Czech border by hiding them in her ski poles. Arrested in 1937 when the Gestapo crushed the group, she would ultimately perish in Ravensbrück at the age of twenty-two. The judgment in her trial concluded that because the accused "was very conscious of her important role as a foreign courier … and of her desire to further world communism and thereby abetting international Jewry, her activities clearly intended to bring harm to the Reich."[17]

An anti-Fascist resistance group of Jewish girls, made up of former members of the League of German-Jewish Youth (*Bund Deutsch-Jüdischer Jugend*), clandestinely worked in Berlin. Led by Eva Mamlok, the group's activities focused on the distribution of antiwar propaganda.[18] Already in 1933, at the age of fourteen, Mamlok had painted the slogan "Down with Hitler" on the exterior wall of the Hertie department store in Berlin. Promptly arrested, she was released from jail after only a few days because of her age. Back on the streets, she once again provoked Nazi ire by placing flowers on the graves of the murdered former Communist leaders, Rosa Luxembourg and Karl Liebknecht. Again arrested, this time she served a longer jail term, but on release continued to distribute anti-Fascist propaganda. From 1939 to 1941, the regime assigned Mamlok and other members of the girls' group to compulsory labor service in a Berlin factory where she recruited other members for resistance efforts. In September 1941, as a result of a denunciation, the Gestapo confiscated incriminating pro-

16. Paucker, *Deutsche Juden*, 233.

17. "Deutsches Reich," in *Im Kampf Gegen Besatzung und 'Endlösung': Widerstand der Juden in Europa, 1939–1945*, ed. Georg Heuberger (Frankfurt: Jüdisches Museum der Stadt Frankfurt am Main, 1995), 20–21; Arnold Paucker, "Jüdischer Widerstand in Deutschland," in Arno Lustiger, *Zum Kampf auf Leben und Tod! Vom Widerstand der Juden 1933–1945* (Munich: Deutscher Taschenbuch Verlag, 1997), 54–55.

18. Ibid., 21.

paganda materials and sentenced Mamlok and her colleagues to confinement for life. Mamlok, however, perished in 1944.[19]

In the Munich area, Berthold Feuchtwanger, the youngest brother of the famous writer Lion Feuchtwanger (author of *Jud Süss*), aided Social Democrat resistance groups by printing and distributing leaflets with titles such as the "Twenty-one Theses against Hitler" and "Hitler is sawing off the branch he's sitting on." In Hamburg, also arrested and tried for the production and distribution of anti-Nazi leaflets, were leaders of the SAP, Albert Kahn and Kurt and Rudolf Saalfeld. In 1934, Emanuel Bruck, the cultural editor of the banned but illegally distributed central organ of the KPD, *The Red Flag* (*Die Rote Fahne*), was sentenced to eight years of hard labor. Taken to Dachau after serving the sentence, Bruck died there in 1942. The Hamburg attorney and KPD member, Herbert Michaelis, was a member of a Communist resistance group that sought to expose the regime's activities in the Spanish Civil War. Arrested for high treason and sentenced to death by the People's Court, Michaelis was executed in Plötzensee prison in June 1943. Another Jewish member of the Hamburg resistance group, Dagobert Biermann, sentenced to six years of hard labor, was taken to Auschwitz in 1943, where he died one month after arrival. Julius Phillippson, the regional director of the ISK for the Berlin, Brandenburg, Saxony, and Thuringia area, was arrested and sentenced to a life term of hard labor for distributing underground anti-Nazi literature and newspapers from abroad.[20]

A 1934 end-of-year Gestapo report based on information submitted by regional offices, attempted to summarize the degree of Jewish participation in Communist and Socialist underground resistance activities. Of the 195 Jewish resistance members the Gestapo were aware of in Germany, the report determined that about half were members of the KPD, while others belonged to organizations such as the Communist Youth, Communist Opposition group (KPO) and Red Help (*Rote Hilfe*), the Communist Red Trade Union Opposition (*Rote Gewerkschafts Opposition*), the SPD, the Socialist Youth Association, the Socialist Workers' Party, or were anarchists. Some were described as being guilty of distributing leaflets or pamphlets such as "The Red Trade Unionist" (*Der Rote Gewerkschaftler*), tearing down Nazi posters, making statements hostile to the regime, or for insulting state leaders, while others were charged with hav-

19. Christina Steenken, "Erinnerung an eine Heldin. Gedenken Widerstand: In Kreuzberg wird ein Stolperstein für Eva Mamlok gelegt," online edition of *Die Tageszeitung* (*www.taz.de*), October 10, 2011.

20. Eschwege, "Resistance of the German Jews against the Nazi Regime," 403–06.

ing committed treason. As this list included only those individuals known to the regime, the total number of Jews engaging in resistance was considerably higher. According to the police, the cities registering the highest number of resistance fighters were Karlsruhe, Frankfurt (Main), Breslau, and Berlin.[21] After arrest and subsequent interrogation of suspects that included torture in order to extract confessions as well as further information about other resistance fighters, Nazi courts meted out sentences ranging from several years of hard labor (which in some cases resulted in death) to execution. Much of the Jewish resistance activity occurred during the first two years of the Third Reich, and by 1935–36, in the aftermath of the anti-Jewish Nuremberg Laws, the police surmised that their harsh measures had the impact of having "taken [Jews'] breath away," as a decline in Jewish resistance activities seemed to have set in.[22]

Nonetheless, clandestine activities did continue. In December 1935, Helmut Hirsch, a twenty-year-old Jewish architecture student, was arrested in Stuttgart for his part in a bomb plot, in which he intended to detonate explosives at the Nuremberg offices of the Streicher publication *Der Stürmer* and at the main train station. Hirsch was sentenced to death in 1937 and executed in June of that year. In 1937 in Berlin, Felix Jonas, the Jewish leader of the illegal *Reichsbanner* local group that had continued to hold meetings and distribute political literature, was arrested. Also in Berlin, the Jewish Social Democrat, Günther Salomon-Salter, was arrested, tried, and sentenced to six years of hard labor for preparing illegal literature and maintaining contact with SPD connections in Denmark. In Frankfurt (Oder), the Jewish SPD leader was arrested because his group continued to hold regular meetings that included listening to Moscow radio broadcasts. In the same city, the Gestapo hunted for Walter Gutmann, a forty-five-year-old Jew sought for having distributed a pamphlet denouncing the Kristallnacht pogrom, entitled "J'accuse—ich klage an." Other activists were arrested in Weimar, Wiesbaden, Mannheim, Heidelberg, Erfurt, Magdeburg, Zeitz, Halle, Bremen, and Dresden. In Heilbronn, during the events of *Kristallnacht* in November 1938, a Jewish family fought back against storm trooper violence by throwing an SA man from their window into the street below.[23]

From within left-wing circles, two groups had emerged during the late 1920s that included many disenchanted former adherents of the KPD and SPD, and young German Jews played key roles in the leadership of these new organiza-

21. Ibid., 406.
22. Ibid., 408.
23. Ibid., 411.

tions. Formed in 1929, the Leninist Organization, "New Beginning" (*Neu Beginnen*) or the "Org," grew rapidly during the first few months of Hitler's takeover, expanding from about one hundred members to nearly five hundred, and boasting a full-time executive staff of some twenty administrative functionaries.[24] Anticipating the rise of Fascism, the Org, even before 1933, had developed elaborate underground tactics that would later help underpin their resistance activities. Org member, Gerhard Bry, recalled that the organization:

learned how to use concealed code in writing and in telephone conversations, shift meeting times and places by pre-arranged rotations that made them different from those agreed upon by phone, arrange for danger signals, avoid being followed, discover tails, shred carbon and other papers ... and many other tricks of the trade.... We also had technical experts in micro-photography, chemists who developed quick burning paper which left little residuals and capsules in which undeveloped microfilm could be carried in the mouth and quickly destroyed, carpenters who built really hard-to-discover hiding places.[25]

Most of the group's opposition to the regime, however, involved primarily the covert distribution of Socialist publications, such as its pamphlet, "*Neu Beginnen*," and the production and distribution of anti-Nazi leaflets. By the mid-1930s, Gestapo arrests of many members and the flight of others caused the decline of the Org.

Similarly, the "Left Opposition" (*Linke Opposition*), whose activities mirrored those of the Org, also included Jewish members in leading positions. Purportedly, this group also produced a brochure entitled "Treatise on the Jewish Question," although no copies have survived. Yet because the Jewish members of both the Org and *Linke Opposition* were thoroughly secularized, their anti-Nazi activities were leftist oriented, and not until after the Kristallnacht pogrom in 1938, did the Jewish members of these groups fight specifically against the anti-Jewish measures of the regime.[26] The German Communist Party, whose membership also included secularized Jews, also did not respond directly to the Nazis' anti-Jewish policies until after 1938.[27] In a special November issue of its publication "The Red Flag," the KPD appealed directly to all Communists, Social Democrats, Democrats, Catholics, and Protestants, and all "decent Germans" to aid the Jews.[28] The headlines of the paper that was

24. Cox, *Circles of Resistance*, 34–35.

25. Gerhard Bry, *Resistance: Recollections from the Nazi Years* (West Orange, N.J.: G. Bry, 1979), 53–54; quoted in Cox, *Circles of Resistance*, 36–37.

26. Cox, *Circles of Resistance*, 48.   27. Ibid., 63.

28. Eschwege, "Resistance of the German Jews against the Nazi Regime," 391.

slipped under doors in the working class district of Berlin urged all to "Oppose the Disgraceful Pogroms against the Jews."[29]

Active in the Socialist Youth Movement, Henny Prax recalled that in Berlin:

many people were involved in anti-Fascist activity, many Jews. They were Social Democrats and Communists. Jews were in the forefront. When Hitler came to power, we went underground. We knew that this thing that had befallen Germany was totally wicked and wrong, and we were prepared to fight it. We formed in groups of people who knew each other. It was highly organized. We had middle-men who passed on news.[30]

Their activities included distributing their own newspapers. "In the early days we tried to give information to the public. Information that wasn't available anymore once the Nazis had taken over." Despite the danger, they found novel ways to distribute leaflets discreetly in public places, leaflets that they had secretly typed until two or three in the morning, in closed, noise-muffled rooms ("we hung blankets over the windows and doors"). The leaflets contained "the news of the world."

Once you were caught doing those things, it wasn't always certain your life would be spared, but we devised things. We made cigar boxes with little springs inside and put the leaflets inside so that if someone opened it, then leaflets would whoosh into the air and people could pick them up. Or we would put leaflets in paper in public toilets, and people would find the leaflets there, and people would have time and privacy to read them. We tied leaflets onto fireworks sticks, and they would go up and the leaflets would fall down in parks. Sometimes we would do these things as people were coming home from work.

Prax was caught, nonetheless, when the Gestapo fingerprinted all employees at the firm where she worked, and her fingerprints matched those found on leaflets. Summoned to Gestapo headquarters, she was held for one week in a small cell in the building's cellar and interrogated. Sleep deprived, subjected to bright lights and incessant interviews, she yielded no information and steadfastly denied knowing the people who were shown to her in photos. Yet each refusal was met with a brisk "smack to the head" that inflicted severe ear drum damage, causing hearing loss. Battered and bruised, she was released after one week, but had revealed nothing.

---

29. Paucker, "Jüdischer Widerstand," 51.

30. USC Shoah Foundation Institute for Visual History and Education, Testimony of Henny Prax, Interview Code 35107.

Jewish Youth Movements

After the various leftist organizations, the second largest group that engaged in resistance work consisted of assorted youth groups. Jewish youth groups experienced tremendous membership growth during the early years of the Third Reich, doubling in number from the Weimar period, so that by 1935 more than one-half of German Jewish youths had joined an organization. Jewish youth groups ideologically reflected the broad spectrum of Jewish political orientations, but most had either Jewish-liberal or Socialist tendencies, while the Zionist youth movement steadily increased in membership and played an ever larger role in preparing youth for emigration to Palestine.[31] Faced with the new reality of the Hitler state, one young activist remembered the turbulent events of 1933 as having "shattered overnight" everything that he had believed in:

Nothing seemed more urgent or more important than to find something that we could hold on to, something that would steady and unite us as we drifted about in a sea of uncertainty ... to restore our sense of direction and our self-confidence ... we needed each other. We needed the comfort of our company, the reassuring knowledge that, expelled as we were, we were not alone.[32]

Clearly the sense of isolation felt by Jews underscored the importance of group membership and the mutual support and protection it offered. Group membership also provided a firmer foundation for resistance.

Zionist groups

Despite the resistance offered by Jews within the leftist and various youth movements described above, many within the German Jewish community between the years 1935–38 grew increasingly discouraged about their future prospects within the Hitler state. Heinrich Stahl, chairman of the Berlin Jewish community in 1938, summed up the pessimism of many with these words: "Let me tell those among our youths who have not yet made up their minds to emigrate that there is no future for the Jews in this country. Whatever changes may be in store, there will probably be no improvement at all for us."[33] From 1933 until 1938, a number of Zionist organizations were also active in the anti-Nazi resistance. While most Zionist organizations primarily engaged in training and

---

31. Paucker, *Deutsche Juden im Kampf um Recht und Freiheit*, 221.
32. Cox, *Circles of Resistance*, 20.
33. Eschwege, "Resistance of the German Jews against the Nazi Regime," 411–12.

preparing young German Jews for eventual life in Palestine, many members of these organizations were also involved in underground political and educational activities. In 1938, however, the regime banned all Zionist organizations, although many continued their activities illegally by going underground.[34]

The Zionist organization *Hechaluz* (the Pioneer) grew into the largest Jewish youth group in Germany after 1933, counting roughly some 15,000 members, with youth group members dominating its leadership ranks. Between 1933 and 1936, *Hechaluz* encouraged 7,000 people to immigrate to Palestine. The desire to leave the Reich became even more intense after 1938, until October 1941, at which time an emigration ban was imposed. Although many *Hechaluz* leaders were deported to the Theresiendstadt ghetto in 1942, the organization continued to be an important point of contact for illegally emigrating Jews as was the affiliated youth group, *Chug Chaluzi*, which would be formed in 1943. Years earlier, beginning in 1933, future leaders of this group, Jizchak Schwersenz and Edith Wolff, had gained valuable organizational experience preparing and training young German Jews for eventual emigration to Palestine. In the face of the Nazi takeover, Zionist planning provided much needed moral support for Jewish youth. Wolff, the child of a Jewish father and Aryan mother, classified by the Nuremberg Laws of 1935 as a first degree *Mischling*, became intensely involved in aiding her fellow Jews by working for the Zionist cause. Even before these activities, she opposed the Nazis by pasting "Poison" stickers obtained from a pharmacy on the card catalog entries for Hitler's *Mein Kampf* in various libraries.[35]

Resistance during the War Years, 1939–45

The Herbert Baum Group

The resistance efforts of the Herbert Baum Group—or more accurately, the individuals and groups affiliated with Herbert Baum—were commemorated in the former German Democratic Republic as the work of Communist anti-Fascist fighters, without much mention of the Jewish composition or Jewish-based motivation of its members. In the Federal Republic, the degree of "Jewish" or

---

34. Ibid., 389.

35. Christine Zahn, "Nicht Mitgehen, sondern weggehen! Chug Chaluzi—eine jüdische Jugendgruppe im underground" in *Juden im Widerstand: Drei Gruppen zwischen Überlebenskampf und Politischer Aktion, Berlin 1939–1945*, Wilfried Löhken and Werner Vathke, eds. (Berlin: Verlag Edition Hentrich, 1993), 160–66.

"Communist" identity of the group was, and today continues to be, debated.[36] Some scholars, such as Wolfgang Wippermann and Arnold Paucker, have firmly maintained that the group must be regarded as a "Jewish" resistance organization. Others who continue to argue that the Baum Groups, and especially their leader Herbert Baum, were principally motivated by Communist influences, nonetheless concede that "the nature and actions of the Baum Group were undeniably shaped by the evolving Jewish consciousness of many of its members."[37]

Herbert Baum and several close friends initially began their anti-Nazi activities soon after Hitler came to power in January 1933, with anti-Fascist and Communist ideology influencing their efforts at that time. Increasingly, however, and especially after 1935 and 1936, their actions became motivated by the regime's measures of persecution and racial exclusion of Jews. Baum had ties to a number of organizations and became affiliated with political groups in 1925 when, at the age of thirteen, he joined the SPD's children's organization, the Red Falcon, and subsequently joined the SPD's youth group, the Socialist Workers Youth. At the age of fifteen, he became a member of the German-Jewish Youth Association, and in 1931 also joined the Communist Youth League. It was during this period that his friendships developed with classmates Martin Kochmann, Sala Rosenbaum, and Marianne Cohn (who would later become his wife). After 1933, Baum and his friends also developed important connections to the German-Jewish Youth League, a non-Zionist youth group. The early activities of these various individuals and groups consisted primarily of communal hiking, staging musical evenings, educational and political discussions, and debates about the ideal of a classless society. Importantly, however, they all also shared the common notion of wanting to engage in some kind of anti-Nazi activity. This resulted mostly in clandestine anti-Fascist graffiti campaigns, producing and distributing leaflets, and in transporting and disseminating banned literature.[38] Some, like Alice and Gerhard Zadek, recalled

36. See Wolfgang Wippermann, "Die Berliner Gruppe Baum und der jüdische Widerstand" in *Beiträge zum Thema Widerstand* (Berlin: Informationszentrum Berlin Gedenk-und Bildungsstätte Stauffenbergstrasse, 2001) 2–4; Cox, *Circles of Resistance*; Konrad Kwiet and Helmut Eschwege, *Selbstbehauptung und Widerstand. Deutsche Juden im Kumpf um Existenz und Menschenwürde, 1933–1945* (Hamburg: Hans Christian Verlag, 1984), 114–39.

37. Cox, *Circles of Resistance*, 164. See also the website of the Berlin-Brandenburg *Landesinstitut für Schule und Medien Berlin-Brandenburg* that discusses the activities of the Widerstandsgruppe Baum: http://bildungsserver.berlin-brandenburg.de/station14.html.

38. Eric Brothers and Michael Kreutzer, "Die Widerstandsgruppen um Herbert Baum," in *Im*

also defacing Nazi newspaper reading-boxes of Streicher's rabidly antisemitic publication, *Der Stürmer*. By simply covering over two letters with black paint in the propaganda slogan so prominently displayed atop each box, "The Jews are our Misfortune" (*Die Juden sind unser Unglück*), the altered wording proclaimed, "The Jews are our Good Fortune" (*Die Juden sind unser Glück*).[39] During 1938 and 1939, a number of the early members of the Baum Group, such as the Zadeks, emigrated.

Three years after the issuance of the 1935 Nuremberg Laws, conditions became even worse for German and Austrian Jews. The March 1938 German annexation of Austria immediately subjected Austrian Jews to all of the Nazis' anti-Jewish legislation. In April, the regime launched measures to "Aryanize" Jewish property. In October, 17,000 "stateless" Jews were expelled from the Reich, followed shortly by the November 9–10, 1938 "Pogrom Night," which saw the looting of Jewish businesses, and the desecration and destruction of synagogues, along with mass arrests and concentration camp incarcerations. Not long after, all Jewish children were expelled from German schools, and as of January 1, 1939, identification cards for Jews became mandatory, and men and women were required to adopt the middle name of "Israel" or "Sara." With the advent of war in September 1939, the regime was ultimately able to radicalize its racial policies within the Third Reich and in the territories it would occupy in the months and years that followed. It was during this period, from early 1939 until mid-1941—a time when Jews were not only subjected to countless new discriminatory laws and regulations, had their freedom of movement curtailed, and were increasingly publicly humiliated—when the Baum Group's inner core was shaped and when their motivations came into focus. Two developments in particular served to crystallize their perspective—the Nazis' introduction of forced labor (which came on the heels of the curtailment of Jewish economic activity) and the prohibition of Jewish youth organizations in the wake of the pogrom.[40]

Because of these conditions, the Baum Group became something of a catch-all organization for members of dissolved groups. New members were rapidly attracted and the group gatherings lessened their sense of isolation.[41] When

Kampf Gegen Besatzung und "Endlösung": Widerstand der Juden in Europa, 1939–1945, ed. Georg Heuberger, 28–29.

39. Alice and Gerhard Zadek, *Mit dem letzten Zug nach England* (Berlin: Dietz, 1992), 109.

40. Brothers and Kreutzer, "Die Widerstandsgruppen um Herbert Baum," 33–35.

41. Kwiet and Eschwege, *Selbstbehauptung und Widerstand*, 117.

in 1940 and 1941, he was forced to work alongside hundreds of other Jewish slave laborers who had been detailed to a special "Jewish section" of the Siemens electric motor plant in Berlin, Herbert Baum, who had been trained as an electrician, found like-minded colleagues who would also become members of his resistance circle.[42] The members of the groups affiliated with Herbert Baum during this period were all relatively young, most were in their early twenties, and numbered around 100. Many were former members of anarchist groups such as the *Schwarze Haufen*, of Jewish youth groups, or of Zionist organizations such as *Hashomer Hazair*, and *Habonim*, which had been formed out of the earlier *Deutsch-Jüdische Wanderbund-Kameraden*. These groups were tolerated initially by the Nazis who, in attempting to remove Jews from the *Volksgemeinschaft* (national community), were trying to force Jews to emigrate. Zionist youth groups, like other Zionist organizations, were, however, dissolved by the regime in 1938, but their former members continued to be closely monitored. Several members of the Baum Group, including its leader, were simultaneously also active in the Communist Youth League. This new cooperation between Zionist and Communist Jews was logical, given the fact that all German Jews were now members of a common persecuted minority, and had by 1939 been deprived of all legal rights, economically and socially ostracized from society, and mercilessly targeted by the regime's increasingly harsh policies.[43]

During the war and particularly with the regime's escalation of its brutal campaign of racial annihilation, the Baum Group—informed by contacts in the army—began to disseminate leaflets in the summer of 1941 that called attention to Nazi atrocities in the East. Typically, the anti-Nazi propaganda material would be left in places where the public could find it, such as in telephone booths. Baum's colleagues made valuable contacts with French foreign laborers with whom they worked in factories, such as the Siemens plant, and through these connections the group was able to secure French and Belgian identity papers.[44] By the spring of 1942, the group decided the time had come to undertake more aggressive action. Convinced that the Nazi attack on the Soviet Union would bring about the collapse of the Third Reich, and that there would be widespread dissatisfaction among a population facing increased hardships, the group reasoned that conditions were ripe for civil war and revolution. It

42. Cox, *Circles of Resistance*, 83.

43. Wipperman, "Die Berliner Gruppe Baum," 4.

44. Brothers and Kreutzer, "Die Widerstandsgruppen um Herbert Baum," 35; also see the website http://bildungsserver.berlin-brandenburg.de/station14.html.

was during this period that they planned their public attack on a prominent Nazi propaganda display in Berlin.[45]

The Assault on the Nazi Anti-Soviet and Antisemitic Exhibition "Soviet Paradise"

On May 8, 1942, propaganda minister Joseph Goebbels staged a propaganda exhibition in a huge hall on a central square in Berlin designed to ridicule the Soviet system and simultaneously identify Jews with Bolshevist ideology. More than 1 million people visited the exhibition, entitled "The Soviet Paradise," which displayed what the Nazis claimed were actual living conditions within the Soviet Union.[46] The pamphlet accompanying the exhibition opened with the text: "Words and pictures are not enough to make the tragedy of Bolshevist reality believable to Europeans." The exhibition itself included a model of the Belorussian city of Minsk depicted through dilapidated shacks, farm houses of rough huts made of straw and mud, complete with manure piles, and all portrayed as typical. Photos of Russian peasants, workers, and soldiers were on display depicting them as primitive brutes in order to illustrate the Nazi claim of the inferiority of the Slavic subhuman Untermenschen. Moreover, a member of the Baum group remembered the exhibition as an attempt to depict a society wherein "nothing [was] newly built" and "the people were all robbers and criminals."[47] The exhibition catalog informed the reader that the inventor of Marxism was the Jew "Marx-Mordochai," that the Soviet state was nothing other than the implementation of that Jewish invention, and that the "Jewish world revolution" had brought this about. Before showing in Berlin in May 1942, the exhibition had earlier that year traveled to Vienna and Prague, where attempts had been made to sabotage the showing. In Berlin, however, on May 18, Baum Group activists firebombed the exhibition and succeeded in burning down a section of it.[48] Berlin firefighters were able to extinguish the flames quickly and prevent further damage. Yet this bold act of protest by a group of underground Jewish activists who dared to challenge the Nazi regime was symbolically one of the most significant acts of defiance undertaken within the Hitler state, and must be regarded as comparable to the more well-known 1943 anti-Nazi illegal leaflet campaign of Hans and Sophie Scholl in Munich.[49] The members of the Baum Group, however, were not simply attempting to destroy the exhibition,

45. Ibid., 37–39.
46. Cox, *Circles of Resistance*, 81.
47. Ibid.
48. Ibid., 82.
49. http://bildungsserver.berlin-brandenburg.de/station14.html.

they were intent on protesting and opposing the Nazi dictatorship. The group was objecting to both the depiction of Slavs as subhuman and the propagandistic linking of Jews and Communists.

The regime's retribution was both swift and severe. The Gestapo uncovered not only those connected with the firebombing, but also located wider circles of activists. The investigation of the Berlin attack immediately revealed that it had been carried out by members of two resistance groups connected to Herbert Baum. The arrests occurred in four phases. The first arrests were made on May 22, 1942, four days after the fire-bombing, and included the four members of the inner circle of the Baum group who worked together in the Siemens plant: Herbert Baum and his wife, Marianne, Gerhard Meyer, and Heinz Rothholz. The next day, Sala Kochmann, as well as two non-Jewish members of Baum's inner circle—Irene Walther and Suzanne Wesse—were taken into custody. Several managed to avoid arrest for a few days, but in early June, Heinz Birnbaum, Hanni Meyer, and Heinz and Marianne Joachim were seized. Only one member of the group escaped. Further arrests soon after swept up all members of the circle around Baum's friend, Joachim Franke. Police discovered that the Franke Group had, in early 1942, written with red paint on a number of factory walls the demand that "Hitler must abdicate" and had also prepared to launch a placard pasting campaign.[50] A second round of arrests on July 8 captured three others from the wider circle of Baum's friends. The third round of arrests focused on the group of individuals around Heinz Joachim.[51] Subsequent arrests followed over the next eighteen months, and most of those arrested were charged with high treason. Ultimately, a total of thirty-two members and supporters of the Baum Group were either executed or murdered by Nazi authorities.[52] Family members and friends were also rounded up and deported to various camps.

The regime determined to set a public example that resistance had severe consequences. On May 27, nine days after the bombing, the Gestapo arrested a large number of Berlin Jews and took them to a collection camp (*Sammellager*). Some were released soon after, but on May 28, the remaining 154 were transported to the Sachsenhausen concentration camp, where they were shot immediately after arrival. Some had previously been active in the Resistance during the 1930s

50. Michael Kreutzer, "Die Suche nach einem Ausweg, der es ermöglicht, in Deutschland als Mensch zu leben," in *Juden im Widerstand: Drei Gruppen zwischen Überlebenskampf und Politischer Aktion, Berlin 1939–1945*, ed. Wilfried Löhken and Werner Vathke (Berlin: Verlag Edition Hentrich, 1993), 123–24.

51. Ibid., 140.

52. Cox, *Circles of Resistance*, 132.

and had already been incarcerated in penitentiaries. The relatives of the 154 were then rounded up and deported to Theresienstadt. Another ninety-six Jews were selected at evening roll call in the Sachsenhausen camp and were shot. In Berlin, a further 250 Jews were rounded up and taken to Sachsenhausen where they were either murdered or shipped to Auschwitz where they perished.[53]

"Underground" Resistance in Berlin

Unable to flee across borders, especially once war began, many Jews in Berlin chose to resist Nazi deportation efforts by going underground internally. Estimates of how many chose this option vary considerably, some suggesting that as many as 7,000 Jews lived underground in Berlin in February 1943; by November 1943 the number was reduced to 5,000–6,000, and by early 1944, it is estimated, a mere 2,000. At the time of the liberation of Berlin, only about 1400 Jews emerged from hiding.[54] Life in hiding was precarious, stressful, and required a great amount of courage, but many were determined to hold out and mutually supported each other. Although it was risky to be seen in public, many did so; some even used public transportation to go to movie houses, visit museums, and frequent restaurants. Some dyed their hair blond in order to appear more Nordic or "Aryan."[55] Others were not so daring. Inge Deutschkron remembered moving frequently to different living quarters, with most being anything but comfortable. Able to sleep at night in a friend's store, she recalled that "we laid mattresses on the floor behind the counter every evening. There was a toilet and washbasin in the basement. We weren't allowed to turn the light on, in case someone thought there had been a break-in. The following morning, we were the first customers to leave the store, so to speak."[56]

In Berlin, many of the Zionist youth organizations continued their activities both legally and conspiratorially, even after the war began. In 1942, one such group, the *Chug Chaluzi* (Circle of Pioneers), organized by Edith Wolff, who persuaded Jizchak Schwersenz, a Zionist youth leader, to go underground in order to save children from deportation, succeeded in creating an underground existence for some forty of its youthful members. The group determined that its mission was to save young lives, and regarded this as a form of political resis-

53. Kreutzer, "Die Suche nach einem Ausweg," 95; Brothers and Kreutzer, "Die Widerstandsgruppen um Herbert Baum," 26–27.
54. Kwiet and Eschwege, *Selbsbehauptung und Widerstand*, 150.
55. Ibid., 155.
56. Inge Deutschkron, *We Survived: Berlin Jews Underground* (Berlin: German Resistance Memorial Center, 2008), 37.

tance against the regime.[57] They were able to overcome extremely difficult obstacles that included finding safe living quarters, securing foodstuffs and false identity papers, but had vital monetary support, receiving 100 marks monthly from the underground *Hechaluz* organization. For security reasons, hiding places had to be changed frequently, and all the while the group carried on its Zionist and Jewish educational activities that included religious ceremonies.[58]

Resistance in Berlin's Jewish Hospital

An extraordinary example of resistance to Nazi efforts to deport and murder Jews in the death camps of Poland is the case of the Jewish Hospital in Berlin. The hospital was staffed by Jewish doctors and nurses who treated and protected Jewish patients, and continued to function—if in a limited capacity—for the duration of the Third Reich. It appears that the hospital was allowed to continue to exist after 1938 because the Nazis recognized that it could potentially provide necessary medical services to the Jewish population if a public health risk, such as an epidemic, were to occur within Berlin's large Jewish community.[59] The hospital later became involved in the Nazis' deportation efforts, as it was used as a collection station (*Sammellager*) for the deportation of Jews to the East. Staff at the hospital, however, defied the regime and protected patients from deportation by issuing medical "deferments" to many of the sick. Some Jewish doctors apparently even resorted to unnecessary surgeries, thereby at least postponing deportations.[60] Many of the hospital staff had *Mischling* status (categories defined by the degree of inherited Jewish blood) or were Jewish partners in racially mixed marriages, and as such were not in immediate danger of deportation. Nonetheless, some hospital staff at times risked severe penalties by defying Nazi regulations and removing the requisite yellow star from their clothing in order to venture occasionally beyond the walls of the hospital.[61] In no small measure did the efforts of the hospital staff make it possible for some 800 people to survive to liberation.[62]

---

57. Marion Kaplan, *Between Dignity and Despair: Jewish Life in Nazi Germany* (New York: Oxford University Press, 1998), 212.

58. Konrad Kwiet and Helmut Eschwege, "Chug Chaluzi—eine zionistische Untergrundorganisation in Berlin," in Arno Lustiger, *Zum Kampf auf Leben und Tod Vom Widerstand der Juden, 1933–1945* (Munich: Deutscher Taschenbuch Verlag, 1997), 70–71; Zahn, "Nicht Mitgehen, sondern weggehen!" 169.

59. Daniel B. Silver, *Refuge in Hell: How Berlin's Jewish Hospital Outlasted the Nazis* (New York: Houghton Mifflin, 2004), 44.

60. Ibid., 68–71.   61. Ibid., 96.

62. Ibid., 161.

Resistance in Austria

As in Germany, so also in Austria. After the 1938 Anschluss (the annexation by the Third Reich), it was the changed political situation, marked by increased discrimination and surveillance, that made it much more difficult for Jews than non-Jews to undertake measures of resistance against the new regime. Nonetheless, here too, many Jews adopted a variety of anti-Nazi positions that can be characterized as resistance, ranging from nonconformist behavior to defiance and oppositional activity. Accordingly, resistance cannot be defined narrowly as armed action, as the Documentation Center of Austrian Resistance cogently argues. The term must include all attempts by Austrian Jews to defy Nazi efforts to "disenfranchise, expel, and annihilate" them, or even to deprive them of the right to "live any sort of decent life as a Jew."[63]

Austrian Jews engaged in defiance of various Nazi anti-Jewish measures, including the refusal to follow specified anti-Jewish regulations, evading roundups and deportations by taking refuge "underground," as well as by illegally crossing borders.[64] This is evidenced by Vienna Gestapo reports which, for instance, for the thirty-day period from early September to early October 1940, reveal that more than 100 Jews were arrested, indicted, and fined for offenses such as curfew violations or for attending theaters and movie houses forbidden to Jews. Subsequent months saw more than fifty Jews arrested on charges of listening to banned foreign radio broadcasts. In 1941, over fifty Viennese Jews were arrested and charged with making treasonous statements or engaging in Communist subversive activities. Hundreds of Jews arrested during 1941 and deported to ghettos in Poland, escaped and made their way back to Austria only to be again arrested and deported. Their reports of conditions in Polish ghettos, however, warned others not to comply freely with Nazi roundup and deportation orders, urging many instead to go underground, to try to live in hiding, or to flee across borders. In 1942, Gestapo reports continue to list the arrests of some eighty Jews trying to cross the border into Hungary, while over fifty were charged with failing to comply with wearing identifying armbands, twenty-two were charged with attempting to pass themselves off as non-Jews, thirty-eight were detained for making forbidden public utterances, and twenty-five were arrested for distributing Communist propaganda. During 1943, more

63. www.doew.at/ausstellung/chapter7_en.html.
64. Wolfgang Neugebauer, *Der österreichische Widerstand, 1938–1945* (Vienna: Steinbauer, 2008), 166.

than 100 Jews still living in hiding in Vienna were discovered, only to be immediately deported to concentration camps, most often Auschwitz. Even in 1944, forty-three individuals living clandestinely under cover were detected and caught. It has been estimated that between 600 and 700 Jews remarkably survived the war (most in Vienna), aided by friends and acquaintances.[65]

Life in hiding was perilous for those who opted to resist Nazi deportation actions by going underground. Yet their numbers increased following the deportations during the fall of 1941, as interviews with survivors reveal that most felt that the so-called resettlement or "evacuations" meant certain death. The clandestine existence of these so-called *U-Boote* (submarines) was fraught with constant fear of discovery. Finding safe quarters, securing the necessary foodstuffs and other provisions, not having access to medical care, concern over hygienic conditions, the inability of normal social interaction, and constant psychological stress took a heavy toll. Moreover, these difficulties only increased as time wore on.[66]

With the 1938 Anschluss, some 130,000 Austrians, mostly Jews, fled the country seeking refuge in nations ranging from France to China. Yet those already politically active in left-wing organizations in their homeland continued to engage in anti-Fascist activity abroad, particularly in France and Belgium, and in 1941 merged to form the anti-German resistance group, *Travail Allemand* (TA). Much of the TA's work consisted of the production and distribution of anti-German propaganda leaflets and newspapers in France and Belgium, but after the German defeat at Stalingrad, a large number of Austrian TA members returned to Austria to organize anti-Fascist efforts there. In helping to support and organize resistance efforts, particularly in Vienna, most were ultimately discovered and arrested. At least ten perished through torture or died in concentration camps.[67] Jews, in general, played leading and active roles in Austrian leftist—especially Communist—organizations, and were heavily represented in the membership ranks of these groups.[68] The German invasion of the Soviet Union in 1941 sparked a marked increase of oppositional activity within both Germany and Austria, much of it involving Jewish members of organized

65. Ibid., 167; Jonny Moser, "Österreichische Juden und Jüdinnen im Widerstand gegen das NS-Regime," in *Widerstand in Österreich, 1938–1945*, Stefan Karner and Karl Duffek, eds. (Vienna: Ludwig Boltzmann-Institut für Kriegsfolgen-Forschung, 2007), 125–32.

66. *Dokumentationsarchiv des Österreichischen Widerstandes* (*DÖW*), ed., Jüdische Schicksale: Berichte von Verfolgten, 2nd ed. (Vienna: Österreichischer Bundesverlag, 1993), 604–6.

67. "Österreich," in *Im Kampf Gegen Besatzung und "Endlösung": Widerstand der Juden in Europa, 1939–1945*, 44–48.

68. Neugebauer, *Der österreichische Widerstand, 1938–1945*, 170.

Communist groups. In the summer of 1943, more than thirty Jewish Communist activists returned to Austria from France, posing as "foreign workers" in order to support resistance within working class circles. Most, however, were ultimately discovered and subsequently murdered in various camps.[69]

Historian Wolfgang Neugebauer points to other forms of Jewish "resistance" in Austria. He poignantly argues that in view of the Nazis' Nuremberg Laws which prohibited so-called "racial defilement"—marriages or sexual relations between Jews and Aryans—and the attendant draconian penalties meted out by the regime, those who knowingly engaged in these unions must certainly be regarded as consciously practicing acts of resistance.[70] The non-Jewish partners in these relationships certainly faced stringent penalties including incarceration; but their Jewish spouses had no judicial recourse, were sent to concentration camps, and could be subjected to the death penalty. Yet, at great personal peril, some defied the regime and married nonetheless.[71]

Mischlinge (partial Jews) were also actively involved in resistance efforts. Unlike full Jews, *Mischlinge* were not deported, but were nonetheless subjected to discrimination (particularly in education), prompting many young *Mischlinge* to engage in oppositional activities. Among the most active of these Austrian resistance groups was the Viennese so-called *Mischlingsliga* (League of Partial Jews), whose members consisted mostly of those deemed *Mischlinge* of the First Degree (two Jewish grandparents) as defined by the Nuremberg Laws, but also included full Jews in its ranks. Initially urged by the banned Austrian Communist Party (KPÖ) to establish a resistance group among Jews affected by the Nuremberg Laws, the League was founded in 1943. After becoming acquainted while working in a munitions factory, the Communist youth group functionary, Otto Ernst Andreasch, and the technician Otto Horn, formed the League, composed of young, educated men and women committed to undertaking anti-Nazi propaganda and various acts of sabotage. Horn recalled that the group's activities included simple traffic disruptions, such as causing short circuits in trolley car wiring that resulted in temporarily delaying trains loaded with workers bound for munitions factories: "This was not just meant to disrupt traffic, but, more importantly, it sent a signal to workers that something was being undertaken against the regime. The propaganda aspect of our work was even more significant."[72] One of the group's first propaganda efforts was

---

69. Moser, "Österreichische Juden," 130.
70. Neugebauer, *Der österreichische Widerstand, 1938–1945*, 167.
71. Ibid., 167–68.   72. Ibid., 171.

the distribution of printed fliers urging the populace to join in the struggle for a free Austria, calling for an armed insurrection to topple the Hitler regime. The group committed more than twenty successful acts of sabotage during 1943–44, including intentionally damaging aircraft engine parts.[73]

Individual activists, such as the Viennese Zionist, Aron Menczer, must also be recognized for their illegal, regime-defying efforts to aid young Austrian Jews attempting to reach Palestine. Menczer, a member of the Zionist youth movement "Gordonia," became director of the "Youth Aliya" in Vienna in September 1939, and thereafter trained and prepared many for a possible future life on a *kibbutz*. In September 1942, however, he too was deported, initially to the Terezin ghetto where he continued to work with youth, in particular counseling some 1,200 children who had been deported from Bialystock. Tragically, in October 1943, he and the entire group of children perished in the gas chambers of Birkenau.[74] Within the Jewish medical community, notable opponents of the Nazis' so-called euthanasia program, such as Viktor Frankl, psychiatric director of Vienna's Rothschild Hospital, and Franzi Dannenberg-Löw, children's caseworker in the Viennese Jewish community, chose noncompliance with the regime's measures designed to terminate the lives of mental patients. Frankl continued to accept Jewish patients, falsifying their medical records and diagnoses in order to protect his charges. Franzi Löw similarly tried to save Jewish children by working to transfer them from other institutions into Frankl's care, attempting thereby to rescue them from the euthanasia killing centers.[75]

As has been evidenced in the preceding pages, Jews in Germany and Austria did indeed actively resist the Nazis on many fronts, and in a multitude of ways during the twelve years of the Third Reich. Moreover, as we have seen, even before 1933, German and Austrian Jews had vehemently opposed and taken steps of resistance against the Nazis and their allies, both as members of political organizations and as members of Jewish cultural associations. In the face of overwhelming force, Jews in Germany and Austria—whether collectively participating in group activities or simply acting as individuals—demonstrated remarkable courage and determination in resisting to the best of their abilities the efforts of the Nazis to denigrate, ostracize, and ultimately physically destroy them.

---

73. Evan Burr Burkey, *Jews and Intermarriage in Nazi Austria* (New York: Cambridge University Press, 2011), 181–83; Neugebauer, *Der österreichische Widerstand, 1938–1945*, 171–73.

74. Neugebauer, *Der österreichische Widerstand, 1938–1945*, 168–69; Ghetto Fighters House Archives, Online Photo Catalog No. 12519, Aron Menczer (iis.infocenters.co.il/gfh/list.asp).

75. Neugebauer, *Der österreichische Widerstand, 1938–1945*, 170.

Dalia Ofer

16   "Three Lines in History?"

Modes of Jewish Resistance in Eastern European Ghettos

My aim is to present resistance as it was conceived by the inmates of the ghettos, by survivors, and by historians. My hypothesis is that the ideas articulated by historiography on Jewish resistance were already expressed by the Jews under Nazi occupation. Under the yoke of Nazism a rather sophisticated understanding of Jewish reality was shared by people of all walks of life, which is evident in the contemporaneous documentation of different genres.

Thus, the issue of Jewish responses to the Nazi genocidal policy was expressed and even deliberated by intellectuals and functionaries in the ghettos. Activism and passivity, armed resistance and passive resistance were the terms used to describe the responses of individual Jews and groups to Nazi persecution and mass murder. Responsibility and conduct of leaders and institutions were all discussed and deliberated in the sources. We read the sources today after gaining historical perspective and with the ability to integrate the findings of the vast research on the Holocaust, the Nazis, and World War II.

I wish to allow the authentic voices of the victims and survivors to be heard on the issue of resistance in the ghettos while incorporating various approaches of historical research

"Three lines in history" is taken from testimonies of activists in the underground movement in Cracow quoting from a talk by Dolek Liebeskind, one of its central protagonists. It expressed his feelings following a successful retaliation attack in the wake of the deportation of Jews from the Cracow ghetto. The

Jewish underground attacked the SS officers club Cyganeria on December 22, 1942, an attack in which a considerable number of Germans were killed and wounded.[1]

Jewish underground fighters felt that they were fulfilling a national mission and redeeming Jewish honor. A mixture of pain, anger, and bewilderment characterized Jewish fighters against Nazism and many Jews who struggled with the Occupation in different ways. The disturbing question of how it was possible to eradicate whole communities with almost no resistance troubled various groups in the Jewish communities. The image of the Jews being led "like sheep to the slaughter" was coined by youth movement leaders, writers, diarists, and others. This biblical metaphor described the ultimate helplessness of Jews when confronting their enemies. The use of the expression in ghettos and camps was either a painful description of Jewish fate and lamentation, a condemnation of the Jewish response to the deportations, or a call to resist and obstruct the killings.[2]

To quote Liebeskind again: "We achieved our goal, we took up arms, unable to allow the idea that thousand of Jews—men, women, and children—were killed so wildly. We did not want to be led like sheep to the slaughter.... History would have claimed that the Jews of Poland died a pitiful death with not even one act of resistance."[3] Like the members of the Jewish underground, others in the ghettos shared the pain of what was considered to be Jewish passivity vis-à-vis the occupier. For example, after the mass deportation from the Warsaw ghetto in the summer of 1942, Yehoshua Perle, a well-known Yiddish writer, wrote *The Destruction of Warsaw*, a text of mourning and pain, a text of horrors. The author declared that no pen, no words could even attempt to

1. For a comprehensive description of the underground in Cracow, see Yael Peled (Margolin), *Jewish Cracow: Resistance, Undergound, Struggle* (Hebrew) (Kibbutz Lohamei Hagetaot: Ghetto Fighters' House, 1993); see also, Leni Yahil, *The Holocuast: The Fate of European Jewry, 1932–1945* (New York: Oxford University Press, 1990), 473.

2. The origin of the expression is in Isaiah 53:6–7; Psalm 44:23. The image of the Jews being led as sheep to the slaughter was mentioned independently in a number of ghettos and in a number of personal diaries. The best known is the call of Abba Kovner on December 31, 1941, in the Vilna Ghetto, in an effort to establish an underground movement. For further discussion see Dina Porat, *The Fall of a Sparrow: The Life and Times of Abba Kovner* (Stanford, Calif.: Stanford University Press, 2009), 68–71. For a challenging approach to the interpretation of this expression, see Yael Feldman and Stephen Bauman, "We Shall Not Die as Sheep Led to Slaughter" (Hebrew), *Ha'aretz* 15 (December 2007).

3. *Hehalutz halohem* 30 (August 20, 1943), in *Hehalutz halohem* (Fighting Pioneer): *The Organ of the Jewish Underground Youth in Cracow* (Hebrew) (Kibbutz Lohamei Hagetaot and Tel Aviv: Ghetto Fighters' House and Hakibbutz Hameuhad, 1984), 76.

describe what happened in the deportation of 300,000 Jews to Treblinka. His description portrayed the brutality and inhumanity of the Germans, Ukrainians, and Jewish policemen, together with the complete helplessness of the Jewish victims. Yet he ended his horrific account with a severe condemnation of the Jewish victims who went to their death like sheep to the slaughter without any thought for their dear ones: "300,000 people lacked the courage to say: No. Each one of them was out to save his own skin. Each one of them was ready to sacrifice even his own father, his own mother, his own wife and children."[4]

Emanuel Ringelblum, who wrote *Polish-Jewish Relations* in hiding after the Warsaw Ghetto Uprising, described how the Germans were deceiving the people in the ghetto. They were unable to imagine this diabolic plan of murder. Diaries, too, expressed the inability to comprehend the criminality of the Nazis.[5] It is important to note that news of the Warsaw Ghetto Uprising, the first organized revolt against the Nazis, reached the isolated ghettos and despite its tragic outcome offered a glimmer of solace in the dark reality. Armed resistance was to redeem Jewish honor, as expressed in the above quotation from Liebeskind, or in the last letter of Mordechai Anielewicz: "The dream of my life has risen to become fact. Self-defense in the ghetto became a reality. Jewish armed resistance and revenge are facts. I have been a witness to the magnificent, heroic fighting of Jewish men in battle."[6]

The Jewish Survivors

In the aftermath of World War II, after long years of subjugation and terror, the people of Europe were seeking images that would comfort their injured national pride. The heroes were to be found among those who fought the Nazis, primarily underground activists, partisans, and soldiers in the Allied armies. Jews participated in underground movements in Western and Eastern Europe

4. Yad Vashem Archives (YVA) M10/AR2/199. Yehoshua Perle, *Hurban Varshe* (The Destruction of Warsaw) was published after the war in *Bletter far Geschichte* 4/3 (July–September 1951): 101–40. The translation is from Saul Friedländer, *Nazi Germany and the Jews 1939–1945: The Years of Extermination* (New York: HarperCollins, 2007), 528, who quoted the translation of David G. Roskies, "Landkentenish: Yiddish Belles Lettres in the Warsaw Ghetto," in *Holocaust Chronicles: Individualizing the Holocaust through Diaries and other Contemporaneous Personal Accounts*, ed. Robert Shapiro (Hoboken, N.J.: Ktav Publication House, 1999), 20–21.

5. Emanuel Ringelblum, *Polish-Jewish Relations during the Second World War* (Jerusalem: Yad Vashem, 1974), 159–64.

6. Nachman Blumental and Joseph Kermish, eds., *Resistance and Revolt in the Warsaw Ghetto: A Documentary* (Hebrew) (Jerusalem: Yad Vashem, 1965), 219–20. The English translation: http://www.jewishvirtuallibrary.org/jsource/Holocaust/Anielewiczlet.html

and served in Allied armies as citizen of their countries. Jews from Palestine (the Yishuv—the Hebrew name for the new Zionist enterprise in Palestine) living under the British Mandate volunteered both for regular British units and also formed a unit known as the Jewish Brigade, which bore the emblems that represented the Jews as a national entity.

The remnants of European Jewry were also seeking their own heroes. The non-Jewish underground movements in Eastern Europe were often anti-Jewish, and many Jews suffered greatly when they tried to get help. This often included Soviet partisan units which ignored the unique situation of the Jews, refused to accept unarmed Jews into their ranks, and did not support the Jewish partisan family units. Nevertheless, Jewish survivors were longing to glorify their own fighting heroes. The bitter memory of how their communities were led as "sheep to the slaughter" was now not only a call of the underground or the lamentation of rabbis and leaders, it was also a deep sense of sorrow, pain, and rage that in many respects expressed a wish to avenge the tragedy.

In the general atmosphere of searching for heroes and in the efforts to establish the narrative of the years of destruction, Jews in Europe, Palestine (Israel), and the Americas looked up to the first heroic armed resistance in all of Europe—the Warsaw Ghetto Uprising. Led by a joint leadership of youth movements, political parties, and the remnants of Jews who were not deported in the summer of 1942, the uprising provided a sense of redemption of Jewish honor. The Jewish fighters were viewed with both amazement and admiration.[7]

Jewish survivors found little consolation in the Allied victory, for which they yearned during the endless years of the war. The extent of destruction and the complete loss of family, friends, and community were revealed after liberation, when stories of the killings and the destruction came to light. The prospects of finding dear ones were minimal but the hopes did not dissipate. Jewish survivors began to put together the stories of their destroyed communities. Despite differences in the details and chronology of each personal experience, there was a common core to the narratives—Jews were murdered helplessly, forgotten, and betrayed by the non-Jewish population, destined to death by the Germans and their collaborators, who were often their own neighbors. Though underground movements were active in many ghettos and Jews mounted different forms of armed struggle against the Nazis, and despite the fact that individual Jews and groups joined the partisan movements in Lithuania, Belarus,

7. Friedländer, *Nazi Germany and the Jews 1939–1945*, 527–28.

and the Ukraine, they were but a small minority among the survivors. In view of the millions who were murdered, members of the organized underground and armed rebellions accounted for only a small fraction.[8]

In the context of such a state of mind and emotional landscape, many survivors were involved in a search for a usable past while taking their first steps toward reconstructing their lives. This intensive search was particularly evident among members of the youth movements and their leadership, many of whom participated in the underground and the resistance movements. This may explain why and how so many Jews, those who were part of the underground or the fighting forces and even those who were not, constructed a narrative that placed armed revolt and armed resistance as the jewel in the crown.[9]

However, reservations about the narrative that placed armed resistance at the center of Jewish heroism were already expressed in the displaced persons camps in Germany. Some named it "the cult of heroism." One of these voices was that of Dr. Faivel Wienderman. Most victims were truly led like sheep to the slaughter, he claimed, but "the true heroism in the days of darkness was not primarily the fighter but the mother who refused to abandon her children and voluntarily accompanied … them until death came. This was Jewish heroism."[10] The need to understand Jewish resistance in a multifaceted manner already emerged in the ghettos and among the survivors. Reading the two concepts mentioned above, one senses the confusion and contested feelings of writers and survivors who on the one hand display empathy and love for the victims and on the other anger and embarrassment. This distraught emotional situation emerged from both the inability to change the scope of the destruction and the humiliation that followed the mass killings. Among survivors, these feelings were often immersed in guilt and doubt: Why am I alive? How is it that I am alive?

A great effort to record the account of the destruction was undertaken by survivors through the historical committees established throughout Europe. Survivors were interviewed and asked for details about their personal experiences and the fate of their families and communities. The goal of the committees was to gather as much information as possible about the destruction and the perpe-

---

8. M. Gefen et al., eds., *The Book of the Jewish Partisans* (Hebrew), 2 vols. (Merhavia: Sifriat Poalim, 1958–59); Yitzhak Cukierman and Moshe Basok, eds., *The Book of the Ghetto Wars: Within the Walls, in the Camps, in the Forests* (Hebrew) (Tel Aviv: Hakibbutz Hameuchad, 1956).

9. Zeev W. Mankowitz, *Life between Memory and Hope: The Survivors of the Holocaust in Occupied Germany* (Cambridge: Cambridge University Press, 2002), 209–13.

10. Ibid., 213.

trators.[11] The outcome presented a complex narrative that reflected the efforts to weave the destruction of the Jews into a European and a Jewish narrative that would provide a usable past and a vision for a constructive Jewish future. In the context of resistance, this narrative could be defined as one that moved from the mundane to the heroic. In the following pages, I shall concentrate on manifestations of resistance in daily life in the ghettos of Eastern Europe, drawing on contemporaneous writings and on survivors' accounts. I will also emphasize the contribution of gender perspective to the understanding of Jewish resistance.

From the Mundane to the Heroic: Different Forms of Jewish Resistance

Forced Labor

As the complex Jewish reality in occupied Europe was revealed and contemporaneous Jewish documentation was studied in depth, many efforts of Jews to preserve their lives were understood as defying the major goal of the Final Solution—the annihilation of all Jews under German control. The term "passive resistance" entered the historical narrative. Was passive resistance an apologia, in contrast to active resistance, and what did passive resistance really mean?

In the chaotic condition of life in the ghettos, where new orders and prohibitions were commonplace and uncertainty was the rule, ghetto residents lived with great awareness of their surroundings and had to be constantly on guard. The daily routine integrated continuously keeping one's eyes open, listening to rumors, and seeking information. The inmates of the ghetto, in the streets and in places of work, had to calculate how to respond to confrontational situations—whether to avoid a clash, comply with demands, or oppose them. Often such decisions had to be made in an instant. This included mundane situations, such as walking on the sidewalk, which was prohibited, doffing one's hat when facing a German soldier, and many more. A central locus where a strategy of compliance and resistance had to be devised was the forced labor in ghettos and camps.[12]

11. For a detailed analysis of the historical committees, see Laura Jockusch, "*Collect and Record! Help to Write the History of the Latest Destruction!" Jewish Historical Commissions in Europe, 1943–1953* (Ph.D. dissertation: New York University, 2007). One example of a monograph written and published in the Landsberg DP camp (near Munich) is Joseph Gar, *The Extermination of the Jews of Kovno* (Kaunas) (Yiddish) (Munich: Association of Lithuanian Jews in the American Zone in Germany, 1948).

12. For a general discussion of Jewish forced labor under the Nazis, see Wolf Gruner, *Jewish*

Although forced labor existed in all ghettos and in special camps, I will give only one example from the Kovno ghetto, from a forced labor site in the suburb of Aleksot, about 8 km outside the city, where an airfield was being built. After the occupation of Lithuania an airfield was constructed near Kovno that was important for transferring wounded soldiers from the Soviet front to the hospital in the city. Some 8,000 workers were provided for work in the airfield in two or three daily shifts. Thus, a large number of ghetto inmates were forced to work on construction of this airfield under difficult conditions. They had to walk some 5 km each way without proper footwear and they worked outside in the cold winter and during hot summer days. The workers were poorly fed and treated harshly by German inspectors (in particular from the summer of 1942 onward when the SS took charge on the airfield).

Ghetto inmates endeavored by all means to avoid assignment to the airfield. They tried to join other work brigades, approached doctors hoping to be released due to health problems, and even tried to hide in the early dawn when the policemen were waking up people to be gathered in the work force columns. Others attempted to use their connections ("vitamins" in the ghetto slang) in the Jewish Council, in particular among the heads of the labor department, to free themselves from the airfield brigade.

However, the quota had to be provided and the thousands who were unable to find a way to escape working at the airfield developed a strategy of minimal work. The proximity of the German or Lithuanian inspector was the key factor. When he was around, people worked and moved their bodies energetically to avoid beatings, but once he was at a distance the slow motion tactic began. While watching carefully the comings and goings of the inspectors, a special coded language was developed to alert the workers that danger arose. A warning call *"ya'ale"* was sounded, a Hebrew expression for calling up a person in the synagogue to the *bema* to read from the Torah scroll. Other coded words were used in different dangerous situations.[13]

Forced Labor under the Nazis: Economic Needs and Racial Aims, 1938–1944 (Cambridge: Cambridge University Press, 2006); see also, *Forced and Slave Labor in Nazi-Dominated Europe: Symposium Presentations* (Washington, D.C.: Center for Advanced Holocaust Studies, United States Holocaust Memorial Museum, 2004); Bella Gutterman, *A Narrow Bridge to Life: Jewish Forced Labor and Survival in the Gross-Rosen Camp System, 1940–1945* (Hebrew) (Jerusalem: Yad Vashem, 2008).

13. The description is based on *The History of the Police in the Vilijampole (Kovno) Ghetto*, a text of some 250 printed pages in Yiddish written in the ghetto and hidden before its destruction, and dug out by survivors who knew about it. It was not available to researchers until the early 1990s. YVA, P P.2414391 ﬥ.ﬡ, 48–54. For more comprehensive descriptions of the Kovno ghetto, see Gar, *The Extermination of the Jews of Kovno*; Leib Garfunkel, *The Destruction of Jewish Kovno* (Hebrew) (Jerusalem: Yad Vashem, 1959).

Analysis of these patterns of behavior demonstrates a complex response to forced labor. In the Kovno ghetto, as in many others, it was generally believed that in order to avoid further deportations the ghetto should be useful to the Germans. If the Germans needed Jewish manpower, they would not kill those who provided it. Thus, work was crucial for survival. Nevertheless, work was also a major factor in the deterioration of peoples' capability to carry on, as illustrated through the conditions in the airfield which were characteristic of the many forced labor venues. Accommodation and avoidance were used interchangeably and reinforced the urge of *überleben*, to outlive the Germans. This very urge provided the means of resisting the daily routine. To establish a semblance of normality in the daily routine was the essence of survival in an abnormal situation.

This tactic of accomplishing the minimum production quota was employed in most of the forced labor installations and, in many respects, it was a way to sabotage the economic projects which the Germans established. The airfield never operated because its construction was never completed. Isaiah Trunk quotes one of the central figures in the department of labor of the Jewish Council, M. Segalshon, who claimed that the productivity of the forced labor was extremely low, and all the economic gains went to the local authorities and individual personnel who exploited the Jews.[14]

Nevertheless, despite the necessity to work and provide for basic needs, people expressed resentment at working for the Germans since it assisted in their war efforts. This was often expressed by youth movement members and in particular by Communists in the ghetto. In this context they used the expression "passive resistance." This can easily be demonstrated through the extraordinary text written by Jewish policemen in the Kovno ghetto, entitled *The History of the Police in Vilijampole (Kovno)*.[15]

It was the task of the Jewish police in the Kovno ghetto to wake the people early in the morning and gather them near the main gate of the ghetto to set off in columns for work. The task was difficult. Some people tried to shirk work and would not get up to join the workers. Therefore, the policemen had to search the apartments for those who were hiding. On many occasions a po-

14. Isaiah Trunk, *Judenrat: The Jewish Councils in Eastern Europe under Nazi Occupation* (New York: Macmillan, 1972), 70; on the issue of sabotage, see also Gutterman, *A Narrow Bridge to Life*, 63.

15. For a description of the genre of the text, see Dalia Ofer, "Swearing-in Ceremony: The Police in the Kovno Ghetto, November 1, 1942," *Partial Answers* 7, no. 2 (June 2009): 229–42. For a more general description of the text and two of its chapters translated into English, see Dov Levin, "How the Jewish Police in the Kovno Ghetto Saw Itself," *Yad Vashem Studies* 29 (2001): 183–207.

liceman who found the hidden person would beat him. The rule of the Kovno ghetto was that people who dodged work were fined and even put into prison. The following description is telling:

One cannot say that the police treated them mildly. It would frequently happen that once such a person had been caught in his hiding place, after an hour's search, he would get a beating. It is, of course, not good and not nice that one Jew should beat another for not wanting to go to slave labor. On the other hand, however, we understand that those who were hiding were not doing so out of idealistic motives of passive resistance but were simply the same ones who were always, under all circumstances, the lazy ones. At such a time, when the labor quota for the airfield was an issue of life and death for the entire ghetto of sixteen thousand Jews, one could not stand on ceremony.[16]

We learn that the Jewish police in the Kovno ghetto had a definition of passive resistance that was accepted positively, and connected to idealistic causes. The writers of the "history" did not elaborate upon it, but they referred to the term as part of common knowledge. From the context of the text, it is clear that what they had in mind was the objection to work for the Germans and assist in their war efforts. The writers themselves were policemen who were also members of the underground in the ghetto. They were involved in spiriting Jews out of the ghetto to the partisans in the nearby forests, and providing the partisans with medicine and other needed supplies.[17] It is therefore clear from the subtext that, in addition to the underground that provided arms for fighting the Germans in the forest, another form of resistance occupied the minds of ghetto inmates— passive resistance that was formulated under the routines of the Occupation. In the context of the above description, this resistance was connected to the objection to work for the Germans; however, from other descriptions, it included many other responses in the daily routine of the ghetto, to which I'll now turn.

16. *The History of the Police in Vilijampole (Kovno)* (Yiddish), YVA, P P.24 14391 .מ.ר, 85. I shall refer to this document henceforth as "Police History." The manuscript has three different page numberings, attesting to the different authors and the times of editing and compilation of the manuscript. I am using the handwritten running numbers probably given by the staff in the archive in Lithuania when they prepared the manuscript for use by researchers. I am also using the English translation by Samuel Schalkowsky who prepared it for publication by the United States Holocaust Memorial Museum (USHMM). I am deeply indebted to Mr. Schalkowsky for long and interesting discussions we had about the text. I will give the page numbers of both the Yiddish original and the still unpublished English translation.

17. On the connection between the Jewish police in the Kovno ghetto and the underground, see Abraham Zvi Brown and Dov Levin, *The Story of an Underground: The Resistance of the Jews of Kovno in the Second World War* (Hebrew) (Jerusalem: Yad Vashem, 1962), 107–08; 233–34; 352–55. On the armed resistance of the Jews in Lithuania, see Dov Levin, *Fighting Back: Lithuanian Jewry's Armed Resistance to the Nazis, 1941–1945* (New York: Holmes and Meier, 1985).

Getting Provisions

The ghetto inmates who were forced to work for the Germans turned this into an opportunity to defy Nazi rules concerning the supply of food to the ghetto.[18] The narrative of the history of the Kovno ghetto police depicts the calculated efforts of the Jewish forced laborers to take advantage of their marching in columns out of the ghetto to the work sites, including the notorious airfield. Reading the description of the waking-up process mentioned above, one senses the gloomy atmosphere of the oppressive, unhappy morning and can almost even feel the heavy footsteps of the unwilling workers as they begin another day of torment. However, while following the march of the thousands of workers to the gate and imagining their gathering in columns and brigades as daylight slowly comes, one notices that the bundles and sacks carried by the workers are filled with food smuggled into the ghetto. While the ghetto worker was complying with the order to go to work, he was simultaneously planning how to overcome the harsh restrictions that almost precluded survival.[19]

Thus, survival was the name of the game, directly opposed to the goals of the occupier. Though the mass killings did not start before the Barbarossa Campaign (June 1941), the Jews in the General Government of Poland who lived under the Nazi yoke from September 1939 were certain that the aim of the Nazis was to starve them to death.[20] The situation became critical after their confinement in the ghettos. Thus the immediate goal of the ghetto's inmates was to get supplies into the ghetto and produce substitutes for the necessary commodities. Considered illegal according to the Germans' rules, this was accomplished by different means whose common strategy was to take advantage of what was seemingly legal, such as going out of the ghetto to forced labor venues, exploiting ghetto guards' greediness, and using the willingness of opportunists to gain Jewish assets and household goods.

In this way individuals smuggled personal goods and household items out of the ghetto and exchanged them for food and other needed merchandise such as

18. On the shortage of food in the occupied East and the allotment for different ethnic groups and forced laborers, see Christian Gerlach, *Krieg, Ernährung, Völkermord: Forschungen zur deutschen Vernichtungspolitik im Zweiten Weltkrieg* (Hamburg: Hamburger Edition, 1998); on the discussion about using Jewish workers or starving them to death, see Christopher R. Browning with contributions by Jürgen Matthäus, *The Origins of the Final Solution: The Evolution of Nazi Jewish Policy, September 1939–March 1942* (Lincoln: University of Nebraska Press, 2004), 151–68.

19. "Police History," 82–90.

20. On the debate about the policy of starvation or exploitation of Jewish labor, see Browning and Mätthaus, *Origins*, 151–68

medicine. It was done with great pain as this ghetto text explains: "This trading in one's movables, the fruit of one's work of many years and one's blood and sweat is one of the silent and most painful chapters of the great, universal tragedy of the Jewish community and of the Warsaw Ghetto."[21] The importance of smuggling was stressed in personal diaries, and in the analysis of the economy of the ghetto written for the Ringelblum Archive.[22] "It should be emphasized most strongly," wrote Tadeusz Szymkiewicz in Warsaw after the destruction of the ghetto, "that the ghetto was supplied with food exclusively through smuggling. Without this the ghetto would much earlier have been subject to self-liquidation, and General Stroop would have had nothing to do."[23] Adam Czerniakow, the head of the Warsaw Judenrat, wrote in his diary on December 8, 1941 that the legal trade in the ghetto amounted to 1,800,000 zloty, while the illegal was 70,000,000–80,000,000 zloty.[24] This trade, which enabled the ghetto to carry on despite starvation (though thousands did die), was another form of resistance by individuals and groups. Thus the individual smugglers and the more organized large smuggling efforts into the Warsaw ghetto were perceived by ghetto inmates as maintaining its lifeline and defying the Germans' goal of starving the ghetto.

Next to the exchange of household items and personal goods, creativity was invested in producing various goods within the ghetto. These activities, too, should be divided into clandestine initiatives by individuals and formal planning by the Jewish ghetto authorities. Both were devised to enable the ghetto to survive. The individuals aimed to provide for the family, work often carried out by women, about which I will elaborate below. In Warsaw, the cemetery or the courthouse were the venues of such exchanges that, in cases of luxurious commodities such as rugs and musical instruments, needed the participation of several agencies and a few stages to accomplish a deal. A whole industry of exchange—a kind of barter economy—was developed from the early months of the establishment of ghettos.

21. Joseph Kermish, ed., *To Live with Honor and Die with Honor!: Selected Documents from the Warsaw Ghetto Underground Archives "O.S." ("Oneg Shabbath")* (Jerusalem: Yad Vashem, 1986), 548. The title of this account is "Flourishing—Branch of Commerce in the Ghetto June 1942." It was written in June 1942, shortly before the mass deportation from the Warsaw ghetto.

22. Ibid., 533–84.

23. Quoted in Barbara Engelking and Jacek Leociak, *The Warsaw Ghetto: A Guide to the Perished City* (New Haven, Conn.: Yale University Press, 2009), 447.

24. Ibid., 448–49; *The Warsaw Diary of Adam Czerniakow: Prelude to Doom*, ed. Raul Hilberg, Stanislaw Staron, and Josef Kermisz (New York: Stein and Day, 1979), 306. Despite these impressive numbers, the death toll in the ghetto was high and people died from starvation. Czerniakow mentioned that of the roughly 400,000 people in the ghetto, 10,000 were persons of means, 250,000 were people who lived by their work, and 150,000 needed assistance.

The planned industry in the ghettos, such as the workshops established through the councils, aimed to produce various items that could be exported from the ghetto, substitutes for products that the ghetto was lacking, and items that could be used to bribe the German and other non-Jewish authorities.[25] Throughout the handling of these different endeavors ghetto inmates and the Jewish authorities had to be constantly on guard. Activities had to be endlessly planned and thought out. Once one avenue of defiance was blocked, a new one had to be created. When the fence around the Warsaw ghetto was replaced by a wall that was harder to climb or cross, for example, new techniques for bringing in flour, sugar, and even milk over the ghetto walls were created.

Spiritual Resistance

Spiritual resistance is defined as the engagement in cultural activities, education, religious observation and study, and other activities that helped ghetto inmates maintain their morale and encouraged their Jewish and human identity. Even before the policy of the Final Solution was comprehended, the horrendous death toll from starvation and diseases challenged people to focus on the preservation of life. The traditional concept of *kiddush hashem* (sanctification of the Name; sanctification of G-d) was adapted to the new dangers and transformed to *kiddush hehaim* (sanctification of life).[26] Essential for the preservation of life was the conviction that there would be a promising future. It was extremely difficult to hold a vision of such a future throughout the ghetto years. The way people were able to conceive of their lives depended upon many different factors, foremost German policy. However, the personality of the German commander of the ghetto and the extent of German intervention in daily life were also central to the ability to devise different strategies of survival. Other factors, such as the strictness of isolation—the ability to contact the Aryan side or Jews in other communities, or to have some access to information on the

25. For an impressive report on such economic initiatives, see Jerzy Winkler, "The Ghetto Combating Economic Servitude," in *To Live with Honor and Die with Honor!* ed. Kermish, 552–84; Trunk, *Judenrat*, 61–144.

26. As exemplified in the saying of Rabbi Yizhak Nissenbaum of Warsaw: "In these times the Sanctification of the Name is practiced by sanctifying life. In the past, when our enemies demanded the soul, the Jew sacrificed his body for the Sanctification of the Name in order to save his soul. Now, when the enemy wants to take the body's life, we must not give him what he wants; rather we must defend the body, preserve life." This quotation is from Saul Esh, "The Dignity of the Destroyed: Towards a Definition of the Period of the Holocaust," in *The Catastrophe of European Jewry: Antecedents, History, Reflections—Selected Papers*, ed. Yisrael Gutman and Livia Rothkirchen (Jerusalem: Yad Vashem, 1972), 25–152.

war from non-German sources—were crucial for a broader understanding of the existential situation of the Jews. Radical hunger and the immediacy of deportations and mass murder were the ultimate signs of the direction in which German policy was heading, and thus the major factor in reconsidering daily routines and tendencies.

It is important to understand the efforts of individuals, groups, and the different institutions in the ghetto to establish an appearance of normalcy. Cultural institutions of all kinds served the goal of spiritual self-determination and the semblance of normality. This was manifested in both the private and the public spheres and became a significant measure of the capability to hold on. As the war continued and ghetto life became prolonged, daily routines were more and more distant from normalcy, though some kind of an illusionary mood developed. The hardships of daily life, on the one hand, and the efforts to adopt perceptions of positive prospects, on the other, could create a kind of escapism. Was this supporting resistance to the main goals of the Nazis or was it a quiescent factor?

In the public sphere it was the responsibility of the Jewish councils and other self-help institutions to provide public kitchens, education, cultural activities, and health and other social services. Without going into a detailed description of each of the services, and despite the great differences between the ghettos in the attitude of their councils, demography, and social culture, the documentation pointed to ghettos in which the public sphere was capable of providing services for a large number of ghetto residents, and to others where it failed to do so. Such services contributed to a mind-set that it would be possible to outlive the Occupation.

Study

Diaries of young people, such as David Sierakowiak from Lodz, Yizhak Rudashevski from Vilna, Tamara from Kovno, and others attest how study in classes or other facilities, and youth movement activities, supported their ability to hold out.[27] Sierakowiak, for example, realized that when he would be able to start school again, "There will finally be an end to the anarchy in my daily

27. David Sierakowiak, *The Diary of David Sierakowiak: Five Notebooks from the Lodz Ghetto*, ed. Alan Adelson (New York: Oxford University Press, 1996); Yizhak Rudashevski, *The Diary of the Vilna Ghetto, June 1941-April 1943* (Hebrew), ed. Percy Matenko (Tel Aviv: Beit Lohamei Hagetaot and Hakibbutz Hameuhad, 1973); Tamar Lazarshon Rostovski, *The Diary of Tamara: Kovno 1942–1946* (Hebrew) (Tel Aviv: Beit Lohamei Hagetaot and Hakibbutz Hameuhad, 1975).

activities and, I hope, an end to too much philosophizing and depression."[28] The establishment of a school, and activity corners for poor and destitute children, by the Dror (freedom) Youth Movement in the Warsaw ghetto provided the option to forget, even for a short while, the hunger and suffering and helped to raise spirits. In August 1940, the Dror Movement established a Hebrew-Yiddish high school: seventy-two pupils studied there and eleven teachers were employed. At the end of 1941, it was expanded to include 120 pupils and thirteen teachers.[29] Members of the movement were convinced that study would assist to overcome the general deterioration of Jewish life under Occupation: "They [street children] should be educated; they should simply be taught to read and write; they should learn Yiddish, Hebrew, and Mathematics. The youth who are already studying, those who already have an education and knowledge, should be taught concern for their brethren and to act with responsibility and solidarity."[30] This quotation attests to the values of Jewish identity and social awareness to which the organizers of the school and children's corners aspired.

Music and Theater

The desire to raise the spirits of the ghetto population was both an interest of the Jewish authorities, of the artists who performed and prepared programs, and of people who longed for moments of escape from ghetto concerns or wanted to assist in reflecting on the ghetto situation with humor and irony. The establishment of orchestras, theater groups, or cabarets in a number of ghettos such as Lodz and Vilna, and the orchestra of the police force in Kovno reflected the understanding of the ghetto councils and the people that depression could become a major enemy in the ghetto. In order to defy the Nazi scheme, it was crucial to avoid depression or apathy following the endless traumas inmates had experienced. Yet, one may ask critically whether it was perhaps the channel by which some of the councils intended to calm down resentment and criticism and turn the ghetto population into a more cooperative public.

Herman Kruk, a refugee from Warsaw, an active member of the Bund movement, and a librarian in the Vilna ghetto, thought that theatrical activity in

28. Sierakowiak, *Diary*, 83, entry for April 22, 1941. See also his entries for the days following April 22, 1941, 83–85.

29. Mark Pulmann (Sever), "In This Hour," *Dror* (May–June 1941), in *Periodicals of the Jewish Underground in Warsaw* (Hebrew), ed. Joseph Kermish, 6 vols. (Jerusalem: Yad Vashem, 1979–1997), 2:387. On the author of the article and the organizer of the high school in the Warsaw ghetto, Mark Pulmann, see volume three of the same edition, 398–99n16.

30. *Dror* 3 (July–August 1940) (previous to the establishment of the Warsaw ghetto), in ibid., 1:39.

the ghetto was a scheme of the Jewish Council to mislead the ghetto residents. When on January 18, 1942, he received the invitation to the first concert in the ghetto, he wrote in his diary that he was offended. Together with his friends from the Bund party they distributed leaflets in the streets of the ghetto declaring: "You don't make theater in a graveyard."[31] The event, they claimed, was intended to please the Germans and the ruling groups in the ghetto—the Jewish police and Jewish Council. No celebration was appropriate in the Vilna ghetto where most of the inmates had been brutally murdered.

However, Kruk, like many others, learned to appreciate the theater and the cultural performances as they provided spiritual support for the ghetto's inmates during the different phases of the ghetto's existence. Nevertheless, on May 23, 1943, in an entry that dealt with a number of topics, including news of the Warsaw ghetto fighting and "its heroic struggle for six weeks now," he reports on the establishment of a small art theater. The title of this section in his diary reads: "Also a Small Art Theater" and begins with "Now we have everything: we lack only one small thing—a small art theater. Now we will have this, too." One cannot escape the bitter irony expressed in this entry. The words, "everything" and "we lack only" are clear evidence of Kruk's ambivalent attitude toward the theater. Moreover, the last section of that day's report described the evacuation of tenants from the first-floor apartments in Rudnicka Street, needed to set up new workshops. The three incidents on the same street are indicative of Kruk's style of criticism.[32]

To conclude, one must stress that learning, membership in youth movements, and listening to music were all part of the social life of the individuals and services provided by the community. All were part of Jewish life before the war, and their emergence in the ghetto reality was a manifestation of how the Jews clung to the patterns of living that were theirs before the Occupation and the war. Despite persecution, hunger, forced labor, loss of homes and assets, and often the corruption of members of the Jewish Council, they did their utmost to preserve a vestige of normal life. During different stages of ghetto life all contributed to the endeavor not to desert the values and habits of regular routines, and to maintain a semblance of order and normality under chaotic and uncertain conditions. These enabled selective compliance with and defi-

31. Herman Kruk, *The Last Days of the Jerusalem of Lithuania: Chronicles from the Vilna Ghetto and the Camps, 1939–1944*, ed. Benjamin Harshav (New Haven, Conn.: Yale University Press, 2002), 174. In the same text, on the concert, see 176; see also "A Year of Ghetto Theater," 449.
32. Ibid., 548.

ance of Nazi rules at the same time, which transpired as the essence of resistance to the central goals of the Nazis—to have their territories free of the Jews.

There were, however, always signs of transformation which brought hope that their fate might change, even after mass deportation and killings. The end of the war was a dominant factor in the mind of the Jews from the end of 1942, when the Nazi advance was halted and news of German losses and captured German divisions reached the ghetto. It was therefore crucial not to give up despite the horrors and the year-and-a-half of mass killings. The challenge to hold on became greater as time passed, and the ability of the decimated ghettos to provide social assistance and solidarity was declining. Should these responses be defined as passive resistance? Did they not display ample activism to outwit the German rules?

Involvement or Indifference: What Was the Measure?

Another manifestation of resistance—which in many respects stands in contrast to the concern and involvement presented above—was the ability to ignore some of the depth of suffering and want in order to go on. The landscape of the ghettos also called for a kind of indifference or numbness to the sufferings surrounding each of the inhabitants. In large ghettos such as Warsaw and Lodz, people had to confront daily scenes of starving people begging for a piece of bread or some donation. The sight of dying people and dead bodies was common in the streets of the Warsaw ghetto. The description of passing over dead bodies and ignoring the cries of the dying and starving has been regularly documented. Much criticism was leveled by social leaders, physicians, and intellectuals at the social injustice in the ghetto, the corruption of ghetto authorities, and the indifference of those who had toward those who had not.[33]

In late 1941, a research project was initiated by the directors of the Ringelblum Archives. The purpose of the project—known by the short title "Two and a Half Years"—was to prepare a number of research papers on various aspects of ghetto life that would add to the collection of documentation on life under German occupation. It covered many aspects: economy, education and culture, religion, children, women, refugees and their lives in the special refugee centers that were set up, resistance to the Occupation regime, testimonies about the

33. The issue of social disparity and the large number of poor plagued all large and medium-sized ghettos.

mass murders, and so forth. The project covered two-and-a-half years of war and aimed to create an infrastructure for future research about the lives of Jews in the German ghettos at large.[34] As part of this effort a questionnaire was sent to a number of intellectuals and activists in the Warsaw ghetto that included questions about the major issue of ghetto life and prospects for the future.

One of the responses was that of Szaul Stupnicki, a reporter for the Yiddish paper *Moment*. Among other issues, he related the indifference that people expressed while bypassing the dead in the streets:

Maybe what I say will sound like a paradox, but I see it as a possible phenomenon. It's a miracle that people do not get depressed, do not break down at these macabre scenes in the streets. That they do not lose their poise at the sight of those crowds of naked, barefoot, starving children in the streets. Were is not for that cruel cold-bloodedness, scenes like these could paralyze whatever processes of life are in us; they would drive people into such a state of depression that it would bring about total resignation which would tow us under. So therefore I define it a positive phenomenon that people in the ghetto have become so hardened, so stone hard, that they pass by the dead and keep fighting for life.[35]

Stupnicki defined such feeling and conduct in these terms: "The stout vitality of the Jewish masses, their dauntless will to survive. Jews don't feel like passive victims but rather as active fighters."[36]

Contribution of Gender to Analysis of Resistance

A major change in defining resistance came in the wake of gender studies and its application to the history of the Holocaust. Gender analysis broadened historical narrative and legitimized the introduction of the perspective of the individual and the individual's subjectivity into the core of the historical analysis of the Holocaust. It also aroused a greater awareness of a methodological issue: how to integrate and disseminate personal documentation such as letters, diaries, post-Holocaust memoirs, and oral history into the historical narrative. These efforts led to the democratization of the field of research. The nuances added new information on women to the conventional knowledge of Holocaust events, while the personal points of view enriched historical narra-

34. Emanuel Ringelblum, *Last Writings: Polish–Jewish Relations, January 1943–April 1944* (Hebrew) (Jerusalem: Yad Vashem and Ghetto Fighters' House, 1994), 6–7; Samuel D. Kassow, *Who Will Write Our History? Emanuel Ringelblum, the Warsaw Ghetto, and the Oyneg Shabes Archive* (Bloomington: Indiana University Press, 2007), 209–84.

35. Discussed in Kermish, *To Live with Honor and Die with Honor!* 738.

36. Ibid., 737.

tives, proving that the absence of women from the narratives had resulted in a partial, incomplete reconstruction of events that prevented a comprehensive interpretation of the Holocaust in general and of resistance in particular. In the following section, I shall deal with two themes: the family unit, which related to the daily routine of life under Occupation, and women in the underground, which suggests the defying of daily routines. Both are topics that emerged as a result of gender awareness.

Patterns of Resistance within the Family

The family was not a subject of research in Holocaust studies until about a decade ago. The efforts to preserve family life, which often failed, constitute one of the significant differences between the ghettos and all other forms of life in Eastern Europe, such as passing as a non-Jew, hiding, life in the forests and in the camps.[37] The history of the Jewish family relates to routines typical of the ordinary life of the individual and society. It entails the detailed handling of day-to-day situations and the use of common sense in ordinary activities that do not demand any exceptional attention of the individual, such as going to work, providing food for the family, leisure time, and more. Everyday lifestyle differs from one society to another and according to class and gender. Daily activities were gendered and thus reflected the hierarchy between men and women (both in the public and private spheres), defined responsibilities, and contributed to the order of routines. These reflected the culturally defined gender roles of Jewish men and women which endowed the two sexes with different skills, knowledge, and expertise.[38]

In the course of the destruction of European Jewry between 1939 and 1945, the family as a social unit and as a personal sanctuary faced unprecedented pressures and duress. The main blow to regular family life was economic discrimination reflected in the loss of working places, businesses, bank accounts, and more. From the outset of the Occupation in Poland and in all occupied countries, Jews lost their economic standing. Thus the regular roles within the family were confused and men in particular were victimized as they were no longer able to provide for their families, thereby losing the most basic feature of male identity. The public sphere became more and more hostile to males,

37. For a more comprehensive discussion of the family in the ghettos, see Dalia Ofer, "Cohesion and Rupture: The Jewish Family in East European Ghettos during the Holocaust," *Studies in Contemporary Jewry* 14 (1998): 143–65.

38. Dalia Ofer and Lenore J. Weitzman, eds., *Women in the Holocaust* (New Haven, Conn.: Yale University Press, 1998), 1.

who were the first targeted by the German occupier, kidnapped for forced labor, mocked and tortured in the streets, and more.

The home was also an unstable haven for both men and women as German soldiers and police could rush into homes violently to confiscate goods and furniture, or just to enjoy maltreatment of Jews. This often included physical injuries and sexual assault by the non-Jewish local followers of the Nazis which degraded the adults and was damaging for the children. Thus any balance in family routine was severely at risk and adjustment to the new situation must have been very painful.

In Poland many Jewish families did not have a male provider since some men served in the army and never came back, while others fled to the new Soviet territories or were sent to forced labor camps. At the outset of the war, all believed that a greater danger confronted men; thus mothers encouraged their young sons to escape and wives often encouraged their husband to leave, at least for a while. In such cases women were left alone to take care of their families, without the necessary skills to cope with the situation and restricted by the Germans' rules that narrowed even more their ability to carry on.

The waves of expulsions from western Poland and from small places to larger centers left many with few of the household belongings which were the basis for sustaining the family. The incarceration in the ghettos worsened the situation even further. Often a few families shared one room, and all families in the apartment shared one kitchen and bathroom facilities. This created a significant change in intimacy within the family and was a cause of tension. In the ghettos, families made great efforts to stay together and devised survival techniques as a unit. This was fundamental in the efforts to maintain normalcy, to adhere to the emotional ties and the cultural values of Jewish and non-Jewish society. Nevertheless, family members had to accommodate themselves to considerable changes in the roles of various members of the family, in particular between the married couple, but no less between children and parents. The tension between the traditional order and the need to alter habits, perspectives, and conventions was characteristic of the family's daily practice. Responsibility for providing for the family had to be shared by all and mother, father, and children had to assist in creating an integrated effort for survival of the family unit. Many records testify to the fact that women had a much stronger voice in the new situation.

This strategy became a major means of resistance to Nazi rules and edicts. In the course of such endeavors adaptation to new roles for each family member was no simple matter and the contribution of each was modified in different phases and circumstances in the ghetto. Both forced labor and the need to employ irregular means to meet the basic needs for the family created a new environment in which women had to extend considerably the boundaries of their conventional responsibilities, without neglecting their traditional responsibilities. Women were often quite inventive in creating situations in which they could disguise themselves as non-Jews, a task that was easier for women than for men. They pretended to be Polish domestic help in Jewish homes (when this was still allowed) and were willing to change external characteristics, such as dyeing their hair, wearing women farmer's dresses, and more. Young girls were smuggled across into the Aryan side and did not hesitate to use feminine gestures to pass through the gate.

In this smuggling by individuals, the role of women was considerable, using what they believed to be their advantages over men. Women were also involved in establishing specific industries and bartering their products with non-Jews or with well-to-do Jews in the ghetto. In the Kovno ghetto women developed the production of scarves made of colorful old textiles they brought into the ghetto. They exchanged the scarves through the ghetto fence for food brought by Lithuanian women. Women knitted scarves and hats from used wool and bartered or sold them. In the report on women written for the Ringelblum Archive by Cecilia Slepak, based on interviews she conducted with sixteen women in the ghetto between December 1941 and the spring of 1942, all but one were married women. A number of women were engaged in smuggling or involved in the illegal exchange of goods from the ghetto with the Aryan side; others engaged in small trade or were doing housework for well-to-do families.[39]

A great burden on Jewish mothers resulted from the traditional order of Jewish family roles. The mother's direct duty focused on caring for the home and the children, but the ability to perform motherly obligations was now enormously limited. Contemporaneous sources disclose the frustration of mothers

39. Cecilya Slepak's research is in the Ringelblum Archive (ARI/49), divided into a number of bands. Her subjects are identified only by an initial. I use the Yad Vashem Archives (YVA) copy JM/217/4 and JM/215/3 (henceforth Slepak, followed by a band number). We have very little information about Slepak. Ringelblum writes that she gained her reputation from her translation of Simon Dubnov's twelve-volume *History of the Jews* into Polish and that she was asked to write about the women in the ghetto. He mentions that she was deported to Treblinka in the first great deportation in the summer of 1942; see Emanuel Ringelblum, *Last Works* (Hebrew) (Jerusalem: Yad Vashem, 1994), 2:223–25. Ringelblum's notes were published in English as *Notes from the Warsaw Ghetto*, ed. and trans. Jacob Sloan (New York: Schocken Books, 1958). The Hebrew version, however, presents the full original Yiddish text.

Dalia Ofer

in view of their inability to provide basic cleanliness, as they observed the deteriorating health of children and adults and were confronted with obstacles to sustaining a fair distribution of food for all family members. Success was always limited.[40]

For Jewish women in particular, the preparation of food represented commitment and love. However, given the appalling scarcity of food, it was an extremely difficult task. In some ghettos, such as Lodz, children of all ages were enlisted to search garbage cans for scraps that could be turned into edible dishes; potato peelings, for instance, became a staple.[41] One should bear in mind that the economic condition of the family was the paramount factor in nourishing it and that there were considerable differences in all ghettos, particularly in Warsaw and Lodz.[42] Therefore, memoirs and diaries of mothers and women who were not on the brink of starvation differed considerably from the testimonies of the impoverished.[43]

In the context of the ability to resist, families that reinforced their bonds were better able to endure life in the ghetto; in such cases, the economic situation of the family was significant. However, this often prevented the younger generation from acting for their self-survival, as they did not want to leave their older parents or the younger offspring. In ghetto society, it was the family that strove for even a semblance of family normalcy. Some families, for instance, went to great lengths to hoard a bit of food for celebrations such as a birthday.[44] In his wartime diary, Avraham Tory describes a bar mitzvah in the

40. For a broader description of the difficulties of mothers, see Dalia Ofer, "Motherhood under Siege," in *Life, Death and Sacrifice: Women and Family in the Holocaust*, ed. Esther Hertzog (Jerusalem: Gefen Publishing, 2008), 41–67.

41. *The Chronicle of the Lodz Ghetto* (Hebrew), translated and annotated by Arie Ben-Menachem and Joseph Rab, 4 vols. (Jerusalem: Yad Vashem, 1986–89), 4, 283.

42. See, for example, the correspondence between Avraham Modechai Rogowy and an official of the Judenrat discussed in "Our Social Injustice to Stand Trial," in *To Live with Honor and Die with Honor!, ed.* Kermish, 317–23; see also, in the same volume, "Of Jews and Being Jewish," 730–34, that includes this passage: "All of you who are great or small in deeds, fight hunger! In Yiddish, Polish and Hebrew, fight hunger! This is our culture, this is being Jewish. There is no other culture now, but succor for ones who fall down in the streets and who die in their homes of hunger," 732–33.

43. See, for example, Helena Szereszewska, *Memoir from Occupied Warsaw 1940–1945* (London: Vallentine Mitchell, 1997), or Mary Berg, *The Diary of Mary Berg: Growing Up in the Warsaw Ghetto*, ed. S. L. Shneiderman; new edition prepared by Susan Lee Pentlin (Oxford: Oneworld, 2006). Both women were of the upper middle class, as compared to accounts from the poor in the ghetto. On this score, see Lea Preiss, *The Impact of the Refugee Problem on Jewish Communal Life in the City of Warsaw and in the Warsaw Ghetto (September 1939–July 1942)* (Hebrew) (Ph.D. dissertation: Hebrew University of Jerusalem, 2006).

44. See, for example, Oskar Singer, who describes both a birthday celebration arranged by his

Kovno ghetto.[45] Holidays were a form of maintaining family unity, when families were able to sit around a Sabbath table, or when Chanukah candles were lit and children received small presents such as a colored ribbon or a small candy.[46] These demonstrated the efforts to maintain family cohesion and negate the forces of rupture—not to forget what normalcy was. This memory in itself was a form of resistance.

Many families were unable to stay together. A number of reasons account for such cases, first and foremost economic want. For example, families of refugees in the Warsaw ghetto who were living in public buildings or in small basements in large apartment buildings were barely surviving. The high death toll among such families left many orphans who frequently became street children, begging or being abused by other adults or older teenage gangs. Some mothers left their children in the staircase of a monastery or orphanage to increase their chances of survival, or if they were completely distressed.[47]

Women in the Underground

Women were part of the underground and armed resistance from its outset.[48] In Eastern Europe, the youth movements were the cradle of underground activities. Following the shock of the Polish defeat, youth movement activities resumed little by little. Many of the adult leaders of the various youth move-

---

wife and the family's participation in making pancakes from potato peels, in *Chronicle of the Lodz Ghetto*, 4:177 and 283, respectively.

45. Avraham Tory, *Surviving the Holocaust: The Kovno Ghetto Diary* (Cambridge, Mass.: Harvard University Press, 1990), 502.

46. *Chronicle of the Lodz Ghetto*, 3:770–72.

47. On the specific difficulties of mothers, see Ofer, "Motherhood under Siege," in *Life, Death and Sacrifice*, 41–67.

48. This section is based on the following literature: Yisrael Gutman, *The Jews of Warsaw, 1939–1943: Ghetto, Underground, Revolt* (Bloomington, Ind.: Indiana University Press, 1982); Lenore Weitzman, "The Kashariyot (Couriers) in the Jewish Resistance during the Holocaust," in *Jewish Women: A Comprehensive Historical Encyclopedia*, ed. Paula Hyman and Dalia Ofer (Jerusalem: Shalvi Publishing Ltd, 2006) (electronic resource); Eli Tzur, "The Forgotten Leadership: Women Leaders of the Hashomer Hatzair Youth Movement at Times of Crisis," in *Gender, Place and Memory in the Modern Jewish Experience: Re-placing Ourselves*, ed. Judith Tuydor Baumel and Tova Cohen (London: Vallentine Mitchell, 2003), 51–66; Naomi Shimshi, "Lunka and Tema: Leading Couriers in the Dror Movement in Poland" (Hebrew), in *Women and Family in the Holocaust* (Bnei Berak: Otzar Hamishpat, 2006), 129–56; Rivka Perlis, *The Pioneering Zionist Youth Movement in Nazi Occupied Poland* (Hebrew) (Kibbutz Lohamei Hagetaot: Beit Lohamei Hagetaot and Hakibbutz Hameuhad, 1987). See also the following entries in *Jewish Women: A Comprehensive Historical Encyclopedia* [electronic resource]: Ziva Shalev, "Altman, Tosia"; Tikva Fatal-Kna'ani, "Czapnik, Liza"; Yael Margolin Peled, "Dranger Dawidson, Gusta"; Sara Bender, "Hazan Ya'ari, Bela"; Neima Barzel, "Grosman, Haika"; Lenore J. Weitzman, "Klibanski, Bronka"; Naomi Shimshi, "Plotniczki, Frumka"; Avihu Ronen, "Poland: Women Leaders in the Jewish Underground during the Holocaust."

ments fled Poland, either because they feared being targeted by the Nazis due to their role in the movements or because they wanted to join the front in eastern Poland. In a number of communities young women assumed leadership of the movement, since the danger for females, as mentioned earlier, was less considerable. Only in the winter of 1940 did the men begin to return and a new kind of dual leadership emerged, of young men and women.

Under the regulations of the Nazi occupation regime, many of the routine procedures of the youth movements were illegal, including more than a few individuals congregating together, moving after curfew, or traveling from one community to another. As all the youth movements had branches throughout Poland, communication between communities was vital to their educational work. The participation of girls in the youth movements' activities was not a novelty. The belief in equality between the sexes was shared by all nonreligious movements. Even among religious youth movements importance was placed upon the activities and services of girls. However, often in prewar reality the ideology of equality was not practiced; so girls and female adolescents had to struggle for their fair share. Nevertheless, the new situation offered some specific opportunities for young females: on the one hand, adapting to male roles, including physical work and later participation in fighting, to which I shall return; and on the other hand, the advancement of feminine traits, such as nurturing and taking special care of refugee youngsters who were strangers in the community and of those whose families had become very poor or dismembered.

Many of the youth who were in the movements before the war did not rejoin; those who did, however, found the gatherings a haven. Barred from their schools, dismissed from places of work, and often unable to comprehend the difficulties that their families confronted, they discovered in these meetings an opportunity to put aside gloom for a few hours and feel a sense of belonging and even hope. Youth movement gatherings produced an intimate mood of comradeship, an important factor in the relations between the members. From a gender perspective, it is interesting to learn that youth movement discourse used family terms such as sisters, brothers, mothers, and fathers.

Following the incarceration in the ghettos, life became increasingly difficult and more young people lost members of their families. In many homes the day-to-day worries of parents about getting provisions and preparing a meal occupied all their faculties and little energy was left for emotional support. As a result, the youth movements' centers (*ken*, "nest" in Hebrew) turned into a real nest, a place to find reassurance, for many even a surrogate family. The leaders, among them many young women, turned the movements' soup kitchens into more than a supplementary source of food. They were also a cultural and educational center which provided members with motherly warmth. Thus we read, in the underground papers and in memoirs, of the maternal character of central leaders such as Zivia, of the Dror Hehalutz movement, who eventually became the leader of the Warsaw ghetto uprising together with Mordechai Anielewitz, Tema Schneiderman from Bialystok, and many others.

Due to the isolation in the ghettos, once mobility was completely forbidden to Jews, young women and members of youth movements, disguised as non-Jews, turned out to be the vital life line of the movement. They were sent as couriers or emissaries (*shlihim* in Hebrew) from one community to another, informing others of the situation, passing underground papers, exchanging messages from the centers, and distributing educational materials. These emissaries remained at their destination for several days or weeks to discuss ideological and educational matters with the local leadership, to oversee educational activity, and, among other things, to plan and lead theoretical seminars for the older members of the branch. In short, they had to represent personally the central leadership, its ideas, programs, and operations. They also became deeply involved in problems connected with the daily life of the members of the movements. These meetings were described as a beacon of light by the groups which the emissaries visited in the ghettos. They provided a sense of belonging to a larger body, strengthened local initiatives, and supplied spiritual encouragement.

When the mass killings began in the East, the couriers passed on the information. When the idea of armed resistance was initially formulated, they were the first to contact the non-Jewish underground to get arms and carry parts of weapons that would be assembled in the ghetto. Leaders of the movement and of the armed resistance valued the contribution of the couriers, as well as those of the other young women who participated in the actual fighting in Warsaw and in the smaller direct clashes in Bialystok and other ghettos. This was also true among the groups of Jewish partisans formed from among members of the youth movements and the underground in the ghettos.

Avihu Ronen discerns a particular form of leadership that developed within the youth movements during this time which he relates to the young age of those leaders, who were in their early twenties. He calls it a "dual leadership," composed of one man and one woman that emerged in many of the Jewish undergrounds in the ghettos. The main reason for this development lay in the family structure of the intimate group in which the male and female youth leaders were viewed by the youngsters as the group's "father" and "mother." During the war, there was an additional reason: romance.[49]

The preceding images may come across as describing triumphant opposition to the policy of persecution. However, one should not read it with any sense of victory. For large numbers of the ghetto population survival was hardly possible even before the deportations and mass killings. Despite creativity, planning, manipulation, and alleviating negative aspects of the situation, the death toll was enormous. In the large ghettos such as Warsaw and Lodz many died of starvation and diseases and many others were killed by the Germans or local collaborators when caught smuggling or when on the Aryan side. The feeling of satisfaction of an individual child or adult who succeeded in bringing home some food, the assistance of self-help activists and the Judenrat to the needy, or the educational enterprise of the Dror youth movement for poor children could not overshadow the anxiety, sadness, and sense that the world of the past had collapsed. The ghetto reality offered few choices, and within this narrow space ghetto inmates endeavored to shape their lives. In the last stages of ghetto life, when dismembering of the ghetto was foreseen, resistance was modified: hiding, passing as non-Jews, and joining the underground, became endeavors to save one's life or to select the manner of death. Even the decision about how to die was itself a form of resistance.

The course historiography has taken can be demonstrated by the writings of Raul Hilberg and Yehuda Bauer, two major scholars of the Holocaust. Hilberg, in his standard work, supported the claim that compliance and accommodation were the traditional behavior of Jews in the Diaspora when faced with dangers: "When confronted by force, a group can react in five ways: by resistance, by an attempt to alleviate or nullify the threat (the undoing reaction), by evasion, by paralysis, or by compliance.... The reaction pattern of the Jews is characterized by almost complete lack of resistance.... Jews were not oriented toward resistance."[50] In the modern era, Hilberg maintained, only the Zionists, who opposed the traditional Diaspora life, suggested other options of behavior.

Many agreed with him and thought that all forms of defiance and avoidance

49. Avihu Ronen, "Poland: Women Leaders," in *Jewish Women: A Comprehensive Historical Encyclopedia.*

50. Raul Hilberg, *The Destruction of European Jews* (Chicago: Quadrangle Books, 1967), 662; see also 663–69; 15–17.

ended up in escapism and an illusionary belief that it would be possible to outlive the Germans. This claim became a major issue in the criticism of the Jewish councils in the first stages of research.[51] Nevertheless, as the complex Jewish reality in occupied Europe was revealed and the contemporaneous Jewish
documentation was studied in depth, the concept of resistance was redefined
and modified. The actions of Jews to preserve life were viewed as actions taken
to defy the major goal of the Final Solution to annihilate all Jews under German control. The expression "passive resistance" became part of the historical
narrative. In the first stage of redefining resistance, Yehuda Bauer suggested
the following: "Any group action consciously taken in opposition to known
or surmised laws, actions, or intentions directed against the Jews by the Germans and their supporters."[52] This definition opposes Hilberg who confined
resistance to the use of force. For Bauer, only paralysis, and in some cases the
collaboration of Jewish leaders, is nonresistance. All actions should be examined in reference to motivation and intention. The Jewish councils, the self-
help organizations, the Jewish youth movements, and the political parties were
among those who affirmed Jewish life.

Considering gender studies, though not directly admitting the consideration, Bauer expands the definition of resistance to include acts of individuals
who either confronted the Nazis directly by force or by verbal provocation, or
acted in defiance of their laws and rules by bringing food into the ghetto, providing for their children, teaching children, and more. In the Hebrew language
there is a term *amidah* that relates to such actions. A literal translation would
be "standing up against"; however, it also expresses a great sense of pride and
self-assurance about the actions one commits. *Amidah* for Bauer includes:

smuggling food into ghettos, mutual self-sacrifice within the family to avoid starvation or worse, cultural, educational, religious, and political activities taken
to strengthen morale, the work of doctors, nurses and educators to consciously
maintain health and moral fiber to enable individual and group survival and, of
course, armed rebellion or the use of force (with bare hands or with "cold" weapons) against the Germans and their collaborators.[53]

51. A fine essay on Philip Friedman discusses this issue and the role of the Jewish councils as
part of the German bureaucracy in the killing process. See Roni Stauber, *Philip Friedman and the
Beginning of Holocaust Research* (Hebrew) (Jerusalem: Yad Vashem, Search and Research, 2005).

52. Yehuda Bauer, *Rethinking the Holocaust* (New Haven, Conn.: Yale University Press, 2001), 119.

53. Ibid, 120. Stauber claims that the foundation for this change was in the work of Philip Friedman who was unable to complete it because of his death in 1960, even before Hilberg's book was
published. See Stauber, *Philip Friedman*, 38–41.

Although in general I agree with Bauer's definition, I would like to stress that the use of a particular word that does not exist in other languages, such as *amidah*, is meaningful for those who understand Jewish culture, but for the majority it is unclear. I therefore maintain the terms "armed" and "unarmed" resistance and explain why unarmed resistance was central and in many respects characteristic of Jewish efforts in confronting the Nazis. Moreover, as we have seen, since the victims realized that the oppressor's main goal was to kill Jews, a central form of resistance emerged from the commitment to preserve life by all possible means. Thus, actions of individuals and groups fell into the category of sanctification of life. Sanctification of life confirmed responses by individuals that demonstrated a conscious resistance to German policy.

When reading Slepak's narrative, Ringelblum's notes, and diaries of women and men, a clear subtext emerges: the activism of women and men was important. The abnormal conditions of the war and Occupation demanded that women become active in promoting the survival of their families in nonconventional ways.[54] Under wartime conditions, particularly in the ghettos, choices were very limited and all were made under the occupier's oppression. However, the women Slepak described and the men who left their writings for posterity did make choices; they were constantly thinking of alternatives. Some choices that Slepak noted were the decision to work and not beg in the streets, to engage in smuggling, to cross over to the Aryan side despite the danger involved, and to establish romantic relations with non-Jews that provided some advantages. Choices emerged as an outcome of both general and specific conditions, an individual's particular personality, and standards. Making choices reflected people's sense of autonomy and activism together with resentment toward the situation forced upon them.[55]

The heroes and heroines of these narratives are individuals who acted according to their resourcefulness and dared to resist the German policy of persecution and annihilation. They were acting out of deep commitment to fulfilling their duties as members of the community, husbands, fathers, wives, sons, daughters, and mothers. From the point of view of the final annihilation, all those endeavors were irrelevant. Yet, in order to understand how people lived in the ghetto and what their patterns of resistance were, one should realize that each phase in the ghetto's reality contained the totality of people's lives.

54. Band 1: Ms. H. and the story of Ms. F., the wife of the shoemaker. For a more detailed description of this woman, see Ofer, "Cohesion and Rupture," 143–65.

55. See also Dalia Ofer, "Gender Issues in Diaries and Testimonies of the Ghetto: The Case of Warsaw," in *Women in the Holocaust*, 143–67.

Avinoam Patt

17   Jewish Resistance in the Warsaw Ghetto

The Warsaw Ghetto Uprising (April 19, 1943–May 16, 1943), the largest mass revolt in a major city in German-occupied Europe, is the defining symbol of Jewish resistance to Nazi oppression during World War II. Immediately after the
war, Holocaust survivors in Europe seized upon the Warsaw Ghetto Uprising as
the basis for Holocaust commemoration activities and the dates of the uprising
have since been linked to annual Holocaust commemoration events in countries around the world. Israel's Knesset selected the 27th of Nisan as the date
for *Yom HaShoah ve-haGevruah* (The Day of Remembrance of the Holocaust and
Heroism) in 1953 to correspond roughly with the Warsaw Ghetto Uprising.[1] The
Warsaw Ghetto Uprising has occupied a central place in the history of the Holocaust and of World War II; as a military encounter, its significance may seem
relatively minor, resulting in a small number of German dead and wounded
over the course of the one month that the Jewish resistance fighters managed
to battle German forces in the ghetto. Nonetheless, during the war, the small
band of Jewish fighters in the Warsaw ghetto had a major impact on Jewish
communities elsewhere in Eastern Europe and on German procedures in the
aftermath of the uprising as well.[2] From the perspective of Jewish history, its
significance has been tremendous, representing perhaps the most well-known
Jewish response to Nazi persecution during the war, serving both as the coun-

1. The date was selected by the Knesset on April 12, 1951, and became law on August 19, 1953. The
actual starting date of the uprising (14th of Nisan) was problematic as it was also the eve of Passover.
Therefore, the 27th of Nisan, when the uprising was still going on, was selected by the Knesset to
take place eight days before Israel's Independence Day (on the 5th of Iyyar).
2. Gerhard Weinberg, "The Final Solution and the War in 1943," in *Revolt Amid the Darkness*
(Washington, D.C.: United States Holocaust Memorial Museum, 1993), 6.

393

terargument to the myth that the Jews of Europe had been "led like sheep to the slaughter" and conversely, reinforcing the mistaken view that the Warsaw Ghetto Uprising represented the only case of armed Jewish resistance in Europe (explicitly given the lie by the other essays in this volume).

If anything, the final resort to armed resistance taken by the rebels in the Warsaw ghetto symbolized the transition from those prior resistance activities that had been attempted to sanctify life in the ghetto, activities included in Yehuda Bauer's definition of "*amidah*," to a realization that the Nazi plan was to eliminate all Jews and that armed resistance signified a means by which Jews might not only take a measure of revenge, but more importantly, die with honor.[3] The rebellion in the Warsaw ghetto was the last chapter written by the Jews in the ghetto (save for those Jews who managed to survive in hiding after the uprising), but it was not the only chapter written by the Jews of Warsaw during the war, nor would it serve us well to read the history of Jewish life in occupied Warsaw as one long prelude to the finale that was the revolt. As Ben Zion Dinur wrote in 1953, "the chapter of the Holocaust and heroism is not only a story of life and death, murder and uprising; it also concerns the daily life of the Jews in the ghettos, of Jewish life in all the countries of Europe from the day the Nazis seized power."[4] According to historian David Engel, Dinur argued for a broader reading of Jewish resistance against the Nazis, not only in the form of armed resistance, but through the documentation of German crimes under the Occupation and the dedication to continuing *Jewish* life under all circumstances. Therefore to understand fully the significance of the Warsaw Ghetto Uprising and armed Jewish resistance in the Warsaw ghetto, this resistance must be understood in the context of broader underground activity in the ghetto, which eventually laid the groundwork for the organization of armed resistance, largely by the leaders of youth movements in the ghettos, who had been engaged in many of the other forms of underground activity before the scope of the Nazi plan for the genocide of the Jews was fully realized. While much can be written about the afterlife of the Warsaw Ghetto Uprising, its postwar significance and symbolism as the basis for subsequent debates about the place of the Holocaust in Jewish history, its place in Jewish history writing about the Holocaust, or about the degree to which Jews "fought back," this chapter attempts primar-

3. Concerning "*amidah*," see Yehuda Bauer, *Rethinking the Holocaust* (New Haven, Conn.: Yale University Press, 2001), 120.
4. Cited in David Engel, *Historians of the Jews and the Holocaust* (Stanford, Calif.: Stanford University Press, 2010), 122.

ily to provide a clear and concise overview of the history of armed Jewish resistance in the Warsaw ghetto, with a focus on the Warsaw Ghetto Uprising in April–May 1943.

From the Outbreak of War to the Creation of the Ghetto in Warsaw

In August 1939, just before the outbreak of the war, the Jewish population of Warsaw was approximately 380,000, or about 30 percent of the city's total population. Jews in Warsaw and throughout Poland anxiously tracked developments in the German Reich over the summer of 1939, as it became increasingly clear that war was likely to break out. With the outbreak of war on September 1, 1939, Jews and non-Jews alike suffered from the indiscriminate bombing of the Luftwaffe. An AJDC (American Jewish Joint Distribution Committee) report in Warsaw estimated 20,000 Jews were killed during the first month of the war, with 7,000 Jews killed in Warsaw alone in September 1939.[5] Thousands of Jewish homes, businesses, factories, and shops were also destroyed in the bombings. In the first weeks of the war, Warsaw's Jewish population fluctuated as a result of mobilization, flight, and the arrival of refugees; by early 1940, the Jewish population of Warsaw swelled to some 400,000 as Jews from areas annexed to the Reich were deported to the Generalgouvernement, and refugees crowded into Warsaw.[6] This only further compounded the scarcity of housing, food, and medical supplies in the city.

On September 23, 1939, Adam Czerniakow, who had served as deputy chair of the Jewish community before the war, was appointed head of the Jewish community by the mayor of Warsaw, Stefan Starzynski. Czerniakow would subsequently be named head of the Warsaw Jewish Council (Judenrat) under the Nazis. As he noted in his diary on that very September day:

5. Cited in Alexandra Garbarini, Emil Kerenji, Jan Lambertz, and Avinoam Patt, *Jewish Responses to Persecution, 1938–1940* (USHMM/AltaMira Press, 2011), 121. AJDC Warsaw Report about work during the thirteen war months from September 1939–October 1940, AJDC Warsaw, USHMMA, Acc. 1999.A.0154, ZIH 210/6. The report also counted 59,000 Jewish homes, factories, workshops, shops, and so forth destroyed by the bombing and fires; the JDC estimated the number of destroyed Jewish homes in Poland at 6,850, including Warsaw—1200; Warsaw district—800; Lublin district—2200; Radom district—1400; and in the Cracow district—650. For the history of AJDC work in Europe during the Holocaust, see Yehuda Bauer, *American Jewry and the Holocaust: The American Jewish Joint Distribution Committee, 1939–1945* (Detroit, Mich.: Wayne State University Press, 1981).

6. Barbara Engelking and Jacek Leociak, *The Warsaw Ghetto: A Guide to the Perished City* (New Haven, Conn.: Yale University Press, 2009), 47–48.

September 23, 1939—For quite a while a shortage of bread. There is no meat. They've started selling horsemeat, praising its taste in the newspapers, even as stock for soup. Mayor Starzyński named me Chairman of the Jewish Community in Warsaw. A historic role in a besieged city. I will try to live up to it—The city was bombed all night long, perhaps more heavily than before. Extensive damage to buildings and great loss of life. Sparks from the gutted railroad station fell on our school. At the office (4 Sienkiewicz Street) shrapnel hit the fifth floor for the second time, demolishing two rooms. We are moving to the fourth floor.[7]

At the beginning of the war, most of the official Polish Jewish leadership either fled Warsaw and the other major cities of Poland for the Soviet Union or places abroad or were captured, imprisoned, and executed. As the historian Israel Gutman has noted, among the leaders who fled at the beginning of the war were the leaders of all of the major Jewish political parties and movements in Poland; from the General Zionists, Moshe Kleinbaum (Sneh), Apolinary Hartglas, and Moshe Kerner; from the Bund, Henryk Erlich and Victor Alter; from Poalei Zion C. S., Anshel Reiss and Abraham Bialopolski; from Mizrachi, Zerah Warhaftig and Aaron Weiss; from Left Po'alei Zion, Yitzhak Leib and Nathan Buksbaum; from Agudat Israel, Yitzhak Meir Levin; and from Betar and the Revisionist party, Menachem Begin.[8] The flight of the leadership during the first week of the war left Warsaw without most of its political leaders (from across the political spectrum) and most directors of Jewish relief organizations.[9]

After the start of the war, however, a number of Zionist youth leaders who had managed to flee to the East made the decision to return to occupied Poland. This was the case among the youth movement leadership of Warsaw, many of whom had fled to Vilna in order to escape the Nazi invasion in September 1939. The leaders of Hashomer Hatzair (including Haim Holtz, Zelig Geyer, Yosef Shamir, Yitzhak Zalmanson, and Tosia Altman who made it to Vilna) decided that "as long as there is a Jewish community in Poland, the movement must be there."[10] While in Vilna at the start of the war, movements like Hashomer Hat-

7. Adam Czerniaków, diary entries for September/October 1939. See Garbarini, et al, *Jewish Responses*, 144. Quoted in Marian Fuks, ed., *Adama Czerniakowa dziennik getta warszawskiego: 6 IX 1939–23 VII 1942* (Warsaw: Państwowe Wydawn. Naukowe, 1983), 48–51 (translated from Polish). Also printed in a slightly differently worded translation in Raul Hilberg, Stanislaw Staron, and Josef Kermisz, eds., *The Warsaw Diary of Adam Czerniaków: Prelude to Doom* (Chicago, Ill.: Ivan R. Dee, 1999), 76–78.

8. Israel Gutman, *The Jews of Warsaw, 1939–1943: Ghetto, Underground, Revolt* (Bloomington: Indiana University Press, 1982), 121.

9. Samuel Kassow, *Who Will Write Our History? Emanuel Ringelblum, the Warsaw Ghetto, and the Oyneg Shabes Archive* (Bloomington: Indiana University Press, 2007), 104–5.

10. Cited in Moshe Arens, "The Jewish Military Organization (ZZW) in the Warsaw Ghetto," *Holocaust and Genocide Studies* 19 (2005): 205.

zair shifted their focus from solely training an elite cadre of movement members for *aliyah* to the land of Israel, to a broader effort to represent the wider Jewish public in the struggle against Nazism, and to an ideological position which would enable them to support the Soviet Union in this struggle.[11] The Hashomer Hatzair movement leadership sent emissaries from Vilna back to the Occupied Zone of Poland, first sending Tosia Altman, later to be followed by Yosef Kaplan, Mordecai Anielewicz, and Josef Kaplan.[12] Likewise, the Dror movement decided at a secret conference in Lvov on December 31, 1939 to send Zivia Lubetkin to Warsaw; she was followed several months later by Yitzhak Zuckerman.[13] While much of the leadership of the Bund fled Warsaw, Abraham (Abrasha) Blum, was one of the few Bund leaders who remained in Warsaw and would eventually become a member of the ZOB. The youth movement leaders who returned to Warsaw were motivated by a sense of responsibility as local leaders, not only to their young *chanichim* (movement members), but to the Jewish community as a whole. These youth movement leaders (like Mordecai Anilewicz, Zivia Lubetkin, Yitzhak Zuckerman, Josef Kaplan, Frumka Plotnicka, Tosia Altman, and Shmuel Breslaw) would play a key role in the formation of the ghetto underground, and eventually the Jewish fighting organization or ZOB. On the other hand, it was a group of Jewish military officers who had participated in the defense of Poland in September 1939, including Kalman Mendelson, a Revisionist and former officer in the Polish Army, David Apfelbaum, Henryk Lipszyc-Lipiński, and Szymon Białoskóra (Białoskórnik), who would form the core nucleus from which developed the Revisionist Zionist fighting organization, the ZZW. Later, along with Leon Rodal, members of Betar, the Revisionist Zionist youth movement, including Perotz Lasker and Pawel Frenkel, joined and helped to organize the group further.[14]

By September 28, 1939, the siege of Warsaw was over, with fully one-quarter of the city's buildings having been destroyed, and as many as fifty thousand citizens killed or injured.[15] As the Wehrmacht entered the city and organized soup lines for the starving population, Jews quickly experienced the changing dynamics of Polish society under German occupation. Emanuel Ringelblum,

11. Raya Cohen, "Against the Current: Hashomer Hatzair in the Warsaw Ghetto," *Jewish Social Studies* 7, no. 1 (Autumn 2000): 67.

12. Arens, "The Jewish Military Organization," 205.

13. Ibid. See also Yitzhak Zuckerman, *A Surplus of Memory: Chronicle of the Warsaw Ghetto Uprising* (Berkeley, Calif.: University of California Press, 1993), 36–40.

14. See Arens, "The Jewish Military Organization"; see too Haim Lazar, *Matsada shel Varsha* (Tel Aviv: Machon Jabotinsky, 1963).

15. Kassow, *Who Will Write Our History?* 106.

the historian, teacher, and social activist who would organize the underground Oyneg Shabes archive in the Warsaw ghetto, described the changing dynamics of social interactions between Polish Jews and non-Jewish Poles in the first month after the Occupation:

If, standing in line for water on Oczki Str. [in Warsaw], or in the Central-Railway Station Tunnel, a quarrel arose over a place, Poles eagerly called a passing-by German soldier or a German railroad worker and, indicating that "this is a Jew," demanded the undesirable neighbor's removal from the line. As a result, Jews were, indeed, led away. The same thing happened in lines for bread, meat, etc. Wishing to please the masses, the Germans made a rule that Jews were not allowed to stand in line. At the bakeries, soldiers appeared to take care of "order," which meant to kick out those who had been pointed out or recognized as Jews.[16]

In addition to the rapid process of social isolation and extreme persecution that quickly unfolded in Warsaw and throughout occupied Poland, the official establishment of the Generalgouvernement, which replaced the German military administration under the leadership of Hans Frank, soon subjected Jews to special decrees that limited them to 2,000 zlotys in cash, blocked their access to bank accounts, limited Jewish use of trains and public transport, instituted the Aryanization of Jewish businesses, and subjected Jews between the ages of fourteen to sixty to random seizure for forced labor.[17] By December 1, 1939, Hans Frank had decreed that all Jews over the age of ten residing in the Generalgouvernement must wear white armbands with a Star of David on the right sleeve of their clothing.[18]

Szmul Zygielbojm, a Bundist leader and member of the first Warsaw Jewish Council (before his escape from Poland in December 1939), detailed the efforts of the Judenrat in Warsaw to intervene and prevent random kidnappings of Jews for forced labor in the fall of 1939 as Jews young and old were seized in the streets to perform hard labor, enduring terrible torture in the process:

We [at the Jewish Community] could not bear to see the humiliation that Jews were kidnapped from the streets the way dogcatchers catch dogs. We tried to figure out how to put an end to this. The Warsaw Jewish Community approached the Gestapo with a proposal: if the German occupation authorities need people for labor, they

---

16. Emanuel Ringelblum, "Polish-Jewish Relations in Occupied Warsaw," October 1939, USHMMA RG 15.079M (ŻIH Ring. I/91), reel 7 (translated from Yiddish). Also printed in a differently worded translation in Joseph Kermish, ed., *To Live with Honor and Die with Honor! Selected Documents from the Warsaw Ghetto Underground Archives "O.S." (Oyneg Shabes)* (Jerusalem: Yad Vashem, 1986), 611–14.

17. Kassow, *Who Will Write Our History?* 106–7.

18. Saul Friedländer, *The Years of Extermination: Nazi Germany and the Jews, 1939–1945* (New York: Harper Perennial, 2008), 38.

should obtain them in an organized fashion; but the kidnapping of people in the street must stop. Let the daily quota of Jews required by the Germans be determined, and the community will provide people.

The Gestapo accepted the proposal on the surface. From that time (November 1939 onward) the Warsaw Jewish Community did, indeed, provide two thousand Jews a day for labor service. But the kidnappings of Jews from the streets did not stop.[19]

The Jewish Council, which had sought to alleviate the suffering of the Jews through random kidnappings for forced labor had now obligated itself to provide 2,000 workers for the Germans daily, even as random seizures continued. For the Jewish public in Warsaw, this seemed to make the Judenrat complicit in German policy, eventually opening a space for an alternative underground leadership in Jewish Warsaw to emerge as the Nazi policy of persecution continued and increased.

Following the occupation of Warsaw, German military leaders discussed the idea of creating a ghetto in Warsaw, although the idea was initially shelved for economic reasons, partly in response to petitions from Jewish leaders in the city, who argued that imprisoning the Jewish population in a ghetto would lead to the rapid spread of disease. On March 27, 1940, however, the Warsaw Judenrat received orders to begin the construction of walls around a "plague-infected area" in the Jewish residential section of Warsaw and, as noted by Czerniaków in his diary, on April 13, 1940, the Jews of Warsaw had even been ordered to pay to build their own ghetto walls.[20]

On Yom Kippur 1940 (October 12), the Jews of Warsaw were informed by announcements made over street megaphones that all Jews in the city would be required to move into the ghetto by the end of the month.[21] Helena Gutman-Staszewska, a Jewish woman living in Warsaw at the time, described the chaos

19. Szmul Zygielbojm, "Kidnapping for Labor," n.d. (ca. December 1939), *Zygielbojm-bukh* (New York: Farlag "Unzer Tsayt," 1947), 142–50 (translated from Yiddish). Also published in a slightly different translation in David Engel, *The Holocaust: The Third Reich and the Jews* (New York: Longman, 2000), 105–6. See Garbarini, et al, *Jewish Responses to Persecution*, 378–80. Zygielbojm (1895–1943) was a prominent Polish interwar Bundist. After leaving Warsaw for New York, he became the Bund's representative in the Polish National Council in London, an advisory body to the Polish Government-in-Exile. Upon hearing news of the destruction of the Warsaw ghetto in the aftermath of the uprising in the spring of 1943, Zygielbojm committed suicide in protest over the world's lack of action to prevent the mass murder of the Jews. Daniel Blatman, "On a Mission against All Odds: Szmuel Zygielbojm in London (April 1942–May 1943)," *Yad Vashem Studies* 20 (1990): 237–71.

20. See Hilberg, Staron, and Kermisz, *The Warsaw Diary of Adam Czerniaków*, 140.

21. See Engelking and Leociak, *The Warsaw Ghetto*, 642; Chaim Kaplan, *Scroll of Agony: The Warsaw Diary of Chaim A. Kaplan* (Bloomington: Indiana University Press, 1999), 208.

that ensued after the announcement of the formation of the ghetto, as Jews living outside the ghetto boundaries would be forced to trade their apartments for living quarters within the ghetto.[22]

The declared boundaries of the Jewish District were continually altered, even over the course of a day there were several changes. In our apartment building [at 20 Chłodna Street] there were 50 Jewish tenants and 10 Christian families. We did not know for sure whether we would be added to the Jewish District because the situation was subject to constant revision. It was on Yom Kippur when the news spread that we would have to move and that we had the right to exchange [our current apartment] for Aryan apartments. Since our building was modern—even the smallest apartments had modern appliances—from the very break of dawn it was as if a siege had begun, like a swarm of locusts. As soon as day broke, there was constant knocking at the door and questions about the exchange. The mood in the courtyard was terrible, some were yelling, some were crying, people were cheating each other, numerous shady characters were lurking about who wanted to take advantage of the situation.... Witnessing all these scenes, I was literally afraid that I would go insane; I left to try to shake it off.

As noted by Chaim Kaplan in his diary, the Jews of Warsaw were gradually being imprisoned in their own dungeon, walls rising before their very eyes: "In all the thoroughfares leading to the 'Aryan' quarters, high walls are being erected.... Before our eyes a dungeon is being built in which half a million men, women, and children will be imprisoned, no one knows for how long" (November 10, 1940). "What we dreaded most has come to us.... We went to bed in the 'Jewish quarter,' and the next morning we awoke in a closed Jewish ghetto, a ghetto in every detail" (November 17, 1940).[23]

On November 15, 1940, German authorities ordered the Warsaw ghetto in the General Government sealed off, creating the largest ghetto in both area and population in Poland. Over 350,000 Jews, approximately 30 percent of the city's population, were confined to about 2.4 percent of Warsaw's total area. Over 120,000 additional refugees would later be sent to the ghetto, bringing its

22. Helena Gutman-Staszewska, Warsaw, "Recollections from the German Occupation, August 1939-November 1940," USHMMA RG 02.208M (ŻIH 302/168) (translated from Polish). Parts of testimony published in Michal Grynberg, ed., *Words to Outlive Us: Eyewitness Accounts from the Warsaw Ghetto* (London: Granta Books, 2004), 25–26, 28. See in Garbarini, et al, *Jewish Responses to Persecution*, 363–64.

23. Kaplan, *Scroll of Agony*, 220–24.

24. Gutman, *The Jews of Warsaw*, 60–61. Estimates of Jewish refugees in Warsaw during the period range from 130,000 (Gutman) to 150,000 (Bauer). Gutman, *The Jews of Warsaw*, 63; Yehuda Bauer, *American Jewry and the Holocaust: The American Jewish Joint Distribution Committee, 1939– 1945* (Detroit, Mich.: Wayne State University Press, 1981), 69. Barbara Engelking and Jacek Leociak

total population to nearly 500,000.[24] The population of the ghetto fluctuated over the course of 1941, both as a result of the influx of refugees into the ghetto from smaller cities and towns in the Warsaw district, and as a result of the staggering death rate within the ghetto caused by starvation and disease.

The sealing of the ghetto left Warsaw's Jews completely isolated and without access to sufficient nourishment—food shortages became the primary concern of the ghetto's inhabitants. The German Transferstelle (transfer authority) controlled the entry of food and other items into the ghetto, limiting Jews to 184 calories of food per day.[25] Under such extreme circumstances, smuggling became the lifeblood of the Jewish people in the ghetto, and the professional smugglers became the ghetto's new elite.[26]

The Judenrat (Jewish Council) assumed a position of significance that the prewar Kehilla never had, directing all aspects of daily life in the ghetto and forming the Jewish administration within the ghetto. The areas of Judenrat responsibility in the ghetto included responsibility for basic nutrition, public health (and prevention of the spread of disease), sanitation (removal of garbage from the ghetto), maintaining public order (police and fire-fighting), housing, and registering the ghetto inhabitants. The Judenrat not only had to administer daily affairs; it also had to ensure compliance with German regulations. It oversaw the establishment of hospitals and clinics, cultural activities and education, welfare and mutual aid institutions, and orphanages. In total, the Warsaw Judenrat numbered about twenty-five departments and 6,000 workers (compared with 530 in the prewar community). The German authorities forbade any direct approach from individual Jews to German officials, requiring all negotiations and interactions to take place under the auspices of the Judenrat.[27] By using the Judenrat as their conduit to control Jewish life in the ghetto, the Germans also successfully deflected much of the direct rage of the ghetto population at the abominable conditions in the ghetto onto the Judenrat itself, and onto the other hated Jewish institution in the ghetto, the Jewish police. The Jewish police, headed by Jozef Szerynski (a Jewish convert to Catholicism), numbered approximately 1,635 policemen, and was responsible for directing traffic, supervising trash collection and sanitation, preventing crime, and adjudicating disputes between Jews in the ghetto.[28] While the Jewish police were subject to the supervi-

---

suggest the peak number of inhabitants of the Warsaw ghetto may have been 460,000 in March 1941. Engelking and Leociak, *The Warsaw Ghetto: A Guide to the Perished City*, 49.

25. Gutman, *The Jews of Warsaw*, 66.   26. Ibid., 68.
27. Ibid., 85.   28. Ibid., 87.

sion of the Polish police, over time it became clear that the Gestapo and the S.D. would pass orders directly to the Jewish police; this became abundantly clear during the mass deportations in July 1942, when the Judenrat was sidelined by the Jewish police who supervised the roundups in direct communication with the German authorities. Beyond the Jewish police, Abraham Gancwajch headed Force 13 (so named for the address of its headquarters at 13 Leszno Street), a unit established under the supervision of the German security police as the Office to Combat Usury and Profiteering in the Jewish Quarter of Warsaw. While Gancwajch engaged in a bitter power struggle with Czerniakow to assume power in the ghetto, arguing that Jews must understand that the Germans would win the war and operate accordingly under this new reality, his office was eventually shut down by Heinz Auerswald (Komisar of the Jewish quarter in Warsaw).[29]

Grass Roots Social Welfare in the Ghetto

Under the extreme conditions created in the ghetto—both in light of the food crisis, the economic crisis, the housing crisis, the public health crisis, and the refugee crisis—the work of social welfare organizations to address all of these issues became critical. Voluntary Jewish organizations that existed before the war to aid the weak and the needy continued to function, augmenting and often exceeding the efforts of the Judenrat to provide for the Jewish public. The Jewish Self-Help (Zydowska Samopomoc Spoleczna [ZSS]; renamed ZTOS in October 1940, then ZSS in November 1941) was funded by the "Joint" [American Jewish Joint Distribution Committee] and worked in cooperation with the Judenrat.[30] The JDC also transferred funds from American contributors to local self-help organizations like TOZ, a health and sanitation organization, and CENTOS, which cared for orphans.[31] The Warsaw Aleynhilf (literally, self-help) organization, was the name for the Jewish relief movement that grew out of the Warsaw-based Coordinating Commission of Jewish Aid and Social Societies in the first days of the war. Emanuel Ringelblum played an important role in the work of the group, which assumed even more prominence in the ghetto, coordinating the grassroots Jewish relief efforts of the house committees and other groups.[32]

29. Ibid., 90–94.
30. For background on the work of the Joint in Warsaw, see Bauer, *American Jewry and the Holocaust*.
31. See Miri Freilich and Martin Dean, "Warsaw," in *The USHMM Encyclopedia of Camps and Ghettos*, 2:76–82.
32. See Kassow, *Who Will Write Our History?* 119.

The house committees were centered in the inner courtyards of the large apartment buildings in the Jewish quarter, which seemed to offer more security from the dangers of the street. As Samuel Kassow suggests, "the house committees quickly became the basis of public life in the Warsaw ghetto," providing communal kitchens, child care, shelter for the sick, and a safe place for social interaction.[33] By April 1940, 778 such committees had been set up in the Jewish quarter of the city, and eventually this number would reach 1,518 covering more than 2,000 houses. The committees received contributions from their members as well as from the ZSS and other organizations.[34] The JDC also worked to alleviate the suffering of Warsaw's Jews and feed the starving population. Because of its international status, access to American resources, and experience on the ground and in cooperative projects, the Joint served as the most important source of support for all Polish Jews. In Warsaw alone between October 1939 and September 1940, the Joint counted 10,101,963 meals distributed.[35] In the course of 1940, the Joint spent over 14,735 million złoty on relief work before dropping to a mere 8 million złoty in 1941.[36] After the American entry into the war in December 1941, AJDC funds from the United States became largely unavailable.

Cultural, Religious, and Educational Activity in the Ghetto

In addition to maintaining social welfare organizations in the ghetto, an active cultural, educational, and religious life continued there, despite the abominable conditions and a German ban on most educational activities. Schools for children in elementary and middle schools functioned, as did vocational training and university-level lectures. Although religious services in the ghetto were officially banned, Jews continued to worship in secret, even as maintaining Jewish religious law became increasingly difficult, and visibly observant Jews were often singled out for the harshest persecution. Emanuel Ringelblum helped found a society for the advancement of Yiddish culture (Yidishe Kultur Organizatsye—YIKOR) in the ghetto. His most important initiative, how-

33. Ibid., 121.
34. Gutman, *The Jews of Warsaw*, 45–47; Saul Friedländer, *The Years of Extermination*, 148.
35. See "Thirteen Months of JDC work in Warsaw," USHMMA Acc. 1999.A.0154 (ŻIH 210/6); Bauer, *American Jewry and the Holocaust*, 72–76; Kassow, *Who Will Write Our History?* 114–15.
36. See Bauer, *American Jewry and the Holocaust*, 73, on official JDC expenditures for 1940; on the crucial role of the AJJDC for ghettos in Poland, see Isaiah Trunk, *Judenrat* (New York: Stein and Day, 1977), 135–42.

ever, was the creation of the Oyneg Shabes underground archive—the secret archive of the Warsaw ghetto. Begun as an individual chronicle by Ringelblum in October 1939, the archive was transformed, after the sealing of the ghetto in November 1940, into an organized underground operation with several dozen contributors.[37] Initially, the archivists would collect reports and testimonies by Jews who had come to the ghetto to seek help from the self-aid organizations. As described by Kassow, Ringelblum organized the Oyneg Shabes archive around the networks of the Aleynhilf—using the refugee points, soup kitchens, house committees, and underground schools to provide the information, documents and testimonies for the archive. Through his new contacts in the Aleynhilf, Ringelblum recruited much of the nucleus of the Oyneg Shabes archive which collected an enormous range of material that included the newspapers of the underground press, documents reflecting all aspects of life in the ghetto, drawings, tram tickets, ration cards, candy wrappers, and theater posters, as well as literature in the form of poems, plays, songs, and stories.[38] After July 22, 1942, the archive documented the great deportation, collecting posters that had called on Jews to assemble for transport and the desperate appeals from those waiting to board deportation trains to Treblinka. These materials and later posters calling for armed resistance in 1943 were crammed into milk cans and buried. Two of Ringelblum's young collaborators on his documentation effort, Josef Kaplan and Shmuel Breslaw of Hashomer Hatzair, would become early leaders of the armed resistance in the Warsaw ghetto.[39]

Youth Movements and the Formation of the Ghetto Underground

Under the German occupation, organized Zionist youth worked to understand more fully the needs of a wider Jewish public. Whereas before the war their activities had been focused on the "elite" among Jewish youth training for *aliyah* to Palestine, during the war their sense of responsibility and range of activities broadened. As part of their educational efforts, Zionist youth movements established kibbutz groups and underground schools in the ghettos. Through continued activity during the war, communication between ghettos,

---

37. For a thorough examination of Ringelblum's work in the Warsaw ghetto, see Kassow, *Who Will Write Our History?*

38. Ibid., 213.

39. For more on the work of Kaplan and Breslaw in the Oyneg Shabes, see ibid., 162–65.

and the establishment of an underground press, Zionist youth groups maintained better organization of their movements than other political groups (which collapsed or were greatly weakened under the weight of German persecution and genocidal policies). Through the broader scope of underground activities during the war, and a network which facilitated the dissemination of knowledge despite the extreme isolation of the ghetto, the youth movements were well-suited to emerge as an alternative leadership in the ghetto and eventually to organize the resistance movement in Warsaw.

Before the scope of the Nazi plan to eliminate European Jewry had been ascertained, however, youth movements within the ghettos worked to improve Jewish morale and rescue what they deemed to be an increasingly alienated, isolated, and demoralized youth suffering bitterly from the persecution and privations of the Occupation. Before the deportations, the Zionist youth movements like Hashomer Hatzair, Dror, and Betar worked among the ghetto population with a particular focus on the youth, forming study groups, schools, and collective social frameworks aimed at elevating the morale of youth in the ghetto, while also providing food and shelter to children and adults. Although exact figures are difficult to establish, Dror He-Halutz counted an estimated 300 *chanichim* in Warsaw; Hashomer Hatzair, 800; Hanoar Hatzioni, 160; and Betar, probably several hundred—one of Betar's eight Warsaw groups had 80 *chanichim*.[40]

As Tuvia Borzykowski wrote in the underground newspaper of the Dror youth movement in 1940, the youth movement sensed that it had a responsibility to take the broken and demoralized youth of Warsaw and save them from the spiritual calamity which the anarchy of the war threatened by providing them not only with education but, more importantly, with a secure social framework:

To remove the children of the street to a warm, friendly environment, to imbue in them as much as possible a concern for their own fate. To instill the feeling of solidarity and responsibility. With song and games to create the youthful atmosphere for the children who have been aged too soon … to awaken in them national feeling, give them a socialist consciousness, to activate them socially to all aspects of Jewish life, to familiarize them with all of the spiritual creation, which the Jewish people have formed throughout time. And finally, to concentrate the best segment of the Jewish youth, which have already received their instruction in our branches, as a front-line avant-garde of the Jewish youth.[41]

40. Gutman, *The Jews of Warsaw*, 135.
41. "Di yidishe yugnt in itstikn moment," article published in Dror underground newspaper in Tammuz 1940. USHMMA, RG 15.079, Ring I–705. Tuvia Borzykowski, whose pennames in the under-

Such dedication to the spiritual state of the young, while instilling solidarity and camaraderie among the members, would suit the movements well when the call for resistance came after the great deportation.

Warsaw functioned as a central point of information gathering for youth movement members, especially women, who managed to travel between ghettos under false identities. Over the course of 1941, movements like Hashomer Hatzair and Betar managed to open agricultural training farms (Hashomer Hatzair in Zarki, near Czenstochowa, and Betar in Hrubieszow). Under the leadership of Peretz Lasker, Betar managed to transfer many of its members from the closed Warsaw ghetto to the movement farm near Hrubieszow, where in the summer and fall of 1941, Betar members worked on the farm, listened to lectures, and engaged in military training.[42] The underground press of the youth movements also served as a key source of information on events throughout Poland, conveying information gathered by intrepid youth movement members that was otherwise denied to the ghetto inhabitants. Access to information about the scope of the German annihilation of the Jews of Eastern Europe after the summer of 1941 played a key role in the formation of the resistance groups in the Warsaw ghetto.

The leaders of the pioneering youth movements who had returned to occupied Poland from Vilna after the start of the war (in the case of Hashomar Hatzair, Tosia Altman, Josef Kaplan, Mordecai Anielewicz, and Shmuel Breslaw) sought to maintain contact with the movement in Vilna, the leadership in Israel, and the Hehalutz office in Geneva. Female members of the underground, like Tosia Altman, Frumka Plotnicka, or Chajke Grossman, for example, played a key role traveling to the various movement branches in the Generalgouvernement and Galicia to assist in organizing the movement and sharing information between parts of occupied Poland. They risked their lives to smuggle ma-

---

ground press of Dror were T. Domski and T. Ben-Zion, was born in Lodz on May 14, 1911. He spent his childhood and youth in Radomsk. Early in his youth he became connected with the Freiheit youth movement, and served as an emissary and lecturer in seminars and summer camps about Yiddish literature and the Jewish labor movements. In the middle of 1940, Tuvia was called to the Dror Hehalutz central offices in Warsaw, and participated in the organization of illegal seminars and the development of widespread educational activities among the youth. He maintained his connections with his community members in Radomsk and even visited them secretly twice. He survived the April 1943 uprising, escaped to the Aryan side, fought in the 1944 Polish uprising and emigrated to Israel in 1949. He died in 1959. See Tuvia Borzykowski, *Between Tumbling Walls* (Tel Aviv: Ghetto Fighters' House and United Kibbutz Movement, 1976).

42. Arens, "The Jewish Military Organization," 212. The beginning of the roundups in the Lublin region in the summer of 1942 led to the closing of the farm, with most members either returning to the Warsaw ghetto or joining the partisans in the forests around Lublin.

terial and information, as well as people, in and out of ghettos, undermining prevailing gender stereotypes which kept women out of positions of leadership in other domains.[43]

These youth movement leaders in turn became the leaders of the ghetto resistance and took the initiative in determining political and social action underground. Before the war, the youth movements were largely dependent on *shlichim* (emissaries) from Palestine in determining policy formation. During the war, however, largely cut off from the outside world and far more independent and autonomous than before, the youth movements functioned as a source of information from the outside world, emerging as an alternative leadership organization to the Judenrat. The youth movement leaders, because they were indeed younger than the other political leaders, were not confronted with the impossibly difficult task of serving on the Judenrat. Nonetheless, the youth movements quickly became highly critical of the Judenrat and Jewish police, often making them the first targets of both their political and physical attacks in the ghetto underground. In many cases, the youth movements were often the first to assess the early Jewish massacres as part of a comprehensive program, and were thus instrumental in the early organization of resistance.[44] The mobility of the youth movement leadership also enabled them to publicize the first news of atrocities in Lithuania, as was the case in Tosia Altman's return from Vilna to Warsaw in late 1941.[45]

43. For more on the role of women as couriers in occupied Poland and in the Resistance more generally, see Dalia Ofer and Lenore Weitzman, eds., *Women in the Holocaust* (New Haven, Conn.: Yale University Press, 1998); Lenore J. Weitzman, "Living on the Aryan Side in Poland: Gender, Passing and the Nature of Resistance," 187–222; Nechama Tec, *Resilience and Courage: Women, Men, and the Holocaust* (New Haven, Conn.: Yale University Press, 2003), 263–65.

44. See Israel Gutman, "The Youth Movement as an Alternative Leadership in Eastern Europe," in Asher Cohen and Yehoyakim Cochavi, eds., *Zionist Youth Movements during the Shoah*, (New York: Peter Lang Publishing, 1995). For example, Zuckerman, Lubetkin, Kaplan, Breslaw, and Anilewicz in Warsaw, Abba Kovner in Vilna, and Chajke Grossman in Bialystok. It should be noted that wartime resistance was not the exclusive province of Zionist youth movements. Bundist and Communist Jewish youth played an active role in resistance, including Abrasha (Abraham) Blum and Marek Edelman of the Bund in Warsaw. Nonetheless, the Bund's attitude to resistance was somewhat equivocal. See Daniel Blatman, *Lema'an Heruteinu ve-Herutchem: ha-Bund be-Polin, 1939–1949* (Jerusalem: Yad Vashem, 1996).

45. Tosia Altman (1918–43) was raised in Włocławek, where her Zionist father ran a store. When the war broke out she fled with other Zionist youth activists, eventually reaching Vilna. From there she returned to occupied Poland, traveling extensively and working to gather and rally youth leaders for clandestine work. She carried news of the onslaught against Jews with her and encouraged Jewish youth to organize resistance. Altman also forged contacts with the Polish and Communist underground organizations and, as an emissary of the Jewish Fighting Organization (ZOB), worked to gather weapons for an armed uprising. Trapped in the ghetto during the April 1943 uprising, she

After the German invasion of the Soviet Union in June 1941, contact between Warsaw and the movement leadership became increasingly difficult. In the case of Hashomer Hatzair, after receiving reports of systematic slaughters of Jews taking place to the East, Tosia Altman traveled to Vilna in December 1941, entering the Vilna ghetto on Christmas Eve together with Haika Grossman.[46] While Altman argued to the movement members there that the movement should focus its efforts on saving the activist core of the movement located in Warsaw, Abba Kovner, leader of Hashomer Hatzair in Vilna, argued that the German slaughter of the Jews in Lithuania and Poland was not local in nature, but part of an overall systematic plan bent on the total slaughter of the Jews of Europe. As Ziva Shalev describes, Tosia Altman was told that a decision had been made among the leadership of the various youth movements in Vilna that the Jews should not go to their deaths without a fight ("Let us not go like sheep to the slaughter," in the words of the manifesto composed by Abba Kovner). Shalev speculates that Altman may have even delivered the Vilna underground's manifesto before the Hashomer Hatzair members in the Warsaw ghetto.[47]

In Warsaw, the leadership of the Jewish public—both the alternate leadership of the youth movements and the official Judenrat leadership—initially met the reports of systematic annihilation skeptically. Still, Hashomer Hatzair began to focus its efforts increasingly on organizing armed resistance. At the last ideological seminar of Hashomer Hatzair held at the end of 1941, Emanuel Ringelblum noted the transition in his journal:

Once, during a break between classes in the Ha-Shomer seminar (I lectured on the history of the Jewish labour movements), Mordecai Anielewicz and Yosef Kaplan called me down into the yard of the building at 23 Nalewki Street.

They let me into a special room and showed me two revolvers. These revolvers, the members of the central leadership explained to me, were to be employed to train youth in the use of arms. This was the first step taken by Ha-Shomer Ha-Za'ir even before the Fighting Organisation was founded.[48]

At the time, individual movements, including Hashomer Hatzair, the Bund, and Betar, began to come to the realization that the reports of murder through-

---

made her way out through the sewers, but was later burned in a fire that broke out in a fighters' hiding place in a Warsaw suburb, captured and killed by the Germans. See Zivia Lubetkin, *In the Days of Destruction and Revolt* (Tel Aviv: Hakibbutz Hameuchad, 1981), 287; Ziva Shalev, "Tosia Altman," jwa.org/encyclopedia (accessed 2/17/2012).

46. Ziva Shalev, "Tosia Altman," jwa.org/encyclopedia (accessed 2/17/2012).

47. Ibid.

48. As cited in Gutman, *The Jews of Warsaw*, 165. See too Emanuel Ringelblum, *Ksovim fun Geto* (Warsaw: Wydawnictwo "Idisz Buch," 1961), 2:147.

out Poland pointed to the systematic nature of the genocide, necessitating a form of resistance that exceeded underground activity and would require the acquisition of arms. Nonetheless, each movement continued to function independently in its efforts to organize resistance. Marek Edelman, one of the leaders of the Bund in the Warsaw ghetto, related after the war that the Bund established "the first fighting organization" together with the Polish Socialists, headed by Bernard Goldstein, Abrasza Blum, and Berek Szanjdmil.[49] Even so, a lack of arms limited the scope of resistance.

At this point, the youth movements began to change the focus of their activities—from maintaining an underground organization directing educational and cultural activities to raise morale for youth in the ghetto, to a concerted effort to begin preparations for armed resistance in the ghetto. The three main branches of the underground—the Socialist-Zionist youth, Betar and the Revisionist Zionists, and the Bund—each worked to organize in the ghetto, usually separately. Efforts to acquire arms during this period were largely unsuccessful due to the inability to establish contacts with the Polish underground that would have led to the acquisition of weaponry.

In mid-March 1942, He-Halutz, the umbrella organization of pioneering Zionist youth groups called a meeting of several political organizations (including Poalei Zion Z.S., Left Poa'lei Zion, the Bund, and He-Halutz) in an attempt to organize a unified resistance organization in response to the alarming reports of systematic killing. According to a later report of Yitzhak Zuckerman (representative of He-Halutz at the meeting), he presented three concrete proposals: establish an overall Jewish fighting organization, maintain collective representation of all the Jewish political parties and youth organizations vis-à-vis the Polish military authorities, create an apparatus in the "Aryan" residential area for the purpose of obtaining arms and organizing workshops to manufacture arms in the ghetto.[50] Zuckerman later related that while the Zionist groups supported the proposal, the Bund felt it was premature to organize a unified fighting organization. Gutman suggests that the Zionist groups believed the Bund had a capability to connect them with the Polish underground outside the ghetto (and access to the necessary arms) which it simply did not possess. Without the participation of the Bund, the proposal to create a unified fighting organization stalled.

49. Gutman, *The Jews of Warsaw*, 165.
50. Ibid., 168. See also Zuckerman, *Surplus of Memory*, 166.

In January 1942, the Polish Workers' Party (PPR) had been established on the Aryan side of Warsaw, comprised largely of members of the prewar Communist party. While the PPR had trouble rousing supporters among Poles on the Aryan side, it did succeed in forming an alliance with the Left Poalei Zion in the ghetto, led by Adolf Berman. In March 1942, the Anti-Fascist Bloc was formed, and was soon joined by Hashomer Hatzair, He-Halutz, Dror, and the Po'alei Zion Z.S.[51] Among the aims of the bloc were an attempt to organize "joint forces for a political and propaganda war against Fascism," and the organization of combat divisions, which came to be known as the bloc's military division.[52] Following the arrest and murder of the leading figure in the battalion, Andrzej Szmidt (Pinkus Kartin), by the Gestapo, however, the bloc largely ceased to exist as of June 1942.[53]

Meanwhile, in the spring of 1942, the Germans had begun to implement the so-called Final Solution in the Generalgouvernement within the framework of Operation Reinhard, sending transports of Jews from the ghettos of Poland to the newly constructed killing centers at Belzec (where killing began in March 1942), Sobibor (May 1942), and Treblinka (July 1942). In his diary, Chaim Kaplan began to report the rumors that hinted at the Nazi genocide of the Jews:

It is reported that the Führer has decided to rid Europe of our whole people by simply having them shot to death.... You just take thousands of people to the outskirts of a city and shoot to kill; that is all.... In Vilna 40,000 Jews were shot to death.... Had [Hitler] not stated that if war erupted in Europe, the Jewish race would be annihilated? This process has begun and will continue until the end is achieved. (February 2, 1942). Worse was to come: I was told by an acquaintance of mine who has seen the official documents that thousands of Jews have been killed by poison gas. It was an experiment to test its effectiveness. (February 23, 1942)[54]

By spring 1942, the details described by Kaplan in his diary became even more specific as he included more detailed rumors regarding transports by rail cars and the execution of Lublin Jews. In June 1942 the news grew even worse and hinted at a more systematic slaughter of the Jews of the Generalgouvernement:

A catastrophe will befall us at the hands of the Nazis and they will wreak their vengeance on us for their final downfall. The process of physical destruction of Polish Jewry has already begun.... Not a day goes by that the Nazis do not conduct a slaughter.... The rumors that reach us from the provincial towns are worse than the tidings of Job.... (June 16, 1942) Every day Polish Jewry is being brought

51. Gutman, *The Jews of Warsaw*, 171.   52. Ibid., 172.
53. Ibid., 175.   54. Kaplan, *Scroll of Agony*, 296–99.

to slaughter. It is estimated ... that three-quarters of a million Polish Jews have already passed from this earth.... Some of them are sent to a labor camp, where they survive for a month at the outside.... Some are shot; some are burned; some are poisoned with lethal gas; some are electrocuted. (June 25, 1942) It has been decreed and decided in Nazi ruling circles to bring systematic physical destruction upon the Jews of the General Government.... The killing of thousands of people has turned into a business that employs many hands. After the souls expire, they strip the corpses. Their clothing, shirts, and shoes are not wasted, but are collected in piles upon piles and turned over for disinfection, mending, and repairs. Hundreds of Jews are employed in these tasks. (July 10, 1942)[55]

Kaplan recorded the sense of bewilderment and confusion on the part of the ghetto's population as the liquidation approached, along with the dashed hopes of survival and the terror of deportation: "There is an instinctive feeling that some terrible catastrophe is drawing near for the Warsaw ghetto, though no one can determine its time or details." (June 20, 1942) Despite a brief moment of optimism that the deportation would be delayed, the announcement of the "resettlement" was devastating for Kaplan: "I haven't the strength to hold a pen in my hand. I'm broken, shattered.... A whole community of 400,000 people condemned to exile." (July 22, 1942)[56]

On July 22, 1942 the great deportation from the Warsaw ghetto to Treblinka began, as German SS and police authorities initiated the process that led to the deportation of approximately 275,000–300,000 Jews from the ghetto by September 12, 1942. Adam Czerniakow, chairman of the Warsaw ghetto Judenrat, decided to commit suicide on July 23, 1942 rather than comply with the deportation order, writing in his final note, "They are demanding that I kill the children of my people with my own hands. There is nothing for me to do but die."[57] As Marek Edelman and Antek Zuckerman, both leaders of the ZOB, later suggested, Czerniakow should not have died alone with the knowledge that "deportation to the East" actually meant death in the gas chambers. Instead they wished that he had called upon Jews in that moment to defend themselves. While Jewish police forces assisted in the first phase of the deportation, which targeted primarily refugees, the elderly, and the homeless, between July 31 and August 14, German forces raided the ghetto to round up Jews, and soon it became clear that the deportation had become a general liquidation. By mid-September, 35,000

---

55. Ibid., 351, 370.

56. See as recorded in http://www.jewishgen.org/yizkor/terrible_choice/tero03.html (accessed February 28, 2012); Kaplan, *Scroll of Agony*, 379.

57. For a detailed account of the deportation, see Engelking and Leociak, *The Warsaw Ghetto: A Guide to the Perished City*, 698–730.

Jews had been selected to remain in the ghetto, while another 25,000 managed to go into hiding.[58]

In the context of the great deportation from the Warsaw ghetto, on July 28, 1942 the Jewish Fighting Organization (Zydowska Organizacja Bojowa—ZOB) was founded by three Zionist youth movements, Hashomer Hatzair, Dror, and Akiva to organize Jewish self-defense and advocate armed struggle against the Germans. The command of the newly established organization consisted of Shmuel Breslaw, Yitzhak Zuckerman, Zivia Lubtekin, Mordecai Tenenbaum, and Josef Kaplan.[59] There was, however, little that the initial group of approximately two hundred members could do, aside from evade deportation and acquire a few pistols and hand grenades from the Polish Communist underground.[60]

Initial discussions among the members of the new resistance group focused on how best to engage in resistance, especially without arms. In the first week of August, the group acquired five pistols and six hand grenades from the Gwardia Ludowa (the Polish Communist underground) and attempted to assassinate the commander of the Jewish Police in the ghetto, Jozef Szerynski. Israel Kanal, a member of Akiva and former Jewish policeman in the ghetto, succeeded in wounding Szerynski, but failed to kill him.[61] The seeming failure to mount meaningful resistance was compounded in August when a group of eighteen members of the underground on their way from Warsaw to Hrubieszow were caught and killed by the Gestapo. The capture of this group and the aid of an informer led the German police to Josef Kaplan, one of the leaders of the underground and a founder of the ZOB, and then to the capture of Shmuel Breslaw, who was also caught and killed trying to follow Kaplan's captors. After the capture of Kaplan, the underground group tried to move its cache of weapons, but this attempt also failed and the weapons were confiscated. In one day, the ZOB had lost two of its leaders and most of its weapons.[62] Antek Zuckerman captured the group's feeling of hopelessness after the loss of Kaplan and Breslaw at a meeting of the ZOB command on September 12:

The words were bitter, heavy and determined. There would be no Jewish opposition. We were too late. The people are gone. When there were hundreds of thou-

---

58. Gutman, *The Jews of Warsaw*, 197.

59. Ibid., 236.

60. Friedländer, *The Years of Extermination*, 520–21.

61. Israel Gutman, *Resistance: The Warsaw Ghetto Uprising* (Bloomington: Indiana University Press, 1994), 155.

62. Ibid., 157.

sands in Warsaw, we could not manage to organize a Jewish striking force—how could we succeed in doing so now when there are only tens of thousands left? The masses did not place their trust in us. We do not have—and probably never will have—weapons. We don't have the strength to start all over again. The nation has been destroyed; our honor trampled upon. This tiny group might yet save us. Let us go out into the streets tomorrow, set the ghetto aflame, and attack the Germans with knives. We will die. It is our duty to die. And the honor of Israel will be saved. In days to come, it will be said: The youth of the hapless people rose up to defend its honor while it could. [63]

On that evening, the remnants of the ZOB decided to postpone immediate action in order to organize, acquire arms, and plan resistance. According to Gutman, "the nucleus of the surviving Z.O.B. was the foundation upon which the eventually broad-based Jewish Fighting Organization was built."[64] As reports regarding the deportations to Treblinka and Auschwitz and the liquidation of Jewish communities throughout Poland filtered into the ghetto, the various underground organizations struggled to create a unified armed resistance group.[65] The left wing and centrist Zionist youth movements (including Hashomer Hatzair, Hehalutz, Gordonia, Left Poa'lei Zion, Po'alei Zion, Z.S., and the General Zionists) joined together with the Communists to form a broad-based public political group, called the Jewish National Committee and an expanded ZOB.[66] The newly formed group resolved to meet any renewed attempt at mass deportation with armed resistance. After lengthy discussions, the Bund agreed to join the ZOB and coordinate its activities with the Jewish National Committee and the Jewish Coordinating Committee with limited political cooperation (thus not betraying its political principles to work with Zionist groups). The ZOB combat units would be organized around political parties and youth groups. Despite complex negotiations to include the Revisionists, in the end the Revisionist Zionists and Betar maintained their own separate independent armed organization, the Jewish Military Union (Zydowski Zwiazek Wojskowski, or ZZW).[67] Ringelblum described a visit to the ZZW headquarters

63. Quoted in Gutman, *The Jews of Warsaw*, 247. Yitzak Zuckerman, "Yemei September 1942," *Yalkut Moreshet* 16 (1972).

64. Gutman, *The Jews of Warsaw*, 248.

65. On August 28, 1942, Gerhard Riegner of the WJC office in Geneva sent his telegram outlining the Nazi intention to eliminate European Jewry to Stephen Wise and the U.S. State Department, but it took several months for the State Department to verify Riegner's alarming message.

66. Friedländer, *The Years of Extermination*, 522.

67. Ibid.; Arens, "The Jewish Military Organization," 212; Kassow, *Who Will Write Our History?* 354.

on Muranowska 7 where he was impressed with the weapons cache the Revisionist group had managed to acquire, mainly through connections with the Polish underground.[68] Pawel Frenkel most likely served as leader of the armed division of the ZZW, while David Wdowinski served as the head of the political committee of the ZZW. A tunnel dug by the ZZW at Muranowska 7 connected the headquarters with the Aryan side of Warsaw, providing easy access to supplies outside the ghetto. As Moshe Arens notes in his article on the ZZW, this enabled the ZZW to acquire an impressive stash of arms, including pistols, grenades, Molotov cocktails, rifles, machine guns, and medical supplies.[69]

The command of the ZOB included Mordecai Anielewicz, commander (Hashomer Hatzair); Yitzhak Zuckerman (Dror HeHalutz), deputy commander; Marek Edelman (Bund), intelligence chief; Yochanan Morgenstern (Po'alei Zion Z.S), finances; Hirsch Berlinski (Left Po'alei Zion), planning; and Michael Rosenfeld (Communist rep.). Arie (Jurek) Wilner represented the ZOB before the military forces in the Polish underground and Dr. Adolf Berman represented the Jewish National Committee before Polish civilian institutions.[70] By late September 1942, the ghetto population had dwindled to approximately 40,000 Jews working in the remaining workshops; the ZOB comprised an estimated 600 members, but by this point had acquired almost full support of the remaining ghetto population who both understood the nature of Nazi policy and came to respect the leadership of the youth movements and fighting organizations.[71]

Anielewicz, born in Wyszkow near Warsaw in 1919, became a leader of Hashomer Hatzair before the war. At the start of the war, he escaped to Vilna with a group of other Hashomer Hatzair leaders before returning to Warsaw in January 1940. During the deportations from Warsaw in July 1942, Anielewicz was in Zaglembie, where he had traveled in an attempt to organize armed resistance in the southwest region of Poland. While he possessed no formal military training, he had been one of the founders of the ZOB in July 1942 and was trusted by the members of the underground as possessing the leadership traits necessary to lead the ZOB in battle. Anielewicz developed a close relationship with Emanuel Ringelblum, as did Josef Kaplan and Shmuel Breslaw, who aided in the activities of the Oyneg Shabbes Archive before their capture in September 1942.[72] Ringelblum and other members of the Oyneg Shabbes executive com-

---

68. See Kermish, *To Live with Honor and Die with Honor*, 597, and Kassow, *Who Will Write Our History?* 354.

69. Arens, "The Jewish Military Organization," 217.

70. Gutman, *The Jews of Warsaw*, 291.   71. Ibid., 293.

72. See Kassow, *Who Will Write Our History?* 162–65.

mittee joined the finance committee of the ZOB to help raise what meager funds could be raised for the resistance.

Once Anielewicz had learned of the mass slaughters, he devoted himself entirely to the cause of armed resistance, forsaking all of the cultural work that had been the arena of the youth movement in the earlier period in the ghetto (seminars, literature discussion, history courses, and other activities). As Kassow notes, Anielewicz came to regret having spent any time not focused on training for armed resistance. In the words of Ringelblum, from this point forward "a paradoxical situation arose." While the adult generation continued to worry about survival, about the possibility of continuing life, it was

the youth—the best, the most beautiful, the noblest element that the Jewish people possessed—who spoke and thought only about an honorable death. They did not think about surviving the war, they did not arrange "Aryan" Papers, they did not get apartments on the other side. Their only worry was about the most honorable death, the kind of death that a two-thousand-year-old people deserves.[73]

In one of its first missions, Eliyahu Rozanski (Hashomer Hatzair) of the ZOB assassinated Jacob Lejkin, the deputy commander of the Jewish Police, who had uniquely devoted himself to the deportation operation. In the words of Ringelblum: "Lejkin, who had allowed power to go to his head and whose dedication to the Germans was boundless, was 'swept out' by the organization to the heartfelt acclamation of the Jewish population."[74] The ZOB next targeted the Judenrat which it deemed to have "collaborated with the conqueror" and assassinated Yisrael First, a Judenrat official in the economic department who had also served as a liaison with the German police.[75] An October 30, 1942 announcement posted by the resistance movement in the ghetto "indicted ... the directing board and the Jewish Council in Warsaw, for collaboration with the invader and for signing the deportation document," as well as those who were exploiting Jewish labor in the ghetto, warning that drastic measures would be "applied with the utmost severity."[76] In conjunction with the six-month anniversary of the great deportation, the ZOB planned a retaliation against the Jewish police for January 22, 1943, calling on the remaining Jews of Warsaw:

---

73. Ringelblum, *Ksovim fun Geto*, 2:148–49, as cited in Kassow, *Who Will Write Our History?* 371.

74. Gutman, *The Jews of Warsaw*, 302. Ringelblum, *Ktovim fun geto*, 2:332.

75. Gutman, *The Jews of Warsaw*, 303.

76. Quoted in Kermish, *To Live with Honor and Die with Honor*, 588; Archiwum Zydowskiego Instytutu Historycznego w Polsce (Archives of the Jewish Historical Institute in Poland), ARII/333, [Public Calls and Notices of the Resistance Movement in the Ghetto] "Announcement."

Jewish masses, the hour is drawing near. You must be prepared to resist, not give yourselves up to slaughter like sheep. Not a single Jew should go to the railroad cars. Those who are unable to put up active resistance should resist passively, meaning go into hiding. We have just received information from Lvov that the Jewish Police there forcefully executed the deportation of 3,000 Jews. This will not be allowed to happen again in Warsaw. The assassination of Lejkin demonstrates that. Our motto should be: All are ready to die as human beings.[77]

At the same time, the ZZW issued a parallel call for resistance:

> We are rising up for war!
> We are of those who have set themselves the aim of awakening the people. Our wish is to take this watchword to our people:
> Awake and fight!
> * * * *
> Our watchword is:
> Not even one more Jew is to find his end in Treblinka!
> Out with the traitors to the people!
> War for life or death on the conqueror to our last breath!
> Be prepared to act!
> Be ready![78]

Before either the ZOB or the ZZW could act on their plans for January 22, 1943, however, SS and police units launched a new *aktion* seeking to round up approximately 8,500 Jews. Following a January 9, 1943 visit to the ghetto by Reichsführer *SS* Heinrich Himmler, where he was surprised to learn that nearly 40,000 Jews had been kept alive as workers, he ordered that the total liquidation of the ghetto take place by February 14, 1943, with the remaining Jews and production facilities transferred to a concentration camp in the Lublin district.[79] On the first day of the roundup, on January 18, 1943, German forces managed to capture approximately 3,000 Jews for deportation to Treblinka, catching the ZOB and ZZW largely off-guard. Among those killed on the first day of the roundup was Yitzhak Giterman, the JDC director and the main organizer of self-help in the ghetto, killed as he ran from apartment to apartment in

77. "Call to Resistance by the Jewish Fighting Organization in the Warsaw Ghetto, January 1943," Archiwum Zydowskiego Instytutu Historycznego w Polsce (Archives of the Jewish Historical Institute in Poland), ARII/333 (cited in Gutman, *The Jews of Warsaw*, 305.) See also Joseph Kermish, ed., *Mered Geto Varshah be-Einei ha-Oyev* (Jerusalem: Yad Vashem, 1966), 589.

78. "Call for Resistance by the Jewish Military Organization in the Warsaw Ghetto, January 1943," Archiwum Zydowskiego Instytutu Historycznego w Polsce (Archives of the Jewish Historical Institute in Poland), ARII/333. See a slightly different translation in Kermish, *Mered Geto Varshah*, 590–91.

79. Gutman, *The Jews of Warsaw*, 329.

his housing block on Muranowska Street to warn Jews of the *aktion*.[80] On the second day of the roundup, the ZOB, under the leadership of Anielewicz, did manage to mount several attacks against German soldiers, in some cases embedding themselves with Jews being marched to the Umschlagplatz for deportation. Anielewicz led a group of Hashomer Hatzair fighters in battle; Yitzhak Zuckerman led a group from Dror and Gordonia that included Zivia Lubetkin and Tuvia Borzykowski; and Marek Edelman, a group from the Bund. Tosia Altman, who had been instrumental as an underground courier for Hashomer Hatzair, was caught in the roundup but managed to escape at the Umschlagplatz with the aid of a Jewish policeman. Although the January revolt failed to prevent the deportation of approximately 5000 Jews, it did teach the Resistance several important lessons: 1) German soldiers would flee when shot upon by Jewish fighters; 2) the tactic of ambush was more successful than open street fighting, which had cost the ZOB some of its top fighters in the January days of battle; 3) the January roundups were an indication that the Germans intended to act upon the final liquidation of the ghetto, leading ghetto inhabitants to construct hundreds of bunkers underneath buildings in the ghetto. The ZOB built its main command bunker at Mila 18, which would serve as headquarters for the April revolt; 4) the ghetto inhabitants would support the ZOB in its efforts to engage in armed resistance against the Germans, having learned from the previous summer that "deportation" likely meant death.[81]

As Dr. Lensky, a physician in the ghetto wrote in his memoirs:

Unfurling the banner of revolt enhanced the underground's stature in the eyes of the remaining Jews. Many who did not even know that an underground existed now saw concrete proof of its deeds. They sensed that the ghetto has an organized force other than the community council (*Judenrat*); a moral force that is fed up with the old methods which brought a "holocaust" down upon the Jews. This organization has chosen a new way of dealing with the Nazis. Hope was revived in the hearts of the doomed. Perhaps the Germans will really not expose their soldiers to danger and will stop sending them to execute operations because Jews are prepared to resist.[82]

Following the January uprising, a period of relative quiet ensued, as German officials debated the proper course of action, with some arguing for complete liquidation of the ghetto and others lobbying for the continued use or transfer

---

80. Ibid., 309–10.
81. See Freilich and Dean, "Warsaw," and Gutman, *The Jews of Warsaw*, 312; 316–17.
82. Gutman, *The Jews of Warsaw*, 319. Dr. Lensky ms. In YVA, 0-33/13-2, 0-33/257, 116.

of the workers in the armaments, leather, and textile factories in Warsaw to other parts of the Generalgouvernment. It is unclear to what extent the January uprising influenced German policy in their approach to liquidating the ghetto, although clearly the final liquidation was delayed beyond Himmler's original February 14, 1943 deadline. The remaining Jews in the ghetto had been convinced that the time had come for armed resistance as their last resort, refusing to believe German assurances that transfer to labor camps at Trawniki or Poniatow would enable them to survive until the end of the war.[83] The remaining population also devoted itself to preparing bunkers in the ghetto, described by Gutman as a type of "bunker mania." In his memoirs, Lensky writes of the period, "one can say without exaggeration that the entire population, from the young to the old, was engaged in preparing hiding places.... No one thought of willingly going to Treblinka. The survivors prepared everything necessary for remaining in hiding for months."[84]

Following the January uprising, the ZOB focused on applying the lessons of January in preparation for the next *aktion*. It was clear to the ZOB that they lacked sufficient weaponry and they thus focused on acquiring funds to purchase arms, while also working to purge any dangerous collaborators from their midst. The earlier approach of dividing fighting units according to movements also weakened the overall effectiveness of the fighting force. In its preparations for what would be the final battle, the ZOB pledged to mix the members of different movements together and create an overall combat structure of twenty-two units, each having approximately twelve to twenty members. Having been caught off-guard in January, the units were now always at the ready. The ZOB also divided the ghetto into three major combat sectors: 1) the Central Ghetto, under the command of Yisrael Kanal with nine units, also where the ZOB command was located; 2) the shop sector, under the command of Yitzhak Zuckerman (replaced by Eliezer Geller before the April revolt) with eight units; and 3) the Brushmakers' Area, under the command of Marek Edelman with five units. The ZOB also improved cooperation with the ZZW during this period, with the two groups agreeing to fight side by side, although when the actual fighting began, the ZZW engaged German forces more directly, with the ZOB choosing to employ the ambush and retreat tactics.[85] The ZZW fortified its positions along Muranowksa Street and the area of the workshops, while also pre-

83. Gutman, *The Jews of Warsaw*, 334.
84. Ibid., 351.
85. Arens, "The Jewish Military Organization," 218.

paring defensive positions at the Umschlagplatz. In this period, some additional arms were acquired by the ZOB through the AK (Armia Krajowa, the Polish Home Army and main Polish resistance movement), including revolvers, grenades, and explosives, while in some cases weapons were actually purchased from German soldiers returning from the Eastern Front or from Poles in Warsaw. Needing funds for the purchase of revolvers on the Aryan side of Warsaw, the ZOB pressured ghetto inhabitants to provide funds and took them from the supply authority of the Judenrat, thereby raising millions of zlotys in this period, according to the memoirs of Marek Edelman.[86] While it is unclear exactly how many fighters the two organizations counted between them, it seems that shortly before the April revolt, the ZOB counted approximately 450–500 members; the ZZW, perhaps 200–250.[87]

Even so, the ZOB was all too aware of the enormous power differential that existed between their meager force and the German war machine. The decision to engage in a last act of resistance against the Germans was not made out of hope that, in some way, lives might be saved, but as a final declaration of human dignity and a refusal to "go like sheep to the slaughter." Commenting on a conversation with ZOB Commander Mordecai Anielewicz, Emanuel Ringelblum wrote, "He gave an accurate appraisal of the chances of the uneven struggle, he foresaw the destruction of the ghetto and the workshop, and he was sure that neither he nor his combatants would survive the liquidation of the ghetto. He was sure that they would die like stray dogs and no one would even know their last resting place."[88] In other words, the final decision to engage in revolt was made as a response both to the hopelessness of the Jewish situation and out of an ultimate desire to preserve the last bit of Jewish honor. Inspired by Yitzhak Lamdan's poem, "Masada," which imagined a return to the desert fortress surrounded by the Romans in the year 73CE and its call that "Masada shall not fall again," the ghetto fighters were determined to make a historical statement in their last struggle against the full force of the mighty German Reich.[89]

---

86. Gutman, *The Jews of Warsaw*, 344.

87. Ibid., 348.

88. Quoted in Kermish, *To Live with Honor and Die with Honor*, 600; in Rachel Einwohner, "Opportunity, Honor, and Action in the Warsaw Ghetto Uprising of 1943," *American Journal of Sociology* 109, no. 3 (November 2003): 650–75.

89. David Roskies notes that the *Dror* movement anthology published in 1940, which would later serve as a "blueprint for the revolt," included Lamdan's famous poem. David Roskies, *Against the Apocalypse: Responses to Catastrophe in Modern Jewish History* (Cambridge, Mass.: Harvard University Press, 1984), 207.

The April Revolt: April 19–May 16, 1943

The ZOB estimated that the Germans would plan for a final liquidation of the ghetto sometime in the spring of 1943. Having learned from the January uprising that the Jews would now resist any efforts for transfer or roundup through armed force, the Germans planned to enter the ghetto with a large military force. They nonetheless seem to have underestimated the size of the Jewish resistance forces.

The final liquidation of the Warsaw ghetto began on Passover Eve, April 19, 1943 (14 Nisan 5703). Approximately 2,000 German soldiers (including SS troops, German police, and army soldiers), commanded by SS Senior Colonel Ferdinand Von Sammern-Frankenegg, entered the ghetto early that morning. While the German forces were surprised by the size of the Jewish resistance, the ZOB and the Jewish fighters were fully prepared for the German liquidation. The day before, the ghetto had begun to receive reports that German forces were massing outside the ghetto. Accordingly, Jews began to gather in their bunkers that night and ZOB fighters, prepared to encounter the German forces in their combat units, mobilized by 2:15 a.m.[90]

When the German troops entered the ghetto, ZOB and ZZW units were waiting for them. The first clash took place between ZOB fighters and German troops at the corner of Gesia and Nalewki as the German soldiers were caught off-guard by a shower of explosives and hand grenades; the ZZW engaged in heavy battles in Muranowska Square, wounding many Germans and seizing a light machine gun. ZOB fighters were so successful in catching the German forces off-guard initially that the German troops retreated to organize a counter-attack, leaving fallen comrades in the street.[91] Stroop reported losing twelve men on the first day of fighting (six SS privates and six Trawniki men).[92] The ZZW sustained many more losses than the ZOB on the first day of battle, although they did manage to raise the Zionist flag and the Polish flag on the highest building in the area, at 17 Muranowska Street, keeping it raised as the symbol of the Resistance for several days.[93] Other ZOB forces engaged German troops in battle at the corner of Zamenhof and Mila streets. Chaim Frimmer, a fighter in one of the ZOB squads positioned at that corner recounted the first en-

---

90. See reports of Borzykowski and Edelman, in Gutman, *The Jews of Warsaw*, 367–68.
91. Ibid., 372.
92. See Stroop Report in *Revolt Amid the Darkness*, 194.
93. Arens, "The Jewish Military Organization," 218.

gagement with German forces as a German column entered the ghetto, attempting to establish a temporary headquarters near the entrance to the ghetto:

A mighty blast within the column was the signal to act. Immediately thereafter grenades were thrown at the Germans from all sides, from all the positions on both sides of the street. Above the tumult of explosions and firing, we could hear the sputter of the German Schmeisser [a German submachine gun] operated by one of our men in the neighboring squad.... The battle lasted for about half an hour. The Germans retreated leaving many dead and wounded in the street ... again my eyes were peeled on the street, and then two tanks came in, followed by an infantry column, when the tank came up to our building, some Molotov cocktails and bombs put together from thick lead pipes were thrown at it. The big tank began to burn and, engulfed in flames, made its way toward the *Umschlagplatz*. The second tank remained in place as fire consumed it from every side.[94]

Thus, on the first day of the revolt, the German forces were forced to fight a well-prepared ZOB and ZZW and to respond to repeated ambushes, a new tactic which served the Jewish fighters far better than the open street fighting of January 1943. As a result of his failures on the first day, Col. Von Sammern-Frankenegg was relieved of his command and replaced by SS Major General Jürgen Stroop, who resolved to engage the Jewish fighters in house-to-house fighting rather than through open street battles. After the war, Stroop, who commanded the final liquidation of the ghetto, blamed von Sammern-Frankenegg for failing to take into account the reports of Jewish resistance.[95] Stroop's detailed report on the fighting and liquidation of the ghetto, while surely inflating Jewish losses and minimizing German casualties, also reveals the stubborn resistance of the Jewish fighters in its day by day account of the April revolt. Stroop reported the capture of 580 Jews on the first day, although the vast majority of the ghetto population managed to evade capture by hiding in bunkers, and in some cases, also engaged German forces in surprise attacks.[96]

On the second day of the revolt, most of the fighting took place in the area of the brushmakers, including five groups from the ZOB and the ZZW fighters, who again sustained heavy losses. At the end of the second day, the ZZW fighters were forced to retreat from their positions on Muranowska Street. They lost most of their fighters on the second and third day of the uprising. Stroop record-

---

94. Gutman, *The Jews of Warsaw*, 372, quoting Aharon Carmi and Chaim Frimmer, *Min Ha-Deleka Ha-Hi*, (Tel-Aviv: ha-Ḳibuts ha-me'uḥad, 1961), 216–17.

95. Ibid., 370; quoting Kermish, *Mered Geto Varshah*, 189. See description in Engelking and Leociak, *The Warsaw Ghetto: A Guide to the Perished City*, 776–77.

96. Gutman, *The Jews of Warsaw*, 376.

ed the loss of two Order policemen, two SS privates, and one wounded Trawniki man on the second day of the operation.[97] On April 21, 1943, under the command of Stroop, the German forces shifted their tactics and, determined not to engage the underground fighters directly, chose to enter the ghetto in less vulnerable small groups of soldiers, chasing resistance fighters and burning and bombing the buildings housing the Jews. This more destructive policy would ultimately be more successful in crushing the revolt, but it also destroyed valuable machinery and equipment the German shop-owners had hoped to preserve. Anielewicz and the command of the ZOB moved to the bunker at Mila 18, which came to house nearly 300 surviving members of the ZOB. Tosia Altman continued to serve as a liaison between the underground bunker and a bunker of wounded ZOB members, which included Arieh Wilner.[98] Altman also communicated events in the ghetto to Yitzhak Zuckerman, who had been sent to the Aryan side of Warsaw to serve as a liaison to the Polish underground before the final liquidation had begun. By the end of the first week of the revolt, the Germans had managed to destroy most of the points of resistance fighting, as the ZOB dug itself underground. During the second week, German soldiers began progressively liquidating the bunkers in the ghetto, encountering and destroying remaining ZOB, ZZW, and "wildcat" fighters who struggled to defend individual bunkers throughout the ghetto.

Nonetheless, on April 23, 1943, in the midst of the fighting, Mordecai Anielewicz, leader of the revolt in the Warsaw ghetto, appreciated the tremendous significance of the moment on a historical level. As he wrote to his comrade Yitzhak Zuckerman stationed on the Aryan side: "Keep well, my dear. Perhaps we shall meet again. Most importantly: the dream of my life has become true. I have been privileged to witness Jewish self-defense in the ghetto in all of its greatness and glory."[99]

In a communique issued on April 23, 1943, signaling a broader appeal to the Polish nation, the ZOB proclaimed its willingness to fight "for your freedom and ours":

Poles, citizens, freedom fighters!
From out of the roar of the cannon with which the German Army is battering our homes, the dwellings of our mothers, children, and wives;

---

97. *Revolt Amid the Darkness*, 195.
98. See Ziva Shalev, "Tosia Altman," jwa.org/encyclopedia (accessed 2/24/2012).
99. See *Sefer Milhamot Ha-Getaot*, 158 (Yad Vashem Archives, O-25/96); translated differently in various sources.

From out of the reports of the machine guns which we have captured from the cowardly police and SS men;

From out of the smoke of fires and the blood of the murdered Warsaw ghetto, we—imprisoned in the ghetto—send you our heartfelt fraternal greetings. We know that you watch with pain and compassionate tears, with admiration and alarm, the outcome of this war which we have been waging for many days with the cruel occupant.

Let it be known that every threshold in the ghetto has been and will be a fortress, that we may all perish in the struggle, but we will not surrender; that, like you, we breathe with desire for revenge for all the crimes of our common foe.

A battle is being waged for your freedom as well as ours.

For your and our human, civic, and national honor and dignity.

We shall avenge the crimes of Auschwitz, Treblinka, Belzec, Majdanek!

Long live the brotherhood of arms and blood of fighting Poland!

Long Live freedom!

Death to the hangmen and torturers!

Long live the struggle for life and death against the occupant.[100]

By the end of the first week of the "ghetto operation," Stroop reported increasing success apprehending the remaining ghetto population: those Jews caught hiding in bunkers, those burned out of buildings in the ghetto, and those discovered in the sewers under the city. On April 24, 1943, Stroop counted 25,500 Jews apprehended; by May 3, 41,806 Jews apprehended, although it is clear that his total numbers were inflated.[101]

On the twentieth day of fighting, May 8, 1943, the central command bunker of the ZOB at Mila 18 was discovered and the Germans began to pipe poison gas into the bunker to flush the Jewish fighters out. Arieh Wilner called upon the fighters to take cyanide pills they had prepared rather than submit to the Germans; most of those in the group, including Anielewicz, did so when they could no longer fight off the gas. A group of six fighters, including Tosia Altman, who had managed to breathe through a concealed opening in the bunker, were found that night by Zivia Lubetkin and Marek Edelman, who helped the group escape from the ghetto via the sewers.[102] Lubetkin later recalled the last moments of her comrades in Mila 18 after the Germans began to pump poison gas into the bunker:

---

100. *Revolt Amid the Darkness* (USHMM, 1993), 193; reprinted from Lucy Dawidowicz, *A Holocaust Reader* (New York: Behrman House, 1976), 357–59.

101. Ibid., Stroop Report, 197.

102. Altman died on May 26, 1943 as a result of a fire that had broken out in a celluloid factory where she was hiding with the surviving fighters from the ghetto on the Aryan side of Warsaw; described by Shalev, "Tosia Altman," jwa.org/encyclopedia (accessed 2/24/2012).

It was the death sentence for one hundred and twenty Jewish fighters. It was not a quick death, either. The Germans used only enough gas to suffocate them slowly. Aryeh Vilner was the first to challenge: "Let us kill ourselves rather than surrender to the Germans alive!" The sound of shots filled the air. The Jewish fighters began taking their own lives. If a pistol didn't fire, its confused and wretched owner would beg a comrade to have pity and shoot him, but no one dared. Berl Broyde, who had been wounded in the hand and was unable to hold a gun, implored his comrades to end his life. Mordecai Anielewicz, who believed that water would remove the lethal effects of the gas, suggested they drench their faces. Someone suddenly discovered a way out of the bunker hidden from the Germans' view. Only a few managed to escape. The others died a slow death of poisoned suffocation.[103]

Most of the remaining fighters were killed in the ghetto.

On May 12, 1943, the Bundist leader Szmuel Zygielbojm committed suicide in London to protest the lack of assistance for the insurgents on the part of Western governments:

I cannot continue to live and to be silent while the remnants of Polish Jewry, whose representative I am, are being murdered. My comrades in the Warsaw ghetto fell with arms in their hands in the last heroic battle. I was not permitted to fall like them, together with them, but I belong with them, to their mass grave. By my death, I wish to give expression to my most profound protest against the inaction in which the world watches and permits the destruction of the Jewish people.[104]

On May 16, 1943, Stroop celebrated the final liquidation of the ghetto by ordering the destruction of the Great Synagogue on Tlomacki Street. After a month of fighting, the ghetto was in ruins. Stroop reported the capture of over 56,065 Jews and the destruction of 631 bunkers, killing 7,000 Jews in the uprising and deporting another 7,000 to Treblinka.[105] Following the final capture of the ghetto by German forces, German SS and police units deported many of those who survived the armed revolt to Treblinka, and sent others to Majdanek and forced labor camps at Trawniki and Poniatowa in the Generalgouvernement. The Warsaw Ghetto Uprising, as the first mass revolt in a major city in German-occupied Europe, became a symbol of Jewish resistance to Nazi oppression, inspiring similar revolts in Bialystok and Minsk, as well as uprisings in Treblinka and Sobibor later in 1943. The Jewish fighters in Warsaw, under-equipped and over-matched, with few weapons and almost no military training, isolated and

---

103. Quoted in *Revolt Amid the Darkness*, 206. Reprinted from Zivia Lubetkin, *In the Days of Destruction and Revolt*, (Israel: Ghetto Fighters' House, 1981), 178–246.

104. Last letter of Szmul Zygielbojm, May 11, 1943, in Yitzak Arad, Yisrael Gutman, Abraham Margaliot, eds., *Documents on the Holocaust* (Jerusalem: Yad Vashem, 1981), 324–27.

105. See Stroop Report in *Revolt Amid the Darkness*, 199.

surrounded by an indifferent and often hostile population, malnourished and diseased, managed to hold off the German forces for as long as the entire Polish Army had in the invasion of Poland at the beginning of the war. But it was not enough.

After the revolt had been crushed, Ringelblum mourned the loss of Anielewicz:

And so died one of the best, one of the noblest, who had from the beginning of his life dedicated himself to the service of the Jewish people, to protect its honor and dignity. The working class will remember that he was one of the few who had, right from the first moment, tried to serve the world revolution and the first proletarian state in the world.[106]

106. Ringelblum, *Ksovim fun Geto*, 2:330, in Kassow, *Who Will Write Our History?* 372.

Esther Gitman

18   Courage to Defy

Jews of the Independent State of
Croatia Fight Back, 1941–45

I will focus on Jewish resistance against the Axis powers and their local collaborators, the Croatian Ustaše, in the Independent State of Croatia (Nezavisna Država Hrvatska, NDH) which, during World War II, also included Bosnia and Herzegovina (BiH). This essay uncovers the available evidence that Jews in NDH exhibited a strong will to resist while the Ustaše, acting under the auspices of Nazi authorities, transported approximately 30,000 Jews to local concentration camps and to German labor or death camps by 1944. Because Jews fought back, 9,500 of them in the NDH survived.

From the start, Pavelić's Ustaše regime combined in cruelty and brutality the worst of Croatian Fascism and German Nazism. Yet archival material and the stories of survivors document the prevalence of resistance. Using these sources, we discover that the annihilation of 75 percent of Jews in the NDH during World War II does not prove an absence of resistance on the part of Jews. We will also examine why most Croatian Jews initially showed a dangerous complacency about their situation at a time when their enemies had a well-developed plan for their annihilation. Moreover, those Jews who did decide to join the Partisans faced considerable difficulties. I begin with a brief outline of the nature of the enemy, the obstacles confronting the Jews, and the absence of strong Jewish leadership. The analysis of these issues will demonstrate why, despite their attempts to defy their enemies, so many Jews perished during the first six months of the war.

426

Historical Background

By November 1940, Hitler was relentlessly pressuring the Kingdom of Yugoslavia to join Germany, Italy, and Japan in the recently concluded Tripartite Pact, thus aligning with its neighbors Bulgaria, Romania, and Hungary. On March 25, 1941, the government of Prince Regent Pavel Karađorđević reached a decision to accept Germany's overtures, and on March 26, Yugoslavia's representatives in Vienna signed the agreement. The ink had not yet dried when vocal objections to the submission arose from various military, political, and social elements. The following day, Belgrade awoke to news of a coup d'état. Several pro-Western military officers and politicians opposed to the pact rallied supporters who paraded through the streets shouting: "Better grave than slave" and "Better war than pact."[1] Elated and inspired by the spirit of defiance and by the military's revolt, the country's Jews among many others felt admiration for their countrymen. Yet their exuberance was short-lived and their hopes quickly dashed.

Hitler reacted forcefully and decisively to this insolence, aiming to destroy Yugoslavia militarily and thus reduce the threat of British air power against the southern flank of the German armies. Moreover, he decided to dismember Yugoslavia politically, using not only Axis military forces but also right-wing Croats and Yugoslavia's other national minorities, especially the half-million Volksdeutsche (citizens of German ancestry). By making Croatia an independent state, Hitler thought he could satisfy widespread separatist feelings among Croats who chafed at what they viewed as Serb domination. Henceforth German agents intensified their subversive activities in Zagreb in preparation for the Wehrmacht's entrance into the city.[2] On April 5, 1941, the Yugoslav kingdom signed an agreement of friendship with the USSR. Its reasons for this move are not entirely clear, although Germany had signed a similar pact in 1939. Rather than being flattered, Hitler questioned the intentions behind this decision.[3] On April 6, 1941, the Axis powers—Nazi Germany, Fascist Italy, Hungary, and Bulgaria—attacked Yugoslavia from four directions; the Luftwaffe meanwhile bombed Belgrade and other cities, killing thousands.

1. Jozo Tomasevich, *War and Revolution in Yugoslavia, 1941–1945: Occupation and Collaboration* (Stanford, Calif.: Stanford University Press, 2001), 47–48.

2. Esther Gitman, *When Courage Prevailed: The Rescue and Survival of Jews in the Independent State of Croatia, 1941–1945* (St Paul, Minn.: Paragon House, 2011), 22.

3. Ante Nazor and Zoran Ladić, *History of Croatians: Illustrated Chronology* (Zagreb: Multigraf, 2003), 350.

On April 10, 1941, the NDH was proclaimed and the Axis partners installed Dr. Ante Pavelić as *Poglavnik* (head) of this entity. Although Mussolini had groomed Pavelić for this role, Hitler readily agreed, knowing that many of his Ustaše supporters were Nazi sympathizers. Moreover, Pavelić's Bosnian birth and his ten years in exile, most of it in Italy, were political liabilities in a nationalist Croatia, making him more malleable for Germany.[4] In return for Croatian territorial gains and "independence" from Serbia, Nazi Germany demanded that Pavelić's regime implement the Nazi-like ideology enshrined in legislation for the "Protection of the Croatian (Aryan) People." With German indulgence, Pavelić and his entourage developed a somewhat idiosyncratic notion of racial purity that encompassed not just the Volksdeutsche and the 6.3 million nominally Slavic Croats but also the 750,000 Bosnian Muslims in the BiH, whom the new state deemed Croats and thus honorary Aryans.[5]

From Zagreb, the Wehrmacht—accompanied by SS troops—marched south, reaching Sarajevo, the capital of BiH, on April 15. The Yugoslav Army collapsed on April 17, and by April 18, the twenty-three-year union of the South Slavs was history, as was the Federation of Jewish Religious Communities of Yugoslavia. The partition of Yugoslavia and the distribution of its territories among Axis partners triggered a civil war that exacerbated the viciousness of anti-Jewish policies. The contest for Yugoslavia involved primarily the Ustaše, both Croat and Muslim, the Četniks, a remnant of the former Royal Serbian Army, the Volksdeutsche, and the Partisans, encompassing diverse ethnic, religious and political affiliations. Three of these four warring parties found common cause in hunting down and murdering Jews; only the Partisans invited Jews to join their ranks and after the capitulation of Italy in September 1943 also shielded thousands of them.[6] Under Axis occupation, Yugoslavia again reverted to a collection of disparate states, all of them plagued by chaos and civil war.[7]

Treating the former Kingdom of Yugoslavia as plunder, Nazi Germany kept its most lucrative regions for itself, while also rewarding its allies, Hungary, Bulgaria, and Italy. Italy annexed "Zone I," a small stretch of land along the

---

4. On Italy's hopes that Pavelić would reward them with territorial gains, see Galeazzo Ciano, *The Ciano Diaries, 1939–1943* (New York: Simon Publication, 2001), 341.

5. See the letter from Edmund Glaise von Horstenau, Germany's plenipotentiary general in Croatia, November 26, 1941, to Colonel Friedrich von Mellenthin, Wehrmacht High Command (OKW). U.S. Department of State, *Documents on German Foreign Policy, 1918–1945* (hereafter DGFP) (Washington, D.C.: 1960–64), Series D, 12:515–17.

6. See Gitman, *When Courage Prevailed*, 23–24 and all of chapter 6.

7. Hrvoje Matković, *Povijest Nezavisne Države Hrvatske* (Zagreb: Naklada P.I.P, 1994), 242.

Adriatic; "Zone II" was jointly controlled by the Italian military and the NDH civil administration. Nonetheless, there was no question as to which Axis partner was in control.

Jews under Attack

The threat of a Nazi attack on Yugoslavia confronted its Jewish citizens with two existential choices: flee the mainland to the Adriatic coast or stay put. The fact that most Jews decided to remain where they were was in no small measure due to the editors of the Jewish weekly newspapers, who calmly suggested to their readers that Yugoslavia was different from other Eastern and Central European countries, where antisemitism was prevalent.[8] Was their reaction a consequence of eternal optimism, or did it come from an acute realization that Europeans were oblivious to their plight and that no other country would accept them? Ivo Goldstein, in *Holocaust in Zagreb,* suggests that Yugoslav Jews might have had reason to doubt that the impending war would have genocidal consequences in Yugoslavia, despite the appearance of some antisemitic pamphlets and street skirmishes.[9] Moreover, most Jews at that point anticipated Hitler's imminent attack on Russia. With such a daunting campaign ahead, why would Germany be diverted by Yugoslavia? Many Croatian and Bosnian Jews, though aware of National Socialist Germany's persecution of their coreligionists, supposed that conversion to Catholicism and Islam would gain them protection.

The Jewish leadership itself advised that the best way to survive was to stay put, to listen to instructions from the authorities, and to keep a low profile until everything had passed. Michael (Mišo) Montiljo—a twelve-year-old boy when the Germans entered Sarajevo—recalls how the members of his community approached their rabbi daily, asking whether they should pack and flee. His answer was always the same: "Stay where you are. It is possible that they may send you to a labor camp and even rough you up a bit. But you would live and return to your homes."[10] These comforting words sounded more reliable and reassuring than the horror stories they had heard from the thousands of transient immigrants who passed through Yugoslavia from countries already invaded by the Nazis. Now they could not conceive of leaving, refusing to be-

8. *Židov,* 37/1938, 8-15/1939.

9. Ivo Goldstein and Slavko Goldstein, *Holokaust u Zagrebu,* [Holocaust in Zagreb] (Zagreb: Novi Liber, 2001), 78–88.

10. Michael Montiljo, Gitman interview, Zagreb, Croatia, January 15, 2003.

lieve that they would experience the same fate their ancestors had experienced in fifteenth-century Spain.[11]

In her memoir, Zdenka Steiner Novak attempted to explain why her wealthy and well-informed father was in no hurry to leave their home in Zagreb: "Our fatal mistake was that of not taking Hitler seriously. During all those years he announced his plans to the world, shouting so loudly that heaven and hell could shake, yet we did not hear or did not want to hear. When it did happen, it seemed so unexpected, like a whirlwind destroying everything in its way with violent blows."[12] It appears that even those who had the financial means and opportunities to escape did not believe that their destiny in Croatia could be as bad as it was elsewhere in Europe.

Yet, in accord with Nazi racial ideology, the NDH set upon purging its Jews in three stages: First, accomplish their economic destruction by dismissing them from all government and civil service posts and by shutting down their private enterprises, thus ensuring their inability to earn a living.[13] Second, demolish their synagogues and cultural institutions, thereby destroying their spirit. Third, give the appearance of legitimacy to murderous acts by charging the Jews with collective responsibility for disseminating lies about the conduct of the government, thus disturbing the public peace and order. In response to their "subversive" conduct, on April 30—twenty days after its creation—the NDH imposed harsh collective measures on Croatian Jews, effectively providing legal justification for their murder and for the punishment of any Croat who assisted them.[14] Meanwhile, the Third Reich initiated and organized the genocide of Jews and other targeted groups throughout the former Yugoslavia, and in some areas where they lacked local collaborators, they were also the executioners. To prepare the ground for the Jewish genocide, the Nazis ensured that anti-Jewish measures were introduced and fully implemented throughout the territories, measures which, if "properly" implemented, would lead to "the annihilation of the Jews."[15] Historian Raul Hilberg singled out Croatia for its efficiency in implementing anti-Jewish policies: within four months, by the end of August 1941, the Ustaše government had Aryanized most Jewish enterprises, prohibited Croa-

11. Goldstein and Goldstein, *Holokaust u Zagrebu*, 95.

12. Zdenka Novak, *When Heaven's Vault Cracked* (Braunton: Devon, 1995), 31.

13. Gitman, *When Courage Prevailed*, 28.

14. National Archives and Records Administration, RG59, 860-H.4016/64, PS/RJH, "Persecution of Jews in Croatia, Zagreb, June 13, 1941." See also *Zbornik Zakona i Naredba Nezavisne Države Hrvatske* (Listing of NDH rules, decrees and regulations) (Zagreb: NDH, 1941).

15. Jaša Romano, *Jevreji Jugoslavije 1941–1945: Žrtve genocida i učesnici narodno-oslobodilačkog rata* (Belgrade: JIM, Published by the Federation of Jewish Communities in Yugoslavia, 1980), 31–32.

tians from intermarrying with Jews, employing female Aryan servants under age forty-five, or raising the Croatian flag, and so on. Hilberg argues that it had taken Nazi bureaucrats more than eight years to think up and implement the model policies, whereas the Ustaše managed to implement them within a few months[16]

Yugoslavia in the Historiography of the Holocaust

Holocaust historiography in the countries of the former Yugoslavia has focused heavily on the rightly notorious atrocities perpetrated by the Axis powers and their local collaborators. After the war the new Yugoslavian government established official Commissions for the Ascertainment of Crimes Committed by the Occupiers and their Local Collaborators against the Jews, whose duties included taking testimonies from Jewish survivors and from those who had relevant information, in order to identify the criminals and bring them to justice. For many years historians have studied these documents with an objective to expose the atrocities. Only after the disintegration of Communist Yugoslavia and the opening of the archives to the general public, has attention been paid to what testimonies and documents reveal about such subjects as the rescue of Jews by non-Jews, the rescue of Jews by other Jews, and Jewish resistance as integral parts of the Holocaust. In recent years, Holocaust historiography has increasingly turned to its victims, in particular letting the survivors tell their own stories. This redirection and broadening of research is a welcome change, expanding attention to the proactive role that individuals as well as groups of Jews played in ultimately defeating their enemies' genocidal ambitions and plans for territorial conquest. Importantly, these studies undermine the commonly held notion that during World War II the Jews went to their death like sheep to slaughter.

Any discussion of resistance first requires an understanding of the concept of resistance. Initially Holocaust historian Yehuda Bauer, for example, defined resistance as "any group action consciously taken in opposition to known or surmised laws, actions or intentions directed against the Jews by the Germans and their supporters." In time, however, Bauer used only one Hebrew term, *amidah*, which he defined as "standing up against" as an appropriate term to describe all forms of resistance.[17] Following Bauer and informed by interviews

16. Raul Hilberg, *The Destruction of the European Jews*, rev. and expanded ed. (New York: Holmes and Meier Publishers, 1985), 711.

17. Yehuda Bauer, *Rethinking the Holocaust* (New Haven, Conn.: Yale University Press, 2002), 119–20.

I conducted with World War II survivors, resistance on the part of Jews in occupied Yugoslavia will be understood here as: any purposeful action undertaken
by individuals or groups of Jews to defy the Nazi and Ustaše racial laws and
their ideology of genocide. The following discussion will focus on the various
ways in which Jews resisted their oppressors: Nazi Germany, the Ustaše, the
Četniks, and the Volksdeutsche militia.

Jews among the Partisans

Young Jews were among many in the post-World War I generation to search
for universal causes that promised to improve the lot of mankind, and in their
case, also that of their fellow Jews. By 1932 the Communist Party of Yugoslavia
had persuaded many of these young Jews that its revolutionary ideals were in
harmony with the centuries-old aspirations for justice for their people.[18] In July
1941, three months into the occupation of Yugoslavia, the Communist Party
decided that the time was ripe to start a popular uprising. Young Jews were
among those who joined when, a few days later, the first partisan units were
formed.

In my conversation with General Vladimir Velebit in 2003, he suddenly
asked: "Why did so few Jews join the Partisans"? Momentarily stunned by his
question, I instinctively responded that I was under the impression that many
Jewish men, as well as women, had rushed to join them.[19] I wondered whether
Velebit was aware that Yugoslavia's Jewish population in 1941 had been less
than 0.46 percent of the total population. Nonetheless, his question lingered in
my mind, and I felt that I had to determine the accuracy of his implied charge,
especially considering that Jews surely had many reasons to fight the occupiers—indeed their lives depended on it. My research ultimately demonstrated the
accuracy of Velebit's observation: in the beginning, only a few hundred Jews
joined the Partisans. However, many reasons prevented them initially from
joining the Partisans in large numbers. First, the German occupation troops and
their local collaborators took strong and almost immediate measures against
Jewish men, aiming to prevent them from joining the Partisans or to block their

18. Eva Nahir, a World War II survivor and one of the leading young Communists of that era,
recalled the prevailing spirit and Communist ideology among many young Jews as a "dream come
true" and their "entry into the human race." Gitman interview, Kibbutz Shaar Hamakim, Israel, August 23, 2003.

19. Vladimir Velebit, Gitman interview, Zagreb, Croatia, February 4, 2003.

escape, especially to the Italian zones or to Palestine. Second, only a limited number of underground channels were open to Jews, and the Partisans, fearful of betrayal by infiltrators, accepted only those who had been known party members before the war. Third, in 1941, Partisans in some regions, for instance in Bačka, required that anyone wanting to join their ranks bear their own arms.

Despite all these difficulties, ninety Jews from Macedonia joined the war of national liberation in 1941. In addition, 277 Jews from communities throughout Yugoslavia were recruited to a special action group responsible for acts of sabotage and diversion in Belgrade, Sarajevo, Zagreb, Subotica, Novi Sad, Sombor, and other cities.[20] Also in 1941, 382 Jews from the territory of Bosnia and Herzegovina joined partisan groups. Poorly armed and unaccustomed to fighting, these Jews soon incurred 300 casualties. Nonetheless, 616 more Jews from various parts of the country joined the struggle in 1942, themselves suffering 118 casualties. Jaša Romano, a Yugoslav historian and a former Partisan, attributes Jews' initially small numbers to their clannishness, which allowed them as a group to be manipulated by their leaders and rabbis into believing that they would not become victims of genocide. There was also a widespread notion that German soldiers would soon be shipped off to the Eastern Front to fight the Soviets. Finally, young Jews were deeply concerned that joining the Partisans would put their family members in danger. Nonetheless, the number of Jews fighting with the Partisans began to swell by the summer of 1942.

Dr. Stjepan Steiner described how, by the beginning of 1942, the Partisans desperately needed physicians. The Ustaše had exempted approximately 170 Jewish physicians from anti-Jewish policies if they agreed to serve with a special NDH medical corps to address an epidemic of endemic syphilis in the mountainous regions in Bosnia. Many of these physicians had a keen desire to join the Partisans, but they feared for the well-being of their families, who were protected from deportation only so long as their relative was in government service. As a ruse, the physicians asked the Partisans to arrange defections that appeared to be abductions by force against the doctors' will. Steiner and his wife, Dr. Zora Goldsmith, joined the Partisans in 1942, after such a staged kidnapping, which took place in broad daylight so that everyone could see how they struggled to escape from the grip of the Partisans. In so doing, they protected the lives of family members, while joining the war and the resistance against the enemy.[21]

---

20. Romano, *Jevreji Jugoslavije 1941–1945*, 202–76. This includes a detailed description of all individuals known to have joined any of the several partisan armies (NOV, NOP, NOB, NOR).

21. Stjepan Steiner, Gitman interview, Zagreb, Croatia, December 16, 2002.

Zlatko Glik, one of several Jews I interviewed in Zagreb, recounted the day in January 1942 when, with the help of leftist activist friends, he joined the Partisans. It was a particularly cold winter, and he had to reach the mountainous region of Moslovačka Gora in Croatia. Glik explained that this area sheltered a small Partisan contingent of forty-two people. Such units were typical: small and effective, comprising largely young people who did not share their real names or personal information. This code made it difficult to determine how many Jews joined the Partisans. Glik chose for himself the name Gorky.

We owe knowledge of instances when this code of secrecy was broken under extenuating circumstances to a 1944 story by Hinko Gottlieb, a Jewish writer who combined such incidents in the following account:

Kaddish in the Forest

That day, at sundown, Žanka, a partisan woman was buried. She was buried where she fell trying to stop an onslaught of Germans and Ustaši.

A grave was dug and they put her in....

Drago, standing near Toša, blurted out:

"Still, we should say Kaddish for her."

"What should we say?" asked the Commander....

"Jewish prayer for the dead," said Drago.

"Why Jewish prayer?" wondered the Commander.

"Because she was Jewish. There are some other Jews here."

"Other Jews? Who is Jewish?"

"I!" "And I!" "And I!" three of them announced.

The Commander was amazed.

"Well then, go on, say the prayer for her as you think is proper."

"Do you know how to say the Kaddish?" Tošo asked Drago....

Three Jewish Partisans, in the heart of Lika, above the grave of their comrade, decided to say Kaddish.

"Go on Drago, say it!" He began: "Jisgadal vejiskadash shemej raba...."

Not knowing the rest, he exclaimed, "When you stand in front of Him tell Him to see what has happened to us. There are not enough of us even to say the Kaddish with you. Amen." "Amen," repeated the twenty-two Partisans.[22]

This story provides a glimpse into the mindset of the young Jews—and their comrades —who were bidding goodbye to a Partisan, a comrade in arms who happened to be a Jewish woman, in a form of resistance against their own fear of oblivion. Memoirs, monographs, diaries and other forms of commentating the Holocaust that I have examined are filled with similar stories.

22. Hinko Gottlieb, "Kadiš u Šumi" [Kaddish in the forest] (Beograd: Jevrejski Almanah, Savez Jevrejskih Opština, 1954), 209–10.

Collective Decisions to Resist the Occupiers Reached after Italy's Capitulation

On September 8, 1943, the day Italy capitulated, the Italian concentration camp on the Island of Rab, officially "Campo di concentramento per internati civili di Guerra—Arbe," held approximately 3,366 Jews and 28,000 Slovene and Croat inmates.[23] Although the Italian Army laid down its arms, the inmates rightfully assumed that within hours the German Army would take over most of the former Italian territories in Croatia. The impending situation would be disastrous for all the former inmates, and especially disastrous for the Jews, who had to find a way to resist the enemy.

The Jewish refugees on Rab immediately called their first general meeting for September 9, in order to decide how to confront their new situation. Those assembled quickly appointed a six-member board to represent them in all negotiations with the outside world. Most decided to place their fate in the hands of the Croatian Partisans, who had already been contacted before the capitulation.[24] Within days, a contingent of Partisans appeared on the island.[25] Based on Italian and German documents and subsequent research, it becomes apparent that, despite the refugees' concerns, the Nazis lacked the manpower required to attack Rab immediately after Italy's capitulation.[26] The resultant period of respite from German attack allowed the Partisans to evacuate all the Jews who wished to leave the island. The Croatian Partisan headquarters issued an order to its marine staff to prepare vessels, as well as a number of trucks to transfer the refugees to Senj on the Dalmatian coast. From there, if necessary, the refugees could march toward the liberated territories.[27]

A group of about 211 Jews chose to remain on Rab, while another group,

---

23. HDA, ZKRZ-GUZ 2235/12-45, box 11, Židovi u logoru na otoku Rabu, žrtve fašizma i taljinskog imperialisma, 1229–58.

24. Jaša Romano, "Jevreji u logoru Na Rabu i njihove uključivanje u Narodnooslobodilački rat" [Jews in the Rab Camp and their participation in the liberation war], *Zbornik* 2 (1973): 1–68.

25. Vlado Stringer, *Jugoslavija 1941–1945* (Beograd: Vojnoizdravački zavod, 1969). Partisan strength peaked at 800,000 in April 1945 at the time the greater portion of Yugoslavia was under Partisan control.

26. Gerhardt Schreiber, *Die Italienischen-Militärinternierten im deutschen Machtbereich 1943–1945* (Munich: edited by Verraten-Verachtet-Vergessen, Militärgeschichtlichen Forschungsamt, Bd. 28, 1990), 93–214.

27. Yad Vashem Archive, JM/24, October 31, 1943, a collection of documents and articles about the period. The National Antifascist Army for the Liberation of Croatia in documents #1444 summarized the "Decision" reached with the Jewish representatives of the camp to evacuate the Jewish refugees from the Island of Rab to the freed territories.

similar in number, took responsibility for their fate when they hired boats with the intention of reaching the Italian shore. Most of the young people among the former Rab inmates joined the Partisans: approximately 1,000 in the Liberation Army's fighting forces and 648 in the auxiliary units, serving as physicians, nurses, teachers, journalists, photographers, administrators, and cooks.[28] Those Jews who could not bear arms—including the sick, the elderly, women, and children—followed the troops into the already liberated territories of Croatia, where they joined large groups of refugees designated "Zbjeg." From the statistical survey conducted by the Partisans, 38 percent were men, 47 percent women, and 15 percent children under fifteen. By the end of the war, the number of Jewish fighters drawn from former Rab inmates reached 1,339, of whom 119 were killed in action and seventeen died from various other causes. Most survived the war.[29] The Army of National Liberation recognized and decorated those Jews who had joined in 1941 and those who distinguished themselves in combat. One hundred and fifty Jews are holders of the Partisan Star: ten are listed as Peoples' Heroes; fourteen reached the rank of general, two as lieutenant general, two as major general, and ten as brigadier general.

The Partisan authorities wished to help the demoralized survivors who were unfit for combat, and this they did by recruiting them to perform various tasks aimed at rebuilding Yugoslavia. The working units were composed of women and the elderly; all of a sudden they felt rejuvenated and their morale soared. I had conversations with Ella Finci Koen, Erna Kaveson Debenić, and Erna Gaon Latinović.[30] All of these women had been sheltered by the Partisans; through talking with them I first began to understand the difficulties they had endured after Italy's capitulation. But I also noticed their enthusiasm even after sixty years, when describing their good fortune in being given the opportunity to live another day as free human beings. They were grateful to the international humanitarian organizations that had cared for them and to ZAVNOH.[31] They had not been forgotten and abandoned after all. The physical and mental activity

---

28. Two hundred and forty-three young Jews freed from Rab formed their own combat unit, known as the Jewish Rab Battalion. Because of strategic reasons as well as concern for individual soldiers' lives, the unit was dissolved; the soldiers were dispersed into other general units.

29. Aleksandar Demajo, "Jevrejski vod u prvoj prekomorskoj brigadi NOVJ." The Jewish battalion was formed in Bari, Italy in the fall of 1943. See *Zbornik* 7, Jevrejski Istorijski Muzej-Beograd (1997): 185–89.

30. Gitman interviews with Ella Finci Koen, Erna Kaveson Debenić, and Erna Gaon Latinović, Jewish Community of Sarajevo, Bosnia-Herzegovina, August 11 and 12, 2003.

31. ZAVNOH, Zemaljsko antifašističkom vijeće narodnog oslobođnja Hrvatske (Anti-Fascist Board People's Liberation of Croatia.)

needed for erecting schools and kitchens and for rebuilding the infrastructure signified renewal. Their hopes for a better future were also encouraged by the supplies and monies they were able to receive from Jewish friends and relatives from southern Italy and Palestine. With help from the Partisans and Allied forces, Jews incarcerated in Korčula and the neighboring islands were transferred to the safety of southern Italy where they stayed till the end of the war.

The Partisans also benefited from young Jews who had fled the occupied territories and found a way to join partisan groups. For example, a group in Bari, Italy, organized the First Overseas Brigade (Prva prekomorska brigada) on the Italian side of the Adriatic Sea. This twenty-two-person platoon, comprising twenty Jews from the former Yugoslavia and two from Pisa, eventually joined the inland forces. In testimony to the postwar National Commission for the Ascertainment of Crimes Committed by the Occupiers and their Local Collaborators against the Jews (hereafter National Commission), Dr. Josip Presburger described the general disillusionment of the approximately 400 Jewish officers and soldiers with the Yugoslav Royal Army because of their swift capture by the Germans. They had legitimate reasons for despair in the Nuremberg POW camps in the heartland of Nazi Germany. All along they were naturally worried about the unknown fate of their families at home. In his testimony, however, Presburger, with a measure of hope, described the first steps of the officers, including non-Jews, in forming an illegal Communist Party cell in the camp. Its primary aim was to instill faith in the coming victory of the Allies and in the subsequent rebirth of Yugoslavia. As a consequence, the officers' despair and disorientation swiftly faded, replaced by the will to live and see their aspirations for a free Yugoslavia fulfilled. In May 1942, the overwhelming majority joined in political, cultural, and professional activities that even further invigorated them. For a time the center of this illegal activity was in room No. 7 of Jewish barrack No. 37, which managed to obtain and hide a radio, enabling the prisoners to listen to Allied broadcasts. They transmitted the edited news through established channels to other barracks.

As the Western Allies advanced eastward, in January 1945, the Jewish POWs were transferred to a camp in Barkenbrugge, near the former Polish border, where the Red Army was swiftly encroaching. One of their groups succeeded in overpowering the German guards, and in March 1945, assisted by Soviet authorities, it reached Yugoslavia through Poland and Romania. The other POWs, less fortunate, walked southward for four weeks under difficult conditions. Nevertheless, most reached their homes. Jews who were repatriated either joined the new Yugoslav Army or were given duties in the country's administration.[32] They resisted the forces of darkness with courage and determination.

Resistance in Concentration Camps

Ervin Miler was seventeen years old in 1941 when he was deported to the NDH Jasenovac labor and concentration camp, where he spent almost four years. His deepest memories of a place he described as hell on earth were of hunger, thirst, and brutal beatings. But his worst enemy was the fear of premature death, before he could tell of his experience of walking for over six months practically barefoot in sackcloth-bandaged feet. The winter of 1941–42 in Europe was one of the coldest in history, and the earth was covered with deep snow. He recalled that for years he could not close his eyes without remembering his constantly wet garments and without seeing the imprints of the sackcloth on his feet that took years to fade away. Ervin did not indicate to what he attributed his survival, but from his testimony it seems that his strong desire to make known the deplorable conditions of torture and hunger played a crucial role.[33]

Đuro Schwarz was another inmate who survived Jasenovac. Invited to testify before the postwar National Commission, he identified himself as one of a group of forty-two gravediggers under the supervision of Haim Danon. Early in the morning they would get into a truck and drive for thirty minutes, then walk under guard through the woods to a large clearing. There, without pause except for harassment and beatings, they would work until four in the afternoon digging large ditches. Danon estimated that such a ditch could contain between 400 and 500 bodies. They constantly feared that they were digging what would be their own graves. In fact two of their comrades, Vilko Schlossberg from Vukovar and a certain Lowy, were buried there. Because of his Aryan wife, Schwartz was eventually released. But he attributed his survival during the early mass killing to his belonging to a group in which Danon, their group leader, had a way of dealing with the Ustaše, especially with the trigger-happy Muslim Mujo.[34]

Edit Armuth, along with her parents and 200 other Jews, decided to stay on

32. Josip Presburger, *Zbornik* 3 (Jevrejski Istorijski Muzej-Beograd Studije, Arhivska i Memoraska Građa, 1975): 225–27.

33. Miler interview, cited in Aleksandar Demajo, "The Jewish Squadron of the First Yugoslav Overseas Brigade in World War II," *Zbornik* 7 (1997): 250–303.

34. HDA, ZKRZ-GUZ 3335/2–45, box 10, Đuro Schwarz testimony.

the Island of Rab after the capitulation of Italy in September 1943 rather than accept evacuation by the Partisans. Eventually, on March 19, 1944, the unopposed Nazis took over the island and captured most of the Jews hidden by the local population. 180 of them were captured and taken to the port of Rijeka for deportation to Auschwitz. Edit was gravely ill but when the camp's Association of Anti-Fascist Women (AFŽ) learned that Edit was one of them long before she arrived at Auschwitz, they accepted her into their inner circle. About these women, she recalled that "their boundless support, nurture and protection during my six-week illness delivered me out of Auschwitz."[35] Edit's strong will to live, bolstered by the group support she received in Auschwitz, gave her an opportunity to tell her own story and those of other Yugoslavian Jews who perished.[36]

In the case of Dr. Ljudevit Rosenberg from Osijek, survival itself seems to have been a form of resistance. After the war, he was frequently interrogated by the Yugoslav secret services OZNA and UDBA about how he survived Auschwitz. He admitted that this question was constantly on his mind, although on one occasion he did remember one life-changing event during his incarceration in Auschwitz. On his birthday, November 1, 1942, Rosenberg, prisoner 61561, was sick with typhus and his temperature rose to 42° Centigrade (107.6° Fahrenheit). While hallucinating that he was 245 meters underground digging coal with other Jews, his mother appeared before his eyes and told him: "My son, you will stay alive." Then she kissed him and disappeared. After this "visit," Rosenberg eagerly awaited a meeting with Rabbi Abrahamson, who was knowledgeable in reading dreams. The rabbi told him something to the effect that he had really spoken to his mother, and from then onward, he who had been condemned to death was condemned to life. Against all odds, Rosenberg's determination to resist and survive Auschwitz kept him alive for one thousand days and nights.

Individuals and Families Made Painful Existential Decisions

Women who saw their fathers, husbands, brothers, and sons living in constant anxiety and fear of deportation insisted that, whenever possible, these men should pack up and leave for the Adriatic coast. But even if difficult deci-

---

35. HDA, ZKRZ-GUZ 2235/45, Box 10, Auschwitz.

36. Vlasta Kovać, "Life after Death" (interview with Dr. Ljudevit Rosenberg), *Kol* (*Voice of the Jewish Communities of Croatia*) 3 (Fall 2000): 49–53.

sions were reached, exit visas were hard to obtain and required a great sacrifice from the rest of a family. In such situations, the family had to decide: whom to send first? Who was the most likely to be deported first, and who was the most likely family member to survive? Once such an arduous decision was reached, men whose families selected them to leave often had great difficulty bidding goodbye to a spouse, children, and old parents. Some decided to stay and wait for new opportunities, which rarely came. The story Jakica Danon told me typifies the mood that prevailed in Sarajevo. His family invested every penny they could scrape together to purchase an exit visa for his father, but he refused to leave until all his family was safe. A few days later, he was taken to Jasenovac concentration camp. Danon and his two sisters, all teenagers, recognizing that time was not on their side, decided to escape from Sarajevo. With other teenagers, they walked by night and rested during the day, carrying forged travel documents in case of detection.[37] These young people who seized the moment to escape often survived.

A young physician, Dr. Stjepan Steiner, along with three other doctors who had been expelled from the hospital where they worked, volunteered to visit Croatian private clinics around Zagreb and ask for contributions of first aid medications. They were successful. The donated supplies were brought to the Jewish community, where the doctors, together with other volunteers, prepared small medical kits. Representatives from Zagreb's Jewish community then welcomed each transport of Jewish deportees passing through the city with these kits, along with refreshments and vital necessities. The deportees—herded eighty to 100 in each railroad car—deeply appreciated these gifts as evidence of human kindness and generosity.[38]

In another case, Eva, after seeing her husband killed and her apartment seized, tried to remain in Zagreb and raise her infant daughter. Constantly on the move in an effort to find daily safe accomodations, after several treacherous months, she and her mother decided to join the Partisans, leaving her daughter, Vesna, for the duration of the war with a Catholic friend who was married to a Jew.[39] It took great courage to leave Vesna, but survival and refusal to accept the fate planned for them by the enemy called for bold and purposful acts of defiance.

37. Jakica Danon, Gitman interview, Sarajevo, Bosnia-Herzegovina, August 9 and 14, 2003.

38. Stjepan Steiner, Gitman interview, Zagreb, Croatia, December 16, 2002. He also mentioned non-Jews who volunteered their assistance to Jews.

39. Eva Grlić, Gitman interview, Zagreb, Croatia, February 2, 2003; Vesna Domany interview, Zagreb, Croatia, February 8, 2003.

The Jewish Communities Assist Their Fellow Jews

Responsibility for NDH concentration camps fell to the section of national supplies at the Ministry of Labor, Industry and Trade; in practice, however, Jewish communities had to undertake the task. The absurdity of the government decree of April 30, 1941 was such that the government aid remitted to the Jewish communities had been generated by obligatory payment of taxes either by Jews or by the owners of their plundered enterprises.[40] The problem, however, was that most of the Jewish assets were confiscated and the plunderers were not ready to relinquish their newly found wealth. All that the Jewish leadership could do was to file useless complaints. But after a while and out of necessity, the Jewish communities which initially took care of their own members decided to change their mode of operation.

Early into the war, the Jewish communities of Sarajevo, Zagreb, Osijek, and Slavonski Brod—among the largest under NDH jurisdiction—recognized that they had much in common and that instead of each one trying to work alone, combining their meager resources would be more effective and lasting.[41] The first joint project of the four communities was to refurbish dilapidated prison facilities the Ustaše had inherited from the previous regime and to search for suitable locations for new camps.[42] To carry out these responsibilities, their most important task was to search for volunteers who had skills to build such facilities.[43] But, more urgently, they needed funds; to obtain them, they were granted permits to send representatives to the Hungarian offices of the humanitarian organization the Joint Distribution Committee (Joint).

But their true endeavor started when the lives of the Jews began to change drastically, as on the nights of August 15 and 16, 1941, when the Jews of the town of Vukovar were captured and locked in the local synagogue. Until November 8 of that year, the Jews of Osijek assumed responsibility for their upkeep as a demonstration that Jews would care for each other. Not only did they sustain the lives of the Jews trapped there, but some, in the confusion, were able to escape and survive.

40. HDA, *Zbirka*, NDH, carton 284, #5201, 7925, 4498, 46432; carton 290, #4839.

41. Avram Pinto and David Pinto, *Dokumenti o Stradanju Jevreja u Logorima NDH* (Sarajevo: Jevrejska Opština Sarajevo, 1972), 45–65. This discussion is based on letters and minutes written by two Croatian judges, Srećko Bujas, president of the District Court of Sarajevo, who was appointed a trustee of the Sephardic community, and Branko Milaković, judge of the District Court of Sarajevo, trustee of the Ashkenazic community.

42. HDA, ZKRZ-GUZ, 2235/2–45, box 10, testimony by Judge Srećko Bujas, 225.

43. AIHRPH (HAD) *Zbirka NDH*, carton 288, no. 3769.

Esther Gitman

Reflecting its mixed culture, Sarajevo had two Jewish communities, the Sephardic and the Ashkenazic. They were assigned to two NDH trustees, Srećko Bujas and Branko Milaković, both judges before the war. Both men performed their tasks as honorable civil servants with no attempt to line their own pockets. Jews displayed similar acts of courage and defiance when large-scale internments began in Sarajevo on the night of September 3, 1941 and continued without respite till the end of November. During this time the Jewish communities of Sarajevo and Slavonski Brod (henceforth Brod) maintained an especially amicable relationship which involved daily correspondence. The two communities developed a plan whereby Jewish volunteers in Brod would welcome the transports from Sarajevo with refreshments, including hot tea, bread, cheese, and sometimes salami, as they passed through the city. These transports varied in size from 400 to over 1,000 deportees who were taken directly from labor camps to the trains. Bujas also asked the volunteers in Brod to provide the inmates with clothing and shoes. On November 7, 1941 the Jewish community of Brod sent Bujas a letter stating: "We are informing you that all the transports from Kruščica concentration camp have passed through Brod. There were about 1,600 people in total, approximately 1,350 women and children and the rest were men. The women and children received milk, tea, bread, and water in this last station. And as soon as we obtain an official authorization from NDH, we will begin collecting clothing and footwear."[44]

At times, the Ustaše gave Bujas a day's notice for an upcoming transport, or they gave him a date and then on purpose arrived a day later. In such cases the volunteers in Brod would be notified and might have to wait for hours, while the tea and the cooked food had to be discarded, especially on hot August and September days. To prevent the waste of precious food and the disappointment, volunteers began to make hard and nourishing cookies that would last for months and which the inmates could take with them. This was yet another small victory of defiance in the constant struggle for survival.[45] Moved by the generosity of spirit exhibited by the volunteers of Brod, many deportees emptied their pockets of hidden money and valuables, handing them over to the volunteers for the purchase of food for later transports. But the Brod community instead donated the money to the impoverished Jews of the Jewish community in Sarajevo. These symbolic gestures of gratitude speak volumes and should certainly be considered acts of resistance.

44. Pinto and Pinto, *Dokumenti o stradanju jevreja u logorima NDH*, 6–7.
45. Ibid., 18 (based on the correspondence between the Sarajevo and Brod communities).

Throughout the years 1942 and 1943, the chief rabbi of Zagreb, Dr. Miroslav Šalom Freiberger, in concert with the president of the community, Dr. Hugo Kon, worked tirelessly on behalf of Jewish children. They searched for donors within Croatia and abroad, especially at the beginning of the war when all their assets were frozen, confiscated, or plundered while their expenses and responsibilities grew exponentially. To this end, they developed a new institutional framework to encourage financial support for the welfare of detainees and inmates, specifically to enable Jews who had converted to Catholicism to provide funds that would not be considered a contribution to their former religion. In addition, Freiberger personally sent individual letters to potential donors like the Catholic Church, to Jewish humanitarian organizations in Switzerland, Turkey, and Portugal, as well as to the International Red Cross, DELASEM, and the Joint in Hungary and in Switzerland, and to the officers of the Italian Army on behalf of children in their occupation zone.[46] Further, Freiberger and Kon asked Archbishop Stepinac to use his Vatican connections to reach officials in the Italian interior ministry regarding exit visas.[47] When an effort to rescue hundreds of children via Turkey failed, rather than succumbing to despair, they undertook small-scale rescue actions. One result, however modest, of all these efforts on the part of many individuals and agencies from mid-1942 to mid-1943 was that eleven children ages five to sixteen left Croatia via Turkey and in April 1942 reached Palestine.[48]

The Zagreb Jewish Community took care of destitute coreligionists in that city and also in the various concentration camps. A canteen opened in May 1941 prepared 334,000 meals and sent 51,000 food packages to concentration camps until it was closed in early May 1945.[49] The Jewish community also provided refreshments and first aid kits to thousands of Jews on the transports from Sarajevo and other locations in BiH which began arriving at the large detention center in Zagreb on July 30, 1941.

Jewish leaders in Zagreb, as elsewhere, were overwhelmed by the financial hardship forced upon them by the regime. Under such duress, on July 2, 1942, Dr. Kon sent a letter (subject: "Request and Suggestion") to Interior Minister An-

46. Romano, *Jevreji Jugoslavije, 1941–1945*, 192–200.

47. Jure Krišto, *Katolička Crkva i Nezavisna Država Hrvatska 1941–1945: Dokumenti* (Zagreb: Hrvatski institut za povijest, dom i svjet, 1998), 136 (document 112: Zagregački nadbiskup Stepinac Kardinalu Maglioneu).

48. Ruth Lipa, "Jews of Yugoslavia to the Aid of Jewish Refugees: Research Pages on the Holocaust" (unpublished Master's Dissertation, Haifa University, Israel, 1986), 231–43.

49. Narcisa Lengel-Krizman, "A Contribution to the Study of Terror in the so-called Independent State of Croatia: Concentration Camps for Women in 1941–1942," *Yad Vashem Studies* 20 (1990): 33.

drija Artuković asking that he "remove from Zagreb all the Jewish newcomers and those without identification cards to a collective resettlement site that he recommended be built."[50] In August of the same year, 1,200 Jews, one of the largest transports, left Zagreb for Auschwitz. We will never know whether the timing of this transport was an unfortunate coincidence or a result of Kon's letter.

Also, in retrospect, we can see that debates were conducted regarding how to best assist Jews. These discussions among the Jews demonstrate that orders were not blindly followed. Dr. Hans Hochsinger, a convert to Catholicism, yet a Jew according to the Ustaše, had reasons to urge the Zagreb leadership to close the Jewish community office and burn all documents pertaining to their members before they become a vile tool in Nazi and Ustaše hands. He also urged the leadership to stop paying the so-called "voluntary contribution" of 1,000 kg gold, as requested by the regime as a down payment for protection. This protection money, Hochsinger argued, could be better used to purchase exit visas for Jews who wished to leave NDH.[51] Hochsinger himself perished in Jasenovac, despite his status as one of Zagreb Archbishop Stepinac's protected Jews.[52] Attempting to fathom the destruction of Europe's Jews nearly two decades later, Raul Hilberg notably condemned the cooperation between the Jewish communities and the Nazis and their collaborating regimes, arguing that both perpetrators and victims drew upon their age-old experience in dealing with each other. The Germans, however, did it with success and the Jews did it with disaster."[53]

Srečko Bujas deserves to be remembered in particular for his great personal care and concern for the welfare of the women and children in the concentration camp in Đakovo.[54] In concert with both branches of Sarajevo's Jewish leadership, Bujas decided to stop sending individual packages to camp inmates on the grounds that they, at best, received empty boxes. Subsequently, the Zagreb and Osijek communities adopted this policy in recognition that they would do the greatest good by serving the impoverished Jews in their communities who depended on them for meals. Nonetheless, the communities mobilized a volun-

50. HDA, RUR 252, Inv. # 29876.

51. Josef Ithai, "Children of Villa Emma: Rescue of the Last Youth Aliyah before the Second World War," in *The Italian Refuge: Rescue of Jews during the Holocaust*, ed. Ivo Herzer (Washington, D.C.: The Catholic University of America Press, 1989), 183.

52. Goldstein and Goldstein, *Holokaust u Zagrebu*, 570.

53. Hilberg, *The Destruction of the European Jews*, 24.

54. JIM, 2698/22/2-2/5, 9. Communication between the trustees of Sarajevo's Jewish community and the community in Zagreb. See also Menahem Shelah, ed., *History of the Holocaust—Yugoslavia* (Jerusalem: Yad Vashem, 1990), 168.

teer effort to contribute food and clothing for detention center inmates in all the NDH Jewish communities. The volunteers also assisted in the preparation of food and its delivery to sick, elderly, and needy Jews.[55]

When in January 1942, 1,830 Jewish women and children, along with fifty Serbian women from Sarajevo, were deported to Đakovo concentration camp, Bujas worked closely with the Jews of Osijek to address their plight. Initially, the volunteers from Osijek worked together with local police on the camp's administration and the internees themselves shared the daily tasks of cooking and maintaining sanitary conditions. Croatian historian Narcisa Lengel-Krizman has eloquently described the unique camp life that resulted from these efforts.

Conditions in the Đakovo camp during the first period cannot be compared with those in any other camp in the Independent State of Croatia run by the Ustaše or the Germans. The district police headquarters allowed individual prisoners to leave the camp in order to purchase necessary goods in the town, to visit the hospital in Osijek for check-ups and to call on relatives and friends. It was also decided that all children under the age of ten would be placed in homes of Jewish families in Osijek and its vicinity. In addition, in certain cases girls and boys, including 16-year-olds, obtained their release from the camp.[56]

The mother's permission was required for a child's placement in a Jewish home. Since each family could take in only one child, siblings had to be separated.[57] Zagreb's Jewish community supplied the camp with thousands of kilograms of food during this period.[58] Due to the combined efforts of all three Jewish communities, the fate of the Ashkenazi Jews of Osijek and that of the Sephardi of Sarajevo were intertwined in this attempt to save Sephardi children from annihilation. The children were placed in Ashkenazi homes. Helping the women and children from Sarajevo became a sacred mission for some Jewish men and women from Osijek. For example, Dr. Zdenko Sternberg related how his parents had purchased papers and documents for their escape to the Italian zone on the black market. However, on the designated day of departure, his father refused to leave, for the reason that, as Zdenko explained to me: "my father was responsible for the supplies that were needed in Đakovo and he re-

55. Charles W. Steckel, *Destruction and Survival* (Los Angeles, Calif.: Delmar Publishing Company, Inc., 1973), 29.

56. Lengel-Krizman, "A Contribution to the Study of Terror," 30.

57. Romano, *Jevreji Jugoslavije, 1941–1945*, 111,184.

58. AIHRPH (HDA) *Zbirka* NDH, itemization of receipts, payment orders, bills of lading, boxes 288, 296, 299, and 300.

fused to leave as long as the issue of the women and children from Sarajevo was not settled."[59] His parents, together with many other Osijek Jews, perished in Auschwitz. The brief ad hoc experiment in Jewish camp management ended abruptly on March 29, 1942, when Ustaše officials from the Jasenovac concentration camp took over the administration of Đakovo. All four major Jewish communities made a supreme effort to assist and rescue as many children and women from Đakovo as possible and up to mid-1942 they were pleased with their success.

However, when the Ustaše arrived at Osijek, they removed the district police and forbade representatives of Osijek's Jewish community from visiting or contacting the camp's internees.[60] Food that was shipped to the camp at great expense rarely reached the inmates; most of it was stolen and the rest was left in the pantries to spoil. In despair, the Jewish leadership from Zagreb wrote to the papal representative Giuseppe Ramiro Marcone and to Archbishop Alojzije Stepinac of Zagreb. Both tried in vain to convince Pavelić to stop the persecution of the Jews.[61] The end of the Đakovo camp came on August 8, 1942, when the first transport with 1,200 Jews left Osijek; among them were 600–700 children, some 300 of whom were originally from Sarajevo. Only forty to fifty Sarajevo children who had been placed in Jewish homes remained in Osijek after the August 1942 deportation.

Due to the threat of additional roundups in Osijek, the leadership of the Jewish community determined that they were no longer in a position to care for the children. Thus they contacted the Jewish community in Split, which was in the Italian occupation zone, to ask whether they would care for the remaining, now orphaned children. Not only did the Split community send a favorable response, they immediately sent individuals to Osijek who were skilled in transferring Jewish refugees across enemy lines. The majority of the Osijek children arrived safely in Split.

Italy's capitulation on September 8, 1943 removed the protection of the Italian army. In anticipation of a Nazi occupation, the Osijek orphans who were transferred to Split, with financial and other assistance from DELASEM (Delegazione Assistenza Emigranti), a humanitarian organization for Jewish emigrants, were transferred to Italy where they joined other Jewish children in

59. Zdenko Sternberg, Gitman interview, Zagreb, Croatia, January 12, 2003.
60. HDA, ZKRZ, GUZ, carton 10, #2235/7bc-45. See also Lengel-Krizman, "A Contribution to the Study of Terror," 38–39.
61. Steckel, *Destruction and Survival*, 28–29, 46.

Villa Emma in Nonantola, a region of Modena.[62] It is clear that without the collaborative efforts of Zagreb, Sarajevo, Osijek, and Brod to save as many human lives as possible, the Ustaše would have inflicted even greater human losses and suffering.[63]

The historiographic literature on the fate of the Jews in occupied Croatia and Bosnia-Herzegovina is filled with thousands of poignant accounts which, while collectively describing a tragedy, also tell stories of courage on the part of individuals and groups that refused to reconcile themselves to the fate their enemies had ordained for them. These stories convincingly convey their indefatigable determination to fight for their personal freedom and that of their country. They relate the deeds of heroic Jews who joined the Partisans and of Jewish community officials who, with relentless determination, searched for ways to improve the living conditions of those who had lost everything. We witness an unconquerable will to live nourished in great part by an irrepressible need to record the atrocities committed against them.

62. Ithai, "Children of Villa Emma," 178–204.

63. JIM, file ŽOZ, 4859, K-65-1/1–172, a letter from Dr. Hugo Kon to the Sarajevo Jewish community.

Ştefan Ionescu

19   Legal Tools Instead of Weapons

Jewish Resistance to the State Takeover of
Urban Real Estate and Businesses during
the Antonescu Regime, 1940–44

I will investigate the different forms of Jewish resistance to the Antonescu regime, focusing on the use of legalities to bypass the process of Romanianization or Aryanization or state takeover of businesses and urban real estate, a
process that aimed to exclude Jews from the local economy and, ultimately,
from society.[1] The use of legal tools, mainly sabotage and judicial contestation
by tens of thousands of Romanian Jews, was resistance to the Holocaust at its
best.[2] If the seizure of Jewish properties, businesses, and jobs, as envisioned

The writing of this chapter was supported by the Claims Conference through a Saul Kagan Academic Fellowship for Advanced Shoah Studies. I would like to thank Professor Debórah Dwork, Professor Leonard Greenspoon, Josh Franklin, and Emily Terrana for their helpful comments on previous drafts of this text.

    1. I will investigate only the Romanianization of urban real estate and businesses. On the Ro-
manianization of jobs, see Ştefan Ionescu, "Implementing the Romanization of Employment in 1941
Bucharest: Bureaucratic and Economic Sabotage of the 'Aryanization' of the Romanian Economy,"
Holocaust Studies: A Journal of Culture and History 16, no. 1–2 (Summer/Autumn 2010): 39–64.

    2. By resistance I understand the enlarged version of the concept *amidah*, which includes vari-
ous forms of opposition to the Antonescu regime, especially the massive use of legalities to disrupt
the process of Romanianization or state takeover of Jewish properties and businesses. During that
time, the regime treated many of the Romanian Jews as "domestic enemies." The official vocabulary
belonged to the realm of warfare and conflict: "domestic enemies," "saboteurs," "infiltration," and
so on. To this governmental assault, Jews refused to (and could not) engage in a military struggle
against the state that had the monopoly of power and violence; they would not have stood a chance
of winning. At the same time, the majority of local Jews were loyal citizens of the state. Instead of
armed opposition, Jews chose to undermine (in an asymmetric struggle) the policy of Romanianization that threatened their livelihoods. In this struggle, Jews' weapons were legal tools and docu-

by Romanianization's social architects, had succeeded, it would have meant starvation, homelessness, forced labor detachments, deportation to Transnistria, and the destruction of Jewish communities.[3] According to contemporary accounts (diaries), Jews considered the struggle to stay alive and preserve their livelihoods (including properties, jobs, and businesses) as resistance to Antonescu's antisemitic policies.[4] Additionally, the Antonescu bureaucrats considered Jews' massive use of legalities as resistance to Romanianization using terms such as "resistance," "opposition," and, most frequently, "sabotage."[5] My study is based on official documents produced by state bureaucrats, judicial bodies, Jewish communities, foreign diplomats, and personal narratives of Romania's inhabitants.[6] I will begin with an overview of the World War II Antonescu regime and its antisemitic policies, especially Romanianization, and a brief history of Jewish responses to these persecutions. I will then explore legal resistance and sabotage as the main forms of Jewish resistance to the Romanianization of urban real estate and businesses.

---

ments, such as real and fictitious contracts, court contestations, foreign citizenships, visas, and Christian identities to protect them from persecution. It seems that the term resistance is the best way to describe this costly and risky effort against Romanianization.

3. Having real estate, jobs, and businesses made Jews "useful" for the national economy and qualified them, in exchange for a fee, to be exempted from forced labor units, which often operated outside their area of residence, and doing heavy work in conditions that endangered their lives. Furthermore, without money to "contribute" to the periodic official requisitions (clothes, household items, public subscriptions), Jews risked deportation to Transnistria. Without informal contributions to Romanian bureaucrats (policemen, militaries from recruiting offices, clerks, and others), Jews exposed themselves to malicious treatment that sometimes could have serious consequences (deportation to Transnistria, for example). Finally, without income from jobs, businesses, or real estate, Jews risked starvation and the impossibility of paying the increasing rent payments demanded by greedy landlords.

4. See, for instance, Maria Banuş, *Sub camuflaj: Jurnal 1943–1944* (Bucureşti: Cartea Românească, 1977), 133–35; Emil Dorian, *Jurnal din vremuri de prigoana: 1937–1944* (Bucureşti: Hasefer, 1996), 208; Mihail Sebastian, *Jurnal: 1935–1944* (Bucureşti: Humanitas, 1996), 327.

5. Sabotage, the authorities' favorite term to describe the Jewish struggle against Romanianization, has an intrinsic resistance meaning. It usually refers to one of the most radical forms of resisting aggressors through the disruption of certain military, economic, and transportation facilities in a conflict situation. In the Romanianization case, Jews engaged in sabotage not as destruction of physical facilities, but in a more sophisticated disruption of the process through the use of various legalities. In this way, Jews managed to reverse or delay the Romanianization of their properties, businesses, and jobs. Jewish sabotage of the Antonescu policy of excluding them from the economy had, thus, an obvious resistance character. See Arhivele Naţionale ale României (ANR), Ministerul Economiei Naţionale (MEN)—Direcţia Secretariat (DS), 52/1941, 135–37.

6. Today judicial archival collections are only partially available. However, thousands of decisions of judicial commissions and courts are available mainly in the National Archives of Romania (ANR). The reports and correspondence of Romanianization bureaucrats, including those referring to judicial proceedings, are available in ANR and the Bucharest Municipal Archives (AMB).

Ștefan Ionescu

The Antonescu Regime and Its Antisemitic Policies—an Overview

As one of the main beneficiaries of the Paris peace treaties at the end of World War I and a major French and British ally in Eastern Europe, Romania found itself increasingly isolated two decades later, in the context of the growing power of Nazi Germany, Fascist Italy, and the Soviet Union. Sensing that the spirit of the era favored nondemocratic regimes and wanting greater personal power, in 1938 King Carol II transformed the country into a dictatorship. Fearing its neighbors, especially the Soviet Union, and hoping to gain German support and marginalize his main domestic competitor, the fascist Iron Guard party, the dictator made economic concessions and adopted similar policies, including antisemitic legislation. Despite these measures, Carol II did not convince Hitler or Mussolini, and in the summer of 1940 Romania suffered several territorial losses (Bessarabia, northern Bukovina, northeastern Transylvania and southern Dobrogea) to the profit of its neighbors who secured German cooperation. As a result, King Carol II lost power to General Ion Antonescu and the Iron Guard. Aiming to secure German support for the return of the lost provinces, Romania joined the Axis powers in November 1940. Half a year later, Antonescu engaged in the anti-Soviet war. Domestically, neither Antonescu nor the Iron Guard wanted to share power, and they soon engaged in serious disputes concerning governance methods and supremacy. These tensions produced a civil war, known as the January (1941) Rebellion. Backed by the army, Antonescu won and ruled Romania until August 1944 with a government of military and civilian technocrats.

Though he was an antisemite responsible for the deportation and destruction of major parts of Jewish communities in Bessarabia and Bukovina—regarded as domestic traitors who sided with the Soviet Union—Antonescu also held honesty and legality in the highest esteem. He believed in law and order (as long as administering them conformed to his ideas about these concepts) and promised a just treatment for "loyal" Jews of the Old Kingdom, whose security he publicly guaranteed to Jewish leader Wilhelm Filderman.[7] This commitment, however, did not prevent Antonescu from deporting thousands of Old Kingdom Jews to Transnistria and agreeing to deport Romanian Jews to the Belzec death camp. Probably prompted by political opportunism, he abandoned the Belzec plan in the fall of 1942. Transnistria, the Soviet region occupied by

7. Ottmar Trașcă, ed., *Chestiunea evreiască în documentele militare române: 1941–1944* (Iași: Institutul European/Institutul Elie Wiesel, 2010), 457; see also ANR, MEN-DS, 48/1940, 108–09.

Romania for approximately two and a half years, became a mass cemetery for many deported and local Jews due to executions, diseases, starvation, and exposure. The Jews who escaped deportation were subjected to requisitions, forced labor, and other forms of discrimination.

Romanianization of the economy was "a very important" part of Antonescu's domestic policies.[8] The Antonescu regime promoted Romanianization as a nation-wide process "purifying" the economy of foreigners, especially Jews, delivering social justice, and reshaping Romanian society on the basis of ethno-nationalism. Romanianization sought to build, empower, and strengthen a productive and efficient ethnic Romanian middle class as the core element of a developed nation state. Ethnic Romanian refugees, civil servants, veterans, members of the bourgeoisie, and skilled workers were the main categories of Romanianization beneficiaries. To achieve his goals, Antonescu distributed the task of implementing Romanianization to three institutions. Thus, the under secretariat for Romanianization, Colonization, and Inventory (SSRCI) and its department, National Romanianization Center (CNR), supervised the expropriation, administration, and distribution of properties. The Ministry of National Economy (MEN) was the driving force behind the Romanianization of businesses and the Central Romanianization Office (belonging to the Ministry of Labor, Health, and Social Work) promoted the Romanianization of employment.

During the four months of power sharing, Romanianization was also a major topic of dispute between Antonescu and the Iron Guard. While the Iron Guard engaged in violent Romanianization of properties and businesses, Antonescu envisioned a gradual and legal elimination of Jews from the economy and society. The Antonescu regime implemented the process mainly through a series of laws, such as the expropriation of rural real estate (October and November 1940), ships (December 1940), and urban real estate (March 1941).

Initiated in the fall of 1940, the program for Romanianization of businesses and real estate closed with the end of the regime in August 1944. Despite multiple attempts, Antonescu's government failed to achieve the complete expropriation of Jewish urban buildings in favor of the state and the subsequent distribution of these properties to ethnic Romanians. The Romanianization of businesses had similar results. A variety of reasons explain these failures, ranging from war mobilization and foreign policy considerations to individual

8. *Trei ani de guvernare: 6 Septembrie, 1940–6 Septembrie, 1943* (Bucureşti: Monitorul Oficial şi Imprimeriile Statului, Imprimeria Naţională, 1943), 143.

451

responses. Technical difficulties arising from the implementation of the process, such as the inefficiency, disorganization, and corruption plaguing public institutions, further contributed to the failure of Romanianization. In the end, Jewish resistance frustrated the hopes of Antonescu's officials for a rapid and smooth Romanianization of urban real estate and businesses. While the authorities blamed local Jews for most of the failures of Romanianization, without the cooperation of gentiles—motivated by friendship, greed, or opportunism—Jews by themselves would never have managed to affect the process significantly.

Jewish resistance to Romanianization took two main forms: legal resistance and sabotage. Both of them consisted of the use of legalities to bypass Romanianization. While legal resistance used legal tools following formal procedures—such as court contestation of expropriation and eviction decisions—sabotage referred to an informal use of legal strategies at the border of, and often beyond, legality. The saboteurs adopted different methods to breach Romanianization, especially camouflage (fictitiously transferring real estate from Jews to gentiles and providing ethnic Romanian names as covers for Jewish companies through joint ventures).[9] Camouflage required creativity and the use of legal loopholes to screen the ownership of properties. Indeed camouflage methods were so sophisticated and widespread that the government adopted specific measures to fight this type of "criminality," including legislation, increased surveillance, special courts, and judicial commissions. In the end, governmental efforts were in vain, and the campaign against camouflage failed. Laws proved ineffective, bureaucrats and controllers were inefficient and corrupt, and judges remained unable to eradicate the pervasive sabotage initiatives.

For Jews, resistance to Romanianization—mainly through camouflage and court contestation—was the only option to preserve their livelihoods during this era of persecution, and they turned to lawyers, bribery, and fictitious transactions to undermine the system. Money purchased legal assistance and protection from forced labor and deportation. Thus, sabotaging and contesting Romanianization in the courts served as resistance to the antisemitic persecu-

9. See, for instance, ANR, MEN-DS, 63/1941, 151; Președinția Consiliului de Miniștrii-Serviciul Special de Informații (PCM-SSI), 77/1938, 28, 30, 33, 36, 41–43; Colecția Documente Comunități Evreiești din România (CDCER), 21/1940, 13; Dumitru Hîncu, *Confidențial: București-Berna. Rapoartele diplomatice ale lui René de Weck 1940–1944* (București: Hasefer, 2002), 35, 39–42, 46; René de Weck, *Jurnal: Jurnalul unui diplomat elvețian în România: 1939–1945* (București: Fundația Culturală Română, 2000), 250.

tions promoted by the state.[10] For many gentiles, camouflaging Jews or helping them to contest the Romanianization of properties and businesses in courts emerged as a great opportunity to make a profit and, sometimes, to help their friends.

The Romanian chapter of the Holocaust has triggered the interest of various scholars, especially after 1989, when the collapse of Communist regimes facilitated limited access to archives. During the last two decades, scholars have explored Romanian antisemitism, racial policies, and the Holocaust.[11] While many of these authors examined crucial aspects of Jewish responses to Antonescu's antisemitic policies, including Jewish resistance, few of them mentioned the strategies of Romanian Jews for resisting the Romanianization of properties and businesses.[12] More generally, how did Jews resist the persecution of the Antonescu regime?

10. ANR, Centrala Evreilor din România (CER), 35/1942; 197/1942; 202/1942.

11. See, for instance, Jean Ancel, *The History of the Holocaust in Romania* (Lincoln, Nebr.: University of Nebraska Press, 2011); Jean Ancel, *The Economic Destruction of Romanian Jewry* (Jerusalem: Yad Vashem, 2007); Viorel Achim, Constantin Iordachi, eds., *România și Transnistria: Problema Holocaustului. Perspective Istorice și Comparative* (București: Curtea Veche, 2004); Dorel Bancoș, *Social și Național în Politica Guvernului Ion Antonescu* (București: Eminescu, 2000); Maria Bucur, *Eugenics and Modernization in Interwar Romania* (Pittsburgh, Pa.: University of Pittsburgh Press, 2002); Dennis Deletant, *Hitler's Forgotten Ally: Ion Antonescu and His Regime: Romania 1940–1944* (Houndmills: Palgrave Macmillan, 2006); Armin Heinen, *România, Holocaustul și logica violenței* (Iași: Editura Universității "Alexandru Ioan Cuza" Iași, 2011); Radu Ioanid, *The Holocaust in Romania: The Destruction of Jews and Gypsies under the Antonescu Regime 1940–1944* (Chicago, Ill.: Ivan R. Dee, 2000); Irina Livezeanu, *Cultural Politics in Greater Romania* (Ithaca, N.Y.: Cornell University Press, 1995); Vladimir Solonari, *Purifying the Nation: Population Exchange and Ethnic Cleansing in Nazi Allied Romania* (Baltimore, Md.: Johns Hopkins University Press, 2010); Marius Turda, *Eugenism și antropologie rasială în România, 1874–1944* (București: Cuvantul, 2008); Leon Volovici, *Nationalist Ideology and Anti-Semitism: The Case of Romanian Intellectuals in the 1930s* (Oxford: Pergamon Press, 1991).

12. Current scholarship still lacks a thorough study of the process of Romanianization. The fact that Romanian archives opened relatively recently and not yet entirely, and that the attention of scholars has been focused on other aspects of the Holocaust—such as mass execution and deportation—might explain this neglect. Several scholars dealt with the topic recently, but their studies just scratched the surface of the rich Romanianization archives. Only one chapter of Bancoș's study on the Antonescu regime has references to Romanianization, especially of Jewish employment. Jean Ancel mentioned disparate cases of court contestation and sabotage of Romanianization, but only as marginal aspects of his general narrative on the economic destruction of Romanian Jews. He also lacked access to key Romanianization collections. Vladimir Solonari examined SSRCI archives, but his work focused on the ethnic cleansing and population exchanges of the Antonescu regime and only one chapter of his book deals with Romanianization; it is mostly focused on Bessarabia and Bucovina, and only two pages refer to the sabotage of Romanianization.

Ştefan Ionescu

Petitioning and Mobilizing the Support of Romanian Officials

Attempting to deflect the antisemitic persecutions unleashed by the Antonescu regime, Jewish leadership petitioned relentlessly to the authorities, emphasizing not only the injustice of these measures, such as Romanianization, but also the negative consequences they could have on the national economy and the possibility of Jews supporting Romania's war effort.[13] Sometimes, these petitions paid off. In 1941, for example, Wilhelm Filderman complained about the abusive interpretation of the Romanianization laws by officials of a Bucharest suburb, who had decided to expropriate the local Jewish cemetery. Soon after, MEN informed the Jewish Funeral Society that the officials had made a mistake, and the cemetery would be returned to them.[14] Furthermore, one year later, the government adopted a law specifically proclaiming that active cemeteries and synagogues could not be expropriated.[15] As various historians have argued, the Jewish lobbying of Antonescu authorities ("the Filderman model") owed its (partial) success to community leaders, who skillfully navigated the domestic, geopolitical, and military context.[16] Other Jewish notables, such as Arnold Schwefelberg, Alexandru Şafran, A. L. Zissu, and Franz von Neumann supported Filderman's actions of mobilizing support from some of Antonescu's officials, royal family members, high clergy, foreign diplomats, and even the Vatican, and contributed to the abandonment of the deportations to Transnistria and the Belzec death camp.[17] Ordinary Jews also struggled on behalf of persecuted members of the community. For instance, the Blumer family mobilized the community's effort and obtained the king's pardon for imprisoned Zionist youth.[18] Additionally, after numerous interventions that followed the opportunistic change of Romania's antisemitic policy from summer-autumn 1942 on,

13. Ancel, *The History*, 168–72; ANR, MEN-DOPCI 80/1941, 259–61; CDCER 1/1941, 3–6, 9, 22, 26; 19/1941, 1–2, 54, 65; MJ-DJ 124/1941, 292–95.

14. ANR, CDCER 1/1941, 19.

15. See the law no. 499 (June 21, 1942) in Lya Benjamin, ed., *Legislaţia antievreiască: Evreii din România între anii 1940–1944* (Bucureşti: Hasefer, 1993), 218–20.

16. Lya Benjamin, *Prigoana şi rezistenţă în istoria evreilor din România: 1940–1944: Studii* (Bucureşti: Hasefer, 2001), 198–276; Heinen, *România, Holocaustul*, 96–107.

17. Ancel, *The History*, 486–509; Alexandru Şafran, *Un tăciune smuls flăcărilor: Comunitatea evreiască din România 1939–1947: Memorii* (Bucureşti: Hasefer, 1996), 80–87 to 97–107; Arnold Schwefelberg, *Amintirile unui intelectual evreu din România* (Bucureşti: Hasefer, 2000), 111, 128, 135–38.

18. Carol Buium Benjamini, *Un sionist în vremea lui Antonescu şi după aceea* (Bucureşti: Hasefer, 1999), 93.

Jewish leaders obtained Antonescu's consent to repatriate Old Kingdom Jews (mostly from Dorohoi) and orphaned children from Transnistria.[19]

Conversion

Facing the persecutions of the Antonescu regime, some Jews chose to convert to other religions, especially to Christian Orthodoxy and Catholicism, as a survival strategy that could be interpreted as resistance.[20] According to Radu R. Rosetti, the minister of education, Antonescu believed that Jews chose to convert to Catholicism to bypass Romanianization laws.[21] The sudden mass of conversions and their implications concerning the status and the properties of such converts threatened to undermine the nation from within, and led Antonescu to adopt a law (March 31, 1941) that forbade Jews from converting to other religions.[22] Sometimes clergy breached this interdiction, triggering complaints from government.[23] Even worse for the Romanian officials, some of the Bucharest Catholic priests who baptized Jews were (ethnic) Hungarians, an unacceptable peril in the context of intense Romanian-Hungarian rivalry. As Antonescu put it: "With this system, all the Jews will be transformed into Hungarians."[24] Even though Jews converted mainly to Christianity, some considered the idea of converting to Islam to avoid the racial laws that excluded them from the economy.[25]

Spiritual Resistance

During the antisemitic persecutions of the Antonescu regime, Jews engaged in what survivors, such as Şafran, called spiritual resistance. This type of resis-

19. Schwefelberg, *Amintirile*, 136.

20. See Şafran, *Un tăciune*, 103; Sebastian, *Jurnal*, 424; sometimes Jews bought fake baptismal certificates. Banuş, *Sub Camuflaj*, 252. After the war, many converts returned to Judaism. ANR, Direcţia Generală a Poliţiei 61/1945, 245–46.

21. Radu R. Rosetti, *Pagini de jurnal* (Bucureşti: Adevărul, 1993), 190.

22. The interdiction covered all recognized religions, even though, in practice, Jews tried to convert to Christian denominations (Orthodoxy and Catholicism). See law no.771 of March 18, 1941. Discussed in Benjamin, Legislaţia, 119–21.

23. According to a report, by January 1942, 1,000 Bucharest Jews registered to convert at a single Roman-Catholic church in Bucharest. See also the petition in favor of Jewish converts sent by the Bucharest Catholic Bishop to SSRCI. ANR, MJ-DJ 116/1942, 21–41, 48–49. Orthodox priests also resented the ban and converted Jews. See Gala Galaction, *Jurnal* (Bucureşti: Albatros, 2000), 4:135, 153.

24. ANR, MJ-DJ, 116/1942, 40.

25. Saşa Pană, *Născut in '02: Memorii, file de jurnal, evocări* (Bucureşti: Editura Minerva, 1973), 598.

tance encompassed primarily organized education (schools, universities) and religious life to support morale during perilous times.[26] Besides education and religious activities, Romanian Jews engaged in other forms of spiritual resistance, such as the creation of art, poetry, music, and theater. Emil Dorian, a Jewish poet from Bucharest, for example, worked on an anthology of Yiddish poetry.[27] Painters and other graphic artists, whose work documented the tragedy of Romanian and Ukrainian Jews, represented a major chapter of spiritual resistance during the Holocaust. Commissioned by the Jewish community, the graphic artist Lazar Zin over two and a half years created fifty-three paintings depicting the funeral monuments of the Sevastopol Jewish graveyard in Bucharest. Despite the protests of the Jewish community, the Antonescu authorities decided to Romanianize the land of the cemetery. The only concession they obtained before the expropriation was permission to relocate graves and headstones to other Jewish cemeteries under the religious supervision of the community.[28]

During his deportation, the painter Arnold Dagani recorded notes and drawings illustrating the life of Jewish deportees in Transnistrian and Ukrainian camps and ghettos. As historian Lya Benjamin noted, these written and graphic records were so important for Dagani that he took special care to save them when he escaped from the slave labor camp of Mihailovka. His fellow inmates and the German guards also recognized their importance, the inmates for their memorial value showing the world their torment, and the guards because of their concern about what could happen if the drawings ended up in the wrong (Allied) hands, enhancing "anti-German propaganda."[29] Other deported artists, such as Aurel Marculescu, carved scenes from the Vapniarka camp life on wood and metal scrap sheets.[30]

Intracommunitarian Help (Aid, Rescue, and Emigration)

According to World War II Jewish leader Schwefelberg, intracommunitarian help "became one form of resistance to the destructive persecutions unleashed

26. Șafran, *Un tăciune*, 73–75; Schwefelberg, *Amintirile*, 142–43; Benjamin, *Rezistența evreiască*, 201–4.

27. See Dorian, *Jurnal*, 177–78, 187, 191–92, 200–01, 205, 207.

28. Benjamin, *Rezistența evreiască*, 268–74; Șafran, *Un tăciune*, 123–25.

29. Arnold Dagani, *Groapa e in livada cu visini*, 2nd ed. (Bucuresti: Hasefer, 2004), 19, 94, 139; Benjamin, *Rezistența evreiască*, 262–68.

30. Benjamin, *Rezistența evreiască*, 260–61.

on the Jewish community."[31] At the initiative of Filderman, the Federation of the Associations of Jewish Communities from Romania (FECE) established the Jewish Aid Commission that helped the victims of Iron Guard violence, collected and distributed aid to needy Jews, forced labor battalions, and deportees to Transnistria.[32]

Several thousand Jews from Poland, Slovakia, and especially Hungary managed to cross the border into Romania (mainly in 1943 and 1944) and secured help from the local community, which sheltered them while they waited for emigration to Palestine. Despite harsh laws punishing such trespasses, the regime closed its eyes and allowed the refugees into Romania on their way to Palestine, hoping at the end of the war to obtain good credentials and material benefits from the emigration of Jews.[33] During the war, emigration became almost impossible for Jews living in German-dominated Europe, since it required money, passports, visas, domestic and foreign connections, and, above all, a country willing to accept Jewish refugees. Few such places existed.[34] In Romania, would-be Jewish refugees faced a slightly better situation. Despite the hardships, most notably lack of money, and German and British opposition, several thousand local and Central European Jews emigrated to Palestine by steamers.[35] Many of these refugees left Romania on ill-equipped, crowded ships acquired from dubious naval companies, because Antonescu refused to allow the Romanian fleet to transport Jews to Palestine. The chicanery of Romanian, Turkish, British, and German officials prevented the Struma and Mefkure, two ships transporting Jewish refugees, from reaching Palestine. They sank in the Black Sea and more than 1,000 people drowned.[36]

31. Schwefelberg, *Amintirile*, 126.

32. Schwefelberg, *Amintirile*, 118, 124–38; Şafran, *Un tăciune*, 86–122; Benjamin, *Rezistenţa evreiască*, 205–10; Itzhak Artzi, *Biografia unui sionist* (Bucureşti: Hasefer, 1999), 90–101.

33. See Deletant, *Hitler's Forgotten Ally*, 225–29; Schwefelberg, *Amintirile*, 118–20, 141; Bernard Politzer, *O tinereţe în România* (Bucureşti: Curtea Veche, 2004), 47–48; Şafran, *Un tăciune*, 133–38.

34. For the difficulties faced by Jews who attempted to escape Nazi-dominated Europe during World War II, see Debórah Dwork and Robert Jan van Pelt, *Flight from the Reich: Refugee Jews 1933–1946* (New York: W. W. Norton, 2009).

35. Ottmar Traşcă and Dennis Deletant, eds., *Al III-lea Reich şi Holocaustul din România: 1940–1944—Documente din arhivele germane* (Bucureşti: Editura INSHR-EW, 2007), 572–797; Ioanid, *The Holocaust in Romania*; Mihai Chioveanu, "The Metamorphosis of Romania Cleansing Nation-State: Reassessing the Immigration Policy during the Holocaust," *Studia Hebraica* 9–10 (2009–2010): 241–66.

36. Struma and Mefkure were sunk by Soviet submarines. Douglas Franz and Catherine Collins, *Tragedy on the Black Sea: The Untold Story of Struma and World War II Holocaust at Sea* (New York: Ecco Press, 2003).

Ștefan Ionescu

Armed Resistance

Organized Jewish armed resistance was not widespread in the Romanian sphere of influence. Rather, Soviet partisan groups—although even their activity was assessed by some historians as "trifling"—managed to maintain a presence in Odessa's catacombs and Transnistria's forests, to harass the occupation authorities and their local collaborators, especially in 1943 and 1944.[37] Official documents and survivor testimonies mention cases of armed resistance by Jews who joined in Soviet partisan groups from 1941 onward.[38]

The lack of armed resistance to Antonescu among Romanian Jews was the result of the specific context of the Jewish community and its relation with the state. Romania was not occupied by Nazi Germany and the regime enjoyed popular support for most of the war years. No significant armed resistance to the Antonescu regime existed among Romanians, except for the Fascist rebellion in January 1941. At the same time, the majority of the Jews were loyal to the state. Then too, Jews believed that an armed resistance strategy would have triggered a general massacre validated by obsession with Jewish domestic treason, which determined the Antonescu government to take Jewish notables as hostages and threaten harsh penalties in case of any military or industrial sabotage.[39] The pogroms (veritable mass murder episodes) that took place in 1940 and 1941, such as the Iasi Pogrom, were publicly justified by alleged Jewish armed subversion against Romanian or German soldiers.[40] Reading about the alleged Jewish attacks against the army in Iasi (June 1941), some better-informed Romanians, such as former Prime Minister Argetoianu, recorded their disbelief in the accusations: "The Yids have no weapons."[41] Despite the anti-semitic slur, Argetoianu was right. Romanian Jews lacked weapons and military organization, key elements for any armed resistance. Furthermore, Jews believed that if they behaved as loyal citizens, the regime would spare them,

37. See, for instance, Alexander Dallin, *Odessa, 1941–1944: A Case Study of Soviet Territory under Foreign Rule* (Iași: Center for Romanian Studies, 1998), 228–33.

38. Discussed in Trașcă, *Chestiunea evreiască*, 271–72; Meir Teich, "The Jewish Self-administration in Ghetto Shargorod," *Yad Vashem Studies* 2 (1958): 247.

39. Discussed in Benjamin, *Legislația*, 332; Schwefelberg, *Amintirile*, 131–32; Șafran, *Un tăciune*, 70–71.

40. Jean Ancel, *Preludiu la asasinat: Pogromul de la Iași, 29 iunie 1941* (Iași: Polirom, 2005); Ștefan Ionescu, "Myths, Narratives, and Patterns of Rumors: The Construction of 'Jewish Subversion' and Retributive Violence in 1940–41 Romania," *Culture and Psychology* 15 (2009): 327–36.

41. Constantin Argetoianu, *Însemnări zilnice*: vol. 9 (21 Aprilie-31 Decembrie 1941): 156, 159, 320. The official investigation failed to uncover any wounded Romanian or German soldiers and attributed the violence to the Fascist provocateurs.

and they tried their best to prevent any pretext for accusations of domestic treason. Only during the last year of the Antonescu regime did things slowly start to change.

For many Jews, the approaching front line (from late 1943 onward) brought fears that Germans and local collaborators might engage in a last-minute massacre. These worries triggered preparations for armed resistance among Jewish leadership and Zionist youth groups, the latter under the influence of envoys from Palestine.[42] In 1943, aiming to rescue the community, Jewish leadership formed a secret committee that reunited representatives of Jewish political parties. The committee established relations with opposition circles connected with the king and former political parties, who were plotting to topple Antonescu.[43] Although potential resisters, especially Zionist youth groups, attempted to hoard weapons and train their members, the results were rather meager. According to Bernard Politzer, one of the Hashomer Hatzair, his organization prepared safe houses and trained its members in self-defense, but managed to gather only three handguns. The arsenal of other Zionist groups was more or less the same. Patriotic Defense, the pro-Communist underground, promised to deliver more weapons to the Zionists at the right time but failed to keep its promise.[44] In the end, there was no need for Jewish armed resistance, because in August 1944, King Michael, together with army generals and a coalition of democratic parties, arrested Antonescu and his aides, and joined the Allies. The Romanian army followed the king and drove German forces out of the country.[45]

Legal Resistance to Romanianization

I have to inform you about a situation that has extremely serious social and moral implications. CNR awarded houses in Bucharest to a number of 4,000 [ethnic] Romanian families. The majority of them are in danger of becoming homeless. They have to leave their current houses on November 10th, and cannot obtain the eviction of the Jews by this time. Jewish tenants of CNR houses have used all the unimaginable means to sabotage the entrance of [ethnic] Romanians in these houses.... During the last days ... the Jews displayed stiff resistance and audacity that

42. See Banuș, *Sub Camuflaj*, 354; Dorian, *Jurnal*, 319, 335; Sebastian, *Jurnal*, 525–26; Schwefelberg, *Amintirile*, 139–40; Buium, *Un sionist*, 87–88; Politzer, *O tinerețe*, 49–50.

43. Schwefelberg, *Amintirile*, 139; Șafran, *Un tăciune*, 90–94.

44. Politzer, *O tinerețe*, 49–51; Artzi, *Biografia*, 113.

45. In the first stage with American air support, and later in collaboration with the Red Army.

went beyond any limit. We are fighting these resistance methods of the Jews, who collaborate with incorrect and dishonest bureaucrats.... Facing Jewish resistance and opposition grounded on the rights awarded them through the eviction legal formalities [stipulated in the expropriation laws] we lack any power of action.... We cannot force the courts to adopt our point of view, because judges are sovereign. (SSRCI confidential memo to Antonescu, 10 November 1941)[46]

Among these different methods of resisting antisemitic persecution, using legalities to preserve properties, businesses, and ultimately lives, played a major role for Romanian Jews. By petitioning the courts against the Romanianization of houses, for example, Jews obtained a reversal of CNR decisions in approximately 10 percent of expropriation cases by September 1943. Even when the state won the majority of these trials, Jewish contestations, together with other structural problems of the regime and its institutions, delayed the enforcement of Romanianization (seizure of properties and their distribution to gentile ownership), through never-ending judicial procedures, until the collapse of the Antonescu regime in August 1944.[47] Jews also won some—it is not yet clear how many—trials against the Romanianization of businesses. Even though they lost particular judicial battles, many Jewish plaintiffs won the Romanianization war in the long run, by preventing complete implementation of the regime's radical policies.

Jewish legal resistance against the seizure of properties and businesses required resourcefulness and its final result was uncertain. Jews needed to decide whether to take the opportunity to contest the expropriation and eviction summons, to study the legislation for loopholes, to contact gentile friends for information, and to appeal in an upper court if the lower court rejected their initial case. If Jews won the trials, they had to hire judicial executors to implement the decisions and get back their Romanianized assets. In order to engage in legal resistance, one needed psychological strength, money, time, and legal knowledge or connections among gentiles. Even after meeting all these conditions, the results of the trials were uncertain. Moreover, the lawyers hired to contest the expropriations sometimes failed to deliver their promises and proved to be greedy profiteers, attempting to get rich at the expense of their clients.[48] Overall, the Jews who engaged in legal resistance confronted a body

46. ANR, MEN-DS, 52/1941, 135–37.
47. See SSRCI's complaints about Jewish legal resistance that delayed their eviction from Romanianized houses, which "created a disheartening situation for ethnic Romanians ... and fueled Jewish hopes and imagination." ANR, MEN-DS, 52/1941, 135–37.
48. Sașa Pană's lawyer alluded to his important connections (allegedly Mihai Antonescu). He

of antisemitic legislation, specific state institutions (such as SSRCI/CNR) with major resources, popular prejudices identifying Jews with domestic traitors, and the hostility and opportunism of bureaucrats.

One of the most widespread methods of legal resistance against the Romanianization of properties was contestation in courts. The laws stipulated the right of the Jews, whose properties had been Romanianized, to contest the expropriation decisions and procedures. Adopting the law for the expropriation of Jewish urban real estate (March 28, 1941), the government established a Central Judicial Commission (CJC) under CNR to review Jews' complaints.[49] Made up of three supreme court judges and assisted by an appeal court judge, the CJC started its activity with great expectations. Appointing only a few judges to deal with this issue, the regime did not expect a massive Jewish response, and probably relied on the restrictive conditions in which Jews could contest the Romanianization of their properties.[50] However, CJC was soon overwhelmed. By January 1942, CJC registered approximately 39,000 cases of contestations against the Romanianization of Jewish urban real estate. According to 1943 data, the government expropriated 75,833 apartments.[51] In certain locations, such as the capital and its metropolitan area, it seems that the proportion of

cashed in and extorted a lot of money while continuously assuring his clients that they were on the right track. This scam lasted until the Antonescu regime collapsed. Pană, *Născut in '02*, 648–49.

49. The law applied to 1940–41 Romania, except Bessarabia and Northern Bucovina, at that time part of the Soviet Union. From the summer of 1941 (when Romania expelled the Red Army) until the spring of 1944 (when the Red Army returned) these two "model provinces" had a special status and were run by governors, who implemented a policy of ethnic purification, including a more radical Romanianization. According to decree law no. 2507 (September 1941), the Romanian laws were extended to Bessarabia and Bucovina, but the governors could suspend these laws anytime. See Solonari, *Purifying the Nation*, 142–67, 256–63; Nicolae Ghimpa, et al., eds., *Codul de Românizare* (București: Editura Ziarului Universul, 1942), 100–101.

50. According to article 13 of law no. 1216 from May 3, 1941 (establishing CNR), Jews could contest the Romanianization of their properties only within thirty days from the moment CNR sent them the takeover notice or within just fifteen days if the assets had been seized before the establishment of CNR. See Ghimpa, et al., *Codul*, 33.

51. A comparison of the number of Romanianized houses (75,833) with the number of contestations (38,202), suggests that Jews contested around 50 percent of the expropriated residences. Keeping in mind that some people owned several apartments (in blocks of flats) and that a "contestation file or case" sometimes referred to buildings with several apartments, the proportion of contesting the expropriation was much higher. Thus, the absolute majority of Jews contested the Romanianization decisions in courts. *Trei ani de guvernare*, 145–46. SSRCI's internal data gives a slightly higher number of Romanianization trials at the eleven appeal courts—39,059 cases. MJ-DJ 39/1943, 84–85. Jews contested not only the Romanianization of their residencies, but also other types of real estate. Preparing for distribution, CNR experts evaluated (in 1941) a group of vineyards, farms, and gardens, and reported that former Jewish owners contested the expropriation of sixty-five (around 70 percent) out of ninety-two Romanianized properties. ANR, MMSOS, 93/1942, 183–85.

contestations was higher than the national average.[52] Unwillingly, the government admitted its failure publicly: "Despite the exceptional value of its magis-
trates and their will to resolve all the contestations, the commission could not
fulfill the goal of fast trials for three reasons: first, there were so many cases,
close to 40,000; second, solving these cases demanded detailed investigations
all over the country; third, the law required a complicated procedure."[53]

Jewish response to the Romanianization of urban properties led the regime
to adopt a new law (no. 313) on January 1942, designed to create an institutional
framework able to cope with the sudden excess of contestations.[54] Thus, the
government dismantled CJC and empowered the appeal courts to establish as
many panels as needed in order to examine the contestations against the Romanianization of properties and businesses.[55] Antonescu officials hoped that
the increased number of panels, located all over the country, and a simplified
judicial procedure would prove more efficient.

Despite the major resources allocated to the task, it amounted to wishful
thinking. Twenty months later, in September 1943, SSRCI reported that the appeal court panels solved only 19,390 (around 51 percent) out of 38,202 cases
of contestations against the Romanianization of urban real estate.[56] According
to official data, Jews won 2,016 cases (around 10.4 percent) out of 19,390 finalized trials, and 18,912 cases were still on trial.[57] The Supreme Court was slightly
more efficient than the appeal courts: it solved 3,549 (56.6 percent) out of 6,265

52. The circumscription of the Bucharest Appeal Court included, besides the capital, several nearby counties (Ilfov, Vlaşca, Ialomiţa, Dâmboviţa, Buzău, Muscel, Prahova) with poorer and smaller
Jewish populations (around one-tenth of the Bucharest Jewish population). While in Bucharest 17,833
apartments had been expropriated, we don't know exactly how many had been Romanianized in
the surrounding counties, but the number cannot be higher than the number of households (several
thousand). By March 31, 1943, the Bucharest Appeal Court had to examine approximately 20,765 cases of contestations and other petitions related to expropriated Jewish real estate (such as requests for
fixing the amount of compensation). MJ-DJ, 51/1942, 2:108–9; CER 33/1941, 307.

53. See the preamble of law no. 313. See Ghimpa, et al., *Codul*, 141.

54. Ibid., 56–63, 141–42.

55. Only the Bucharest Appeal Court established seven Romanianization panels. ANR, MJ-DJ,
51/1942, 2:109.

56. *Trei ani de guvernare*, 146.

57. These SSRCI data (released in late 1943) do not match—possibly due to editorial errors. The
confidential reports sent by prosecution offices and courts to MJ confirm that around half (or even
higher in some areas) of the Romanianization contestations remained unsolved after two years of
judicial procedures and that Jews won around 10 percent of contestations. For example, by March
31, 1943, Jews won 921 (10.3 percent) out of 8,857 cases resolved (44.5 percent) at the Bucharest Appeal Court, while 11,033 trials (55.5 percent) had been postponed. ANR, MJ-DJ 51/1942, 2:109. According to other SSRCI reports (contradicting the published data), by September 1943 the appeal courts
resolved 28,758 cases and only 10,301 remained to be examined, especially at the appeal courts in
Czernowitz, Chisinau, Galati, Iasi, and Sibiu. ANR, MJ-DJ, 39/1943, 83–84.

complaints against the decisions of the appeal courts Romanianization panels.[58] Moreover, SSRCI declared that it could not distribute the Romanianized real estate for ownership until all contestations were solved, thus establishing the legal status of those properties.[59] The prospects were not very encouraging for Romanianization. In more than two years of activity, the various judicial bodies solved only 51 percent of the contestations of the Romanianization of Jewish real estate.

Clearly, the Romanianization panels needed more time to resolve all these cases. But time was running out for the Antonescu government, and during the last year of the regime things got worse for the Romanianization bureaucrats. Especially from spring 1944 onward, many institutions—including the Iasi and Bucharest appeal courts and CNR branches—relocated from major cities to the countryside, due to the entrance of the Red Army into Romanian territory (Moldova) and the Allied bombing campaign. These measures further delayed Romanianization activity.[60]

The massive court battles against the Romanianization of residencies suggests that some sort of widespread information effort must have taken place within the Jewish community. This vital information spread quickly among ordinary Jews, who embraced promising legal strategies, such as claiming the status of exempted and deserving Jews.[61] Lawyers played a crucial role in identifying legal strategies of resisting Romanianization.[62] According to Sasa

58. ANR, MJ-DJ 39/1943, 85.   59. *Trei ani de guvernare*, 146.

60. The relocation sites—usually small towns—did not have the facilities to host as many institutions with their substantial logistics and personnel, which further slowed down the judicial process (insufficient space for archives and offices, interruptions of communications and transportation, and so on). ANR, SSRCI-Direcția Controlului (DC), 73/1944, 9–18.

61. According to law no. 143/1943, three main categories of Jews could be assimilated with ethnic Romanians from a legal point of view. First, Jews who had volunteered to serve in the Romanian army and had fought on the frontline in the Second Balkan War and World War I; second, Jewish soldiers of the Romanian army who had been awarded citizenship during World War I for their bravery; third, those Jews who "proved themselves useful and faithful to the Romanian nation through their devotion and exceptional deeds or through their constant and praiseworthy activity." A special commission (made of a Bucharest Appeal Court judge, a SSRCI delegate, and a public lawyer designated by the government) was charged with assessing potentially deserving Jews. See Benjamin, *Legislația*, 234–43. There was a precedent for the favorable treatment of deserving Jews before 1943. The March 1941 law (no. 842) exempted several categories of Jews (article no. 5) from the expropriation of real estate and stipulated (article no. 6) that Jews who proved exceptional devotion and brought exceptional services to Romania would also be exempted. Law no. 143/1943 followed up this norm and enlarged the sphere of "benefits" for deserving Jews—from property rights to urban houses to all rights. See Ghimpa, et al., *Codul*, 16–18.

62. For instance, CER legal experts read carefully *Pandectele Românizării*, the only journal dedicated to the Romanianization project (discussing its theory, legislation, and jurisprudence). ANR,

Pana's testimony, if Jews did not find reasons to fight against expropriation decisions, lawyers provided them with such pretexts.[63] The fact that several Jewish leaders, such as Filderman and Schwefelberg, were brilliant lawyers with a personal history of legal interventions in favor of the Jewish community, even at the international level, suggests that they might have spread awareness about legal resistance methods.

The archival evidence indicates that Jewish leaders were involved in the campaign of legal contestations against Romanianization policies, particularly those targeting communal properties. Besides beseeching authorities and mobilizing gentile support, Jewish leaders struggled to avoid the expropriation of their community's assets—schools, hospitals, and cemeteries—by using various legalities. FECE, and later Centrala Evreilor din Romania (CER)—a centralized organization modeled after the Nazi Zentrallelverein with the aim of controlling Romanian Jews, which replaced FECE in December 1941—supported the legal struggle against the Romanianization of communal, welfare, and NGO properties.[64] CER sometimes provided lawyers to contest the Romanianization of houses belonging to impoverished members of the community who solicited help.[65] Jewish leaders from Bucharest also disseminated among countrywide communities legal strategies on how to paralyze or delay the Romanianization of properties, by avoiding legal acts that might have been interpreted as consent to expropriations.[66] In May 1942, at the request of CER, two law experts—including Bucharest Law School professor Anibal Teodorescu—sent written consultations on the expropriation of Jewish real estate to CER's branch in Cernowitz and to an NGO engaged in legal battles with CNR at the local appeal court.[67] CER continued the correspondence with its branches about legal resistance to Romanianization until the end of the regime.[68]

CER, 33/1942, 14–25. L. Sorin, "Rolul jurisprudenței în legile de Românizare," *Almanahul Evreiesc* (1943/1944): 119–20.

63. Pană, *Născut în 02*, 648.

64. CER's legal department contested the expropriation of Jewish communal properties, including those of NGOs in front of Romanianization panels and lobbied for them before the government. ANR, CER, 14/1942, 13; CER 16/1942, 159; CDCER 1/1941, 3–6, 19, 26; see also *Centrul pentru Studierea Istoriei Evreilor din România* (CSIER), III 379/1939–1942, 67, 88–90, 92, 99, 103.

65. For the cases when CER refused to intervene on behalf of expropriated individual Jews, see ANR, CER, 16/1942, 3; for cases when CER provided legal assistance, see CSIER, III 379/1939–1942, 41, 57.

66. ANR, CDCER, 21/1941, 9; CER 16/1942, 25, 28–29, 79, 83, 159, 162, 231bis, 247–48bis, 280–81, 326, 421, 468, 484, 501, 503, 505, 516, 540–41, 574–75.

67. See CER's letter (May 1942) to the Czernowitz Jewish community. ANR, CER, 20/1942, 365.

68. See CER's correspondence with its branches from Botosani and Dolj counties in 1943 and 1944. CSIER, III 320 B/1943, 129; III 321/1944, 77.

Jews engaged in legal resistance against the Romanianization of their businesses as well. A typical case illustrates the legal resistance of local Jews to the government's plan to eliminate them from the economy through administrative measures. As a result of a denunciation, in May 1942, the registry of commerce's judge erased the company owned by Leah Rosenstein, a Jewish woman from Bucharest.[69] Refusing to accept this injustice, she went to court in May 1943 and obtained a cancellation of the decision, and the reregistration of her company. Prompted by new complaints, the registry of commerce's judge decided, again, to erase the company, arguing that, in the meantime (December 1943), Rosenstein sold her commercial patrimony to an ethnic Romanian, and thus she could not own the business. This was a harsh interpretation of legal texts, since the businesswoman sold only the patrimony (assets, logistics, copyrights, and so on) and not the entire company—a strategy often used by Romanian Jews to escape the administrative pressures to Romanianize their businesses.[70] Undeterred, she appealed to the court against the new decision and the case was on trial again. Suspecting that Rosenstein would win again, MEN complained that the case tied their hands: "No [administrative] measure can be adopted until the court rules."[71] In the end, the only thing MEN could do was to monitor the trial. Besides attesting to Jewish legal resistance, this case confirms that courts enjoyed some autonomy, and sometimes decided in favor of Jewish plaintiffs.

Other reports mentioned similar cases all over the country. The Jewish owners of businesses targeted by various Romanianization policies (erasures of companies or restrictions against acting in particular domains of the economy) complained to courts against malicious decisions and sometimes won.[72] As MEN officials noticed, there were no legal provisions to force Jews to Romanianize their companies by selling them to ethnic Romanians. The administrative pressures (import-export bans, restrictions to making any legal changes to the company, and so on) used against Jewish entrepreneurs often failed to produce the desired effects.[73]

69. When entrepreneurs wanted to establish a company or to change the legal status of an existing one, they needed to go to the registry of commerce, where a delegate judge supervised any commercial legal procedures in order to make sure they conformed to the current legislation.

70. Because there were no laws stipulating the mandatory erasing of an existing Jewish company, the National Bank of Romania complained that the Romanianization of Jewish businesses through special loans awarded by the Romanian credit institute to ethnic Romanian buyers was a joke and, in fact, financed the Jews with Romanianization funds. ANR, MEN-DOPSF, 10/1941, 61–79.

71. ANR, MEN-DOP-SIF 1/1940, 191.

72. See, for instance, similar cases from Roman, Bacău, Galați, Iași, and Timișoara counties. ANR, MEN-DOP-SIF 1/1940, 189, 190, 192, 221–22, 227–28; MJ-DJ 111/1943, 19–22, 112–14.

73. ANR, MEN-Direcția Comerț Interior (DCI), 46/1941, 9.

Ștefan Ionescu

The court decisions in favor of Jewish entrepreneurs worried Romanianization officials and triggered a lot of tensions between them and the members of the judiciary, who refused to conform to the demands of the era. These bureaucrats urged the government to intervene and order the courts to rule in favor of Romanianization. For instance, complaining about the implications of the Timis Appeal Court's decision that canceled the administrative prohibitions adopted against a Jewish businessman, MEN warned MJ that, "The generalization of such jurisprudence ... would prevent the elimination of Jews from commerce with alcohol."[74] There was no consensus among bureaucrats on how to react toward Jewish legal resistance. For instance, MEN blamed the passivity of the local chamber of commerce, which should have pursued the case more aggressively in court. Other cases attest to the constant preoccupation of MJ bureaucrats with the results of trials in which courts reversed the Romanianization of businesses. MEN and MJ officials were not the only ones frustrated by Jewish legal resistance. The ministry of interior officials inquired about the possibility of adopting administrative measures against Jewish plaintiffs. These cases reflect a general perception among bureaucrats that confidential administrative measures were more efficient than the ambitious but vague laws that allowed multiple (mis-) interpretations and enabled Jewish resistance.[75]

At the current stage of research, it is not entirely clear why, despite official pressures, certain judges recognized the rights of local Jews and ruled against Romanianization. The regime pressured courts and public attorney offices to act in its favor not only in cases involving Jews and Romanianization, but also in trials implicating gentiles.[76] But not all judges and prosecutors complied, and the pressure was neither overwhelming nor ubiquitous.[77] According to the testimony of military prosecutor Florea Olteanu, he was never pressured by superiors during the Antonescu regime, and could rule in favor of Jews indicted for breaching forced labor laws.[78] Sometimes bribes and nepotism influenced the decisions of judges and prosecutors in ordinary trials, and this might have

74. ANR, MEN-DOP-SIF 1/1940, 219; MJ-DJ 111/1941, 111–14.
75. ANR, MEN-DOP-SIF 1/1940, 199, 219; MEN-DOPSF, 10/1941, 80–81.
76. Nichifor Crainic, *Zile albe-zile negre: Memorii* (București: Gândirea, 1991), 350.
77. Complaining about Jewish legal resistance to evictions from CNR houses, the SSRCI director sent a confidential memo to Antonescu, decrying his powerlessness to influence court decisions "because judges are sovereign." ANR, MEN-DS 52/1941, 135–37. Antonescu and public prosecutors complained of the courts' leniency in cases of economic sabotage. Rosettti, *Pagini de jurnal*, 195.
78. Florea Olteanu, *Un procuror incomod: interviu* (București: Fundația Academia Civică, 2011), 16–18.

happened in Romanianization cases as well.[79] Paradoxically, during the Antonescu dictatorship, judges still benefited from a certain autonomy—perhaps because judges' "irremovability" (a sort of tenure) abolished during the Iron Guard regime had been reestablished in October 1941—that allowed them to disagree with the government.[80] Various subjective factors favored the partial success of Jewish legal resistance to Romanianization, ranging from judges' professional ethics, to corruption, opportunism, and fear of postwar retribution by the Allies. While courts reversed Romanianization throughout the Antonescu regime—especially after the defeat of the Iron Guard rebellion in January 1941[81]—many of these reversals took place from 1942 onward, a time when the Nazi victory appeared uncertain and Allied warnings that Axis officials would be held accountable for the persecution of Jews impressed Romanian elites.[82] It seems that Romanianization followed the evolution of the war and of the Antonescu regime's radicalism toward the Jews. Once the prospects of a victorious short war in the East vanished, many officials of the Antonescu regime, perhaps even judges, lost their zealousness in persecuting Jews.

As legal scholar Jens Meierhenrich has persuasively shown in his recent book *The Legacies of Law: Long-Run Consequences of Legal Development in South Africa: 1652–2000*, the existence of legal norms and institutions, even illiberal ones, can help make democracy work in a non-democratic society.[83] To a certain extent, this was also the case with the Antonescu regime and his Romanianization policy. The existence of pubic legal provisions (such as laws, exemptions,

---

79. See Argetoianu, *Însemnări*, 10:391; Olteanu, *Un procuror incomod*, 23; Cristian Scarlat, ed., *Diplomați Germani la București 1937–1944: Din memoriile Dr. Rolf Pusch, atasat de legație și dr. Gherhard Stelzer, consilier de legație* (București: Editura, All, 2001), 167.

80. The irremovability (tenure) system was designed to protect judiciary power from the executive's pressures, giving the judiciary, at least in theory, freedom of decision in trials. *Trei ani de guvernare*, 284. On the importance of the decisions to remove tenure from judges during the Iron Guard regime and in the fall of 1944 (by the post-Antonescu Communist minister of justice), see the diary of Constantin Năvârlie, a supreme court magistrate. Constantin Năvârlie, *Între abandon și crucificare: România 1944–1946* (Craiova: Editura de Sud, 2000), 30, 54; MEN-DS 52/1941, 135–37.

81. Sometimes, courts restituted the Romanianized properties to Jews even during the Iron Guard regime, but these were rare instances. In Târgu Neamț, for example, in December 1940, Jewish owners obtained the restitution of three pieces of real estate that they sold under threat to local Iron Guard members. ANR, CDCER, 3/1940, 33–45. In general, during the four months when the Iron Guard shared power with Antonescu, the members of the judiciary were afraid of the Fascists' violence that targeted politicians and bureaucrats. ANR, MJ-DJ, 124/1941, 1:259–60.

82. See Heinen, *România, Holocaustul*, 100–101, 205; Șafran, *Un tăciune*, 24; Schwefelberg, *Amintirile*, 135.

83. Jens Meierhenrich, *Legacies of Law: Long-Run Consequences of Legal Development in South Africa: 1652–2000* (Cambridge: Cambridge University Press, 2008).

and procedures) and judicial structures (such as courts, different jurisdiction levels allowing appeals, judicial commissions, and bar associations), before and during World War II, created some sort of an autonomous judiciary and enabled members of persecuted groups (mainly the Jews) who possessed a tradition of litigation to defend their rights using legal tools.

For instance, Jewish legal resistance was facilitated by structural factors of the regime and its judiciary, because the regime did not adopt the most radical anti-Jewish legislation possible. Contrary to the Anglo-Saxon legal system based on precedents, the Romanian judiciary was modeled on the French (continental) legal system by which judges had to obey the legal texts strictly but not judicial precedents. The antisemitic laws had boundaries and Antonescu did not cross a certain line. Some categories of privileged Jews were exempted from Romanianization, and Jews were allowed to contest expropriation decisions and procedures. The regime also avoided excluding all Jews from the business sector and never ordered a seizure of all Jewish companies. Antonescu worried that a radical Romanianization would paralyze the economy during the war effort, that the Axis might lose the war or negotiate a peace compromise with unforeseen implications for Romania, and he believed in an idea of justice and a rule of law. All of these moderated the antisemitic policy.[84]

The success of legal battles by Jews aiming to reverse or postpone his Romanianization of properties was facilitated not only by an insufficient number of judges, complicated formalities, professional ethics, vague and incomplete legislation, opportunism, and corruption, it was also aided by the tensions and poor cooperation between courts and state institutions. Frustrated by the slow pace of Romanianization trials and by CNR complaints, MJ urged the courts to speed up the rhythm of solving the cases involving Romanianized properties and businesses.[85] At the same time, Romanian general staff requested MJ to instruct appeal courts to demand tougher standards and rules for the evidence of plaintiffs trying to prove they belonged to the exempted or deserving Jewish categories.[86] While CNR and MJ complained about the courts' inefficiency and

84. "The preamble of the law that instituted more Romanianization panels at the appeal courts stipulated that it did so "In order to defend the idea of justice." See Ghimpa, et. al., *Codul*, 142; CD-CER 19/1941, 45; Traşcă, *Chestiunea evreiească*, 457; ANR, MEN-DS 48/1940, 108–09; MEN-DOPSF, 10/1941, 61–81.

85. ANR, MJ-DJ, 39/1943, 39–40, 80, 83; MJ-DJ 111/1943, 10, 15–18.

86. The Romanian general staff wanted MJ to instruct the courts to require Jewish plaintiffs claiming exempted status on military grounds (such as heirs of wounded, dead, or decorated veterans) to show original military documents (more difficult to obtain during World War II), instead of

benevolence towards Jews, the courts blamed Romanianization bureaucrats for delaying the judicial procedures. Thus, CNR did not transfer indispensable individual files for the examination of Romanianization cases to the judiciary. In June 1942, for example, the Cluj Appeal Court (relocated in Sibiu) accused CNR of failing to send the documentation for all 1,500 contestations against the expropriations of Jewish real estate, thereby forcing its Romanianization panels to postpone the trials for the third time.[87] Despite MJ pleas for expediency, little progress was made. In 1943, appeal court judges continued to complain that CNR was late in sending them the expropriation documents and did so only after repeated requests. Even when CNR sent the files, the majority of them were incomplete. Also, because fiscal authorities did not send their data on time, the courts could not assess the value of the disputed properties.[88]

Sabotage

The State versus the Saboteurs of Romanianization: Uncovering and Repressing Sabotage

An alternative and a supplement to legal resistance, the sabotage of Romanianization (usually through camouflage) was a widespread pattern of action among Jews and gentiles in World War II Romania.[89] While legal resistance did not necessarily require the collaboration of a gentile, sabotage usually did. Contrary to judicial contestation, a legitimate behavior according to existing legislation, sabotage posed serious risks for those who practiced it. Camouflage was not an ideal arrangement, but rather a complex situation with unforeseen complications. Sometimes gentile businessmen who agreed to camouflage Jewish properties changed their minds and violated the initial agreement. Other gentile saboteurs refused to return the camouflaged businesses to the legitimate Jewish owners.[90] Still: the motivations were not always malicious. Ac-

---

using corroborating eyewitness testimonies, "as the majority of special [Romanianization] panels permitted so far." ANR, MJ-DJ, 128/1942, 61–62, 65–66.

87. ANR, MJ-DJ, 128/1942, 155–56, 159.

88. ANR, MJ-DJ, 39/1943, 86–87.

89. Sabotage of Romanianization should be distinguished from "economic sabotage," which was a different and more generic crime. Any entrepreneur, regardless of his ethnicity, could be held liable of perpetrating this crime if his actions affected the national economy by failing to supply its company with raw materials or failing to deliver its products, firing employees without approval, refusing to accept new orders, and so on. See the "Surveillance and the Defense of the National Economy Law" (no. 3122 of 14 September 1940), *Monitorul Oficial* 214 (September 14, 1940): 5395.

90. See, for instance, the case of Matei Gall's parents and their Christian partner. Matei Gall,

cording to postwar testimonies, several ethnic Romanians sabotaged the process simply to help their Jewish friends.[91]

All breaches of Romanianization rules warranted punitive action and the government attempted to curb sabotage. As the situation proved pervasive, Antonescu's obsession with repressing sabotage grew. The authorities issued instructions on how to uncover camouflage, constantly investigated suspect companies, and promulgated special provisions to punish the breaches of policy.[92] For Antonescu, the legal provisions already implemented to punish breaches were utterly ineffective.[93]

On March 13, 1942, the government therefore adopted a specific law (no. 196) for fighting the camouflage of Jewish goods, rights, and interests and for repressing the sabotage of Romanianization. The statute identified the "crime of sabotaging Romanianization" and demanded severe penalties. Sabotage included "camouflage" (the concept itself was not clearly defined) of Jewish goods and interests, in any form or acts by any person.[94] Proclaiming a repressive law was one thing. Implementing it was quite another. In spite of the public image of a vigorous offensive against the sabotage of Romanianization, the execution of the policy failed. Creating repressive institutions targeting the sabotage of Romanianization seemed tangible in theory. In reality, it proved an onerous task to persuade the public to collaborate in rooting out the breaches of Romanianization.

Established in 1942 to carry out the anticamouflage law (no.196), the Special Judicial Commissions to Fight the Camouflage of Jewish Properties, Rights, and Interests, in short the (anti) Camouflage Commissions (CCs), functioned as the

---

Eclipsa (Bucureşti: Du Style, 1997), 267; also Zaharia Stancu, *Zile de lagăr*, 2nd ed. (Bucureşti: Socec & Co.: 1945), 96–97.

91. See Constantin Th. Sapatino, *Trăiri, Trăiri ... de-a lungul unui veac* (Bucureşti: Romfel, 1994), 76; Banuş, *Sub Camuflaj*, 112; Solly Border, *Între două lumi cu un român american* (Bucureşti: Aldo Press, 2007), 11.

92. ANR, MMSOS, 80/1941, 2:31–38, 58–59; MMSOS, 296/1941, 35–41; MEN-DOPSIF, 1/1940; MEN-DS, 18/1941, 56.

93. ANR, MEN-DOPSF, 1/1940, 171–72. The November 1940 law implementing the Romanianization of private jobs punished companies engaged in sabotage of Romanianization of employment, not individuals. While the sanctions were severe—confiscation or liquidation of the company—the judicial procedure was long and complicated. The only punishment stipulated by the March 1941 law (on the expropriation of urban real estate) was that Jewish perpetrators lost their right to receive the compensations promised by the state in exchange for the expropriated real estate.

94. The criminal punishment for sabotaging the Romanianization of property and business was hard labor (imprisonment) for five to fifteen years. The material penalty was confiscation of the property or business in favor of CNR, if both partners of the transaction, or only the Aryan one, refused to "confess" to sabotage. If both partners, or only the Jewish one, confessed sabotage, the property or business was returned to the rightful owner. See Ghimpa, et al., *Codul*, 121–25.

major institutions to eradicate the camouflage of Jewish properties and busi-nesses.[95] The CCs investigated the transfers of properties (companies, shares, or real estate) from Jewish owners to ethnic Romanians or other gentiles, con-cluded between September 1940 and March 1942, in order to establish its real or camouflaged nature.[96] In addition to investigating property and business transfers, the CCs had to examine transactions between the Jews and gentiles they suspected of camouflage, most especially following up on the reports of Romanianization bureaucrats or various denunciations.

The Romanian authorities expected great results from the CCs. As we see from the records of one of these CCs attached to SSRCI, its early activity seemed to confirm official expectations. Most of this CC's rulings (some 2,585 decisions out of 3,585) have survived. Covering the period from mid-1942 to May 1944, these judicial rulings, referring to 2,030 transactions, provide a comprehensive overview of the activity of such commissions.[97] They reveal that the process of uncovering camouflage began to lose momentum after only a few months. The number of uncovered camouflages dropped significantly. It began at 22.4 percent in the first months of activity (June–September 1942) and declined to a worrying—for the government—9.2 percent two years later (in spring 1944). Overall, this CC uncovered camouflage in 9.3 percent of the cases it examined.[98] What could be the explanation for these results? Did camouflage actually di-

95. Three CCs were organized around SSRCI and they comprised four members. One represented the National Bank of Romania (BNR): the other three were legal experts, usually judges. The presi-dent of each CC was a judge from the Bucharest Appeal Court (designated by the ministry of jus-tice), and the other two members came from tribunals or lower courts (designated by SSRCI with the agreement of MJ). Public attorneys and members of administrative courts were also eligible to participate in the CCs. See articles 12–19 of law no. 196 in Ghimpa, et al., *Codul*, 118–21. See also *Trei ani de guvernare*, 147.

96. The government suspected that after Antonescu came to power in September 1940, many Jews transferred their properties and businesses to various gentiles, or they bought properties from gentiles using gentile accomplices' names. Law 196 (March 1942) therefore required the partners of all transfers involving Jewish goods (or in favor of Jews) conducted between September 1940 and March 1942 to submit special declarations to the CCs about the real or camouflaged nature of the transactions. The state offered a certain "incentive": if both partners of the transaction, or only the Jewish one, confessed to sabotage, the property would return to the initial owner. This legal incen-tive did not protect Jewish owners from the subsequent expropriation of that returned property, and the evidence suggests that, of course, the majority of saboteurs did not confess.

97. See ANR, SSRCI-Direcția Drepturilor Statului (DDS)—Comisia de Camuflaj (CC), 452bis/1941–502/1944. The decisions of several hundred CCs were canceled, and sometimes a ruling referred to several transactions.

98. During some months, such as August–September 1943, there was only one conviction (2.5 percent of all decisions) for camouflage. SSRCI-DDS-CC 486/1943. Overall, this CC uncovered 188 (9.3 percent) cases of camouflage out of 2,030 transactions it examined.

minish so much in less than two years? Did the saboteurs of Romanianization, now accustomed to the new repressive legislation and practices, somehow find methods to avoid detection? A close scrutiny of the antisabotage laws, procedures, and jurisprudence from the epoch, as well as a study of contemporary personal documents, suggests that the saboteurs of Romanianization learned how to bypass anticamouflage laws and judicial practices.

In spite of their aggressive title, the (anti-)camouflage commissions failed to uncover the breaches of Romanianization. Judicial procedures moved at a sluggish pace and the hearings and follow-up procedures often took more than a year (sometimes even two). Romanianization bureaucrats blamed the camouflage commissions for their inefficiency, arguing that certain judges delayed the decision-making process significantly. For instance, SSRCI people discovered that a particular camouflage commission took over a year to finalize a decision because some of its members (judges) neglected to elaborate on relevant information and left documentation unsigned.[99]

Overall, the commissions seldom uncovered camouflage of Romanianization. Indeed, the system offered them little latitude to do so. The two parties (or their lawyers) of the transaction presented their case with accompanying documents to prove their claims. The commission's only method of uncovering camouflage was to investigate if the buyer had "the appropriate financial means" to purchase the Jewish company or real estate in question. This criterion was too blunt an instrument to handle the complexity and ambiguity of the camouflage, and if the saboteurs of Romanianization refused to confess, the commission had to proclaim the transaction valid. It is thus no surprise that the CC uncovered camouflage in just 9.3 percent of cases.

On the other hand, diaries, memoirs, and interviews reported camouflage as a much wider practice. For example, of the available twenty diaries of residents of Romania who described the process of Romanianization, 50 percent mentioned the sabotage of Romanianization.[100] This ratio is closer to that of

---

99. ANR, SSRCI-DDS-CC, 471/1942. The MJ also requested public attorney offices to keep detailed statistics of prosecuted sabotage cases.

100. I consulted twenty diaries written by residents of World War II Romania, which referred to Romanianization. Seven diarists were Jewish: Banuş, *Sub camuflaj*; F. Brunea-Fox, *Oraşul măcelului* (Bucureşti: Hasefer, 1997); B. Brănişteanu, *Jurnal*, 3 vols. (Bucureşti: Hasefer, 2003–2006); Dagani, *Groapa*; Miriam Korber-Bercovici, *Jurnal de ghetou: Djurin, Transnistria, 1941–1943* (Bucureşti: Kriterion, 1995); Dorian, *Jurnal*; Sebastian, *Jurnal*. Thirteen diaries were written by non-Jewish authors: Dumitru Amzar, *Jurnal Berlinez* (Bucureşti: România Press, 2005); Argetoianu, *Însemnări zilnice*; N. D. Cocea, *Jurnal* (Bucureşti: Editura Politică, 1970); Petru Comarnescu, *Pagini de jurnal*, 3 vols. (Bucureşti: Noul Orfeu, 2003); Gala Galaction, *Jurnal*, 5 vols. (Bucureşti: Albatros, 1999–2003); Ioan

the camouflages uncovered by one CC during its first month of activity (22.4 percent) than to the CC's average during its entire existence (9.3 percent over almost two years). Additionally, confidential reports produced by German, Swiss, and French diplomatic representatives in Bucharest referred frequently to the issue of camouflage and corruption that plagued the process of Romanianization.[101] A comparison of all these data suggests that, even though we will never be able to quantify it precisely, a large proportion of the population engaged in sabotaging Romanianization; at least 22 percent, probably much more, of all cases of Romanianization.[102]

The Antonescu regime permitted some Jews more space to maneuver with regard to the Romanianization of properties during the second part of the war. A 1943 law (no. 143), for instance, allowed "deserving" Jews the legal status of ethnic Romanians, which preserved their property rights. The same law exempted Jews married to ethnic Romanian partners from the expropriation of urban real estate by donating the property to their ethnic Romanian partners or their offspring. Obviously, the majority of Romanian Jews could not fit into these narrow categories.[103] Nevertheless, these more liberal Romanianization regulations, paralleling the regime's opportunistic softening of its antisemitic policies from 1942 onward, created hope for local Jews that they might survive Romanianization and the war's terrible tragedies, after all.[104] In general, the ambiguous nature of legislation, which lacked clarity and consistency and stipulated many exceptions, facilitated the sabotage of Romanianization.

Hudită, *Jurnal Politic*, 14 vols (București, Pitesti: Roza Vânturilor, Institutul European, Lucman, Paralela 45, Editura Pro, Comunicare.ro, 1998–2011); Paul Mihail, *Jurnal: 1940–1944* (București: Paideia, 1999); Constantin Rădulescu-Motru, *Revizuiri și adăugiri*, 8 vols. (București: Floarea Darurilor, 1996–2001); Miron Radu Paraschivescu, *Jurnalul unui cobai: 1940–1954* (Cluj-Napoca: Dacia, 1994); Rosetti, *Pagini de jurnal*; Constantin Sănătescu, *Jurnal* (București: Humanitas, 1993); Alice Voinescu, *Jurnal* (București: Albatros, 1997); René de Weck, *Jurnal*. Ten (four Jewish and six non-Jewish) out of the twenty diarists mentioned the sabotage and camouflage of the process.

101. Hincu, *Confidențial*, 34–35, 39, 41, 69; Carol Iancu, ed., *Shoah in Romania: Evreii în timpul regimului Antonescu. Documente diplomatice Franceze inedite* (Iași: Polirom, 2001), 153, 166, 168–69, 175, 180; see Trașcă and Deletant, *Al III-lea Reich*, 335, 385–88, 698.

102. Perhaps more than half of Romanianization cases were camouflage, keeping in mind the self-censorship of diarists living in a dictatorship and at risk of a police search at any time. For the diarists' self-censorship and fear that authorities might uncover their notes, see Pană, *Născut in 02*, 634; Korber-Bercovici, *Jurnal de ghetou*, 118–19; Banuș, *Sub camuflaj*, 315–16.

103. According to historian Lya Benjamin, thirty-three Romanian Jews were assimilated with ethnic Romanians between July 1943 and July 1944. During World War I, 286 Jewish soldiers obtained Romanian citizenship for their bravery. The number of Jewish volunteers who fought in Romania's wars is still unclear. See Benjamin, *Legislația*, 234–43.

104. See article 3, paragraphs A and B of the decree law no. 143/March 9th, 1943, published in *Monitorul Oficial* 58 (10 Martie 1943): 2038–42.

These ambiguities, particularly the exceptions, enabled multiple interpretations of the same law.[105]

Sabotaging the Romanianization of Urban Real Estate

The saboteurs used different methods, some more ingenious than others, to bypass the Romanianization of houses. Fictitious transfers or rentals of Jewish properties to gentiles, preventing potential beneficiaries from visiting the Romanianized houses (still inhabited by former Jewish owners), and destroying the signs installed by CNR on the Romanianized houses, emerged as some of the most creative types of sabotage.

Among the various types of fraud used by the saboteurs of Romanianization, one in particular straddled the borders of legality: requests by the same person or family for numerous residencies. Although such behavior was not a crime in itself, the authorities suspected that fraudulent intentions lay behind these ethnic Romanians' applications. Romanianization officials suspected that the applicants were motivated not by the need to obtain a family accommodation, but by the desire to speculate on the real estate by subletting to other less entrepreneurial gentiles, or even to Jews. By September 1942, more than 50,000 requests for only 4,000 available Jewish houses had been submitted to CNR. This avalanche of demands from would-be Romanianizers compelled SSRCI to publish a press release urging the public to denounce those who requested accommodations from CNR without proper justification. The most outrageous example quoted by SSRCI was the case of a citizen who submitted thirty-two applications for Jewish houses.[106]

Some ethnic Romanians submitted many applications because they felt entitled to many apartments. An army officer, a major from Bucharest, for example, requested nineteen houses. He claimed to deserve them because of his brave conduct on the battlefield and the hardships endured by his large family. He also complained about the abuses of the distribution process, when CNR bureaucrats allegedly awarded residences to undeserving citizens, such as busi-

105. Numerous and inconsistent definitions of who was Jewish, who was exempted from Romanianization, and deadline extensions were among the ambiguities and exceptions that enabled misinterpretation of Romanianization laws. Trașcă, *Chestiunea evreiască,* 311–50; see Trașcă and Deletant, *Al III-lea Reich,* 385–86; ANR, MEN-DS, 63/1941, 127; see also MEN-DOPCI, 79/1941, 35–41; MEN-DOPCI, 86/1941, 195–99; MJ-DJ, 114/1941, 1:29–30, 96, 100–10.

106. See "O comunicare a CNR-ului în legătură cu închirierile de imobile," *Viața:* 507 (September 14, 1942): 5. Even after September 1941, things continued to move slowly, and CNR complained to Antonescu that the avalanche of requests (more than 50,000) prevented a rapid distribution of Romanianized houses to ethnic Romanian beneficiaries. See MEN-DS, 52/1941, 135–37.

nessmen and liberal professionals. As a good and deserving Romanian, the officer resented the selection process, and accused the CNR of using "a Judeo-Masonic style." Ironically enough, greedy Romanianizers such as this one suspected even the institution that was the leader in robbing the Jews, CNR, of being "contaminated by Jewish and Masonic influence."[107]

Another way of sabotaging the Romanianization of residences consisted of maneuvers to slow down the process of eviction of Jewish owners and tenants and of renting properties to ethnic Romanian beneficiaries. While Romanian Jews could pursue certain legal avenues in order to avoid eviction from their expropriated apartments, Antonescu's officials soon outlawed "unorthodox" methods of resisting the eviction and threatened the stubborn Jewish "saboteurs" with severe punishments. What exactly were these unorthodox methods of resisting eviction? For one, Jews refused to accept the preview visits of their homes by potential beneficiaries of Romanianized residences, who needed to see the houses before choosing what they liked. Noting this pattern, the authorities charged those who refused access with criminal behavior. They also accused of sabotage Jewish owners and tenants who destroyed the details about the house and the preview visiting hours posted on the doors.[108]

Although widely employed, these methods of breaching Romanianization posed serious risks for the saboteurs. The press reported many such cases in the summer of 1942. Outraged by the "difficulties" faced while trying to choose a house from the available Romanianized residencies, numerous would-be Romanianizers complained to the press. Newspapers publicized these cases, and urged the authorities to punish "Jewish audacity" and "defiance" in the toughest way possible. In August 1942, one journalist demanded the deportation of the Jewish offenders to a "lice-infected area of Russia."[109] As a result of this public outcry, CNR inspectors investigated the Romanianized apartments still inhabited by Jews. The vigilance of the inspectors proved successful; CNR immediately boasted its first "victories" on this domestic front. The newspapers announced that several Jewish Bucuresteni had been evicted and interned in camps.[110]

107. ANR, PCM-SSI, 90–1941, 43–49.

108. "Evrei sancționați pentru că au împiedicat vizitarea apartamentelor ce se închiriază," *Timpul* 1898 (August 21, 1942): 6.

109. Probably he thought of Transnistria, the former Soviet area where many Jewish deportees died of typhus during the Antonescu regime. See "Note și comentarii," *Viața* 477 (August 15, 1942): 3.

110. See, for instance, "Evrei evacuați pentru neafișarea biletului de închiriere," *Timpul* 1901 (August 24, 1942): 9 and "Evrei evacuați pentru refuz de afișare a biletelor de închiriat," *Viața* 486 (August 25, 1942): 3.

Personal documents of Jewish survivors confirm that the procedure of distributing Romanianized houses could have led to serious consequences for Jews still living in their own house. If a bargain-hunting Romanianizer found a reason to denounce or threaten a Jew with a real or imaginary accusation of sabotage, the Jew risked harsh punishment. Ethnic Romanian beneficiaries were obviously eager to move into Jewish houses despite being weary of competition, and suspicious of potential sabotage or legal resistance.[111]

For gentiles, too, sabotaging the Romanianization of properties held danger. Ethnic Romanian beneficiaries of CNR houses were, for example, responsible for a form of sabotage that Antonescu's bureaucrats found particularly annoying. To their dismay, some Romanianization profiteers showed their gratitude for obtaining expropriated Jewish houses by subletting them to Jewish tenants, thus breaching the goal of the Romanianization project. Uncovering these sabotages, CNR bureaucrats referred them to the police, urging the eviction of such undeserving ethnic Romanians.[112] Many gentiles engaged in various acts of camouflage despite these dangers. Taking so many risks for something one could have obtained "honestly" by following the Romanianization procedures appeared incomprehensible to others. One journalist, for example, argued that "Christians who camouflaged Jewish fortunes made a mistake. They could have seized those Jewish fortunes in an honest way."[113]

Besides the initiatives of individual Jews, there were other causes for the failure of Romanianization of real estate. These pertained mainly to the structural deficiencies of the organizations in charge of the process, such as SSRCI/CNR. These institutions confronted internal weaknesses—insufficient, incompetent, and corrupt personnel, poor management, and frequent leadership changes—that crippled their performance. After numerous denunciations complaining about the problems plaguing SSRCI/CNR, Antonescu appointed several commissions to examine the effectiveness of the leading Romanianization institution. The results of these investigations revealed a somber reality at CNR.

An audit team from the ministry of finance (MF) investigated CNR and issued a substantial report in December 1941 attesting to its chaotic organization and processes:

111. For example, see the testimony of Hefter Avraam from April 9, 1945 collected during the investigation of World Jewish Congress in post-Antonescu Romania. CSIER, III-Congresul Mondial Evreiesc (CME), fișa no. 46; also Dorian, *Jurnal*, 231; Banuș, *Sub camuflaj*, 55–56.

112. ANR, PCM-SSI, 90/1941, 164–65.

113. This article attracted the attention of Emil Dorian, who recorded it in his diary. Dorian, *Jurnal*, 232.

It lacks an internal organization plan and coordination between its various sub-departments.... Clerks do not know their precise tasks ... It is inefficient.... From a quantitative and, especially, a qualitative perspective, CNR does not have the necessary personnel.... Because of the great urgency to establish this institution, personnel were recruited hastily ... and at random.... CNR has insufficient employees.... Due to technical and legal problems, as well as organizational deficiencies, CNR experienced considerable delays in seizing expropriated goods. Expropriations were made through different laws, at different times, for different categories of goods, some of them even before the establishment of CNR. These laws referred to different procedures and institutions, which sometimes did not yet exist.... Another problem is to avoid deterioration of the expropriated assets which have not been yet inventoried and seized. A long period of time passed between the moment of expropriation of real estate and taking over the property, a period which enabled uncontrolled deterioration.[114]

The future looked bleak for CNR. The audit team concluded that without appropriate supervision, CNR's assets would erode quickly, and the state still had to compensate former owners and personnel who supervised and administered those goods. Struggling with all of these organizational problems, it is no wonder that CNR performed poorly in seizing the Romanianized properties. In February 1942, the MF found that CNR managed to take over only 334 of a total of 30,000 Jewish buildings expropriated all over the country. This data showed that the Romanianization of Jewish real estate advanced extremely slowly. Legal formalities, an insufficient number of technical experts to make evaluations, unreliable inventories, contestation in courts by Romanian Jews, and other technicalities delayed the process. Since the proclamation about the expropriation of Jewish urban real estate (March 1941), CNR had seized only a small fraction of the expropriated buildings for full-fledged ownership—230 out of 17,000 in Bucharest—that could be rented to ethnic Romanians. Outside the capital, Romanianization fared even worse: during the same period, CNR seized only 114 buildings out of 13,000. Furthermore, Romanianizaton bureaucrats engaged in more outrageous abuses outside of Bucharest than in the capital itself. The same report mentioned that in Dorohoi county, for example, the winners of the public auctions for renting the Romanianized properties "were the members of the auction committee."[115]

---

114. ANR, MF-CSIS, 412/1942, 2–119.
115. ANR, MF-CSIS, 413/1942, 52–58; 221–23.

Ştefan Ionescu

Sabotage of the Romanianization of Businesses

Just as with the expropriation of Jewish real estate, the Romanianization of the business sector faced a lot of difficulties, especially sabotage. Camouflage through the association between Jewish and ethnic Romanian partners represented one of most successful forms of sabotage of the Romanianization of companies. Authorities complained a great deal about this sabotage method and about the difficulty in uncovering it. Although at the beginning of the Antonescu regime this type of business contract looked like a promising way to exclude Jews from the economy, by 1942 the authorities became disenchanted with it, and even planned to forbid such partnerships completely. The reason for this change of policy was the growing suspicion that such associations were often a cover for a breach of Romanianization, and that the real intention of business partners was to bypass the antisemitic restrictions, not to advance the Romanianization of the company.

In the summer of 1942, a MEN internal memo assessed the pressing problem of the camouflage of Jewish businesses through the growing number of "associative-participatory" companies, and advocated tough legislation against it. The associative-participatory company was a legal way of organizing private enterprises. Facing various legal and administrative limitations that restricted their participation in economic life, Jewish entrepreneurs engaged in creative strategies to safeguard their businesses.[116] The Romanianization officials noticed that, suddenly, the associative-participatory business, a type of company rarely used, became widely employed. After detailed examination of this issue, they reached the conclusion that this type of company was formed because the law did not stipulate any obligation to register the new associates. In this way, the Jews bypassed the Romanianization laws.[117]

In just a few years, Romania witnessed a burst of associative-participatory companies. In this way, Jewish entrepreneurs escaped the legal restrictions of Romanianization. Worried by the extent of this type of "systematic" sabotage, SSRCI bureaucrats advocated tougher measures against it. "We have written the current draft law which nullifies all the associative-participative contracts made since September 1940 that have Jewish partners, and forbids them in the future."[118]

116. If they were single business owners or shareholders, Jewish entrepreneurs could neither register new companies nor modify the existing ones.

117. Titus Dragoş, ed., *Românizarea: Înfăptuiri: 6 Decembrie 1941-6 Decembrie 1942* (Bucureşti: Tipografia Curierul Judiciar, 1942), 38–39.

118. ANR, MEN-DOP-SIF, 1/1940, 171–72.

Afraid that SSRCI's suggestions would paralyze economic life, the government did not follow the urging of radical bureaucrats; as a result associative-participatory companies with Jewish partners continued to function. Even though the increasing regulation and surveillance of this genre of business produced some results, massive registration failed to prevent the sabotage problem.[119] In May 1943, for example, SSRCI urged MEN to adopt more radical measures against Jewish businessmen associated with ethnic Romanians, in order to counter yet another sabotage method. SSRCI noticed that some ethnic Romanian partners withdrew from their business associations with local Jews who thus remained the only legal partner in those companies. SSRCI complained that it lacked the necessary legal mechanisms to act against the ingenious Jewish entrepreneurs.[120] According to MEN, the SSRCI was correct: this type of sabotage was a systematic practice.[121] The subsequent measures adopted by the Antonescu regime, which included several special directives, suggest that it was indeed widespread.[122]

No matter how valuable official documents might be in portraying the camouflages of Romanianization, they somehow offer only an external perspective on this issue. The human stories behind the dry narratives of Romanianization reports and press accounts were recorded in the private documents of both Jews and gentiles in World War II Romania.[123] One such case was Matei Gall, survivor of a mass execution in Transnistria.[124] Returning to Romania in spring 1944, Gall hid in Bucharest and Deva for several months, until the collapse of the Antonescu regime. In his memoirs, he depicted several episodes of the camouflage of Jewish companies by ethnic Germans who succeeded in breaching the Romanianization laws in those cities:

I was shocked ... by the weird economic collaborations between Jews and Germans. In spite of the racial laws, I found small companies that belonged to Jews in practice, while legally they functioned under the cover of the German names of the co-owners.... I bumped into a similar case in Bucharest, during the period when I

---

119. By December 1942, 34,000 associative-participatory companies and other associative enterprises filed declarations on the ethnic origin of their associates. See Dragoş, *Românizarea*, 38–39.

120. ANR, MEN-DOP-SIF, 1/1940, 248.

121. ANR, MEN-DS, 70/1941, 10–15.

122. See SSRCI's "ministerial decisions" no. 23,681 of 7 September 1942 and no. 24,491 of September 14, 1942. Dragoş, *Românizarea*, 38.

123. See Sapatino, *Trăiri, trăiri*, 76; Politzer, *O tinereţe*, 30; Border, *Între două lumi*, 10–11.

124. The son of a middle-class Jewish family from Deva, Gall joined the Communist (underground) Party and, in 1942, he and the Communist inmates of Jewish origin were deported to Transnistria (Vapniarka and, later, Râbniţa).

had to hide in the house of ... a Jewish lawyer ... who lived with a beautiful German woman from Transylvania.... I found the secret of the lawyer's prosperity. Since the racial laws had been implemented he could not practice his profession.... In the new context, a business couple was created between the Jewish lawyer and his German girlfriend. They registered a company using the name of the Aryan lady, and started to make various products for the Romanian and German armies. Being of good ethnic origin, she obtained the necessary orders from the army.[125]

Foreign observers also noticed the successful camouflage of Jewish businesses in World War II Bucharest. René de Weck, the head of the Swiss legation in Bucharest, recorded in his diary the camouflage conducted by his girlfriend's sister. This was done in association with a Jewish businesswoman from Bucharest, who managed to save her tailor workshop from Romanianization.[126] Other diplomatic documents mentioned the illegal practices of sabotaging the Romanianization of companies. Jacques Truelle, for example, the chief French diplomat in Bucharest, reported to his superiors that numerous Jewish entrepreneurs camouflaged their businesses with the help of ethnic Romanian accomplices. Furthermore, Truelle argued that Germans purchased many Jewish companies, using ethnic Romanians as fictitious buyers.[127] One of the most outrageous cases of sabotage reported by the French diplomat concerned the former chief of Romanianization, General Eugen Zwiedeneck. Zwiedeneck functioned as the head of SSRCI from April–December 1941. He was fired for making serious mistakes. "This bureaucrat," Truelle recorded, "decided that the best way to Romanianize several companies and real estate was to transfer them to his wife."[128] Overall, it seems that personal relations, such as friendship, were decisive for mutual participation. The engineer Constantin Sapatino, for one, got involved in camouflage at the request of Mr. Steinberg, a Jewish businessman whose father was a former employee and a good friend of Sapatino's father.[129]

Facing the sudden excess of decrees aimed at excluding them from the local economy and society, Jews responded with massive resistance. Instead of weapons—as using weapons would have triggered a general massacre in the context of the widespread obsession with Jewish domestic treason—Romanian Jews employed strategies of resistance developed throughout history. Thus,

125. Gall, *Eclipsa*, 268–69.

126. René de Weck, *Jurnal*, 250.

127. The January 14, 1942 letter of Jacques Truelle, the head of the French Legation in Romania, to Admiral Darlan, the secretary of France's foreign affairs, can be found in Iancu, *Shoah*, 168–69.

128. Iancu, *Shoah*, 169.

129. Sapatino, *Trăiri, trăiri*, 76.

they engaged in lobbying to secure the support of political and religious authorities, conversion, spiritual resistance, intracommunitarian aid, rescue, and emigration. Additionally, in the last months of the regime, Jews, especially Zionist youth groups, prepared for armed resistance against a potential last-minute pogrom.

Though by the end of the Antonescu regime (August 1944), Romanianization had taken a harsh toll on the Jews—houses had been expropriated, Jewish owners evicted, and buildings rented to gentiles—the authorities failed to achieve a complete Romanianization of real estate and businesses. Antonescu's bureaucrats were frustrated in their efforts to seize all Jewish buildings targeted for Romanianization, not to mention their distribution to deserving ethnic Romanians. The reasons for this failure ranged from Romania's involvement in World War II, and the implications of this enterprise, to the structural problems of the Romanian economy. The international events that tipped the war in the Allies' favor and the concerns triggered among local elites because of that outcome softened the antisemitic policies of the Antonescu regime, including Romanianization. Two of the main domestic reasons for the partial failure of the process were the *illegal* (sabotage) and *legal resistances* to Romanianization conducted by Jews, often in collaboration with gentiles. Legal resistance consisted mainly of tens of thousands of contestations against the Romanianization of houses, which brought the reversal of expropriations—around 10 percent—or the delay of Romanainization up to the collapse of the regime. Until these judicial procedures were finalized, the regime could not distribute real estate for ownership. The court system worked slowly and sometimes issued contradictory decisions.

Some Jewish entrepreneurs also obtained in court the reversal of the Romanianization of their businesses. The Antonescu regime hesitated to adopt radical laws for the Romanization of businesses fearing that such action would paralyze the economy during the war. State bureaucrats tried to increase the penetration of ethnic Romanians into the business sector using special loans for would-be Romanianizers and administrative restrictions against Jews and other ethnic minorities, but these efforts were in vain. The illegal resistance—sabotage—through camouflage consisted of fictitious transactions of real estate and companies from Jews to gentiles, which prevented their Romanianization. Overall, the Romanian Jews' massive use of legalities (judicial contestations and camouflage) against the state takeover of their properties, together with other structural problems of the regime and its institutions, and the international events that tipped the scale in the Allies' favor, led to a partial failure of the process.

The cases of sabotage and legal resistance illustrate the range of perspectives on Romanianization and the chasm between ideology and everyday reality. The majority of ethnic Romanians failed to conform to official expectations. While many ethnic Romanians agreed with the idea of "redistribution" of Jewish wealth in their favor, many of these supporters did not follow the official procedures for the distribution of the spoils. They wanted to profit from redistribution much earlier than official participation would have entailed, and often found it more profitable to sabotage the process, or decided to help their Jewish friends. Thus, the gentile response to Romanianization was rather ambivalent and often, directly or indirectly, helped Jewish resistance.

Sabotage and legal resistance played a vital role in the survival of Romanian Jews, who managed, with major costs and risks, to reverse, paralyze, or delay the Romanianization of their houses and businesses. When King Mihai and the coalition of opposition parties toppled Antonescu, in August 1944, it was clear that the Romanianization project, as envisioned by its theoreticians, had failed.

Yehuda Bauer

20 Jewish Resistance in the Ukraine and Belarus during the Holocaust

What exactly is meant by "Jewish Resistance?" In parts of Europe, especially in the West, many Jewish individuals joined resistance movements for a variety of reasons. Were these cases of resistance by Jews, or Jewish Resistance? Do we speak only of armed resistance, or do we include unarmed resistance by Jews not able to use firearms but only so called "cold" weapons (knives, clubs, pitchforks, and other implements)? Do we include or exclude unarmed reactions, such as morale-building activities, flight, hiding, organized smuggling into ghettos, social welfare, or religious activities, all of which were intended to react to this murderous persecution? There was no such thing as "passive" resistance, because the term resistance already denotes activity rather than passivity. It seems essential to define our terms of reference in as clear a manner as possible.

It is proposed here that in the conditions of World War II, given the Nazi-German policies of absolute terror and mass murder, any Jewish action, whether by a group or by an individual, that ran counter to real or perceived Nazi-German policies, has to be regarded as active nonacceptance of such policies, that is, resistance. That includes unarmed resistance, such as smuggling food into ghettos; social welfare; educational efforts; keeping religious traditions that were forbidden; underground political activities including publication of newspapers, leaflets, or books; keeping diaries; and more. It also includes, of course, physical resistance, whether with firearms or "cold" weapons—clubs, knives, and so on. This general statement is true for the Ukraine and Belarus as it is for other German-occupied areas.

We will differentiate here between areas that had been part of the Soviet

Union before 1939, and the areas of what then was eastern Poland (today western Ukraine and western Belarus), occupied by the Soviets in September 1939, as a result of the nonaggression treaty between the Soviet Union and Nazi Germany. According to Soviet estimates, in 1941 there were some 2.4 million Jews in the whole of the Ukraine, out of a general population of some 42 million. In Belarus, the estimate is close to 700,000, out of a general population of 10,589,000, for a total of roughly 3.1 million.[1] Of these, in eastern Ukraine (pre-1939 borders), about 700,000 Jews remained under German rule; the figure for eastern Belarus is 240,000. For western Ukraine, the estimate is that some 840,000 Jews remained under German occupation; for western Belarus, the figure is 350,000–360,000. The total number of Jews under German rule in all of the Ukraine and Belarus comes to roughly 2.1 million. In the eastern parts of the two countries, about 20,000–25,000 survived altogether; in the western areas the figure is similar, between 15,000 and 20,000. The total is therefore about 40,000–45,000.[2] The figures indicate a survival rate of 1–2 percent.

By 2011, no detailed research had been done on most of the eastern areas, with the exception of Minsk, the capital of Belarus. Some material exists on Vitebsk (also in Belarus) and a few Ukrainian cities, as well as a number of published memoirs by survivors. Neither the Germans nor the local population in the two countries evinced any interest in the internal affairs of the Jewish communities, so that there is little documentary material available about them. Historical research on the western areas is more advanced than on the eastern ones. Reliance on postwar testimonies, while no doubt problematic, is yet important, because a number of testimonies, independently obtained and in agreement with each other, are a reliable source. At the same time, one has to realize that, while the number of survivors is small, in the aggregate it amounts to tens of thousands of people, most of whom testified as to their fate. On the other hand, we have no evidence from 98 percent of the people involved. Most of the survivors were young, and probably energetic and more determined than others may have been, so that the testimonies we have may not represent the experiences or the attitudes of those who were killed.

1. Shalom Cholawsky, *The Jews of Bielorussia During World War II* (Amsterdam: Harwood Publishers, 1998), 3:305; Gershon D. Hundert, ed., *The YIVO Encyclopedia of Jews in Eastern Europe* (New Haven, Conn.: Yale University Press, 2008), 140–42. Soviet statistics are not reliable—quite a number of Jews sought to hide their ethnicity, and there was also considerable movement from the areas under discussion into Russia.

2. Yizhak Arad, *The Holocaust in the Soviet Union* (Lincoln: University of Nebraska Press and Yad Vashem, 2009), 521–25.

The German invasion of the Soviet Union that began on June 22, 1941 (Operation Barbarossa) was initially highly successful, though the first doubts in German generals' minds about the prospect of a German victory arose already in the course of July. By August, all of the western, formerly Polish, territories in the Ukraine and Belarus were in German hands. From then on, the German advance became increasingly more difficult and therefore slower. That gave people, especially in the eastern sectors, and especially Jews, who thought they were in immediate danger from the invaders (though they had no idea of what the Germans intended to do to them) an opportunity, limited though it was by the chaos that reigned in the Soviet Union in those days, to flee into the interior of the country. Many young men had been drafted into the Red Army, either prior to the outbreak of hostilities, or during the first few days of the invasion; but only a few survived, largely because all Soviet Jewish POWs who could be identified as such were selected out of the general number of prisoners and killed.

The mass murder of Jews, especially in the eastern areas, happened very quickly. It was executed by the four special task groups (Einsatzgruppen A–D) of the SS, by Order Police (Ordnungspolizei) battalions, by other special units of the SS under the direct command of Heinrich Himmler, head of the SS, and many army units. In most small places, the Germans did not bother to set up either ghettos or Jewish councils (Judenräte, or Aeltestenräte [Councils of Elders]). They ordered all Jews to assemble at a certain point, led them out of the villages or townships on some pretext or other—usually telling them that they were being relocated for forced labor—and killed them. Only in larger cities were Jewish councils set up for a short time, usually after a first wave of mass murder, and then the elimination process continued; it included the Judenräte members as well. The Jews were taken by surprise, as no one had imagined that a total annihilation of all people defined as Jews was possible. The mass murder proceeded in quick stages. While the speed was tremendous, it nevertheless differed slightly in different areas, as the German commanders had considerable leeway as to when to apply the consensual policy of the genocide of the Jews.

In the eastern areas, and especially in the Ukraine, the annihilation of the Jews was especially rapid. It was therefore extremely difficult for the Jews to organize and maintain some kind of social or communal life, even if a Judenrat was appointed at first. Jewish communities as such did not exist in the Soviet Union—they had been abolished subsequent to the Bolshevik revolution.

Jews had been atomized by the regime, and while a Jewish nationality was recognized and registered as such on identity cards that every Soviet citizen had to carry, by 1939 there were no Jewish communal organizations in existence. There were, however, in 1941, remnants of cultural institutions—such as a declining number of primary schools teaching in the Yiddish language, but devoid of any specific Jewish content (beyond the inclusion of some classic Yiddish writers who emphasized class differences, at least in Soviet eyes). Jewish intellectuals had to be careful not to be branded as bourgeois nationalists. In effect, therefore, there was no Jewish leadership that could take charge in organizing any kind of Jewish reaction to the murderous onslaught of the Germans and their local collaborators. The paradox consists in the fact that in many cases Jews were forced to establish a kind of communal framework, for a short, transitional period, until they were killed.

In pre-1939 Soviet Ukraine, there was little armed opposition to the Germans. This was partly due to the fact that the region is agricultural, with no significant mountain ranges or forested areas. However, the main cause was that many among the peasant population had no reason to love the Soviet regime, which had been responsible for mass death, exile, and incarceration of millions in a ruthless rush to industrialization that created an artificial starvation in order to export huge amounts of grain in return for industrial equipment from the West (1930–33). Also, the rapid advance of the Germans caused many Ukrainians to expect a Soviet defeat and a long-term imposition of German rule in their country. Many tended to accommodate themselves to this new situation. Thousands of Ukrainians joined auxiliary forces set up by the Germans that participated actively in the killing of their Jewish neighbors. There were Ukrainians who supported the Soviet regime and established underground cells, mainly in the cities, and there were some "red" villages of Soviet sympathizers, opponents of the Germans, who were therefore more friendly to Jews. But these were a small minority; the majority of the population either collaborated in the persecution and murder of the Jews, or were afraid—rightly so, one must add—for their own lives and those of their families. They tried not to get involved in any kind of activity, positive or negative, with the foreign occupiers. Yet, large numbers of Ukrainians had been recruited into the Red Army prior to the German occupation, their families remaining under the Germans, and there developed a natural tendency to hope for a Soviet victory. These were contradictory tendencies, but the majority of Ukrainians, especially at the beginning of the German occupation, had no sympathy for the plight of their

Jewish neighbors. It was this attitude, which can be characterized as veering between being uninvolved to being actively hostile, that explains the almost total annihilation of the Jews in pre-1939 Soviet Ukraine. In this situation, Jews found themselves in a trap: armed resistance was almost out of the question, and unarmed reactions were next to impossible. The attitude of the Ukrainians became increasingly hostile toward the Germans after the German defeat at Stalingrad in early 1943, and as a result of the imposition of forced labor, locally and then in Germany. By that time, however, there were practically no Jews left.

In all the vast areas of eastern Ukraine, the slaughter of the Jews was quick and total. Some examples will demonstrate this. The areas administered by the civilian administration in eastern Ukraine, as of September 1941, were included in the Reichskommissariat Ukraine, ruled by Erich Koch, a violent and sadistic Nazi. Many Jews had resided in the "Generalbezirk" (province) of Zhitomir, but many also had managed to flee before the area was occupied. Thus, in the town of Zhitomir, which had a prewar population of some 30,000 Jews, only a third remained behind. The town was occupied on July 9, 1941, and a ghetto was established, about which we know little. It was liquidated on September 19 by a subunit of Einsatzgruppe C, with the help of the Ukrainian militia set up by the Germans. Two hundred and forty artisans and workers were left alive; they were murdered shortly afterwards. Berdichev was another town with a long Jewish history. Some two-thirds of the prewar Jewish population, or 16–17,000, remained behind. The town was captured on July 7, 1941; a ghetto established on July 25; on September 4, 1,500 young Jews were shot. Of the rest, 12,000 were killed on September 15. Those who remained, somewhere between 2,000 and 2,500 Jews, were murdered on November 3.[3]

The case of the large city of Dnipropetrovsk (Dnepropetrovsk in Russian) is typical. Of approximately 100,000 Jews who lived there among about half a million inhabitants, some 70,000 managed to flee before the Germans occupied it on August 25, 1941. The German Order Police battalion no. 314 and local Ukrainian militia killed most of the remaining Jews between October 13 and 16, about seven weeks after the Occupation began. Many Jews tried to hide, and German documentation shows that the Occupation authorities spent a great deal of effort trying to catch and murder them. Almost no one escaped. Most who remained, about 5,000, were shot in December; several hundred artisans were kept alive

3. Ibid., 168–70

for a few more weeks. There was no time to organize anything, neither unarmed nor armed resistance. There is evidence that one Jewish member of a Soviet underground cell participated in blowing up a bridge, was caught, and executed.[4]

The areas to the east of the Reichskommissariate Ukraine and Ostland (covering much of Belarus and a portion of northwestern Ukraine) were under military administration until the German defeat there. There was no difference between the east Ukrainian areas under military command and the areas to the west as regards the treatment of Jews. They were murdered by the same forces—Einsatzgruppe C, police battalions (especially no. 314), and Ukrainian militias, with the active support of the Wehrmacht (the German Army). Take the fate of the Jews in Kharkiv (Russian: Kharkov), for example, which was occupied by the Germans on October 23, 1941 and had a population of 833,000 in 1939, of whom an estimated 130,000 were Jews. Of these, 20,000 remained under German occupation, but only 10,271 registered as Jews—the others tried to hide. The local collaborationist Ukrainian administration ordered a Judenrat to be selected. The Germans created a ghetto for the Jews, who had to move there on December 16, obviously in order to facilitate their annihilation. They were killed during the first half of January 1942—according to German figures, over 21,000. On April 10, 1942, the Germans reported that there were still some Jews in hiding, but that the "Ukrainians ... have reported Jews in hiding, or families who housed them; these are being arrested each day. With a few exceptions, the attitude of the population of Kharkov to the Jews is absolutely negative."[5]

Mariupol, a harbor town on the Sea of Azov, was captured by the Germans on October 6, 1941, and on October 20, its 8,000 to 9,000 Jews were killed. The same applied to Kiev, the Ukrainian capital. Out of the approximately 160,000 Jews in the city, some 100,000 managed to flee before the German occupation, which occurred on September 19, 1941. Between September 24 and 28, a Soviet sabotage group that had remained behind blew up a number of houses in which German military offices had been established. In retaliation, the Germans decided to kill all Kiev Jews. On September 29, over 33,000 Jews were murdered, in the Babi-Yar ravine on the outskirts of the city; this was followed by a manhunt for the rest. A small number of Ukrainians and Russians hid Jews, but most collaborated in finding them and delivering them to the Germans. There was no time for any type of organized response.[6]

4. Ibid., 179–82, 501, 554.   5. Ibid., 190–92. The quotation is on page 192.
6. Ilya Ehrenburg and Vasily Grossman, *The Black Book* [*Chornaya Kniga*] (Jerusalem: Tarbut, 1970).

The same pattern can be found in the Crimea, which was occupied by the Germans between October 30 and November 16, 1941. Basically, all the Jews in the Crimea, some 45,000, were killed by early January 1942. The murderers were Einsatzgruppe D, police battalions, the army, and local Russian, Ukrainian, and Tartar collaborators. Again, the elimination process was so swift that there was no possibility of any kind of Jewish unarmed resistance.

The southern area of the Ukraine was occupied by Romanian troops, with German help, and presents a different picture. Romania was ruled by the Fascist dictator Ion Antonescu, who was informed of the impending invasion of the U.S.S.R. on January 14, 1941, by Hitler. Romania joined the Germans when they invaded on June 22, 1941. It had had to cede its northern provinces, Bessarabia and Bukovina (populated by Ukrainians, Romanians, Jews, and others) to the Soviets in 1940, and was now eager to reacquire these areas. The Antonescu regime was violently anti-Jewish. There was an explicit decision to kill as many Jews in the two provinces as possible and deport the rest to an area that the Romanians called Transnistria, between the rivers Dniestr (the northern boundary of Bessarabia) and the Bug, an area of the southern Ukraine that the Germans gave to Romania. It also included the harbor city of Odessa, which was occupied by the Romanians and the Germans on October 17, 1941. There were 320,000 Jews in that area, of whom some 200,000 lived in Odessa. Many Jews managed to flee before the fall of the area to the Germans and Romanians, but 115,000 were caught in Odessa and 80,000 in the other areas. On October 22, Soviet sabotage caused a major explosion in the new Romanian headquarters, killing the Romanian general in command and many other officers. The Romanian reaction was to kill Jews, perhaps following the example of Kiev a month previously. Tens of thousands were killed in the most horrific fashion (many of them burnt to death), a ghetto was established (with no Judenrat) that was liquidated in stages, and some 30,000 Jews were deported to three death traps in Transnistria—Bogdanovka, Akmecetka, and Domanovka, where almost all of them died of starvation, epidemics, and planned murder. A remnant, some five hundred people, hid in the underground catacombs and sewers of the city, and some of them survived. Again, there was no possibility of any kind of resistance, especially as most of the local Ukrainian population was hostile. Of the 80,000 local Jews remaining under Romanian-German occupation outside of Odessa, some 10,000 were killed more or less immediately. The others, mainly Ukrainian Jews in the southern part of Transnistria, were quickly murdered or starved to death, very largely by Romanians, partly also by local German settlers whose families had lived in the area since the early nineteenth century. Obviously, in such circumstances no unarmed or armed resistance was possible, and no significant help came from the Ukrainian population.

Over 300,000 Jews lived in Bessarabia and Bukovina—the majority, 205,000, in Bessarabia. Some fled, or were deported into the Soviet interior (because they were considered to be anti-Soviet, and that saved their lives), but between at least 230,000 and 240,000 remained. During the first two months of the Romanian occupation, about 90,000 Jews were brutally killed by Romanian forces, Ukrainian neighbors, and Germans. In the summer of 1941—after an agreement between the Romanian and German military leadership regulating the deportation of Bessarabian and Bukovina Jews to Transnistria had been signed at Tighina, a town on the Dniestr, on August 30, 1941—close to 150,000 Jews were deported into the area. This was followed in 1942 by a few thousand more, mainly from areas within Romania proper, for a total of some 160,000. Ninety thousand of these were to die there before liberation. For technical reasons, most of the deportees were forced into the northern part of Transnistria and placed in ghettos and camps by the Romanian rulers. The idea was to wait until the Germans had established their control over the Ukraine and then deport the Jews over the Bug, to be killed there by the Nazis. In the meantime, they would do forced labor. Terrible conditions, lack of food, lack of even minimal housing, random killing by Romanian soldiers, policemen, and others, and typhoid epidemics greatly reduced their number. However, the Romanian administration was corrupt, and there was a minimum of time for the Jews to organize and try to improve their condition. For instance, in the two larger ghettos in the area, in the towns of Shargorod and Mogilev Podolski (Ukrainian: Mohiliv Podilskyi), there were Judenräte that managed to alleviate the suffering and enable survival.

Today, Shargorod is a small town (3,500 inhabitants) in southern Ukraine; during the war, some 6,000 Jews were deported there (in October and November 1941), largely from Bukovina; in addition, there were 1,500 local Ukrainian Jews. After they were already on their way, some of the deportees managed to organize themselves and, mainly by bribing corrupt Romanian officials, avoided the mass killings that took place on other deportation routes. By December, a leadership representing the four groups that had been deported from different locations in Bukovina had to arrange for 7,000 people to live in just 337 primitive, almost all-wooden, buildings. The head of the ghetto, Dr. Meir Teich, recruited the help of engineers, doctors, and other experts from among the deportees, and managed to organize the community. During the first harsh winter (1941–42), hundreds died in a typhoid epidemic (including twelve of the twenty-seven doctors). But a health department was set up that kept the ghetto and its inhabitants clean. During the second winter, only four people died; none during the third. Schools were organized; an orphanage began collecting the many orphans; a soap "factory" was established—all in the face of the hostility of Ukrainian collaborators and Romanian corruption. There were exceptions—some Romanian officials turned out to be friendly, and the ordinary Ukrainian population in the area, especially the women, did provide some help and sympathy. Teich and two committee members established contact with a group of Soviet partisans in a nearby forest, and by 1943 were already able to supply them with medicines and other materials. Where did they get the means for all this? One of the groups of deportees managed to smuggle their community's money chest into the ghetto. From January 1942 onward, they began receiving help from the Romanian Jewish community's Bucharest center, mainly in the form of goods that the government agreed to have shipped into Transnistria. This became significant after Stalingrad, when Romania began looking for a way out of the war. Contrary to draconian rules established by the authorities, the ghetto leaders managed to sell the goods they received and with the proceeds bought essential food and medicines. Hundreds of men had to do forced labor under harsh conditions and some died as a result, but there was no comparison between that and the hell holes where tens of thousands of Jews were killed in the southern part of the province. In the end, almost all of the Jews still alive after the first months in the ghetto survived, although the Soviet liberators who came in March 1944 were no less brutal than some of the Romanians had been.[7]

The other example is that of Mogilev Podolski, which had a population of some 20,000 locals in 1941. Long columns of Jewish deportees from Bessarabia and Bukovina arrived there in the autumn of 1941, after many had been killed by Romanian troops on the way. The Romanian authorities only gave up to 3,000 permits for Jews to stay in the town, but in fact 15,000 stayed on, in addition to the 5,000 local Ukrainian Jews. Lack of minimal housing, food, and medicine, and a typhoid epidemic during the first winter killed more than 3,500 people. 3,000 more were banished from the town, but most of these made their way back after a time. The situation in Shargorod was repeated here, ex-

7. M(eir) Teich, "Haminhal hayehudi haotonom ibegetto Shargorod (Transnistria)," *Yad Vashem Studies* 2 (1958): 203–36; Yad Vashem Archive (YVA), Ball-Kadduri Collection, 10/185.

cept that the numbers were higher. From the beginning, Siegfried Jägendorf, an engineer, stood out as organizer, and then head of the ghetto that the Romanians created there. By the summer of 1942, 17,000 Jews inhabited the ghetto and, as in Shargorod, intensive work in creating health care, providing soup kitchens for the needy, and insisting on fairness and equality in recruiting the forced labor demanded by the authorities saved many lives. Jägendorf managed to persuade the Romanians to let him organize a large group of experts and workers who not only repaired electricity and sewage, but also established a metal foundry called "Turnatoria," all of which enabled him to create income for the community that improved the standard of living. In time, and especially after the Antonescu regime realized that Germany might not win the war (this happened even before the battle of Stalingrad), the Romanians abandoned the idea of pushing the Jews beyond the Bug into German hands. Most of the Jews incarcerated in the ghetto survived the war.

There were other cases like these in northern Transnistria—as opposed to the mass killing that occurred in the south and in Odessa—but one must also stress that there was help from the outside, mainly from the Jews of Romania proper. One has to emphasize the importance of leadership: the moving spirit was the central personality in Romanian Jewry, the lawyer Wilhelm Filderman, who utilized internal political disagreements in the Antonescu regime to help persecuted Jews all over Romania, but especially in Transnistria. The International Red Cross was also persuaded to intervene, in the person of Eugene Kolb, its representative in Bucharest, and the Catholic Church (an important minority of Romanians were Roman Catholics), in the person of Papal nuncio Andrea Cassulo, was moved to visit Transnistria in the later stages of Romanian rule there.[8]

There is some evidence of Jewish membership in Soviet partisan activities late in 1943 and early 1944, but there was no massive participation, though Jewish communities, including the two discussed here, helped partisan detachments in their areas. The reason was probably that the deportees were foreigners in the area, whereas the partisans relied on local Ukrainians and people who were parachuted in or infiltrated from the unoccupied Soviet Union.

---

8. Siegfried Jägendorf, *Jägendorf's Foundry* (New York: Harper-Collins, 1991); Jean Ancel, *Transnistria, History and Document Summaries*, vol. 1 (Goldestein-Goren Diaspora Research Center, Tel-Aviv University, 2003); Aleksands I. Kruglov, *Katastrofa Ukrainskogo Evreistva, 1941–1944* (Karavella, Kharkov: Entsiklogodichenskii Spravodnik, 2001); Wendy Lower, *Nazi Empire-Building and the Holocaust in the Ukraine* (Chapel Hill: University of North Carolina Press, 2005).

Can the activities of Jewish councils such as those presented here in these two locations (and there were additional ones) be considered unarmed resistance? It appears that the answer is positive: the official Romanian policy aimed at the annihilation of the Jews and the activities of the councils were intended to achieve opposite ends. There was no possibility of armed resistance, so that the preservation of Jewish life was the only reaction that had any chance of success. It succeeded in some places and failed in others, but success was, it seems, due to a long history of Jewish communal organization—a tradition people could draw on—and in part the result of leadership by individuals who managed to get the support of their communities (not very easily, and against occasional opposition). Clearly these are cases of Jewish resistance, as the people involved identified with either Jewish ethnicity or religion.

One should differentiate between four regions with different characteristics and fate: eastern (that is, pre-1939 Soviet) Ukraine, Romanian-occupied Transnistria, eastern (pre-1939 Soviet) Belarus, and the formerly Polish areas of today's western Ukraine and western Belarus (the Polish name for those territories was *kresy*, that is, "borderlands").

Contrary to most of eastern Ukraine, eastern Belarus is an area of thick forests and swamps; only the border region between the two countries, known as Polesie—basically, the swampy and forested area of the river Pripet—forms an exception. Western Polesie lies in the *kresy*. The Germans occupied eastern Belarus during the first weeks of Operation Barbarossa, and mass killings took place in the main cities; but not all Jews were killed in the capital, Minsk (occupied by the Germans on June 28, 1941). There, a ghetto was established (July 20), the fourth-largest in Europe, with about 84,000 people (a second ghetto, separated from the first, was set up for 35,000 German Jews who were deported there on November 11, 1941, and killed in July 1942 and March 1943). Elsewhere, for a short time, there were ghettos in cities such as Vitebsk, Orsha, Mogilev, and Bobruisk as well, but they were all liquidated in October–November 1941. The Minsk ghetto was decimated by mass killing actions on November 7, 1941 and March 2 and July 28, 1942, but some thousands were left alive because Jewish labor was needed in the central German institutions in the city, and the numbers appear to have been too large for immediate total liquidation. The last Jews were not killed until 1943.

This situation enabled Minsk Jews to develop institutions and organize unarmed and armed resistance. As in the Ukraine, there were no Jewish communities in Soviet Belarus—they had been abolished by the Communist regime in

1918–19. But by force of circumstances, communities developed. In Minsk, the Germans quite randomly appointed a Judenrat, headed by a former middle co-op store official, Ilya Mishkin, who happened to have learned German. Mishkin organized a hospital, some schooling, social welfare, and tried to get food smuggled into the ghetto. From day one, Mishkin also collaborated closely with an underground set up by a Jewish Communist refugee from Warsaw, Hersh Smolar. A parallel underground Soviet anti-German group in the city, led by a Jew, was uncovered by the Germans, who also discovered that there was a Jewish underground leader in the ghetto whose assumed name they knew. Mishkin managed to save Smolar by presenting the Germans with a disfigured Jewish corpse with Smolar's bloodied false identity card shoved into its trousers; the Germans swallowed the story. Mishkin was killed in February 1942, but his successor, a refugee from Vilno (Vilnius) called Moshe Yaffe, continued his policies. When the Germans ordered all Jews to report to a major square on July 28 in preparation for their murder, Yaffe was commanded to calm the crowd. Instead, he yelled out to them that they were going to be killed, and they should hide. He was killed on the spot.

The Minsk Jewish underground succeeded in smuggling some 7,500 people, men, women, and children, into the surrounding dense forests. They were led out of the ghetto mostly by Jewish children, who could move with greater ease than adults. Soviet partisan units accepted some of them, but most of them died there, of sickness, pursuit by Germans and local collaborators, or in battle; an unknown number survived. The Minsk underground was, arguably, numerically the most significant case of Jewish armed resistance during the Holocaust. It was Jewish resistance, but once they reached the Soviet partisans, they became cases of resistance of Jews, as the majority of the fighters in the units they joined were non-Jews.[9] There is a great deal of evidence about individual Jews in other places in eastern Belarus who were active in the anti-German underground and in Soviet partisan detachments, but no attempt has been made, as of 2011, at a historical analysis in this regard.

The situation in the *kresy* was very different. There were an estimated 1.2 to 1.3 million Jews there before the war; relatively few managed to flee before the swiftly advancing German armies. Einsatzgruppen and other units murdered mainly men at first wherever they could, but quickly moved forward

9. Barbara Epstein, *The Minsk Ghetto* (Berkeley: University of California Press, 2008); Hersh Smolar, *The Minsk Ghetto* (New York: Holocaust Library, 1984); Dani Zayets, *Getto Minsk Vetoldotav leor hateyud hachadash* (Ramat Gan: Bar Ilan University Press, 2000).

with the Wehrmacht. In the Ukrainian south there were two main provinces, Volhynia to the north, and eastern Galicia in the south and west. There was only one major city, Lwow (Ukrainian: Lviv), some medium-sized towns, and many small townships with a high proportion of Jews called "*shtetlach*" (Yiddish: small towns, singular—*shtetl*). In most, but not all of them, ghettos were created, subjected to the usual brutal persecution; but in quite a number of them, the mass murder took place only a year after the Occupation, in the summer and fall of 1942. In others, the killings took place in stages, so that again, there was a minimum of time to organize some sort of life and engage in unarmed resistance. It is impossible to generalize, as there were communities where social cohesion collapsed totally, where Judenräte turned out to be corrupt traitors, and where the Germans and their Ukrainian helpers were able to use Jewish agents to prevent any kind of meaningful social life from developing. A typical case of this kind is the shtetl of Kremenets (Polish: Krzemieniec) in Volhynia, where the Germans concentrated some 14,000 in a ghetto that was subjected to extreme starvation, and the two successive Judenrat heads were despicable characters (Dr. Bronfeld and Itzik Diamant). Another case, though less extreme, was that of the *shtetl* of Buczacz in eastern Galicia, where there were, ultimately, some 13,000 Jews (Judenrat head—Baruch Kramer).[10] Yet another larger place was Czortkow, also in east Galicia (Judenrat head—Dr. Haim Ebner).[11] Such Judenrat heads were viewed very negatively by survivors, though they did provide some minimal help to groups of inhabitants. But there were a number of places, for example, Tuczyn, Rokitno, and Sarny in Volhynia, or Starachowice, Skalat, Zborow, Kosow Huculski and others in east Galicia, where the Jewish councils did all they could to protect the Jewish population as long as they could, by trying to provide aid to the forced laborers, by providing minimal social welfare, and in some cases (Zborow—head of Judenrat—Janek [Ja'akov] Fuchs; Tuczyn) by aiding the armed resistance.[12]

Armed resistance in the two Ukrainian provinces in the south was, it would seem, possible only in the woody and swampy areas of Polesie in northern Volhynia and near the Carpathian mountains in the south of Galicia. In central and southern Volhynia, there were no Soviet partisans to whom the Jews could have fled and the Ukrainian population was nationalistic, anti-Jewish,

---

10. Yehuda Bauer, "*Buczacz and Krzemieniec,*" *Yad Vashem Studies* 33 (2005): 245–306.

11. Martha Goren, *Kolot min ha'ya'ar hashachor* (Rehovot, Israel: private publication, 2009).

12. Yehuda Bauer, *The Death of the Shtetl* (New Haven, Conn.: Yale University Press, 2009), passim; Shmuel Spector, *The Holocaust of Volhynian Jews, 1941–1944* (Jerusalem: Yad Vashem, 1990).

and anti-Polish. In 1942–44, the Ukrainian Insurgent Army (UPA—Ukrainska Povstanska Armia) killed any Jews it could find, and in 1943–44 engaged in genocidal massacres of some 40,000 Poles. Contrary to logic, however, Jews engaged in armed resistance in quite a number of places, without any hope, of course, of standing up to the Germans and the Ukrainians. In some places, there were underground groups that aimed at armed resistance, but the Germans, with their superior tactics, prevented it. In Sarny, for instance, where a rebellion was planned, with the agreement of the Judenrat head, Shmaryahu Gershonok, they were persuaded to desist after hearing the assurances from the local German commander that nothing would happen. On the morning of that assurance, August 26, 1942, the ghetto was liquidated. Nevertheless, between 1,000 and 1,500 Jews managed to escape from the barbed-wire enclosure into which they had been put, and from the shooting pits, and many joined the partisans in Polesie. A few dozen kilometers away, in Rokitno, on that same August 26, 1942, the Jews were called to assemble (they numbered 1,630), supposedly for a check of their identity papers. Three sides of the square in which the Jews were concentrated were surrounded by German and Ukrainian forces armed to the teeth, but one side was still open. A very tall woman, Mindl Eisenberg, nicknamed "Mindl Cossack," saw a troop of armed Ukrainians approaching that side and yelled out "Jews, they are coming to kill us" (or, "Jews, run"— there are different versions of this). As a result, a totally spontaneous, chaotic flight ensued of those who were able to act, and several hundreds (estimates vary between 400 and 900) escaped to the nearby forests. Hundreds more were machine-gunned, and the rest shipped to Sarny to share the fate of the Jews there. Most of those who escaped joined the Soviet partisans. A group of escapees fled to a forest next to three Polish villages; the villagers helped them, as they themselves were defending themselves against UPA militias. When these militias then burned down the villages, the Polish peasants joined the Jews in the forest.[13]

The Judenrat in Tuczyn, led by Getzel Szwarcman, a graduate of a right-wing Zionist group, organized an uprising (September 24, 1942), after it became clear to them that the Germans would kill everyone. They did so, even though the Ukrainian peasantry around them was hostile, expecting to pillage their homes after the killing. With just a few firearms, and mainly "cold" weapons,

---

13. Bronislaw Janik, *Bylo Ich Trzy* (Warszawa: Wydawactwo Panstwowe, 1970); Yehuda Bauer, "Sarny and Rokitno in the Holocaust" in *The Shtetl, New Evaluations*, ed. Steven T. Katz (New York: New York University Press, 2010), 253–89.

they fought the attackers and burned down their own homes. Some 2,000 of the 3,000 Jews in the township fled to the nearby forest. Most of them were hunted down by Ukrainian and German forces, and some, especially women and children, had no alternative but to surrender and go back to Tuczyn to be killed. The local population, Ukrainians and Poles, refused to help them. A small number of them managed to reach Soviet partisans, who were a long distance away. Some managed to hide with peasants. Only seventeen people survived.[14]

Whereas Volhynia, except for the north, has no mountain ranges or thick forests, eastern Galicia is more wooded. The province was annexed to German-occupied central Poland (the so-called "Generalgouvernement") in August 1941, and its SS commander, Fritz Katzmann, made it his business to annihilate the Jews there. The largest concentration of Jews was in the city of Lwow (Lviv) with a prewar population of 340,000, of whom 110,000 were Jews. About 6,000 were killed immediately after the Germans conquered the city (June 30, 1941), in two pogroms (July 1–3 and July 25–27). At the end of July, a Judenrat was appointed by the Germans, whose head was Dr. Joseph Parnas. Parnas refused a German demand to supply them with Jewish forced labor; he was murdered in October. A ghetto was set up by December 15. The next Judenrat head, Abraham Rotfeld, died in February 1942, and Henryk Landsberg was appointed in his place. The rabbis of Lwow tried to persuade Landsberg not to agree to a German order to make lists of people to be deported "to the East," because by that time there was an understanding that that meant death. Landsberg refused because, he said, if the Germans took people at random the outcome would be even worse. In March 1942, 15,000 people were deported to the death camp of Belzec, where they were asphyxiated by gas. However, Landsberg did oppose the Germans and unsuccessfully tried to avoid further slaughter; he was hanged from the balcony of the Judenrat. The last head of the Judenrat, Eduard Eberson, was more pliant, but he and his colleagues were murdered nevertheless in January 1943. The Germans liquidated the ghetto in stages; most people were killed in the camp they set up on the outskirts of the city, at Janowska Street; the final liquidation began on June 1, 1943. However, the Germans met resistance. Young Jews had acquired some firearms and there were exchanges of gunfire. Little is known about who exactly organized the resistance, which was obviously quite hopeless, and how the few handguns used were obtained, because there were almost no survivors. We do know that two youngsters, Tadek Dotorsky and Michael Hofmann, gradu-

---

14. Shalom Cholawsky, "Parashat Tuczyn," *Yalkut Moreshet* 2 (1964): 81–95; Shmuel Spector, *The Holocaust of Volhynian Jews, 1941–1944*, 212–16; Arad, *The Holocaust in the Soviet Union*, 499.

ates of Zionist youth movements, led two of the groups that resisted. The slaughter of the last remnants, about 10,000 people, was completed toward the end of June.

There was what has been termed here unarmed resistance. The Judenrat, whose first head was a courageous resister, tried to set up soup kitchens and organize other elements of social welfare, as well as a health program of sorts though, as we have seen, it could not openly oppose the Germans—no official administration in Poland, Polish, or Jewish, could. Some people hid in the sewers, and a small number of Poles assisted them.[15]

The story of the many towns, townships, and villages in eastern Galicia with a high percentage of Jews is varied. Unarmed resistance has been mentioned regarding a number of them, and many more instances could be given. Yet there was also armed resistance, although the conditions for such actions were very adverse. Thus, in Buczacz, which has been mentioned as a place where there were clear signs of a disintegration of Jewish society, three resistance groups developed nevertheless, aided by a member of the Judenrat. One of the groups waited too long to act, and when it did its actions came too late to have an impact; a second took revenge on Polish and Ukrainian Jew-baiters, and thus possibly helped by persuading non-Jews to hide and not to betray Jews to the Germans; a third defended itself and fought and lost a battle against Ukrainians and Germans.[16] In Zborow, a group of resisters fought and lost another fight in a labor camp against Germans.[17] A group led by a woman resister, Anda Luft, escaped from the large town of Stanislawow (now called Ivaniv Frankivsk), and fought several engagements against superior German forces, until it was annihilated.[18] On the other hand, in a *shtetl* such as Kosow Huculski, with a Judenrat that tried its best to help, and which lies in the foothills of the forested Carpathian range, there was no armed resistance at all.

Who organized the various forms of resistance in the *kresy*? Unarmed resistance was almost always the work of people who had been active in social causes before the war, and that includes elected officials of prewar communities who composed the majority of the Judenräte under the Germans; also other

15. Leon (Weliczker) Wells, *The Death Brigade* (*Janowska Road*) (New York: Macmillan, 1963); Eliyahu Yones, *Smoke in the Sand: The Jews of Lvov in the War Years, 1939–1944* (Jerusalem: Gefen, 2004); Iakov Khonigsman, *The Catastrophe of Jewry in Lvov* (Lviv: Aholem-Aleichem Jewish Society, 1997).

16. Bauer, "Buczacz and Krziemieniec," 295–97.

17. Bauer, *The Death of the Shtetl*, 107–11.

18. Aharon Weiss, "Haproblematika shel hahitnagdut hayehudit hameurgenet," *Dapim leheker Tkufat HaSho'ah* 12 (Haifa: Haifa University Press, 1995), 206–8.

former activists, as well as former youth movement members. Armed resistance was almost always organized by graduates of youth movements, mostly Zionist, of various political colorings. Also, the youth movement of the prewar Socialist, anti-religious and anti-Zionist Bund, by 1938–1939 the most important Jewish political party in Poland, was active, but the Bund was relatively weak in the *kresy*. There were of course no Jewish political groups of any kind in eastern Ukraine or Belarus. Jewish Communists were a tiny group, but were, naturally, active in the pre-1939 Soviet areas. The underground movement in Minsk was initiated and led by Communists, and there were a few Communists who were active in the *kresy* as well. Religious groups and leaders were conspicuously absent in all this.

There was a considerable difference between the developments in the Ukrainian and the Belorussian areas of the *kresy*. Unarmed resistance was fairly universal: attempts, sometimes partial only, at social organization, education, food smuggling, attempts at flight, and hiding, can be documented for a large number of *shtetlach*, as well as for larger centers. The case of the only larger city in the Belarussian area, Brest-Litovsk, is typical. It is estimated that by 1939 there were 30,000 Jews in the city. It was the first to be conquered by the Germans when they invaded on June 22, 1941 (Soviet soldiers defended the city fortress even long after the Germans had advanced hundreds of kilometers further east; the last commander of the Soviets was a Jewish NCO, a fiddler, Zalman Stanski. In the end, they surrendered and were all killed by the Germans). In July, there occurred the mass killing of about 5,000 young men, making any unarmed or armed resistance very difficult. On November 15, a ghetto was created with about 14,000 inmates. The Judenrat, led by a merchant, Hersh Rosenberg, tried its utmost to organize help. A small group of doctors tried valiantly to fight epidemics. The Germans starved the people, so that any kind of cultural activity became impossible—when one starves, one does not play Beethoven, even when one has a violin. "Those who are sentenced to die, do not smile." There was no education and only very minimal religious life. But there were two underground groups, one led by Communists, one by Zionists. Jewish agents of the Germans, who were promised food and life (these promises were of course not kept), betrayed them and they were liquidated prior to the annihilation of the ghetto.[19] In the *shtetl* of Baranowicze, which became a German military center, there were 12,000 Jews (the Germans always evicted Jews

19. Yehuda Bauer, *Rethinking the Holocaust* (New Haven, Conn.: Yale University Press, 2001), 149–58; the quotation is from Moshe Smolar, *Neevakt ial Chayai* (Tel-Aviv: Moreshet, 1978), 66.

from smaller places and villages into slightly larger towns). The Judenrat, let by Ovsiei Isaacson, a Zionist, but composed of people from different groups (leftist Zionist and Bund, mainly), established order with a Jewish police group that became part of the armed underground; schooling was organized, an efficient health service prevented the outbreak of epidemics, care for the elderly was provided—all in an atmosphere of German terror, executions, and lack of food (the Judenrat supported smuggling). Isaacson was murdered in March 1942, because he refused to supply the Germans with a list of elderly people whom the Germans obviously wanted to kill. His successor, a former owner of a bicycle shop, Shmuel Yankelewicz, continued his predecessor's policies and escaped to the forest after his wife and child were killed during an attempt organized by him to rescue a number of Jewish families. He survived and died much later in Israel. His successor tried to organize an escape of a remnant of Jews in the town and died in the attempt. Three armed underground groups united into one, but by pure mischance an attempt at rebellion in July 1942 failed—in a way, luckily, because the Germans in retaliation would have killed every Jew in the ghetto. As it was, a relatively large number of members of the underground, including its head, Eliezer Lidovsky (another graduate of a left-Zionist youth movement), escaped to the forests and managed to find Soviet partisans who accepted most of them. The relatively large number of survivors, some 2.5 percent of the original ghetto inhabitants, makes it possible to reconstruct the story.[20]

Similar developments occurred in many places in the west Belorussian north. Unarmed resistance, in the sense of communal solidarity expressing itself in social activities of the kind described above, was much more common there than in the south. This was due partly to the fact that, in this backward region, Jews had historically developed a fairly stable communal life. Armed resistance was aided by the fact that this is a thickly forested and swampy area, with impenetrable jungle-like undergrowth, and that many local Jews knew their way in these forests. Both unarmed and armed responses were helped by the more friendly attitude to Jews of the Belorussian peasantry (itself the result, possibly, of the fact that the standard of life of the Jews was similar to that of the peasants). Many Jews earned at least part of their living by various agricultural pursuits, and at the same time were rooted in Jewish traditions originating in religion, though by World War II a majority of Jews had moved

20. Yehuda Bauer, *"Jewish Baranowicze in the Holocaust," Yad Vashem Studies* 31 (2003): 95–151.

away from orthodoxy. Research has estimated that in this region there were some sixty-four *shtetlach* with resistance groups, and that some 23,000 Jews managed to escape into the forests.[21] The problem was that the mass murder of the Jews took place in 1941–42, when the Soviet partisan movement in Belarus (where most of the Soviet partisans operated) was still in its infancy, so that there were no armed groups in the forest that Jews could have joined. Those that did exist deteriorated into armed brigands, looters, and thieves, and killed large numbers of Jews trying to find refuge in the forests. Only in May 1942, did the Soviets establish a High Partisan Command in unoccupied Soviet territory that began to establish some order in the occupied areas. Commanders were parachuted in; basic radio communications were set up—very inefficiently, in many cases—and discipline was imposed. That did not always help, as many commanders were often drunk, and women were often forced into sexual slavery.[22] Nevertheless, antisemitism diminished, and more Soviet detachments accepted Jews into their ranks. Some of the higher commanders were Ukrainians.[23] These commanders were Communists of course, who proved friendly to Jews; but others, too, tried to prevent antisemitic incidents, mostly because the Soviets wanted to avoid any interethnic difficulties. Lower ranks and many ordinary partisans, Russians, Belorussians, and Ukrainians, however, still harbored hostility toward Jews.

It was Soviet policy to establish partisan groups on the basis of the Soviet territorial divisions, so that in Belarus, for instance, the detachments were "Belorussian," whatever their ethnic composition was; ethnic, or national, units, were not permitted. Jews, of course, wanted to fight in Jewish detachments, primarily to avoid antisemitism. Contrary to established Soviet policy, several Jewish detachments were formed, and at least two of them, the Bielski and Zorin groups in the Naliboki jungle forests, maintained themselves until liberation (which happened in June–July 1944, as a result of the great Soviet offensive that caused the disintegration of the German Central Front). Tuvia Bielski was the son of millers in a tiny village. He and his three brothers (one of them still a child) organized and developed a unit that devoted itself to saving Jewish lives.

21. Cholawsky, *The Jews of Bielorussia*, 294.

22. For a critical view of the Soviet partisan movement in Belarus, based on a solid source basis, see Bogdan Musial, *Sowjetische Partisanen, 1941–1944, Mythos und Wirklichkeit* (Paderborn: Ferdinand Schöningh, 2009).

23. Such as the famous Sidor (Sydyr) A. Kovpak, who offered to rescue Jews in places that his forces occupied on their way from Belarus to east Galicia to blow up German oil installations; or Aleksandr A. Saburov, and a number of others.

It accepted every Jew, man, woman, or child. Bielski accommodated himself to Soviet usage, made alliances with (sometimes quite antisemitic) commanders of Soviet units, and obtained the support of the commanding officer of the region, Vassily Y. Chernishev ("Platon"), a Russian. Fighting the Germans and their local collaborators as other units did, he also set up a village-type settlement in the depth of the forest that supplied essential services to the surrounding Soviet units: bakery, laundry, health services, a metal shop where firearms were repaired, and so on. When liberation came, he led some 1,200 Jews out from the forest.

Semyon Zorin was a baker from Minsk, possibly even a party member, with a Belorussian friend, whose rescue from a German camp he engineered with the help of a Jewish girl. The two men established a unit in the forest, but they fell out because Zorin wanted to rescue Jews fleeing from the Minsk ghetto. He took many of them to the Naliboki forest, not very far from Bielski, and developed a Jewish unit there. He too saved several hundred Jews. The higher command agreed to all this because the Jewish commanders in their turn also agreed to accept non-Jews into their units, though their numbers were small. A third Jewish unit developed from two ghetto rebellions, in Nieswiez (actually, this was the first Jewish armed rebellion against the Germans anywhere in Europe, on July 21, 1942, led by Shalom Cholawsky) and in Kleck, with the decisive help of a Ukrainian commander. Cholawsky obtained arms by digging up a mass grave of Soviet soldiers massacred by the Germans, who had been buried with their arms. The Jews took the rifles and munitions, cleaned them, and ended up with some thirty-five rifles, which was a precondition for them joining the partisans. Similar tactics were used in some other places too.[24] The unit was disbanded in 1943 and its members were assigned to general Soviet detachments, as the high commanders demanded.

As German policies toward the local population became more brutal and the Soviet armies drew nearer, many locals joined the partisan movement which, according to official Soviet statements, numbered, in 1944, some 360,000 fighters. The proportion of Jews in the Belorussian partisan movement, which was quite high at first (in 1942, probably about 10 percent), diminished. This was also the result of the many casualties among the veteran partisans. It is estimated that of the roughly 23,000 Jews who escaped into the Belorussian forests, some 15,000 fought as partisans; the rest tried to maintain themselves in hiding.[25]

24. Sjalom Cholawski (Cholawsky), *Soldiers From the Ghetto* (Amsterdam: Harwood, 1998).
25. Cholawsky, *The Jews of Bielorussia*, 292–309; Sjalom Cholawski (Cholawsky), *Meri velochama*

The importance of unarmed and armed Jewish resistance in the areas dis-cussed here lies in the fact that significant parts of a population taken com-pletely by surprise by the German decision to murder all of them, responded by a refusal to accept that verdict of death. As shown above, only minimal re-sponse was possible in the vast areas of the pre-1939 Soviet territories occupied by the Germans, because of the speed with which the mass killing was orga-nized and executed. In northern Transnistria, under the corrupt rule of Roma-nian Fascists, the stay of execution allowed unarmed resistance to take place. In the formerly Polish territories (the *kresy*), especially in the forested areas of Belarus, unarmed and armed resistance was massive. It is difficult to find par-allels elsewhere to this Jewish unarmed resistance to what was quickly recog-nized as what we would call today "an immediate genocidal threat," especially regarding morale-building activities. Armed resistance in the many small ghet-tos of the region was hopeless, and yet took place—not everywhere, to be sure, but in many ghettos. The remnants fought back in the forests.

---

partizanit (Jerusalem: Yad Vashem, 2001). This large volume, unfortunately available only in He-brew, details more or less all the underground Jewish organizations in Belarus, and describes in detail Jewish participation in Soviet partisan warfare.

Hana Kubátová

21   Jewish Resistance in Slovakia, 1938–45

"Slovakia is our only homeland, it is here that we want to live, work, establish things and, if needed, suffer with our Christian fellow citizens, share the same destiny and die." This statement composed by Jews from Žilina, a city in the northwest of the country, expressed Jewish loyalty to Slovakia and its newly established autonomous government.[1] The Jewish minority in Slovakia—136,737 according to the 1930 census—voiced their loyalty on numerous occasions following the autonomy declaration of the Slovak land (*Slovenská krajina*) on October 6, 1938.[2] Autonomy, however, marked an outburst of political antisemitism.[3]

I will examine the life of the Jewish community in Slovakia between fall 1938 and spring 1945, that is, between the declaration of autonomy and the fall of the wartime state. I will analyze the survival mechanisms of this minority that was gradually stripped of its rights. Hence, I will focus on Jewish resistance in Slovakia—and by resistance I understand not only rebellion against the oppressive regime but also, for example, the struggle against individual and collective feelings of lethargy and resignation. Research on Jewish resistance and revolt has until now emphasized two issues: activities of the Working Group (Pracovná skupina), a secret Jewish rescue organization, and the involvement of Jews in

---

1. Slovenský národný archív (hereafter SNA), fund Úrad predsedníctva vlády, box 2, file 614/38.

2. *Naučný slovník aktualít* (Praha: L. Mazáč, 1939), 96.

3. For more on the Jewish minority in autonomous Slovakia, see especially Eduard Nižňanský, *Židovská komunita na Slovensku medzi československou parlamentnou demokraciou a slovenským štátom v stredoeurópskom kontexte* (Prešov: Universum, 1999); Ivan Kamenec, *Po stopách tragédie* (Bratislava: Archa, 1991), 19–46. The English translation of the book is available under the title *On the Trail of Tragedy: The Holocaust in Slovakia* (Bratislava: Hajko & Hajková, 2007).

the Slovak National Uprising, an armed insurrection against the Germans and the collaborating government in Slovakia.[4] Both play an important role in the history of Jewish resistance in Slovakia and their significance exceeds their geographical limitations. Here, however, I will place these events in a larger context of resistance and revolt, and attempt to portray the mood of the endangered Jewish community during this historical period.

First of all I would like to clarify possible terminological difficulties. The independence of the wartime state of Slovakia was declared on March 14, 1939. According to the constitution, adopted on July 21, 1939, its official name was the Slovak republic. However, with the exception of legal documents and diplomatic correspondence, the name Slovak state was generally preferred. Consequently, I will refer to the wartime state as the Slovak state, although this might not be technically correct. Moreover, aiming for a better transparency of the text, when speaking about Slovak Jews, I will mean all Jews of Slovakia, regardless of their actual Slovak, Hungarian, or other nationality.

The history of the wartime state and the Holocaust in Slovakia continues to be a contentious issue both in the historiography and for the Slovak public. This is a result of several factors, but I will limit myself to discussing only one of those factors. The wartime state—a state fatally connected with the Holocaust—remains the only historical (though not legal) antecedent of today's Slovakia. The negative sides of the wartime Slovak state, described by its constitution as the fulfillment of the nation's and God's aims, were suppressed in its historical evaluation.[5] Not surprisingly, this also led to the relativization of

4. See for example: *Aktivity ilegálnej židovskej Pracovnej skupiny počas holokaustu na Slovensku*, zborník príspevkov zo seminára (Bratislava: Dokumentačné stredisko Holokaustu, 2007); *Židé v boji a odboji: rezistence československých Židů v letech druhé světové války*, ed. Zlatica Zudová-Lešková (Praha: Historický ústav Akademie věd České Republiky, 2007); Jozef Jablonický, Židia v rezistencii na Slovensku, in *Pracovné jednotky a útvary slovenskej armády 1939–1945, VI. Robotný prápor*, ed. Dezider Tóth, (Bratislava: Zing Print, 1996), 161–66; Juraj Špitzer, "Jewish Opportunities for Resistance and Revolt in the Years 1939–1945 (as in Case of Novaky Camp)" in *The Tragedy of the Jews of Slovakia: 1938–1945 : Slovakia and the "Final Solution of the Jewish Question*," ed. Waclaw Dlugoborski, et al., (Oswiecim: Auschwitz-Birkenau State Museum; Banská Bystrica: Museum of the Slovak National Uprising, 2002), 257–76; Gila Fatran, "The 'Working Group,'" *Holocaust and Genocide Studies* 8, no. 2 (1994): 164–201; Gila Fatran, *Boj o prežitie* (Bratislava: Slovenské národné múzeum—Múzeum židovskej kultúry, 2007); Oskar Neumann, *Im Schaten des Todes: Ein Tatsachenbericht vom Schicksalskampf des slovakischen Judentums* (Tel Aviv: Olameinu, 1956); *Holokaust na Slovensku. 8. Ústredňa Židov (1940–1944). Dokumenty*, ed. Katarína Hradská (Bratislava: Dokumentačné stredisko holokaustu; Zvolen: Klemo, 2008); *Holokaust na Slovensku. 3. Listy Gisely Fleischmannovej (1942–1944). Snahy Pracovnej skupiny o záchranu slovenských a európskych židov. Dokumenty*, ed. Katarína Hradská (Bratislava: Nadácia Milana Šimečku—Židovská náboženská obec, 2003); Yehuda Bauer, *Jews for Sale? Nazi-Jewish Negotiations, 1933–1945* (New Haven, Conn.: Yale University Press, 1994), 91–101.

5. *Slovenský zákonník*, 1939, ústavný zákon 185/1939, Sl.z.

the Holocaust. Juraj Špitzer, leader of the Jewish military unit in the Slovak National Uprising against the Germans, and a Holocaust survivor, explains this revisionist process as follows:

The death camps did not exist; they are only a Jewish invention. The Nazis did not kill only Jews. Everything was done under German pressure. We provided only the record-keeping; we only guarded them, put them in carriages and passed them on to the Germans. We do not know what happened to them later on; it was none of our business. There were exceptions. They stayed in camps where they worked and produced goods; they even had kindergartens and orchestras; they played in the theatre. They did not resist when being taken. The principle that the victim must collude in his own liquidation is given as evidence of cooperation and collaboration. More people left than returned.[6]

Although I would argue that Holocaust denial does not occupy an important place in Slovak postwar historiography, relativization, including deflecting political responsibility for the Holocaust on others—either Germans or Jews—is a widespread and dangerous issue. My goal is to contribute to the historiography of the Holocaust in Slovakia by presenting historical evidence that argues against the cooperation and collaboration of the victims.

Autonomy

In November 1938, a month into Slovakian autonomy, the government decided to deport poor Jews and Jews without Czechoslovakian citizenship twenty kilometers into territory ceded to Hungary as a reaction to the result of the First Vienna Arbitration.[7] Altogether, approximately 7,500 Jews were forcibly transported from the country, including children, elderly, and pregnant women.[8] Despite the chaotic nature and the early halt to the whole action, it "clearly indicated to Jewish citizens that the territory of autonomous Slovakia was no longer a safe place for them."[9] Moreover, though no anti-Jewish legislation was adopted during this period, various motions indicated that it would only be a matter of time before such legislation would be passed.[10]

6. Špitzer, "Jewish Opportunities for Resistance," 260.

7. This order was later changed and "only" Jews without Czechoslovakian citizenship and the homeless were to be deported.

8. Nižňanský, *Židovská komunita na Slovensku medzi československou parlamentnou demokraciou a slovenským štátom v stredoeurópskom kontexte*; Kamenec, *Po stopách tragédie*, 19–46.

9. Kamenec, *Po stopách tragédie*, 29.

10. Ibid., 33–37.

The November 1938 Vienna Arbitration was the first foreign political defeat for the autonomous government. Accordingly, Slovakia lost to Hungary 10,307 km² of its territory and 879,697 inhabitants, including a sizable number of Jews.[11] When the country received its independence on March 14, 1939, approximately 89,000 Jews lived in Slovakia and comprised about 4 percent of the total population of about 2,709,000 inhabitants. In addition to the over 2 million Slovak majority, the wartime state was also inhabited by roughly 128,000 Germans, 94,000 Czechs, almost 80,000 Ruthenians, 67,000 Hungarians, and 27,000 Roma.[12]

As I have already mentioned, the Jewish minority instinctively expressed loyalty, together with assurances of being "sincerely willing to cooperate in making the Slovak lands thrive."[13] It would be false to interpret expressions of loyalty solely as manifestations of submission; they also indicated willingness to cooperate with the new establishment. Historian Yeshayahu Jelinek maintains that in the period between the country's independence and the spring 1942 deportations: "There was no trace of even slight resistance on the part of the Jewish leadership. The leaders and the general public neither expected nor imagined what the future held in store for them. The Zionist movement concentrated its efforts on arranging emigration to Palestine for those interested. Others tried to find different means of emigration. Only those Jews with left-wing affiliations prepared themselves for positive action."[14] By "left-wing affiliations," Jelinek means especially the underground Communist movement.[15] The two Zionist Socialist youth movements, Hashomer Hatsair and Makkabi Hatsair, should be counted in as well. Jewish political parties were dissolved by January 1939 but, at this point at least, Jews did not give up their political aspirations. With the state's approval they established the Jewish Central Office for the Land of Slovakia (Židovská ústredná úradovňa pre krajinu Slovensko), an organization aiming to become the representative of Slovak Jewry. Because of its Zionist orientation, however, it faced opposition from the Orthodox, the predominant religious affiliation of Slovak Jewry.[16] The Jewish Central Office's

11. Seznam obcí a okresů republiky Česko-slovenské, které byli připojeny k Německu, Maďarsku a Polsku: stav ke dni 28. listopadu 1938 (Praha: Státní úřad statistický, 1938), 5–6. According to the statistics, 45,292 were of the Jewish religion while 26,227 indicated Jewish as their nationality. *Naučný slovník aktualít*, 96.

12. *Naučný slovník aktualít*, 479.   13. *Židovské noviny* (November 4, 1938): 1.

14. Yeshayahu Jelinek, "The Role of the Jews in Slovakian Resistance," *Jährbücher für Geschichte Osteuropas* 15:3 (1967): 416–17.

15. Ibid., 417.

16. According to Gila Fatran, the "massively Orthodox affiliation of Slovakian Jewry was largely

main tasks were "the organization of vocational training for manual work for those who were hit by the first anti-Jewish measures, and of the emigration of refugees and the problems of youth."[17] Educational and training activities organized for Jews during this period, however, not only aimed to prepare Jews for emigration but sought to prevent resignation and feelings of despair, an important precondition for surviving the intensifying discrimination that was to follow.

Emigration was a way out of the trap called the "Jewish question" and, at least initially, emigration plans were supported by the government. As elsewhere, however, emigration was a costly matter and many Jews simply lacked the funds needed to obtain the foreign money that was needed not only to pay for the minimum capital that every receiving country requested from Jews but also to start life anew.[18] As the historian Ivan Kamenec summarizes it, for "an average Jewish citizen—merchant, artisan, farmer, or laborer—emigration with family was in the years 1939 and 1940 still a bigger problem and risk than staying in Slovakia."[19] Some Jews left for Palestine but neighboring Hungary was also a target area. This was not only because of its geographical proximity but also because it offered relative safety until 1944. By summer 1940, approximately 6,000 Jews left Slovakia.[20]

Sociologist Peter Salner points out that very soon after the proclamation of autonomy, both individual and collective activities were launched that aimed at saving individuals and families. Among these activities, Salner counts baptism "as an important step not only towards saving bare life but also providing satisfactory existence both for individuals and whole families."[21] Especially during the 1942 roundups, "early" baptism could have saved a convert from deportation. For example, the constitutional law of May 1942, while sanctioning the ongoing deportations, also exempted three categories of individuals— those granted a presidential and ministerial exemption, those living in a mixed

a reflection of the *fin de siècle* situation; it was more a carryover of their forebears' tradition than an identification with the anti-Hasidic and anti-Zionist ultra-Orthodox Weltanschauung of the community leaders. Many ostensible adherents of formal Orthodoxy actually sympathized with the Zionist cause; others were assimilated Jews. Organized Zionists, however, were a minority in all streams of Slovakian Jewry." Fatran, "The 'Working Group,'" 165.

17. Livia Rothkirchen, "Slovakia: II, 1918–1938," *The Jews of Czechoslovakia: Historical Studies and Surveys* (Philadelphia: Jewish Publication Society of America; New York: Society of the History of Czechoslovak Jews, 1968), 1:115.

18. Kamenec, *Po stopách tragédie*, 51–52.   19. Ibid., 53.
20. Ibid., 54.
21. Peter Salner, *Prežili Holokaust* (Bratislava: Veda, 1997), 38–39.

marriage, and those baptized before March 14, 1939.[22] Moreover, as James Mace Ward established in his research on the presidential exemptions, apart from those who were "clearly useful to the Slovak state," President Tiso primarily exempted "Christian 'Jews.'" Of the direct exemption holders on the 1942 census, "90% had undergone baptism; of these, over three quarters had done so before 14 March 1939, one-quarter before 30 October 1918. Only 6% of the direct exemption holders still identified their religion as Jewish."[23]

The Wartime Slovak State

In April 1939, only a month after the country declared its independence—though this independence remained valid only on paper—the government of the newly established state adopted its first codification of "a Jew." Accordingly, a Jew was a person of Jewish faith. Interestingly, despite the country's ties with Catholicism, this codification limited the power of baptism, one of the very foundations of Christianity. To paraphrase the decree itself, a Jew was not considered a Christian or a non-Jew if baptized after October 30, 1918.[24] Such persons remained Jewish according to the state.[25] The same applied to those without a religion but with at least one parent being of Jewish religion and to those married or living in partnership with Jews after this decree became valid—and to children of mixed unions.

The September 1941 codification of "a Jew," by contrast, sought to introduce a racial theory. According to the government decree that became infamously known as the "Jewish Codex," "a Jew" was a person with at least three racially Jewish grandparents and "a part Jew" was a person with two racially Jewish grandparents.[26] The so-called Jewish Codex, to an extent a summary of already valid anti-Jewish measures, banned marriages between Jews and non-Jews (and Jews and half-Jews). Furthermore, it also criminalized extramarital sexual relations with a person known to be Jewish.

In the course of its existence, the wartime republic issued dozens of laws and decrees, gradually depriving Jews of all their economic, religious, civil,

22. Slovenský zákonník, 1942, ústavný zákon 68/1942, Sl. z.

23. James Mace Ward, "'People Who Deserve It': Jozef Tiso and the Presidential Exemption," *Nationalities Papers* 30:4 (2002): 583.

24. On this date the Martin Declaration was adopted, approving the entry of Slovakia into the newly established Czechoslovakian state.

25. Slovenský zákonník, 1939, nariadenie 63/1939, Sl. z.

26. Slovenský zákonník, 1939, nariadenie 198/1941, Sl. z.

and human rights. Already in 1939, for example, Jews were expelled from state services and their employment as doctors, pharmacists, and lawyers was severely limited. Jewish soldiers were transferred into special labor divisions and eventually all their military ranks were taken away from them. At this point it was already clear that an important component of what was termed the so-called "solution of the Jewish question" would include stripping Jews of their economic rights—or to say it more boldly, stealing their property. In spring and early summer 1939, first drafts of this discriminating solution were adopted. These decrees gradually started the Aryanization—or rather Slovakization—process in the wartime state.

The first so-called Aryanization law became effective in June 1940. Despite the fact that it was only enforced for three months, 229 Jewish businesses were liquidated and an additional fifty were Aryanized. The second so-called Aryanization law of November 1940 introduced important changes. It denied any form of cooperation between the Jewish owner and the new Aryan business "partner." Even in cases of partial Aryanization, the role of the former Jewish owner was only nominal. The second so-called Aryanization law was also much more thorough and radical. By January 1, 1941, out of the total number of 12,300 Jewish businesses, 9,935 were liquidated and 2,223 Aryanized.[27] The looting of Jewish property was not only an attack on Jewish rights, it also paved the way to later deportations. In other words, the Aryanization process created a mass of unemployed Jews now unable to support their families and—paradoxically as it may sound—they created a social problem that the state "solved" by deporting them outside of the country. Hence, being economically stable was, together with "early" baptism, a second condition that helped Jews not to be deported, at least in 1942.

For reasons I will touch upon later, it is difficult to examine the mood of the Jewish community vis-à-vis the increasing discrimination they were facing. A source that might shed light on this—despite the methodological obstacles connected with interpreting it—is the monthly situational reports written by district councils and gathered by the Slovak version of the Gestapo between 1940 and 1945. The Central Security Office (Ústredňa štátnej bezpečnosti), officially established on January 1, 1940, gathered information about all components of the society, including the political situation, Communists and Socialists, state

27. Ľudovít Hallon, "Arizácia na Slovensku 1939–1945," *Acta Oeconomica Pragensia* 15, no. 7 (2007): 154.

organizations, the economic and social situation, religious conditions, national minorities—and the Jews. Though one has to be very careful when interpreting these situational reports, they do provide informational value.

According to 1940 reports, for example, Jews adapted quickly to the new situation as the wartime state was established, and refrained from disclosing their opinion on domestic or international matters in public.[28] This is far from surprising given the position they were in. Even a small change in their behavior could have been used as a pretext for further anti-Jewish actions. Besides, even the majority population to a large extent kept to itself when it came to voicing their opinion on political issues.

When it comes to anti-Jewish laws, district authorities reported that Jews calmly accepted the various norms and decrees against them.[29] Now this might be interpreted as a sign of passivity; however, it was the only possible reaction if one wanted to avoid further repression. Moreover, such "opinion passivity" in public spaces did not have to reflect their actual stance and, very often, discussions about important issues were held only in the relative safety of religious institutions and private homes. Officials were aware of this and consequently banned Jews from gathering in the evenings.[30] Furthermore, this passivity does not mean that Jews were not thinking about their future. In the peak of the Aryanization process, for example, reports were issued that indicated dissatisfaction and feelings of uncertainty among Jews "particularly because young Jews are entirely without work. They wander through the city without work and ask what they will do in winter and how they will live if they do not work in the summer."[31] Many were certain that, "more radical measures will be adopted, the elderly are paralyzed by this—some are apathetic. This is not the case with young Jews."[32]

The first wave of deportations that took place between March and October 1942 was accompanied by fear and even panic among Jews. At this point in the process of "solving" the Jewish question, some Jews tried to escape deportation, either by fleeing from the country or by hiding.[33] As rumors spread that deportations would be renewed, situational reports remarked that Jews were becoming increasingly nervous.[34] The position of Jews became more and more difficult, since "the strictest possible controls are conducted and each, even

28. SNA, 209–752–8, SNA, 209–761–1.

29. SNA, 209–763–7.

30. SNA, 209–865–3.

31. SNA, 209–761–3.

32. SNA, 209–748–4

33. Ibid.

34. SNA, 209–752–10, SNA, 209–761–11.

the smallest, misdemeanor is punished with the strictest financial punishments .... In more serious cases ... immediately a deportation request will be issued."[35]

The German-Slovak talks that took place in late July 1940 brought not only important changes in the government but also an adoption of so-called Christian (or Slovak) National Socialism. Closer personal and ideological ties also further increased anti-Jewish discrimination. To speed up the process of robbing Jews of their property, the Slovak Diet delegated its legislative powers in solving the Jewish question and hence authorized the government to prepare all measures for Aryanization. In September 1940, a centralized institution was established, the Central Economic Office (Ústredný hospodársky úrad), concentrating the agenda and jurisdiction for implementing anti-Jewish measures. Furthermore, a central Jewish organization was established on September 26, 1940 and consequently, all remaining Jewish organizations and associations were abolished. The Jewish Central Agency (Ústredňa Židov, ÚŽ), a Slovak version of a Judenrat, was the first Jewish council outside Germany and Poland.[36] Membership in this organization was mandatory for all Jews living in Slovakia.

The man behind the creation of this organization was a young, twenty-nine-year-old SS Hauptsturmführer Dieter Wisliceny, the German "adviser" (berater) on Aryanization and the Jewish question in Slovakia. Wisliceny was one of almost twenty German "advisers" in the highest political, economic, and administrative institutions in Slovakia and their presence was a result of the Salzburg talks and one of the most direct interferences in the Slovak sovereignty.[37]

The department of special affairs of the Jewish Central Office proved to be crucial for the future of the Slovak Jews. It was this organization—together with its head Karl Hochberg, defined by historians as a "bureaucrat longing for power"[38]—that was supposed to "ensure the precise and swift implementation of Wicliceny's orders."[39] The ambitious SS Hauptsturmführer defined his ultimate aim concisely as "Aryanization—concentration—deportation."[40] It was

---

35. SNA, 209–USB–521

36. Yehuda Bauer, *Rethinking the Holocaust* (New Haven, Conn.: Yale University Press, 2002), 176.

37. Katarína Hradská, *Nemeckí poradcovia na Slovensku v rokoch 1940–1945: Prípad Dieter Wisliceny* (Bratislava: Academic Electronic Press, 1999), 16.

38. Gila Fatran, "The Struggle for Jewish Survival During the Holocaust," in *The Tragedy of the Jews of Slovakia: 1938–1945: Slovakia and the "Final Solution of the Jewish Question,"* ed. Dlugoborski, et al., 145.

39. Fatran, "The 'Working Group,'" 166.

40. As quoted in Katarína Hradská, "The Influence of Germany on the 'Solution of the Jewish

the establishment of this department together with individuals like Karl Hochberg that, "exasperated the local activists who joined the ÚŽ in order to help and rescue fellow Jews, and who regarded their membership in this contrived institution as the embodiment of a mission and commitment to work for Jewish survival."[41] This group of Jewish activists, referred to as the Working Group, the Shadow Government, or by the German equivalent "Nebenregierung" was as diverse as the Jewish community in Slovakia, including Zionists and Orthodox, as the inner circle of the organization illustrates. Members were Michael Dov Weissmandel, an Orthodox rabbi, liberal Rabbi Armin Frieder, architect Andrej Steiner, assimilated lawyer Tibor Kováč, treasurer Wili Fürst, and Oskar Neumann, a secular Zionist.[42] It was headed by Gisi Fleischmann, "the only woman to be a member of a major Judenrat in Europe, with the possible exception of Cora Berliner in Germany."[43] As we will see, the greatest test of this secret organization came with the spring 1942 deportations.

1942 Deportations

The so-called Jewish Codex of September 1941 was "one of the most cruel anti-Jewish legislations in modern European history."[44] Although it is certainly true that to some extent the code only summarized already existing anti-Jewish norms, it introduced one important novelty: racial understanding of the Jewish question, as we have indicated earlier.

In October 1941, a Slovak delegation led by the president-priest Jozef Tiso paid an official visit to Hitler in his field headquarters in east Prussia.[45] Despite the fact that it was mainly a courtesy visit, options to deport Jews of Slovakia were discussed. In a more concrete way, deportations were openly discussed in December of the same year, when the Slovak Prime Minister and Minister of Foreign Affairs Vojtech Tuka agreed to meet with the German Ambassador Hans Ludin to deport Jews with Slovak state citizenship to occupied Poland.

Deportations began in March 1942 when 999 girls and young women from

---

Question' in Slovakia," in *The Tragedy of the Jews of Slovakia: 1938–1945: Slovakia and the "Final Solution of the Jewish Question,"* ed. Waclaw Dlugoborski, et al., 90.

41. Fatran, "The 'Working Group,'" 166.

42. Gila Fatran, "Pracovná skupina: pokus o záchranu," *Aktivity ilegálnej židovskej Pracovnej skupiny počas holokaustu na Slovensku*, 7.

43. Bauer, *Rethinking the Holocaust*, 177.

44. Kamenec, *Po stopách tragédie*, 125.

45. Katarína Hradská, "Jozef Tiso v Hitlerovom hlavnom stane a na Ukrajine roku 1941 vo svetle nemeckých dokumentov," *Historický časopis* 51, no. 4 (2003): 686–91.

the eastern Šariš-Zemplín county were deported to Auschwitz. By April 1942, when the Jewish family transports began, almost six thousand Jews had already been deported. Before October 1942, when the deportations were discontinued, approximately 58,000 Jews had been forcibly transported to the death camps. Somewhere between 200 and 800 of them would survive.[46]

Protests against deportations came from different sides and were surely motivated by different reasons. In April 1942, for example, Slovak bishops issued a proclamation, in which they voiced their concern about the fate of Jewish converts. Their letter from the following year, March 1943, was more critical toward the regime and protested against discriminatory measures based on collective guilt.[47] Efforts to put a halt on deportations came also from the most endangered people, the Jewish minority. On March 5, 1942, two Jewish religious organizations, Central Office of the Autonomous Orthodox Jewish Religious Community and the Jeshurun Federation of the Religious Communities (Zväz židovských náboženských obcí Ješurun), sent a memorandum to the President-Priest Jozef Tiso, protesting against the planned deportations on various grounds. Their memorandum entails only "purely objective arguments" and points toward legal, economic, and social issues connected with deportations. Concretely, leaders of the two aforementioned communities stress that deportations are against both international laws and the laws of the country. They also rightly observe that deportations would economically harm the country and mass numbers of dislocated Jews would also cause a social problem. In other words, authors of the memorandum used pragmatic arguments against deportations. They did, however, also include one other argument as well: "We Jews are considered enemies of the Slovak state; we are not. But even if we were, we respectfully point out that even nations living in a real war situation do not use such methods against members of a hostile nation living in their territory.[48] On the following day, March 6, 1942, Rabbi Frieder sent a memorandum to the president in the name of the rabbis in Slovakia. Rather than being pragmatic, it was more of an emotional cry:

In despair we cry out to you, Mr. President, the supreme judge of this state, confident that His Honor, as well, believes in the Supreme Judge who is above him. As servants of Almighty God, we humbly request in our desperate straits: hear our

---

46. Kamenec, *Po stopách tragédie*, 195–96.

47. *Vatikán a Slovenská republika, 1939–1945, Dokumenty*, ed. Ivan Kamenec, Vladimír Prečan, Stanislav Škovránek (Bratislava: Slovak Academic Press, 1992), 105–08, 138.

48. United States Holocaust Memorial Museum, fund RG-57.001M, Slovak documents related to the Holocaust, 1939–45, reel 17, microfilm picture 484–88.

voices and answer us, for we are in great distress. Did not one God create us, and do we not all owe a final accounting to Him? Have mercy on us, on our families, on our wives, on our men, on our children and our elderly, who pour out their hearts with tears and pray to our Father in Heaven for salvation. Hoping for His mercy, we place our fate in your hands.[49]

As Rabbi Frieder remarked "on reading these words, written from the heart, even a person with a heart of stone would be moved."[50] Both memoranda were left unanswered by the president. The government reacted in its own way: an order was issued to investigate the background of the first memorandum.

In spring 1942, the Working Group was joined by Rabbi Michael Dov Weissmandel and it was he who suggested bribery as a means to achieve a moratorium on deportations. Members of the Working Group selected several corrupt Slovak officials in high-ranking positions, including, for example Anton Vašek, the director of section 14 at the interior ministry, and Izidor Koso, director of the ministry of interior. In the middle of July 1942, the group approached Dieter Wisliceny who asked for $50,000 in return for not renewing deportations. Although this $40,000 to $50,000 was provided to him, Wisliceny, like other Slovak politicians, played a double game. From a historical perspective, the interruption of deportations in October 1942 was less a result of bribery, as Rabbi Weissmandel believed, and more a consequence of several other factors including, for example, changes in the international situation or growing interventions. Besides, by October 1942, the majority of Jews who were still in Slovakia held a presidential or ministerial exemption and were thus economically important to the state.[51]

The Working Group tried to use bribery as a means to save not only Slovak but European Jews as well. According to the so-called Europa Plan, Jews from German-controlled Europe were supposed to be exchanged for money and goods. This plan, however, was also unsuccessful.[52]

The Slovak National Uprising

Disappointed with the government's inability to suppress the increasing partisan activities, on August 29, 1944, the Wehrmacht entered the western borders of Slovakia and triggered an armed rebellion. What became known as the

---

49. Emanuel Frieder, *To Deliver Their Souls: The Struggle of a Young Rabbi during the Holocaust* (New York: Holocaust Library, 1987), 69.
   50. Ibid.   51. See also Bauer, *Jews for Sale?* 97.
   52. Fatran, "The 'Working Group,'" 173–77.

Slovak National Uprising was caused by and included different groups, both Communist and civic. Already in December 1943, the Slovak National Council (Slovenská národná rada) was established. It later declared itself the supreme body of the uprising and took upon itself all legislative, governmental, and executive power until the reestablishment of Czechoslovakia. Though its chances of victory were virtually nonexistent, partisans did make some important initial advances. In the territory controlled by the partisans—the central parts of Slovakia with Banská Bystrica as the heart of rebel territory—the Slovak National Council abolished all anti-Jewish laws, including Aryanization transfers.

The situation differed in territories seized by the advancing Germans. With the assistance of the newly formed Emergency Units of the Hlinka Guard (Pohotovostné oddiely Hlinkovej gardy), the Germans quickly began to hunt down Jews as the Sicherheitsdienst now took upon itself responsibility for the Jewish question. On September 5, 1944, it established a new Slovak government. In one of its first decisions, the new government decided to concentrate all remaining Jews in the former labor camp Sereď, now transformed into a German concentration camp. Unlike the Germans who ran the country, the new Slovak government wanted to keep Jews as a labor force in Slovakia.

According to sources, out of the 89,000 Jewish community members, less than 20,000 lived in Slovakia before the Germans renewed deportations on September 30, 1944.[53] By that time, much of the territory that had formerly rebelled was under German occupation. Until March 1945, approximately 12,300 Jews had been deported in thirteen transports, most of them to Auschwitz, others to Ravensbrück, Sachsenhausen, Bergen-Belsen, and Theresienstadt.

There were three Jewish concentration and forced labor camps in Slovakia between 1942 and 1944: Sereď, Vyhne, and Nováky. All three camps were opened during the uprising, giving Jews the opportunity to join the partisans. More than 1,500 Jews joined the uprising, fighting on all fronts of the armed rebellion. Out of forty-six larger partisan units, Jews fought in thirty-two of them.[54] Jews constituted 10 percent of the 16,000 partisans.[55] Moreover, around 250 men from the Nováky camp formed a Jewish partisan unit, "the only compact partisan unit formed by fighters of Jewish descent."[56] Juraj Špitzer summarizes the importance of the Jewish partisan unit as follows:

---

53. Ladislav Lipscher, *Židia v slovenskom štáte 1939–1945* (Bratislava: Print-servis, 1992), 161–62.
54. Ibid., 207.   55. Ibid., 211
56. Ibid., 204.

The origin and history of the unit from the Jewish work camp in Novaky proves that in the years 1939–1945 the Jews did not accept the fate determined by their liquidators, that from the very beginning of persecution, they expressed resistance and that together with the Slovak nation fought with "weapons in their hands" on the fronts of the Slovak National Uprising and, after its suppression by the German soldiers, in the mountains, till the end of the war and the freedom of the nations of Czechoslovakia.[57]

Though the Germans were the masters of the country at this point, the scale of their actions would not have been possible without Slovak assistance.[58] Let us note that more than 1,000 Jews were killed in Slovakia.[59]

According to official propaganda, the armed rebellion was the work of the Czechs and the Jews. Consequently, the hate campaign against members of these communities was intensified. The daily *Slovák*, for example, the official newspaper of the state party, claimed that "A Jew remains a Jew even if he is hanged; he will never change and we have every reason to look upon the Jew as the saboteur of the nation."[60] In a similar tone, the *Slovák* explained that the Uprising started when the "Czechs and Jews joined the wealthy Slovaks, bolshevik partisans, to help them enslave the Slovak nation."[61] The propaganda drew a picture in which the Czechs and Jews betrayed the nation and for which they will be "punished by the horrible consequences of their traitorous actions. Beasts in human skin who have found pleasure in the killing of innocent women and children, they will forever be marked throughout history with the black seal of shame."[62]

In the last stages of the war, the Working Group attempted one last rescue operation. Very soon after the German occupation of Hungary in March 1944, information about planned deportations of Hungarian Jews to Auschwitz reached Slovakia. The plausibility of these reports was supported by testimonies of two Slovak Jews who managed to escape Auschwitz, Alfred Wetzler and Walter Rosenberg, alias Rudolf Vrba. On their arrival in Žilina, they gave a vivid account of the systematic killing of Jews in the Auschwitz-Birkenau camp complex. Gisi Fleischmann and Tibor Kováč presented a proposal to the Germans, according to which merchandise worth 7 million Swiss francs would be handed over to the Germans, if they allowed 7,000 Jews to emigrate to Swit-

57. Špitzer, "Jewish Opportunities for Resistance," 274.

58. Especially the special emergency units of the Hlinka Guard (Pohotovostné oddiely Hlinkovej Gardy).

59. *Slovenské národné povstanie: Dokumenty*, ed. Vilém Prečan (Bratislava: Vydavateľstvo politickej literatúry, 1965), 457.

60. *Gardista* (March 9, 1944): 5.   61. *Slovák* (September 3, 1944): 1.

62. Ibid., 2.

zerland. As Gila Fatran observes, the Working Group unfortunately did not learn from the rumors that warned about the arrival of Eichmann's best man to Slovakia, Alois Brunner, a man who promised to solve the Jewish question not from behind his desk, but in the field.[63] And so he did. Following the 1944 deportations, approximately 10,000 Jews survived the last months of the war, most of them by hiding. At this point, it would not have been possible to hide without assistance from the majority population.

By the end of World War II, the once flourishing Jewish community of Slovakia shrank by two-thirds when compared to its prewar numbers. This was the result of the so-called Final Solution, the Nazi attempt to annihilate European Jewry. Though undoubtedly a Nazi German plan, the Slovak government played a significant role through its active collaboration.

I have examined the Jewish community of Slovakia with respect to its resistance to Nazi and Slovak government repression. While it is true that Jews did not revolt until 1944, they resisted degradation and oppression in numerous ways. In the early stages of the war, escape and baptism were options, though limited ones. At this point, as I have indicated, many Jews believed that this was "just" another phase, like many before, that they simply needed to wait out. Morever, at least until 1940, emigration for Jews was more risky than staying in Slovakia. To prevent feelings of despair and helplessness, educational and training courses were organized. These should also be understood as tools of survival. By the summer of 1941, the Working Group was formed by Jewish activists who wanted to prevent the projected deportations and did not give up when their plans did not work out. Finally, the armed rebellion of 1944 gave Jews an option to fight the Nazis, just as it gave one to the ethnic Slovaks: "In 1942, Jews in Slovakia did not resist deportation for the same reasons why the European nations—including the Slovak one—did not fight fascism in 1942. When they did, the Jews did the same. Nothing more and nothing less!"[64]

63. Martin A. Lee, *The Beast Reawakens: Fascism's Resurgence from Hitler's Spymasters to Today's Neo-Nazi Groups and Right-Wing Extremists* (New York: Routledge, 2000), 149; Hans Safrian, *Eichmann und seine Gehilfen* (Frankfurt am Main: Fischer Taschenbuch Verlag, 1997), 309; Fatran, "The 'Working Group,'" 190.
64. Juraj Špitzer, *Nechcel som byť žid* (Bratislava: Kalligram, 1994), 253.

Gábor Kádár, Christine Schmidt van der Zanden,
and Zoltán Vági

22 Defying Genocide

Jewish Resistance and Self-Rescue in Hungary

For a variety of reasons, armed Jewish resistance was virtually nonexistent in Hungary during the Holocaust. This does not mean that the Jews gave up. The Holocaust claimed approximately 500,000 Hungarian Jewish lives between 1941 and 1945. The number of victims surely would have been higher if many of the persecuted—in groups and individually—had not defied the perpetrators' genocidal intentions by disobeying the German and Hungarian authorities' orders, going into hiding, escaping, supplying, and rescuing themselves and their brethren. We will survey these examples of defiance and prove that there were tens of thousands of Hungarian Jews who tried to take their fate into their own hands.

Historical Framework: The Holocaust in Hungary

In the spring of 1944, the Hungarian Jews were the largest surviving Jewish community in Nazi-dominated Europe.[1] They had survived, that is, but were far from being unharmed. Starting in 1938, the government and parliament launched an incrementally radicalizing and discriminatory anti-Jewish legislation program. Between May 1938 and March 1944, more than twenty antisemitic

1. The most comprehensive work on the Holocaust in Hungary is Randolph L. Braham, *A népirtás politikája—a Holocaust Magyarországon* [The politics of genocide: the Holocaust in Hungary], vols. 1–2 (Budapest: Belvárosi Könyvkiadó, 1997).

laws and about 260 disenfranchising governmental decrees were passed and issued.[2] Between 1941 and 1944, the anti-Jewish policies claimed tens of thousands of lives due to the deportation of some 18,000–20,000 Jews of "unsettled citizenship" to German-occupied territories, the January 1942 mass killing committed by Hungarian gendarmerie and military units, and the so-called labor service, in which able-bodied Jewish males of military age were compelled to perform unarmed forced labor for the army.

As a result, on the eve of the German occupation, between 760,000 and 780,000 citizens fell under the so-called Jewish laws. Despite the events described above, large masses of Jews enjoyed unusual security in Nazi-dominated Europe. From 1942 to 1944, Regent Miklós Horthy, Prime Minister Miklós Kállay, and their circle sought a way out of the war and the alliance with Germany. They made tentative attempts to enter into a cease-fire with the Western Allies. As part of this strategy, they defied German demands and refused to isolate, ghettoize, and deport Jews, at the same time that the Nazis and their collaborators were deporting European Jews to death camps by the hundred thousands. *Halutz* envoy Rafael Benshalom managed to get to Budapest illegally from Slovakia in January 1944. After living underground for years, he was shocked by the degree of freedom enjoyed by the Hungarian Jews he encountered. "For me, in Europe of 1944, this seemed like a fantasy ... Jews who sought entertainment could still visit coffeehouses, cinemas and theaters. While in Poland, hundreds of thousands of Europe's Jews were being annihilated and the whole world lived in fear."[3]

This situation changed radically when Germany occupied Hungary on March 19, 1944. Hitler's intention to "solve the Jewish problem" in Hungary was among the reasons for the occupation, but it was by far not the most important one. Hitler (quite justifiably) was afraid that the country would try to follow Italy and jump ship. Moreover, the *Führer* wanted to exploit Hungary's military and economic resources to the greatest possible extent.

With the occupying forces arrived *SS-Obersturmbannführer* Adolf Eichmann, head of the Jewish subsection (IV/b/4) of the Reich Security Main Office (*Reichssicherheitshauptamt*) and his special team, the *Sondereinsatzkommando Eichmann*. It only consisted of around twenty officers and was supported by

2. László Karsai, "Magyarországi zsidótörvények és rendeletek 1920–1944" [Anti-Jewish law and decrees in Hungary, 1920–1944], *Századok* 6 (2004): 1287–88.

3. Rafi Benshalom, *We Struggled for Life: The Hungarian Zionist Youth Resistance during the Nazi Era* (Jerusalem: Gefen, 2001), 8–10.

a few dozen guards, secretaries, and drivers. Eichmann was fully aware that with such a small force, it would be impossible to seek out, round up, guard, and deport nearly 800,000 people scattered around a country of 66,000 square miles. He knew perfectly well that the key to success lay in the cooperation of the Hungarian authorities. Consequently, Eichmann was pleasantly surprised to realize that the newly appointed government, led by the pro-Nazi former ambassador to Germany Döme Sztójay, was more than ready to collaborate in the anti-Jewish campaign. Particularly instrumental was the state secretary of the ministry of the interior László Endre, whom Eichmann later recalled as "his best friend."

As a result of the smooth, often enthusiastic and initiating collaboration of the Hungarian government, public administration, and law enforcement agencies, the anti-Jewish campaign unfolded at lightning speed. Between mid-April and mid-June, Jews were totally disenfranchised, plundered, and forced into ghettos, collection camps, or other forms of residences. Between May 15 and July 9, more than 437,000 Jews from the countryside were deported. Ninety-seven percent were taken to Auschwitz-Birkenau. Moreover, between April and August 1944, the German security police deported between 11,000 and 12,000 additional Jews with little to no involvement by the Hungarian authorities. Thus, altogether close to 450,000 people were deported during this period.

Jews disappeared from the countryside by early July. According to the Eichmann-Endre plan, the last action would have been the deportation of the Budapest Jews. However, Regent Horthy halted the operation at this point. The reasons behind this decision are multiple and include the deteriorating military situation, increasing international protests (for example, from Pope Pius XII and President Roosevelt), and the now widely circulated documents describing mass murder at Auschwitz-Birkenau. Apart from the Budapest Jews and the labor service battalions (who were not included in the spring-summer mass deportation campaign), Hungary was *Judenrein*, "free of Jews." For the time being, the remaining Jews were safe.

After this, Horthy's attempts to extricate Hungary from the war intensified. In response, the Germans removed him and placed the extreme right-wing Ferenc Szálasi and his Arrow Cross movement in power on October 15–16, 1944. The deportations were launched again. In November and December, 50,000–60,000 Budapest Jews and labor servicemen were handed over to the Germans. To the Nazis' great astonishment, Szálasi, a devoted antisemite who permitted his paramilitary troops to commit a series of mass murders in the first weeks of his rule, ended up prioritizing his diplomatic objectives over the *Endlösung*. Since he craved diplomatic recognition from the neutrals (Switzerland, Sweden, Spain, and the Vatican), he was open for requests from these countries' representatives on issues related to the Jews. Yielding to their demands, he stopped the ongoing deportations in late November. (Smaller transports were sent to the Reich until December.) Against the Germans' explicit will, the Arrow Cross government set up two ghettoes in Budapest in November and December: one for those having diplomatic protection (the "international ghetto") and one for the rest (the "large ghetto"). Both were liberated by the advancing Soviet army in January 1945.

Armed Resistance and the Lack Thereof

For the emergence of considerable Jewish armed resistance (outside the camps), the following basic conditions needed to be present: weapons; people capable of carrying arms; significant non-Jewish resistance; time to set up organizations; topography (forests, swamps, streets of a big city, and so forth); and, finally, the mindset of the victims. This latter factor included information regarding the Nazis' basic intentions and the conviction that armed resistance was the only way to escape, at least to a death chosen by the victims and not the perpetrators.

In Hungary, none of the above conditions were in place. There were no arms available. In the regions where serious resistance movements emerged (for example, in France and the former Polish, Soviet, and Yugoslav territories), usually large armies had been destroyed by the German war machinery.[4] This resulted in a vast amount of scattered weaponry that could be obtained by the resistance, both Jewish and gentile. Hungary was occupied by the Germans without a shot fired. What's more, there were no fighters. Most Jewish men of military age served as labor servicemen under tight military guard, usually far away from their communities. The overwhelming majority of the ghettos' population consisted of women, children, the elderly, and the sick.

There was also no relevant gentile resistance. While Jews in other parts of Europe generally fought within the framework of or in connection with gentile resistance groups, in Hungary there were no significant armed anti-Nazi movements. The activity of organizations such as the Hungarian Front, the Lib-

---

4. Asher Cohen, *A Haluc ellenállás Magyarországon 1942–1944* [The Halutz resistance in Hungary, 1942–1944] (Budapest: Balassi, 2002), 117.

eration Committee of the Hungarian National Uprising, and some Communist cells was more symbolic than effective. Plenipotentiary of the German Reich SS-General Edmund Veesenmayer's remark aptly characterized the Hungarian resistance: "One day in Yugoslavia is more dangerous than a year in Hungary."[5]

In addition, there was simply no time. The German tanks rolled into Hungary on March 19, and in only three and a half months, Jews disappeared from the countryside and the Budapest Jews were spared only at the last minute. While it was almost nine years after Hitler came to power that German Jews were ordered to wear the yellow star (September 1941), Hungarian Jews were marked seventeen days after the German occupation (April 5, 1944). While the Greek Jews were crammed into ghettos two years after the German and Italian occupation, in Hungary the ghettoization commenced on the twenty-ninth day of German military presence (April 16, 1944). Whereas it took the Germans fifty-three days (July 22–September 12, 1942) to deport approximately 275,000 Warsaw Jews to Treblinka, Eichmann and the collaborating Hungarian authorities deported more than 430,000 people in only fifty-six days (May 15–July 9, 1944). The uprising in Warsaw broke out in the third year of the ghetto's existence (April 1943), the Bialystok revolt started two years after the ghetto was set up (August 1943), and the Czestochowa Jews first offered armed resistance following three and a half years of suffering and almost two years of ghetto life (January 1943). The ghettos in Hungary existed for only a few weeks. The longest-lasting ghettos were located in Budapest, and these stood for six to eight weeks.

Unlike Eastern Europe, in Hungary there were no immense forests and swamps. The only territory apt for (vastly theoretical) partisan warfare was the Carpathians in the eastern and northeastern reaches of the country. Since these regions were the closest to the advancing Soviet army, the Jews of these territories were the first to be deported by the perpetrators. One of the most important factors for the lack of armed resistance was that the minds of Hungarian Jews were not set for it. After years of suffering under Nazi oppression, the Eastern European ghetto fighters and partisans knew precisely that the Germans' aim was their annihilation. In Hungary, Jews were relatively safe until the March 1944 German occupation. When the ghettoization and deportation started, the overwhelming majority of "ordinary" Jews had no idea what was awaiting them (while the Jewish leaders were quite well-informed about the realities of the genocide).

5. Cited by Braham, *A népirtás politikája–a Holocaust Magyarországon*, 1080.

However, this was not the only circumstance that differed radically from the Eastern European situation of 1942–1943. There the Jews took up arms on the threshold of death. The ghetto uprisings usually broke out when the Germans decided to liquidate the ghetto and deport or immediately kill its inhabitants. Jewish slave laborers in Sobibor and Treblinka, and the Birkenau *Sonderkommando,* revolted when they came to the conclusion that the Nazis were about to execute them and survival did not appear as a likely option anymore. When the destruction of Hungarian Jews started in the spring of 1944, the Soviet army was in front of the Carpathian Mountains, and the first Russian units reached Hungary in late August. In the days of the Arrow Cross takeover (October 15–16), the Red Army was 150 miles from Budapest and launched the offensive to occupy the capital in a few weeks. Liberation was within arm's reach for the Jews. Survival was not against the odds at all. The dilemma was no longer "To die with hands held high or to die fighting." It was rather "To fight and die or to gain time and live." It is no surprise that the illegal *Halutz* youth, the only group that was not only acutely aware of the Nazis' genocidal plans, but also had the experience and means to perform armed resistance, decided not to revolt. Their standpoint was succinctly summarized by *Hashomer Hatzair* member Imre (Yitzak) Herbst: "I don't want a kibbutz in Palestine to be named after me; I want to live in it."[6]

However, even within these conditions, a few instances of armed resistance occurred, almost exclusively in the last months of 1944 during the Arrow Cross regime in Budapest.[7] Immediately after the Arrow Cross takeover on October 15–16, a few labor servicemen obtained weapons and put up resistance in Népszínház Street and Teleki Square. They were quickly crushed by Arrow Cross and SS forces.[8] The young Zionists were also engaged in a few firefights. Historian and former resistance fighter Zvi Erez identified six such cases, five of which were defensive acts.[9] The arms were usually obtained on the black market: they were bought from soldiers who had deserted or those who had stolen weapons from military warehouses.[10] Later the *halutzim* received a larger amount of arms from the gentile underground.[11]

6. Avihu Ronen, *Harc az életért. Cionista ellenállás Budapesten—1944* [Fight for life: Zionist resistance in Budapest, 1944] (Budapest: Belvárosi, 1998), 33.

7. Robert Rozett, "Jewish and Hungarian Armed Resistance in Hungary," *Yad Vashem Studies 19* (1988): 285–88.

8. Braham, *A népirtás politikája—a Holocaust Magyarországon,* 1088.

9. Interview with Zvi Erez. István Gábor Benedek and György Vámos, *Tépd le a sárga csillagot* [Tear off the yellow star] (Budapest: Pallas, 1990), 40.

10. Cohen, *A Haluc ellenállás Magyarországon 1942–1944,* 62.

11. Interview with Zvi Erez. Benedek and Vámos, *Tépd le a sárga csillagot,* 39.

Hungarian Jews were also involved in armed resistance outside Hungary. The *Sonderkommando* that revolted in Birkenau on October 7, 1944 had hundreds of Hungarians in their ranks.[12] One of them was Péter Zoltán, a physician from Munkács. Before the uprising, he told a woman from the neighboring camp section: "Maybe one of you will survive. Go home, even if for a single day, and take revenge."[13] Dr. Péter was killed in the revolt. Occasionally, Hungarian Jews deported to Birkenau showed serious physical resistance in the face of death. For example, on May 26, hundreds tried to break out of the closed sector of crematorium V. The SS gunned down all of them. Two days later there was a similarly unsuccessful attempt. As a reaction, *Standortältester* Rudolf Höss ordered that electricity in the barbed wire fence remain switched on throughout the night.

Some labor servicemen joined the partisans. Vilmos Baumann, for example, spent months with the Polish resistance before he was caught by the Germans.[14] Miklós Grósz escaped his labor service units and joined a Russian partisan group only to be imprisoned by the Soviet military authorities in September 1944.[15] Some of the labor servicemen liberated by the Yugoslav partisans around the copper mines of Bor also joined resistance fighters' ranks. Granted, they were not deployed in armed conflicts. Out of the 1,200 Hungarian soldiers of the so-called Petőfi Brigade in Tito's partisan army, at least 200 came directly from Hungary. Some of them were Jews. Hungarian Jews participated in the French resistance movement as well. The infamous Nazi propaganda poster known as *L'Affiche Rouge* (Red Poster) showed pictures of the Communist Manouchian Group. Among them were three Hungarian Jews: József Boczor (Joseph Boczow), Tamás (Thomas) Elek, and Imre (Emeric) Glasz. They participated in derailing Wehrmacht and SS trains and launched hand grenade attacks against German soldiers. They were captured, tortured, and executed.

Organized Defiance: The Zionists

The above-mentioned cases of armed resistance were heroic, albeit marginal and isolated instances. The majority of Jewish actions of defiance in Hunga-

12. According to Filip Müller, a survivor of the revolt, there were 450 Hungarian Jews in the Sonderkommando. Filip Müller, *Eyewitness Auschwitz: Three Years in the Gas Chambers* (Chicago: Ivan R. Dee, 1999), 132–33.
13. Hungarian Jewish Archives (HJA), DEGOB Protocols no. 385.
14. Ibid., no. 3255.
15. Ibid., no. 3528.

ry, both organized and individual, were unarmed.[16] The only group to perform organized rescue and resistance was the Zionists. The movement's membership was very small but by far its influence exceeded its size during the Holocaust.

The two main, opposing branches of religious Hungarian Judaism, the conservative Orthodox and the so-called Neologue (reform) groups, agreed on few issues. Condemning Zionism was one of them. At the center of the patriotic Neologue ethos was the conviction that Jews are "Hungarians of the Mosaic Faith" who do not wish to belong to any other nation. For the Orthodox communities, the Zionist movement was much too secular to be acceptable. Hungarian-born founder of political Zionism Theodor Herzl met nothing but refusal in his home country. It is little wonder that he once called the Hungarian Jews "a desiccated branch on the tree of Jewry."[17]

Therefore, between the two world wars, Zionism was a marginal, factious movement in Hungary, rejected by the majority of Jews. The movement gained strength in 1939 due largely to two factors. First, in the territories annexed to Hungary between 1938 and 1941 (Transylvania, Carpatho-Ruthenia, and the so-called Upper and Southern Provinces), the Zionist movement was significantly stronger than in the heartland. Following the annexations, the Zionists from the new territories joined the Hungarian movement. The other source of "reinforcement" came from Jewish groups fleeing from areas and territories under Nazi occupation, arriving in Hungary mostly illegally. The most definitive impact was made primarily by young people with extensive organizational and resistance experience.[18]

The Zionist movement operating in Hungary in 1944–45 had three poles: the young Zionists (*halutzim*), the so-called Kasztner group, and the Palestine Office. Their concepts and strategies regarding the responses to persecution differed greatly. The *halutzim* are usually viewed as the undisputed heroes of the Holocaust, while Kasztner's controversial story still ignites emotions and fiery debates today.

---

16. See more on the Hungarian Jewish responses in Gábor Kádár, Zoltán Vági, and László Csősz, *The Holocaust in Hungary. Evolution of a Genocide. Documenting Life and Destruction: Holocaust Sources in Context* (Washington, D.C.: United States Holocaust Memorial Museum, 2013).

17. Cited by Raphael Patai, *The Jews of Hungary: History, Culture, Psychology* (Detroit, Mich.: Wayne State University Press, 1996), 345.

18. The strength of the Hungarian Zionist movement is estimated between 2,000 and 6,500 before territorial gains, and 10,000–12,000 after. The data published in the literature is summarized in Attila Novák, *Átmenetben. A cionista mozgalom négy éve Magyarországon* [In transition: four years of the Zionist movement in Hungary] (Budapest: Múlt és Jövő, 2000), 199.

The *Halutz* Movement

Zionist youth organizations had few members.[19] Even so, they carried out significant resistance activities, predominantly unarmed actions due to the circumstances mentioned above. The *halutzim* did not have a single organization, but a network of groups dominated by left-wing movements, such as *Hashomer Hatzair* and *Dror Habonim*. Jewish youth fleeing from Slovakia and Poland between 1942 and 1944 assumed leading roles. When they arrived in Hungary, they already had a substantial past in the movement, which was why their parent organizations selected them to organize Zionist youth in Hungary.[20] Many leaders of the Hungarian youth organizations were being called up for labor service. Their positions were soon taken over by the newly arrived members from abroad. They mostly came without their families, had nothing to lose, and were accustomed to living illegally. The Zionist youth were quick to adapt to extreme situations and good at enduring the physical and psychological hardships of an illegal existence—attributes obviously linked partially to their age, which ranged from eighteen to twenty-six. Therefore it is not surprising that the most organized underground resistance and rescue work was carried out by the *halutzim*. The most prominent leaders and members were Márton Elefánt (Mose Alpan), Rafael Friedl (Benshalom), Imre Herbst, Sándor (Simha) Hunwald, Perec Révész, József Mayer, Endre Grósz (David Gur), Ernő Teichmann (Efra Agmon), among others.[21]

During the German occupation, they rescued, hid, and provided false documents primarily for their own friends and family. They assisted many people in reaching Slovakia, Romania, and the Yugoslav areas. According to Asher Cohen's estimates, counting the Romanian border only, about 7,000 people made it across.[22] Following the example of the Jewish resistance in Poland, the Zionist youth organizations built hiding places in caves, cellars, out-of-the-way buildings, and abandoned apartments, predominantly in Budapest. However, these could not shelter a great number of people. Some of the hiding places were

19. The number of the *halutzim* fluctuated between a few hundred and a thousand members. Many escaped toward Romania; others left in the transport organized by Kasztner. Only a few dozen people were active from the German occupation to the liberation. Cohen, *A Haluc ellenállás Magyarországon 1942–1944*, 125.

20. Recollection of Moshel Alpan, United States Holocaust Memorial Museum Archives (USHMM), RG 50.120*03.

21. For their biographies, see David Gur, *Brothers for Resistance and Rescue: The Underground Zionist Youth Movement in Hungary during World War II* (Jerusalem: Gefen, 2007).

22. Cohen, *A Haluc ellenállás Magyarországon 1942–1944*, 85.

discovered and raided by Hungarian law enforcement, especially during the Arrow Cross era. On December 16, 1944, when the shelter on Hungária Boulevard was attacked, the guard, Ernő Székely of the *Maccabi Hatzair* movement, opened fire on the invaders. Székely was shot and killed; those in the shelter were arrested.[23]

The *halutzim* also organized illegal trips to the countryside ghettos.[24] Their main aim was to provide false papers to the members of their movements and to take them to Budapest. However, at many places they also tried to inform the ghetto inmates of what was awaiting them, and they offered false papers to those who were ready to flee. They were mostly unsuccessful. Béla Grünwald tried to convince his parents to leave with him. "They did not accept illegality," remembered Grünwald four years later. "And they reprimanded me, saying 'Those Poles [i.e., the Polish *Halutz* refugees] confused your head.' My parents thought that only the villages would be evacuated, but the city ghettos would remain, and they could stay in Nyíregyháza."[25]

The scope of the Zionist youth's rescue activities gradually widened. As time passed, they extended their help to Jews outside the Zionist movement as well. However, their priorities remained the same. Moshe Alpan, one of their leaders, was quite frank about their policy: "We had to implement a cruel practice. One Jew is not equal to another.... Therefore if I had the chance to save three people and risk one belonging to the inner circles, I had to let the chance go. We had to keep alive the people of the inner circle by all means."[26]

Their document-forging workshops were particularly crucial in their work, which was framed by the wide-scale rescue missions of the diplomatic corps. The Swiss, Swedish, Spanish, papal, and Portuguese diplomatic missions and the Red Cross issued thousands of protective documents. These were forged and distributed by the Zionists on an ever-expanding scale. This activity gained new momentum when the *halutzim* moved their headquarters into the so-called "Glass House" on Vadász Street, which was under Swiss protection. "If Wallenberg issued 150 safe conducts, we made a thousand. If the Swiss Lutz issued 8,000 documents, we made 20,000," recalled Moshe Alpan.[27] According to David Gur, who

23. Ibid., 159, 183; Gur, *Brothers for Resistance and Rescue*, 233.

24. According to David Gur, the young Zionist emissaries visited 200 destinations in the countryside, mainly ghettos. Gur, *Brothers for Resistance and Rescue*, 14.

25. Cited by Attila Novák, "Ellenállás vagy önmentés? Adalékok az 1944—es magyarországi cionista ellenállás problémájához" [Resistance or self-rescue? Data on the problem of the 1944 Zionist Resistance in Hungary], *Századok* 1 (2007): 155.

26. Ibid., 154–55.

27. Interview with Moshe Alpan. Benedek and Vámos, *Tépd le a sárga csillagot*, 61.

led the forging operations, the Zionist youth produced approximately 120,000 fake documents.[28] This work had negative consequences as well. The value and protective power of the documents reproduced in large volume was "devalued," and the Arrow Cross militiamen often mistook even the authentic documents for forged ones. Nevertheless, on many occasions the fake papers saved the lives of the persecuted. The *halutzim* did not always distribute the papers for free. Their rescue operations cost money, and the financial backing was partially created through selling the documents they produced.[29] They provided papers for the Communist underground as well, which incidentally included many Jewish members (for instance, György Aczél, Endre Ságvári, among others).[30]

The young Zionists carried out their bravest actions following the Arrow Cross takeover. Often wearing military or Arrow Cross uniforms and weapons, they displayed forged documents to save people from the hands of the militiamen. These acts, of course, were extremely risky. Right after the Arrow Cross takeover, *Hashomer* member Ernő Teichmann was cruising the streets in a railway officer's uniform. A boy from his hometown recognized him and started to yell that he was Jewish. People surrounded him and handed him over to two passing Arrow Cross militiamen, who drew their guns and took Teichmann away. After walking a few blocks they put away their weapons and set him free. They turned out to be Zionists on a mission as well.[31] Yet not every incident ended so fortunately. Many *halutzim* were arrested and tortured. Every so often, their comrades conducted daring and successful rescue actions at the prisons to set them free. Others, like *Hashomer* leader Simha Hunwald, were killed.

The *halutzim* also made substantial contributions to the child rescue operations of the International Red Cross that extended its protection to about 6,000 children in over fifty children's homes. Many of these places were protected and supplied by the young Zionists.[32] They participated in the Red Cross's efforts to supply the prisoners of the Budapest "large" ghetto as well.

28. Interview with David Gur. Ibid., 81.

29. László Karsai, "Lőni vagy túlélni?" [Shoot or survive?] *Beszélő* 7–8 (1999): 111; Novák, "Ellenállás vagy önmentés? Adalékok az 1944–es magyarországi cionista ellenállás problémájához," 157–58.

30. Bauer distinguishes between "Jewish resistance" and "resistance by Jews." Yehuda Bauer, *Rethinking the Holocaust* (New Haven, Conn.: Yale University Press, 2001), 137–39. Obviously in the case of the Communists, the latter is dominant.

31. Avihu Ronen, *Harc az életért. Cionista ellenállás Budapesten—1944*, 207. Interview with Rafael Friedl. Benedek and Vámos, *Tépd le a sárga csillagot*, 103. Interview with Ernő Teichmann. Benedek and Vámos, *Tépd le a sárga csillagot*, 119.

32. Asher Cohen, *A Haluc ellenállás Magyarországon 1942–1944*, 137–45.

The Kasztner Group

In his *Rethinking the Holocaust*, Yehuda Bauer contemplates a theoretical scenario regarding the head of the Lodz Jewish Council, Chaim Rumkowski. In this imaginary turn of events, the Soviet troops reached the city earlier than they actually did, the Lodz ghetto had been liberated, and Rumkowski's strategy of ruthlessly carrying out the German orders to save the ever-decreasing ghetto population had proven successful. "If so," asks Bauer, "Would we have erected a statue in his memory, as a hero of the Jewish people, or would we have sentenced him to death for having knowingly caused the murder of thousands upon thousands of helpless Jewish children, old people, and sick people?"[33] Zionist leader Rezső Kasztner's role has raised similar questions in past decades, even without a counterfactual scenario.

Established in early 1943, the Budapest Relief and Rescue Committee served to unify the Zionist groups operating in Hungary. Ottó Komoly, an engineer, was appointed as its president, and its executive vice-president was Rezső Kasztner, a lawyer and journalist from Kolozsvár.[34] In the Zionists' international flow of information, the Rescue Committee became an important link. Kasztner and his colleagues handled the lion's share of supporting and hiding Jews who fled to Hungary to escape the Holocaust raging in Nazi Europe. The financial base for their operations was provided by international Jewish organizations (for example, the Jewish Agency for Palestine and the American Jewish Joint Distribution Committee).[35]

Following the occupation, the members of the Kasztner group made an immediate decision about the strategy to follow: they would negotiate with everyone who could significantly influence the fate of the Hungarian Jews. Ottó Komoly took it upon himself to try to foster contact with the Hungarian authorities. Rezső Kasztner and Jenő (Joel) Brand were assigned the German line, that is, the difficult and controversial task of negotiating with Eichmann's *Sonderein-*

33. Bauer, *Rethinking the Holocaust*, 132.
34. Today, Cluj-Napoca, Romania.
35. For details about the 1944 activities of the Rescue Committee, the Nazi-Jewish negotiations and the Kasztner affair, see for example Braham, *A népirtás politikája—a Holocaust Magyarországon*, 1012–101; Yehuda Bauer, *Jews for Sale? Nazi-Jewish Negotiations, 1933–1945* (New Haven, Conn.: Yale University Press, 1994), 172–209; Gábor Kádár and Zoltán Vági, *Self-financing Genocide: The Gold Train, the Becher Case and the Wealth of Hungarian Jews* (Budapest: Central European University Press, 2004), 209–44. For a sizable bibliography of the literature on the topic, see Randolph L. Braham, *A magyarországi holokauszt bibliográfiája* [Bibliography of the Holocaust in Hungary] (Budapest: Park, 2010), vols. 1–2, 472–80.

satzkommando. In May, a glimmer of hope emerged that the deportation of the Hungarian Jews might be thwarted when Eichmann made his notorious offer to exchange "blood for goods." According to this plan, Brand would be provided the opportunity to travel to a neutral country and contact the leaders of "world Jewry" and the Western Allied powers. Brand's task was to convey Himmler's offer. According to this offer, 1 million Jews would have been released if the Western Allies would have shipped ten thousand trucks and large amounts of goods (soap, coffee, tea) to the Third Reich. Himmler's tentative inquiries about a separate peace agreement were in the background of this surprising offer. The *Reichsführer-SS*, who was becoming more and more independent in Nazi Germany, was seeking to establish contact with the West in pursuit of a potential pact signed behind Hitler's back. One such attempt was the infamous "blood for goods" deal, founded on an absurd assumption that fit the Nazi worldview completely: Himmler thought that the path toward the Anglo-American leaders was via "world Jewry." The Zionists, unaware of this background, saw this operation as the only option for rescuing Hungarian Jews. However, the attempt turned out to be a failure: Brand was arrested by the British, who thought he was an enemy spy. In the shadow of the failed operation, Kasztner was carrying out a far more realistic series of negotiations on a smaller scale with Eichmann. The increasingly complex Budapest talks were gradually slipping out of the grip of the irresolutely inflexible Eichmann. Control was progressively taken over by *SS-Obersturmbannführer* Kurt Becher, Himmler's economic envoy to Hungary.

Kasztner's problems were heightened when on June 20, at the peak of the negotiations, two Hungarian Jewish paratroopers from Palestine, sent to the country by the British army, knocked on his door. Emil Nussbacher and Ferenc Goldstein came to Hungary to collect information for the Allies and to help the remaining Hungarian Jews. They crossed the border on June 9 with a third comrade, Hannah Szenes, who was arrested right away. The secret police was following Nussbacher and Goldstein, too. Kasztner and the Relief Committee were navigated into an extremely fragile situation: the appearance of the British fighters could have destroyed the bargain they made with the Nazis behind the Hungarians' backs. Nussbacher was soon arrested and Goldstein turned himself in—probably partially due to Kasztner's pressure. Nussbacher later escaped; Goldstein was killed in a German concentration camp, and Hannah Szenes was executed by the Arrow Cross in November. The paratroopers' action turned out to be heroic, but rather futile: they did not fire a single bullet, nor did they save one Hungarian Jewish life.

As a result of the negotiations, the so-called "Kasztner train" left Budapest on June 30, 1944. It carried certain prominent religious and secular Jewish figures (writers, artists, rabbis, Zionist leaders) and their family members (including some relations of Brand, Kasztner, and Komoly), in addition to a number of other passengers who got in from various lists (Neologues, Orthodox, Zionists, among others), Polish and Slovak refugees, orphans, and those who actually raised the vast amount of money to be paid to the SS. The train transported its passengers to a special section constructed inside the Bergen-Belsen camp. According to the subsequent negotiations between the Nazis and the Jews, the first group of "Kasztner Jews" (more than 300 people) reached neutral Switzerland safely in August 1944. The rest (about 1,370 people) reached Swiss soil in December.

The assessment of Kasztner's actions remains controversial today.[36] There are some who think that the rescue of a few people had to be paid for by the death of many, because Kasztner made a deal with the Nazis that as long as he facilitated deportations smoothly, the chosen few could leave the country. He held back the precise information he had about the genocide in order to achieve this goal. He even sacrificed the lives of the paratroopers. After the war he whitewashed some of his accomplices, especially Becher.[37]

It is indisputable that Kasztner had precise information about Auschwitz, and did not try to disseminate it.[38] Even SS-Obersturmbannführer Rudolf Höss, who at that time was in charge of the annihilation of Hungarian Jews in Auschwitz, heard about Kasztner. While he was in Budapest to organize the transports to Birkenau, Eichmann told him about a certain "Zionist leader" with whom he had "many prolonged conversations." "It was interesting to hear that this Jewish leader knew all about Auschwitz, the number of Jews rounded up and the selection for extermination," wrote Höss in his memoirs.[39] It is also a fact that he gave favorable testimonies on behalf of SS officers after the war.[40]

36. See, for example, the heated debates in the Hungarian journal *Élet és Irodalom* in 2004 and 2008.

37. This opinion was the center of Judge Benjamin Halevi's decision in the 1953–55 State of Israel versus Malkiel Grünwald case (known as the Kasztner case). Kasztner testified not as a defendant, but as a witness in a libel suit. This case was initiated by the government against a right-wing publicist, Malkiel Grünwald, for accusing Kasztner, a state employee, of collaboration with the Nazis. Judge Halevy agreed with Grünwald and stated that Kasztner "sold his soul to Satan."

38. Randolph L. Braham, *A népirtás politikája—a Holocaust Magyarországon*, 794–96.

39. Steven Paskuly, ed., *Death Dealer: The Memoirs of the SS-commandant at Auschwitz* (New York: Da Capo Press, 1996), 242.

40. For Kasztner's effort to rescue Becher from prison, see Kádár and Vági, *Self-financing Genocide*, 219–44.

Interviewed in hiding in Argentina during the 1950s by Dutch Nazi journalist Willem Sassen, Eichmann remarked: "[Kasztner] agreed to help keep the Jews from resisting deportation—and even keep order in the collection camps—if I would close my eyes and let a few hundred or a few thousand young Jews emigrate illegally to Palestine. It was a good bargain. For keeping order in the camps, the price of 15,000 or 20,000 Jews—in the end there may have been more—was not too high for me. And because Kastner [sic] rendered us a great service by helping keep the deportation camps peaceful, I would let his groups escape."[41] It is clear that Eichmann was not completely truthful: he was not in a position to decide whether or not to let Jews go, since this was a political decision made above him. However, his words cannot be totally swept aside either. Out of all his recollections (interrogation by the Israeli police, testimonies at his trial, memoirs written in captivity, and so forth), he was the most likely to have spoken honestly on the Sassen tapes. He was in hiding, without threats or pressure, and talking to a Nazi comrade. If he ever told the truth, it was to Sassen.

On the other hand, without a doubt, Kasztner managed to rescue more than 1,600 Jews on his train. The significance of this should not be underestimated: ever since Jewish emigration was stopped in October 1941, this was the first sizable group allowed to leave the territory of the Third Reich with the Nazis' permission. Probably—as many pro-Kasztner authors state—he had some share in the decision that in late June approximately 15,000 people were not taken to Auschwitz, but to Lower Austria, where 75 percent of them survived the war.[42]

Even if the existence of an Eichmann-Kasztner agreement (to save the few through keeping the masses quiet) is not completely proven, it cannot be disputed that Kasztner did select those who could survive. Hannah Arendt called this practice "morally disastrous."[43] However, in many cases, the act of rescue went hand in hand with deciding who can stay alive. Kasztner's partner in leading the Relief and Rescue Committee, Ottó Komoly, also participated in compiling the train's passenger list. He was well aware of the tormenting issue Arendt pointed out two decades later. "I feel a dreadful moral disgust,"

41. *Life* (December 5, 1960).

42. In early June, SS-Brigadeführer Blaschke, the mayor of Vienna, requested workers from Kaltenbrunner, the head of the RSHA, to work in the military production plants in the area. Kaltenbrunner told this to Eichmann, for whom the request came in handy because he could then appeal to this transport as a concession in his negotiations with Kasztner.

43. Hannah Arendt, *Eichmann in Jerusalem: A Report on the Banality of Evil* (New York: Viking Press, 1963), 117.

he wrote in his diary on April 25, 1944, when he was informed that his name was on the emigration list.[44] Swiss Vice-Consul Carl Lutz, savior of thousands, holder of the title Righteous Among the Nations by Yad Vashem, also had to select. The Arrow Cross authorities forced him to appear at detention sites and single out the holders of fake Swiss protective documents. Lutz knew what was awaiting those whose documents he labeled as forged: "The disapproval of a certificate was equal to the holder's death sentence," he wrote later.[45] No wonder he was torn by the decisions. As he put it in his diary: "It makes me insane when I abruptly have to decide who to save. Where is God?"[46] Sometimes Lutz's wife, Gertrud, also participated in this horrendous task. "We were like judges issuing death sentences," she recalled later about the selection.[47] As we have mentioned, the *halutzim* also had preferences for whom to save. Nevertheless, no one has accused Komoly, Lutz, or the Zionists of moral collapse or collaboration with the Nazis. Komoly had the same information Kasztner had; still there was never a question raised about why he did not try to spread it. Komoly is without a doubt a martyr: while he was spearheading the child rescue operations of the Red Cross, he was murdered by the Arrow Cross in Budapest. The dark irony of the situation is that accusations against Kasztner perhaps would not have been raised had he been killed during the Holocaust.

Execution or statue? Bauer has asked regarding Rumkowski. Kasztner got both. In the wake of the trial, he was shot and killed in front of his Tel Aviv home in 1957. Honoring his memory, there is a plaque in the garden of the Dohány Street Great Synagogue in Budapest.

The Palestine Office

The third pole of the Zionist movement was the Palestine Office, which also followed an independent strategy. Established for the task of coordinating emigration to Palestine, it was an important Zionist center. Similar to the Rescue Committee, it included representatives of various Zionist groups. Headed by Miklós Krausz, the Office resolutely opposed Kasztner's strategy, rejecting the option of negotiating with the Nazis. For this reason, Krausz sought and found

44. Ottó Komoly's diary. Yad Vashem Archives (YVA), P31/44.

45. Cited by Theo Tschuy, *Becsület és bátorság. Carl Lutz és a budapesti zsidók* [Honesty and bravery: Carl Lutz and the Jews of Budapest] (Budapest: Well-Press Kft, 2002), 213.

46. Cited in Júlia Sárközy, "A magyar zsidókat mentő svájci Carl Lutz" [The Swiss Carl Lutz, rescuer of Hungarian Jews], *Népszabadság* (January 19, 2005).

47. Cited by Theo Tschuy, *Becsület és bátorság. Carl Lutz és a budapesti zsidók*, 214.

relations with international diplomatic bodies. His activities became particularly important in the summer of 1944. He had the Palestine Office relocated into the so-called Glass House at 29 Vadász Street, and managed to have it placed under Swiss diplomatic protection. Although eventually nothing came of the emigrations that he was pushing for, the Glass House still provided shelter for several thousand Jews, and became one of the primary bases of the underground activity of the *halutzim*.

Krausz's most important action was to forward the eyewitness account of Birkenau escapees (the so-called Auschwitz Protocols) to Switzerland in mid-June 1944.[48] Through this channel, the information finally made it to the world media: many articles were published in British, American, Swedish, and Swiss newspapers on the horrific fate of the deported Jews. This also contributed to the international pressure that made Horthy eventually stop the deportations in early July.

Lethal Authenticity or Action with *Amidah*? The Jewish Council

In his 1979 study, Raul Hilberg analyzes the role of the Jewish councils and the practice that they usually were appointed from among the pre-occupation leadership of the communities: "It is that authenticity of the Councils which made them all the more lethal ... Jewish authenticity aided German authority; bread, soup kitchens, and sewing machines became fasteners in the German destructive machine."[49] On the contrary, Yehuda Bauer assessed the council's community organizing activity as resistance. He coined the term *amidah* (Hebrew for "standing up against") to define a wide spectrum of Jewish resistance during the Holocaust from cultural activities to armed revolt.[50] In his opinion, "many [councils] acted with *amidah*—trying to preserve their dignity as long as possible, trying to obtain food, trying to preserve health, protect the children and infirm, support cultural activities and other morale building projects—and ultimately failing."[51] The activity of the Central Jewish Council in Hungary incorporated both lethal authenticity and *amidah*.[52]

---

48. Braham, *A népirtás politikája—a Holocaust Magyarországon*, 78889.

49. Raul Hilberg, "The Judenrat: Conscious or Unconscious 'Tool,'" in *Patterns of Jewish Leadership in Nazi Europe 1933–1945*, ed. Yisrael Gutman and Cynthia J. Haft (Jerusalem: Yad Vashem, 1979), 34–38.

50. Bauer, *Rethinking the Holocaust*, 120.

51. Ibid., 134.

52. The Hungarian *Judenrat* was transformed several times and its name also went through some

The Jewish Council was established by Eichmann during the days following the German occupation.[53] Soon, the Hungarian government gained legal
control over the body. Theoretically, the Council had a statewide sphere of com-
petence, but in practice, its operation was restricted to Budapest. In the countryside, the local Hungarian (and occasionally German) authorities also set up
councils. These operated for a few weeks only, and naturally ceased to exist
once the Jews (among them, the Council members) were deported.

Until the Arrow Cross era, the strategy and policy of the Jewish Council were
shaped by a small circle of pre-occupation community leaders headed by bank-
er and wholesaler President Samu Stern. They were the representatives of the
integrated, acculturated, and wealthy Budapest Jewish upper middle class that
headed the Hungarian Neologue (reform) communities before the German occupation. They were allies of the moderate right-wing, conservative groups of
the Horthy regime's political elite, and devoted adherents of the regent. They
were Hungarian patriots, faithful to their country and its legal system.

It was exactly that law-abiding attitude that prevented them from financially supporting the Polish, Slovak, and German Jews who had illegally escaped
to Hungary and lived in the country in hiding or with fake papers.[54] However,
those who obtained legal refugee status from the authorities (and were mostly
imprisoned in internment camps) were provided financial aid by this leadership. Stern and his circle sharply refused to break the law and finance rescue
and aid work performed in Slovakia.[55] They made this decision not from self-
contained abidance of the law, but rather from a conviction that illegal actions
would negatively affect the entire community. They thought that their primary
obligation was to protect the local Jews. With all its concomitant cruelty, this

---

changes. From March 21 to April 22 it was called the "Central Council of the Hungarian Jews," from
April 22 to the liberation it was the "Interim Executive Board of the Association of Jews in Hungary."
To simplify the description, we will call the organization "Jewish Council."

53. For issues concerning the history and activities of the Jewish Council, see, for example, Braham, *A népirtás politikája—a Holocaust Magyarországon*, 430–972; Judit Molnár, *Csendőrök, hivatal-
nokok, zsidók. Válogatott tanulmányok a magyar holokauszt történetéből* [Gendarmes, officials, Jews:
selected studies on the Hungarian Holocaust] (Szeged: Szegedi Zsidó Hitközség, 2000), 131–81; Vági,
Csősz, and Kádár, *The Holocaust in Hungary*, 254–64; Gábor Kádár and Zoltán Vági, "Compulsion of
Bad Choices—Questions, Dilemmas, Decisions: The Activity of the Hungarian Central Jewish Council in 1944," in *Jewish Studies at the Central European University V*, ed. András Kovács and Michael
Miller (Budapest: Central European University Press, 2009); and the books and articles listed in Braham, *A magyarországi holokauszt bibliográfiája*, 412–21.

54. Braham, *A népirtás politikája—a Holocaust Magyarországon*, 103.

55. Ibid., 99. See also the American Joint Distribution Committee (AJDC), December 8, 1943, AJDC
Archives Saly Mayer Collection, File 38.

reasoning was logical: until March 1944, it seemed feasible that the Hungarian Jews would survive the war.

After the German occupation, the strategy of the Council was rooted in the Stern circle's prewar policies of legality. It stood on two pillars. One was—in Stern's words—"running a race with time." They were hoping that Germany would be defeated before the deportation was completed. The expectation was again not completely unfounded, but it turned out to be unrealistic in the face of the most effective deportation operation of the Holocaust. The other was the conviction that the result of any large-scale revolt or disobedience would inevitably end in the crushing of the whole community. Stern and his circle wanted to keep the Jews unharmed until the fall of Nazis, and they thought avoiding "illegal" activity (that is, activities against the measures of the Nazis and their Hungarian henchmen) was the only way to do so. Therefore, the strategy implied the complete fulfillment of the orders and the constant reassurance of the masses in the Council's official journal, as well as demanding total obedience from them. "Lethal authenticity" was in full swing. On April 13, Stern himself wrote the following in the *Journal of Hungarian Jews*: "we stress that all the decrees and orders of the authorities must be obeyed immediately, precisely, without complaints and murmuring."[56]

This strategy also included another controversial, if not tragic, element: the question of information. The Jewish leaders were well-informed about what was happening in Europe even before the German occupation.[57] After the war, Stern did not deny that he understood the Nazi agenda: "I knew about their deeds in all occupied countries of Central Europe and I knew that their activity was a long series of plunder and murder ... I knew their habits, acts, their dreadful reputation."[58] The information kept flowing in after the destruction of the Hungarian Jews started. The Auschwitz Protocols were probably obtained by the Council in May 1944, but at the beginning of June they certainly had them in hand. Disseminating this information to the Jewish population would have been problematic for practical reasons (censorship, traveling restrictions, and other restraints), but not at all impossible.[59] However, for a long time the Council did not even distribute the documents to those they could access and

---

56. *Magyar Zsidók Lapja* (April 13, 1944).

57. Braham, *A népirtás politikája—a Holocaust Magyarországon*, 1087–88.

58. Recollection of Samu Stern. HJA, DEGOB Protocols no. 3627.

59. Kádár and Vági, "Compulsion of Bad Choices—Questions, Dilemmas, Decisions: The Activity of the Hungarian Central Jewish Council in 1944," 85–86.

who would have been able to use them effectively: Horthy's circles, the diplomatic corps, and the churches. Instead, for weeks, they did nothing except translate the documents, as if the governments and diplomatic corps did not have translators of their own.

What would have happened if the Council had somehow informed the masses about what was awaiting them? Probably they would not have given credence to it. Even if they had, armed resistance—for the above listed reasons—would have been out of the question. The answer of the authorities to a hypothetical escape wave probably would have been mass execution. Nevertheless, 75–80 percent of those deported to Auschwitz were gassed upon arrival. This rate of mortality could hardly have been surpassed by retributive executions following any hypothetical wave of collective disobedience. No mass murder triggered by escape or resistance would have been more devastating than Auschwitz.

The general strategy of Stern's Council was not completely baseless but proved tragically mistaken. However, it is clear that the assessment of one of the first Hungarian Holocaust experts, Jenő Lévai, is not accurate. He saw the Council as an "enthusiastically collaborating, expert organization, which later obeyed [the Nazis'] orders and fulfilled all their wishes humbly and with exaggerated goodwill."[60] In the general framework of this failed strategy, acting with *amidah*, the Council did everything in its capacity to ease the situation of the Jews. With ever more enormous efforts and ever decreasing financial means, it organized the provisioning and housing of about 200,000 Budapest Jews. It arranged health care for the sick and the tending of the elderly. Trying to provide psychological and spiritual sustenance, it kept open the city's synagogues and upheld religious life.

In fact, the Council actually did more than that. Once in a while, it was even able to step out of the general framework of the legal concept. It cooperated with the illegal rescue work of the Zionists. In the first phase of the Nazi-Jewish negotiations, a major part of the sum to be transferred to the Nazis was produced by the Council.[61] It made more than one room of its Síp Street headquarters available to the Zionists, creating a relatively safe place for their rescue actions since the building was under SS "protection," that is, for a while Hungarian authorities were not even allowed to enter. The illegal work was per-

60. Jenő Lévai, *Zsidósors Magyarországon* [Jewish fate in Hungary] (Budapest: Magyar Téka, 1948), 76.
61. The Kasztner report, YVA, 015H/35; recollection of Hansi Brand. USHMM RG 52, Box 72.

formed in the so-called information office of the Council, which served as a de facto cover institution for the Kasztner group and the *halutzim*.

It seems that after the bitter experiences of the destruction of the Jews in the countryside, the Council was ready to give up its aversion to armed resistance. In the early fall of 1944, it hatched daring plans with gendarme Lieutenant Colonel László Ferenczy, who had previously directed the countryside deportations. With changes to the anti-Jewish policy, Ferenczy tried to make the Council forget his lethal role in the deportations and intended to appear as the "savior of Jews" The extremely risky idea (which derived from a consultation with Regent Horthy as well) was that the Hungarian authorities would seemingly agree to the recommencing of deportations, and they would order the gendarmerie and some military units to the capital. Since the Germans would think that the troops were arriving in the city for the deportations, they would not hinder the gathering. At this point, anti-Nazi officers would replace the commanders of the troops, who would turn their weapons against the Germans. This plan was completely baseless for many reasons and was wiped out by the flow of events, but clearly indicates how the Council involved itself in underground activities. An even more ambitious idea was developed in the second half of September, when the Council made tentative attempts to contact those circles that they hoped would organize armed resistance: the Hungarian Front. They started to develop a plan to arm the labor service companies and attack the Germans.[62] However, this plan was also aborted.

After the Arrow Cross takeover, the Council was reshaped. Although on paper Stern remained the president, the body was actually led by Lajos Stöckler and a high ranking official of the Council, Miksa Domonkos. Their activity saved many lives during the days of the Budapest ghettos. Some authors have claimed that it was the young Zionists who fed the ghetto at the end of 1944 and early 1945.[63] In reality, it was predominantly the result of the Jewish Council's efforts that most of the 70,000 inmates did not starve to death before the Red Army broke down the ghetto plank. Stöckler and his colleagues tirelessly negotiated with the diplomatic corps, the Red Cross, and the municipality of Budapest to secure the food supply for the Jews locked up in the ghettos in the middle of the war-torn city.[64] Miksa Domonkos deserves special mention for his

---

62. Braham, *A népirtás politikája—a Holocaust Magyarországon*, 1087–88.

63. Gur, *Brothers for Resistance and Rescue*, 16. See also the debate between David Gur and László Karsai on the topic in the July–August 1999 and November 1999 issues of *Beszélő*.

64. Karsai, "Lőni vagy túlélni?" 112–13.

actions during the ghetto days. Dressed in his army captain's uniform, wearing no yellow star, he passed himself off as a ministry of defense officer. With his firm demeanor, he forced the withdrawal of the Arrow Cross gangs on several occasions. Together with Stöckler, Domonkos turned up wherever he was needed and, displaying extraordinary personal courage, organized life in the ghetto to the last day.

Individual Defiance

Mendel Jutkovics was a shoemaker from the Carpatho-Ruthenian city of Iza.[65] He escaped from the local ghetto the night before the deportation because, as he recalled in 1945, "I decided I'm not going to go through all that." He hid in the forest for a few days, but then he was arrested and deported to Auschwitz. He survived the selection and was assigned to the Golleshau subcamp. He fled from there, too, but was caught again. He was severely beaten up, but avoided execution.[66] Another who tried his hardest to avoid deportation was dentist Béla Horvát, from the Transylvanian city of Nagyvárad.[67] He and his family did not put on the yellow star and refused to move into the ghetto. However, they were arrested and deported.[68] The Steiner family was luckier: they managed to get out of the Nagyvárad ghetto and, through an adventurous journey, fled to Romania.[69] Izidor Schönwirth at first wanted to escape from the Ungvár ghetto.[70] He decided to stay, however, since he did not want to be separated from his elderly parents. After losing his family in Birkenau and surviving several concentration camps, Schönwirth finally escaped in early 1945, when an Allied air attack hit the Nordhausen subcamp where he was working.[71] Ernő Klein fled from his labor service unit a few days before the Arrow Cross takeover. He came to Budapest where he was hidden by Vilmos Faragó, a baker. Faragó did not help only him, but also Klein's brother who escaped from his unit as well.[72] These are only a few of the thousands of examples illustrating how individual Hungarian Jews decided to defy orders and tried to save themselves.

In 1945–1946 more than 3,600 testimonies were recorded from about 5,000

---

65. Today: Iza, Ukraine. 66. HJA, DEGOB Protocols no. 2367.

67. Today: Oradea, Romania.

68. Béla Ötvös, *Porrá és hamuvá* [*Dust and ash*] (Nagyvárad: Pelikán, 1997), 24–66.

69. Reuven Tsur, *Menekülés a gettóból* [Escape from the ghetto] (Noran: Budapest, 2005).

70. Today: Ushgorod, Ukraine. 71. HJA, DEGOB Protocols no. 9.

72. Ibid., no. 1160

survivors by the Hungarian Jewish aid organization, the National Committee for Attending Deportees (DEGOB).[73] Although, for a variety of reasons, the sample cannot be considered strictly representative from a sociological or a historical point of view, the sheer amount of testimonies (about 2 percent of all survivors) enables us to draw some conclusions regarding the general behavior patterns of the Hungarian Jews. It should be emphasized that the processing of data provided in the protocols has only just begun, and only preliminary results are at our disposal. Yet, we will use this database to outline some tendencies of individual defiance.[74]

Similar to those in other occupied countries, the majority of Jews in Hungary accepted the increasingly intense persecution in a passive manner. At the same time, a regional and temporal difference can be observed in terms of resistance opportunities and inclinations. Out of the 4,238 cases of disobedience, self-rescue, and resistance mentioned in the DEGOB protocols, only 422 (9.9 percent) happened in the countryside before and during the ghettoization and deportation. Figure 22-1 presents a closer look at these cases. One of the reasons why the number of cases of defiance is small is that the testimonies generally focus on the events in the camps. However, the reasons are also rooted in the general circumstances of the summer deportations in the countryside. A wide range of factors worked against defiance tendencies there, including the fact that Jews were under-informed about the aim of ghettoization and deportation. Another reason was the lighting speed of the anti-Jewish campaign. Moreover, the vast majority of the gentile population showed indifference or animosity toward the Jews.

If we take a look at the same population (those deported from the countryside in spring and summer), we see that the number of cases skyrocketed in the

73. The documents can be found in the HJA. They are also online at www.degob.hu and www.degob.org.

74. For this purpose, we will use the following terms in the following sense: *Undertaking conflict for oneself or others*: verbal or written protest against the disenfranchisement, humiliation, aggression of oneself or others; attempt to achieve better assignment, more food, and other essentials in ghettos and camps for oneself or others; and so forth. *Minor offense committed for oneself or others*: smuggling and stealing food, medication, clothes for oneself or others; hiding own or other's property; resting at work, helping others rest at work; and so forth. *Major offense for oneself or others:* avoiding selection in camps or helping others avoid selection in camps; changing identity in ghettos and camps or helping others change identity in ghettos and camps; breaking tools and machines to get rest or to sabotage production; and so forth. *Flight, hiding, violence*: refusing to wear the yellow star and going underground; not obeying the labor service draft; escape from ghettos, camps, death marches, cattle cars; hiding with or without false papers; physical violence against guards, militiamen, and so forth, while escaping and hiding; and so forth.

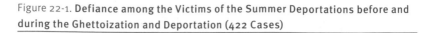

Figure 22-1. Defiance among the Victims of the Summer Deportations before and during the Ghettoization and Deportation (422 Cases)

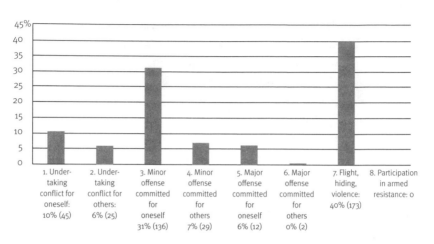

Nazi concentration camps (figure 22-2). It seems that those who tended to be passive before and during the deportation were much more eager to defy the Nazi regime in the concentration camps. The loss of family members, the constant proximity of death, and deteriorating circumstances instilled the will to resist in many prisoners. As we can see, more than half of the cases (52 percent) fall into the category of minor offences. This predominantly meant stealing food and clothing. The second largest category (18 percent) is flight and hiding. Out of these 445 cases only thirty (6.7 percent) happened in Auschwitz. The overwhelming majority occurred in the camps where the deportees were taken from Birkenau. Many took advantage of the mayhem of the last weeks when the concentration camp system was collapsing and the SS was transporting Jews from one camp to another in an increasingly chaotic way. Many Hungarian Jews fled from death marches and trains, and still others escaped from the camps and industrial plants where they arrived under lax security. Some resisted by sabotaging war production in German military plants.[75] Occasionally, they even resisted physically in the camps, as mentioned above.

Returning to Hungary, we can assert that in contrast to the summer situ-

75. See, for example, HJA, DEGOB Protocols no. 51, 81, 174, 509, 588, 704.

Figure 22-2. **Defiance among the Victims of the Summer Deportations in the Nazi Concentration Camps (2,425 Cases)**

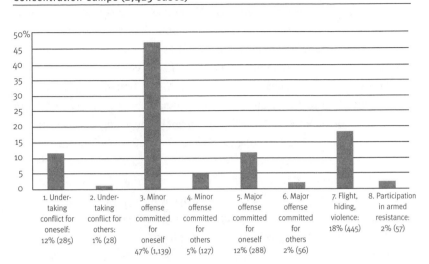

1. Under-taking conflict for oneself: 12% (285)	2. Under-taking conflict for others: 1% (28)	3. Minor offense committed for oneself 47% (1,139)	4. Minor offense committed for others 5% (127)	5. Major offense committed for oneself 12% (288)	6. Major offense committed for others 2% (56)	7. Flight, hiding, violence: 18% (445)	8. Participation in armed resistance: 2% (57)

ation in the countryside, there were many Jews in the capital during the Arrow Cross era who opposed the authorities and moved away from obedience. In this they were greatly helped by the size of the capital, the chaos of the siege, the rapid disintegration of public conditions, and the successful rescue work of neutral embassies. For a variety of reasons, the gentile population's willingness to engage in rescue activities also increased considerably when compared to rescue activity during the countryside deportations.[76] This logically led to a rise in Jewish self-rescue as well.

The DEGOB database does not provide satisfactory information regarding the Budapest Jews, since it predominantly contains the stories of Jews who were deported. However, other sources clearly reveal that Jewish defiance happened on a mass scale during the winter of 1944–45 in Budapest. On October 28, Edmund Veesenmayer reported to Berlin that there were 200,000 Jews remaining in Budapest.[77] In November–December about 40,000 of them were

76. See more on the gentile responses to the Holocaust in Kádár, Vági, and Csősz, *The Holocaust in Hungary. Documenting Life and Destruction: Select Sources of the Holocaust.*

77. Veesenmayer's report to the Ministry of Foreign Affairs. October 28, 1944. Randolph L. Braham, ed., *The Destruction of Hungarian Jewry I–II. A Documentary Account* (New York: World Federation of Hungarian Jews, 1963), 520.

deported to the western border and to Germany.[78] In January 1945, the "large" Budapest ghetto had approximately 70,000 inmates.[79] Roughly another 20,000 people were liberated in the "international" ghetto.[80] A few hundred to a thousand people were in hospitals outside the ghetto. This means that if we take Veesenmayer's estimation into consideration, about 70,000 people (200,000 minus 40,000 minus 70,000 minus 20,000) were "missing." Even if the plenipotentiary's data were exaggerated, it is certain that tens of thousands went into hiding under the Arrow Cross regime in Budapest. This is backed up by numbers published by the statistical department of the World Jewish Congress in 1946. According to these, 119,000 Jews were liberated in Budapest, therefore at least 30,000 people survived the last days of the war in hiding.[81] This was obvious to the Arrow Cross authorities as well. On December 23, 1944, Minister of the Interior Gábor Vajna issued a decree according to which "many of the Jews obliged to move into the ghetto are in hiding in the capital."[82] The decree stipulated that they immediately report to the ghetto.

Within the 3,629 analyzed protocols, 4,238 cases of disobedience, (self-)rescue, and resistance of different degree are documented (see figure 22-3). This is a significantly high number even if we consider that the database consists only of survivors' testimonies; in other words, we do not hear the voices of those who were murdered. It is clear that not everyone who resisted survived, but to survive one usually had to perform defiance of some form. Therefore those who came back from deportation saw liberation *partially* because they decided not to give up. According to the chart, minor offences constitute almost half of all the acts of defiance, while flight and hiding amount to almost 25 percent. If we put minor and major offences together, we can state that disobeying and breaking

78. See the detailed calculation in Tamás Stark, *Zsidóság a vészkorszakban és a felszabadulás után 1939–1955* [Jews during the Holocaust and after the liberation] (Budapest: Magyar Tudományos Akadémia, 1995. Történettudományi Intézete, 1995), 28.

79. According to the report of the ghetto administration, on January 8, 1945, there were 62,949 adults and 6,759 children in the ghetto. Muster-roll of the ghetto. January 8, 1945. Holocaust Memorial Center (Budapest, Hungary) (HMC), RG Gy-13, Box 13.

80. According to Wallenberg, in mid-December 35,000 Jews were in the international ghetto. Report of Wallenberg on the situation of Hungarian Jews. December 12, 1944. Raoul Wallenberg, *Letters and Dispatches* (New York: Arcade Publishing—United States Holocaust Memorial Museum, 1995), 265. The extensive evacuations from here to the large ghetto started in late December. Arrow Cross Deputy Prime Minister Jenő Szőllősi testified that about 18,000 people were taken from the international ghetto to the large one. Éva Teleki, *Nyilas uralom Magyarországon* [Arrow cross rule in Hungary] (Budapest: Kossuth, 1974), 143.

81. Braham, *A népirtás politikája—a Holocaust Magyarországon*, 1246.

82. Ibid., 950–51.

Figure 22-3. **All Defiance Cases from the DEGOB Database (4,238 Cases)**

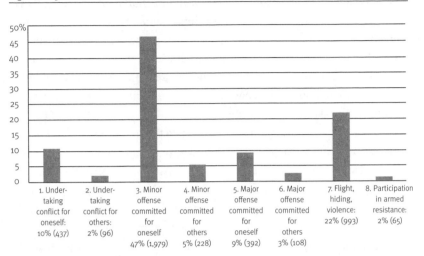

laws and regulations make up two-thirds (64 percent) of the cases. However, the ratio of acts for other people is quite low (8 percent). Therefore the results of our preliminary investigations suggest that the most successful survival strategy was a mixture of going against the rules, trying to flee, and being self-centered.

The Armenian defenders of Musa Dagh held out for fifty-three days against the Turkish armed forces in 1915. Most of them survived the battle and escaped, but this victory made no difference in the larger scheme of events: the Turkish government fulfilled its genocidal plans. The Herero warriors of southwestern Africa took up arms against the German colonial army in 1904, but could not stop General von Trotha's troops from wiping out most of their people. Genocidal regimes are usually overthrown by outside forces: the mass murder of Cambodians was stopped by the Vietnamese army that defeated Pol Pot; the Hutu government was crushed by the Rwandan Patriotic Front; Karadzic, Mladic, and Milosevic were bombed to the negotiating table by NATO. Neither Tito, nor the French *maquis*, nor even Stauffenberg and the best officers of the *Wehrmacht* were able to halt Hitler. The mass murder against Slavs, Gypsies, and Jews could only be stopped by the complete military defeat of Nazi Germany.

Still, across Europe tens of thousands of Jews took up arms against the Nazis. In the Baltics, Ukraine, and Belorussia 20,000 to 30,000 Jews fought in partisan units.[83] Thousands participated in the Yugoslav and French resistance movements. Jewish fighters shot at Nazis or their collaborators in Italy, Slovakia, and Greece as well.[84] Armed Jewish groups operated in Algeria, supporting the invading Allied forces.[85] Approximately 100 ghettos saw the formation of Jewish self-defense organizations.[86] In at least fifty of them, significant armed resistance was carried out. Revolts broke out in the killing centers of Treblinka, Sobibor, Birkenau, and twenty slave labor camps, including *Sonderkommando 1005* of the Janowska camp in Lemberg.[87]

Jews were by far the most actively resisting victim group in the Nazi concentration camp universe. There was no considerable armed resistance by POWs, political prisoners, or other persecuted groups. Around 5 million Soviet POWs, adult men trained to fight, were captured by the Germans. Almost 60 percent of them died in captivity. Many escaped, some even tried to break out of the camps, but still we have no knowledge of relevant armed resistance by them. More than 200,000 Allied troops and 1.8 million French soldiers were taken by the Germans in World War II. They performed a few brilliant escapes, but they did not cause any trouble to the Third Reich. The camp resistance in Buchenwald, dominated by political prisoners, waited with their rebellion until the very last day of the camp's existence. The Auschwitz underground organization was preparing a general uprising for two years. But it never took place. Thus the Jewish *Sonderkommando* revolted alone in Birkenau. Besides typhus, it was only Jews who killed SS men in Auschwitz until the arrival of the Red Army.

Few Jews on few occasions defied the German and Hungarian Nazis with arms in hand. Yet, it seems, that Jews were the most active resisting group in Hungary as well. Hundreds of them tried to break through the barbed wires of Birkenau. Hundreds of others were involved in (albeit sometimes controversial) rescue actions, and tens of thousands, individually, thwarted the genocidal plans by hiding, fleeing, and undermining the power of the perpetrators in every possible way.

83. Israel Gutman, ed., *Encyclopedia of the Holocaust* (New York: Macmillan Publishing Company, 1990), 1111.
84. Bauer, *Rethinking the Holocaust*, 137–39.
85. As discussed in Gutman, *Encyclopedia of the Holocaust*, 1265.
86. Ibid., 1268.
87. Yisrael Gutman and Shmuel Krakowski, *Unequal Victims: Poles and Jews during the Holocaust* (New York: Holocaust Library, 1986), 106.

Robert Jan van Pelt

23 Resistance in the Camps

In Memory of Rudi Vrba (1924–2006)

Primo Levi once compared the core reality of the death camps to a Gorgon, the mythological being that turned all men who approached it into stone.[1] When I began to think about the topic of "Jewish resistance in the camps," I felt paralyzed. Should I take a narrow definition, which limits resistance to open revolts such as those undertaken by the Jews in Treblinka and Sobibor, the *Sonderkommando* of crematorium 4 in Auschwitz, or the group of Warsaw Jews who resisted in the undressing room of crematorium 2 in Auschwitz, killing one SS man and wounding a second? It would be a topic that might just be covered in the nine thousand words available to me. Or should I take a wide definition, and include all acts that countered the camp's purpose to break the inmates morally and destroy them physically? In that case, I ought consider the whole gamut of defiance as it arches from open revolt to small acts like sharing a piece of bread with a comrade, or the act of keeping oneself clean and one's head high—and struggle with tricky questions such as whether a voluntary death in order not to be separated from friends or family, or survival at any cost, or suicide may also count as acts of resistance, as Holocaust-survivor Meir Dworzecki suggested in a paper given at the Yad Vashem Conference on Manifestations of Jewish Resistance held in Jerusalem in 1968.[2] Or should I adopt a Goldilocks strategy by opting for

1. Primo Levi, *The Drowned and the Saved*, trans. Raymond Rosenthal (New York: Simon and Schuster, 1986), 83f.
2. Meir Dworzecki, "Day-to-day Stand of the Jews," in *Jewish Resistance during the Holocaust:*

a middle ground, and follow Auschwitz-survivor Hermann Langbein, who in his book-length study on resistance in the camps defined resistance as "actions, or preparations for actions, that were undertaken in order to thwart or mitigate management campaigns directed against all inmates or a group of them."[3]

What about "the camps"? Between 1933 and 1945, Jews suffered, died, and possibly resisted in so many different kinds of camps: *Arbeitslager* (labor camps), *Auffangslager* (absorption camps), *Durchgangslager* (transit camps), *Firmenlager* (company camps), *Judenarbeitslager* (labor camps for Jews), *Judenlager* (Jews' camps), *Judenumsiedlungslager* (Jewish resettlement camps), *Konzentrations-lager* (concentration camps), *Polizeihaftlager* (police detention camps), *Sammel-lager* (assembly camps), *Sonderlager* (special camps), *"Vernichtungslager"* ("extermination camps"—set in quotation marks because the category did not officially exist), *Zwangarbeitslager* (forced labor camps), and so on. What about the non-German camps where Jews were imprisoned? What about the *camps d'accueil* (reception camps), *camps d'internement* (internment camps), *camps de séjour* (sojourn camps) and *camps de transit* (transit camps) in France, or the camps in Hungary, Romania, and other countries that persecuted Jews? Should I try to cover all of these camps? Should the topic limit itself to life *in* the camps, or does it also include the situation of those who, like almost all who arrived in Treblinka, Sobibor, Belzec, Chelmno, and Auschwitz-Birkenau, never were properly admitted to those camps as inmates, but who were upon arrival immediately murdered?

Having observed over many years the way men make buildings and the way men run organizations, I have been able to reconstruct the making of Auschwitz as a physical environment, and the operation of Auschwitz as an organization. But I have never observed a domain of degradation that begins to approximate the condition of life in a German death camp. Like almost all academics, I am one of those whom Auschwitz survivor Primo Levi addressed in his poem "Shemà," written in 1946—one of those who live secure in warm houses and "who return at evening to find / hot food and friendly faces," and therefore never will be able to understand the being "Who fights for a crust of bread / Who dies at a yes or no."[4] One year before Auschwitz became one of

---

Proceedings of the Conference on Manifestations of Jewish Resistance, ed. Meir Grubsztein, trans. Varda Esther Bar-On a.o. (Jerusalem: Yad Vashem, 1971), 152–81.

3. Hermann Langbein, *Against All Hope: Resistance in the Nazi Concentration Camps, 1938–1945*, trans. Harry Zohn (London: Constable, 1994), 52.

4. Primo Levi, "Shemà," in *Collected Poems*, trans. Ruth Feldman and Brian Swan (London: Faber and Faber, 1988), 9.

the final destinations of the Jews of Europe, the French-Jewish academic Marc Bloch argued that historians could nurture the historical sensitivity that allowed them to know the past "from within" by studying the vibrancy of human life around them. "It is always by borrowing from our daily experiences and by shading them, where necessary, with new tints that we derive the elements which help us to restore the past." Historians who did not understand that the observation of life around them was the basis of all historical understanding "would be wise to renounce all claims to that of a historian."[5] Bloch only confirmed what five years earlier the British philosopher and historian Robin George Collingwood had argued in one of his lectures given at Oxford. "If we raise the question, Of what can there be historical knowledge? The answer is, Of that which can be re-enacted in the historian's mind."[6] This view squared with that of the Italian philosopher, historian, and critic Benedetto Croce who, in 1938, had posited the thesis that historical evidences can only be understood if "they stimulate and hold fast in me the memory of states which are mine." The experience and the state of mind of historians were crucial to their understanding. "History does not come to us from without but lives within us."[7] So how can historians, using their experience and their reason, understand anything about a situation that is beyond experience and beyond reason? And if, miraculously, some who lived in such a world were able to transcend it through a posture of defiance and one or more acts of resistance, how could a historian who has never witnessed a miracle recognize and understand this?

When the Greek hero Perseus decided to kill the Gorgon Medusa, he knew that he was to approach her walking backwards, observing a vague reflection of the outline of her body in the mirror of the Aegis, the polished silver shield lent to him by Athena, goddess of reason. Therefore I might try to encounter the immense and impossible topic of "resistance in the camps" by walking backwards, by taking as my point of departure not the question of "resistance," but the inverse: what was the onslaught that the deportees and inmates suffered in the camps, and which they sought to resist? I will use as my Aegis a classic tool of analysis, typology. Typological analysis seeks to understand an aspect of the world by comparing and contrasting different "ideal types."[8] An

5. Marc Bloch, *The Historian's Craft*, trans. Peter Putnam (New York: Knopf, 1953), 44.

6. Robin George Collingwood, *The Idea of History* (Oxford: Clarendon Press, 1946), 302.

7. Benedetto Croce, *History as the Story of Liberty*, trans. Sylvia Sprigge (London: George Allen and Unwin Ltd., 1949), 19f.

8. Max Weber, *The Methodology of the Social Sciences*, ed. Edward A. Shils and Henry A. Finch (New York: The Free Press, 1997), 88.

ideal type is an abstraction constructed on the basis of the observation of actual phenomena considered from a particular viewpoint with the aim to answer a particular question. As a theoretical construct, an ideal type represents a great variety of actual examples that share certain similarities emphasized in the type. Well-known is the attempt by the Italian philosopher Giorgio Agamben to analyze "the camp" as a spatial-social-political type by comparing it to three other spatial-social-political types: "the nation," "the state," and "territory." Agamben defined the essence of the camp as "the materialization of the state of exception"—that is, it is an extraterritorial place within the territory of a state where some or all rights of either citizens or foreigners or both are suspended. To Agamben the camp is "dislocating localization" that emerged when the three constituent elements of the old trinity of "nation," "state," and "territory," which had structured the classic nation state, began to drift apart.[9]

While Agamben's understanding of the camp has proven useful to understand the place, purpose, and function of the camp within society, the fact that he did not subdivide this ideal type within subtypes is problematic. In a recent effort, I proposed a scheme framed by Agamben's understanding and inspired by typologies proposed by Hannah Arendt, the French historians Joël Kotek and Pierre Rigoulot, and the German academics Axel Dossmann, Jan Wenzel, Kai Wenzel, and Thomas Kühne.[10] In my model, I distinguish five ideal types (which may be understood as subtypes of Agamben's single ideal type of the camp), giving them, following the lead of Arendt, Kotek, and Rigoulot, the traditional designations of the afterlife: "Paradise," "Hades," "Purgatory, "Hell," and "Gehenna." Paradise is the place in which individuals are encouraged or forced to surrender some of their rights to a larger community; in Hades a per-

9. Giorgio Agamben, "What Is a Camp?" in *Means without End: Notes on Politics*, trans. Vincenzo Binetti and Cesare Casarino (Minneapolis, Minn.: University of Minnesota Press, 2000), 40, 43; also Giorgio Agamben, *Homo Sacer: Sovereign Power and Bare Life*, trans. Daniel Heller-Roazen (Stanford, Calif.: Stanford University Press, 1998), 166–80.

10. Hannah Arendt, "The Concentration Camps," *Partisan Review* 15, no. 7 (July 1948): 743–63; Hannah Arendt, *The Origins of Totalitarianism* (New York: Harcourt, Brace and Company, 1951); Joël Kotek and Pierre Rigoulot, *Le siècle des camps: Détention, concentration, extermination—Cent ans de mal radical* (Paris: J. C. Lattès, 2000); Axel Dossmann, Jan Wenzel, and Kai Wenzel, "Barackenlager: Zur Nutzung einer Architektur der Moderne," in *Auszug aus dem Lager: Zu Überwindung des modernen Raumparadigmas in der politischen Philosophie*, ed. Ludger Schwarte (Berlin: Akademie der Künste/Transcript Verlag, 2007), 220–45; Thomas Kühne, *Belonging and Genocide: Hitler's Community, 1918–1945* (New Haven, Conn.: Yale University Press, 2010); Robert Jan van Pelt, "Paradise / Hades, Purgatory, Hell / Gehenna: A Political Typology of the Camps," in *The Routledge History of the Holocaust*, ed. Jonathan Friedman (London: Routledge, 2011), 191–202; see also Michal Aharony, "Hannah Arendt and the Idea of Total Domination," *Holocaust and Genocide Studies* 24: 2 (2010): 193–224.

son's legal rights are suspended; in Purgatory the moral person comes under attack; in Hell one's individuality is at stake. Finally, Gehenna is the place of physical death.

Paradise

The first ideal type, Paradise, denotes the system of what one might label (for lack of better words) as "betterment" or "optimization" camps. These became, first in nineteenth-century North America and later also in Europe, a hallmark of the will to transform and renew society by removing people—especially young people—for some time from the evils of the city to what one assumed to be the unspoiled margins of the inhabited world. These camps were sites of idealism and aspiration. In North America they included religious revival camps like the Salem Camp Meeting in Covington, Georgia; the Philosopher's Camp in the Adirondacks; the Boy Scout and Girl Guide camps; and the summer camps organized by the YMCA, YWCA, and other organizations devoted to the spiritual and physical well-being of urban youth.[11] In Weimar Germany countless groups that were part of the *Jugendbewegung* organized *Lager* where German youth, under leadership of charismatic *Führer*, could commune with nature and each other. Since the 1920s there were, of course, also camps specifically created to reform Jewish youngsters. These were the *Hachsharot* (Preparation) camps organized and run by the *Hechalutz* (The Pioneer) Zionist youth movement to train young people who sought to settle in Palestine, the *Kvutzot* (Groups) and *Kibbutzim* (Gatherings) that were created not only in Palestine, but also within the European Diaspora, and the various training farms.

All these betterment camps—both non-Jewish and Jewish—were conceived as smaller or greater acts of resistance against the seductions of urban civilization. They represented a romantic revolt against decadence and the whole pattern of bourgeois values and conventions in general and, in the case of Jewish camps, the debilitating political, social, and economic conditions of the Diaspora. Nurturing a spirit of revolt, it is not surprising that the esprit-de-corps and sense of belonging young Jews had experienced in these places played a vital part in their attitude of defiance during the Holocaust. In his studies on Warsaw Jewry during the Holocaust and Jewish Resistance, Israel Gutman has stressed the crucial role of the Jewish youth movement in organizing the resistance against the Germans. "Between the two wars, the Jewish youth move-

11. See Charlie Haley, *Camps: A Guide to 21st-Century Space* (Cambridge, Mass.: MIT Press, 2009).

ments had fashioned a special image of youth and woven a network of intimate and stable relations with their organizational frameworks. In addition to their devotion to ideology, some of the movements placed emphasis on education toward communal living at some future time. Thus a causal relationship developed between ideological identification and personal comradeship." When the German occupation began, these ties were not broken. In fact, the bonds of comradeship strengthened as, in a situation of great scarcity, young people increasingly practiced communal living. In addition, they witnessed the helplessness of the adults, most of whom had lost so much and who felt unable to protect their families, and they saw collapse of the traditional Jewish parties. "The sense of comradeship had been so firmly established that it was able to withstand the unprecedented conditions that now arose.... Members of the youth movements were able to preserve their consciousness of being part of human society and thus to remain undefeated by the general sense of isolation."[12] Mordecai Anielewicz, the leader of the Jewish Fighting Organization in the Warsaw Ghetto, his deputy, Izhak Zuckerman, and the majority of members of the JFO had received training in the *Hechalutz* movement. After the war Zuckerman claimed that, among the inhabitants of the Warsaw ghetto, only the members of *Hechalutz* had "the fortitude to see things as they were, the Jewish reality as it was. This was our education in exile, in the chapters of the *Hechalutz* (the pioneer movement): to attempt in every possible manner, and with every intellectual resource, to alter the existing order of things—both human in general and Jewish in particular."[13]

Including an albeit short discussion on the significance of the Jewish Youth Movement in general and the legacy of the Zionist training camps in the history of Jewish resistance may seem to stretch the intended scope of this essay. Yet it is a necessary corrective if we desire to understand the topic of the camps in its full range. I would like to push the envelope even further, and suggest some kind of theoretical Möbius strip, which is a surface that has only one side and one boundary. It may be correct to say that the Holocaust culminated in the camps—although, for the record, I note here the recent challenge of this position by Timothy Snyder.[14] It may be equally correct to say that the Holocaust

12. Yisrael Gutman, *The Jews of Warsaw, 1939–1943: Ghetto, Underground, Revolt* (Bloomington: Indiana University Press, 1982), 133, 143.

13. Izhak Zuckerman, "The Jewish Revolt," in *The Fighting Ghettos*, ed. Meyer Barkai (Philadelphia: Lippincott, 1962), 5.

14. Timothy Snyder, "Holocaust: The Ignored Reality," *The New York Review of Books* 56, no. 12 (July 16, 2009): 14.

arose from the camps: the German betterment camps, created by the Nazi regime—camps that, in a fundamental manner, represented the first assault on
the Jews because a sojourn in these camps were a precondition for membership
in German society—and Jews were not welcome.

To understand Nazi Paradise it is necessary to understand the self-identification of the Nazis as being part of the revolt of youth against a set of old and
established orders, both international order and domestic. As far as international politics was concerned, the Nazi view of the world was inspired by a concept first coined by Fyodor Dostoyevsky: namely that Germany was a nation
of continual protest—"against the Roman world, ever since Arminius,—against
everything that was Rome and Roman in aim, and subsequently—against everything that was bequeathed by ancient Rome...."[15] Dostoyevsky's understanding of German history and destiny as a continuous revolt against the European order influenced the editor of the first German edition of Dostoyevsky's
complete works: Arthur Moeller van den Bruck. In the wake of the Great War,
Moeller van den Bruck argued that Germany was a young, fertile, and restless
nation that had sought to find a place in a world divided up and controlled by
old, wealthy, and satisfied nations like Great Britain and France—nations that
refused to provide Germany with the space and resources it needed. Germany
was young because it had no wealth but it had the ability, will, and energy of
its people, and that was what the old nations feared and hated.[16] These ideas
shaped the Nazi desire to create a New Order in Europe centered on the "New
Germany," which was to be known as "The Third Reich," a concept also coined
by Moeller van den Bruck.[17]

As far as domestic politics was concerned, the Nazis also were a movement
dedicated to youthful revolt—but in this case against a class-ridden, politically, economically, and socially fragmented society. National Socialism was
to reeducate and resocialize Germans into a unified, strong, and racially pure
Volksgemeinschaft (national community), and optimization camps located at
the margins were to be the primary tools of this transformation.[18] These camps

15. Feodor M. Dostoievsky, *The Diary of a Writer*, trans. Boris Brasol (New York: George Braziller, 1954), 727.

16. Arthur Moeller van den Bruck, "Das Recht der jungen Völker," in *Das Recht der jungen Völker: Sammlung politischer Aufsätze* (Berlin: Verlag der Nahe Osten, 1932), 157–71; also Gerwin Stroibl, *The Germanic Island: Nazi Perceptions of Britain* (Cambridge: Cambridge University Press, 2000), 102ff.

17. Arthur Moeller van den bruck, *Das dritte Reich*, ed. Hans Schwarz (Hamburg: Hanseatische Verlagsanstalt, 1931).

18. See Dossmann, Wenzel, and Wenzel, "Barackenlager," 220ff.

included those run by the *Deutsches Jungvolk*, the *Hitler-Jugend*, the *Arbeitsdienst*, the *Wehrmacht*, camps run by many professional organizations for their members. In the official ideology, these camps were presented as symbols of the collective will of the nation to renew itself, true "communities of fate" that resembled those that had existed in the trenches of the Great War. The practical aim, however, was to use the camps as a tool to introduce within the existing civil society a new social order based on the idea of *Kameradschaft* (comradeship)—which, as such, was a not necessarily harmful concept that also inspired the various non-Nazi Youth movements, including, as we have seen, Zionist youngsters. But in the case of the Nazi camps, comradeship came to serve the Nazi aim of totalitarian domination and which, as the historian Thomas Kühne has argued, created the social type that proved capable of unleashing the Holocaust. Some key elements made this possible. In addition to the physical isolation of the camps from cities and towns, which they shared with betterment camps created by other organizations, a few additional elements gave the Nazi betterment camps their own specific character which made them radically different from the autonomous, anarchic, and spontaneous communities of the *Hachsharah* camps.[19] These elements included a strict hierarchy, a tight schedule without down time that organized every minute of the day, uniforms, no possibility of any privacy, the jettison of all customs of civility and decorum, and the careful cultivation of a series of enemies that allowed the group to congeal. The most important of these enemies was, of course, "the Jew."[20]

An excellent introduction to the way these camps worked and the impact of life within them on the behavior and values of the inmates can be found in the memoir written in 1939 by the German refugee Raimund Pretzel, who lived in England under the adopted name Sebastian Haffner. A convinced anti-Nazi, Pretzel had been forced in the autumn of 1933 to receive obligatory ideological training in a camp for candidates for the second state examination for lawyers who sought to become members of the judiciary. Pretzel entered the camp, located some thirty-five miles south of Berlin, in a spirit of critical opposition. Yet he noticed that camp life quickly erased his ability to resist, changing him (and all the others), if not into enthusiastic Nazis, then "certainly into usable Nazi material." The key to this transformation was "the trap of comradeship." This comradeship, modeled on that of soldiers in the trenches, destroyed the sense

19. Israel Oppenheim, "Hehalutz in Poland between the Two World Wars," in *Essential Papers on Zionism*, ed. Jehuda Reinharz and Anita Shapira (New York: New York University Press, 1996), 240ff.
20. Kühne, *Belonging and Genocide*, 42ff.

of individual responsibility as it demanded a surrender of all sense of dignity and insisted on a total conformity with the group. Pretzel noted that after some weeks of "comradeship," a group of aspiring judges had morphed into "an unthinking, indifferent, irresponsible mass" in which no one—Pretzel included— was willing to stand out. Yet, in exchange, each and every one was relieved of a sense of responsibility for his own actions. This was the dark, demonic aspect of the comradeship in the betterment camps. Pretzel realized that each of these camps was a microcosm of the new Germany: everywhere Germans willingly embraced comradeship as the model of a new society, exchanging "the delicate, hard-to-reach fruits of freedom for the juicy, swelling, close-at-hand intoxication of general, undiscriminating, vulgar comradeship."[21] Pretzel noted that those who live in a "comraded" condition lost their grasp on reality.

Hannah Arendt reflected in the second, expanded edition of *The Origins of Totalitarianism* (1966) on the way a totalitarian environment like the one that existed in the Nazi version of Paradise made people become delusional. The key is the loneliness that arises when people have no privacy. In such a situation, they lose their ability to relate both to those around them and to the reality in which they find themselves. The distinction between fact and fiction, which allows people to judge the reality of experience, and the distinction between true and false, which is a basic standard of thought, collapse in such an environment. "The self-coercion of totalitarian logic destroys man's capacity for experience and thought just as certainly as his capacity for action."[22] Arendt stressed that we are able to experience reality in so far as we are in the company of other people who are different from us, but whom we trust, and who either challenge or confirm our experiences. Yet in a situation of totalitarian domination, these people are absent. "In this situation, man loses trust in himself as the partner of his thoughts and that elementary confidence in the world which is necessary to make experiences at all. Self and world, capacity for thought and experience are lost at the same time."[23]

The practice of comradeship and the desire to confirm and strengthen its bonds carried the obligation to break, at times to transgress, not only the conventions of society but even the most elementary norms of human conduct.

---

21. Sebastian Haffner, *Defying Hitler: A Memoir*, trans. Oliver Pretzel (New York: Farrar, Straus and Giroux, 2002), 257ff.

22. Hannah Arendt, *The Origins of Totalitarianism*, new edition (New York: Harcourt, Brace and World, 1966), 474.

23. Ibid., 477.

This made one in the eyes of one's comrades a "man amongst men." From 1941 onwards, the intoxication of comradeship was to shape too many German men into genocidal killers. Places that had been created as communities of fate ended up forging a nationwide community of complicity.[24]

Hades

The second ideal type of camp is "Hades." In Greek mythology, Hades was the main part of the underworld. It was a gloomy realm of shadows, but not a place of torture and punishment. Through the ideal type of Hades, I refer to all the various internment camps established in order to get out of the way bothersome and undesirable elements such as refugees, stateless people and asocials. Established outside of the penal system, and imprisoning people who had not been convicted in a normal judicial procedure in which a definite crime entails a predictable penalty, these internment camps annihilated, in the words of Hannah Arendt, the "juridical person" in human beings. The inmates had lost their civil rights.[25] In the late 1930s and in the 1940s, hundreds of thousands of Jews spent longer or shorter times in Hades. The sections of the German concentration camps where, after the November Pogrom, German-Jewish and Austrian-Jewish men were kept belong to this category, as well as the camps for German-Jewish and Austrian Jewish refugees in France, the Netherlands, Switzerland, and other countries, or the internment camps in the Soviet Union for stateless Jewish refugees from German-occupied Poland who refused in 1940 to become Soviet citizens. In general, Jews did not resist internment in those camps. The Hungarian-Jewish exile Arthur Koestler, who had fled Germany for France in 1933, allowed himself to be interned in Le Vernet. In 1941, in safety in England, he reflected on the passivity with which the internees had accepted their fate. "Men of exemplary courage and daring, after having been labeled 'refugees' and beaten out of three or four countries, went about as if carrying an invisible leper's bell.... Combative idealism became a squashy inferiority complex, and martyrdom a neurosis."[26] Of course, resisting internment meant, in general, running the risk of *refoulement* (expulsion) to Nazi Germany or the German-occupied territories.

---

24. See Kühne, *Belonging and Genocide*, 55ff.

25. Arendt, "The Concentration Camps," 752; Asher Cohen and Yehoyakim Cochavi, eds., *Zionist Youth Movements During the Shoah* (New York: Peter Lang, 1995).

26. Arthur Koestler, *Scum of the Earth* (London: Jonathan Cape, 1941), 88f.

What did resistance in Hades look like? As the key issue in Hades was the destruction of the juridical person, resistance encompassed every effort to restore the rights of the inmates. Both Jewish nongovernment organizations like HICEM and non-Jewish organizations like the American Friends Service Committee were crucial in the effort to provide the inmates of the internment camps in Vichy France legal advice, and helped them to obtain the stack of papers that allowed them to leave the camps in order to emigrate to the United States. Their activities did not stop until the German occupation of southern France in November 1942. In the case of the Polish Jews interned in 1940 in camps in Arctic Russia and Siberia, the ultimately successful effort to restore their rights and ensure their release was undertaken from July 1941 onward by representatives of the Polish government-in-exile in London.[27] Even if their attempts to help were unsuccessful, the presence of these representatives of the outside world within the camps gave the inmates some measure of confidence that they had not been forgotten, and some measure of hope that, at some future date, they might be released—that is if the foreign consuls who issued the visas were willing to cooperate.

The inmates interned in the camps that can be (loosely) arranged under the type of Hades not only had to bear the assault on their rights and their hopes, they also faced an assault on their personality. After the beginning of the German invasion in May 1940, the French authorities interned the Austrian-Jewish refugee Soma Morgenstern in a camp for "enemy aliens" near Audierne, Brittany. He escaped after a little more than two weeks, making his way first to Marseilles, then to Casablanca, and finally to the United States. There he wrote a memoir of his time in Audierne and his subsequent flight. "Much has been talked, chattered, written and smeared about the suffering in concentration camps, but none has observed the greatest danger of this mass grave of the mind, above all the mind. How can one explain that people locked up in dungeons do not disintegrate as quickly (and some do not do so at all) as people in a concentration camp?" To Morgenstern the key issue was the tyranny of the present—a tyranny that arose from the total uncertainty about the future and led to a destruction of "the softest tissue of life": memory. "There is a plenitude of the present. Not a crack opens up to allow in a bit of past and a bit of future. That is why one loses one's memory. One does not have any time to appropriate

27. See Debórah Dwork and Robert Jan van Pelt, *Flight from the Reich: Refugee Jews, 1933–1946* (New York: Norton, 2009), 218–44.

one's own impressions, one's own thoughts, one's own feelings. That is why these collapse into oblivion the moment they are born. To remember means to find. One can only find in the past. In the present one can only lose. And a concentration camp is full of the present. Full to the level of madness."[28]

On February 11, 1943, the Dutch-Jewish student David Koker was arrested and interned in a *Judenauffangslager* (reception camp for Jews) that had been created in the Herzogenbusch (aka Vught) concentration camp in the German-occupied Netherlands. Initially, the conditions in this internment camp were somewhat relaxed: the inmates were not put to work. David decided to keep a diary in an effort to maintain a grasp on reality. On March 1, he noticed that camp life had drained him of all content. "It's impossible to express how empty I am here. Everything I always thought about, all my 'positions,' which were always *associated* to all the phenomena of reality that cropped up, they are gone and gone. There's nothing left besides camp life." On May 23, he noticed that "the loss of memory is a general feature here.... Thoughts keep going around in the same circle. Our receptiveness lies open and shrinks and hardens at the surface. Because life has become a nothingness, a void." On June 3, he came back to his mental state once again. "Our feelings are like skin that has been stretched very tight—you get that with wounds sometimes—and then becomes insensitive and oversensitive at the same time." The internees had lost their spontaneity. "People vitrify here, as it were. They hold on to everything they used to have, but it is as if they were objects in a museum." David noted that he would like to believe that it was possible to transcend the situation in which he found himself, to transcend mere endurance, and live "actively" in the camp, adopting a "proud, exalted attitude." But this was "difficult, too difficult," and he feared it would destroy his health. "Hibernation is better."[29]

Yet recording not only the events of camp life in his diary, but also tracking his own struggle to hold on to them, David did not retreat into hibernation. He chose to resist the subtle but certain destruction of personality that internment brought. His diary was a tool of resistance because it expressed his own hope that, at some future date, he would be free, regain the self that he had lost in the camp, and reconnect to his former existence. "You can allow all your feelings to freeze; when this has ended you can thaw them out and then they'll

28. Soma Morgenstern, *Flucht in Frankreich: Ein Romanbericht*, ed. Ingolf Schulte (Lüneburg: zu Klampen, 1998), 50, 289.

29. David Koker, *At the Edge of the Abyss: A Concentration Camp Diary, 1943–1944*, ed. Robert Jan van Pelt, trans. Michiel Horn and John Irons (Evanston, Ill.: Northwestern University Press, 2012), 82, 126, 201, 206f.

live again," he wrote on June 3. He believed that while few experiences became conscious, they were nevertheless not lost. "Everything will be stored in our unconscious mind and will manifest itself after the war. To activate that un- conscious experience must be the task of this diary." Every entry was not only a testimony to his faith in his own future as a thinking and feeling person, but also in a future for the friends from whom he had separated. Key to his strategy of rebuilding a life after his liberation would be to resume "those relationships after the war in their original form." Yet this would be difficult, as the expe- rience of his non-Jewish friends had been so different from his own. He also despaired at times about his ability to reconnect to his girlfriend, Nettie David, who had avoided arrest and deportation by going into hiding. "This morning I became conscious of why I'm writing my diary. A thought that I'm already quite unable to grasp but is irrefutably true: this diary reaches beyond the end of the war!" he wrote on March 6. "I could be reading from it to Nettie, with an image available to me, an image full of remarkable things, full of the most as- tonishing as well as incomprehensible facts. Reading from it to Nettie is a big, heavy thought, charged with tenderness."[30] In keeping his diary, David made an incredible leap of faith: despite all the evidence that the Germans would realize their project to make a Jew-free Europe, David followed the example of Abraham who, in the words of Saint Paul, "against hope, believed in hope."[31]

The question, of course, is whether David Koker's act of keeping a diary be- longs to our story or not. The noun "resistance" has a couple of meanings. The first one provided by the *Oxford English Dictionary* is as follows: "The action of resisting, opposing, or withstanding someone or something." David's devotion to preserve his mind and his hope by recording his experiences certainly fits this wide definition. But what about the second entry found in the *OED*: "Orga- nized (in later use usually covert) opposition to an invading, occupying, or rul- ing power; (an organized body of) individuals engaged in such opposition"?[32] In his study on resistance in the Nazi concentration camps, Hermann Langbein clearly excluded from resistance actions aimed to maintain the morale, health, or life of oneself, or perhaps a few chosen comrades. The non-Jewish Auschwitz survivor Langbein had been a member of the International Brigade in Spain; he had been incarcerated in Auschwitz as a political prisoner, and he under-

---

30. Ibid., 207, 132.

31. Epistle to the Romans, 4:18; see also Avishai Margalit, *The Ethics of Memory* (Cambridge, Mass.: Harvard University Press, 2002), 154ff.

32. "Resistance," in *The Oxford English Dictionary*, 2nd ed., 20 vols., ed. John A. Simpson and Edward S. C. Weiner (Oxford: Clarendon Press, 1989), 13:717.

stood resistance politically, that is in terms of the second definition given in the *OED*. While he admitted that within the camps private actions such as sharing bread with a comrade or an escape to seek liberty represented enormous feats and often tokens of enormous strength and heroism, they did not fit his definition of resistance. When David wrote his diary, he did not seek to create a protective wall around the consciousness of all inmates, or even a group of them, but only around his own. To Langbein, diary writing would therefore not have counted as an act of resistance unless, as with the example of the organized effort of Emanuel Ringelblum and his *Oyneg Shabes* group in the Warsaw ghetto, it aimed at a general political goal.

I am sympathetic to Langbein's limitation because it fits the classic understanding of human existence as a *shared* reality. I touched on this issue in my discussion on Paradise, but would like to expand on it. In *The Human Condition*, written in response to the Holocaust, Hannah Arendt observed that "appearance—something that is being seen by others as well as by ourselves—constitutes reality.... The presence of others who see what we see, hear what we hear assures us of the reality of the world and ourselves."[33] As we have seen in the discussion on Paradise, Arendt postulated that Nazism denied that the human world is a shared world. It sought to reduce human beings to isolated monads who could then be assembled into a mass. Camps were a tool to create such conditions of isolation, loneliness, and massification—that is, a forced gathering that did not allow for any separation between one person and the other. In this, Nazism went beyond traditional tyrannies that sought to destroy the public realm and thus isolate human beings. Traditional tyrannies, Arendt argued, did not touch the private realm. "Political contacts between men are severed in tyrannical government and the human capacities for action and power are frustrated. But not all actions between men are broken and not all human capacities are destroyed. The whole sphere of private life with the capacities for experience, fabrication, and thought are left intact." Yet under Nazism the private domain was also destroyed. "Total terror leaves no space for such private life and the self-coercion of totalitarian logic destroys man's capacity for experience and thought just as certainly as his capacity for action.... Totalitarian domination as a form of government ... bases itself on loneliness, on the experience of not belonging to the world at all, which is among the most radical and desperate experiences of man."[34] If we take Arendt as our guide, it

33. Hannah Arendt, *The Human Condition* (Chicago: University of Chicago Press, 1958), 50.
34. Arendt, *The Origins of Totalitarianism*, new edition, 474f.

appears that Langbein's definition of resistance as one of common action aiming at a common goal would make sense if the camps had been instruments of traditional tyrannical government. In that case, resistance would be a tool to reestablish within conditions of oppression a public domain, and hence the possibility of action. Yet because the camp regime was the ultimate embodiment of a totalitarian continuum that also sought to destroy the private realm, any action that defends even the most intimate sphere must be considered as resistance. In preserving his mind and the reality of his experience, David resisted the aims of the SS—and so did anyone else who attempted to preserve their inner core against the assault of camp life by means of some disciplined activity like, for example, regular religious observations.

When Arendt introduced the typology of the camps as Hades, Purgatory, and Hell, she noted that in each of these types "the human masses sealed off in them are treated as if they no longer existed, as if what happened to them were no longer of any interest to anybody, as if they were already dead and some evil spirit gone mad were amusing himself by stopping them for a while between life and death before admitting them to eternal peace."[35] This certainly applied to all those people considered superfluous and candidates to be interned in Hades: refugees, stateless people, and so on. But in the case of Jews, the situation was worse. Nazi antisemitism, formally embodied in the Nuremberg Laws, denied Jews the basic dignity of being human. Stateless persons might obtain citizenship, refugees might obtain asylum, but Jews were not really human. "Daily, for years on end, we could read and hear that we were lazy, evil, ugly, capable only of misdeed, clever only to the extent that we pulled one over on others," Auschwitz survivor Jean Améry observed after the war. "By their very presence, our bodies—hairy, fat, and bow-legged—befouled public swimming pools, yes, even park benches. Our hideous faces, depraved and spoilt by protruding ears and hanging noses, were disgusting to our fellow men, fellow citizens of yesterday. We were not worthy of love and thus also not of life. Our sole right, our sole duty was to disappear from the face of the earth."[36] Jews were depicted as belonging to a different species. They were defined as subhumans and made to feel like subhumans. For that reason the separation from the rest of society that came with the internment in Hades was for a Jew different than for a non-Jew. To the latter, it meant a separation from other human

35. Arendt, "The Concentration Camps," 750.
36. Jean Améry, *At the Mind's Limits: Contemplations by a Survivor on Auschwitz and its Realities*, trans. Sidney Rosenfeld and Stella P. Rosenfeld (Bloomington: Indiana University Press, 1980), 86

beings; for the former it meant confirmation of one's status as a subhuman, a confirmation, in the words of the French-Jewish philosopher Emmanuel Levinas, of living a life that was irrelevant to the rest of the world. When in a German prisoner-of-war camp Levinas and other Jewish soldiers were separated from the non-Jewish soldiers, he experienced this separation as an absolute rupture. "We were no longer part of the world," he noted afterwards. "Our comings and goings, our sorrow and laughter, illnesses and distractions, the work of our hands and the anguish of our eyes, the letters we received from France and those accepted for our families—all that passed in parentheses." Having been defined as "Jews," Levinas and the other Jewish prisoners-of-war had become "beings without language…. How can we deliver a message about our humanity which, from behind the bars of quotation marks, will come across as anything other than monkey talk?" Significantly, the only being that refused to accept the division thus created within the human species was a member of another species: a wandering dog that the Jewish prisoners-of-war named Bobby. "He would appear at morning assembly and was waiting for us as we returned, jumping up and down and barking in delight. For him, there was no doubt that we were men." Levinas concluded: "This dog was the last Kantian in Nazi Germany."[37]

When she conceptualized the internment camps as Hades, Arendt stressed that key to the understanding of Hades was that the great majority of the inmates of the camp "had done nothing whatsoever that, either in their own consciousness or the consciousness of their tormentors, had any rational connection to their arrest." Political prisoners or criminals locked up in the camps knew that there was a relationship between their beliefs or actions, and their imprisonment. Jews did not have that privilege. They could not but experience their fate as haphazard. Yet, as Arendt observed, because they were innocent in every sense, they proved "the most suitable for thorough experimentation in disenfranchisement and destruction of the juridical person."[38]

If in the internment camps grouped under the label of Hades the arbitrariness applied to the reasons for incarceration, there existed most often still some vestige of an intelligible social order within the camp itself. In Vught, the inmates had some possibility to organize their own lives, and it provided space for mutual solidarity of the prisoners against their jailers. The very small mea-

---

37. Emmanuel Levinas, "The Name of a Dog, or Natural Rights," in *Difficult Freedom: Essays on Judaism*, trans. Seán Hand (Baltimore: Johns Hopkins University Press, 1990), 153.

38. Arendt, "The Concentration Camps," 753f.

sure of autonomy given to the inmates also allowed those who wished to do so to define their own position in the camp. On March 15, Koker wrote in his diary that he wanted to assert himself and "associate with anyone who's highly placed, regardless of his quality. An ambition of the lowest kind."[39] He did not like the "crude pushiness" he had discovered in himself, but in Vught old-time manners were of little value, and so he made a concerted effort to be on friendly terms with the chief camp clerk, the German-Jewish inmate Arthur R. Lehmann. It paid off: when in July 1943 David discovered that his younger brother Max was on a list of people to be deported to Poland—which in this case meant the Sobibor death camp—he approached Lehmann and Max's name was taken off the list.[40]

Purgatory

At least for Jews, the possibility of agency exercised by David Koker on behalf of his brother was lost in the group of camps understood as "Purgatory." When she coined Purgatory as a class of camps, Arendt referred to the classical concentration camps as places where, in addition to a destruction of the juridical person, inmates also faced a sustained assault on their moral person. The concentration camp did not offer space for solidarity between the prisoners because of the manner in which the SS had organized and divided the inmates in arbitrary hierarchies. These hierarchies included many inmate functionaries, but also equally arbitrary categories that were supposed to divide "criminals" from "politicals," "homosexuals" from "asocials," "gypsies" from "Jehovah Witnesses," and so on. Arendt observed that in the concentration camps, "the gruesome and grotesque part of it was that the inmates identified themselves with these categories, as though they represented a last authentic remnant of their juridical person." The divisions were actually quite arbitrary, producing an "eternally shifting though pedantically organized edifice." Arendt noted that the only reason that it had any appearance of solidity was the fact "that under any and all circumstances the Jews were the lowest category."[41] The system was designed to pit every person against the other, and all against the Jews.

Primo Levi recounted that he had entered the Auschwitz concentration camp with the expectation of finding solidarity, and was shocked when he discovered it did not exist within the camp. He began with a short philosophical

---

39. Koker, *At the Edge of the Abyss*, 143.   40. Ibid., 219.
41. Arendt, "The Concentration Camps," 754.

reflection. "Perhaps for reasons that go back to our origins as social animals, the need to divide the field into 'we' and 'they' is so strong that this pattern, this bipartition—friend/enemy—prevails over all others." He expected to find "a terrible but decipherable world, in conformity with that simple model which we atavistically carry within us—'we' inside and the enemy outside, separated by a sharply defined geographic frontier." Yet this did not happen. "The world into which one was precipitated was terrible, yes, but also indecipherable: it did not conform to any model; the enemy was all around but also inside, the 'we' lost its limits, the contenders were not two, one could not discern a single frontier but rather many confused, perhaps innumerable frontiers, which stretched between each of us." In Auschwitz he did not encounter solidarity among inmates. There was no sense that they were bound to each other as "companions in misfortune." Instead, the prisoners had to struggle against each other. "This brusque revelation, which became manifest from the very first hours of imprisonment, often in the instant form of a concentric aggression on the part of those in whom one hoped to find future allies, was so harsh as to cause the immediate collapse of one's capacity to resist."[42] Levi noted that, as a result of the terrible conditions within the camp, every inmate who had not (yet) fallen to the bottom faced every day calls for solidarity. "The presence at your side of a weaker—or less cunning, or older, or too young—companion, hounding you with his demands for help or with his simple presence, in itself an entreaty, is a constant in the life of the Lager. The demand for solidarity, for a human word, advice, even just a listening ear, was permanent and universal but rarely satisfied. There was no time, space, privacy, patience, strength."[43]

Time, space, and privacy: the camps provided none of those. The German sociologist Wolfgang Sofsky has described how in the concentration camps one could not plan anything. The inmates lived in "a universe of total uncertainty, one in which submissiveness is no shield against even worse outcomes. It forces its victims together into an aggregate, a mass; it stirs up differences and erects a social structure marked by extreme contrasts." The great likelihood of an immediate, radical change of one's circumstances—including the possibility of death—prevented the creation of community. "Terror reduces the field of human consciousness to the passing moment." Except for inmate functionaries—and in the concentration camps Jews were not admitted to those exalted ranks—prisoners did not have an opportunity to take their bearings, to plan

42. Levi, *The Drowned and the Saved,*, 36ff., 78.
43. Ibid., 78.

ahead, to have agency. This prevented any significant acts of solidarity. "Terror has an immediate dissociative impact," Sofsky observed. "Because it eradicates the ability of the person to act, it also eliminates social trust, cooperation, and mutual aid."[44] In addition, the camp did not provide the space and privacy to gather oneself. The inmates were jammed together in overcrowded barracks, sharing bunks with two or three others. This crowding resulted in a situation in which each inmate struggled with every other inmate, and in which all were totally isolated. "Each prisoner lay alone, for himself or herself, in the midst of the mass—powerless to protest, to pull back, to move.... Nowhere is the forlornness of the individual greater than in an atomized, densely packed mass, where each is eager to grab the place and space of the other." In such conditions, a prisoner did not mourn the death of his neighbor, but welcomed it, as it provided, if only for a moment, a bit of extra space, or a bit of extra bread. A prisoner could not mourn the death of his neighbor because the latter was anonymous to the former. "The other people were not individuals whose stories you knew," Sofsky noted. "The mass made the other person faceless; it robbed the individual of the possibility to relate to another person, and thus also to himself or herself." The result was a serially coerced mass, structured on mistrust and animosity, that lacked the fabric of reciprocity and all possibility of solidarity. "Where there is nothing to share, except at the cost of common destruction and doom, solidarity lacks a material basis. Hunger, deprivation, and the pressure of annihilation ravaged social relations, inciting individuals to ruthless self-interest, pitting them one against the other. In the coerced mass, the other person was not indifferent to you—he or she was a potential enemy who cheated you in a bartered exchange, betrayed you to superiors, or stole your last crust of bread."[45]

Resistance to the destruction of the moral person must, therefore, be found in attempts to show solidarity within conditions designed and operated to deny the very possibility of solidarity, understood as the quality of unity among different people who form a community.[46] In the situation that existed in the concentration camps, there was no room for any unity of the inmate community as a whole. Inmates looked on passively as others were killed. Polish Auschwitz survivor Tadeusz Borowski recorded that when trucks full of naked women on

44. Wolfgang Sofsky, *The Order of Terror: The Concentration Camp*, trans. William Templer (Princeton, N.J.: Princeton University Press, 1997), 17, 88.

45. Ibid., 70f., 155, 24f., 162f.

46. "Solidarity," in *The Oxford English Dictionary*, 15:972.

the way to the gas chambers passed by a formation of ten thousand prisoners that included himself, the women called out for help: "'Save us! We are going to the gas chambers! Save us!' And they rode slowly past us—the ten thousand silent men—and then disappeared from sight. Not one of us made a move, not one of us lifted a hand."[47] There was no room for solidarity between the two groups that had been separated by barbed-wire fences as if in separate universes. Neither was there room for the partial unity among all the inmates as far as the distribution of resources—both material as well as emotional and spiritual—was concerned. If there was some possibility of solidarity, it might exist at the level of subgroups, or subgroups of subgroups, or subgroups of subgroups of subgroups—that is, among inmates who lived in the same barracks, or who shared the same bunk. During the debate in the Yad Vashem Conference on Manifestations of Jewish Resistance held in Jerusalem in 1968, Meir Dworzecki recalled the way he had survived nine camps. "In the camps I lived a 'cooperative' life with one of my comrades—that is we shook hands on a pledge to help one another and to share all the 'good' and all the travail in the camps. I helped him and he helped me. He would steal a potato and I would steal a beet.... So we lived together and together we survived all the camps. His name is Lillienheim."[48] The pairing of two inmates was a normal occurrence in the camps. Primo Levi credited his survival to his partnership with Charles Conreau.[49] "Stable pairing was the most common type of interpersonal relationship pattern," the sociologist Elmer Luchterhand observed in his pathbreaking study on inmate behavior in the concentration camps. "With all of the raging conflict in the camps, it was in the pairs that the prisoners kept alive the semblance of humanity. The pairs gave relief from the shame of acts of acquiescence and surrender. The pairs provided expertise in the survival skills known as 'organizing.'"[50] Men found a comrade, and women adopted a "camp sister," or a surrogate "camp mother."

But does the solidarity shown within pairs constitute resistance? In my discussion of Hades, I cited Langbein's definition of resistance as an organized

47. [Tadeusz Borowski], "Auschwitz, Our Home, A Letter," in Janusz Nel Siedlecki, Krystyn Olszweski, and Tadeusz Borowski, *We Were in Auschwitz* (New York: Welcome Rain Publishers, 2000), 129.

48. Meir Dworzecki, "Debate," in *Jewish Resistance during the Holocaust*, ed. Meir Grubsztein, 190.

49. Myriam Anissimov, *Primo Levi: Tragedy of an Optimist*, trans. Steve Cox (Woodstock, N.Y.: The Overlook Press, 1999), 207.

50. Elmer Luchterhand, "Prisoner Behaviour and Social System in the Nazi Camp," *International Journal of Social Psychiatry* 13 (1967): 259f.

activity with far-reaching, essentially political goals: "In this context the aid given to a friend and spontaneous actions are not included in our definition of active resistance."[51] Yet in the same way that the key issue of loneliness under totalitarianism made a private act of keeping a diary in order to maintain one's grasp on reality an act of resistance, sharing one's life with another human being subverted the aim of the camp to reduce all inmates to monads. Such a communality may have been carefully considered and formalized in some kind of explicit agreement. It also may have depended on the very spontaneity that Langbein rejected as the opposite of the carefully considered and executed acts of resistance that were of interest to him. Arendt believed that spontaneity (from the Latin *sponte*, meaning "of your own will"), that is the possibility to act, to begin something new that is not determined by necessity or precedent, is one of the essential elements of the human condition. "The new always happens against the overwhelming odds of statistical laws and their probability, which for all practical purposes amounts to certainty; the new therefore always appears in the guise of a miracle. The fact that man is capable of action means that the unexpected can be expected of him, that he is able to perform what is infinitely improbable. And this again is possible only because each man is unique."[52] Totalitarian government sought to destroy the possibility of spontaneity, and the camps it established were designed to make spontaneity impossible.[53] They were designed to make generosity absurd. In *If This Is a Man,* Levi described four inmates who had extremely egoistic personalities and, in the case of three of them, had also developed survival strategies that allowed them to prosper in the camp—as the perfect slaves. All four of them lived without a trace of generosity towards others.[54] Albert Camus postulated that a spirit of generosity is, at its core, spontaneous and, as such, an act of revolt that "unhesitatingly gives the strength of its love and refuses injustice without a moment's delay. Its merit lies in making no calculations, distributing everything that it possesses to life and living men.... Its purest outburst, on each occasion, gives birth to existence. Thus it is love and fecundity or it is nothing at all."[55] Hence the very spontaneity and generosity of the small acts of solidarity and support between friends and comrades must be defined as acts

51. Langbein, *Against All Hope*, 51f.   52. Arendt, *The Human Condition*, 178.
53. Arendt, *The Origins of Totalitarianism*, 455.
54. Primo Levi, *If This Is a Man*, trans. Stuart Woolf (New York: The Orion Press, 1959), 106–16.
55. Albert Camus, *The Rebel: An Essay on Man in Revolt*, trans. Anthony Bower (New York: Knopf, 1954), 271.

of revolt and resistance. As Luchterhand noted, those pairs were also the nuclei of organized resistance—if and when it occurred. "For the minority that had some contact with an underground, it was in the pair that man and organization usually met. In the pair, the politics of resistance survived, found form and technique, and in some places began to grow."[56]

When Arendt formulated the way Purgatory murdered the moral person, she focused on what is, in the final analysis, the key issue of human solidarity—one that transcends the solidarity of inmate to inmate, and also embraces bystanders and perpetrators: it is the common solidarity of all human beings as mortals. "The Western world has hitherto, even in its darkest periods, granted the slain enemy the right to be remembered as a self-evident acknowledgment of the fact that we are all men (and *only* men).... The concentration camps, by making death itself anonymous ... robbed death of the meaning which it had always been possible for it to have. In a sense they took away the individual's own death, proving that henceforth nothing belonged to him and he belonged to no one. His death merely set a seal on the fact that he had never really existed."[57] On very rare occasions the SS allowed an inmate to die a martyr's death—perhaps not so much out of respect for the man who died, but as a means to terrorize those who had to continue living. Primo Levi told how he and the other inmates were forced to attend the execution of a prisoner who had helped to prepare the *Sonderkommando* uprising in Auschwitz-Birkenau. The fact that a few hundred prisoners, "helpless and exhausted slaves like ourselves, had found in themselves the strength to act," puzzled Levi. The inmate who was to be hanged had not only been in contact with the rebels in Birkenau, but he was credited with having carried arms into Monowitz, "plotting a simultaneous mutiny among us." Levi knew that no one would have dared to join. "But everybody heard the cry of the doomed man, it pierced through the old thick barriers of inertia and submissiveness, it struck the living core of man in each of us: '*Kamaraden, ich bin der Letzt!*' (Comrades, I am the last one!). I wish I could say that from the midst of us, an abject flock, a voice rose, a murmur, a sign of assent. But nothing happened. We remained standing, bent and grey, our heads dropped, and we did not uncover our heads until the German ordered us to do so."[58]

But yet. If Levi and the other prisoners had been unable to muster the most

56. Luchterhand, "Prisoner Behaviour and Social System in the Nazi Camp," 260.
57. Arendt, "The Concentration Camps," 756.
58. Levi, *If This Is a Man*, 176f.

elemental moral fiber and show "the last one" a sign of solidarity in the hour of his death, Levi did know that this was not to be the end. One could try to survive, and begin to regain one's moral person by bearing witness. In keeping his eyes and ears opened while he attended the execution, Levi did in fact resist the destruction of the moral person in himself. "For many of us the hope of survival was identified with another, more precise hope: we hoped not to live *and* tell our story, but to live *in order* to tell our story," he wrote twenty years after his return from Auschwitz. "Each of us survivors, as soon as we returned home, transformed himself into a tireless narrator, imperious and maniacal."[59] Thus, when he returned home, he immortalized the "last one."

Hell

Levi's memoir allows the reader to follow his journey through Purgatory, but it only offers occasional glimpses into the aspect of the camp that Arendt identified as "Hell"—that is those concentration camps normally referred to as death camps. "Once the moral person has been killed, the one thing that still prevents men from being made into living corpses is the differentiation of the individual, his unique identity." In the death camps, people were transformed "into specimens of the human beast" through the destruction of each person's unique identity. Arendt found it difficult to write about it. "The killing of man's individuality, of the uniqueness shaped in equal parts by nature, will, and destiny, which has become so self-evident a premise for all human relations that even identical twins inspire a certain uneasiness, creates a horror that vastly overshadows the outrage of the juridical-political person and the despair of the oral person."[60]

When he was admitted to Auschwitz, Levi got an inkling of what this meant. After being stripped, shaved, and tattooed, he realized he and the other deportees "had reached the bottom. It is not possible to sink lower than this; no human condition is more miserable than this, nor could it conceivably be so. Nothing belongs to us anymore; they have taken away our clothes, our shoes, even our hair; if we speak, they will not listen to us, and if they listen, they will not understand. They will even take away our name." Without anything to link him to his former life, the prisoner had become "a man whose life or death

59. Primo Levi, "Note to the Theatre Version of *If This Is a Man*," in *The Black Hole of Auschwitz*, trans. Sharn Wood (Cambridge: Polity Press, 2005), 24.
60. Arendt, "The Concentration Camps," 757ff.

can be lightly decided with no sense of human affinity, in the most fortunate of cases, on the basis of pure judgment of utility. It is in this way that one can understand the double sense of the term 'extermination camp,' and it is now clear what we seek to express with the phrase: 'to lie on the bottom.'"[61] Yet, as the rest of his memoir reveals, Levi did not remain on the bottom. As a chemist he was useful, and his living and working conditions were so much better than the ordinary inmate's that he could preserve a minimal sense of identity, individuality, and spontaneity. He never became one of the so-called *Muselmänner*—the almost nonmen whom Arendt described as "ghastly marionettes with human faces, which all behave like the dog in Pavlov's experiments, which all react with perfect reliability even when going to their own deaths, and which do nothing but react."[62] Arendt never witnessed the *Muselmänner*. She learned about their existence from descriptions by camp survivors. Levi did witness firsthand the fate of those who had lost all signs of individuality and, as a result, all ability to act spontaneously. "Their life is short, but their number is endless; they, the *Muselmänner*, the drowned, form the backbone of the camp, an anonymous mass, continually renewed and always identical, of non-men who march and labour in silence, the divine spark dead within them, already too empty to really suffer. One hesitates to call them living: one hesitates to call their death death, in the face of which they have no fear, as they are too tired to understand."[63]

Could one prevent becoming oneself from becoming a *Muselmann*? Levi described a certain Steinlauf who, twenty years earlier, had been a sergeant in the Austro-Hungarian army. Steinlauf told Primo that, "precisely because the Lager was a great machine to reduce us to beasts, we must not become like beasts." The only way to do so was to continue to act in a civilized manner. "So we must certainly wash our faces without soap in dirty water and dry ourselves on our jackets. We must polish our shoes, not because the regulation states it, but for dignity and propriety. We must walk erect, without dragging our feet, not in homage to Prussian discipline but to remain alive, not to begin to die." Yet, Levi couldn't accept it. "The wisdom and virtue of Steinlauf, certainly good for him, is not enough for me."[64] To Levi, no strategy proposed could prevent the descent toward the bottom, the transformation of Man into *Musel-*

---

61. Levi, *If This Is a Man*, 21f.
62. Arendt, *The Origins of Totalitarianism*, new edition, 455.
63. Levi, *If This Is a Man*, 103.
64. Ibid., 39f.

mann. He was convinced that all those who had become *Muselmänner* had the same story: they didn't have the disposition to adapt, or, if they did, they had bad luck when they became inmates. "On their entry into the camp, through basic incapacity, or by misfortune, or through some banal incident, they are overcome before they can adapt themselves; they are beaten by time, they do not begin to learn German, to disentangle the infernal knot of laws and prohibitions until their body is already in decay, and nothing can save them from selections or from death by exhaustion."[65] If this is true, then we are entering here a realm in which resistance to the destruction of individuality was only an option to the few fortunate ones who arrived in the camp with the training and the inner disposition that allowed them not to be fully crushed by the initiation and the violence that characterized the subsequent period of quarantine, and who had the luck not to be at the wrong place at the wrong time. Is resistance still resistance when it has become, essentially, an aspect of luck?

On the Threshold of Gehenna

If there were some options of resistance in Hades, and very few in Purgatory, the situation in Hell was dire. This applied to both Jewish and non-Jewish inmates of the camps—with the situation for the former always worse, and the options for any form of resistance more limited. What were the options in Gehenna—the Chelmno killing installations, the Operation Reinhard death camps (Belzec, Sobibor, and Treblinka) and the bunkers and crematoria in Auschwitz that were solely dedicated to the destruction of human life—or to be more specific, *Jewish* life—itself? This question has three aspects: first of all, there is the passivity of the Jewish deportees, who arrived in those places and chose not to resist. Second, there are the choices for the members of the *Sonderkommandos*, the Jewish slave workers forced to participate in the operation of those killing machines. Finally, in the case of Auschwitz, there are the choices of those inmates who were not members of the *Sonderkommandos*, but who might have chosen to make an effort to intervene.

Before we begin, it is good to recall that Arendt did not define the type Gehenna. In her typology, the sequence of Hades, Purgatory, and Hell represented intensification of totalitarian domination, the destruction of the juridical person, the moral person, and individuality. The final destruction of the body

65. Ibid., 103.

was, in a sense, implied in all three types because in each of these categories of camps the inmates were treated "as if they were already dead."[66] Kotek and Rigoulot added Gehenna as a fourth type, and I endorse it with the provision that Gehenna is not a simple continuation of the triad Hades-Purgatory-Hell. It occupies a separate category: both historically and typologically there is a discontinuity between the internment, concentration, and death camps on the one hand, and the annihilation installations on the other. In the case of Gehenna, those murdered were generally not inmates, but people who had lived, until the moment they were locked in the deportation trains, a life that had something of the semblance of being normal. Most of them had experienced the destruction of their rights, but in the ghettos or transit camps they still had preserved their moral person, their individuality, and with that their ability to act spontaneously. But, as we know, only very few of them chose to do so upon their arrival in Gehenna. Perhaps the most famous example is the one-woman revolt of Franceska Mann (or it might have been Lola Horowitz), a dancer who had been a performer at the Melody Palace nightclub in Warsaw. When Ms. Mann (or Ms. Horowitz) entered the undressing room of crematorium 2 on October 23, 1943, she found the resolve and the strength to grab the gun of an SS man, and kill him. Yet most did not revolt, did not protest. In the case of Auschwitz, there is evidence of only four other cases where one or a few Jews openly resisted the SS near or in the gas chambers. This brings us to the other reason that there exists a gap between our discussions of the forms of resistance that emerged from Paradise and occurred in Hades, Purgatory, and Hell, and the resistance in Gehenna. It concerns the heavy metaphysical and emotional load this topic carries—a burden circumscribed by the allegation that Jews collaborated with the Germans in their own destruction.

"On the day when crime puts on the apparel of innocence, through a curious reversal peculiar to our age, it is innocence that is called on to justify itself," wrote Camus. Both Nazism and Communism had initiated a new epoch in history by justifying murder through ideology. "Yesterday, it was put on trial; today it is the law." In the face of such nihilism there was only one moral response: rebellion. Camus understood revolt as a double act: the rebel says "no" to the unacceptable condition of one's life and "yes" to some value that one is not willing to surrender because it is the core of one's identity. Therefore, "what was, originally, an obstinate resistance on the part of the rebel, becomes the

66. Arendt, "The Concentration Camps," 750.

rebel personified." Camus proposed that revolt was the key to a communal solidarity that transcended the loneliness brought about by totalitarianism. "Suffering is individual," Camus observed. "But from the moment that a movement of rebellion begins, suffering is seen as a collective experience—as the experience of everyone.... Rebellion is the common ground on which every man bases his first values. I *rebel*—therefore we *exist*."[67]

Camus's proposition that rebellion is the origin and essence of human existence provides the background for the bitter allegation that has shaped all discussions of Jewish resistance since the 1960s: did Jews collaborate in their own destruction? Did they go as sheep to the slaughter? When I discussed Paradise, Hades, Purgatory, and Hell, the question of a specific Jewish passivity was not relevant, because non-Jews experienced in those camps the assaults on their juridical and moral persons, and on their individuality. They were, in most cases, in a better situation to resist those assaults, as they were, unlike Jewish inmates, in most cases not at the bottom of the camp hierarchy. It is critically important to note therefore that most non-Jewish inmates did *not* resist. But when we consider Gehenna, we must acknowledge the fact that, apart from a few exceptions, this was a world designed and made exclusively for the destruction of Jews. Thus it is proper to pause here, and consider the allegation that in Gehenna Jews went as sheep to the slaughter and, in doing so, proved themselves unworthy of physical or even spiritual solidarity.

The opening shot occurred in a short editorial that introduced Bruno Bettelheim's "The Ignored Lesson of Anne Frank" published in the November 1960 issue of *Harper's Magazine*. "The remarkable essay which follows poses a question which has received little public discussion since World War II: Why and how did millions of people quite passively go to their death in Nazi concentration camps, putting up scarcely more than token resistance? Dr. Bruno Bettelheim's controversial answer to this question may disturb some readers but we believe it has acute significance for contemporary society and therefore deserves a wide hearing."[68] With this note to the reader, the question that has either explicitly or implicitly framed most discussions of Jewish resistance in the Nazi camps acquired a place in the public realm. Bettelheim was a German-born psychoanalyst who had been interned for eleven months in the Dachau and Buchenwald concentration camps before his emigration to the United States in 1939. In *Harper's*, Bettelheim postulated that the key reason for the

---

67. Camus, *The Rebel*, 11f., 20, 28.
68. Editorial, *Harper's Magazine* 221, no. 1326 (November 1960): 45.

vast scale of the Holocaust was that, in the face of increasing danger, Jews had attempted "to go on with life as nearly as possible in the usual fashion." Wishful thinking and disregarding the possibility of one's own death shaped the attitude of the victims. Clinging as much as possible to their routines, they tried to roll with the punches they received. Bettelheim suggested that the SS began to consider the possibility of annihilation when they saw how the Jews accepted ever greater degrees of degradation without resistance. "Thus in the deepest sense the walk to the gas chamber was only the last consequence of a philosophy of life-as-usual." The Jews, he argued, should have taken stock of the situation, reevaluating all of what they had done, believed in, and stood for. Invoking the example of the Blacks in South Africa who were willing to march against the forces of *Apartheid*—an admittedly not too felicitous comparison for which he was to receive much criticism—Bettelheim suggested that the Jews of Europe "could at least have marched as free men against the SS, instead of groveling, at first; then waiting to be rounded up for their own extermination, and finally walking to the gas chambers."[69]

Bettelheim had raised a question that proved timely. The Eichmann Trial, which began on April 11, 1961, confronted the world not only with a full picture of the German war against the Jews, but also with few testimonies that spoke of Jewish revolts, and many testimonies that suggested Jewish passivity in the face of death. One of the few witnesses who fitted the conventional idea of a hero, JFO deputy commander Izhak Zuckerman, was asked why only the Warsaw ghetto had revolted, and he had no answer. The Israeli writer Keshev Shabbetai attended the trial that day, and when the proceedings were over, he overheard two young native-born Israelis or *Sabras* comment on Zuckerman's testimony. "Why did they let themselves be slaughtered?" one asked. The other responded: "I should think that it was the Jewish exile cowardice at work.... I can't see any other explanation." Shabbetai decided to take action and so wrote the book *As Sheep to the Slaughter?* in which he described the desperate situation of the Jews who did revolt and the resources of other Europeans under German rule who did not revolt. Shabbetai's book was adopted by the Israeli Ministry of Education, and by 1962 the issue of Jewish compliance and resistance had become an obligatory two-hour session in all high schools in Israel. Israeli youth could read how, for example, millions of Soviet prisoners of war had not resisted their annihilation, and they were taught to ask not "Why

69. Bruno Bettelheim, "The Ignored Lesson of Anne Frank," *Harper's Magazine* 221, no. 1326 (November 1960): 46ff.

did [the Jews] not revolt?" but "How did it happen that they nevertheless and in spite of everything were left with enough strength, enough faith, enough free will to stand against the enemy in the way they did stand? Out of what rock was this nation hewn?"[70]

The public debate on this question acquired an academic dimension as the result of the publication of Raul Hilberg's massive *The Destruction of the European Jews* which, from its appearance in 1961, was to create a standard of Holocaust scholarship. Hilberg had given little attention to Jewish resistance. During the Holocaust, "Jews were not oriented toward resistance," he wrote in his conclusion. "They took up resistance only in a few cases and at the last moment."[71] While prominent non-Jewish historians welcomed Hilberg's book as a major achievement, Jewish historians were accusing Hilberg of defamation of the dead and falsification of history.[72] Just at the time that the Jewish rage about Hilberg's book had subsided, Hannah Arendt's *Eichmann in Jerusalem* (1963) appeared, which put some of the blame for the enormous mortality of Jews at the feet of the Jewish leadership.[73] The result was a new controversy that convulsed the American Jewish intellectual community.

The members of the generation that had experienced the Holocaust first hand had raised the question of resistance. But the next generation, that of young people who had not experienced the Holocaust, addressed the question head-on, and without nuance or mercy. During the Eichmann trial the young *Sabras* of Israel listened with astonishment to the testimonies of the witnesses broadcast on national radio. And they expressed puzzlement at the lack of agency of their parents and teachers. In March 1966 a twenty-five-year old French Jew took ownership of the question in an interview published in *Le Nouveau Candide* entitled "Les Juifs: ce qu'on n'a jamais osé dire" ("The Jews: what no one ever dared to say"). The occasion of the interview was the forthcoming publication of the historical novel *Treblinka*. Its author, Jean-François Steiner, was the son of a man who had been murdered in a satellite camp of Auschwitz. In the interview he admitted that he had decided to write *Treblinka* "because I felt, not the indignation I had been taught, but the embarrassment of being a child of this people of whom six million allowed themselves to be led

70. Keshev Shabtai, *As Sheep to the Slaughter?* (Bet Dagan: Keshev Press, 1962), 8, 60.

71. Raul Hilberg, *The Destruction of the European Jews* (Chicago: Quadrangle Books, 1961), 663

72. Oscar Handlin, "Jewish Resistance to the Nazis," *Commentary* 34, no. 5 (November 1962): 399; Ber Mark, "Falsifying the Jewish Resistance," *Jewish Currents* 17, no. 4 (April 1963), 17.

73. Hannah Arendt, *Eichmann in Jerusalem: A Report on the Banality of Evil* (New York: Viking, 1963), 111.

to the slaughter like lambs." Worse: in Treblinka, as in Belzec and Sobibor, "the victims themselves, the Jews, made themselves into the accomplices of their own extermination. In Treblinka, as in all the other extermination camps, the Germans had designed 'the machine,' as they referred to the methods of extermination, in such a way that it would almost run itself. It is the Jews who did everything."[74] Steiner believed that in Treblinka the compliance, collusion, and complicity of Jews in the killing process had been greatest, but also the ultimate heroic response of those Jews, the revolt of August 2, 1943, had been most notable. When, a few weeks after the interview, Steiner's novel appeared, it carried as an epigraph a Hasidic saying: "A man must descend very low to find the force to rise again." This crude dialectic between the deepest abyss and the highest pinnacle structured the book. "Physically weakened and morally broken, the Jews had let themselves be led to death like a flock of animals to the slaughterhouse, had let themselves be transformed into accomplices in the extermination of their people.... Just when the abdication was total, when all values had ceased to exist, when their humanity had almost left them, the Jews, rousing themselves at the bottom of the abyss, began a slow ascent which death alone would stop."[75]

Treblinka became a best-seller in Europe and North America. It found praise amongst critics. One of France's most influential thinkers, Simone de Beauvoir, unequivocally endorsed the book. In an essay that was appended to *Treblinka* as a preface, she recalled the reproach with which the Israeli *Sabras* had confronted the survivors during the Eichmann trial. Steiner's book was their answer. "That [the Jews] were capable of such an uprising shows that their helplessness in the face of their executioners was not the expression of some secret blemish, some mysterious malediction. This book demonstrates brilliantly that it was due to the circumstances. It is not their initial helplessness that must astonish us, but the way they finally overcame it." According to de Beauvoir, the publication of *Treblinka* marked a breakthrough in the world's understanding of what had occurred in the camps. "Steiner has tried to understand and to make us understand. He has fully achieved this purpose."[76]

The few surviving witnesses disagreed. In an open letter published in the

74. Pierre Démeron and Jean François Steiner, "Les Juifs: Ce qu'on n'a jamais osé dire," *Le Nouveau Candide* (14–20 March 1966); as quoted in Samuel Moyn, *A Holocaust Controversy: The Treblinka Affair in Postwar France* (Waltham, Mass.: Brandeis University Press, 2005), 4, 6.

75. Jean François Steiner, *Treblinka*, trans. Helen Weaver (New York: New American Library, 1979), xxvi, 138f.

76. Simone de Beauvoir, "Preface," in Steiner, *Treblinka*, xxiif.

daily *Ma'ariv*, Israeli Treblinka survivors denounced the book. The Czech-Jewish engineer Richard Glazar wrote an open letter to Steiner. He credited him for having drawn attention to Treblinka, a place that had been almost forgotten. Yet, beyond that, *Treblinka* was a catastrophe. Glazar accused Steiner of having understood nothing, nothing at all of the place. The whole book was a "literary concoction," and his thesis in which a descent to the "lowest depths of cowardice" had allowed for the ascent towards the heights of the revolt was absurd. "Cowardice, shame, bravery? These concepts had different content in Treblinka.... Yes, I also sometimes have the unpleasant feeling that I let those dear to me go to the slaughter 'just like that.' But that is how I feel today, when I can choose coffee or tea for breakfast, jam or marmalade, rolls or bread.... As for you, today, Jean, I know of another type of terrible human cowardice and weakness, namely when a person is unable to admit that his ideas fail to stand up to reality."[77] Thus a member of the survivor generation poured contempt on the reconstruction undertaken by someone of the second generation, implying that no one who had not been in Treblinka would be able to understand and represent it.

It appears that those who had some judgment on the issue agreed with Glazar's premise. When in 1968 scholars met in a conference organized by Yad Vashem to discuss Jewish resistance in the Holocaust, not a single one of thirty papers was devoted to resistance in the camps.[78] This, of course, could be the luck (or in this case lack of luck) of the draw. More significant is the way resistance is almost totally absent in the most profound meditation ever made on the world of the death camps: Claude Lanzmann's nine-hour movie *Shoah* (1985). *Shoah* focusses on the process of annihilation. Commenting on the depiction of the camps in Lanzmann's masterpiece, Auschwitz survivor Elie Wiesel observed in a review published in the *New York Times* that "in this death industry, all the wheels seemed well oiled, all the participants were in their places. The killers killed, the spectators observed, the victims fell, the children were hurled into flaming pits. It was as if, since the beginning of Creation, things had to happen this way."[79] Wiesel's language reflects the great epic *and* mythic force of the movie as it depicts the Holocaust as a historical catastrophe

77. Richard Glazar, "Treblinka as Seen and Described in Writing," Yad Vashem Archive, 0.33/1152, as quoted in Moyn, *A Holocaust Controversy*, 138.

78. Discussed in Grubsztein, *Jewish Resistance during the Holocaust*.

79. Elie Wiesel, "A Survivor Remembers Other Survivors of *Shoah*," in *Claude Lanzmann's Shoah*, ed. Stuart Liebman (Oxford: Oxford University Press, 2007), 69.

not safely buried in the past, but one that in the lives of the witnesses continues to exist as a contemporaneous event in the present, throwing, through the presence of the absence of the six million victims and their offspring that were never born, long shadows into the future. It is a *Mythos* in which resistance has no place.

The question Bettelheim posed in 1960 has remained, in various incarnations, with us. Even when we do not seek to answer it, we do not seem able to escape it, and with it the need to come to a judgment. But, as we enter the last circle, we had better suspend judgment. Even Bettelheim, who had harshly censored and almost mocked deportees' behavior in his article in *Harper's Magazine*, came to realize this. In 1977, during the first San Jose Conference on the Holocaust, Bettelheim called on students of that epoch to give the deportees who had entered the gas chambers without protest "the last recognition that could be theirs and grant them the last dignity we can accord them: to face and accept what their death was all about." If Bettelheim had focused in 1960 on the few who had chosen to resist, seventeen years later he had come to the realization that those who did not also deserved their place in our histories. "Certainly those few who finally fought for their survival and their convictions, risking and losing their lives in doing so, deserve our admiration; their deeds give us a moral lift. But the more we dwell on these few, the more unfair we are to the memory of the millions who were slaughtered—who gave in, did not fight back—because we deny them the only thing which up to the very end remained uniquely their own: their fate."[80] It is not clear what brought about Bettelheim's change of heart. But I think that he might have understood that in asking innocence to justify itself, he had adopted the perspective of the murderers. Nevertheless, even if the question is obscene, we want to know the answer. Can innocence justify itself? I think it can, and would like to turn for such a justification to the reflections of someone who was sent to Auschwitz, who did submit, who did not protest, who was lucky not to be sent to the gas chambers, and who not only survived, but struggled for a decade to find a way to represent to those who were not there the conditions that made the deportees accept their fate: the Hungarian-Jewish Auschwitz survivor and author Imre Kertész.

In the spring of 1944, the fourteen-year-old Kertész was arrested, deported to Auschwitz, and after passing the selection, taken to Buchenwald to end up in *Arbeitskommando* Troeglitz, a satellite camp near the town of Zeitz in which

---

80. Bruno Bettelheim, "The Holocaust—One Generation Later," in *Surviving and Other Essays* (New York: Knopf, 1979), 93f.

over 4,000 inmates slaved to build a plant that was to use locally mined lignite coal for the production of synthetic gasoline. He survived this ordeal, returned to Budapest, and became a translator. In 1960 he began work on a novel that he conceived as a *Bildungsroman* in which the adolescent György comes of age in concentration camps. Kertész's aim was to represent life within a totalitarian society: for him, there were essential continuities between life in the German camps and life in communist Hungary. Key to that life was the principle of adaptation. On Christmas day 1963 he noted in his diary that "today's human being ... only adapts himself." Such a person was, at its core, a being without reality, and therefore he could not be made the object of art. "Functional life that is devoid of reality cannot serve as artistic material. Nothingness flickers through his fate, because this fate lacks all meaning, in which lies the possibility of tragedy."[81] Kertész started to lose his confidence that a novel could encompass the reality of the camp as its inmates were, in his words, beyond tragedy.

A few months later he jotted down in his diary a few terse entries on the way the desire to adapt to circumstances turned life against itself. "Conformism [occurs] when man does not look for harmony with reality, but with the facts. What is reality? In short: ourselves. What are facts? In short: absurdities. The combination of both, in short: a moral life, destiny. Or: no connection, the acceptance of facts, a series of coincidences and one's adaptation to it." This was the life of the conformist, a person who has no center, and who consists of a "void of facts."[82] Slowly he began to articulate the core idea of the novel. In May 1965 he recorded in his diary that he had found a possible title: *Sorstalanság* [Fatelessness]. "What do I refer to as fate? In any case, the possibility of tragedy." Totalitarianism, however, denied the possibility of tragedy. "If we are experiencing as reality a determinism that is imposed on us instead of a necessity that arises from our own—relative—freedom, I designate this as fatelessness."[83] This sense of fatelessness now began to shape the story in which, at the beginning of the novel, György's father dutifully reports for the labor camp, and György himself does not resist his arrest and his initial detention at a custom post. When he and a large group of other Jews were marched through Budapest to a holding pen, he noticed how one of the arrested made his escape, and then a couple of others. "I myself took a look around, though more for the fun of it, if I may put it that way, since I saw no other reason to bolt, though I

81. Imre Kertész, *Galeerentagebuch*, trans. Kristin Schwamm (Reinbek: Rowohlt, 2002), 8f.
82. Ibid., 15.   83. Ibid., 16.

believe there would have been time to do so; nevertheless, my sense of honor proved the stronger."[84] His honor told him to stay in line, to accept his fate. A few days earlier, his uncle Lajos had told him that the boy was to be "part of the shared Jewish fate," and that this fate was one of "unbroken persecution that had lasted for millennia" and that György had to accept "with fortitude and self-sacrificing forbearance."[85] Having accepted the burden of Jewish fate— which was to turn out to be at the same time a fatelessness on an individual level—György felt it as a question of honor not to leave the line.

In October 1969, Kertész noted in his diary that he was about to begin with the story of the protagonist's arrival in Auschwitz. One and a half years later, he still struggled with the key part: the arrival. There were many accounts of this key episode in every survivor's life. Almost all of them stressed two things: first of all, they did not know where they had arrived; secondly, things happened so fast that they had no opportunity to collect and organize themselves. Kertész didn't trust these accounts. With a magnifying glass, he began to study reproductions of photos made by SS officers Ernst Hoffman and Bernhard Walter during the arrival of a group of deportees from Hungary in the spring of 1944.[86] He noticed "smiles, confidence, trust. Yes, provided that under the conditions of totalitarianism a person wants to remain alive, he will contribute with such an attitude to the preservation of totalitarianism: this is the simple trick of the organization."[87] The deportees had cooperated with the SS. In 2002, when he gave his Nobel lecture in Stockholm, he came back to this moment of discovery. "I saw lovely, smiling women and bright-eyed young men, all of them well-intentioned, eager to cooperate." Survivors, he told his audience, desired to forget that, upon arrival, they had chosen to accommodate to the situation as best as they could—a behavior that actually smoothed the operation of the death camp. Hence they had repressed the memories to cover their arrival with a simplistic narrative in which they were robbed of agency. But they were wrong: they had chosen to cooperate. "And when I thought how all this was repeated the same way for days, weeks, months and years on end, I gained an insight into the mechanism of horror; I learned how it became possible to turn human nature against one's own life."[88]

---

84. Imre Kertész, *Fatelessness*, trans. Tim Wilkinson (New York: Vintage International, 2004), 55f.
85. Ibid., 20.
86. Israel Gutman and Bella Gutterman, eds., *Auschwitz Album* (Jerusalem: Yad Vashem, 2002).
87. Kertész, *Galeerentagebuch*, 29f.
88. Imre Kertész, "Eureka: The 2002 Nobel Lecture," *World Literature Today* 77: 1 (April-June 2003): 6.

Now Kertész became able to complete the novel that he had begun ten years earlier. In *Fatelessness*, not only György but all victims try to adapt to the increasingly impossible situations they find themselves in, and in doing so they subject themselves to the perverse rationality of the camp, smoothing the process of their own destruction. Kertész's description of the arrival in Auschwitz-Birkenau and the selection not only illustrates his insight, but also allows us to understand the key event in which accommodation became the default choice of the victims. As the deportation train came to a halt in Auschwitz-Birkenau, György noticed that "some, women especially, hastily freshened up, smartened themselves, combed their hair." Of course, they wanted to look good as they entered a new and unknown environment. When the doors of the freight cars opened, they faced shaven-headed inmates dressed in the striped duds of criminals who were to help them disembark. György, who had never seen convicts before, was frightened of being in such close contact to people he had only heard about in stories. "Their faces did not exactly inspire confidence either: jug ears, prominent noses, sunken, beady eyes with a crafty gleam. Quite like Jews in every respect. I found them suspect and altogether foreign looking." Compared to them, the smartly dressed and trim SS men appeared to be "anchors of solidity and calm in the whole tumult." All the arrivals seemed eager to impress the Germans. "I immediately heard, and moreover agreed with, the exhortation from many of the adults amongst us that we should try to do our bit by cutting questions and good-byes short, within reason, so as not to give the Germans the impression of such a rabble." And when an old woman in her confusion seemed to obstruct the smooth movement of the line-up of people, György overheard her son telling her that she should follow instructions as they would soon be meeting again, and having said that, he turned to an SS man standing nearby saying "*Nicht wahr, Herr offizier?*" while he smiled at the German with "a knowing and, in a way, somewhat conspirational smile."[89] Thus the deportees lined up, subjected themselves to the selection, and what awaited them beyond—assimilating themselves into the absurd rationality of Auschwitz that embraced both the SS perpetrators and victims, erasing in a diabolical alchemy the distinctions between innocence and guilt.

For Kertész, the submission of the deportees to the whole process that had begun with their arrest in Hungary and culminated in the selection in Auschwitz-Birkenau was a given that could not be changed. Hence those who arrived in the camp were "fateless" people—that is, people who moved step by

89. Kertész, *Fatelessness*, 77f., 80.

step toward the gas chambers. Yet it was not a destiny without dignity. At the end of *Fatelessness*, Kertész returned to the way the deportees had behaved. In the summer of 1945, upon his return to Budapest, György met his Jewish neighbors, Mr. Steiner and Mr. Fleischman. They had survived in the city, and tried to tell the boy what had happened to them as a sequence of events "that came about." György objected to such a language because it removed the history from the linearity of time that people live. "It was not quite true that the thing 'came about'; we had gone along with it too," György told his neighbors. While every minute someone might have decided not to take that next step, it "would have been just as senseless as doing nothing, yet again and just as naturally." As a result, there was no resistance. "Everyone took steps along as he was able to take a step; I too took my own steps, and not just in Birkenau, but even before that . . . ." Mr. Fleischman got angry, beat his chest with his fist, and bawled "So it's us who're the guilty ones, is it? Us, the victims!" György did not deny it, but tried to explain that it was not a crime to have submitted and not revolted. "All that was needed was to admit it, meekly, simply, merely as a matter of reason, a point of honor, if I might put it that way."[90]

Indeed, there was honor in not quitting the line, in not revolting. It was an aristocratic sense of honor that few in the democratic modern societies of the West understand, an act of resistance against the utilitarian principles that set comfort and happiness above pride and principle, an acceptance of a code of honor that reaches back to simpler times, when people were still able to see the unity of all things, understood the place of suffering within that whole, and embraced the tragedy that comes with it as the key to human greatness. Having submitted to his fateless destiny as a matter of honor, a small miracle occurred: György's life became, in the story Kertész told, the stuff of tragedy, of tragedy regained. In *Fatelessness*, Kertész brought an end to at least one aspect of the debilitating "sheep to the slaughter" discourse by transforming György's submission into a work of art.

I qualified Kertész's achievement because the plot of *Fatelessness* depended not only on the innocence of the protagonist, but also on his ignorance. Most of those who were led to the gas vans in Chelmno and the gas chambers in Belzec, Sobibor, Treblinka, and Auschwitz-Birkenau were ignorant of what awaited them. But in the case of Auschwitz, some were not. There were, first of all, individual prisoners who, after some time in the camp, were considered "useless mouths" by the SS, and were sent to the gas chambers. There are no records

90. Ibid., 258, 260.

that these inmates rebelled, but their resignation can be understood when we consider that most of them were physically weakened to such an extent that they did not have the energy to revolt. In addition, the numbers of inmates sent from the camp to the gas chambers were relatively small: one or two truckloads at most. There were never enough of them to make any credible gesture; if, by some miracle, they had had the will, energy, and numbers, what would have been the alternative? A gruesome death by hanging amid the barracks.

Yet, in the history of the Holocaust in Auschwitz, there is an instance in which a very large group of inmates, most of whom were in reasonable physical condition, were sent to the gas chambers, knowing what awaited them. It concerns the liquidation of the 4,000 Jews from the Czech family camp during the night of March 7, 1944. In the historiography of Jewish resistance in the Holocaust, that night represents a nadir. The Czech family camp had been established on September 9, 1943, when 5,006 Jews of all ages arrived from the Theresienstadt ghetto and were admitted to section BIIb of Auschwitz-Birkenau without having undergone selection. These Jews were allowed to keep their clothes and hair. This unusual event occurred twice again on December 16 and 20, when a total of 2,962 Jews from Theresienstadt were admitted to what now was known as the Czech family camp. In the context of Auschwitz, this seemed to be a stable situation; so stable that the then well-known educator Alfred (Fredy) Hirsch established a children's program in Block 31.[91]

In early March, David Schmulewski, who was the liaison between the Jewish resistance groups in Auschwitz-Birkenau and the largely non-Jewish resistance group in the Auschwitz main camp, heard that the crematoria were to be brought into readiness to kill and incinerate 4,000 people on the night of March 7. It was clear that it was going to be the Czech Jews—some 4,000 had died during the months of imprisonment—and the SS expected that it would be a difficult operation. Schmulewski contacted Walter Rosenberg (who was to adopt the name Rudi Vrba after his escape from Auschwitz), who had some freedom of movement in the camp and who was in contact with the family camp. When Schmulewski told him about the upcoming liquidation and the nervousness of the SS, Vrba explained that it made sense. In his memoir *I Cannot Forgive* (1963), he remembered that Schmulewski told him: "It's not going to be easy, gassing those people. They're not an innocent mob off the train. They know what happens here. They could make a fight of it. Now go on, and tell them everything I

91. See Nili Keren, "The Family Camp," in *Anatomy of the Auschwitz Death Camp*, ed. Yisrael Gutman and Michael Berenbaum (Bloomington: Indiana University Press, 1994), 428–40.

have said." As he left to inform the inmates of the Czech camp, Vrba considered that their only chance would be if the inmates of other sections, and especially of the Auschwitz underground, would join them. But why would they do so? "It was easy to say that the resistance would rise and join them; but it was demanding a tremendous sacrifice. Already these men had survived in the face of fantastic odds. With every day their chances of living increased.... Would these hardened prisoners, who had seen a million die in their time, risk everything for the sake of 4,000 Czechs? Or would they, perhaps, be fighting for something much greater? For the demolition of Auschwitz itself, for instance?" Two days later it had become clear that it was unlikely that the Czech camp would rise. Schmulewski made a last appeal. He told Vrba that he was absolutely sure that they were going to be killed, but that they would find help if they did revolt. "I cannot ask our fellows to throw away their lives for a lost cause," Schmulewski told Vrba. "But if the Czechs rise, if they make a worthwhile fight of it, they will not fight alone. Hundreds of us, perhaps thousands, will be beside them and with a bit of luck we could smash this whole stinking outfit." Key to the uprising was to find a leader. Schmulewski identified Hirsch. Vrba got in contact with Hirsch, who listened to him attentively. "'But Rudi,' he said in something like a whisper, 'what about the children?'" Vrba had anticipated his response, and told him that the children would die with or without an uprising. At least, Hirsch and the other Jews could trigger an uprising that might destroy the killing installations. "Think of it that way," he told Hirsch, "a few hundred die today because nobody can save them. But tens of thousands of other youngsters will live." Hirsch faced a moral abyss. "How can I march off to fight for my own skin and leave them to be butchered? Don't you see they trust me? They need me!" Vrba reminded him: "They're doomed, Fredy. You can't save them. Think of others." Hirsch asked for an hour to make up his mind, and used this time to take poison. In the end, the Czech camp did not rise. That night the Czech Jews were killed and their bodies were cremated. The next morning Vrba met one of the *Sonderkommandos* of the crematoria, Filip Müller. "They just walked straight into the gas chambers," Müller reported. "No resistance?" "We were waiting for it, but it never came. Had they started a fight we would have joined them. I suppose they were thinking of the children." "No protests at all?" "Nothing to speak off. Three girls made a fight of it and had to be beaten in. That was all."[92]

In his own memoir, *Auschwitz Inferno*, Müller recorded that the protests

---

92. Rudi Vrba and Alan Bestic, *I Cannot Forgive* (London: Sidgwick and Jackson and Gibbs and Phillips, 1963), 185, 189, 191,196.

were worthy of record. When the Czech women and children entered the undressing room, they pleaded with the SS: "We want to live!" "We want to work!" It did not make a difference. When they were beaten into the gas chambers, they sang the Czechoslovak national anthem and the Zionist anthem "Hatikvah." He also recorded that he was so emotionally overwrought that he joined the group in the gas chamber. Yet he was not to die with them. A few girls recognized him. "We understand that you have chosen to die with us of your own free will, and we come to tell you that we think your decision is pointless," she told Müller. "*We* must die, but you still have a chance to save your life. You have to return to the camp and tell everybody about our last hours." Then the girls dragged him to the still open door, and handed him to an SS man who shouted at Müller: "You bloody shit, get it into your stupid head: *we* decide how long you stay alive, when you die, and not you. Now piss off, to the ovens!"[93]

The memory of March 7, 1944, is without doubt the biggest trauma in the history of Auschwitz. It is a story that offers no consolation. In Lanzmann's movie *Shoah*, the sequence on the liquidation of the Czech family camp ends the narrative about the camps. As the viewer-witnesses, exhausted after almost eight hours of footage, witness Vrba's agony as he relives his confrontation with Hirsch or Müller's tears as he relives the utter despair that made him enter the gas chamber with the Czech Jews, they look into the bottom of the pit. In a nine-hour epic in which there are very few moments of decision, the dilemmas faced by Hirsch and Muller stand out—and do not allow for any satisfactory resolution. Vrba recalled that, when he found Hirsch dying, he called the French-Jewish inmate Dr. Kleinmann, and asked him to save Hirsch as he was key to the uprising of the Czech Jews. Kleinmann told him that Hirsch wouldn't be on his feet for a long time to come. "It would be better to leave things as they are, and do nothing."[94] Kleinmann's advice echoes in my imagination as I try to come to a conclusion about the story of the Czech family camp: it may be better to leave things as they are, and stop trying to make sense of it.

Gehenna

Gehenna represents the core of the machinery of death, that began, as Hilberg so well explained in *The Destruction of the European Jews*, with their

93. Filip Müller (with Helmut Freitag), *Auschwitz Inferno: The Testimony of a Sonderkommando*, trans. Susanne Flatauer (London: Routledge and Kegan Paul, 1979), 113f.
94. Claude Lanzmann, *Shoah: An Oral History of the Holocaust* (New York: Pantheon, 1985), 162.

identification as Jews. It was a world that few people not involved in the construction and operation of the killing installations knew about. As Lanzmann's *Shoah* reveals, there were enough Germans who did know that strange things were going on in certain places named Auschwitz, Belzec, or Chelmno, but who were prudent enough not to ask any questions. "You couldn't talk about that. Unless you were tired of life, it was best not to mention that," railway official Walter Stier told Lanzmann.[95] There were enough Polish villagers who realized what was happening in Chelmno or the Operation Reinhard camps, but they had neither the will nor the military resources to stop the operation. In the case of Auschwitz, however, there was a group that might have undertaken an attempt to destroy the crematoria and thus slow down the industrial-scale killing of Jews that had begun in the summer of 1942 in bunkers 1 and 2 west and northwest of Birkenau, and that had acquired a technological sophistication in the spring of 1943 with the completion of crematoria 2, 3, 4, and 5.[96] Within the Auschwitz concentration camp existed a well-organized resistance movement known as the *Kampfgruppe Auschwitz* (Battle Group Auschwitz).[97] Both the core and the majority of the Battle Group Auschwitz were Roman Catholic Polish prisoners, and there is evidence that the majority of them were infected with the murderous antisemitism of the SS.[98] In addition, their goal, like the goal, for example, of the Buchenwald resisters, was to improve living conditions for the inmates—especially in the main camp, which was largely occupied by non-Jewish prisoners. The Auschwitz resistance had considerable success in this effort, and in 1943 the mortality of registered inmates declined dramatically. "They considered it a great victory on their side," Vrba recalled in *Shoah*. "And that improvement of living conditions within the concentration camp was perhaps not so against the policy of the higher echelons of SS ranks as long as it did not interfere with the objective of the camp, which was production of death on the newcomers who were not prisoners of the camp." This, then, explains the unwillingness of the Auschwitz resistance to take the initiative

95. Ibid., 135.

96. In my numbering of the crematoria, I use the system used by the SS, who referred to the crematorium in the Auschwitz *Stammlager* as crematorium 1, labeling the four crematoria in Auschwitz-Birkenau with numbers 2–5. Many inmates, however, use a different numbering system, ignoring the crematorium in the *Stammlager* and labeling the crematoria in Birkanau with numbers I, II, III, and IV.

97. See Hermann Langbein, "The Auschwitz Underground," in *Anatomy of the Auschwitz Death Camp*, 485–502; also Józef Garlinski, *Fighting Auschwitz: The Resistance Movement in the Concentration Camp* (London: Julian Friedmann, 1975).

98. Langbein, *Against All Hope*, 146, 185.

in an uprising when it became clear that the Czech family camp was doomed. Vrba recalled that when he reported to the resisters that Hirsch had committed suicide, "they gave me bread for the people—yes, bread, and onions—and said that no decision had been made and I should come later for instructions." A gift of bread and onions remained the limit of their participation in the fate of the Czech Jews." By March 8, 1944, Vrba had learned the bitter lesson that "the Resistance in the camp is not geared for an uprising but for the survival of the members of the Resistance."[99]

The unwillingness of the Battle Group Auschwitz to risk its members' safety on behalf of the Jews who were killed on arrival, or even those who, like the Czech Jews, had been part of the inmate population, also applied to the fate of the *Sonderkommandos*. Initially, the *Sonderkommandos* were killed regularly, but from 1943 their situation stabilized somewhat because the SS needed their technical expertise in running the crematoria, and with this stabilization also came some contacts between a resistance group formed within the crematoria, and the Battle Group Auschwitz. Yet their perspective differed radically: by the spring of 1944 the members of the *Sonderkommandos* knew that the SS would kill them either if the killings came to an end or if the camp were abandoned because of the approach of the Red Army, while the members of the Battle Group Auschwitz knew that they would be saved if they would lie low. In May 1944, just before the beginning of the Hungarian Action and at a time that the Red Army was advancing through Poland, members of the resistance group in the crematoria contacted the Battle Group Auschwitz with the request to join in a general uprising that would perhaps save Hungarian Jewry and certainly give the *Sonderkommandos* a fighting chance for survival.[100] But, as *Sonderkommando* Salmen Lewenthal wrote in his secret diary (which he buried in a jar near crematorium 3, and which was found in October 1963), the Battle Group Auschwitz was not interested. "A great offensive had started in the East. It was evident that Russians were each day getting closer to us. The others came to the conclusion that this whole undertaking was perhaps unnecessary, that perhaps it were better to wait a little more until the front came nearer still, until the Germans lost heart and the disorganization among the military increased." Lewenthal conceded that, from their perspective, they acted rationally: "They did not feel the threat of being made away with." They could play for time. But

---

99. Lanzmann, *Shoah*, 151f., 165f.

100. See Eric Friedler, Barbara Siebert, and Andreas Kilian, *Zeugen aus der Todeszone. Das jüdische Sonderkommando in Auschwitz* (Lüneburg: Zu Klampen Verlag, 2002), 223–81.

this did not apply to the *Sonderkommandos*. "We believed that the Germans would want at all costs to obliterate all traces of their crimes committed till now. They would not be able to do this otherwise than by killing our entire Kommando, leaving not a single one alive."[101] When, in July 1944, the Hungarian Action had come to an end, and the *Sonderkommandos* feared imminent liquidation, they approached the Battle Group Auschwitz again, and were told to postpone a revolt planned for July 27. By then the *Sonderkommandos* realized that they stood alone. On September 6, one of them, Salmen Gradowski, wrote in a letter to be buried close to crematorium 3: "We, the Sonderkommando, had long since wanted to put a stop to our horrible work which we were forced to do under threat of death. We wanted to do great things. But people from the camp, a section of the Jews, Russians, and Poles, have restrained us with all might and have forced us to put off the date of our mutiny. That day is approaching. It may happen today or tomorrow. I am writing these words in a moment of the greatest danger and excitement."[102] The Battle Group Auschwitz was not going to intervene.

In Auschwitz-Birkenau, but also in Chelmno, Belzec, Sobibor, and Treblinka, the Jews who were forced to operate the killing installations were isolated from the rest of the world in both a physical and, perhaps even more importantly, spiritual way. They lived a life of "forced culpability" and "forced complicity." In *The Rebel*, Camus observed that "he who kills or tortures will only experience the shadow of victory: he will be unable to feel that he is innocent. Thus he must create guilt in his victim so that, in a world that has no direction, universal guilt will authorize no other course of action but the use of force and give its blessing to nothing but success. When the concept of innocence disappears from the mind of the innocent victim himself, the value of power establishes a definitive rule over a world in despair."[103] The *Sonderkommandos* in Chelmno, the Operation Reinhard Camps, and in the Auschwitz crematoria knew that their lives depended on the continued arrival of deportees. It led, as Glazar told Lanzmann, to "a feeling of hopelessness, of shame.... We were the workers in the Treblinka factory, and our lives depended on the whole manufacturing process, that is, the slaughtering process at Treblinka."[104] In a world

---

101. Salmen Lewenthal, "Diary," in *Amidst a Nightmare of Crime: Manuscripts of Members of Sonderkommando*, ed. Jadwiga Bezwinska (Oswiecim: The State Museum at Oswiecim, 1973), 154f.

102. Gradowski, "Letter," in ibid., 77.

103. Camus, *The Rebel*, 155.

104. Lanzmann, *Shoah*, 147f.

so far lower than Purgatory, there was no space for a solidarity with the victim. The *Sonderkommandos* wanted to live. "The truth is that one wants to live at any cost, one wants to live because one lives, because the whole world lives," Lewenthal wrote in his diary. "I must speak the truth here, that some of that group have in the course of time so entirely lost themselves that we ourselves were simply ashamed. They simply forgot what they were doing [illegible] and with time [illegible] they got so used to it that it was even strange [that one wanted] to weep and complain; that [illegible] such normal, average [illegible] simple and unassuming men [illegible] of necessity get used to everything so that these happenings make no more any impression on them. Day after day they stand and look on how tens of thousands of people are perishing and [do] nothing."[105] The *Sonderkommandos* were unwilling to risk their lives for people who did not resist.

The liquidation of the Czech family camp was an exception. On that particular occasion, the Auschwitz *Sonderkommandos* were willing to rise up against the SS. This was not only because there were some chances of success if the Czech Jews revolted. They were in relatively good shape and they had preserved some esprit de corps, but also the *Sonderkommandos* feared that the liquidation of the Czech family camp heralded the end of the killing of Jews in Auschwitz, and therefore their own liquidation. The *Sonderkommandos* declared that they would join the Czech Jews if they chose to make a last stand. In his memoir Müller recorded that the Chief Kapo of the crematoria, Kaminski, told him that if the Czech Jews would begin an uprising in their own camp by burning the barracks, they could rely on the *Sonderkommandos* joining in. "On our part we shall attempt to destroy the crematorium buildings and finish off our tormentors. With a bit of luck we'll manage to escape into the mountains."[106] But, as we have seen, the Czech Jews did not rise while still in their camp. Even when they arrived in the crematorium yard, the *Sonderkommandos* were still prepared to join them if and when they resisted. In his diary, Salmen Gradowski wrote: "We hoped, we believed, that it would happen today, that today would be the final day that we had awaited impatiently. We expected that the despairing mass would unfold at the edge of the grave the standard of struggle, and, hand in hand, we would join them in the unequal battle. We would ignore the fact that it was impossible to thus attain our freedom or remain alive. It was our greatest chance to end our dismal life heroically." Gradowski and the other

105. Lewenthal, "Diary," 139.
106. Müller, *Auschwitz Inferno*, 102.

Sonderkommandos were disappointed when they saw them descend from the trucks. The Czech Jews entered the crematorium resigned and without protest. "It did not take long before all stood naked in the Bunker [gas chamber], and they faced death calmly and without resistance or struggle."[107]

With the exception of March 7, 1944, the *Sonderkommandos* never came close to an uprising to save a group of deportees. Three groups of them, however, did stand up against the Germans when it became clear that they were themselves in mortal danger: the *Sonderkommandos* of Treblinka revolted on August 2, 1943; the *Sonderkommandos* of Sobibor revolted on October 14; the *Sonderkommandos* of crematorium 4 in Auschwitz-Birkenau revolted on October 7, 1944. The stories that tell of the preparations are the stuff of high drama and, unavoidably so, entertainment. I mention novels like Jean-François Steiner's *Treblinka*, Ian Macmillan's *Village of a Million Spirits* (2000), or Michael Lev's *Sobibor: A Documentary Novel of the Sobibor Uprising* (2007); movies like Jack Gold's *Escape from Sobibor* (1987) and Tim Blake Nelson's drama *The Grey Zone* (2001). Then there is, for our youngest generation, Team Raycast's video game *Sonderkommando Uprising* (2010). In this context, we do not have to go into details. It suffices to say that, in the end, some *Sonderkommandos* stood up and refused to go like "sheep to the slaughter." In the case of the Treblinka and Sobibor uprisings, the uprisings saved the lives of some dozens of people, who after the war testified about what had happened in the camps. The uprisings also brought an end to the operation of the camps, but they would have been closed anyway. In the case of the Auschwitz uprising, the result was total failure: while the uprising resulted in the destruction of crematorium 4, the killings in the gas chambers had wound down already, and the SS was ready to decommission the killing installations. The revolt did not lead to the salvation of the *Sonderkommandos* of crematorium 4. Only one of them, Müller, survived.

Salami, Sandwiches, and Milk

When Perseus finally reached the Gorgon Medusa, he had to take action. Not taking his eyes from his shield, he pulled his sword, and, without ever looking the monster in the face, cut off her head.

In the morning of March 8, 1944, when he heard that the Czech Jews had

---

107. Salmen Gradowski, "Im Herzen der Hölle," *Theresienstädter Studien und Dokumente* 6 (1999): 134f.

been killed, Vrba realized that the only effective way left to resist the killing operations in the gas chambers was through an escape. "I then decided to act, in what was called by the members of the Resistance anarchic and individualistic activity—like escape, and leaving the community, for which I was co-responsible by that time." Vrba revolted, not only against the Germans, but also against the discipline of the Battle Group Auschwitz. "The decision to escape, in spite of the policy of the Resistance movement at that time, was formed immediately," he told Lanzmann. "I started to press on with the preparations for the escape together with my friend [Alfréd] Wetzler, who was extremely important in this matter ... As far as I was concerned, I think that if I successfully manage to break out from the camp and bring the information to the right place at the right time, that this might be a help, that I might manage, if I succeed, to bring help from outside."[108] The particular urgency was, however, not the result of having lost faith in the willingness of the Battle Group Auschwitz to do anything to stop the killing of Jews in the crematoria. In March 1944, both Müller and Vrba had noticed the construction of a new railway spur connecting the main railway lines with Auschwitz-Birkenau. In addition, Vrba learned from Müller that the crematoria were being overhauled, and that the SS ordered the construction of incineration ditches close to the crematoria. "The Nazis, we estimated, were preparing to kill at least a million people," Vrba wrote in 1963. "As the clues filtered through us, we realized who were destined to break all records. It was the Hungarians whom most of us had thought were reasonably safe." When SS men began joking about the imminent supply of Hungarian salami, Vrba had the confirmation he needed. "I knew then that this was my moment. For almost two years I had thought of escape, first selfishly because I wanted my freedom; then in a more objective way because I wanted to tell the world what was happening in Auschwitz; but now I had an imperative reason. It was no longer a question of reporting a crime, but of preventing one; of warning the Hungarians, of rousing them, of raising an army one million strong, an army that would fight rather than die."[109] Vrba and Wetzler escaped on April 7, 1944. A few weeks later the two were debriefed by members of the Slovak Jewish community. The resulting report found its way to key members of the Hungarian Jewish community.

After Perseus had cut off Medusa's head, he returned the Aegis, the silver

---

108. Lanzmann, *Shoah*, 165f.
109. Vrba and Bestic, *I Cannot Forgive*, 197f.

shield, to Athena, and also offered her the Gorgon's head. Athena attached the head as a trophy to the Aegis. In June 1944, a summary of the report reached Dr. Gerhart Riegner, the representative of the World Jewish Congress in Berne. On June 24, Riegner gave a copy to Roswell D. McClelland of the War Refugee Board. That same day McClelland telegraphed the most salient points to Washington. On July 3, 1944, the *New York Times* carried, on page 3, a short article written by its Geneva correspondent, Daniel T. Brigham. Entitled "Inquiry Confirms Nazi Death Camps," the article reported the existence of two "extermination camps" in Auschwitz and Birkenau in Upper Silesia where between April 1942 and April 1944 "more than 1,715,000 Jewish refugees were put to death" in specially designed "execution halls" that could kill up to 8,000 people per day by means of cyanide gas. The article reported that the killing had not come to an end. Since April some 400,000 Hungarian Jews had been shipped to these camps, and it was estimated that some 30 percent of those deportees had already been killed.[110] By that time, President Franklin D. Roosevelt, Pope Pius XII, and King Gustav V of Sweden had already appealed to Hungarian Regent Admiral Miklós Horthy to stop the deportations to Auschwitz. On July 7, Horthy ordered the trains to stop. Now over 260,000 Hungarian Jews who had been destined for Auschwitz found themselves in a strange limbo. Most of them would survive the Holocaust.

After Perseus had cut off Medusa's head.... At some point the parallels break down. The legend has it that from the slain body of the Gorgon arose Pegasus, the winged horse. In 1944 no Pegasus was to emerge from the Gorgon's body. I wrote: "In June 1944 a summary of the report reached Dr. Gerhart Riegner." In an age of telephone and telegraph, it took *two months* for the Vrba-Wetzler report to reach the free world. What if it had reached Washington in early May— before the trains from Hungary began to arrive in Auschwitz? Another 450,000 Jews might have been saved. This "might have been" is not, in the words of the late Sidney Hook, a ghostly echo of what Vrba and Wetzler once hoped for, but an objective possibility that was missed because of the perplexing attitude of the Hungarian-Jewish Zionist leader Rudolf Kastner.[111] After Vrba and Wetzler had been debriefed in the Slovak town of Zilina, they were assured that Kastner would follow up. "He knows how to handle the situation," they were told by officials of the Jewish community. "He's a man of vast experience." A

---

110. Daniel T. Brigham, "Inquiry Confirms Nazi Death Camps," *New York Times* (July 3, 1944): 3.

111. Sidney Hook, *The Hero in History: A Study in Limitation and Possibility* (New Brunswick, N.J.: Transaction Publishers, 1992), 86.

smart lawyer and a well-known fixer, Kastner was used to sparring verbally with opponents in the legal chancelleries, the courts, and backrooms, supporting his arguments with legal opinions, written evidence, and other documents as needed. Faced with the opportunity to save more than 700,000 lives, Kastner did what he knew best to do: he approached his adversary, *SS-Obersturmbannführer* Adolf Eichmann, showed him the Vrba-Wetzler report, and asked the man charged with sending Hungarian Jewry to Auschwitz for a reply. But Eichmann was not an adversary, but an enemy. He offered Kastner a train that he could fill with 1,684 Hungarian Jews of his choice. The train would bring them to a neutral country. "Kastner paid for those 1,684 lives with his silence," Vrba bitterly observed in the epilogue to his memoir. "[Kastner] admitted that Eichmann had told him he did not want another Warsaw. He did not want a repetition of that twenty-seven day battle during which 33,000 men, women and children held at bay thousands of Wehrmacht and S.S. troops, armed with tanks and cannon." As to the 140 other trains that went to Auschwitz? When Vrba heard that trains with deportees had begun to pass through Zilina in the direction of Poland, he raged in frustration. "What are they doing? What's Kastner doing? What in Christ's name is happening?" A Jewish official assured him: "They're doing what they can. Last night they sent sandwiches down to the transports and milk for the children." Compared to the bread and onions supplied by the Battle Group Auschwitz to the Czech Jews, the sandwiches and milk may be considered a small improvement. The official gave the nineteen-year-old Vrba some well-meant counsel: "You must keep calm. They know best. They're clever men, cleverer than you or I."[112]

Clever men living in the relative comfort of Budapest trying to understand and respond to the seemingly absurd reality described in the Vrba-Wetzler report: how could they have gotten it right? Also they must have seen the Gorgon, and frozen—or at least it is clear that they stopped thinking. "Irony with little satire is the non-heroic residue of tragedy, centering on a theme of puzzled defeat," Canadian literary critic Northrop Frye once observed.[113] At the end of an essay that cleverly sought to map Jewish resistance as it arose from the camps (Paradise), unfolded in the camps (Hades to Gehenna), and either occurred or did not occur from the remnants of civilized society to the camps (Washington, Vatican City, Stockholm, and Budapest), a sense of puzzled defeat might perhaps be appropriate.

112. Vrba and Bestic, *I Cannot Forgive*, 250, 263, 251f.
113. Northrop Frye, *Anatomy of Criticism* (Princeton, N.J.: Princeton University Press, 1971), 224.

Contributors

CECILIE FELICIA STOKHOLM BANKE is senior researcher and head of the Research Unit in Holocaust and Genocide Studies at the Danish Institute for International Studies in Copenhagen. She was visiting professor and Fulbright scholar-in-residence at the Strassler Center for Holocaust and Genocide Studies at Clark University during the fall of 2010 and a visiting scholar at the Remarque Institute at New York University in October 2007.

YEHUDA BAUER was born in Prague and moved to Israel with his family in 1939. He has spent his life as a historian and scholar of the Holocaust. He is the former director of the International Institute for Holocaust Research, Yad Vashem, Jerusalem, and now serves as its academic advisor. He is the author of many books, including *Jews for Sale?*, *The Impact of the Holocaust*, *A History of the Holocaust*, and *Rethinking the Holocaust*.

STEVEN BOWMAN is currently professor of Judaic Studies at the University of Cincinnati. Recipient of several Fulbright and NEH awards, he was recently Miles Lerman Fellow at the U.S. Holocaust Memorial Museum. His publications include *The Jews of Byzantium, 1204–1453*, *Jewish Resistance in Wartime Greece*, and most recently *The Agony of Greek Jewry during World War II*.

NATHAN BRACHER is professor of French at Texas A&M University. For the past fifteen years, he has focused on the ways in which French writers, intellectuals, and media narrate the past. In addition to codirecting seven NEH Summer Seminars on the legacy of World War II in France, he has published numerous articles and two books in the field: *Through the Past Darkly: History and Memory in François Mauriac's "Bloc-notes"* and *After the Fall: War and Occupation in Irène Némirovsky's "Suite française."*

Contributors

DEBÓRAH DWORK is Rose Professor of Holocaust History and the founding director of the Strassler Center for Holocaust and Genocide Studies at Clark University. Among Dwork's many award-winning publications are *Children with a Star* and three volumes cowritten with Robert Jan van Pelt: *Auschwitz*; *Holocaust: A History*; and *Flight From the Reich: Refugee Jews, 1933–1946*.

TUVIA FRILING is a senior research fellow at the Ben-Gurion Research Institute of Ben-Gurion University of the Negev. In 2003–04 he served as vice-chairman of the "International Commission of the Holocaust in Romania," which was headed by Elie Wiesel. In 2009, he was awarded the "Cultural Merit Award in Rank of Commander" by Romanian President Traian Basescu. Among his many publications are *Arrow in the Dark: David Ben-Gurion, the Yishuv Leadership and Rescue Attempts during the Holocaust; An Answer to a Post-Zionist Colleague; The Israelis and the Holocaust; "Who Are You, Leon Berger?" The Story of a Kapo in Auschwitz, History, Memory and Politics*.

ESTHER GITMAN, as a toddler, managed to escape with her mother in August 1941 from Nazi- and Ustase-occupied Sarajevo into the Italian Zone of Occupation on the Adriatic. For decades, she gave little thought to her survival, but in 1999 she left her successful business to pursue a Ph.D. in Jewish history at the City University of New York. In 2002 she was awarded a Fulbright grant to Croatia and in 2005 she received her Ph.D. from CUNY. She is the author of *When Courage Prevailed: Rescue and Survival of Jews in the Independent State of Croatia, 1941–1945*.

PATRICK HENRY received his Ph.D. in French from Rice University. He taught at Whitman College 1976–2002. Since his retirement, he has taught courses on the literature and film of the Holocaust and on the literature of peace. His most recent book is *We Only Know Men: The Rescue of Jews in France during the Holocaust*, which was published in France in 2010 as *La Montagne des Justes*. He has been a speaker for the Jewish Foundation for the Righteous since 2000.

ŞTEFAN IONESCU received his Ph.D. from the Strassler Center for Holocaust and Genocide Studies, Department of History, at Clark University. He teaches at the Rodgers Center for Holocaust Education, Department of History, at Chapman University. His most recent publication is, "Implementing the Romanianization of Employment in 1941 Bucharest: Bureaucratic and Economic Sabotage of the 'Aryanization' of the Romanian Economy," in Thomas Kühne and Tom Lawson, eds., *The Holocaust and Local History*.

596

GÁBOR KÁDÁR is the senior researcher of the Hungarian Jewish Archives. He teaches Holocaust history and comparative genocide studies at ELTE University, Budapest. His major publications include *Gold Train:Chapters from the History of Jewish Wealth*, *Self-financing Genocide: The Gold Train, the Becher Case and the Wealth of Hungarian Jews*, and *Robbing the Dead: The Economic Annihilation of the Hungarian Jews*.

HANA KUBÁTOVÁ has studied the public mood and attitude toward the so-called Jewish question in Slovakia, 1938–45. She has been the recipient of prestigious scholarships and fellowships, including the Israeli Government Scholarship, the Felix Posen Doctoral Fellowship, the Marie Curie Fellowship, and the Charles H. Revson Foundation Fellowship. She teaches at Charles University.

DIETER KUNTZ is a program officer in the University Programs Division of the Center for Advanced Holocaust Studies at the U.S. Holocaust Memorial Museum. He was editor of *Deadly Medicine: Creating the Master Race*. He has taught courses in European and modern German history, as well as on the Holocaust, at the University of Iowa and the University of Kansas, and continues to teach the online course "Hitler and Nazi Germany" for the University of Kansas. He has coedited the popular university classroom teaching volume *Inside Hitler's Germany: A Documentary History of Life in the Third Reich*.

ARIELLA LANG received her Ph.D. in Italian from Columbia University in 2003. She currently works at the Institute for the Study of Human Rights at Columbia University. She has published numerous articles in Italian Jewish Studies and her recently published book, *Converting a Nation: A Modern Inquisition and the Unification of Italy*, explores religious and national identity in nineteenth-century Italy. She was recently a fellow at the U.S. Holocaust Memorial Museum.

BEREL LANG is professor emeritus of philosophy and humanistic studies at State University of New York at Albany. He has been a visiting professor of philosophy at Wesleyan University, Hebrew University, and the University of Connecticut. He has received fellowships from the National Endowment for the Humanities, the American Council of Learned Societies, and the American Philosophical Association. He is the author or editor of twenty-one books, including *Act and Idea in the Nazi Genocide*, *The Future of the Holocaust*, *Holocaust Representation: Art Within the Limits of History and Ethics*, *Heidegger's Silence*, and *Philosophical Witnessing: The Presence of the Holocaust*.

Contributors

NANCY LEFENFELD, an independent scholar who lives in Maryland, has conducted extensive research on the subject of Jewish rescue in France during the Holocaust. The main focus of her work has been the smuggling of Jewish children from France into Switzerland. She has recently published *The Fate of Others: Rescuing Jewish Children on the French-Swiss Border.*

YEHUDI LINDEMAN, a child survivor of the Holocaust, was separated from his family in the fall of 1942 and spent the next thirty months in hiding in about fifteen different locations in rural Holland. He is a retired professor of English at McGill University and the founder and past director of Living Testimonies, the Holocaust Video Archive at McGill. He is the author of *Shards of Memory: Narratives of Holocaust Survival,* and, with Irene Lilienheim Angelico, *The Third Seder: A Haggadah for Yom Hashoah.*

JOANNA BEATA MICHLIC is a social and cultural historian and director of the HBI (Hadassah Brandeis Institute) Project on Families, Children, and the Holocaust at Brandeis University. She also teaches in the Department of History at Bristol University. Her major publications include *Neighbors Respond: The Controversy about Jedwabne,* coedited with Antony Polonsky; *Poland's Threatening Other: The Image of the Jew from 1880 to the Present*; and *Bringing the Dark to Light: The Memory of the Holocaust in Postcommunist Europe.* Her current single-authored book projects are *Jewish Childhood in Poland: Survival and Transformation in the Wartime and Early Postwar Realities, 1939–1950* and *More Than the Milk Of Human Kindness: Jewish Survivors and Their Polish Rescuers Recount Their Tales, 1944–1949.* She is the recipient of many academic awards and fellowships, most recently the Rothschild Foundation (Hanadiv) Europe Visiting Fellowship, Birkbeck College, London in spring 2012.

RICHARD MIDDLETON-KAPLAN is professor of English and Humanities and Distinguished Chair of Teaching Excellence at Harper College in Palatine, Ill., where he teaches Literature of the Holocaust. In 2004, he was a fellow at the Northwestern Summer Institute on the Holocaust and Jewish Civilization. His essays have appeared in *Modern Fiction Studies* and *Leviathan.* Articles are forthcoming in *Levinas and Twentieth-Century Literature* and the journal *Peace Research.*

DALIA OFER received her B.A., M.A., and Ph.D. degrees from Hebrew University in Jerusalem. She was a post-doctoral fellow at Harvard's Center for Judaic Studies and a visiting scholar at Brandeis University. She is currently Max and

Rita Haber Emeritus Professor of Holocaust and East European Studies at the Avraham Harman Institute of Contemporary Jewry, the Melton Center for Jewish Education, and the Hebrew University of Jerusalem. She received the Jewish Book Award for her 1990 study, *Escaping the Holocaust: Illegal Immigration to the Land of Israel* and was a Jewish Book Award finalist in two categories, Holocaust and women, for her coedited (with Lenore Weitzman) volume, *Women in the Holocaust*. She recently published *Holocaust Survivors: Resettlement, Memories, Identities*, edited with Françoise S. Ouzan and Judy Tydor Baumel-Schwartz.

AVINOAM PATT is the Philip D. Feltman Professor of modern Jewish history at the Maurice Greenberg Center for Judaic Studies at the University of Hartford, where he is also director of the Museum of Jewish Civilization. He is the author of *Finding Home and Homeland: Jewish Youth and Zionism in the Aftermath of the Holocaust* and coeditor (with Michael Berkowitz) of a collected volume on Jewish Displaced Persons, *We Are Here: New Approaches to the Study of Jewish Displaced Persons in Postwar Germany*. He is coauthor of a recently published source volume, entitled *Jewish Responses to Persecution, 1938–1940*.

CHRISTINE SCHMIDT VAN DER ZANDEN earned her Ph.D. in history from Clark University in 2003, in the first-ever doctoral program in Holocaust and genocide studies. Her most recent research has focused on a comparative study of rescue and resistance in France and Hungary during the Holocaust. She has contributed dozens of entries to the recently published first volume of *The Encyclopedia of Camps and Ghettos, 1933–1945*, which won the 2009 National Jewish Book Award. Schmidt is currently an adjunct assistant professor of history at the University of Maryland University College and at Gratz College.

NICK STRIMPLE has served on the faculty of the University of Southern California's Thornton School of Music since 1996, where he maintains an active career as composer, conductor, scholar, and teacher. The author of two critically acclaimed books and many articles on choral and sacred music, he is also known internationally for his work with Holocaust-related music. He has served as consultant to several museums, including the Los Angeles Museum of the Holocaust and Warsaw's Museum of the history of Polish Jews.

NECHAMA TEC is professor emerita of sociology at the University of Connecticut. She was born in Lublin, Poland, and survived the Holocaust thanks to Polish Catholics. She is the author of *Dry Tears: The Story of a Lost Childhood*;

When Light Pierced the Darkness: Christian Rescue of Jews in Nazi-Occupied Poland; *In the Lion's Den: The Life of Oswald Rufeisen*; *Resilience and Courage: Women, Men, and the Holocaust*; and, with Christopher Browning, *Letters of Hope and Despair*. Several of her books have received prestigious awards and have been nominated for Pulitzer Prizes and National Book Awards. In 2002, she was appointed by President Bush to the Council of the United States Holocaust Memorial Museum. In 2008, Edward Zwick adapted her book, *Defiance: The Bielski Partisans*, into the award-winning film, *Defiance*. Her most recent book is *Resistance: Jews and Christians Who Defied the Nazi Terror* (2013).

ZOLTÁN VÁGI is the deputy chair of the Center for Social Conflict Research at ELTE University, Budapest. He is currently researching the fate of the Hungarian Jews in Auschwitz, and the forms and appearance of Hungarian and regional antisemitism in the nineteenth and twentieth centuries. His major publications include *Self-financing Genocide: The Gold Train, the Becher Case and the Wealth of Hungarian Jews* (with Gábor Kádár).

ROBERT JAN VAN PELT is university professor in the school of architecture at the University of Waterloo in Ontario. In 2000, he served as an expert witness for the defense in the civil suit brought by British Holocaust denier David Irving against Deborah Lipstadt and Penguin Books. He has authored nine books, including three on Holocaust history with Debórah Dwork. Most recently he published an English-language, critical edition of David Koker's concentration camp diary written in KL Herzogenbusch (aka Vught).

HANS DE VRIES graduated in political and social sciences from Amsterdam University. Since 1975, he has been a staff member of the Netherlands Institute for War, Holocaust, and Genocide Studies (NIOD). Among his many publications is a complete revision of *The Underground Press, 1940–1945*.

SUZANNE VROMEN is professor emerita of sociology at Bard College where she taught for twenty-two years. She was living in Belgium when the Germans invaded the country in 1940. After a year under Nazi occupation, with her family she succeeded in escaping and finding refuge in the Belgian Congo. At Bard College, she cofounded the Women's Studies Program in 1979 and directed it for eight years. She is the author of *Hidden Children of the Holocaust: Belgian Nuns and Their Daring Rescue of Young Jews from the Nazis*.

Index of Names

Index of Names

Index of Names

Index of Names

Index of Names

Index of Names

Index of Names

Subject Index

Jewish Resistance against the Nazis was designed in Meta Serif with Meta display and composed by Kachergis Book Design of Pittsboro, North Carolina. It was printed on 50-pound Sebago and bound by Maple Press of York, Pennsylvania.